THE (CRIM) SOLUTION

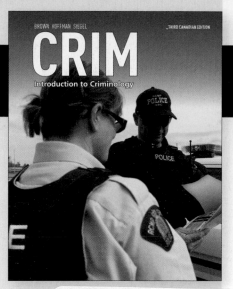

BROWN HOFFMAN SIEGEL — THIRD CANADIAN EDITION

CRIM
Introduction to Criminology

Print

CRIM delivers all the key terms and all the content for the **Introduction to Criminology** course through a visually engaging and easy-to-review print experience.

Digital

MindTap®

MindTap enables you to stay organized and study efficiently by providing a single location for all your course materials and study aids. Built-in apps leverage social media and the latest learning technology to help you succeed.

ACTIVATE
MindTap

ACTIVATE MINDTAP TODAY!

1. Ask your instructor for the **Course Key** for your course—enter it below for safe keeping.

   COURSE KEY *from your instructor*

2. Go to **www.nelson.com/student**
3. In the box labelled "Register," enter the **Course Key** provided by your instructor.
4. Register as a new user OR log in, if you already have a NELSONbrain account.
5. To access your online resource, click on the "Open" button.
6. When prompted with "I have an Access Code" message, enter the Access Code printed below.

   ACCESS CODE

   Gently scratch off foil with coin to reveal your access code.

1 Open the Access Card included with this text.

2 Follow the steps on the card.

3 Study.

Student Resources

- Interactive eBook
- Flashcards
- Review Cards
- Matching Activities
- Multiple Choice Quizzes
- Chapter Videos
- Scenario-Based Activities
- Critical Thinking Questions

Students: **www.nelson.com/student**

Instructor Resources

- Access to All Student Resources
- Instructor Companion Site
- Updated Test Bank
- PowerPoint® Slides
- Image Library
- Instructor's Guide

Instructors: **www.nelson.com/instructor**

NELSON EDUCATION

CRIM, Third Canadian Edition

by Gregory P. Brown, Ron Hoffman, and Larry J. Siegel

VP, Product and Partnership Solutions:
Anne Williams

Publisher, Digital and Print Content:
Leanna MacLean

Executive Marketing Manager:
Amanda Henry

Content Development Manager:
Suzanne Simpson Millar

Photo and Permissions Researcher:
Indu Arora

Production Project Manager:
Christine Gilbert

Production Service:
MPS Limited

Copy Editor:
Karen Rolfe

Proofreader:
MPS Limited

Indexer:
MPS Limited

Design Director:
Ken Phipps

Managing Designer:
Franca Amore

Interior Design:
Cathy Mayer

Interior Images:
image of courtroom – Izzy Schwartz/Photodisc/Getty Images; image of pile of business paper files - Nuk2013/Shutterstock.com

Cover Design:
Cathy Mayer

Cover Image:
Fred Lum / The Globe and Mail

Compositor:
MPS Limited

Library and Archives Canada Cataloguing in Publication

Siegel, Larry J.
[Criminology]
     CRIM / Gregory P. Brown, Ron Hoffman, Larry J. Siegel.—Third Canadian edition.

Revision of: Criminology : the core / Larry J. Siegel, Gregory P. Brown, Ron Hoffman.—1st Canadian ed.—Scarborough, Ont.: Thomson Nelson, © 2006.
Includes bibliographical references and index.
ISBN 978-0-17-656246-5 (paperback)

     1. Criminology—Textbooks.
2. Crime—Canada—Textbooks.
I. Brown, Gregory P. (Gregory Paul), author II. Hoffman, Ron, 1952–, author III. Title. IV. Title: Criminology.

HV6025.S55 2016   364
C2015-907343-X

ISBN-13: 978-0-17-653168-3
ISBN-10: 0-17-653168-8

About the Cover: RCMP officers look over photos of a possible suspect in the June 4, 2014 shooting deaths of three RCMP officers and the wounding of two others in Moncton, New Brunswick. After a two-day manhunt, in which the frightened residents of the New Brunswick city were in lockdown, police arrested Justin Bourque, 24, and charged him with three counts of murder, and two of attempted murder. In October 2014, Bourque was sentenced to 75 years in prison, the longest such sentence in Canadian history.

CRIM
Brief Contents

AP Photo/The Canadian Press, Adrian Wyld

Zurijeta/Shutterstock.com

AP Photo

NEL

CRIM Contents

THE CANADIAN PRESS/Ryan Remiorz

© North Wind Picture Archives/Alamy

Fotosenmeer/Shutterstock.com

© ACE STOCK LIMITED/Alamy

© Royalty-Free/Masterfile

Winnipeg Sun

© Saed Hindash/Star Ledger/Corbis

© NARONG SANGNAK/epa/Corbis

Photo by Rex Features/CP Photo

Minerva Studio/Shutterstock.com

© Oleksiy Maksymenko/Alamy

© Alex Slobodkin/iStockPhoto, Bank note image used with the permission of the Bank of Canada

© MARKA/Alamy

© Pictorial Press Ltd / Alamy Stock Photo

We're very pleased and proud of *CRIM*, Third Canadian Edition. We have made many additions to the text. We have substantially updated the chapter materials, and added a new Chapter 14, The Challenge of Crime in the 21st Century: A Global Criminology. Chapter 14 introduces students to the new reality of the global, transnational, and digital nature of crime, as well as the problems this poses in investigating, responding to, and preventing crime. We believe *CRIM* gives criminology and criminal justice students the tools they need to understand the different strains of criminological theory and their different applications to addressing real-world problems. At the same time, we've written *CRIM* to make the content accessible, interesting, and meaningful for students, including movies that raise questions of theories (in *Criminology at the Movies*), practitioners who use criminology in the work they do (in *Career Connections*), and programs and policies that apply the ideas of criminological theory to real-world problems and crime (in the *Theoretical Applications* boxes). We hope that students, including our own students, enjoy this book and its explicitly Canadian focus. If they enjoy it, read it, and find the material interesting, then we have done part of our job in educating the next generation of criminologists and criminal justice professionals.

Student Engagement: Review, Reinforce, Reflect.

Learning Objectives, presented at the beginning of each chapter, are now aligned with revised Bloom's taxonomy, and incorporate one application and one analysis outcome in each chapter.

New: Chapter Summary. Each chapter now ends with a summary of the chapter's main concepts. Formerly part of the *Chapter in Review* cards, the summary is now part of the chapter itself, providing immediate review and reinforcement for students after they read the chapter.

New: Discussion Questions. Along with the revised end-of-chapter focus, Discussion Questions provide a reinforcement of chapter concepts as well as an opportunity to reflect on them. Students consider a scenario or thought-provoking situation that could occur in the students' lives or careers, and apply theoretical concepts they've learned to answer

these questions. They can be used for group discussions, class discussions, or individual learning.

Restructured: Chapter in Review cards. These perforated pages can be pulled out of the text for students to use as quick study tools. In the Third Canadian Edition, they have been restructured to focus on recall and retention of the main objectives and concepts in the text, giving students their own resource for practice and self-test.

The first page of each Chapter in Review card now includes the Learning Objectives and key terms with definitions from that chapter.

New: For the second page, a quick Quiz has been written so students can give themselves a quick self-test, further reinforcing the chapter concepts. Answers are provided.

Synopsis of Criminological Theories: These perforated cards, located at the end of the Chapter in Review cards, summarize major criminological theories, providing students with another quick reference as they prepare for class and tests.

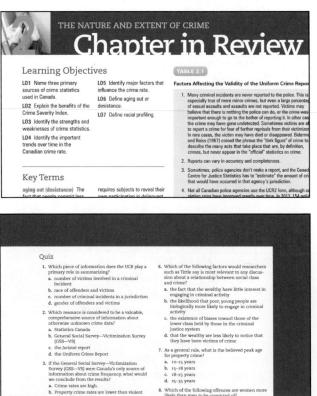

Feature Boxes

New: Every chapter includes a *Criminology at the Movies* feature, which helps students bring to life the issues dealt with by criminological theory. Examples include *Fruitvale Station*, *Clockwork Orange*, *True Story*, *Scarface*, and *Blow*.

New: In *Career Connections*, students are introduced to their future peers—people like them who work in the criminal justice system, from police officers and correctional officers to policy planners and the CEO of an insurance adjustment firm.

New: Toward the end of most chapters, *Theoretical Applications* features give students the chance to read about how academic theories are translated into real results in the field of criminal justice. At the end of each feature the student is asked to consider, in the role of a criminal justice professional, how he or she would approach the situation using a specific theory perspective.

Policy and Practice in Criminology features have been retained in this edition. Select chapters include this feature and provide additional links of theory and application, by looking at real-world issues on a broad scale. Examples include how youth crime is dealt with in Canada within a broader historical context (Chapter 2), and the *Gladue* decision in 1996 regarding restorative justice in Canada's Aboriginal communities (Chapter 8).

Crime and Criminology

Learning Objectives

LO1 Identify the field of study of criminology.

LO2 Recognize the key theorists in the development of the discipline of criminology.

LO3 Summarize the major theoretical perspectives in criminology and the focus of each.

LO4 Identify the subareas that constitute the discipline of criminology.

LO5 Explain how the definition of behaviours as deviant or criminal can change over time.

LO6 Explain the origins of British common law and interpret its relationship to contemporary Canadian criminal law.

LO7 Analyze the relationship between *mens rea* and *actus rea* in the determination of criminal offences.

LO8 Evaluate the ethical issues in conducting criminological research with individuals who are engaged in criminal activities.

Arctic-Images/Getty Images

LO1 Introduction

On the morning of April 15, 2014, Calgary woke to news of the worst mass murder in the city's history. In an as yet unexplained attack, Matthew de Grood, a 22-year-old University of Calgary psychology grad and soon to be law school student, stabbed and killed five young people attending a barbecue and house party near the campus. An invited guest, de Grood had completed his evening shift at a local grocery store and arrived at the party shortly before midnight on Monday, April 14. According to witnesses at the party, de Grood mingled with the 15 to 20 guests in attendance who by that time had moved the party indoors. Shortly after 1:00 a.m., and without warning, de Grood grabbed a large knife from within the home and attacked and repeatedly stabbed five of the party-goers. Responding to a 911 call logged at 1:22 a.m., police arrived at the scene to find University of Calgary students Josh Hunter, 22, and Jordan Segura, 23, and Alberta College of Art & Design student Zachariah Rathwell, 21, already dead inside the home. Kaiti Petras 23, a former Mount Royal University student and aspiring dance teacher, and Lawrence Hong, 27, another UC student, were found alive, but later died of their injuries. De Grood fled the home after the attack, but was quickly arrested by police a short distance from the scene.[1]

At a news conference later the same day, Calgary Police Chief Rick Hanson described the crime scene as "horrific," and confirmed that Matthew de Grood was indeed the son of Calgary Police Inspector Douglas de Grood, a respected, 33-year veteran of the police service. Speaking for himself and his wife Susan, a heartbroken Douglas de Grood said, "We are shocked and devastated, and we are trying to make sense of what happened. We are deeply saddened for what the families and friends of the victims are going through. Your lives have been turned upside down. We know words cannot begin to ease your suffering ... We hope someday we will have answers as to why this happened. Regardless, it won't bring the victims back, but we would give anything to do just that."[2]

The tragic events of the Calgary mass murder are an extreme example, but they are representative of the complex problems and issues that face criminologists and shape their field of study. What causes a person to commit such a horrific act? Are there any common characteristics about the situations (e.g., time of day, location, gender, or age of victims) in which mass killings happen? Do we have a role in helping the families and friends of the victims deal with their grief? How can we help communities heal after such a tragedy? How can we use our knowledge about mass murders to reduce the risk of them happening in the future?

Such questions about crime and its control have spurred the development of criminology, an

Matthew de Groot, 23, is accused of savagely stabbing and killing five young people at a house party in Calgary. What could cause an otherwise quiet, mild-mannered university student, community volunteer, and son of a Calgary Police Inspector to commit such an act? Were there any warning signs? Does he have some kind of physical or mental illness? Did something in the social environment, perhaps among friends or family, trigger this rage?

Stuart Dryden/Calgary Sun/QMI Agency

Dressed like the *Rambo* movie character, with ammunition belt slung across his chest, a pump-action shotgun across his back, and M305 semi-automatic rifle in hand, on June 4, 2014, Justin Bourque set out on a killing spree in a Moncton, New Brunswick, neighbourhood. Three RCMP officers died as they tried to intervene; two others were wounded.

academic discipline that makes use of scientific methods to study the nature, extent, cause, and control of criminal behaviour. Unlike political figures and media commentators, whose opinions about crime may be coloured by personal experiences, biases, and election concerns, criminologists must remain objective as they study crime and its consequences. For example, some politicians have sought to capitalize on public fear by advocating restrictive immigration laws. However, criminologists John Hagan and Alberto Palloni have conducted objective, scientific research that shows that immigrants are actually less involved in crime than citizens and, by many measures of personal well-being, do better than citizens.[3]

Criminology is an interdisciplinary science. Criminologists hold degrees in a variety of diverse fields, most commonly sociology, but also criminal justice, law, political science, psychology, anthropology, economics, health studies, and the natural sciences. For most of the 20th century, criminology's primary orientation was sociological, but today it can be viewed as an integrated approach to the study of criminal behaviour.

LO2 A Brief History of Criminology

The scientific study of crime and criminality is a relatively recent development. During the European Middle Ages (1200–1600), people who violated social norms or religious practices were believed to be witches or possessed by demons.[4] It was common practice to use torture to extract confessions. Those convicted of violent or property crimes (e.g., theft, fraud) suffered extremely harsh penalties, including whipping, branding, maiming, and execution. For example, between 1575 and 1590, Nicholas Remy, head of the Inquisition in the French province of Lorraine, ordered 900 sorcerers and witches burned to death. According to Anne Llewellyn Barstow in her book *Witchcraze: A New History of the European Witch Hunts,* estimates of the number of individuals tortured or burned to death during the European Inquisition period (the 15th, 16th, and 17th centuries) range from 100 000 to possibly several millions.[5]

criminology
The scientific study of the nature, extent, cause, and control of criminal behaviour.

interdisciplinary
Involving two or more academic fields.

Even as Europeans began to establish colonies in North America, the rooting out of witches imposed strict standards of control over the behaviour of the early settlers. For more information about the causes and consequences of the Salem witch hunts, check out the link at http://www.nationalgeographic.com/features/97/salem.

Classical Criminology

By the mid-18th century, social philosophers began to argue for a more rational approach to punishment. They sought to eliminate cruel public executions, which were designed to frighten people into obedience. Reformers stressed that the relationship between crime and punishment should be balanced and fair. This more moderate view of criminal sanctions can be traced to the writings of an Italian scholar, Cesare Beccaria (1738–1794), who was one of the first scholars to develop a systematic understanding of why people committed crime.

Beccaria believed in the concept of utilitarianism, which maintains that punishment should increase the total amount of happiness in the world. For Beccaria, the purpose of punishment was not to seek revenge but rather to better society. It would deter others from committing crimes, and prevent criminals from repeating their crimes. To deter crime, punishment must be swift, certain to occur if the law is broken, and severe enough to deter any future law-breaking behaviour. Beccaria also believed that the law should set out what the punishments for different crimes are, that punishments should be proportional to the severity of the crime, and that they should be public, to

deter (warn) citizens about what would happen to law breakers.[6] The goal of law is to provide "the greatest happiness shared among the greatest number" while punishing those who break the law and threaten the collective pursuit of happiness.[7]

The writings of Beccaria and his followers form the core of what today is referred to as classical criminology. As originally conceived in the 18th century, classical criminology theory had several basic elements:

1. In every society, people have free will to choose criminal or lawful solutions to meet their needs or settle their problems.

2. Criminal solutions may be more attractive than lawful ones because they usually require less work for a greater payoff.

3. A person's choice of criminal solutions may be controlled by his or her fear of punishment.

4. The more certain, swift, and severe the punishment, the better able it is to control criminal behaviour.

utilitarianism
A doctrine positing an action is right if it promotes the greatest happiness of the greatest number of people. Individuals who break the law threaten the ability of the rest of us to enjoy our freedom and the pleasures we work for. Punishment should increase the total amount of happiness in the world because it will prevent criminals from repeating their crimes and it deters others from committing crimes. Utilitarians believe that legal systems can be designed that maximize individual freedom and allow everyone to pursue their pleasures.

classical criminology
The theoretical perspective suggesting that (1) people have free will to choose criminal or conventional behaviours; (2) people choose to commit crime for reasons of greed or personal need; and (3) crime can be controlled only by the fear of criminal sanctions.

Cesare Beccaria (1738–1794) argued that the effectiveness of criminal justice depended more on the certainty and swiftness of punishment, rather than on its severity.

Auguste Comte attempted to discover the successive stages through which the human race evolved. He believed that in the beginning man was not much superior to the great apes, but evolved to the state at which he found the civilized society of Europe of his time.

© James W. Porter/CORBIS

The classical perspective influenced judicial philosophy, and sentences were geared to be proportionate to the seriousness of the crime. Executions were still widely used but gradually came to be employed for only the most serious crimes. The catch phrase was "let the punishment fit the crime."

Positivist Criminology

During the 19th century, a new vision of the world challenged the validity of classical theory and presented an innovative way of looking at the causes of crime. The scientific method was beginning to take hold in Europe and North America. Scientists were using careful observation and analysis of natural phenomena to explain how the world worked. New discoveries were being made in biology, astronomy, and chemistry. If the scientific method could be applied to the study of nature, then why not use it to study human behaviour?

© Mary Evans Picture Library

Auguste Comte (1798–1857) was a French philosopher, known as the founder of the discipline of sociology and the doctrine of positivism.

Auguste Comte (1798–1857), considered the founder of sociology, argued that societies pass through stages that can be grouped on the basis of how people try to understand the world in which they live. People in primitive societies believe that inanimate objects have life (e.g., the sun is a god); in later social stages, people embrace a rational, scientific view of the world. Comte called this the positive stage, and those who followed his writings became known as positivists.

Positivism has two main elements:

1. Positivists see human behaviour as a function of external forces that are often beyond individual control. Some are social, such as wealth and class; others are political and historical, such as war and famine. Personal factors, such as an individual's brain structure and biological makeup or mental ability, also influence human behaviour.

2. Positivists rely on the scientific method. They would agree that an abstract concept such as "intelligence" exists because it can be measured by an IQ test. They would challenge a concept such as the "soul" because it cannot be verified by the scientific method.

Early Positivism

The earliest "scientific" studies examining human behaviour now seem quaint and primitive. Physiognomists, such as J.K. Lavater (1741–1801), studied the facial features of criminals and found that the shape of ears, nose, and eyes and the distances between them were associated with antisocial behaviour. Phrenologists, such as Franz Joseph Gall (1758–1828) and Johann K. Spurzheim (1776–1832), studied the shape of the skull and bumps on the head and concluded that these physical attributes were linked to criminal behaviour.

By the early 19th century, abnormality in the human mind was being linked to criminal behaviour patterns. Philippe Pinel, one of the founders of French psychiatry, coined the phrase *manie sans delire* to denote what eventually was referred to as a psychopathic personality. In 1812, an American, Benjamin Rush, described patients with an "innate preternatural moral depravity."[8] English physician Henry Maudsley (1835–1918) believed that insanity and criminal behaviour were strongly linked.[9] These early research efforts shifted attention to brain functioning and personality as the key to criminal behaviour.

positivism
The branch of social science that uses the scientific method of the natural sciences and suggests that human behaviour is a product of social, biological, psychological, or economic forces.

Viennese physician Franz-Joseph Gall (1758–1828) believed that a person's character and mental capacity could be determined by studying the skull. Different areas of the skull corresponded to various aspects of a person's personality as shown in the image above.

Biological Determinism

In Italy, Cesare Lombroso (1835–1909), known as the "father of criminology," began to study the cadavers of executed criminals in an effort to determine scientifically how criminals differed from noncriminals. His research soon convinced Lombroso that serious and violent offenders had inherited criminal traits. These "born criminals" suffered from "atavistic anomalies"; physically, they were throwbacks to more primitive times when people were savages and were believed to have large, thick skulls; large ears; enormous jaws; and a thick, protruding brow; along with "an absence of feelings of shame, honour or pity" common to carnivores and savages who devour raw flesh.[10] Lombroso's version of criminal anthropology was brought to North America via articles and textbooks that adopted his ideas.[11]

Although Lombroso's version of strict biological determinism is no longer taken seriously, some criminologists have recently linked crime and biological traits. Because they believe that social and environmental conditions also influence human behaviour, the term biosocial theory has been coined to reflect the assumed link between physical and social traits and their influence on behaviour.

biosocial theory
Approach to criminology that focuses on the interaction between biological and social factors as they relate to crime.

Sociological Criminology

At the same time that biological views were dominating criminology, another group of positivists was developing the field of sociology to study scientifically the major social changes that were taking place in 19th-century society. The foundations of sociological criminology can be traced to the work of pioneering sociologists L.A.J. (Adolphe) Quetelet (1796–1874) and (David) Emile Durkheim (1858–1917).[12]

Quetelet was a Belgian mathematician who (along with a Frenchman, Andre-Michel Guerry) used social statistics that were just being developed in Europe to investigate the influence of social factors on the propensity to commit crime. In addition to finding a strong influence of age and sex on crime, Quetelet uncovered evidence that season, climate, population composition, and poverty were also related to criminality.[13] He was one of the first criminologists to link crime rates to alcohol consumption.[14]

BASTIEN.   CHOFFRON.   LAUCERNE.   LEMESLE.

Early positivists believed that the shape of the skull was a key determinant of behaviour. These drawings from the 19th century illustrated "typical" criminally shaped heads.

Emile Durkheim (1858–1917)

According to Emile Durkheim, criminality was the result of cultural or societal forces as opposed to being rooted in the individual. He viewed crime as inevitable and even necessary because it is functionally useful in maintaining a healthy society. In part it does this by reaffirming boundaries between what is considered "good" and "bad" behaviour in society.[15] For example, society's response to crimes such as child abuse, impaired driving, domestic violence, and theft reinforces our concept of what is right and what is wrong. Moreover, the collective nature of society's response promotes social solidarity and cohesion. Crime is also a way to inject new ideas into society, preventing stagnation and encouraging adaptation.

In his famous book *The Division of Labor in Society*, Durkheim described the consequences of the shift from a small, rural society, which he labelled "mechanical," to the more modern "organic" society with a large urban population, division of labour, and personal isolation.[16] From the resulting structural changes flowed anomie, or norm and role confusion. An anomic society is in chaos, experiencing moral uncertainty and an accompanying loss of traditional values. People who suffer anomie may become confused and rebellious. Might the dawning of the "Internet age" create anomie in our own culture?

The Chicago School

The primacy of sociological positivism was secured by research begun in the early 20th century by Robert Ezra Park (1864–1944), Ernest W. Burgess (1886–1966), Louis Wirth (1897–1952), and their colleagues in the sociology department at the University of Chicago. The scholars who taught at this program created what is still referred to as the Chicago School in honour of their unique style of doing research.

These urban sociologists examined how neighbourhood conditions, such as poverty levels, influenced crime rates. They found that social forces operating in urban areas created a crime-promoting environment; some neighbourhoods were "natural areas" for crime.[17] In urban neighbourhoods with high levels of poverty, the fabric of critical social institutions, such as the school and the family, became undone. Their traditional ability to control behaviour was undermined, and the outcome was a high crime rate.

Chicago School sociologists argued that crime was not a function of personal traits or characteristics, but rather a reaction to an environment that was inadequate for proper human relations and development. Thus, they challenged the widely held belief that criminals were biologically or psychologically impaired or morally inferior. Instead, crime was

sociological criminology
Approach to criminology, based on the work of Quetelet and Durkheim, that focuses on the relationship between social factors and crime.

anomie
A lack of norms or clear social standards. Because of rapidly shifting moral values, the individual has few guides to what is socially acceptable or expected.

Chicago School
Group of urban sociologists who studied the relationship between environmental conditions and crime.

High poverty levels in a neighbourhood can influence crime rates.

Fighting in front of children can lead to children who are less able to trust and feel secure in the idea that their world and the authority figures in it will be stable and long lasting.

a social phenomenon and could be eradicated by improving social and economic conditions.

Socialization Views

During the 1930s and 1940s, another group of sociologists began conducting research that linked criminal behaviour to the quality of an individual's relationship to important social processes, such as education, family life, and peer relations. They found that children who grew up in homes wracked by conflict, attended inadequate schools, or associated with deviant peers became exposed to pro-crime forces. One position, championed by criminologist Edwin Sutherland, was that people learn criminal attitudes from older, more experienced law violators. Another view, developed by Chicago School sociologist Walter Reckless, was that crime occurs when children develop an inadequate self-image, which renders them incapable of controlling their own misbehaviour. Both of these views linked criminality to the failure of socialization—the interactions people have with the various individuals, organizations, institutions, and processes of society that help them mature and develop.

socialization
Process of human development and enculturation. Socialization is influenced by key social processes and institutions.

Conflict Criminology

In his *Communist Manifesto* and other writings, Karl Marx (1818–1883) had sown the seeds for a new approach in criminology.[18] Documenting the oppressive labour conditions prevalent during the rise of industrial capitalism, he was convinced that the character of every civilization is determined by its mode of production—the way its people develop and produce material goods. The most important relationship in industrial culture is between the owners of the means of production, the capitalist bourgeoisie, and the people who do the actual labour, the proletariat. The economic system controls all facets of human life; consequently, people's lives revolve around the means of production. The exploitation of the working class, he believed, would eventually lead to class conflict and the end of the capitalist system.

Although these writings laid the foundation for a Marxist criminology, it was not until the social and political upheaval of the 1960s, fuelled by the war in Vietnam, the civil rights movement, and the anti-establishment "hippie" counterculture, that conflict theory took hold. Young sociologists, interested in applying Marxist principles to the study of crime, began to analyze the social conditions that promoted class conflict and crime.

Karl Marx (1818–1883)

What emerged from this intellectual ferment was a Marxist-based radical criminology that indicted the economic system which produced the conditions that support a high crime rate. The Marxist tradition has played a significant role in criminology ever since.

LO3 Contemporary Criminology

These various schools of criminology, developed over 200 years, have been constantly evolving. Classical theory has evolved into modern rational choice theory, which argues that criminals are rational decision makers. They use available information to choose criminal or conventional behaviours, and their choice is structured by the fear of punishment. Lombrosian theory has evolved into contemporary biosocial and psychological views. Criminologists no longer believe that a single trait or inherited characteristic can explain crime, but some are convinced that biological and psychological traits interact with environmental factors to influence all human behaviour, including criminality. Biological and psychological theorists study the association between criminal behaviour and factors such as diet, hormonal makeup, personality, and intelligence. (See Figure 1.1.)

The original Chicago School vision has been updated in social structure theory, which maintains that the social environment directly controls criminal behaviour. According to this view, people at the bottom of the social structure, who cannot achieve success through conventional means, experience anomie, strain, failure, and frustration; they are the most likely to turn to criminal solutions to their problems. The social process view is also still prominent. Some theorists believe that children learn to commit crime by interacting with and modelling their behaviour after others they admire; others find that criminal offenders are people whose life experiences have shattered their social bonds to society.

The writings of Marx and his followers continue to be influential, and have given birth to a number of contemporary variants of conflict criminology, including feminist criminology and peacemaking criminology. The inherently unfair economic structure of advanced capitalist countries, such as Canada and the United States, is the engine that creates inequality and disadvantages among different social groups, and drives the crime rate.

conflict theory
The view that human behaviour is shaped by interpersonal conflict and that those who maintain social power will use it to further their own ends.

rational choice theory
The view that crime is a function of a decision-making process in which the potential offender weighs the potential costs and benefits of an illegal act.

social structure theory
The view that disadvantaged economic class position is a primary cause of crime.

CLASSICAL/ CHOICE PERSPECTIVE
Situational forces
Crime is a function of free will and personal choice. Punishment is a deterrent to crime.

BIOLOGICAL/ PSYCHOLOGICAL PERSPECTIVE
Internal forces
Crime is a function of chemical, neurological, genetic, personality, intelligence, or mental traits.

STRUCTURAL PERSPECTIVE
Ecological forces
Crime rates are a function of neighbourhood conditions, cultural forces, and norm conflict.

PROCESS PERSPECTIVE
Socialization forces
Crime is a function of upbringing, learning, and control. Peers, parents, and teachers influence behaviour.

CONFLICT PERSPECTIVE
Economic and political forces
Crime is a function of competition for limited resources and power. Class conflict produces crime.

INTEGRATED PERSPECTIVE
Multiple forces
Biological, social-psychological, economic, and political forces may combine to produce crime.

FIGURE 1.1

Criminology Perspectives

Some contemporary criminologists are now combining elements from each of these views into complex integrated theories of criminal career development. Each of the major perspectives is summarized in Figure 1.1.

LO4 What Criminologists Do: The Criminological Enterprise

Regardless of their background or training, criminologists are primarily interested in studying crime and criminal behaviour. Their professional training, occupational role, and income are derived from a scientific approach to the study and analysis of crime and criminal behaviour.

Several subareas exist within the broader arena of criminology. Taken together, they make up the criminological enterprise. Criminologists may specialize in a subarea in the same way that psychologists might specialize in a subfield of psychology, such as child development, perception, personality, psychopathology, or sexuality. Some of the more important criminological specialties are described in the following sections and summarized in Figure 1.2.

Criminal Statistics

The subarea of criminal statistics involves measuring the amount and trends of criminal activity. How much crime occurs annually? Who commits it? When and where does it occur? Which crimes are the most serious?

Criminologists interested in criminal statistics try to create **valid** and **reliable** measurements of criminal behaviour. For example, they create techniques to analyze the records of police and court agencies. They develop methods such as questionnaires to measure the percentage of people who actually commit crimes but escape detection by the justice system. They also develop techniques to identify the victims of crime: how many people are victims of crime and what percentage report crime to the police? The study of criminal statistics is one of the most crucial aspects of the criminological enterprise because without valid and reliable data sources, efforts to conduct research

valid
Actually measuring what one intends to measure; relevant.

reliable
Producing consistent results from one measurement to another.

SUBAREA	PRIMARY FOCUS
CRIMINAL STATISTICS	**Gathering valid crime data** Devising new research methods Measuring crime patterns and trends
SOCIOLOGY OF LAW	**Determining the origin of law** Measuring the social, historical, political, and economic factors that change laws and society
THEORY CONSTRUCTION	**Predicting individual behaviour** Understanding the cause of crime rates and trends
CRIMINAL BEHAVIOUR SYSTEMS	**Determining the nature and cause of specific crime patterns** Studying violence, theft, organized, white-collar, and public order crimes
PENOLOGY	**Studying the correction and control of criminal behaviour**
VICTIMOLOGY	**Studying the nature and cause of victimization** Aiding crime victims
PUBLIC CRIMINOLOGY	**Informing and educating the public and politicians about crime** Ensuring that decisions about crime and crime prevention are well-informed

FIGURE 1.2

The Criminological Enterprise

on crime and create criminological theories would be futile.

The Sociology of Law

The sociology of law is a subarea of criminology concerned with the role social forces play in shaping criminal law and the role of criminal law in shaping society. Criminologists study the history of legal thought in an effort to understand how criminal acts, such as theft, sexual assault, and murder, evolved into their present form.

Often criminologists are asked to join the debate when a new law is proposed to outlaw or control a particular behaviour. For example, in response to increasing demands from parents, teachers, and police, and against the backdrop of the tragic cyberbullying-related suicides of Amanda Todd and Rehtaeh Parsons, in November 2013 the attorney general of Canada introduced Bill C-13, the *Protecting Canadians from Online Crime Act*, designed to make it a criminal offence to distribute intimate images without consent, and to provide police with new legal powers to retrieve data from electronic transmissions (phone, Internet) when they have "reasonable grounds to suspect" that a crime may have been committed.[19] Though many parents, teachers and the police applauded the new bill, critics, including Amanda Todd's mother, argue that concerns about cyberbullying are being used to mask other provisions of the bill that would provide the police with broad new powers to request access to virtually any kind of electronic transmission data, including tax records, online business transactions, personal email and social media, even cell-phone and automobile GPS applications.[20] According to University of Ottawa criminologist Valerie Steeves, tougher laws are not the answer to dealing with cyberbullying, and she argues that increased police surveillance will be perceived by kids as "a profound lack of trust on the part of adults" and that "overzealous adults may 're-define' many of their day to-day communications as bullying."[21] According to Michael Spratt of the Canadian Criminal Lawyers' Association, "Bill C-13 … represents a dangerous and in our opinion unconstitutional pattern of erosion of privacy.[22] Criminologists also participate actively in updating the content of criminal law, helping lawmakers respond to changing times and conditions. For instance, computer fraud, cyberbullying, theft from automated teller machines, Internet scams, identity theft, copyright issues related to downloading music and videos from the Internet, distribution of child pornography over the Internet, and trafficking in human organs are behaviours that did not exist when criminal law was originally conceived. The law

A 35-year-old Dutch man was charged with enticing a Grade 7 student into exposing her breasts online, then distributing the images, which were used by others to bully and threaten the young teen.[23]

must be constantly revised to reflect cultural, societal, and technological adaptations of common acts.

For example, in December 2013, in a unanimous decision, the Supreme Court struck down Canada's prostitution laws, accepting the argument made by three sex trade workers that the laws violated their rights to safety and security under s.7 of the *Charter of Rights and Freedoms*. The court gave the government one year to rewrite the prostitution laws in a way that did not violate the *Charter*. In June 2014 the Harper government introduced Bill C-36 making the purchase or communication to purchase the services of a sex worker a criminal offence, along with making it illegal to advertise sex services in either media or verbally in a public place. While winning support from Tory MP's, REAL Women of Canada and some police officials, sex trade workers and constitutional rights advocates argue the new law will make sex work even more dangerous, as prostitutes are forced to come up with more devious and secretive ways to protect clients from police scrutiny.[24] Simon Fraser University criminologist John Lowman agrees, and notes that the last time this approach to aggressively targeting johns was tried, in the Downtown Eastside neighbourhood of Vancouver, "that area became the killing fields of Vancouver. Where Mr. [Robert] Pickton picked up most of the 49 victims that we think he is responsible for murdering."[25] Criminologists can help make the determination when a law should be changed, updated, or eliminated.

Developing Theories of Crime Causation

From the beginning, criminologists have wondered why people engage in criminal acts even though

Edwin Sutherland (1883–1950) graduated from the University of Chicago in 1913 with a PhD in Sociology and Political Economy. In 1924, Sutherland published one of the first textbooks in American criminology, but is best remembered for his "differential association theory" of crime, which was first unveiled in *Principles of Criminology* in 1939. Sutherland argued that pro-criminal attitudes and criminal behaviours are learned in the same way we learn anything: from others around us. Differential association theory is the foundation of contemporary social learning theories of criminal behaviour, and of correctional treatment practice.

Edwin Sutherland (1883–1950)

---

their behaviour may result in harsh punishment and social disapproval. Some criminologists with a psychological orientation view crime as a function of personality, development, social learning, or cognition. Others investigate the biological correlates of antisocial behaviour and study the biochemical, genetic, and neurological linkages to crime. Sociologists look at the social forces producing criminal behaviour, including neighbourhood conditions, poverty, socialization, and group interaction.

Understanding the true cause of crime remains a difficult problem. Criminologists are still unsure why, given similar conditions, some people choose criminal solutions to their problems while others conform to accepted social rules of behaviour.

Understanding and Describing Criminal Behaviour

Another subarea of criminology involves research on specific criminal types and patterns: violent crime, theft crime, public order crime, organized crime, cybercrime, and so on. Numerous attempts have been made to describe and understand particular crime types. Marvin Wolfgang's famous 1958 study, *Patterns in Criminal Homicide*, is considered a landmark analysis of the nature of homicide and the relationship between victim and offender.[26] Edwin's analysis of business-related offences helped coin a new phrase, white-collar crime, to describe economic crime activities of the affluent.

Penology

The study of penology involves the correction and control of known criminal offenders. Some criminologists are advocates of rehabilitation; they direct their efforts at identifying effective treatment strategies for individuals convicted of law violations. Others argue that crime can be prevented only through a strict policy of social control; they advocate measures such as capital punishment and mandatory sentences. Criminologists also help evaluate correctional initiatives in both institutional and community correctional settings to determine if they are effective and how they impact people's lives.

Victimology

Criminologists recognize the critical role of the victim in the criminal process and that the victim's behaviour is often a key determinant of crime.[27] Victimology includes the following areas of interest:

- Using victim surveys to measure the nature and extent of criminal behaviour and calculate the actual costs of crime to victims
- Calculating probabilities of victimization risk

---

white-collar crime
Illegal acts that capitalize on a person's status in the marketplace. White-collar crimes may include theft, embezzlement, fraud, market manipulation, price fixing, and false advertising.

penology
Subarea of criminology that focuses on the correction and control of criminal offenders.

rehabilitation
Treatment of criminal offenders aimed at preventing future criminal behaviour.

capital punishment
The execution of criminal offenders; the death penalty.

mandatory sentences
A statutory requirement that a certain penalty shall be carried out in all cases of conviction for a specified offence.

victimology
The study of the victim's role in criminal events.

- Studying victim culpability in the precipitation of crime
- Designing services for crime victims, such as counselling, compensation, and restorative justice programs

Victimology has taken on greater importance as more criminologists focus attention on the victim's role in the criminal event.

Public Criminology

In response to public misinformation and misunderstandings about crime and crime prevention, a "public criminology" has developed, where criminologists take on an active role in communicating directly with the public through public presentations and the mass media and social media. The goal of a public criminology is to make sure that the public and politicians are well informed when making decisions about responding to crime.[28]

TABLE 1.1

John Hagan's Breakdown of Deviance and Crime

Kind of Deviance	Severity of Social Response	Perceived Harmfulness	Degree of Agreement	Examples
Consensus crimes	Severe	Extremely harmful	Consensus	Homicide; incest
Conflict crimes	Punitive	Somewhat harmful	Conflict	Drugs; prostitution; gambling
Social deviations	Indeterminate	Potentially harmful	Uncertainty	Mental illness; delinquency
Social diversions	Mild	Relatively harmless	Apathy	Fads and fashions

Source: From HAGEDOR. *Sociology 4/E.* © 1990 Nelson Education Ltd. Reproduced by permission. www.cengage.com/permissions

LO5 Deviant or Criminal—How Criminologists Define Crime

Criminologists devote themselves to measuring, understanding, and controlling crime and deviance. How are these behaviours defined, and how do we distinguish between them?

Criminologists view deviant behaviour as any action that departs from the social norms of society.[29] Deviance thus includes a broad spectrum of behaviours, ranging from the most socially harmful, such as rape and murder, to the relatively inoffensive, such as body modification or cross-dressing. A deviant act becomes a crime when it is deemed socially harmful or dangerous; it then will be specifically defined, prohibited, and punished under criminal law.

Criminologist John Hagan developed a useful breakdown for understanding the relationship between deviance and crime (see Table 1.1).[30] Some kinds of behaviours or practices, such as body tattooing and piercing, may be unusual, but are viewed by most of us as relatively harmless; this is an example of what Hagan calls a "social diversion." Other kinds of deviant behaviour, perhaps resulting from mental illness, may be seen as potentially more threatening or dangerous to the public, and so bring forth a stronger societal response such as commitment to a hospital, or community supervision; Hagan terms this type of deviance "social deviation." "Conflict crimes" are kinds of deviance that a society has defined in law as criminal, but there is still not a lot of agreement about whether these acts are really criminal; marijuana use is a good example. Finally, some kinds of deviance virtually everyone agrees are wrong, cause severe harm, and are criminal; Hagen calls these acts, such as child abuse or murder, "consensus crimes."

Hagan points out that what is considered deviant or criminal can change over time and can be culturally specific; for example, running lottery games (like the Irish Sweepstakes) used to be illegal in Canada (a conflict crime), but such a practice is now considered, at worst, a social diversion, and same-sex relationships are still considered illegal in some countries while in Canada they are not.

deviance
Behaviour that departs from the social norm but is not necessarily criminal.

crime
An act, deemed socially harmful or dangerous, that is specifically defined, prohibited, and punished under criminal law.

Colorado and Washington legalized sales of marijuana for recreational use in 2014. More than two-thirds of Canadians say our marijuana laws should be "softened"; nearly 40 percent say its use should be legalized.[31]

Charles Knowles/Shutterstock.com

Photo courtesy of John Hagan

John Hagan, one of the best known criminologists in the world, graduated from the University of Alberta in 1974 with a PhD in Sociology. He is a member of the Royal Society of Canada (1988), and between 1974 and 2004 taught sociology, criminology, and law at the University of Toronto, where he was appointed Professor Emeritus of Law and Sociology in 2004.

In a May 1990 article in the *Canadian Review of Sociology and Anthropology*, Dr. Hagan first revealed his ground-breaking "power-control theory" of crime, which has become a major focus of theory and research in modern criminology. Later, in *Crime and Disrepute* (1994),

John Hagan

Hagan developed a framework for understanding different kinds of deviance, ranging from "social deviations" through "consensus crimes." A recipient of many international awards and honours, Dr. Hagan has published more than 20 books and numerous articles in the field of criminology. In 2009 Dr. Hagan was awarded the prestigious Stockholm Prize in Criminology.

Dr. Hagan is currently John D. MacArthur Professor of Sociology and Law at Northwestern University in Chicago.

Criminologists are often concerned with the concept of deviance and its relationship to criminality. The shifting definition of deviant behaviour is closely associated with our concepts of crime: Where should society draw the line between behaviour that is merely considered deviant and unusual, and behaviour that is considered dangerous and criminal? For example, when does sexually oriented material stop being merely erotic and suggestive (deviant) and become obscene and pornographic (criminal)? Can a clear line be drawn separating sexually oriented materials into two groups, one that is legally acceptable and a second that is considered depraved or obscene? And if such a line can be drawn, who gets to draw it?

Though crimes may be defined as acts that are socially harmful or dangerous, criminologists still differ over what acts are truly "harmful" and who decides that they are "dangerous." As you may recall, professional criminologists usually align themselves with one of several schools of thought or perspectives. Each of these perspectives maintains its own view of what constitutes criminal behaviour and what causes people to engage in criminality. A criminologist's choice of orientation or perspective thus depends, in part, on his or her definition of crime.

consensus view
The belief that the majority of citizens in a society share common values and agree on what behaviours should be defined as criminal.

criminal law
The written code that defines crimes and their punishments.

conflict view
The belief that criminal behaviour is defined by those in a position of power to protect and advance their own self-interest.

The three most common concepts of crime used by criminologists are the consensus view, the conflict view, and the interactionist view.

The Consensus View of Crime

According to the consensus view, crimes are behaviours that all elements of society consider to be repugnant. The rich and powerful as well as the poor and indigent are believed to agree on which behaviours are so repugnant that they should be outlawed and criminalized. Therefore, criminal law—the written code that defines crimes and their punishments—reflects the values, beliefs, and opinions of society's majority. The term *consensus* implies general agreement among a majority of citizens on what behaviours should be prohibited by criminal law and hence be viewed as crimes.[32]

This approach to crime implies that it is a function of the beliefs, morality, and rules that are inherent in Western civilization. Ideally, the laws apply equally to all members of society regardless of wealth, social status, or power.

The Conflict View of Crime

The conflict view depicts society as a collection of diverse groups—such as owners, workers, professionals, and students—who are in constant and continuing conflict. Groups able to assert their political power use the law and the criminal justice system to advance their economic and social position. Criminal laws, therefore, are viewed as acts created to protect the haves from the have-nots. Conflict

In the 2007 Hollywood film *The Brave One* Jodie Foster plays Erica Bain, a young woman who witnesses her fiancée murdered by three violent thugs. Traumatized and seeking vengeance, Erica buys a handgun illegally. Then, while shopping at a convenience store, Erica is caught up in the midst of an attempted robbery, and uses her gun to kill the robber. What follows is a series of vigilante killings by Erica of thugs and pimps who cross her path, all while she searches for her fiancée's killers. Befriending the police detective investigating her fiancée's case, who comes to suspect Erica in the vigilante killings, the film culminates in a violent confrontation in which Erica kills two of the men responsible for her fiancée's murder, and is about to kill the third when the detective convinces her to put down her pistol—and instead gives her his own weapon to finish the execution—in order make it look like he confronted the killers who will also be made out to be responsible for the vigilante killings.

Though movie-goers applaud the actions of the Jodie Foster character, criminologists and criminal justice professionals are concerned about the popularity of movies like *The Brave One* that appear to promote taking the law into your own hands. Criminologists point that the promotion of vigilantism runs counter to one of the most basic principles of our legal system, that crimes are offences against the State (not the individual victim), and only the State has the right to punish the offender. Both Beccaria and Durkheim, and our own Parliament of Canada for that matter, observe that another basic principle of our legal system is that no one is above the law—the law applies equally to everyone, regardless of their position—and that it is critical for social stability that the rule of law be obeyed by all, and that there be confidence that the law will prevail.

---

criminologists often contrast the harsh penalties exacted on the poor for their "street crimes" (break and enter, robbery, and theft) with the minor penalties the wealthy receive for their white-collar crimes (securities violations and other illegal business practices). Although the poor go to prison for minor law violations, the wealthy are given lenient sentences for even the most serious breaches of law.

According to the conflict view, the definition of crime is controlled by wealth, power, and position and not by moral consensus or the fear of social disruption.[33] Crime, according to this definition, is a political concept designed to protect the power and position of the upper classes at the expense of the poor. Even laws prohibiting violent acts, such as robbery, sexual assault, and murder, may have political undertones. Banning violent acts ensures domestic tranquility and guarantees that the anger of the poor and disenfranchised classes will not be directed at their wealthy capitalist exploiters. Spousal assault may be inspired by the capitalist system's devaluation of women, which may increase their vulnerability to this act. The conflict view of crime, then, includes the following in a comprehensive list of "real" crimes:[34]

- Violations of human rights due to racism, sexism, and imperialism
- Unsafe working conditions
- Inadequate child care
- Inadequate opportunities for employment and education and substandard housing and medical care
- Crimes of economic and political domination
- Pollution of the environment
- Price-fixing
- Police brutality
- Assassinations and war making
- Violations of human dignity
- Denial of physical needs and necessities, and impediments to self-determination
- Deprivation of adequate food and blocked opportunities to participate in political decision making*

> **interactionist view**
> The belief that those with social power are able to impose their values on society as a whole, and these values then define criminal behaviour.

The Interactionist View of Crime

According to the interactionist view, the definition of crime reflects the preferences and opinions of people who hold social power in a particular legal

---

*Reprinted with the permission of The Free Press, a Division of Simon & Schuster, Inc., from *Outsiders: Studies in the Sociology of Deviance* by Howard S. Becker. Copyright © 1963 by The Free Press. Copyright (c) renewed 1991 by Howard S. Becker. All rights reserved.

jurisdiction. These people use their influence to impose their definition of right and wrong on the rest of the population. Criminals are individuals that society labels as outcasts or deviants because they have violated social rules. In a classic statement, sociologist Howard Becker argued, "The deviant is one to whom that label has successfully been applied; deviant behaviour is behaviour people so label."[35] Crimes are outlawed behaviours because society defines them that way, not because they are inherently evil or immoral acts.

The interactionist view of crime is similar to the conflict perspective in that behaviour is outlawed when it offends those with sufficient social, economic, and political power to make the law conform to their interests or needs. However, unlike the conflict view, the interactionist perspective does not attribute capitalist economic and political motives to the process of defining crime. Instead, interactionists see criminal law as conforming to the beliefs of "moral crusaders" or moral entrepreneurs, who use their influence to shape the legal process as they see fit.[36] Laws against pornography, prostitution, and drugs are believed to be motivated more by moral crusades than by capitalist sensibilities. Consequently, interactionists are concerned with shifting moral and legal standards.

A Definition of Crime

The definition of crime affects how criminologists view the cause and control of illegal behaviour and shapes their research orientation. Because of their diverse perspectives, criminologists have taken a variety of approaches in explaining crime's causes and suggesting methods for its control (see Figure 1.3). Considering these differences, we can take elements from each school of thought to formulate an integrated definition of crime such as the following:

> Crime is a violation of societal rules of behaviour as interpreted and expressed by the criminal law, which reflects public opinion, traditional values, and the viewpoint of people currently holding social and political power. Individuals who violate these rules are subject to sanctions by state authority, social stigma, and loss of status.

This definition combines the consensus view that criminal law defines crimes, the conflict perspective's emphasis on political power and control, and the interactionist concept of stigma. Thus, crime as defined here is a political, social, and economic function of modern life.

No matter which definition of crime we embrace, criminal behaviour is tied to criminal law. It is therefore important for all criminologists to have some understanding of the development of criminal law, its objectives, its elements, and how it evolves.

FIGURE 1.3

The Definition of Crime

Consensus view
- The law defines crime.
- Agreement exists on outlawed behaviour.
- Laws apply to all citizens equally.

Conflict view
- The law is a tool of the ruling class.
- Crime is a politically defined concept.
- "Real crimes" are not outlawed.
- The law is used to control the underclass.

DEFINITION OF CRIME

Interactionist view
- Moral entrepreneurs define crime.
- Crimes are illegal because society defines them that way.
- Criminal labels are life-transforming events.

Crime and Criminal Law

The concept of criminal law has been recognized for more than 3000 years. Hammurabi (1792–1750 B.C.), the sixth king of Babylon, created the most famous set of written laws of the ancient world, known today as the Code of Hammurabi. Preserved on basalt rock columns, the code established a system of crime and punishment based on physical retaliation ("an eye for an eye"). The severity of punishment depended on class standing: If convicted of an unprovoked assault, a slave would be killed, whereas a free person might lose a limb.

More familiar is the Mosaic Code of the Israelites (1200 B.C.). According to tradition, God entered into a covenant or contract with the tribes of Israel in which they agreed to obey his law (the 613 laws of the Old Testament, including the Ten Commandments), as presented to them by Moses, in return for God's special care and protection. The Mosaic Code is not only the foundation of Judeo-Christian moral teachings but also a basis for the Canadian legal system. Prohibitions against murder, theft, and perjury preceded, by several thousand years, the same laws found in Canada today.

Though ancient formal legal codes were lost during the Dark Ages, early German and Anglo-Saxon societies developed legal systems featuring monetary compensation for criminal violations. Guilt was determined by two methods. One was compurgation, in which the accused person swore an oath of innocence with the backing of 12 to 25 oath helpers, who would attest to his or her character and claims of innocence. The second was trial by ordeal, which was based on the principle that divine forces would not allow an innocent person to be harmed. It involved measures such as having the accused place his or her hand in boiling water or hold a hot iron. If the wound healed, the person was found innocent; if the wound did not heal, the accused was deemed guilty. Another version, trial by combat, allowed the accused to challenge the accuser to a duel, with the outcome determining the legitimacy of the accusation. Punishments included public flogging, branding, beheading, and burning.

LO6 Common Law

After the Norman conquest of England by William the Conqueror in 1066, royal judges began to travel throughout the land, holding court in each county several times a year. When court was in session, the royal administrator, or judge, would summon a number of citizens who would, on their oath, tell of the crimes and serious breaches of the peace that had occurred since the judge's last visit. The royal judge would then decide what to do in each case, using local custom and rules of conduct as his guide. Courts were bound to follow the law established in previous cases unless a higher authority, such as the king or the pope, overruled the law.

The present English system of law came into existence during the reign of Henry II (1154–1189), when royal judges began to publish their decisions in local cases. Judges began to use these written decisions as a basis for their decision making, and eventually a fixed body of legal rules and principles was established. If a new rule was successfully applied in a number of different cases, it would become a precedent. These precedents would then be commonly applied in all similar cases—hence the term common law. Crimes such as murder, break and enter, arson, and sexual assault are common-law crimes whose elements were initially defined by judges. They are referred to as *mala in se*, or inherently evil and depraved. When the situation required, the English Parliament enacted legislation to supplement the judge-made common law. Crimes defined by Parliament, which reflected existing social conditions, were referred to as *mala prohibitum*, or statutory crimes.

Canada inherited English common law and standardized crimes such as murder, break and enter, arson, and sexual assault by putting them in statutory form in *Criminal Code*. As in England, whenever common law proved inadequate to deal with changing social and moral issues, the Canadian Parliament supplemented it with legislative statutes, creating new sections of the *Criminal Code*. Table 1.2 lists a number of crimes that were first defined in common law.

Contemporary Criminal Law

Under Canadian law there are two main types of criminal offences: summary conviction and indictable. The distinction is based on seriousness. Summary conviction offences are the least serious and include crimes like causing a disturbance of the peace, theft under $5000, and fraudulently obtaining transportation. The maximum penalty for a summary conviction

---

Code of Hammurabi
The first written *Criminal Code*, developed in Babylonia about 1780 B.C.

Mosaic Code
The laws of the ancient Israelites, found in the Old Testament of the Judeo-Christian Bible.

precedent
A rule derived from previous judicial decisions and applied to future cases; the basis of common law.

common law
Early English law, developed by judges, that became the standardized law of the land in England and eventually formed the basis of criminal law in Canada.

statutory crimes
Crimes defined by legislative bodies in response to changing social conditions, public opinion, and custom.

summary conviction offence
A minor offence punishable by a fine of up to $5000, six months in jail, or both.

TABLE 1.2

Common-Law Crimes

Crimes	Examples
Crimes Against the Person	
First-degree murder. Unlawful killing of another human being that is planned and deliberate.	A woman buys some poison and pours it into a cup of coffee her husband is drinking, intending to kill him. The motive—to get the insurance benefits of the victim.
Manslaughter. Unlawful killing of another human being committed in the heat of passion caused by sudden provocation.	A man, taunted in front of his co-workers by the man who is having an affair with his wife, grabs an iron bar and uses it to beat and kill his wife's lover.
Infanticide. Unlawful killing of her newly born child by a female person who, at the time, is not fully recovered from the effects of giving birth or the effect of lactation, and whose mind is thereby disturbed.	A new mother, suffering from a severe postpartum depression and fearful she may physically hurt her three-week-old baby, drowns the infant in the bathtub, in the belief that the baby will return to God and be safe from any harm the mother might do.
Assault. Threat of or actual use of force against another without his or her consent.	Leaving a bar at closing time after a night of drinking, a university student accuses his girlfriend of flirting with other men, and slaps her in the face.
Sexual assault. An assault of a sexual nature against another without his or her consent.	After a party a man offers to drive a young female acquaintance home. He takes her to a wooded area and, despite her protests, forces her to perform oral sex on him.
Robbery. Use of violence or the threat of violence to steal from a person or property.	A man armed with a hunting knife enters a gas bar and demands that the attendant hand over all the cash in the till.
Inchoate (Incomplete) Offences	
Attempt. An intentional act or omission for the purpose of committing a crime that is more than mere preparation or planning of the crime. The crime is not completed, however.	A person intending to kill another person places a bomb in the intended victim's car so that it will detonate when the ignition key is turned. The bomb is discovered before the car is started. Attempted murder has been committed.
Conspiracy. Voluntary agreement between two or more persons to undertake to commit an indictable offence.	Two men meet and, on paper, draw out a plan and a list of materials necessary to kidnap an elderly woman. The two are guilty of conspiracy.
Crimes Against Property	
Break and enter. To break in and enter a place with the intent to commit an indictable offence.	Intending to steal a DVD player and any other easy-to-carry electronic equipment, a young man breaks a window and enters another's house.
Arson. Intentional or reckless damage by fire or explosion of another's property.	A man, upset that his boss did not give him a raise, goes to his boss's house and sets fire to it.
Theft. Without permission or right, to take or convert to one's own use property that belongs to another person.	While in the bookstore, a young woman spots a book she wants, but she doesn't have enough money to purchase it, so she slips it into her purse and walks out of the store.

is six months in jail and/or a fine of $5000, though there are a few exceptions, like the crime of assault where the maximum time in jail is 18 months. Indictable offences are the most serious, and include crimes like theft over $5000, robbery, aggravated sexual assault, and murder. Indictable offences are more severely punished, with maximum prison terms ranging from two years to life, and many indictable offences carry mandatory minimum sentences, like sexual assault with a weapon, which carries a minimum sentence of four years imprisonment. For a third category of offences, hybrid offences like forcible confinement of a person, public incitement of hatred, mischief over $5000, or possession of more than 30 grams of marijuana, the prosecuting Crown Attorney will decide, based on the facts, whether to try the case as a summary conviction offence with a less serious penalty, or an indictable offence with a serious penalty.[37]

Regardless of their classification, acts prohibited by criminal law constitute behaviours considered unacceptable and impermissible by those in power. People who engage in these acts are eligible for severe sanctions. By outlawing these

indictable offence
A serious offence punishable with maximum prison terms ranging from two years to life.

hybrid offence
An offence where the crown attorney decides whether to try the case as a more minor summary conviction offence, or a more serious indictable offence.

behaviours, a society expects to achieve a number of social goals:

- *Enforcing social control.* Those who hold political power rely on criminal law to formally prohibit behaviours believed to threaten societal well-being or to challenge their authority. For example, Canadian law incorporates centuries-old prohibitions against the following behaviours harmful to others: taking another person's possessions, physically harming another person, damaging another person's property, and cheating another person out of his or her possessions. Similarly, the law prevents actions that challenge the legitimacy of the government, such as planning its overthrow, collaborating with its enemies, and so on.

- *Discouraging revenge.* By punishing people who infringe on the rights, property, and freedom of others, the law shifts the burden of revenge from the individual to the state. This principle of law dates from the Norman conquest of England in 1066, and the idea that, since the king owns all of England and everything in it including its people, all offences are offences against the "king's peace," and punishment of the offence is therefore the right only of the king. Today, prosecutors in criminal trials are referred to as crown attorneys to reflect the role they traditionally played as representatives of the monarch. Although state retaliation may offend the sensibilities of many citizens, it is greatly preferable to a system in which people would have to seek justice for themselves.

- *Expressing public opinion and morality.* Criminal law reflects constantly changing public opinions and moral values. *Mala in se,* or inherently evil and depraved crimes such as murder and sexual assault, are almost universally prohibited; however, the prohibition of legislatively created *mala prohibitum,* or statutory crimes such as traffic offences and gambling violations, changes according to social conditions and attitudes. Criminal law is used to codify these changes.

- *Deterring criminal behaviour.* Criminal law has a social control function. It can control, restrain, and direct human behaviour through its sanctioning power. The threat of punishment associated with violating the law is designed to prevent crimes before they occur. During the Middle Ages, public executions drove this point home. Today criminal law's impact is felt through news accounts of long prison sentences.

- *Punishing wrongdoing.* The deterrent power of criminal law is tied to the authority it gives the state to sanction or punish offenders. Those who violate criminal law are subject to physical coercion and punishment.

- *Maintaining social order.* All legal systems are designed to support and maintain the boundaries of the social system they serve. In medieval England, the law protected the feudal system by defining an orderly system of property transfer and ownership. Laws in some socialist nations protect the primacy of the state by strictly curtailing profiteering and individual enterprise. Our own capitalist system is also supported and sustained by criminal law. In a sense, the content of criminal law is more a reflection of the needs of those who control the existing economic and political system than a representation of some idealized moral code.

LO7 The Elements of a Crime

In order for a crime to occur, the state must show that the accused committed the guilty act, or *actus reus,* and had the *mens rea,* or criminal intent, to commit the act. The *actus reus* may be an aggressive act, such as taking someone's money, burning a building, or shooting someone; or it may be a failure to act when there is a legal duty to do so, such as a parent's neglecting to seek medical attention for a sick child. The *mens rea* (guilty mind) refers to an individual's state of mind at the time of the act or, more specifically, the person's intent to commit the crime.

actus reus
An illegal or "guilty" act. It may be an affirmative act, such as killing, or a failure to act when legally required to do so.

mens rea
A "guilty mind"; the intent to commit a criminal act.

For most crimes, both the *actus reus* and the *mens rea* must be present for the act to be considered a crime. For example, if Denise decides to kill Carl and then takes a gun and shoots Carl, Denise can be convicted of the crime of murder, because both elements are present. Denise's shooting of Carl is the *actus reus;* her decision to kill Carl is the *mens rea.* However, if Denise only thinks about shooting Carl but does nothing about it, the element of *actus reus* is absent, and no crime has been committed. Thoughts of committing an act do not, in themselves, constitute a crime. Let us now look more closely at these issues.

Actus Reus

To satisfy the requirements of *actus reus,* guilty actions must be voluntary. Even though an act may cause harm or damage, it is not considered a crime if it was done by accident or was an involuntary act. For example, it would not be a crime if a motorist obeying all the traffic laws hit a child who had run into the street. If the same motorist were drinking or speeding, then this action would be considered a crime because it was a product of negligence. Similarly, it would not be considered a crime if a babysitter accidentally dropped a child and the child died. However, it would be considered manslaughter if the sitter threw the child down in anger or frustration and the blow caused the child's death. In some circumstances of *actus reus,* the use of words is considered criminal. For example, according to the Canadian *Criminal Code* (R.S. 1985), if a person makes a speech or distributes literature that incites hatred against an "identifiable" group distinguished by colour, race, religion, or ethnic origin, that person is guilty of an illegal act, punishable by up to two years in prison.[38]

Typically, the law does not require people to aid people in distress, such as entering a burning building to rescue people trapped by a fire. However, failure to act is considered a crime in certain instances:

1. *Relationship of the parties based on status.* Some people are bound by relationship to give aid. These relationships include parent–child and husband–wife. If a husband finds his wife

In November 2007, Dennis Robert White, 30, was found guilty of second degree murder in the shooting death of artist/skateboarder Lee Matasi, 23, outside a Vancouver nightclub in the early morning hours of December 3, 2005. Witnesses described how White angrily confronted Matasi outside the nightclub, pushing him and hitting him in the head with a handgun. A physical struggle ensued, during which the firearm discharged into the air, and then fell or was knocked to the ground. White retrieved the handgun and shot Matasi in the chest—though witnesses, most of whom were intoxicated at the time—gave contradictory evidence as to whether Matasi was standing, or sitting on the ground as the Crown claimed, when he was shot. White fled the scene, but was arrested shortly thereafter by police. In June 2009, White appealed the conviction and life sentence, arguing that the trial judge had erred in allowing the jury to consider his running from the scene as evidence of intent to cause murder, and the jury should have been instructed to also consider a conviction for manslaughter, which is the unplanned, unintentional homicide of another, and carries a lesser penalty. The B.C. Court of Appeal rejected White's argument, ruling that although the trial judge's charge to the jury was incomplete, White's flight from the scene "was of little significance" given the other facts of the case. White appealed the case to the Supreme Court of Canada, but in a March 2011 decision the Supreme Court upheld the B.C. Court of Appeal ruling, finding that post-offence conduct can be taken to be evidence of intent when the jury is properly cautioned to interpret it in the context of the other facts of the case and especially in the White case, where the accused apparently showed no hesitation before fleeing the scene.[39]

unconscious because she took an overdose of sleeping pills, he is obligated to try to save her life by seeking medical aid. If he fails to do so and she dies, he can be held responsible for her death.

2. *Imposition by statute.* Some laws require that any adult must provide assistance by reporting suspected physical, sexual, or emotional abuse of a child.

3. *Contractual relationships.* These relationships include lifeguard and swimmer, doctor and patient, and babysitter and child. Because lifeguards have been hired to ensure the safety of swimmers, they have a legal duty to come to the aid of drowning persons. If a lifeguard knows a swimmer is in danger and does nothing about it and the swimmer drowns, the lifeguard is legally responsible for the swimmer's death.

Mens Rea

In most situations, for an act to constitute a crime, it must be done with criminal intent, or *mens rea*. Intent, in the legal sense, can mean carrying out an act intentionally, knowingly, and willingly. However, the definition also encompasses situations in which recklessness or negligence establishes the required criminal intent.

Criminal intent also exists if the results of an action, although originally unintended,, are certain to occur. For example, when the Tsarnaen brothers planted a bomb at the finish line of the 2013 Boston Marathon, they did not intend to kill any particular person. Yet the law would hold that the brothers or any other person would be substantially certain that people in the surrounding area would be killed in the blast, and the Tsarnaens therefore had the criminal intent to commit murder and terrorism.[40]

Absolute Liability

Though common-law crimes require that both the *actus reus* and the *mens rea* must be present before a person can be convicted of a crime, several crimes defined by statute do not require *mens rea*. In these cases, the person accused is guilty simply by doing what the statute prohibits; intent does not enter the picture. These absolute liability crimes, or public welfare offences, include violations of health and safety regulations, traffic laws, and hunting or fishing out of season. For example, a person stopped for speeding is guilty of breaking the traffic laws regardless of whether he or she intended to go over the speed limit or did it by accident. The underlying purpose of these laws is to protect the public; therefore, intent is not required.[41]

Criminal Defences

When people defend themselves against criminal charges, they must refute one or more of the elements of the crime of which they have been accused. A number of different approaches can be taken to create this defence.

First, defendants may deny the *actus reus* by arguing that they were falsely accused and that the real culprit has yet to be identified. Second, defendants may claim that although they engaged in the criminal act of which they are accused, they lacked the *mens rea* (intent) needed to be found guilty of the crime.

If a person whose mental state is impaired commits a criminal act, it is possible for the person to excuse his or her criminal actions by claiming that he or she lacked the capacity to form sufficient intent to be held criminally responsible. Mental disorder, automatism, intoxication, and ignorance are types of excuse defences. For example, the defence of automatism was successfully used in the *Joudrie* (1996) case. Dorothy Joudrie claimed to be in a state of automatism when she shot her husband Earl Joudrie, chairman of the board of Canadian Tire and Gulf Canada Resources, six times. The Calgary court accepted the argument by Dorothy Joudrie's lawyers that she was not criminally responsible for the murders.[42]

Another type of defence is justification. Here the individual usually admits committing the criminal act but maintains that he or she should not be held criminally liable because the act was justified. Among the justification defences are necessity, duress, self-defence, and entrapment. For example, in *R. v. Ruzic* (1998),[43] the accused (Ruzic) used the defence of duress, claiming she smuggled two kilograms of heroin into Canada because she had been told by a man that if she didn't do it her elderly mother living in Belgrade would be beaten up or even killed. On appeal, first to the Ontario Court of Appeal (1998) and then to the Supreme Court of Canada (2001), Ruzic's acquittal was upheld.

Persons standing trial for criminal offences may thus defend themselves by claiming that they did not commit the act in question, that their actions were justified under the circumstances, or that their behaviour can be excused by their lack of *mens rea*. If either the physical or mental elements of a crime cannot be proven, then the defendant cannot be convicted.

In recent years, Canadian defence lawyers have tried to convince the courts that some women accused of the murder of their male partners may have been acting out of self-defence after having suffered years of emotional or physical abuse. The accompanying Policy and Practice in Criminology feature discusses the "battered woman" defence in detail.

The Evolution of Criminal Law

Criminal law is constantly evolving in an effort to reflect changing circumstances in society. For example, in response to the September 11, 2001, terrorist attacks in the United States, the Canadian government introduced the *Anti-Terrorism Act* (Bill C-41)

Canada's growing population of seniors is an increasingly frequent target of telephone scams, theft, cheque forgery, breach of trust, and violent crime.

to amend the *Criminal Code* so that terrorist groups could be more easily identified and investigated, through the use of electronic surveillance, suspected terrorists and their associates could be detained for up to 72 hours without charge, and individuals who have knowledge about the activities of a terrorist group would be required to report that knowledge to authorities.[44]

Similarly, after public calls for more accountability for crimes committed against senior citizens who are often uniquely vulnerable to being victimized, in 2012 the Government of Canada enacted the provisions of Bill C-36, the *Protecting Canada's Seniors Act*, designed to introduced the victim's age, personal circumstances, and health and financial situation as aggravating circumstances to be considered by judges in sentencing.

Sometimes legal changes are prompted by highly publicized cases that generate fear and concern. For example, a number of highly publicized cases of criminal harassment or "stalking" (including the murder of Arlene May in Toronto in 1996) prompted the Canadian government to amend the *Criminal Code* in 1997 and again in 2002 to implement penalties of up to ten years in prison for engaging in stalking behaviour.[45]

absolute liability crimes
Illegal acts in which guilt does not depend on intent, or *mens rea*. They are usually acts that endanger the public welfare, such as violations of health and safety regulations.

excuse defence
Criminal defence based on a lack of criminal intent (*mens rea*). Excuse defences include mental disorder, automatism, intoxication, and ignorance.

justification defence
Criminal defence that claims an illegal action was justified by circumstances and therefore not criminal. Justification defences include necessity, duress, self-defence, and entrapment.

A LANDMARK CASE: THE "BATTERED WOMAN" DEFENCE

In September 1986, Angelique Lyn Lavallee, a 22-year-old Manitoba woman, was charged with the second-degree murder of her common-law spouse, Kevin Rust. Lavallee admitted to shooting Rust in the back of the head in the midst of a "boisterous party" being held at their home. According to Lavallee, Rust confronted her in an upstairs bedroom and pushed and slapped her. Rust then handed her a .303 rifle kept in the home and a shot was fired through the screen in the bedroom window. Rust chambered a second shell and handed it to Lavallee, with the threat "Wait till everybody leaves, you'll get it then." Meaning to scare Rust off, Lavallee fired the rifle, hitting Rust in the back of the head as he left the bedroom, killing him.

At her trial, Lavallee's lawyer argued that her action was a case of "self-defence" as defined in Section 34(2) of the *Criminal Code*, which states:

(2) Every one who is unlawfully assaulted and who causes death or grievous bodily harm in repelling the assault is justified if
   (a) he causes it under reasonable apprehension of death or grievous bodily harm from the violence with which the assault was originally made or with which the assailant pursues his purposes, and
   (b) he believes on reasonable and probable grounds, that he cannot otherwise preserve himself from death or grievous bodily harm.

The introduction of this defence was surprising; in the past, the courts had required that (1) the perceived harm be "imminent" (about to occur or actually underway) and that (2) there be no means to escape or avoid the harm. Indeed, Lavallee's actions did not appear to meet either test; Rust was leaving the room to go back to the party when he was killed, removing the imminent threat of harm, and providing Lavallee the opportunity to leave the bedroom and the house to seek help.

Lavallee's lawyer introduced evidence at trial that from the very beginning of their relationship, Lavallee was frequently physically abused by Rust, and made several trips to the hospital as a result. Friends of the couple testified to their "stormy" relationship and to the recurring physical abuse of Lavallee.

Lavallee's lawyer capped the defence argument with expert testimony from psychiatrist Dr. Fred Shane, who testified that Lavallee demonstrated the symptoms of "battered woman syndrome." Dr. Shane explained that, like other women characterized by this syndrome, Lavallee had "been terrorized by Rust to the point of feeling trapped, vulnerable, worthless and unable to escape the relationship despite the violence." Based on their past experiences, battered women know that their abusers will make good on their threats, but they feel helpless to escape the inevitable physical assault. For battered women, then, attacks are always "imminent" and, at some point, will probably be fatal.

The Manitoba jury acquitted Lavallee, in large part based on Dr. Shane's testimony that battered woman syndrome characterized the actions of the accused in the case. However, the acquittal was overturned by the Manitoba Court of Appeal, on the ground that Dr. Shane's testimony was "unnecessary and superfluous," as the facts of the case spoke for themselves; and his comment that he found the accused "credible" was improper, given that Lavallee did not testify, and so her credibility could not be tested in cross-examination. The Court of Appeal recommended the Crown proceed with a lesser charge of manslaughter.

On May 3, 1990, the Supreme Court of Canada restored Lavallee's acquittal on the basis that Dr. Shane's testimony was relevant to the issue of self-defence—and the "battered woman syndrome" was therefore accepted as a legitimate defence to homicide and other forms of bodily harm committed in self-defence.

Since the *Lavallee* decision, Canadian courts accept that "battered woman syndrome" is a legitimate criminal defence, as evidenced by a growing number of cases in which the defence has been used (e.g., *R. v. Bennett*, 1993; *R. v. Bear*, 1999; *R. v. Hernando*, 2009; *R. v. Knott*, 2014).

CRITICAL THINKING

1. What standard should the courts use to determine whether the defence of battered woman syndrome is valid? Should the syndrome of "battering" be restricted to women?

2. Is it fair to punish someone suffering from severe emotional trauma who committed a murder in the same manner as someone who killed for money? Why or why not? Should motive influence punishment?

Sources: Canadian Legal Information Institute, *R. v. Lavallee* [1990] 1 S.C.R. 852 at http://www.canlii.org.ca/cas/scc/1990; Martha Shaffer, "The Battered Woman Syndrome Revisited: Some Complicating Thoughts Five Years after R. v. Lavallee," *University of Toronto Law Journal*, 47 (1997): 1–33.

Similarly, the 1988 murder of 11-year-old Christopher Stephenson by a convicted pedophile who had recently been released from a nearby federal prison led the Ontario government to enact "Christopher's Law" (Sex Offender Registry, 2000), which requires convicted sex offenders living in Ontario to report to their local police service on an annual basis, and to notify the police within 15 days of any change in address.[46] The future direction of Canadian criminal law remains unclear. Certain actions, such as crimes by corporations and political corruption, will be labelled as criminal and given more attention. Other offences, such as recreational drug use, may be reduced in importance or removed entirely from the criminal law system. In addition, changing technology and its ever-increasing global and local roles in our lives will require modifications in criminal law. For example, technologies such as automated teller machines, smart phones, and the Internet have already spawned a new generation of

In early May 2014 the bodies of two women were found in a home in Whalley, a suburb of Surrey, BC. The deaths raised public cries for the hiring of more police officers to protect the community, and only days later the city's police services committee endorsed a plan to increase the number of officers to be hired in 2014 from 12 to 30.

However, according to Michael Booth, a reporter for the Vancouver area newspaper *The Tri-Cities Now*, the deaths of the two women were the result of a family tragedy, and had nothing to do with gangs, home invasions, or drugs—and the hiring of more police officers will make no difference in preventing tragedies like this.

Instead, Booth argues, we need to get community members more involved in supporting each other to improve safety—by joining together in neighbourhood groups, by getting to know one another, by keeping an eye out for each other's homes, children, and the neighbourhood as a whole. Only in this way he argues "can we create environments where the bad guys do not feel comfortable and will move on to other, less risky communities."

If you look carefully, public and media discussions about crime often unknowingly reflect the ideas of criminological theories. Which theory do you think underlies Booth's argument?

Source: An organized community can fight crime just as effectively as cops by Michael Booth, The Now Newspaper, May 8, 2014, from http://www.thenownewspaper.com/opinion/300244911.html

Vancouver Sun

criminal acts such as theft of access numbers, software piracy, identity theft, and distribution of child pornography. As the information highway sprawls toward new expanses, computer networks advance, and biotechnology produces new substances, criminal law will be forced to address threats to the public safety that today are unknown.

LO8 Ethical Issues in Criminology

A critical issue facing criminology students involves recognizing the field's political and social consequences. All too often criminologists forget the social responsibility they bear as experts in the area of crime and justice. When government agencies request their views of issues, their pronouncements and opinions may become the basis for sweeping social policy.

The lives of millions of people can be influenced by criminological research data. Debates over firearms control, decriminalization of marijuana possession, and mandatory sentences are ongoing and contentious. Some criminologists have argued successfully for social service, treatment, and rehabilitation programs to reduce the crime rate;

others consider these a waste of time, suggesting instead that building more prisons, coupled with tough criminal sentences, can bring the crime rate down. By accepting their roles as experts on law-violating behaviour, criminologists place themselves in a position of power. The potential consequences of their actions are enormous. Therefore, they must be both aware of the ethics of their profession and prepared to defend their work in the light of public scrutiny. Major ethical issues include what to study, whom to study, and how to conduct those studies:

- *What to study.* Criminologists must be concerned about the topics they study. It is important that their research not be directed by the sources of funding on which research projects rely. The objectivity of research may be questioned if studies are funded by organizations that have a vested interest in the outcome of the research. For example, a study on the effectiveness of home alarm systems to stop break and enters may be tainted if the funding for the project comes from a security company or alarm manufacturer whose sales may be affected by the research findings.

- *Whom to study.* Another ethical issue in criminology concerns selection of research subjects. Too often criminologists focus their attention on the poor and minorities while ignoring middle-class white-collar crime, organized crime, and government crime. For example, a few social scientists have suggested that criminals have lower intelligence quotients than the average citizen and that because the average IQ score is presumed to be lower among some minority groups, their crime rates are therefore high.[47] This was the argument made in *The Bell Curve,* a popular but highly controversial book written by Richard Herrnstein and Charles Murray.[48] In Canada, the availability of funding has led to a flood of research studies about crime in Aboriginal communities, unfairly depicting these communities as crime "hot spots," while ignoring other issues and the many positive aspects of life in Aboriginal communities.[49]

• *How to study.* A third area of concern involves the methods used in conducting research. One issue is whether subjects are fully informed about the purpose of research. For example, when European-Canadian and visible-minority youngsters are asked to participate in a survey of their behaviour, are they told in advance that the data they provide may later be used to demonstrate racial differences in their self-reported crime rates? Criminologists must also be careful to keep records and information confidential in order to maintain the privacy of research participants. In studies that involve experimentation and treatment, care must be taken to protect those subjects who have been chosen for experimental and control groups. For example, is it ethical to provide a special program for one group while depriving others of the same opportunity just so they can later be compared? Conversely, criminologists must be careful to protect subjects from experiments that may actually cause harm. An examination of the highly publicized "Scared Straight" program, which brings youngsters into contact with hard-core felons in a prison setting, found that participants may have been harmed by their experience. Rather than being frightened into conformity, subjects actually increased their criminal behaviour.[50] Finally, criminologists must take extreme care to ensure that research subjects are selected in a random and unbiased manner.[51]

Summary

Criminology is the scientific approach to the study of criminal behaviour and society's reaction to law violations and violators. It is essentially an interdisciplinary field; many of its practitioners were originally trained as sociologists, anthropologists, lawyers, psychologists, economists, political scientists, historians, health scientists, and natural scientists.

Criminology has a rich history, with roots in the utilitarian philosophy of Beccaria, the biological positivism of Lombroso, the sociological theory of Durkheim, and the political philosophy of Marx.

The criminological enterprise includes subareas such as criminal statistics, the sociology of law, theory construction, criminal behaviour systems, penology, victimology, and public criminology

Criminologists believe in one of three perspectives: the consensus view, the conflict view, or the interactionist view. The consensus view holds that criminal behaviour is defined by laws that reflect the values and morals of a majority of citizens. The conflict view states that criminal behaviour is defined in such a way that economically powerful groups can retain their control over society. The interactionist view portrays criminal behaviour as a relativistic, constantly changing concept that reflects society's current moral values. According to the interactionist view, behaviour is labelled as criminal by those in power; criminals are people society chooses to label as outsiders or deviants.

Criminal law is a set of rules that specify the behaviours society has outlawed. Criminal law serves several important purposes: It represents public opinion and moral values, it enforces social controls, it deters criminal behaviour and wrongdoing, it punishes transgressors, and it banishes private retribution.

Canadian criminal law traces its origin to the English common law. In the Canadian legal system, lawmakers have codified common-law crimes into the *Criminal Code.* Every crime has specific elements. In most instances, these elements include both the *actus reus* (guilty act) and the *mens rea* (guilty mind)—the person's state of mind or criminal intent.

At trial, a defendant may claim to have lacked *mens rea* and, therefore, not be responsible for a criminal action. One type of defence is excuse for incapacity, such as mental disorder, automatism, or intoxication. Another type of defence is justification by reason of self-defence or entrapment.

Criminal law is undergoing constant reform. Some acts are being decriminalized—their penalties are being reduced—while penalties for others are becoming more severe.

Ethical issues arise when the questions criminologists choose to study appear biased or exclusionary. These issues may cause serious consequences because their findings can significantly impact individuals and groups.

Discussion Questions

1. What are the specific aims and purposes of criminal law? To what extent does criminal law control behaviour? Do you believe that the law is too restrictive? Not restrictive enough?

2. If you ran the world, which acts, now legal, would you make criminal? Which criminal acts would you legalize? What would be the likely consequences of your actions?

3. Beccaria argued that the threat of punishment controls crime. Are there other forms of social control? Aside from the threat of legal punishment, what else controls your own behaviour?

4. Would it be ethical for a criminologist to observe a teenage gang by hanging with them, drinking, and watching as they steal cars? Should the criminologist report that behaviour to the police?

READY TO STUDY?

IN THE BOOK, YOU CAN:

✔ Check your understanding of what you've just read by reading the Summary at the end of each chapter.

✔ Rip out the Chapter in Review card at the back of the book to have the key terms and Learning Objectives handy, and complete the quizzes provided (answers are at the bottom of the back page).

ONLINE YOU CAN:

✔ Stay organized and efficient with MindTap—a single destination with all the course material and study aids you need to succeed. Built-in apps leverage social media and the latest learning technology. For example:

✔ ReadSpeaker will read the text to you.

✔ Flashcards are pre-populated to provide you with a jump start for review—or you can create your own.

✔ You can highlight text and make notes in your MindTap Reader. Your notes will flow into Evernote, the electronic notebook app that you can access anywhere when it's time to study for the exam.

✔ Prepare for tests with quizzes.

Go to www.nelson.com/student to access these digital resources.

The Nature and Extent of Crime

Learning Objectives

LO1 Name three primary sources of crime statistics used in Canada.

LO2 Explain the benefits of the Crime Severity Index.

LO3 Identify the strengths and weaknesses of crime statistics.

LO4 Identify the important trends over time in the Canadian crime rate.

LO5 Identify major factors that influence the crime rate.

LO6 Define aging out or desistance.

LO7 Define racial profiling.

Introduction

Shortly after 7:00 A.M. on the morning of Saturday, November 8, 2014, two construction workers found the bloodied and broken body of 16-year-old Rinelle Harper lying on a pathway beneath the Midtown Bridge in Winnipeg. The teen had been attacked shortly after midnight on Friday, by two men who lured her beneath the bridge and repeatedly sexually assaulted her, leaving her for dead by the side of the river after a vicious beating with a baseball bat. Disturbingly, the attack on Rinelle Harper appeared to represent another in a long series of brutal attacks on, and even murders of, young Aboriginal women in the Winnipeg area. In an unusual move, Rinelle's parents and Winnipeg police agreed to release the teen's name and photograph to the press in order to put a face to the brutal crime, and to bring forth witnesses. By Tuesday, police had arrested two suspects, 20-year-old James Hudson and a 17-year-old youth, in connection with the attack on Rinelle Harper as well as another sexual assault and beating of a 23-year-old woman the same night. The suspects have been charged with attempted murder, aggravated sexual assault, and sexual assault with a weapon. Rinelle Harper was released from hospital on 14 November 2014.[1]

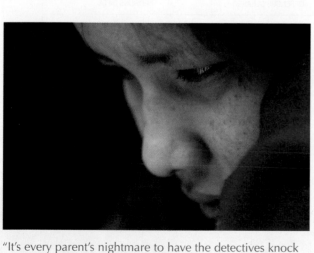

"It's every parent's nightmare to have the detectives knock on your door," Julie says in an interview with the family at the hotel where the teen is recovering. "They asked us if Rinelle was our daughter. [An officer] told us that she had been lying by the river, on the sidewalk, and that now she was on life support. She was an unknown female all day. I forget what they said next. I was in shock" (K. Carlson, "Rinelle's Recovery: 'We Want Our Hearts to Be Peaceful,' Family Says," *The Globe and Mail* (November 21, 2014), at http://www.theglobeandmail.com/news/politics/rinelle -harper-and-family-figuring-out-what-to-do-next-after-attack/ article21687719.)

Stories like these help convince most Canadians that we live in a violent, crime-ridden society that is becoming increasingly dangerous. Are Canadians justified in their fears? Are crime rates actually rising or falling? What types of crime are the most common? Who commits crimes? Where do most crimes occur? What does the future hold? To answer these and similar questions, criminologists have devised elaborate methods of crime data collection and analysis. Without accurate data on the nature and extent of crime, it would not be possible to formulate theories that explain the onset of crime or to devise social policies that facilitate its control or elimination.

In this chapter, we review how data are collected on criminal offenders and offences and what this information tells us about crime patterns and trends. We also examine the concept of criminal careers and discover what available crime data can tell us about the onset, continuation, and termination of criminality. We begin with a discussion of the most important sources of crime data.

LO1 Sources of Crime Statistics

The Uniform Crime Report

First introduced in 1962, the Uniform Crime Report (UCR) is a listing of the number of criminal offences that occurred in each police agency's jurisdiction, the clearance status of each reported offence, and the number of persons charged (see Figure 2.1). Every police agency in Canada is required each month to complete the survey.[2] Completed UCR surveys are forwarded to the Canadian Centre for Justice Statistics, where the information is grouped together or "aggregated" to get a total of the number of crimes reported across Canada, in each of the provinces, and for the larger cities. In 1988, a new version of the survey was created, UCR2, referred to as the "incident-based" survey, to capture more detailed

Uniform Crime Report (UCR)
A yearly crime report used by all police agencies in Canada.

UCR2
Revised crime-reporting system introduced in the mid-1980s. It collects detailed information about accused persons, victims, location, and weapons involved in each criminal incident. Most of the larger police agencies use the UCR and the UCR2.

FIGURE 2.1

Uniform Crime Report, Crime Statistics

Canadian Centre for Justice Statistics

Form "C" – Crime Statistics

Confidential when completed

Month of

Complete and **return this copy to Statistics Canada** in the enclosed envelope on or before the 15th of the month

Si vous préférez ce questionnaire en français, veuillez cocher ☐

Date submitted		
Day	Month	Year

Signature of head of department

INFORMATION FOR RESPONDENTS

Authority:
Statistics Act, Revised Statutes of Canada, 1985, Chapter S19

Objective:
This survey was designed to produce an indicator on the incidence of crime in Canadian society. The information is used by federal and provincial policy makers as well as public and private researchers. The data are also widely disseminated by the media for purposes of general public information.

Confidentiality:
Statistics Canada is prohibited by law from publishing any statistics which would divulge information obtained from this survey that relates to any identifiable respondent/individual without the previous written consent of that respondent/individual. The information reported on this questionnaire

will be treated in confidence, used for statistical purposes and published in aggregate form only. The confidentiality provisions of the Statistics Act are not affected by either the Access to Information Act or any other legislation.

Correspondence:
If you require assistance in the completion of this questionnaire or any questions regarding the survey, please contact the;

Policing Services Program,
Canadian Centre for Justice Statistics,
Statistics Canada
Ottawa, Ontario
K1A 0T6,
Telephone: 1-800-387-2231

OFFENCES	Reported or known to police	Un-founded	Actual Number	OFFENCES CLEARED		PERSONS DATA				
						Adults		Young offenders		
				By charge	Otherwise	Charged		Charged		Not Charged
						Male	Female	Male	Female	
1	2	3	4	5	6	7	8	9	10	11
HOMICIDE * TOTAL 001										
Murder, First degree 002										
Murder, Second degree 003										
Manslaughter 004										
Infanticide 005										
ATTEMPTED MURDER – TOTAL 006										
ROBBERY TOTAL 018										
Firearms 019										
Other offensive weapons 020										
Other Robbery 021										

8-1000-92.1: 1998-09-09   STC/CCJ-140-60100

* (See Supplementary Homicide instructions on page four)

Statistics Canada   Statistique Canada

Canadä

FIGURE 2.1 *(Continued)*

- 2 -

OFFENCES	Reported or known to police	Un-founded	Actual Number	OFFENCES CLEARED		PERSONS DATA				
				By charge	Otherwise	Adults Charged		Young offenders Charged		Not Charged
						Male	Female	Male	Female	
1	2	3	4	5	6	7	8	9	10	11
BREAKING AND ENTERING TOTAL 022										
Business premises 023										
Residence 024										
Other Break and Enter 025										
THEFT – MOTOR VEHICLE TOTAL 026										
Automobiles 027										
Trucks 028										
Motorcycles 029										
Other Motor Vehicles 030										
THEFT OVER $5,000 TOTAL 031										
Bicycles 032										
From motor vehicles 033										
Shoplifting 034										
Other thefts over $5,000 035										
THEFT $5,000 AND UNDER TOTAL 036										
Bicycles 037										
From motor vehicles 038										
Shoplifting 039										
Other thefts $5,000 and under . 040										
HAVE STOLEN GOODS 041										
FRAUDS TOTAL 042										
Cheques 043										
Credit Cards 044										
Other frauds 045										
PROSTITUTION TOTAL 046										
Bawdy house 047										
Procuring 048										
Other prostitution 049										

8-1000-92.1: 1998-09-09

FIGURE 2.1 *(Continued)*

- 3 -

OFFENCES	Reported or known to police	Un-founded	Actual Number	OFFENCES CLEARED		PERSONS DATA				
				By charge	Otherwise	Adults		Young offenders		
						Charged		Charged		Not Charged
						Male	Female	Male	Female	
1	2	3	4	5	6	7	8	9	10	11
GAMING AND BETTING TOTAL 050										
Betting house 051										
Gaming house 052										
Other gaming and betting offences 053										
OFFENSIVE WEAPONS TOTAL 054										
Firearms usage 055										
Weapons possession 056										
Trafficking import/export 057										
Other weapon offences 058										
OTHER CRIMINAL CODE (EX. TRAFFIC) – TOTAL 059										
Arson 060										
Bail Violations 061										
Counterfeiting currency 062										
Disturb the peace 063										
Escape custody 064										
Indecent Acts 065										
Kidnapping 066										
Public Morals 067										
Obstruct public peace officer .. 068										
Prisoner unlawfully at large ... 069										
Trespass at night 070										
Mischief (property damage) over $5,000 071										
Mischief (property damage) $5,000 and under 072										
Other Criminal Code Offences 073										
HEROIN TOTAL 074										
Possession 075										
Trafficking 076										
Importation/Production 077										
COCAINE TOTAL 078										
Possession 079										
Trafficking 080										
Importation/Production 081										
OTHER DRUGS TOTAL 082										
Possession 083										
Trafficking 084										
Importation/Production 085										

8-1000-92.1: 1998-09-09

FIGURE 2.1 *(Continued)*

- 4 -

OFFENCES	Reported or known to police	Un-founded	Actual Number	OFFENCES CLEARED		PERSONS DATA				
				By charge	Otherwise	Adults		Young offenders		
						Charged		Charged		Not Charged
						Male	Female	Male	Female	
1	2	3	4	5	6	7	8	9	10	11
CANNABIS TOTAL 086										
Possession 087										
Trafficking 088										
Importation 089										
Production 090										
OTHER FEDERAL STATUTES TOTAL (EX. TRAFFIC) 095										
Bankruptcy Act 096										
Canada Shipping Act 097										
Customs Act 098										
Excise Act 099										
Immigration Act 100										
Firearms Act 101										
Other Federal Statute Offences 102										
PROVINCIAL STATUTES (EX. TRAFFIC) TOTAL 103										
Liquor Acts 104										
Securities Act 105										
Other Provincial Statutes 106										
MUNICIPAL BY-LAWS (EX. TRAFFIC) 107										

SPECIAL *

991										
992										
993										
994										
995										

SUPPLEMENTARY HOMICIDE RETURN

In view of the importance of homicide statistics, it is requested that the following supplementary information be supplied for all homicides occurring in your jurisdiction. Statistics Canada will send the investigating police force a Homicide Return for completion and return to Statistics Canada. The names of victim(s) and person(s) charged must equal the actual number of offences and persons charged as reported for Items 002 to 005 – Form "C".

Offence	Date of offence	Location of offence	Victim(s)	Person(s) charged

8-1000-92.1: 1998-09-09   ***TO BE UTILIZED FOR SPECIAL SURVEYS OR NON-APPLICABLE OFFENCES**

Source: Adapted from Statistics Canada website, Definition, Data Sources and Methods Module, SDDS 3302, Uniform Crime Reporting Survey, Uniform Crime Reporting, Version 1.0, Reporting Manual (http://www.statcan.gc.ca/imdb-bmdi/documenf3302_D7_T1_V1-eng.pdf).

information about each criminal incident, including the characteristics of victims and accused; the location, date, and time of day of the incident; use and type of weapons; type of property stolen; and so forth. Most of the larger police agencies, accounting for about 70 percent of all crimes, now also report information using the UCR2, which was revised and updated in 1998 (UCR 2.1) and 2004 (UCR 2.2) in order to reflect new changes in the law and types of offences.[3] The UCR surveys are the most widely cited sources of Canadian criminal statistics.

Every year, the Canadian Centre for Justice Statistics publishes *Canadian Crime Reports,* a summary of the data collected from the UCR surveys.[4] The crime data are reported in large tables, using three different methods. First, the number of crimes reported to the police are expressed as raw figures (e.g., 543 murders occurred in 2012). Second, crime rates per 100 000 people are computed. That is, when it is reported that the homicide rate was 2.0 in 2012, this means that two people in every 100 000 were murdered between January 1 and December 31, 2012. This is the equation used:

$$\frac{\text{Number of reported crimes}}{\text{Total Canadian population}} \times 100{,}000 = \text{Rate per } 100{,}000$$

Third, the Canadian Centre for Justice Statistics computes changes in the number and rate of crime over time. For example, the number of homicides in Canada decreased by about 6.7 percent between 2002 and 2012, from 582 to 543.

The accuracy of the data reported on the UCR surveys is, however, suspect. Research indicates that fewer than half of all crime victims report incidents to police. Nonreporters may believe that the victimization was "a private matter," that "nothing could be done," or that the victimization was "not important enough."[5] In the case of so-called "white-collar" crime and environmental crimes, many victims may not know they have been victimized, or who in the corporate world they should blame—and police agencies rarely have the resources or expertise required to investigate these complicated types of crimes.[6]

There is also evidence that local police agencies make errors in their reporting practices. Some agencies may define crimes loosely—for example, reporting an aggravated assault on a woman as an attempted murder—whereas others pay strict attention to the UCR reporting guidelines.[7] Some local police departments make unintentional but systematic errors in UCR reporting, and others may deliberately alter reported crimes to improve their department's public image. Police administrators interested in lowering the crime rate may falsify crime reports by, for example, classifying a break and enter as a trespass.[8] Ironically, what appears to be a rising crime rate may be simply an artifact of improved police record-keeping ability.[9]

Methodological issues also contribute to questions regarding the validity of UCR data. The complex scoring procedure used on the UCR surveys means that many serious crimes are not counted. For example, during a robbery of a gas bar, the offender strikes the clerk with an iron pipe. The robber runs out the door and steals an automobile parked at the gas pump. Although the offender has technically committed robbery, aggravated assault, and motor vehicle theft, because robbery is the most serious offence, it would be the only one recorded in the UCR.[10] The most common issues affecting the validity of the UCR are summarized in Table 2.1.

Every month, Statistics Canada and the Canadian Centre for Justice Statistics publish the *Juristat* report, which contains articles, special studies, and statistics about crime in Canada. *Juristat* can be found in most college and university libraries, and many of the articles are available free online at http://www.statcan.ca.

LO2 Crime Severity Index

Recognizing the limitations of UCR surveys, and in an attempt to enhance the quality of the data collected on crime in Canada, a third instrument, the Crime Severity Index, was introduced in 2009. (See Table 2.2.) The Crime Severity Index was the first major change in the method of reporting of police-reported crime statistics since the collection

TABLE 2.1

Factors Affecting the Validity of the Uniform Crime Reports

1. Many criminal incidents are never reported to the police. This is especially true of more minor crimes, but even a large percentage of sexual assaults and assaults are not reported. Victims may believe that there is nothing the police can do, or the crime was not important enough to go to the bother of reporting it. In other cases, the crime may have gone undetected.[11] Sometimes victims are afraid to report a crime for fear of further reprisals from their victimizer. In rare cases, the victim may have died or disappeared. Biderman and Reiss (1967) coined the phrase the "dark figure" of crime to describe the many acts that take place that are, by definition, crimes, but never appear in the "official" statistics on crime.[12]

2. Reports can vary in accuracy and completeness.

3. Sometimes, police agencies don't make a report, and the Canadian Centre for Justice Statistics has to "estimate" the amount of crime that would have occurred in that agency's jurisdiction.

4. Not all Canadian police agencies use the UCR2 form, although completion rates have improved greatly over time. In 2013, 154 police agencies across the ten provinces and three territories reported complete data, covering approximately 99 percent of the Canadian population. Most agencies that do complete the UCR2 are urban, and so the data may not be representative regionally or nationally.

5. If an accused commits multiple crimes during one incident, only the most serious offence is recorded. For example, if a man sexually assaults, robs, and murders a victim, only the murder is recorded. Consequently, many lesser crimes go unreported.

6. All criminal incidents are not counted the same way. For example, one incident is counted for each separate occurrence of a property crime, such as theft, no matter how many victims are involved. But in the case of violent crime, one incident is counted for each victim involved in the occurrence.

Source: Samuel Perreault, Police-reported crime statistics in Canada, 2012, "Police-reported Crime Statistics in Canada," 2012 Juristat (July 2013) Statistics Canada Cat. no. 85-002-X. *Measuring Crime in Canada: Introducing the Crime Severity Index and Improvements.*

TABLE 2.2

Offences Making the Largest Contributions to the Crime Severity Index

Offence	Percent
Breaking and entering	24.9
Theft under $5000	12.4
Robbery	11.2
Theft of a motor vehicle	7.1
Mischief	6.4
Fraud	5.5
Sexual assault – level 1	2.5
Assault – level 1	2.4
Assault – level 2	2.4
Homicide	2.3

Source: Marnie Wallace John Turner, Anthony Matarazzo and Colin Babyak, *Measuring Crime in Canada: Introducing the Crime Severity Index and Improvements to the Uniform Crime Reporting Survey 2009*, (Ottawa: Statistics Canada), Catalogue no. 85-004-X, at http://www.statcan.gc.ca/pub/85-004-x/85-004-x2009001-eng.htm (accessed 17 October 2015).

Victim Surveys

The second source of crime data is surveys that ask crime victims about their encounters with criminals. Because many victims do not report their experiences to the police, victim surveys are considered a method of getting at the unknown figures of crime.

General Social Survey—Victimization Survey (GSS—VS)

Beginning in 1988, and in 1993, 1999, 2004, 2009 and most recently in 2014, Statistics Canada has conducted the General Social Survey—Victimization Survey. About 20 000 Canadians are asked to complete a 30-minute interview over the telephone, covering their personal, self-reported experiences with criminal victimization and spousal violence. The data collected by the national GSS—VS is the most comprehensive source of information about victimization in Canada. Because of the care with which the samples are drawn and the high completion rate, the GSS—VS data are considered a relatively unbiased, valid estimate of

Crime Severity Index
A yearly crime report used by all police agencies in Canada that measures both volume and severity of crime across the country.

General Social Survey—Victimization Survey (GSS—VS)
National study carried out in 1988, 1993, 1999, 2004, 2009, and 2014, by Statistics Canada, which surveys approximately 20 000 Canadians about their personal experiences of criminal victimization.

of these data began in 1961. In the past, the crime rate was heavily influenced by the large number of less serious offences, which research has shown often went unreported. Additionally, these less serious crimes were assigned exactly the same weight as more serious crimes. What was needed was a method to capture the overall picture of trends in crime severity. The Crime Severity Index helps determine the severity of police-reported crime in relation to the past and to Canada overall. The mechanics involve assigning a "seriousness" weight to each type of offence that is derived from actual sentences handed down by courts in all provinces and territories, with more serious crimes being assigned higher weight than less serious ones. The overall Crime Severity Index, and separate breakdowns for the Violent Crime Severity Index and the Non-Violent Crime Severity Index, is reported annually by Statistics Canada. It should be noted that the new index does not replace, but rather complements, existing measures of crime.[13]

all victimizations for the target crimes included in the survey.[14]

Findings and Validity of the GSS—VS

According to the latest available data from the 2009 survey, 27 percent of Canadians said that they had been a victim of a crime in the previous 12 months. Theft of personal property (34 percent), theft of household property (13 percent), vandalism (11 percent), break-ins (7 percent), and theft of motor vehicles/parts (5 percent) accounted for 70 percent of incidents recorded by the GSS—VS. Violent incidents, namely physical assault (19 percent), sexual assault (8 percent), and robbery (4 percent) accounted for the remaining self-reported incidents.[15] Interestingly, only about one-third of these incidents were actually reported to police.[16] The reason for such discrepancies is that fewer than half of violent crimes, and only about one-third of personal theft crimes (e.g., theft of money from a purse) and household thefts (e.g., lawn ornaments) are reported to police. Victims seem to report to the police only crimes that involve considerable loss or injury. If we are to believe GSS—VS findings, the official UCR statistics do not provide an accurate picture of the crime problem because many crimes go unreported to the police.

Overall, victimization rates in Canada have remained stable since 2004. However, the rate of theft of personal property increased 16 percent, up from 93 incidents per 1000 people in 2004 to 108 incidents in 2009.[17]

Victimization over the Internet is a growing concern to the justice system, and the GSS—VS is providing some useful information about the scope of the problem in Canada. According to the 2009 data, 7 percent of adult Internet users (those 18 years or older) reported they had been a victim of cyberbullying at some point in their lives; threatening or aggressive emails or messages were the most common type of cyberbullying reported, and younger adults (17 percent), single persons (15 percent) and those accessing social networking sites (11 percent) were the most common victims. One in ten (10 percent) adults surveyed reported that a child in their household, usually a female (71 percent), had been a victim of cyberbullying.[18] The relationship between cyberbullying victims and the bully for both adults and children, as measured by the GSS—VS, is shown in Figure 2.2.

Validity of the GSS—VS

Like the UCR and GSS, the GSS—VS may also suffer from some methodological problems. As a result, its findings must be interpreted with caution. Among the potential problems are the following:

- Overreporting due to victims' misinterpretation of events. For example, a lost wallet may be reported as

---

FIGURE 2.2

Cyberbullying Victims, Adults and Children, in Canada

(a) Adult Internet Users Who Self-Reported Cyberbullying, by Relationship to the Bully, 2009

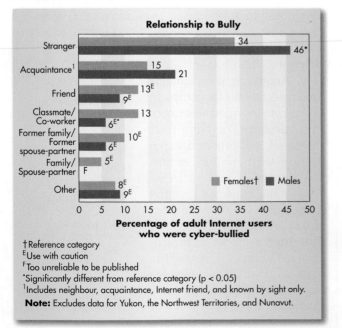

† Reference category
E Use with caution
F Too unreliable to be published
*Significantly different from reference category (p < 0.05)
1 Includes neighbour, acquaintance, Internet friend, and known by sight only.
Note: Excludes data for Yukon, the Northwest Territories, and Nunavut.

(b) Adults with a Child Victim of Cyberbullying in Their Household, by Relationship to the Bully, 2009

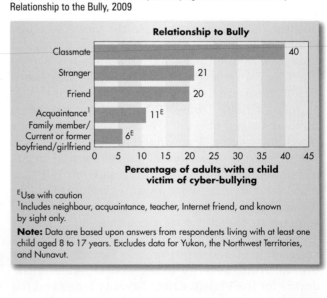

E Use with caution
1 Includes neighbour, acquaintance, teacher, Internet friend, and known by sight only.
Note: Data are based upon answers from respondents living with at least one child aged 8 to 17 years. Excludes data for Yukon, the Northwest Territories, and Nunavut.

Source: Perreault, Samuel. Self-reported Internet victimization in Canada, 2009 (Juristat, September 2011). Statistics Canada catalogue no. 85-002-X.

stolen, or an open door may be viewed as a break-and-enter attempt.

• Underreporting due to the embarrassment of reporting crime to interviewers, fear of getting in trouble, or simply forgetting an incident.

• Inability to record the personal criminal activity of those interviewed, such as drug use or child abuse; murder is also not included, for obvious reasons.

• The GSS—VS does not record crimes committed in the workplace, forms of organized crime, and corporate crimes.

• Sampling errors, which produce a group of respondents who do not represent the nation as a whole.[19]

Self-Report Surveys

Self-report surveys ask people to reveal information about their own law violations. Most often, self-report surveys are administered to groups of subjects through a mass distribution of questionnaires. The basic assumption of self-report studies is that the assurance of anonymity and confidentiality will encourage people to describe their illegal activities accurately. Nowadays, Internet-based surveys are usually used to collect the information. Self-reports are viewed as a mechanism to get at the "dark figures of crime," the figures missed by official statistics. Figure 2.3 illustrates some typical self-report items.

Most self-report studies have focused on juvenile delinquency, bullying behaviour, and youth crime, for three reasons.[20] First, the

self-report survey
A research approach that requires subjects to reveal their own participation in delinquent or criminal acts.

29. In the past year, have YOU DONE any of these to someone else at your school?

FIGURE 2.3

Self-Report Survey Questions

Source: North Bay Police Service School Safety Survey 2012. Prepared by: Institute for Applied Social Research (IASR), Nipissing University. Reprinted with permission.

	Never	Once or Twice this Year	Once or Twice a Month	Once or Twice a Week	Every Day
Pushed/shoved/tripped/spit on someone	○	○	○	○	○
Physically hit (slapped/punched/kicked) someone	○	○	○	○	○
Threatened to hurt someone	○	○	○	○	○
Threatened to hurt someone if they didn't give you something of theirs (e.g. money, cell phone, iPod, clothing, etc.)	○	○	○	○	○
Touched or grabbed someone in a sexual way	○	○	○	○	○
Made someone do something they didn't want to do	○	○	○	○	○
Kept bugging someone or harassing someone	○	○	○	○	○
Spread rumours about someone	○	○	○	○	○
Made fun of someone, insulted them, called them names	○	○	○	○	○
Excluded someone from friends, activities on purpose	○	○	○	○	○
Sent hurtful information or pictures about someone to other people over the Internet, Facebook, MSN or on a cellphone	○	○	○	○	○
Made fun of someone because of their colour or the culture they come from, or their sexual orientation	○	○	○	○	○
Stole something from someone	○	○	○	○	○
Deliberately broke or damaged something that belonged to someone else	○	○	○	○	○
Drove someone in a vehicle when you had been drinking alcohol or were on drugs	○	○	○	○	○

school setting makes it convenient to test thousands of subjects simultaneously because they all have the means to respond to a research questionnaire (pens, desks, Internet access, and time). Second, because school attendance is universal, a school-based self-report survey represents a cross-section of the community. Finally, juveniles have the highest reported crime rates; measuring delinquent and bullying behaviour, therefore, is a key to understanding the nature and extent of crime.

Self-reports are not restricted to youth crime, however. They are also used to examine the offence histories of prison inmates, drug users, and other segments of the population, including college and university students.[21] Also, because most self-report instruments contain items measuring subjects' attitudes, values, personal characteristics, and behaviours, the data obtained from them can be used for various purposes, including testing theories, measuring attitudes toward crime, and computing the association between crime and important social variables, such as family relations, educational attainment, and income.[22]

Self-Report Findings

In general, self-reports, like victimization surveys, indicate that the number of people who break the law is far greater than the number projected by official statistics. Almost everyone questioned is found to have violated some law at some time.[23] Furthermore, self-reports dispute the notion that criminals and delinquents specialize in one type of crime or another; offenders seem to engage in a "mixed bag" of crime and deviance.[24]

Self-report studies typically indicate that the most common offences are truancy; alcohol abuse; trespassing; shoplifting, or theft under $50; fighting; marijuana use; and damage to the property of others. What is surprising is the consistency of these findings in samples taken around the United States and in Canada. Table 2.3 contains data from a self-report study included in the National Longitudinal Survey of Children and Youth started in 1994–95. This long-term national survey includes about 1800 children 12 to 13 years of age, and shows that, consistent with other studies, females are less likely than males to engage in delinquent acts against property or to engage in aggressive behaviours such as fighting, sexual assault, or arson.[25]

As Table 2.3 shows, 56 percent of males and 30 percent of females 12 to 13 years of age report "some" or a "high" level of involvement in delinquent acts against property. The fact that 56 percent of the males and 30 percent of the females report that they have

Gender Differences in Self-Report Delinquency at Age 12–13, 1996–97

Type of Delinquent Behaviour	Gender	Level of Delinquency			
		None	Some	High	Total
Delinquent acts involving property	Females	70%	23%	7%	100% (967)
	Males	60%	27%	13%	100% (964)
Aggressive behaviour	Females	71%	22%	7%	100% (981)
	Males	44%	40%	16%	100% (974)

Source: Adapted from Statistics Canada publication JURISTAT, Catalogue 85-002, Vol. 21, No. 4 page 3, http://www.statcan.gc.ca/bsolc/olc-cel/olc-cel?catno=85-002-x&lang=eng

committed aggressive acts of a criminal nature against others suggests that violence and property crime may be widespread and not restricted to a few "bad apples."

Accuracy of Self-Reports

Although self-report data have profoundly affected criminological inquiry, some important methodological issues have been raised about their accuracy. Critics of self-report studies frequently suggest that it is unreasonable to expect people to candidly admit illegal acts. This is especially true of those with official records, who may be engaging in the most criminality. At the same time, some people may exaggerate their criminal acts, forget some of them, or be confused about what is being asked. Some surveys contain an overabundance of trivial offences, such as shoplifting small items or using false identification, often lumped together with serious crimes to form a total crime index. Consequently, comparisons between groups can be highly misleading.

The "missing cases" phenomenon is also a concern. Even if 90 percent of a school population voluntarily participate in a self-report study, researchers can never be sure whether the few who refuse to participate or are absent that day comprise a significant portion of the school's population of persistent high-rate offenders. Research indicates that offenders with the most extensive prior criminality are also the most likely to "be poor historians of their own crime commission rates."[26] It is also unlikely that the most serious chronic offenders in the youth population are the most willing to cooperate with university-based criminologists administering self-report tests.[27] Institutionalized youths, who are not generally represented in the self-report surveys, are not only more delinquent than the general youth population, but also are considerably more misbehaving than the most delinquent youths identified in the typical self-report survey.[28] Consequently, self-reports may measure only nonserious, occasional delinquents while ignoring hard-core chronic offenders who may be institutionalized and unavailable for self-reports.

LO3 Evaluating Crime Data

Each source of crime data has strengths and weaknesses. The UCR surveys and the Crime Severity Index are carefully tallied by Statistics Canada and the Canadian Centre for Justice Statistics and contain data on the number of murders and people arrested, information that the other data sources lack. However, the UCR omits the many crimes victims choose not to report to police, and it is subject to the reporting caprices of individual police departments.

The GSS—VS includes unreported crime and important information on the personal characteristics of victims. However, the data consist of estimates made from relatively limited samples of the total Canadian population, so that even narrow fluctuations in the rates of some crimes can have a major impact on findings. It also relies on personal recollections that may be inaccurate. The GSS—VS does not include data on important crime patterns, including murder and drug abuse.

Self-report surveys can provide information on the personal characteristics of offenders, such as their attitudes, values, beliefs, and psychological profiles, that is unavailable from any other source. Yet, at their core, self-reports rely on the honesty of criminal offenders and drug abusers, a population not generally known for accuracy and integrity.

Although their tallies of crimes are certainly not in synch, the crime patterns and trends these sources record are often quite similar.[29] For example, all three sources generally agree about the personal characteristics of serious criminals (such as age and gender) and where and when crime occurs (such as urban areas, nighttime, and summer months). In addition, the problems inherent in each source are consistent over time. Therefore, even if the data sources are incapable of providing a precise and valid count of crime at any given time, they are reliable indicators of changes and fluctuations in yearly crime rates.

What do these data sources tell us about crime trends and patterns?

LO4 Crime Trends

Crime is not new to this century. Historical data from Statistics Canada show that the crime rate in Canada grew steadily from 1886 through to the beginning of World War I in 1914. During World War I the crime rate declined, but immediately after the war the increase resumed, reaching a peak in 1939, just prior to the beginning of World War II.[30] During World War II and into the 1950s, the crime rate remained below prewar levels. However, in the late 1950s and early 1960s the Canadian crime rate began a steady increase that continued until the 1990s. Since the early 1990s, both the number and rate of crime have been steadily declining. Between 1991 and 1998, the crime rate declined by 22 percent and, according to the Canadian Centre for Justice Statistics, both the overall Crime Severity Index and the traditional police-recorded overall crime rate declined again in 2012, matching similar declines in the previous five years[31] (see Table 2.4). Even youth crime, a continuing source of public concern, has been declining since 2001, including a 7 percent decrease in 2012.[32]

Trends in Violent Crime

The violent crimes reported in the UCR survey include homicide, attempted murder, sexual assault, assault, robbery, and abduction. In 2012, 119 000 violent crimes were reported to police, a rate of around 1190 per 100 000 Canadians. According to the Canadian Centre for Justice Statistics, the Violent Crime Severity Index decreased by 3 percent in 2012, and

TABLE 2.4

Overall Crime Severity Index and Traditional Police-Reported Crime Rate, Canada, 2000–2010

| Year | Total Crime Severity Index | | Police-Reported Total Crime Rate Per 100 000 Population | |
	Index Number	Percentage Change from Previous Year	Total Rate	Percentage Change from Previous Year
2000	106.7	−4	7607	−1
2001	105.3	−1	7587	0
2002	104.1	−1	7512	−1
2003	106.8	3	7770	3
2004	104.1	−3	7600	−2
2005	101.3	−3	7325	−4
2006	100.0	−1	7244	−1
2007	95.2	−5	6899	−5
2008	90.4	−5	6617	−4
2009	87.6	−3	6442	−3
2010	82.7	−6	6137	−5
2011	77.4	−6	5756	−6
2012	75.0	−3	5588	−3

Source: Adapted from Statistics Canada, Adapted from Shannon Brennan and Mia Dauvergne, "Police-reported Crime Statistics in Canada," 2010, Juristat, July 2011 Statistics Canada Cat. No. 85-002-X, Tables 1A and 1B, pp. 24, 25. Component of Statistics Canada catalogue no. 85-002-X

Born in 1959 in Lachute, Quebec, Paulson joined the Canadian Armed Forces in 1977 at the age of 18, and went on to win his wings as a fighter pilot and instructor in Moose Jaw, Saskatchewan. Paulson joined the RCMP in 1986 in Chilliwack, British Columbia, where he served in various locations in BC at the municipal, provincial, and federal level. His experience included work in homicide and organized crime investigation, along with Aboriginal and community policing. In 2005, Paulson transferred to RCMP National headquarters in Ottawa where he worked in the Major and Organized Crime Intelligence Branch and National Security Criminal Operations. In 2008, he was promoted to assistant commissioner, National Security Criminal Investigations, and later also served as assistant commissioner, Contract and Aboriginal; Policing Services. In November 2010, Paulson was appointed deputy commissioner, Federal Policing. His appointment as commissioner of the RCMP in 2011 came at a turbulent time, with internal allegations of sexual harassment among officers, criminal investigations of politicians, and growing fears of domestic and international terrorism.

> In November 2011, Bob Paulson became the 23rd commissioner of the RCMP, Canada's national police force.

Commissioner Paulson is married, with two sons and two daughters and is, of course, fluently bilingual. He is also member of the Executive Committee of Interpol.

---

the traditional police-reported violent crime rate also decreased by 3 percent, following decreases in each of the previous five years (see Table 2.5).[33]

Assaults account for more than half (54 percent) of violent crime. Uttering threats is the next most frequently occurring form of violent crime, accounting for 17 percent of the total, followed by robbery (8 percent), criminal harassment (5 percent), and sexual assault (5 percent). After peaking in the mid-1970s, the national homicide rate generally declined until 1999 and has been relatively stable ever since.[34] The number of homicides committed with a firearm has been declining since the 1970s (see Figure 2.4). The use of handguns surpassed rifles or shotguns for the first time in 1991 and by 2006, three times as many victims were killed with a handgun than with a rifle or shotgun.[35]

Even though the official crime data tell us that the violent crime rate has been declining for the past decade, highly publicized cases like the fatal shooting of Zaid Athir Youssef, 17, and Michael Menjivar, 15, outside an Etobicoke, Ontario, school in October 2014 by another 17-year-old youth help convince the general public that Canadian society is growing more violent and crime ridden. Politicians sometimes seize on these tragedies to advocate a quick fix for what is seen to be a growth in violence—ban violent videogames, give police more powers, and prohibit rap and heavy metal music with violent lyrics. Can such measures possibly deter violence such as occurred in the Etobicoke murders?

TABLE 2.5

Violent Crime Severity Index and Traditional Police-Reported Violent Crime Rate Per 100 000 Population, Canada, 2000–2010

	Violent Crime Severity Index		Police-Reported Violent Crime Rate Per 100 000 Population	
Year	Index Number	Percentage Change from Previous Year	Total Rate	Percentage Change from Previous Year
2000	97.8	−2	1494	4
2001	97.2	−1	1473	−1
2002	96.2	−1	1441	−2
2003	97.6	1	1435	0
2004	96.0	−2	1404	−2
2005	98.5	3	1389	−1
2006	100.0	2	1386	0
2007	97.7	−2	1352	−2
2008	94.9	−3	1331	−2
2009	94.1	−1	1318	−1
2010	88.9	−6	1287	−2
2011	85.4	−4	1231	−4
2012	81.4	−5	1190	−3

Source: Adapted from Shannon Brennan and Mia Dauvergne, "Police-reported Crime Statistics in Canada," 2010, Juristat, July 2011 Statistics Canada Cat. No. 85-002-X, Tables 1A and 1B, pp. 24, 25. Component of Statistics Canada catalogue no. 85-002-X Juristat ISSN 1209-6393, Police-reported crime statistics in Canada, 2012 by Samuel Perreault Canadian Centre for Justice Statistics Released on July 25, 2013, pp.26–27.

FIGURE 2.4

Homicide in Canada: Homicide Rates Peaked in the 1970s

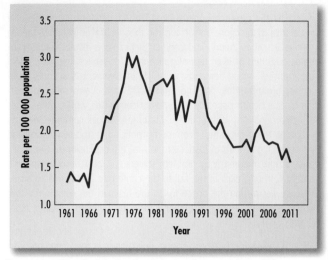

Source: Adapted from Statistics Canada website, http://www.statcan.gc.ca/daily
-quotidien/101026/dq101026a-eng.htm.

Trends in Property Crime

The property crimes reported in the UCR include theft, break and enter, fraud, motor vehicle theft, and possession of stolen goods. Thefts under $5000 are the most common type of property crime committed in Canada and in 2012 they accounted for 42 percent of all property crimes. Interestingly, although they are still prevalent, the rate has dropped 33 percent since 2002.[36]

Trends in Victimization

The rate of victimization in Canada has remained relatively unchanged over the past decade with just over one-quarter of the population aged 15 years and older reporting being a victim of a crime. The majority of crimes reported in 2009 were nonviolent including theft of personal property (34 percent), theft of household property (13 percent), vandalism (11 percent), break-ins (7 percent), and theft of motor vehicles/parts (5 percent); these accounted for 70 percent of incidents recorded by the GSS—VS. Violent incidents, namely physical assault (19 percent), sexual assault (8 percent), and robbery (4 percent), have been stable but highest among youth. Single people are more likely to be victims as opposed to those who are married, and sexual assault rates are higher among females than males. Not surprisingly, physical assault has been highly associated with alcohol and drug use.[37]

What the Future Holds

It is always risky to speculate about the future of crime trends because current conditions can change rapidly. But contemporary criminologists such as Marc Ouimet may have provided some important clues. Ouimet explains that Canadian property crime rates began to level off in the 1980s, as the youth population aged 15 to 24 began to decline in numbers.[38] Ten years later, this same large group or "cohort" of youth, now 25 to 34, moved out of the prime risk years for committing violence, coinciding with the decline in violent crime that began in 1991.

Peter Carrington's research shows that as the Canadian population continues to age, crime rates will continue to decrease right through the year 2041, when decreases will begin to slow down. Until another large youth cohort comes along, like the baby boom, it is likely that Canada will continue to have relatively low crime rates.[39]

While overall in Canada crime rates may continue to decrease, the aging of the baby boomers is having other impacts on the crime rate, in particular in changing the nature of the kinds of crimes that police must respond to. The oldest of the Canadian baby boomers are now in their late 60s, and the youngest are in their early 50s. Most of the members of this age group are now well established, have good incomes, own their own homes, have numerous credit cards, and are looking for good investments to assure their retirement income. Law-enforcement experts point to increases in the number of complaints about telemarketing scams, Internet fraud, and identity theft,

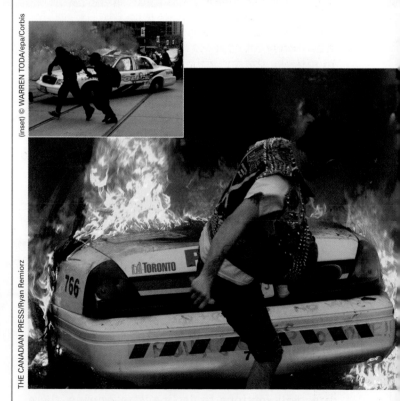

(inset) © WARREN TODA/epa/Corbis

THE CANADIAN PRESS/Ryan Remiorz

G-20 protesters join in trashing a Toronto police cruiser. Those who participated and were later apprehended by police were likely charged with the property crime of mischief—wilful damage to the property of another.

A September 2014 report published by the Fraser Institute, a conservative public policy think tank, argues that with a crime rate falling since the early 1990s, Canadians need to begin questioning why police expenditures and the number of police officers continues to grow. The report's author, Livio Di Matteo, reports that between 2001 and 2012, the number of police officers per 100 000 people in Canada grew by 8.7 percent, while at the same time the crime rate decreased by 26.3 percent. (See Figure 2.5.) The *Ottawa Citizen* reports that since 1997, the "cost of policing in Canada has more than doubled, outpacing the increase in spending by all levels of government." A recently released report (2014) by the Council of Canadian Academies observes that in the 21st century, police must learn to rely on other partners in the "safety and security web," such as organizations, including private companies. The Council also calls for the increased professionalization and use of evidence-based practices—including hiring police officers as specialists, rather than requiring every new recruit to do three or four years on the road as a general duty officer. There appears to be general agreement among recent reports on policing that, in future, some police tasks (e.g., speeding enforcement, serving summonses, scientific forensic identification, community liaison, etc.) will be done by less-qualified, less well paid non-sworn staff.

Beginning in the late 1970s, the call for police to move away from a strictly professional, top-down crime control/detection approach to a more decentralized, community-oriented problem-solving approach, driven by the research findings based on criminological theories like social disorganization, social control theory, broken-window theory, routine activities theory, and conflict theory. As a result, today as little as one-third or even less of police calls for service involve criminal occurrences—while demands for police involvement in schools, community organizations, fire and ambulance calls, alarm calls, addressing mental health issues, other types of committee works, other types of noncriminal disputes, and "quality of life" issues continue to climb year after tear. Advocates of community policing, restorative justice, and peacemaking models of justice argue that the expansion of the police role to that of community problem solvers is a positive development, and may in part explain the fall in the crime rate. Critics would argue that we are paying the police to do the tasks in the community that others could do more cheaply, and focus on building a leaner, more professionalized police services.

What do you think: what role should police place in the 21st century?

Sources: Kelly Egan, "Wasting Time of $90K Cops a Crime That Needs to End," *Ottawa Citizen* (25 November 2014) http://www.pressreader.com/canada/ottawa-citizen/20141126/281590943877001/TextView (accessed 17 October 2015); Livio Di Matteo, "Police and Crime Rates in Canada," *A Comparison of Resources and Outcomes* (September 2014); Richard R. Johnson and Trisha N. Rhodes, "Urban and Small Town Comparison of Citizen Demand for Police Services," *International Journal of Police Science & Management*, vol. 11 iss. 1 (Spring 2009): 27–38, doi: 10.1350/ijps.2009.11.1.107.

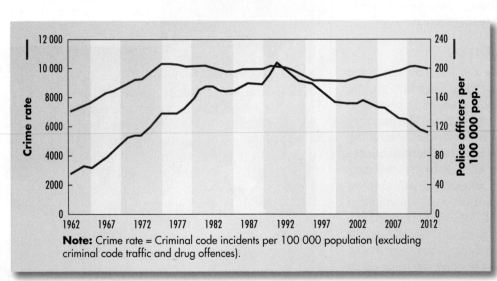

Note: Crime rate = Criminal code incidents per 100 000 population (excluding criminal code traffic and drug offences).

FIGURE 2.5

Police Resources and Crime Rate, 1962–2012

Source: Statistics Canada, 2014: table 1: Statistics Canada, CANSIM Tables 510001, 510026

along with mounting concerns about elder abuse, as early indications of what could be serious problems as the baby boomers mature into old age.[40]

Although Carrington's predictions that crime rates will continue to decline is reassuring, there is no way of telling what unanticipated future changes may influence crime rates. The overall recorded crime rate is forecast to fall to 85 percent of its 1999 level by 2026 and to 81 percent by 2041 (see Figure 2.6). Technological developments such as the rapid expansion of e-commerce have created new classes of crime. Concern about the environment in rural areas may produce a rapid upswing in environmental crimes ranging from vandalism to violence.[41] Terrorism, both at home and abroad, will put new demands on law enforcement.

FIGURE 2.6

Actual and Forecast Recorded Rates of Three Categories of Crime, Canada, 1999–2041

Source: Carrington (2001), "Populating Aging and Crime in Canada, 2000–2041,"*Canadian Journal of Criminology*, 43(3), 331–56. Reprinted with permission from *Canadian Journal of Criminology*

LO5 Crime Patterns

To gain insight into the nature of crime, criminologists look for stable crime rate patterns. If crime rates are consistently higher at certain times, in certain areas, and among certain groups, this knowledge might help explain the onset or cause of crime. For example, if criminal statistics show that crime rates are consistently higher in poor neighbourhoods in large urban areas, then crime may be a function of poverty and neighbourhood decline. If, in contrast, crime rates were spread evenly across the social structure, this would provide little evidence that crime has an economic basis; instead, crime might be linked to socialization, personality, intelligence, or some other trait unrelated to class position or income. In this section we examine traits and patterns that may influence the crime rate.

The Ecology of Crime

Most reported crimes occur during the warm summer months of July and August. During the summer, teenagers and young adults, who usually have the highest crime levels, are out of school and have greater opportunities to commit crime. People also spend more time outdoors, making them easier targets. Two exceptions to this trend are murders and robberies, which occur frequently in December and January (although rates are also high during the summer). Robbery rates increase in the winter partly because the Christmas shopping season means more money in the cash registers of potential targets.[42] Repeat break-and-enter attempts tend to occur at the same time of day as the previously successful break and enter.[43]

Crime rates also may be higher on particular days of the month than at any other time. Government pension and social assistance cheques typically arrive at the end of the month, and with them come increases in activities such as breaking into mailboxes and accosting recipients on the streets. Also, people may have more disposable income at this time, and the availability of extra money may relate to behaviours associated with crime, such as drinking and gambling.[44]

Weather effects, such as temperature swings, may also affect violent crime rates. Crime rates increase with rising temperatures up to a point (about 30 °C), but then begin to decline, perhaps because it becomes too hot for physical exertion.[45] However, the rates of some crimes, such as domestic assault, continue to increase as temperatures rise.[46]

Use of Firearms

According to international criminologists Franklin Zimring and Gordon Hawkins, the proliferation of handguns and the high rate of lethal violence they cause is the single most significant factor separating the crime problem in the United States from the rest of the developed world.[47]

In contrast, Canada has a long history of firearms control legislation dating back to 1892. Canada put in place some of the toughest firearms control legislation in the world, requiring all Canadians who want to purchase a firearm to pass the Canadian Firearms Safety Course (CFSC), to pass a written examination on firearm safety, and to submit to a screening process and background check in order to then acquire a Possession and Acquistion Licence (PAL) before being permitted to purchase a nonrestricted firearm (e.g., a hunting rifle or shotgun); additional restrictions and requirements were put in place for those wishing to acquire a restricted firearm (e.g., handgun, automatic rifle).[48] Public calls for additional restrictions on firearms led to the passage of the *Firearms Act* in 1995 which, among other provisions, created a national Firearms Registry, requiring that all individual firearms be registered with the Firearms registrar in each province. However, the Firearms Registry provisions of the new legislation were revoked in April 2012, no longer requiring owners of nonrestricted firearms to register each individual weapon in their possession.[49]

In Canada (Figure 2.7) firearm-related homicides have been on the decline since the early 1970s, and

FIGURE 2.7

Firearm-Related Homicide, Canada, 1972–2012

Source: Component of Statistics Canada catalogue no. 85-002-X, Juristat ISSN 1209-6393. Firearms and violent crime in Canada, 2012, by Adam Cotter. Canadian Centre for Justice Statistics. Released on April 23rd, 2014 p.8

¹Includes homicides committed with any other weapon (e.g., knife, club, blunt instrument), as well as homicides committed without the use of a weapon (e.g., physical force). Excludes homicides where the weapon used was unknown.

in 2012 the use of a firearm accounted for only about one-third of homicide deaths. Firearm-related robberies have been on the decline since 1991, and the current rates of firearm-related robbery reported by police are the lowest on record. Overall, firearm-related violent crimes decreased by 27 percent between 2009 and 2012. See Figure 2.8.[50]

Social Class and Crime

Criminologists can't agree on whether there is a direct link between social class and crime. Crime statistics show that the poor, those with little education, and those with menial jobs are more likely to be arrested, convicted, and incarcerated, especially for "**street crimes**" such as assaults, prostitution, and theft. After all, common sense tells us that people at the lowest rungs of the social structure have the greatest incentive to commit crimes. Those unable to obtain desired goods and services through conventional means may decide to resort to so-called instrumental crimes such as theft and other illegal activities—for example, selling narcotics—to obtain them, or perhaps they may take out their rage, frustration, and anger against society by committing "expressive" violent crimes such as sexual assault or murder.[51]

street crimes
Crimes such as robbery, assault, sexual assault, theft, and murder that often occur in public places, and are easy to detect.

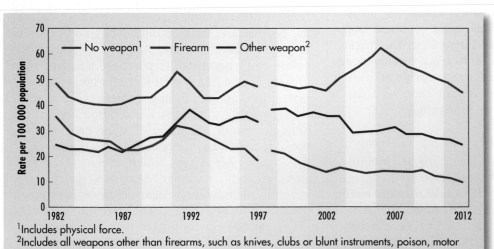

FIGURE 2.8

Robbery, by Type of Weapon, Canada, 1982–2012

Source: Adam Cotter, Firearms and violent crime in Canada, 2012, (Juristat), April 23, 2014, Canadian Centre for Justice Statistics, Statistics Canada catalogue no. 85-002-X, P. 14

¹Includes physical force.
²Includes all weapons other than firearms, such as knives, clubs or blunt instruments, poison, motor vehicles, ligature, or fire.
Note: Revisions have been applied to robbery back to 1998. As such, there is a break in the data series between 1997 and 1998 and any comparisons between the two time series should be made with caution.

Among Canada's cities, Regina reported the highest homicide rate (3.84 per 100 000 population) in 2013. This was followed by Winnipeg (3.24) and Thunder Bay (2.46). "One homicide is too many," Regina Police Chief Troy Hagen told reporters … that homicides are "very hard to prevent" because, unlike many other crimes, police are called only afterward. Their frequency also speaks to the work needed in helping at-risk children, and addressing addictions and mental illness, he said.

Source: Quote is from "Regina deadliest Canadian city; Sask. second among provinces; 2013 homicide statistics show rate here higher, despite national declines," *Leader Post* [Regina, Sask] 02 Dec 2014: A.1.

Official statistics confirm that victimization rates for both males and females in inner-city, high-poverty areas are generally higher than those in suburban or wealthier areas.[52] Studies using aggregate police statistics (arrest records) have consistently shown that crime rates in lower-class areas exceed those in wealthier neighbourhoods. Another "official" indicator of a class–crime relationship comes from surveys of prison inmates, which consistently show that prisoners were members of the lower class and unemployed or underemployed in the years before their incarceration.

But do those in the lowest social class positions really commit more crimes? Or, because they are poor, uneducated, and powerless, are they just more likely to get caught, convicted, and sent to jail? Some criminologists suggest that the relationship between official crime and social class is a function of law-enforcement practices, not actual criminal behaviour patterns. Police may devote more resources to poor areas, and consequently apprehension rates may be higher there. Others observe that middle- and upper-class Canadians probably commit just as many crimes as those in the lower classes, but these suite crimes, such as fraud, embezzlement, stock market manipulation, and price fixing, are much harder to detect.[53]

Class and Self-Reports

Self-report data have been used extensively to test the class–crime relationship. If people in all social classes self-report similar crime patterns, but only those in the lower class are formally arrested, that would explain higher crime rates in lower-class neighbourhoods. However, if lower-class people report greater criminal activity than their middle- and upper-class peers, it would indicate that official statistics accurately represent the crime problem.

Surprisingly, self-report studies generally do not find a direct relationship between social class and youth crime.[54] Socioeconomic class is related to official processing by police, courts, and correctional agencies, but not to the actual commission of crimes. While lower- and middle-class youths self-report equal amounts of crime, lower-class youths have a greater chance of getting arrested, convicted, and incarcerated and becoming official delinquents.[55] More than 30 years ago, Charles Tittle, Wayne Villemez, and Douglas Smith concluded that little if any support exists for the contention that crime is primarily a lower-class phenomenon. They argued that official statistics probably reflect class bias in processing lower-class offenders.[56]

Weighing the Evidence for a Class–Crime Relationship

Tittle's research has sparked significant debate. Many self-report instruments include trivial offences such as using false identification or drinking alcohol. Their inclusion may obscure the true class–crime relationship because affluent youths frequently engage in trivial offences such as petty theft, using drugs, and simple assault. Those who support a class–crime relationship suggest that if only serious indictable offences are considered, a significant association can be observed.[57] Studies showing middle- and lower-class youths to be equally delinquent rely on measures weighted toward minor crimes (e.g., using false identification or skipping school); when serious crimes, such as break and enter and assault, are compared, lower-class youths are significantly more delinquent.[58] There is also debate over the most appropriate measure of class. Should it be parents' income? Occupation? Educational attainment? Findings may be skewed if the measurement of class used is inappropriate or invalid.

> **suite crimes**
> Crimes such as price-fixing, insider trading, embezzlement, and improper disposal of toxic waste that often occur behind closed doors in corporate boardrooms and offices, and are hard to detect.

aging out (desistance)
The fact that people commit less crime as they mature.

Like so many other criminological controversies, the debate over the true relationship between class and crime will most likely persist. The weight of recent evidence seems to suggest that serious, official crime is more prevalent among the lower classes, whereas less serious, self-reported crime is spread more evenly throughout the social structure.[59] Income inequality, poverty, and resource deprivation are all associated with the most serious violent crimes, including homicide and assault.[60] Communities that lack economic and social opportunities also produce high levels of frustration; their residents believe that they are relatively more deprived than residents of more affluent areas and may turn to criminal behaviour to relieve their frustration.[61] In these communities, family life is disrupted, and law-violating youth gangs thrive in a climate that undermines adult supervision.[62] Conversely, when the poor are provided with economic opportunities via welfare and social assistance, crime rates drop.[63]

Nonetheless, although crime rates may be higher in lower-class areas, poverty alone cannot explain why a particular individual becomes a chronic violent criminal; if it did, the crime problem would be much worse than it is now.[64]

LO6 Age and Crime

There is general agreement that age is inversely related to criminality—the older you are, the less likely you are to engage in criminal activity.[65] Regardless of economic status, marital status, race, sex, or other factors, younger people commit crime more often than their older counterparts. Research indicates this relationship has been stable across time periods ranging from the early 1900s to the present era.[66] Figure 2.9 shows the relationship between age and crime.

Official statistics tell us that young people are arrested at a disproportionate rate to their numbers in the population; victim surveys generate similar findings for crimes in which assailant age can be determined. Whereas people aged 12 to 17 collectively make up about 8 percent of the total Canadian population, they account for about 20 percent of all criminal charges. The rate at which youth are charged for crimes of violence is double the adult rate; and the charge rate for youth accused of property crimes is more than triple the adult rate. In the case of motor vehicle theft, youth aged 15–18 years account for 30 percent of those accused of motor vehicle theft, and three-quarters of those charged are under the age of 25.[67]

As a general rule, property crime is a young person's activity, peaking at around age 16, and dropping off significantly after age 20. Violent crime peaks at about age 18, but persists much longer, dropping off in frequency only after about age 35.[68]

Older Canadians, those over the age of 55, are particularly resistant to the temptations of crime; they make up about 22 percent of the population but account for only 4 percent of those charged with a criminal offence. Males aged 55 and over are most frequently arrested for impaired driving, theft, and common assault; females over 55 are most frequently arrested for theft, fraud, and impaired driving.[69] Even those convicted and put in prison experience the effects of age, as research shows that offenders over the age of 40 who have been released from prison are less likely to commit additional crimes, compared to younger offenders.[70] There has been little change in the crime rate for older Canadians for the past 25 years. The fact that people commit less crime as they mature is referred to as aging out or desistance.

Why does aging out occur? One view is that there is a direct relationship between aging and crime. Psychologists note that young people, especially the indigent and antisocial, tend to discount the future.[71] They

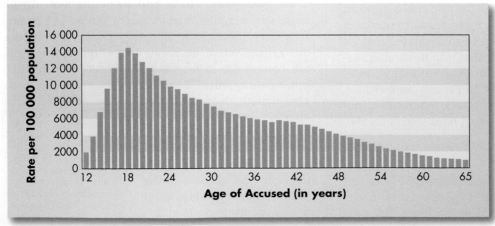

FIGURE 2.9

Visual Depiction of Crime Data by Age

Source: Shannon Brennan, Police-reported crime statistics in Canada, 2011 (Juristat, July 24, 2012), Statistics Canada catalogue no. 85-002-X, p. 20

The "Geezer Bandit," believed to be somewhere between 60 and 70 years of age, is suspected by the FBI of robbing as many as 16 banks in Southern California between 2009 and 2011. Despite the offer of a $20 000 reward for information about him, the Geezer Bandit remains at large.

are impatient, and, because their future is uncertain, they are unwilling or unable to delay gratification. As they mature, troubled youths are able to develop a long-term life view and resist the need for immediate gratification.[72] Kids may view crime as fun, a risky but exciting social activity. As they grow older, life patterns such as job and marriage become inconsistent with criminality; people literally grow out of crime.[73]

James Q. Wilson and Richard Herrnstein argue that aging out is a function of the natural history of the human life cycle.[74] Deviance in adolescence is fuelled by the need for conventionally unobtainable money and sex and reinforced by close relationships with peers who defy conventional morality. At the same time, teenagers are becoming independent from parents and other adults who enforce conventional standards. They have a new sense of energy and strength and are involved with peers who are similarly vigorous and frustrated. Adults, on the other hand, develop the ability to delay gratification and forgo the immediate gains that law violations bring. They also start wanting to take responsibility for their behaviour and to adhere to conventional mores, such as establishing long-term relationships and starting a family.[75] Research shows that young people may turn to crime as a way to solve the problems of adolescence, including loneliness, frustration, and fear of peer rejection. As they mature, conventional means of problem solving become available and their life experience helps them seek out nondestructive solutions to their personal travails.[76]

Although most people age out of crime, some do pursue a criminal career. Yet even career criminals eventually slow down as they age. Crime is too dangerous, physically taxing, and unrewarding (and

punishments too harsh and long lasting) to become a long-term way of life for most people.[77] By middle age, many of even the most chronic offenders terminate their criminal behaviour.

Gender and Crime

Crime is for the most part a male activity. In 2011, 81 percent of cases in adult criminal court in Canada involved a male accused. Women accounted for 19 percent of accused. Offences for which males had the highest involvement included sexual assault (98 percent), other sexual offences (97 percent), and weapons offences (91 percent). On the other hand, females were most highly represented in cases of theft (35 percent), prostitution (34 percent), and fraud (30 percent).[78] Significantly, the pattern of sex differences in criminal activity is consistent across different societies, and over time.

Why are there gender differences in the crime rate? Early criminologists pointed to biological and psychological differences between males and females to explain the differences in crime rates. They maintained that because females were physically weaker and psychologically more passive, they were less likely to commit crimes. Cesare Lombroso argued that a small group of female criminals lacked "typical" female traits of "piety, maternity, undeveloped intelligence, and weakness."[79] Lombroso's theory became known as the masculinity hypothesis; in essence, a few "masculine" females were responsible for the handful of crimes that women commit.[80]

Some criminologists still consider trait differences a key determinant of crime rate differences. For example, some criminologists link antisocial behaviour to hormonal influences by arguing that male sex hormones (androgens) account for more aggressive male

Rates of female violence are rising faster than rates for males. One reason may be the breakdown of the old stereotype that girls don't display aggression.

THE CANADIAN RESPONSE TO YOUTH CRIME

Despite the overall decline in the youth crime rate, there are still calls by the public and media to "get tough" on youth crime. The summer of 2010 saw the first release of the Youth Crime Severity Index (Table 1) and the Youth Violent Crime Severity Index (Table 2). Based on the same concept as the general Crime Severity Index (CSI) offences received a weight based on their seriousness.[85]

As can be seen in Table 1, overall both the seriousness and the number of crimes committed by youth has been declining since 2003, with the police- reported youth crime rate declining by 20 percent between 2009 and 2012.[86]

In addition, despite media calls for action on youth crime to the contrary, the rate of violent crime committed by youth declined by 28 percent between 2003 and 2012, as shown in Table 2.[87]

Historically, the public response to youth crime in Canada is one of controversy and contradiction. The first federal act designed to specifically address youth crime was the *Juvenile Delinquents Act* (JDA), passed in 1908. Under the JDA, youth were not charged with crimes. Instead, young people who came into conflict with the law were brought before the court to plead "true" or "not true" to the charge of being a "delinquent" in need of treatment and supervision. Even youth accused of minor transgressions such as truancy, running away from home, underage drinking, or just being incorrigible could be declared delinquent and institutionalized or put on probation. Unfortunately, the *parens patriae* basis of the JDA, where the state takes on the role of parent for children in need of guidance and treatment, meant that youth had very few legal rights and no way to challenge the decisions of the courts.

© Ocean/Corbis

TABLE 1

Youth Crime Severity Index and Rate of Youth Accused of Police-Reported Crime, Canada, 2000–2012

Year	Youth Crime Severity Index		Police-Reported Youth Crime Rate Per 100 000 Population	
	Index Number	Percentage Change from Previous Year	Total Rate	Percentage Change from Previous Year
2000	103.5	4	6914	7
2001	106.0	2	7159	4
2002	101.1	−5	6945	−3
2003	106.0	5	7280	5
2004	100.8	−5	6959	−4
2005	97.3	−4	6596	−5
2006	100.0	3	6812	3
2007	101.6	2	6783	0
2008	96.2	−5	6578	−3
2009	96.6	0	6594	0
2010	90.5	−5	6187	−6
2011	83.4	−9	5599	−10
2012	78.1	−6	5224	−7

Source: Samuel Perreault, "Police-reported Crime Statistics in Canada," 2012 Juristat (July 2013) Statistics Canada Cat. no. 85-002-X.

TABLE 2

Youth Violent Crime Severity Index and Rate of Youth Accused of Police-Reported Violent Crime, Canada, 2000–2012

Year	Youth Violent Crime Severity Index		Police-Reported Youth Violent Crime Rate Per 100 000 Population	
	Index Number	Percentage Change from Previous Year	Total Rate	Percentage Change from Previous Year
2000	89.3	7	1944	13
2001	91.4	2	1984	2
2002	87.3	−5	1898	−4
2003	92.6	6	1961	3
2004	87.8	−5	1925	−2
2005	94.1	7	1895	−2
2006	100.0	6	1960	3
2007	102.2	2	1956	0
2008	96.3	−6	1904	−3
2009	97.8	2	1895	0
2010	94.9	−3	1854	−2
2011	89.2	−6	1764	−5
2012	83.0	−7	1639	−7

Source: Samuel Perreault, "Police-reported Crime Statistics in Canada," 2012 Juristat (July 2013) Statistics Canada Cat. no. 85-002-X.

By the late 1960s it was clear that the JDA needed to be replaced by legislation that could better address the growth in youth crime taking place at the time, a consequence of the baby-boom children now maturing into teenagers. After years of debate and many versions of the statute, the *Young Offenders Act* (YOA) was proclaimed law in April 1984. The new act did away with the status of "juvenile delinquent" so that young people could now be held accountable for the specific criminal offences they had committed. At the same time, the YOA introduced legal rights similar to those held by adults. Still, under the YOA children and young persons were to receive special consideration, in the form of guidance and treatment and lighter sentences for their crimes. Unfortunately, in attempting to make youth accountable for their crimes, while at the same time providing for shorter sentences to encourage rehabilitation, the YOA failed to satisfy both the "get tough" and the "child saver" camps. Research showed that too many youth convicted of minor offences were placed in custody.[88] The media consistently point to high-profile cases of violent crime as evidence that we needed to get tough on youth crime.

On April 1, 2003, the **Youth Criminal Justice Act (YCJA)** became law, introducing the "justice model" to deal with crimes committed by young people. According to this model and to the "Declaration of Principle" that guides the YCJA, crime prevention through rehabilitation, in combination with the application of meaningful consequences, should be the goal of the youth justice system. To achieve this goal, alternative measures to avoid criminal charges and sentences of custody for minor offences are emphasized, while at the same time "fair and proportionate accountability" will ensure that serious crimes committed by youth are punished with stiffer sentences. In addition, youth will be afforded enhanced protections to ensure that their legal rights are protected.

Will the YCJA end the controversy about how to deal with youth who commit crimes? Not likely. Sociologist Bernard Schissel argues that young people have become a sort of scapegoat for a growing fear of crime in society, an easy target to blame for a host of society's ills and fears.[89] Others observe that youth crime is only a symptom—of social inequality and poverty, lack of educational resources, lack of perceived opportunity, and inadequate parenting. Despite the success of the YCJA in decreasing use of judicial sanctions as well as reducing the number of youth in custody, while at the same time supporting a reduction in the youth crime rate, still critics call for a "get tougher" on youth crime approach.[90] In 2012, passage of the federal government's *Safe Streets and Communities Act* introduced a number of amendments to the YCJA, including stricter provisions meeting the standards for release on bail for youth charged with serious offences; tougher sentencing principles for violent or repeat offenders; and the requirement that the Crown consider an adult sentence for any youth aged 14 years or older charged with murder, attempted murder, manslaughter, or aggravated sexual assault, among other amendments.

> **Youth Criminal Justice Act (YCJA)**
> Law that provides for a range of alternate measures to divert minor cases out of the courts and out of custody sentences, but will mean stiffer sentences for serious crimes.

CRITICAL THINKING

1. Do you think there is a youth crime problem in Canada? Why or why not?

2. What do you think is the most effective way to deal with youth crime? Should we treat youth exactly the same as adults? Why or why not?

Source: Bernard Schissel, *Social Dimensions of Canadian Youth Justice* (Toronto: Oxford University Press, 1993); Bernard Schissel, *Blaming Children: Youth Crime, Moral Panics and the Politics of Hate* (Halifax, Fernwood Publishing, 1997); W. Gordon West, "Reconstructing Canadian Moral Panic: Youth and School Violence," in Thomas O'Reilly-Fleming (ed.), *Post Critical Criminology* (Scarborough, Ontario: Prentice-Hall, 1996); Thomas Gabor, "Methodological Orthodoxy or Eclecticism? The Case of Youth Violence," *Canadian Journal of Criminology* 42 (2000): 77–83; Jim Hackler and Wasanti Paranjape, "Juvenile Justice Statistics: Mythmaking or Measure of System Response," *Canadian Journal of Criminology*, 25 (1983): 209–26; Peter Carrington, "Factors Affecting Police Diversion of Young Offenders: A Statistical Analysis," Report to the Solicitor General Canada, 1998; Robert Hoge, D.A. Andrews, and Alan Leschied, "Tests of Three Hypotheses Regarding the Predictors of Delinquency," *Journal of Abnormal Child Psychology* 22 (1994): 547–59. http://www.justice.gc.ca/eng/cj-jp/yj-jj/ycja-lsjpa/sheets-feuillets/amend-modif.html

THE CANADIAN PRESS/Nathan Denette

Police officers stand by as a lockdown was ordered at Central Technical School in Toronto after at least one shot was reportedly fired shortly after 1 p.m. in a stairwell of the school on the afternoon of September 30, 2010. Do we need tougher laws to deal with youth violent crime?

behaviour; thus, gender-related hormonal differences can explain the gender gap in the crime rate.[81]

However, by the mid-20th century, most criminologists understood gender differences in the crime rate as a function of socialization. Female criminals were described as troubled individuals, alienated at home, who pursued crime as a means of compensating for their disrupted personal lives.[82] The streets became a "second home" to girls whose physical and emotional adjustment was hampered by a strained home life marked by conditions such as absent fathers or overly competitive mothers. The relatively few females who commit violent crimes report having home and family relationships that are more troubled than those experienced by males.[83]

In the 1970s, liberal feminists focused their attention on the social and economic role of women in society and its relationship to female crime rates.[84] They suggested that the traditionally lower crime rate for women could be explained by their "second-class" economic and social position. They predicted that as women's social roles changed and their lifestyles became more like those of men, their crime rates would converge.[91] Though much progress has been made in addressing the economic and social inequality of women in Canadian society, working women still make only three-quarters the money men make, often for doing the same work; continue to shoulder the burden for most childrearing and housework; and are much more likely than males to live in poverty.[92]

Crime rates are still considerably higher for males than for females. However, criminologists have pointed to rapid increases in the female violence rate as evidence of a troubling trend. Between 1991 and 2011, the rate of females charged with violent crimes has increased by 35 percent, while the male rate has decreased by 32 percent.[93] More disturbing, other research on youth crime shows that rates of overall crime and especially violent crime may be increasing much more rapidly for girls than boys, as much as two or three times faster.[94]

LO7 Race and Crime

There is not a lot of Canadian research about the link between race and crime. In fact, due to the sensitivity of the issue, most Canadian police and correctional agencies do not collect or publish data that link racial characteristics with crimes. Criminologist Scot Wortley reports that government statistics show that blacks and especially Aboriginal people are overrepresented in the criminal justice system.[95] However, it is difficult to carry out research into the reasons that these racial groups are overrepresented: Do they commit more crimes, or are these groups just more likely to be targeted for arrest, conviction, and incarceration?

In 2007/2008, Aboriginal adults accounted for 22 percent of admissions to sentenced custody, while representing only about 3 percent of the Canadian population.[96] Rates of violent crime are especially high on First Nations reserves.

Causes of Racial Disparity

Racial differences in the crime rate remain an extremely sensitive issue. Research shows that suspects who are poor, visible minority, and male are more likely to be formally arrested than suspects who are white, affluent, and female.[97] Some critics charge that police

Aileen Wuornos. Her life and crimes, including the murders of seven men, were depicted in the 2003 movie *Monster*.

Karla Homolka. Convicted of manslaughter in the murders of Lesley Mahaffy and Kristen French, she claimed she was a victim and unwilling accomplice of the killer, Paul Bernardo.

© AF archive / Alamy Stock Photo

Based on a true story, *Fruitvale Station* (2013) depicts the last day in the life of Oscar Grant, a 22-year old black man killed by police on New Year's Day 2009. Travelling with friends to New Year's celebrations in San Francisco, Grant gets into a fight with another man on the train. The San Francisco Bay Area Rapid Transit Police (BART) are called and are waiting on the Fruitvale Station platform when Grant and five of his friends exit the train. While witnesses captured the scene on video using their cell-phones, two BART police officers, Johannes Mehserle and Anthony Pirone, confronted Grant and his friends, pushing them to the ground. Witnesses and the recorded video testify to the fact that Grant and his friends did not resist the police officers. However, while Officer Mehserle is attempting to handcuff Grant, a gunshot is heard, and Grant is shot in the back. Mehserle later claims that he meant only to Taser Grant, but drew the wrong weapon and instead shot and killed Grant. Officer Mehserle was convicted in July 2010 of involuntary manslaughter in the killing. Protest-ers rioted after the verdict was brought down, claiming racial bias in the court deliberations, and that the death of yet another young black man was not taken seriously. Mehserle ended up serving only 11 months of his two-year sentence: he later applied for reinstatement with the BART, but was refused. Pirone was fired in June 2010 for his part in escalat-ing the situation that led to the killing. In May 2014, the five friends who were with Oscar Grant the night of the killing won a $175 000 civil suit against the San Francisco Bay Area Rapid Transit Police for exces-sive use of force and illegal detainment.

Criminologists have long recognized that criminal justice system is guilty of racial bias in who gets arrested by police, how they get arrested, whether they make bail once arrested, who actually goes to trial, who gets convicted, and how they are treated while in prison. The important question now is: what can we do about racial bias in the criminal justice system? Most would agree that better information and training for those working in the criminal justice system is an important step, so that they understand that racial characteristics (skin colour most often) are unre-lated to criminal behaviour: while poverty, living in crime-ridden neigh-bourhoods, and lack of educational and employment opportunities *are* related to criminal behaviour; people living in these types of conditions are at greater risk for engaging in criminal activities but it has nothing to do with their physical characteristics.

officers may use "racial profiling" to target certain visible minority groups for arrest.[98] For example, a 2005 study conducted by Scot Wortley in Kingston, Ontario, found that a young black male was 3.7 times more likely to be stopped and questioned by police than a Caucasian, and an Aboriginal person was 1.4 times more likely to be stopped than a Caucasian.[99] In a 2007 survey of black, white and Chinese resi-dents of Toronto about their personal experiences of being stopped and questioned by police, Wortley and Owusu-Bempah found that blacks were more likely to report being stopped and searched by police, with 23 percent of black males reporting being stopped and questioned within the previous two years., com-pared to 8 percent of white males and 6 percent of Chinese males. Black males were also much more likely to be physically searched by police.[100]

While UCR data may reflect discriminatory police practices, Aboriginal people are arrested for a dispro-portionate amount of violent crime, such as assaults and murder, and it is improbable that police discretion alone could account for these proportions. It is doubtful that police routinely ignore white killers and robbers, while arresting violent Aboriginal offenders. Many criminologists today concede that recorded racial differ-ences in violent crime arrest rates cannot be explained away solely by racism or differential treatment within the criminal justice system.[101] To do so would be to ignore the social problems that may explain why crime is more frequent in some racial groups.

Racism and Crime

How, then, can racial patterns be explained? Most explanations focus on the impact of economic depri-vation, social disorganization, subcultural adapta-tions, and the legacy of racism and discrimination on personality and behaviour.[102]

Aboriginal people in particular have suffered through a long history of inequality and racism in Canada that has left long-lasting emotional scars.[103] The legacy of the past is still an element of daily life in Aboriginal communities, undermining faith in social and political institutions and weakening confidence

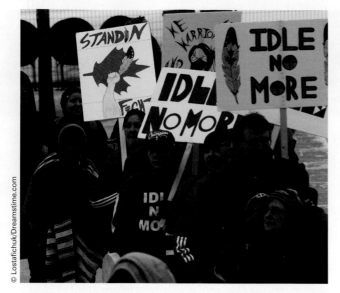

© Lostafichuk/Dreamstime.com

Beginning in December 2012, the "Idle No More" movement started with four Saskatchewan women getting together to discuss the federal government's Bill C-45, an omnibus bill that could have far-reaching consequences for Aboriginal treaty rights. Using Twitter at #IdleNoMore, their comments generated debate and discussion among both Aboriginal and non-Aboriginals about the status of Aboriginal rights in Canada, including the treatment of Aboriginal people by the criminal justice system, and ultimately generated a social movement and protests that spread throughout Canada during 2013.

in the justice system. Such fears are supported by empirical evidence that Aboriginal people, both male and female, are treated more harshly by the criminal justice system than members of virtually any other group. There is also evidence that Aboriginal people are more likely than whites to be incarcerated for committing the same crimes, and are much less likely to be granted parole. It is possible that some judges view many Aboriginal offenders as "poor risks," considering them more likely to reoffend than white offenders.[104] Yet, Aboriginal victims of crime receive less public concern and media attention than white victims.[105]

Is Convergence Possible?

Considering these overwhelming social problems, is it possible that racial crime rates will soon converge? One argument is that if economic conditions improve in minority communities, then differences in crime rates will eventually disappear.[106] A trend toward Aboriginal self-government, underway since the late 1980s, may help reduce race-based crime rate differentials.[107]

Computerized Crime Mapping in Policing and Criminological Theory

By the late 1990s, a growing number of police and other law enforcement agencies began employing techniques to permit computerized crime mapping such as geographical information systems (GIS) computer software to map crime data. Responding to public criticism and a number of high-profile

Halifax Regional Police

In 2014, Hamilton Police Service launched a new online crime mapping tool that allows residents to search when and where certain types of crimes have occurred in the city.

Source: Sunnie Huang, CBC News, "Hamilton Police Launch Online Crime Map," (17 November 2014) at http://www.cbc.ca/news/canada/hamilton/news/hamilton-police-launch-online-crime-map-1.2837957 (accessed 19 October 2015).

studies[108] that showed traditional police strategies were ineffective in preventing or reducing crime, and making use of new developments in computerized information systems, police agencies around the world began to adopt an "evidence-based" approach to policing, making use of the mountains of data they collect to begin to map out where and when crimes were being committed, and to use this information to develop new strategies for deploying police resources to reduce crime, including the identification of "hot spots."[109] At the same time, law enforcement use of spatial crime data created a renewed interest in "environmental criminology," the study of where crime and victimization take place, and how geographical places shape opportunities for criminal behaviour and victimization, including social disorganization theory, routine activities theory, and situational crime prevention.[110] Environmental crime theories are the foundation for many contemporary crime prevention and reduction programs, including most community policing strategies.

Today, the use of GIS systems in law enforcement is common practice, and is used to determine the spatial deployment of personnel and other resources; locate detachments and community policing offices; identify drug distribution networks; map the locations of specific crimes, including serial occurrences; identify "hot spots" and other high-risk areas; and monitor in real time what is taking place in the field, including the movements and locations of officers.

Summary

There are three primary sources of crime statistics: the Uniform Crime Reports, based on police data accumulated by the Canadian Centre for Justice Statistics; self-reports from criminal behaviour surveys; and victim surveys. The Crime Severity Index, based on the UCR data, was introduced as a new, overall measure of crime in 2009. The Crime Severity Index helps determine the severity of police-reported crime in relation to the past and to Canada overall. The mechanics involve assigning a "seriousness" weight to each type of offence that is derived from actual sentences handed down by courts in all provinces and territories, with more serious crimes being assigned higher weight than less serious ones.

Each data source has its strengths and weaknesses. The UCR, based only on crimes reported to the police, tends to underrepresent the total amount of crime, including white-collar and environmental crime. Self-reports from criminal behaviour surveys, often conducted with young people, tend to overrepresent minor crimes such as vandalism or shoplifting, and downplay involvement in serious crimes such as sexual assault. Victim surveys may more validly represent minor types of crimes such as theft or vandalism that victims did not report to police, but more serious crimes may be underrepresented, due to victims' fear of disclosing traumatic events or fear of getting in trouble themselves either from authorities or from those who committed the crime.

The data sources show stable patterns in the crime rate. Ecological patterns show that crime varies by season and by urban versus rural environment. There is also evidence of gender and age gaps in the crime rate: Men commit more crime than women, and young people commit more crime than the elderly. Crime data show that people commit less crime as they age, but the significance and cause of this pattern are still not completely understood.

Similarly, racial and class patterns appear in the crime rate. However, it is still unclear whether these are true differences or a function of discriminatory law enforcement known as racial profiling.

Evidence-based policing makes use of crime and other organizational data to make better use of police resources to in order to prevent and investigate crimes. Computerized crime mapping using GIS allows police to map out the location of crimes, identify hot spots and other areas of concern, and deploy and track use of police resources.

computerized crime mapping The use of police data and geographical information systems (GIS) computer programs to construct and analyze digital maps representing the spatial location of crimes, for the purpose of planning police use of resources to prevent and reduce crime.

Discussion Questions

1. Would you answer honestly if a national crime survey asked you about your criminal behaviour, including underage drinking and drug use? If not, why?

2. How would you explain gender differences in the crime rate? That is, why do you think males are more violent than females?

3. Assuming that males are more violent than females, does that mean that crime has a biological rather than a social basis (because males and females share a similar environment)?

4. UCR data tell us that crime rates are higher in large cities than in small villages. What does that tell us about the effect of TV, films, and music on teenage behaviour?

READY TO STUDY?

IN THE BOOK, YOU CAN:

✔ Check your understanding of what you've just read by reading the Summary at the end of each chapter.

✔ Rip out the Chapter in Review card at the back of the book to have the key terms and Learning Objectives handy, and complete the quizzes provided (answers are on the bottom of the back page!).

ONLINE YOU CAN:

✔ Stay organized and efficient with MindTap—a single destination with all the course material and study aids you need to succeed. Built-in apps leverage social media and the latest learning technology. For example:

✔ ReadSpeaker will read the text to you.

✔ Flashcards are pre-populated to provide you with a jump start for review—or you can create your own.

✔ You can highlight text and make notes in your MindTap Reader. Your notes will flow into Evernote, the electronic notebook app that you can access anywhere when it's time to study for the exam.

✔ Prepare for tests with quizzes.

Go to www.nelson.com/student to access these digital resources.

Victims and Victimization

© ZUMA Press Inc / Alamy Stock Photo

Learning Objectives

LO1 Define victimology.

LO2 Identify major problems faced by victims of crime.

LO3 Identify major risk factors for being victimized.

LO4 Explain the victim precipitation theory, lifestyle theories, and routine activities theory.

LO5 Describe how Canadian society has attempted to provide care for victims of crime.

LO6 Identify victims' services programs.

LO7 Explain the importance of advocacy for rights of victims.

LO8 Interpret the research on the effectiveness of programs designing to prevent victimization.

Introduction

As one newspaper article recently noted, Rehtaeh Parsons was the most famous victim in Canada and her name has become synonymous with a national effort to create and enforce laws around bullying, pornography, consent, and how police respond to allegations of sexual assault. In November 2011, when she was 15 years of age, Rehtaeh attended a house party and while she was leaning out a window to vomit, a photograph was taken of a 16-year-old boy penetrating her from behind. The boy was smiling and giving a thumbs-up to the camera. In September 2014 the now 20-year-old who snapped the picture pleaded guilty to one count of manufacturing child pornography while the now 19-year-old male in the photo is awaiting trial for distributing the image. This is little comfort to Rehtaeh Parsons and her family.

In the days following the infamous party, the photo quickly spread around Rehtaeh's school. Her parents believe the constant bullying from her peers together with police indifference eventually led to Rehtaeh taking her own life. In the aftermath of her death, her name and her plight has become an international symbol for sexual exploitation in the digital age.

In a strange irony, because the police felt they had insufficient evidence to charge her assailant with sexual assault, they proceeded by way of laying charges relating to child pornography. Yet because

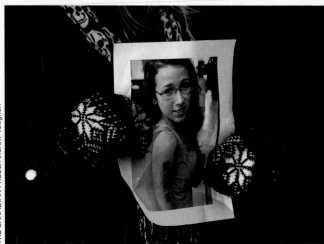

In the aftermath of Rehtaeh Parsons' death, her name and her plight has become an international symbol for sexual exploitation in the digital age.

of a media ban in child pornography cases her story and her name could not be revealed, leading Rehtaeh's mother to comment, "By taking the power of her name away, they're stripping her of her voice a second time." According to Halifax freelance reporter Ryan Van Horne, the law "is unjust in this case and should be ignored." "Rehtaeh Parsons' name brings power to any discussion about sexual consent, cyberbullying, and suicide prevention."[1]

"It's hard to overstate the impact of Rehtaeh Parsons's name throughout Canada. "I think everybody who has heard this story, seen this story, were shocked, were saddened," Prime Minister Stephen Harper said after her death. Rehtaeh's story has resulted in many calls (and increased government funding) to a Halifax, Nova Scotia, rape crisis centre; federal legislation to better address online exploitation; and a six-month investigation of the police response in her case.[2]

The horrific acts carried out by Rehtaeh's assailants and those who bullied her afterward illustrate the terrible impact crime can have on victims, their families, and society in general. Why do some people become targets of criminal acts? Is victimization a matter of chance, or are there ways victims can somehow deflect or avoid criminal behaviour? What can be done to protect victims and, failing that, what can be done to help them in the aftermath of crime?

LO1 Defining Victimology

The Code of Hammurabi is considered one of the first known attempts to establish a written code of conduct. Hammurabi was the king of Babylon, the commercial centre for most of the civilized world in approximately 2000 B.C.[3] The Code of Hammurabi was created to provide the necessary order and stability essential for commerce. It established rules regarding certain offences, sexual relationships, interpersonal violence, code of ethics, and other issues. The idea that society should assist victims of crime can be traced back to the Code of Hammurabi, which stipulated that when a person was robbed or murdered, the city in which the crime occurred would compensate the victim or the victim's heirs for their losses. The Code is recognized as the first law establishing the rights of victims. Such concern would not resurface until the latter half of the 20th century. In the intervening years, crime evolved from relationship between an offender and a victim to that of an offender and the state, with the victim playing the role of witness for the state. That is, a crime is considered to have been committed against the state, not the victim. The victims' rights movement in Canada grew out of the feminist movement and the response to women victimized by domestic violence and sexual assault. The 1980s saw the emergence of victims' organizations such as Victims of Violence, Citizens United for Safety and Justice, and the now defunct Canadians Against Violence Everywhere Advocating for Its Termination (CAVEAT), which lobbied government to recognize the rights of victims and brought about changes that will be discussed later in this chapter.[4]

DID YOU KNOW?

- Victimology is the branch of criminology that examines the nature and extent of crime victimization.

- The total economic loss from crime victimization amounts to billions of dollars annually.

- Victims may suffer long-term trauma, including post-traumatic stress disorder.

- Many victims become fearful and go through a fundamental life change.

- People who are victims may be more likely to engage in antisocial acts themselves.

For many years, crime victims were not considered an important topic for criminological study. Victims were viewed as the passive recipients of a criminal's anger, greed, or frustration; like eight-year-old Victoria Stafford, they were considered to be people "in the wrong place at the wrong time." Stafford went missing on the afternoon of April 8, 2009, while walking home from Oliver Stephens Public School in Woodstock, Ontario. Surveillance camera footage from a nearby high school showed Victoria walking away from the school engaged in conversation with a woman. The woman, who was identified as Terri-Lynne McClintic, 18, and boyfriend Michael Rafferty, 28, both received life sentences for abducting, sexually assaulting, and brutally beating Stafford to death. At McClintic's trial she intimated that she had never intended to steal a child that fateful afternoon.[5]

In the late 1960s, a number of pioneering studies found that, contrary to popular belief, the victim's own behaviour is important in the crime process. Victims were found to influence criminal behaviour by playing an active role in a criminal incident, as when an assault victim initially provokes an eventual attacker. Victims can also play an indirect role in a criminal incident, as when a person adopts a lifestyle that continually brings him or her into high-crime areas.

The discovery that victims play an important role in the crime process has prompted the scientific study of victims, or victimology. Criminologists who focus their attention on crime victims refer to themselves as victimologists.

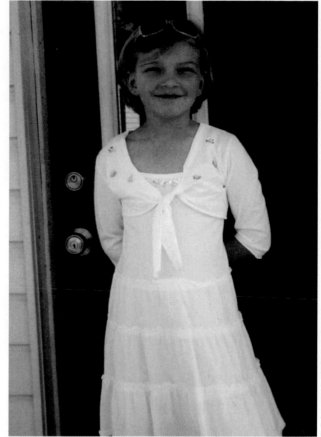

THE CANADIAN PRESS/Dave Chidley

On July 19, 2009, police found "suspicious remains" in a secluded country field near Mount Forest, Ontario, which were later identified as those of Victoria Stafford, a Grade 3 student who was abducted and murdered. Is it possible to protect children from such irrational acts, or is victimization a random event that can happen to anyone at any time?

In this chapter, we examine victims and their relationship to the criminal process. First, using available victim data, we analyze the nature and extent of victimization. We then discuss the relationship between victims and criminal offenders. In this context, we look at various theories of victimization that attempt to explain the victim's role in the crime problem. Finally, we examine how society has responded to the needs of victims and consider the special problems they still face.

LO2 Problems of Crime Victims

The General Social Survey (GSS) gathers data on social trends to monitor changes in the living conditions and well-being of Canadians over time and to provide information

victimology
The study of the victim's role in criminal events.

victimologists
Criminologists who focus on the victims of crime.

on specific social policy issues of current or emerging interest. Victimization is one of the topics covered at five-year intervals with the objective of better understanding how Canadians perceive crime and the justice system and their experiences of victimization. A sample of about 25 000 Canadians are asked about reported and unreported victimization, including experiences of crime, violence and abuse by current or past spouse or partner, use of services available to help victims of abuse or crime, fear of crime, crime prevention, and social disorder and experiences of discrimination. The GGS on Victimization (GSS—VS) data complements police-reported crime, capturing information that does not come to the attention of the police and is not counted in official crime rates. The survey produces estimates of the extent to which persons are the victims of eight types of offences. In 2004 and 2009, the GGS on Victimization survey questions concentrated on eight types of criminal victimization: assault, sexual assault, robbery, theft of personal property, break and enter, theft of household property, motor vehicle/parts theft, and vandalism.[6]

The results from the 2009 GGS on Victimization survey revealed that about 25 percent of Canadians aged 15 and over were the victim of a crime in 2009 (7.4 million), about the same percentage as in 2004.[7] Being the target or victim of a sexual assault, a break and enter, or an assault is a terrible burden that can have considerable long-term consequences. In this section we explore some of the effects of these incidents.

Economic Loss

Given that only about one-third of all crimes are reported to police, it is difficult to arrive at a figure representing the real costs of crime in Canada in any given year. Based on GGS on Victimization survey data, the Department of Justice estimates that crime cost Canadians $70 billion in 2003, or $2200 for every man, woman, and child in Canada every year.[8] As can be seen in Figure 3.1, more than two-thirds of the

FIGURE 3.1

Costs of Crime in Canada

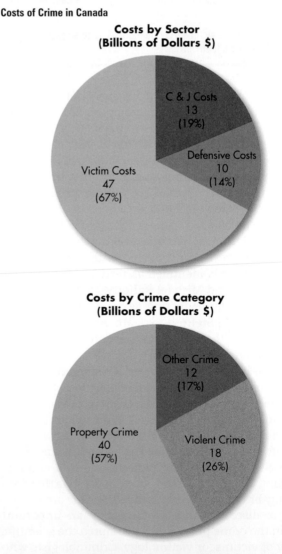

Costs by Sector (Billions of Dollars $)

- C & J Costs 13 (19%)
- Defensive Costs 10 (14%)
- Victim Costs 47 (67%)

Costs by Crime Category (Billions of Dollars $)

- Other Crime 12 (17%)
- Violent Crime 18 (26%)
- Property Crime 40 (57%)

Source: *JustResearch, 2005, Issue No. 12*, Figures: Costs of Crime in Canada an Update, page 58, http://www.justice.gc.ca/eng/pi/rs/rep-rap/jr/jr12/jr12.pdf, Department of Justice Canada, 2005. Reproduced with the permission of the Department of Justice Canada, 2015

Milkovasa/Shutterstock.com

Home invasions can have severe psychological effects, particularly in seniors, including feeling unsafe and fear and distrust of others.

FIGURE 3.2

THE CANADIAN NEWS FRASER INSTITUTE

COST OF CRIME SKYROCKETS

(CANADA)—Despite a dropping crime rate, crime cost Canadians $85 billion in 2009 including $47 billion incurred by crime victims due to stolen property, lost health and more.

POLICING ↑43%

LEGAL AID ↑34%

PRISONS, PAROLE, ETC ↑32%

2002   2012

Reprinted by permission of The Fraser Institute.

the crime is handled callously, with innuendos or insinuations that they were somehow at fault. They have difficulty learning what is going on in the case; property is often kept for a long time as evidence and may never be returned. Some sexual assault victims report that the treatment they receive from legal, medical, and mental health services is so destructive that they can't help feeling revictimized.[13] Victims may also suffer economic hardship because of wages lost while they testify in court and find that authorities are indifferent to their fear of retaliation if they cooperate in the offenders' prosecution.[14]

DID YOU KNOW?

- Males and females are equally likely to be the victim of a crime. Women are much more likely to be the victim of a sexual assault or personal theft, while males are more likely to be the victim of a physical assault or robbery.

- The poor are much more likely than the affluent to be the victims of violent crime; the wealthy are more likely to be the targets of personal theft.

- Younger, single people are more often targets than older, married people.

- Some people and places are targets of repeat victimization.

costs of crime are borne directly by victims, estimated at $47 billion annually, including the value of property stolen or damaged, pain and suffering, lost time from work, and health-care costs (see Figure 3.2).[9]

Police, court, and correctional services costs for dealing with crime are estimated at $13 billion each year, with the remainder of the costs of crime, $10 billion, spread out over various crime prevention measures including alarm systems and security services. Add it all up, and the total costs of crime ($70 billion) are more than every level of government in Canada spends each year on education.[10]

In terms of the costs of various types of crime, as can also be seen in Figure 3.1, property crime, including victim costs, criminal justice system costs, and prevention, is the most expensive type of crime, estimated to cost Canadians $40 billion in 2003. Violent crime is next, costing Canadians an estimated $18 billion that year, followed by "Other" types of crime (including drug and traffic offences) at $12 billion.[11]

In addition to the annual costs, victims may suffer long-term losses in earnings and occupational attainment. Research by Ross Macmillan shows that Americans who suffer a violent victimization during adolescence earn about US$82 000 less than nonvictims; Canadian victims earn $237 000 less. Macmillan reasons that victims bear psychological and physical ills that inhibit first their academic achievement and later their economic and professional success.[12]

System Abuse

The suffering endured by crime victims does not end when their attacker leaves the scene of the crime. They may suffer more victimization by the justice system.

While the crime is still fresh in their minds, victims may find that the police interview following

Long-Term Stress

Victims may suffer stress and anxiety long after the incident is over and the justice process has been forgotten. For example, girls who were psychologically, sexually, or physically abused as children are more likely to have lower self-esteem and be more suicidal as adults than those who were not abused.[15] Children who are victimized in the home are more likely to run away to escape their environment, which puts them at risk for juvenile arrest and involvement with the justice system.[16]

Stress does not end in childhood. Spousal abuse victims suffer an extremely high prevalence of depression, post-traumatic stress disorder (an emotional disturbance following exposure to stresses outside the range of normal human experience), anxiety disorder, and obsessive-compulsive disorder (an extreme preoccupation with certain thoughts and compulsive performance of certain behaviours).[17] One reason may be that abusive spouses are as likely to abuse their victims psychologically with threats and intimidation as they are to use physical force; psychological abuse can lead to depression and other long-term disabilities.[18]

post-traumatic stress disorder Psychological reaction to a highly stressful event; symptoms may include depression, anxiety, flashbacks, and recurring nightmares.

Theo Fleury: Playing With Fire is a 2012 documentary based on a 2009 book of the same title. The documentary describes the painful, tragic, and inspiring life of a hockey superstar. Known for his unpredictable and aggressive behaviour on and off-ice, Fleury played for the Calgary Flames in the 1990s, and later the Colorado Avalanche, New York Rangers, and Chicago Blackhawks. His book and movie document how he squandered nearly $50 000 million on drugs, alcohol, and strippers. In 2009 he revealed that as a teenager he had been sexually assaulted by Graham James, a former coach in the Western Hockey League, which contributed to his drug, alcohol, and mental health problems. Since retiring from the NHL, Fleury has been a spokesperson for tougher sentencing for sexual predators and continues to offer support and comfort to those who suffered a similar fate. In a poignant scene in the film, Fleury comforts a young boy at one of his book signings who revealed that he had also been abused and it easy to see how such abuse will have lasting effects on this young man. The film sheds light on the culture of hockey in Canada where "hockey is glorified to the extent that its victims, be they male players who are sexually assaulted or hazed or young girls in the community who are raped by junior hockey players and coaches, are marginalized and ostracized for criticizing the cultural institution of hockey."

From a criminologist's perspective, the film and life of Theo Fleury clearly demonstrate the long-term effects of victimization and may also explain why he engaged in such antisocial behaviour off the ice. Fleury's age, gender, and social status fit the characteristics of victims of crime and also those of his abuser, who was known to him. Reports of abuse such as that experienced by Fleury are not unusual. The question is why have steps not been taken to prevent such abuse from happening? What measures can be taken to protect young boys from being victimized? What would you do?

Some victims are physically disabled as a result of serious wounds sustained during episodes of random violence, including a growing number who suffer paralyzing spinal cord injuries, and while the health-care system may cover the costs of any required medical procedures, many victims must live with severe long-term emotional and physical consequences.[19]

Fear

People who have suffered crime victimization remain fearful long after their wounds have healed. Even if they have escaped attack themselves, hearing about another's victimization may make people timid and cautious. For example, women who are being abused by their partner may be fearful of reporting the abuse to authorities, especially when they read media reports about women who have been stalked and murdered by their partners following disclosure of the abuse to police.[20]

Victims of violent crime are the most deeply affected, fearing a repeat of their attack. There may be a spillover effect in which victims become fearful of other forms of crime they have not yet experienced; people who have been assaulted develop fears that their house will be burglarized.[21] Many

go through a fundamental life change, viewing the world more suspiciously and less as a safe, controllable, and meaningful place. These people are more likely to suffer psychological stress for extended periods of time.[22]

Communities may live in fear when news of a violent incident grips the neighbourhood. Sometimes local incidents become national news. Beginning in September 2009, Ontario Provincial Police began the search for a male suspect who had tied up and sexually assaulted two women after breaking into their homes in the tiny community of Tweed, Ontario. Then, in November 2009, in a seemingly unrelated incident, Marie-France Comeau, 37, a corporal in the Canadian Armed Forces stationed at CFB Trenton, was found sexually assaulted and murdered in her Brighton, Ontario, home, about an hour's drive west of Tweed. On 28 January 2010, Jessica Elizabeth Lloyd, 27, who worked for the local school bus company as a schedule coordinator, was found sexually assaulted and murdered in her home on Highway 37, about 25 kilometres south of Tweed. In October 2010, Colonel Russell Williams, base commander at CFB Trenton and a decorated air-force officer, pled guilty in the first-degree murders of Marie-France Comeau and Jessica Elizabeth Lloyd, in two separate counts

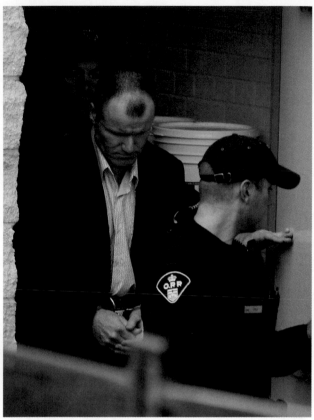

Steve Russell/GetStock.com

Escorted by police, Russell Williams leaves a Tweed-area courthouse after pleading guilty to the murders of Marie-France Comeau and Jessica Elizabeth Lloyd.

of sexual assault and forcible confinement, and in more than 80 break and enters and attempted break and enters in Tweed and the surrounding area in which women's underwear and other clothing was stolen.[23]

Antisocial Behaviour

There is growing evidence that crime victims are more likely to commit crime themselves. Being abused or neglected as a child increases the odds of being arrested, both as a juvenile and as an adult.[24] Young people, especially those who were physically or sexually abused, are much more likely to smoke, drink, take drugs, and become involved in criminal activities than are nonabused youth (see Figure 3.3). Incarcerated offenders report significant amounts of post-traumatic stress disorder as a result of prior victimization, which may in part explain their violent and criminal behaviours.[25]

The abuse–crime phenomenon is referred to as the cycle of violence.[26] Research shows that both boys and girls are more likely to engage in violent behaviour if they were (1) the target of physical abuse and (2) exposed to violent behaviour among adults they know or live with, or exposed to weapons.[27]

cycle of violence
Victims of crime, especially childhood abuse, are more likely to commit crime themselves.

The Nature of Victimization

How many crime victims are there in Canada, and what are the trends and patterns in victimization? According to the 2009 GSS—VS, about 7.4 million Canadians, or just over one-quarter of the population, reported being a victim of a criminal incident in the preceding 12 months. This proportion was essentially unchanged from that reported in 2004.

Patterns in the victimization survey findings are stable and repetitive, suggesting that victimization is

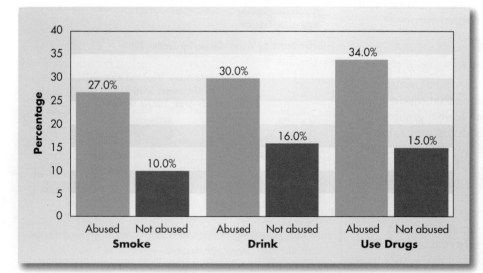

FIGURE 3.3

Percentage of U.S. Male High School Students (Grades 9–12) Reporting Smoking, Drinking, or Using Drugs, by Physical/Sexual Abuse Status

Notes: Smoke: smoked at least several cigarettes in the past week; Drink: drank at least once a month; Use drugs: used illegal drugs at least once in the past month. The survey was an in-class questionnaire completed by 3162 boys in grades 5–12 at a nationally representative sample of 265 public, private, and parochial schools from December 1996 to June 1997. The survey included roughly equal samples of adolescent boys in grades 5–8 and 9–12. All responses were weighted to reflect grade, region, and race and ethnicity.

Source: Cathy Schoen et al., *The Health of Adolescent Boys: Commonwealth Fund Survey Findings* (New York: Commonwealth Fund, 1998). Figure prepared by the Center for Substance Abuse Research, University of Maryland, College Park.

not random but a function of personal and ecological factors. The stability of these patterns allows judgments to be made about the nature of victimization; policies can then be created in an effort to reduce the victimization rate. Who are victims? Where does victimization take place? What is the relationship between victims and criminals? The following sections discuss some of the most important victimization patterns and trends.

LO3 The Social Ecology of Victimization

According to a 2009 Statistics Canada report on victimization,[28] the risk of being a victim of a violent crime increases for those who are often engaged in evening activities outside the home, such as working nights, visiting friends, or going out to bars. Men and women are equally likely to be victims, though of different types of crime: women are more likely to be victims of sexual assault; males are more likely to be victims of assault or robbery. Marital status is another factor impacting on victimization. Single people, either never-married or those who are separated or divorced, are at the highest risk of victimization. Neighbourhood characteristics also affect the chances of victimization. Those living in cities, especially in Western Canada, have higher rates of both personal and household victimization.[29]

More recent studies have suggested that there is substantial evidence that victims and offenders in violent crimes have many characteristics in common. For example, both share certain individual, neighbourhood, and situational characteristics. They tend to live in socially disorganized neighbourhoods and engage in risky lifestyles and violent offending behaviours in similar proportions. These findings highlight the overlapping factors associated with victimization and offending in non-lethal violent personal crimes.[30]

The Victim's Household

The GSS—VS tells us that in Canada, low-income households are at a higher risk for violent victimization. On the other hand, households that reported an annual income of $60 000 or more have a greater risk of personal property theft. Individuals and families living in semidetached, row, and duplex homes have the highest risk for household victimization, while apartment dwellers and those living in single-family dwellings have the lowest rates. Tenants have higher rates of household victimization than homeowners.

Changes in population characteristics and economic changes in Canadian society may account for the victimization patterns. As individuals' incomes and buying power continue to grow, and as more and more Canadians reside in large urban centres, personal and household theft may be expected to increase. At the same time, as the divide between the poor and the rich grows, criminal activities associated with violence will remain common in poorer, low-income neighbourhoods.

Victim Characteristics

Social and demographic characteristics also distinguish victims and nonvictims. The most important of these factors are gender, age, social status, marital status, and race.

Gender

As Figures 3.4 and 3.5 show, gender affects victimization risk: While males and females are equally

FIGURE 3.4

Self-Reported Violent Victimization and Theft of Personal Property by Gender, 2009—Rate per 1000 Population Age 15 Years and Older

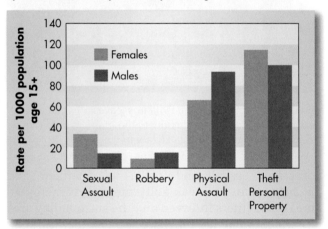

Source: Adapted from Statistics Canada publication JURISTAT—Criminal Victimization in Canada, 2009, Summer 2010, Vol. 30, No. 2, page 22, http://www.statcan.gc.ca/pub/85-002-x/2010002/article/11340/tbl/tbl4-eng.htm

FIGURE 3.5

Victimization by Violent Crime, by Gender, 2009

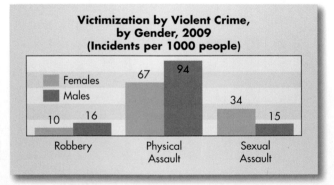

Source: Adapted from Statistics Canada publication JURISTAT, vol. 30, no. 2, 2010, Figure: Victimization by violent crime, by gender, 2009 (incidents per 1,000 people). URL: http://www4.hrsdc.gc.ca/.3ndic.1t.4r@-eng.jsp?iid=61. Human Resources and Skills Development Canada, 2010. Reproduced with the permission of the Minister of Public Works and Government Service Canada, 2012.

FIGURE 3.6

Criminal Victimization and Age

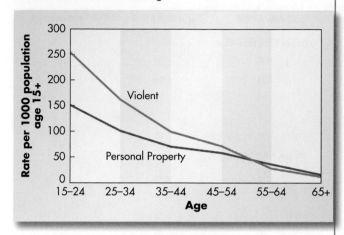

Source: Adapted from Statistics Canada publications JURISTAT, vol. 25, no. 7, and Vol. 30, No 2, 2009, retrieved on HRDSC Website, http://www4.hrsdc.gc.ca/.3ndic.1t.4r@-eng .jsp?iid=61. Human Resources and Skills Development Canada, 2010. Reproduced with the permission of the Minister of Public Works and Government Service Canada, 2012.

likely to be victimized, the victimization rates are different depending on the crime. Females are nearly three times more likely than males to be a victim of a sexual assault and are also more likely to be victims of personal theft. Males, on the other hand, are at greater risk of being a victim of a robbery or a physical assault.

Age

Victim data reveal that young people face a much greater victimization risk than do older persons. As Figure 3.6 shows, victim risk diminishes rapidly after age 25. The elderly, who are thought of as the helpless targets of predatory criminals, are actually much safer than their grandchildren. People 65 and over, who make up 15.7 percent of Canada's population (nearly one in six Canadians),[31] account for only 2 percent of violent victimizations; young people ages 15 to 24, who make up about 13 percent of the population, typically account for more than 30 percent of victimizations. For example, the 15-to-24 age group is about four times more likely to be sexually assaulted than people ages 45 to 54 (see Figure 3.7).[32]

Social Status

The poorest Canadians, those with the lowest level of reported household income, are also the most likely victims of sexual assault and physical assaults (see Table 3.1). Although the poor are more likely to suffer violent crimes, the wealthy are more likely targets of personal theft crimes such as muggings and theft of belongings. Perhaps the affluent, who sport more expensive attire and frequent trendy restaurants and theatres, attract the attention of thieves (See Table 3.2).

Marital Status

Marital status also influences victimization risk. Never-married and separated/divorced males and females are victimized more often than married people. Widows and widowers have the lowest victimization risk. This association between marital

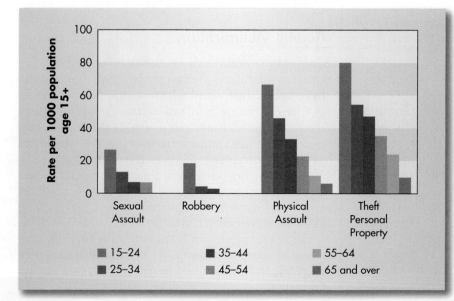

FIGURE 3.7

Self-Reported Violent Victimization and Theft of Personal Property by Age, 2009—Rate per 1000 Population Age 15 Years and Older

Note: Due to small numbers, it is not possible to calculate some rates for older age groups.

Source: Adapted from Statistics Canada publications JURISTAT, vol. 25, no. 7, and Vol. 30, No 2, 2009, retrieved on HRDSC Website, http://www4.hrsdc.gc.ca/.3ndic.1t.4r@-eng .jsp?iid=61. Human Resources and Skills Development Canada, 2010. Reproduced with the permission of the Minister of Public Works and Government Service Canada, 2012.

TABLE 3.1

Criminal Victimization Rates by Household Income Group, Canada, 2004—Household Income in Dollars

	0–14 999	15 000–29 999	30 000–39 999	40 000–59 999	60 000 and over
	rate per 1000 population[1]				
Total violent victimization	156	104	105	94	106
Physical assault[2]	102	68	77	66	80
Sexual assault[3]	38[E]	24[E]	19[E]	21	16
Robbery	17[E]	12[E]	F	7[E]	9[E]
Personal property theft	71	76	92	81	116
	rate per 1000 households				
Total household victimization	160	223	257	267	300
Break and enter	41	36	50	41	42
Motor vehicle theft	21[E]	42	39	49	56
Theft of household property	59	84	93	93	104
Vandalism	39	60	74	84	98

[E] use with caution, coefficient of variation is high (16.6% to 33.3%)
F too unreliable to be published
1. Rates calculated per 1000 population aged 15 and over.
2. Includes incidents of spousal physical assault.
3. Includes spousal sexual assault.

Note: Figures may not add to total due to rounding.

Source: Adapted from Statistics Canada publication Household Income and Victimization in Canada, 2004, Catalogue 85F0033MWE, no. 20, http://www.statcan.gc.ca/pub/85f0033m/85f0033m2009020-eng.pdf

status and victimization is probably influenced by age, gender, and lifestyle:

1. Many young people, who have the highest victim risk, are actually too young to have been married.

2. Young single people also go out in public more often and sometimes interact with high-risk peers, increasing their exposure to victimization.

3. Widows and widowers suffer much lower victimization rates because they are older, interact with older people, and are more likely to stay home at night and to avoid public places.

Race and Ethnicity

Compared to European Canadians, visible minorities and recent immigrant groups are more likely to experience hate crimes.[33] Also, as can be seen in Figure 3.8, Jews and Muslims reported considerably higher rates of hate crimes than Catholics and those of other religions.

Morton Beiser reports that while Southeast Asian refugees to Canada were more likely to experience more subtle forms of racism (e.g., rudeness or insulting remarks), 11 percent reported acts of vandalism directed against their ethnic community as a whole, and 5 percent of the study group had been physically

threatened/manhandled or had personal property defaced with racial graffiti.[34]

Why do these discrepancies exist? Because of income inequality, racial and ethnic minority group members are often forced to live in deteriorated urban areas beset by alcohol and drug abuse, poverty, racial discrimination, and violence. Consequently, their lifestyle places them in the most "at risk" population group.

Repeat Victimization

Does prior victimization enhance or reduce the chances of future victimization? Individuals who have been crime victims have a significantly higher chance of future victimization than people who have remained nonvictims.[35] Households that have experienced victimization in the past are the ones most likely to experience it again in the future.[36]

What factors predict chronic victimization? Most repeat victimizations occur soon after a previous crime has occurred, suggesting that repeat victims share some personal characteristic that makes them a magnet for predators.[37] For example, children who are shy, physically weak, or socially isolated may be prone to being bullied in the schoolyard.[38] David Finkelhor and Nancy Asigian have found that three

TABLE 3.2

Self-Reported Violent Victimization and Theft of Personal Property by Selected Demographic Characteristics, 2009

Characteristics	Sexual Assault Number (1000s)	Sexual Assault Rate[1]	Robbery Number (1000s)	Robbery Rate[1]	Physical Assault Number (1000s)	Physical Assault Rate[1]	Total—Violent Incidents Number (1000s)	Total—Violent Incidents Rate[1]	Theft of Personal Property Number (1000s)	Theft of Personal Property Rate[1]
Sex										
Female[†]	472	34	146	10	945	67	1563	112	1609	115
Male	204[E]	15[E]*	222	16	1277	94*	1704	125	1372	101
Age										
15 to 24[†]	307	69	209[E]	47[E]	757	169	1273	284	898	200
25 to 34	161[E]	35[E]*	56[E]	12[E]*	545	118*	761	165*	642	139*
35 to 44	92[E]	19[E]*	43[E]	9[E]*	413	86*	548	114*	578	121*
45 to 54	96[E]	18[E]*	F	F	316	59*	444	84*	487	92*
55 to 64	F	F	F	F	118	29*	156	39*	257	63*
65 and over	F	F	F	F	73[E]	17[E]*	84[E]	19[E]*	118	27*
Marital status										
Married[†]	131[E]	9[E]	66[E]	5[E]	677	48	874	62	1112	79
Common-law	82[E]	26[E]*	F	F	335	105*	440	137*	442	138*
Single	385	54*	237	34*	1011	143*	1633	231*	1207	171*
Widowed	F	F	F	F	F	F	F	F	26[E]	19[E]*
Separated/divorced	74[E]	40[E]*	36[E]	19[E]*	184[E]	99[E]*	293	158*	192	103*
Household income										
Less than $20 000[†]	41	29[E]	F	F	148	103	212	147	112	78
$20 000 to $39 999	85[E]	26[E]	F	F	246	75	364	112	302	93
$40 000 to $59 999	83[E]	22[E]	F	F	294	76	406	105	343	89
$60 000 to $99 999	138[E]	22[E]	72[E]	12[E]	536	86	746	120	633	102
$100 000 or more	220[E]	31[E]	113[E]	16[E]	598	83	932	129	1037	143*
Aboriginal identity										
Aboriginal people[†]	63[E]	71[E]	F	F	123	141[E]	204	232	127	145
Non-Aboriginal people	612	23*	347	13	2081	78*	3039	114*	2838	107
Immigrant status										
Immigrant	F	F	F	F	244	43	355	62	477	84
Non-immigrant	598	27	334	15	1977	90*	2909	133*	2502	114*
Visible minority										
Visible minority[†]	F	F	F	F	189[E]	51[E]	279[E]	76[E]	376	102
Non-visible minority	604	25	332	14	2009	85*	2945	124*	2578	109
Sexual orientation[2]										
Heterosexual[†]	509	20	262	10	1779	71	2550	102	2483	99
Homosexual	F	F	F	F	F	F	108[E]	405[E]*	F	F
Activity limitations										
Limited in activities[†]	229	27	173[E]	20[E]	832	96	1234	143	916	106
No limitation	445	24	194	10*	1384	73*	2023	107*	2060	109

[†] reference category
* significantly different from reference category (p < 0.05)
1. Rates are calculated per 1000 population age 15 years and older.
2. Data for those who self-identified as bisexual have been suppressed due to the unreliability of the estimates.

Note: Excludes responses of "Don't know" and "Not stated." Excludes data from the Northwest Territories, Yukon, and Nunavut, which will be published at a later date.

Source: Adapted from Statistics Canada publication JURISTAT – Criminal Victimization in Canada, 2009, Summer 2010, Vol. 30, No. 2, page 22, http://www.statcan.gc.ca/pub/85-002-x/2010002/article/11340/tbl/tbl4-eng.htm

FIGURE 3.8

Police-Reported Hate Crime by Type of Religion, Canada, 2006

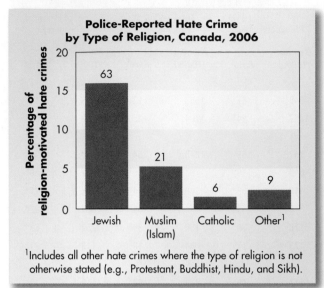

Police-Reported Hate Crime by Type of Religion, Canada, 2006

Percentage of religion-motivated hate crimes

- Jewish: 63
- Muslim (Islam): 21
- Catholic: 6
- Other[1]: 9

[1] Includes all other hate crimes where the type of religion is not otherwise stated (e.g., Protestant, Buddhist, Hindu, and Sikh).

Source: Adapted from Statistics Canada publication Hate Crime in Canada, Catalogue 85F0033MWE2008017, vol. 29, no. 3, http://www.statcan.gc.ca/pub/85f0033m/2008017/c-g/5200138-eng.htm

specific types of characteristics increase the potential for victimization:[39]

1. *Target vulnerability.* The victims' physical weakness or psychological distress renders them incapable of resisting or deterring crime and makes them easy targets.

2. *Target gratifiability.* Some victims have some quality, possession, skill, or attribute that an offender wants to obtain, use, have access to, or manipulate. Having attractive possessions such as a leather coat may make one vulnerable to predatory crime.

3. *Target antagonism.* Some characteristics increase risk because they arouse anger, jealousy, or destructive impulses in potential offenders. Being gay or effeminate, for example, may bring on undeserved attacks in the street; being argumentative and alcoholic may provoke barroom assault.

Source: VIOLENCE AND VICTIMS by UNIVERSITY OF NEW HAMPSHIRE. Copyright 1996 Reproduced with permission of SPRINGER PUBLISHING COMPANY, INC. in the format Textbook and Other Book via Copyright Clearance Center.

Repeat victimization may occur when the victim does not take defensive action. For example, if an abusive husband finds out that his battered wife will not call the police, he repeatedly victimizes her; or if a hate crime is committed and the police do not respond to reported offences, the perpetrators learn they have little to fear from the law.[40]

The Victims and Their Criminals

The victim data also tell us something about the relationship between victims and criminals. Victims report that most violent crimes were committed by a single offender, almost always male, between the ages of 18 and 34. In the majority of violent victimization incidents (sexual assault, assault), the perpetrator was known to the victim, as either a family member (37 percent) or a friend/acquaintance/other (36 percent). For example, in the winter of 2014, a six-year-old girl from Paul Band First Nation west of Edmonton had been kidnapped, sexually assaulted, and found naked in the snow by family members. RCMP arrested and charged a 21-year-old male with attempted murder, aggravated sexual assault, and kidnapping.[41] Although the case is currently before the courts, the accused was known to the family and to the little girl. Unlike violent victimization, there does not appear to be a relationship between robbery victims and their assailants. According to the 2009 GGS on Victimization survey, in a majority of robbery incidents the perpetrator was a stranger.[42]

Victimization commonly occurs within families, and involves parents, children, and extended family.

Theories of Victimization

For many years, criminological theory focused on the actions of the criminal offender; the role of the victim was virtually ignored. However, more than 50 years ago, scholars began to realize that the victim was not simply a passive target in crime, but someone whose behaviour can influence his or her own fate, who "shapes and molds the criminal."[43] These early works helped focus attention on the role of the victim in the crime problem and led to further research efforts that have sharpened the image of the crime victim. Today a number of different theories attempt to explain the causes of victimization.

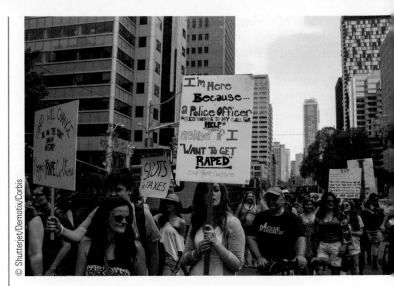

In 2011, while addressing Osgoode Hall Law students on personal safety, Toronto police officer Michael Sanguinetti advised, "Women should avoid dressing like sluts in order not to be victimized." The officer's remarks ignited a firestorm of controversy and set off an international movement referred to as "SlutWalking" to respond to what many believe is a culture in which it is considered acceptable to blame the victim.

Source: Ed Pilkington, "SlutWalking gets rolling after cop's loose talk about provocative clothing" Guardian.com, (6 May 2011) http://www.theguardian.com/world/2011/may/06/slutwalking-policeman-talk-clothing (accessed 5 October 2015).

DID YOU KNOW?

- Victim precipitation theory suggests crime victims may trigger attacks by acting provocatively.
- Some experts link victimization to high-risk lifestyles.
- Some people live in places that are magnets for criminals.
- The routine activities approach suggests that the risk of victimization may be an interaction among suitable targets, ineffective guardians, and motivated criminals. Victims present attractive targets with insufficient protection to motivated criminals.

LO4 Victim Precipitation Theory

According to victim precipitation theory, some people may initiate the confrontation that eventually leads to their injury or death. Victim precipitation can be either active or passive.

Active precipitation occurs when victims act provocatively, use threats or fighting words, or even attack first.[44] Marvin Wolfgang's pioneering 1958 study of U.S. police homicide records was the first attempt to systematically explore victim precipitation. Examining homicides that occurred between 1948 and 1952, he found that 26 percent of homicides resulted from victim precipitation.[45] Studies like Wolfgang's reinforced the notion that victimization theories must include the role of the victim. However, they also helped pave the way for another debated referred to as "victim-blaming." In 1971, Menachem Amir suggested that female sexual assault victims often contribute to their attacks by dressing provocatively or pursuing a relationship with the perpetrator.[46] Amir's findings are controversial, and Canadian courts have taken a strong stand in finding that "implied consent" is not a defence in the case of sexual assault, regardless of the actions or attire of the victim.[47] Critics have suggested that the singular focus on victim behaviours was a step backward for victim's rights and diverted attention from the social and cultural factors that influence both victims and offenders.[48]

Active precipitation might also help explain the controversial phenomenon known as "suicide by cop" where individuals deliberately act in a threatening way with the aim of provoking a lethal response from a police officer. In a study of officer-involved shootings between 1998 and 2007, Kris Mohandie found that, of 707 incidents, 36 percent resulted from suicide-by-cop situations. Mohandie's research revealed that suicide by cop is an effective

victim precipitation theory
The view that victims may initiate, either actively or passively, the confrontation that leads to their victimization.

active precipitation
Aggressive or provocative behaviour of victims that results in their victimization.

means of ending one's life but it is also very dangerous in that there is a one-in-three chance that some other party will be injured or killed in any suicide by cop incident.[49]

In contrast, **passive precipitation** occurs when the victim exhibits some personal characteristic that unknowingly either threatens or encourages the attacker. The crime can occur because of personal conflict—such as when two people compete over a job, promotion, love interest, or some other scarce and coveted commodity. For example, a woman may become the target of intimate violence when she improves her job status and her success results in a backlash from a jealous spouse or partner.[50] In other situations, although the victim may never have met the attacker or even known of his or her existence, the attacker feels menaced and acts accordingly.[51]

Passive precipitation may also occur when the victim belongs to a group whose mere presence threatens the attacker's reputation, status, or economic well-being. For example, hate crime violence may be precipitated by immigrant group members' arriving in the community to compete for jobs and housing. Research indicates that passive precipitation is related to power: If members of the target group can establish themselves economically or gain political power in the community, their vulnerability will diminish. They are still a potential threat, but they become too formidable a target to attack; they are no longer passive precipitators.[52] By implication, economic power reduces victimization risk.

Lifestyle Theories

In 1978, Michael J. Hindelang, Michael R. Gottfredson, and James Garofalo published *Victims of Personal Crime: An Empirical Foundation for a Theory of Personal Victimization* in which they suggested that victimization risk was a function of lifestyle.[53] Victimization risk is increased by behaviours such as associating with young men, going out in public places late at night, and living in an urban area. Conversely, one's chances of victimization can be reduced by staying home at night, moving to a rural area, staying out of public places, earning more money, and getting married. The basis of such lifestyle theories is that crime is not a random occurrence, but rather a function of the victim's lifestyle.

passive precipitation Personal or social characteristics of victims that make them "attractive" targets for criminals; such victims may unknowingly either threaten or encourage their attackers.

lifestyle theories The view that people become crime victims because of lifestyles that increase their exposure to criminal offenders.

High-Risk Lifestyles

People who have high-risk lifestyles have a much greater chance of victimization. For example, young runaways are at high risk for victimization; the more time they are exposed to street life, the greater their risk of becoming crime victims.[54]

Teenage males have an extremely high victimization risk because their lifestyle places them at risk both at school and once they leave the school grounds.[55] They spend a great deal of time hanging out with their friends and pursuing recreational fun.[56] Their friends may give them a false identification so they can go drinking in the neighbourhood bar. They may hang out in taverns at night, which places them at risk because many fights and assaults occur in places that serve liquor. Those who have a history of engaging in serious delinquency, getting involved in gangs, carrying weapons, and selling drugs have an increased chance of themselves being a target of serious violence.[57]

AP Photo/Pier Paolo Cito

Lifestyle risks continue into young adulthood. College and university students who spend several nights each week partying and who take recreational drugs are much more likely to be victims of violent crime than those who avoid such risky academic lifestyles.[58]

Because almost every Canadian will one day become a crime victim, victim/witness assistance programs (VWAP) have been developed across Canada to help victims deal with the stress they may endure when they or their family members become crime victims. Available to both children and adults, the programs provide emotional support and referrals to community agencies, case information and court preparation, needs assessment, and intervention.

Deviant Place Theory

According to deviant place theory, victims do not encourage crime, but are victim prone because they reside in socially disorganized high-crime areas where they have the greatest risk of coming into contact with criminal offenders, irrespective of their own behaviour or lifestyle.[59] Consequently, there may be little reason for residents in lower-class areas to alter their lifestyle or take safety precautions because personal behaviour choices do not influence the likelihood

of victimization.[60] Neighbourhood crime levels may be more important for determining the chances of victimization than individual characteristics.

Deviant places are poor, densely populated, highly transient neighbourhoods in which commercial and residential properties exist side by side.[61] The commercial establishments provide criminals with easy targets for theft crimes, such as shoplifting. Successful people stay out of these stigmatized areas. They are home to "demoralized kinds of people" who are easy targets for crime: the homeless, the addicted, the mentally ill, and the elderly poor.[62]

People who live in more affluent areas and take safety precautions significantly lower their chances of becoming crime victims; the effect of safety precautions is less pronounced in poor areas. Residents of poor areas have a much greater risk of becoming victims because they live in areas with many motivated offenders; to protect themselves, they have to try harder to be safe than do the more affluent.[63]

Routine Activities Theory

Routine activities theory was first articulated in a series of papers by Lawrence Cohen and Marcus Felson.[64]

Cohen and Felson assume that both the motivation to commit crime and the supply of offenders are constant.[65] Every society will always have some people who are willing to break the law for revenge, greed, or some other motive. The volume and distribution of predatory crime (violent crimes against a person and crimes in which an offender attempts to steal an object directly) are closely related to the interaction of three variables that reflect the routine activities of the typical North American lifestyle:

1. The availability of **suitable targets**, such as homes containing easily saleable goods

2. The absence of **capable guardians**, such as police, homeowners, neighbours, friends, and relatives

3. The presence of **motivated offenders**, such as a large number of unemployed teenagers

Source: Crime and everyday life by FELSON, MARCUS Copyright 1998 Reproduced with permission of SAGE PUBLICATIONS INC BOOKS in the format Textbook and Other Book via Copyright Clearance Center.

deviant place theory
The view that victimization is primarily a function of where people live.

routine activities theory
The view that victimization results from the interaction of three everyday factors: the availability of suitable targets, the absence of capable guardians, and the presence of motivated offenders.

suitable targets
Objects of crime (persons or property) that are attractive and readily available.

capable guardians
Effective deterrents to crime, such as police or watchful neighbours.

motivated offenders
People willing and able to commit crimes.

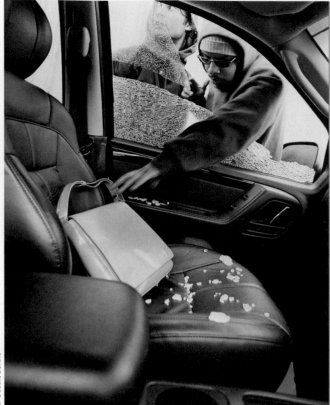
© Ocean/Corbis

Leaving valuables in open view is an invitation to potential criminals.

The presence of these components increases the likelihood that a predatory crime will take place. Targets are more likely to be victimized if they are poorly guarded and exposed to a large group of motivated offenders such as teenage boys.[66] The interacting components of routine activities theory are illustrated in Figure 3.9.

Cohen, Felson, and Land argue that crime rates in the United States increased between 1960 and 1980 because the number of adult caretakers at home during the day (guardians) decreased as a result of increased female participation in the workforce. While mothers are at work and children in child care, homes are left unguarded. Similarly, with the growth of suburbia and the decline of the traditional neighbourhood, the number of familiar guardians such as family, neighbours, and friends diminished. At the same time, the volume of easily transportable wealth increased, creating a greater number of available targets.[67] Skyrocketing drug use in the 1980s created an excess of motivated offenders, and the rates of some crimes, such as robbery, increased dramatically. Falling crime rates in the 1990s would be explained by a robust economy, which decreases the pool of motivated offenders, and the growing number of police officers, which increases guardianship. The Canadian experience has been much the same.

FIGURE 3.9

Routine Activities Theory

Lack of capable guardian
- Police officers
- Homeowners
- Security systems

Motivated offenders
- Teenage boys
- Unemployed
- Addict populations

CRIME

Suitable targets
- Unlocked homes
- Expensive cars
- Easily transportable goods

Sue O'Sullivan, Federal Ombudsman for Victims of Crime

Sue O'Sullivan, a 30-year law-enforcement veteran and former deputy chief of police for the Ottawa Police Service, began her term as Canada's federal ombudsman for victims of crime on 16 August 2010. O'Sullivan has served in Patrol, Criminal Investigative Services, and Operations Support and has been a member of the Leadership in Counter Terrorism Alumni Association, a group of senior professional executives who work together to influence local, national, and international counter-terrorism strategy, and has acted as an adviser to the auditor general of Canada on national security in Canada—the 2001 Anti-Terrorism Initiative Audit.

Throughout her career, O'Sullivan has continually advocated to increase the efficiency of services to victims. O'Sullivan has been recognized for her leadership both within the service and in the community. Her honours include the Governor General's Officer of the Order of Merit of the Police Forces Award, the Queen's Golden Jubilee Medal, the Governor General's Exemplary Service Medal, and the House of Commons Leadership Award (Ottawa-Center), the YM-YWCA Women of Distinction Award, the St. Joe's Women's Centre Quality of Life Award, and the Circle of Canadians Community Service Award. She holds a B.A. in Law and Sociology with a subtitle in Criminology and Corrections from Carleton University and is a graduate of the Police Leadership Program (Ontario Association of Chiefs of Police and the University of Toronto).

As the Ombudsman for Victims of Crime, O'Sullivan speaks with victims on a daily basis, answering their questions, addressing their complaints, and helping them by reviewing important issues and making recommendations to the federal government on how to improve its laws, policies, and programs, to better support victims of crime. Her current challenges include ensuring that her recommendations for strengthening Bill C-32, the Canadian Victims Bill of Rights, are adopted.

Routine Activities and Lifestyle

Routine activities theory and the lifestyle approach have a number of similarities. They both assume that a person's living arrangements can affect victim risk and that people who live in unguarded areas are at the mercy of motivated offenders. These two theories both rely on four basic concepts: (1) proximity to criminals, (2) time of exposure to criminals, (3) target attractiveness, and (4) guardianship.[68]

Based on the same basic concepts, these theories share the following predictions: People increase their victimization risk if they (1) live in high-crime areas, (2) go out late at night, (3) carry valuables such as an expensive watch, (4) engage in risky behaviour such as drinking alcohol, and (5) are without friends or family to watch or help them.[69] For example, young women who drink to excess in bars and fraternity houses may elevate their risk of rape because (1) they are easy targets and (2) their attackers can rationalize sexually assaulting them because they are intoxicated. Intoxication is sometimes used to try to make it seem as though the victim is responsible for the crime.[70] Conversely, people can reduce their chances of repeat victimization if they change their lifestyle and adopt crime-suppressing routines such as getting married, having children, or moving to a small town.[71]

LO5 Caring for the Victim

Victim surveys tell us that almost every Canadian over the age of 15 will one day become the victim of a crime, such as theft or break and enter, and in the aftermath may suffer financially and experience mental stress or even physical hardship.[72] Surveys show that upward of 75 percent of the general public have been victimized by crime at least once in their lives. As many as 25 percent of the victims develop post-traumatic stress syndrome, with symptoms that last for more than a decade after the crime occurred.[73]

Helping the victim to cope is the responsibility of all of society. Law enforcement agencies, courts, and correctional and human service systems have come to realize that due process and human rights exist not only for the criminal defendant but also for the victim of criminal behaviour.

In Canada, recognition of the rights of victims in the criminal justice process dates from the 1970s, when criminal injuries compensation programs were first introduced to provide limited compensation to victims of violent crime.[74] Victim–offender reconciliation programs (VORPs) began to be implemented in the mid-1970s. However, it was not until the 1980s and 1990s, under pressure from women's advocacy groups and victims' rights organizations, that the rights of victims were explicitly expressed in criminal justice legislation, policies, and practice.

There were also legislative changes that recognized the rights of victims. In 1983, Bill C-127 introduced the new offence of sexual assault, which included significant provisions for more equitable and humane treatment of victims, including recognition that sexual assault happens to both women and men; removal of spousal immunity; disqualification of evidence from the victim's background unless it is proven to be directly relevant; and introduction of new rules of evidence regarding consent, corroboration, and recency of complaint.[75] In 1988, the *Criminal Code* was amended to permit the introduction of a victim impact statement at the sentencing stage, and included an explicit definition of "victim" for this purpose, as follows:

> Criminal Code S. 722(4)
>   Definition of "victim"—For the purposes of this section, "victim," in relation to an offence
>   (a) means the person to whom harm was done or who suffered physical or emotional loss as a result of the commission of the offence; and
>   (b) where the person described in paragraph (a) is dead, ill or otherwise incapable of making a statement referred to in subsection (1), includes the spouse or any relative of that person, anyone who is in law or fact the custody of that person or is responsible for the care or support of that person or any dependant of that person.

Source: Criminal Code

In 1995, further revisions to the *Criminal Code* were introduced that now require courts to consider victim impact statements at the time of sentencing. In 1999, Bill C-79 introduced a broader definition of "victim" as "the victim of an alleged offence." Bill C-79 included additional amendments that require officials in the criminal justice system to ensure "the safety and security of any victim of or to the offence," including considerations in relation to granting bail and imposing special conditions on a bail release.[76]

Other recent changes to the *Criminal Code* that involve victim rights include the use of publication bans to protect the identity of sexual assault victims and children, the use of videotaped testimony for children who are victims or witnesses, the imposition of victim surcharges as an additional component of sentencing in order to fund victim assistance programs, the ordering of restitution for victims, and victim notification of "faint hope clause" hearings for offenders serving a life sentence.[77] The *Corrections and Conditional Release Act*, which governs the operations of the Correctional Service of Canada, now contains provisions for the release of information to victims regarding the institution in which the offender is located and any releases from custody and their location. In addition, victims are notified of parole board hearings and are allowed to attend and introduce a victim impact statement for

CP PHOTO/Nathan Denette

MADD Canada's aim is to offer support services to victims, heighten awareness about the dangers of driving impaired by alcohol and/or drugs, and save lives and prevent injuries on our roads.

consideration in parole decision making.[78] Numerous acts, regulations, and policies in each of the provinces and territories contain additional provisions for the support and protection of victims and victims' rights.

DID YOU KNOW?

MADD Canada provides the following services for victims:

- Court accompaniment
- Helping victims know their rights under the law
- Referrals
- Emotional support
- Annual Candlelight Vigil of Hope and Remembrance and Victims' Weekend
- Memorial Wall
- On-line Tribute to Victims
- Advocating for victim rights in law

Source: Victim Services, MADD Canada. Reprinted with permission by MADD Canada.

The Office of the Federal Ombudsman for Victims of Crime was created in 2007 as an independent resource for victims in Canada. The mandate of the office is to ensure the federal government meets its commitments to victims by addressing their needs, promoting their interests, and making recommendations to the federal government on issues that negatively impact victims. According to Sue O'Sullivan, Federal Ombudsman for Victims of Crime, "The Government of Canada has made victims of crime a priority, and we will continue to contribute to that important work by helping victims directly and by actively promoting positive, system-wide change."[79] In addition to the Office of the Federal Ombudsman for Victims of Crime, since 1999 the federal government has operated the Policy Centre for Victim Issues with the goal of promoting research on, new initiatives for, and awareness of victims and victims' rights.

LO6 Victim Service Programs

A wide variety of victim service programs have been developed throughout Canada. These programs are organized on a variety of government levels and serve a variety of clients. We will look briefly at some prominent forms of victim assistance operating in Canada.[80]

Victim Compensation

One of the goals of victim advocates has been to lobby for legislation creating crime victim compensation programs.[81] As a result of such legislation, victims may apply to provincial agencies to receive financial compensation for expenses incurred as a consequence of injuries or death resulting from a criminal offence. Compensation may be provided for medical bills, loss of wages, loss of future earnings, and counselling. In the case of death, the victim's survivors may receive burial expenses and aid for loss of support.[82] Personal and household property losses are not normally compensated.

Court Services

Among the victim services now provided through the court system, victim witness assistance programs (VWAP) play a key role in providing information, assistance, and support to victims and witnesses of crime. VWAP programs provide a range of services, including crisis intervention/counselling, referrals to community agencies, emotional support, information about the progress of the case, hearing dates, bail conditions, and court preparation and support. Some provinces have also implemented domestic violence court (DVC) programs that bring together police, Crown attorneys, VWAP staff, probation staff, and others to ensure coordination in prosecution efforts, to ensure the safety and needs of domestic assault victims and their children, and to monitor court outcomes.[83]

Public Education

More than half of all victim programs include public education programs that help familiarize the general public with their services and with other agencies that help crime victims. In some instances, these are

IT SHOULDN'T HURT TO BE A CHILD
CANADIAN CENTRE FOR MISSING CHILDREN

Canadian Centre for Missing Children

The Canadian Centre for Missing Children has a number of services available to victims of crime and families of missing children.

primary prevention programs, which teach methods of dealing with conflict without resorting to violence. For example, school-based programs present information on spousal and dating abuse, followed by discussions of how to reduce violent incidents.[84]

Crisis Intervention

Most victim programs refer victims to specific services to help them recover from their ordeal. Clients are commonly referred to the local network of public and private social service agencies that can provide emergency and long-term assistance with transportation, medical care, shelter, food, and clothing. In addition, more than half of all victim programs provide crisis intervention for victims who feel isolated, vulnerable, and in need of immediate services. Some programs counsel at their offices, while others visit victims in their homes, at the crime scene, or in the hospital.

Victim–Offender Reconciliation Program (VORP)

Victim–offender reconciliation programs use mediators to facilitate face-to-face encounters between victims and offenders. The first VORP in North America was established in Kitchener, Ontario, in 1974. The aim is to engage in direct negotiations that lead to restitution agreements and, possibly, reconciliation between the two parties involved.[85] With the support of the Crown attorney and the court, professionally trained staff are used to facilitate mediation for a wide range of property crimes and simple assaults.[86]

compensation
Financial aid awarded to crime victims to repay them for their loss and injuries; may cover medical bills, loss of wages, loss of future earnings, and/or counselling.

crisis intervention
Emergency counselling for crime victims.

victim–offender reconciliation programs
Mediated face-to-face encounters between victims and their attackers, designed to produce restitution agreements and if possible reconciliation.

LO7 Advocacy for Victims' Rights

Victim advocates argue that crime victims have legal rights that should assure them basic services from the government.[87] Just as the defendant has the right to counsel and a fair trial, society is also obliged to ensure basic rights for law-abiding citizens. These rights range from adequate protection from violent crimes to victim compensation and assistance from the criminal justice system. In 1988, and again in 2003, the federal, provincial, and territorial justice ministers recognized these rights in a "Canadian Statement of Basic Principles of Justice for Victims of Crime," which states that

1. Victims of crime should be treated with courtesy, compassion, and respect.

2. The privacy of victims should be considered and respected to the greatest extent possible.

3. All reasonable measures should be taken to minimize inconvenience to victims.

4. The safety and security of victims should be considered at all stages of the criminal justice process and appropriate measures should be taken when necessary to protect victims from intimidation and retaliation.

5. Information should be provided to victims about the criminal justice system and the victim's role and opportunities to participate in criminal justice processes.

6. Victims should be given information, in accordance with prevailing law, policies, and procedures, about the status of the investigation; the scheduling, progress, and final outcome of the proceedings; and the status of the offender in the correctional system.

7. Information should be provided to victims about available victim assistance services, other programs and assistance available to them, and means of obtaining financial reparation.

8. The views, concerns, and representations of victims are an important consideration in criminal justice processes and should be considered in accordance with prevailing law, policies, and procedures.

9. The needs, concerns, and diversity of victims should be considered in the development and delivery of programs and services, and in related education and training.

10. Information should be provided to victims about available options to raise their concerns when they believe that these principles have not been followed.

Source: *Canadian Statement of Basic Principles of Justice for Victims of Crime, 2003*, http://www.justice.gc.ca/eng/pi/pcvi-cpcv/pub/03/princ.html. Department of Justice Canada, 2003. Reproduced with the permission of the Minister of Public Works and Government Services Canada, 2011.

Assuring victims' rights involves an eclectic mix of advocacy groups—some independent, others government-sponsored, and some self-help. Advocates can be especially helpful when victims need to interact with the agencies of justice. For example, advocates can lobby police departments to keep investigations open as

target hardening
Making one's home or business crime-proof through the use of locks, bars, alarms, and other devices.

Minister of Justice Peter MacKay speaks about the Victims Bill of Rights legislation, in Mississauga, Ontario, in 2014.

well as request the return of recovered stolen property. They can demand that prosecutors and judges provide protection from harassment and reprisals by, for example, making "no contact" a condition of bail. They can help victims make statements during sentencing hearings as well as probation and parole revocation procedures. Victim advocates can also interact with news media, making sure that reporting is accurate and that victim privacy is not violated.

On 3 April 2014, Prime Minister Stephen Harper announced the introduction of Bill C-32, the Victims Bill of Rights Act to recognize the rights of victims of crime. If passed, this new legislation would ensure statutory rights to information, protection, participation and restitution, and ensure a complaint process is in place for breaches of these rights. According to Federal Ombudsman for Victims of Crime, Sue O'Sullivan, the bill contains a number of measures that will improve the system for victims of crime in Canada.

She has vowed to continue to make recommendations to further strengthen the bill and to address those areas that have been neglected as the bill works its way through the parliamentary system.[88]

LO8 Efforts to Avoid Victimization

Although the general public mostly approves of the police, fear of crime and concern about community safety have prompted many people to become their own "police force," taking an active role in community protection and citizen crime-control groups.[89] The more crime in an area, the greater the amount of fear, and the more likely residents will be to engage in self-protective measures.[90] Research indicates that a significant number of crimes may not be reported to police simply because victims prefer to take matters into their own hands.[91]

One manifestation of this trend is the concept of target hardening, or making one's home and business crime-proof through the use of locks, bars,

Campaigns such as "lock it or lose it" are meant to combat high rates of automobile thefts.

alarms, and other devices.[92] Commonly used crime-prevention techniques include a fence or barricade at the entrance; a doorkeeper, guard, or receptionist in an apartment building; an intercom or phone to gain access to the building; surveillance cameras; window bars; warning signs; and dogs chosen for their ability to guard property. The use of these measures is inversely proportional to perception of neighbourhood safety: People who fear crime are more likely to use crime-prevention techniques.

Although the true relationship is still unclear, there is mounting evidence that people who protect their homes are less likely to be victimized

THEORETICAL APPLICATIONS

In a 2014 article, *Toronto Star* reporters investigated sexual assaults on campuses across Canada. In one of the many interviews that were conducted by reporters, an 18-year-old first-year student at Queen's University described how her boyfriend pinned her on his bed, choked her with his hands, then grabbed her hair and forced her to perform oral sex. It was the middle of the day, in the fall of 2011. "We had been kind of fooling around and I was in my underwear and then he pinned me down. . . . I was screaming and saying no. . . . Once I was being choked I couldn't say no anymore," she recalls. Eventually notifying her department at Queen's, she asked for help from a school counsellor. She said both the university and the counsellor let her down. She did not report the assault to police. Her story makes her among as many as one in five young women who experts estimate will experience some form of sexual assault during their time at college or university.

A year later, in the fall of 2012, she wrote to her department at Queen's describing how she was dealing with a high level of stress as a result of the assault. When she came to Queen's she had a 92 percent average, but since the incident she couldn't sleep, eat, or focus on her school work. In the weeks leading up to her writing the letter, she had seen a counsellor once, but her next three appointments were cancelled, making her feel like she was being told she wasn't in urgent need of help. "I have felt a little as though I am drowning," she wrote in her 2012 letter to her department. Feeling depressed and with no other option but to leave the school, two weeks before Christmas break that

year, she walked to the shores of Lake Ontario at 3 A.M., took off all her clothing, jumped off a pier into the freezing water and waited to see if she wanted to die. After two minutes, limbs numb, she pulled herself out. She told her family and got the help she needed, she says.

The Queen's university incident was among a dozen of similar incidents *Star* reporters heard from across the country. School administrators; professors; residence advisers, rape crisis centres; and police, parents, and friends of victims were interviewed. They spoke of sexual assaults that took place at parties, in dorm rooms and in apartments rented by students, far away from the security lamps schools provide to make a walk on campus safe. The assaults have derailed the academic careers of women attending top institutions across the country and left them shaken, confused, anxious, and depressed.

As a police officer assigned to the crime prevention unit of the local police department, you have been contacted by a university in your jurisdiction to respond to escalating incidents such as those described above. How do the different theories of victimization (victim precipitation, lifestyles, routine activities, and lifestyle), attempt to explain why female students are being victimized and how would these theories influence what advice you would give to university administrators?

Source: Excerpt from article in Star written by Emily Mathieu and Jayme Poisson, Canadian post-secondary schools failing sex assault victims, Nov 20 2014, The Star, http://www.thestar.com/news/canada/2014/11/20/canadian_postsecondary_schools_failing_sex_assault_victims.html (accessed 24 December 2014). Reprinted with permission.

by property crimes.[93] One study conducted in the United States found that people who install burglar alarms are less likely to suffer burglary than those who forgo similar preventive measures.[94]

Community Organization

Some communities have organized on the neighbourhood level against crime. Citizens have been working independently and in cooperation with local police agencies in neighbourhood patrol and block-watch programs. These programs organize local citizens in urban areas to patrol neighbourhoods, watch for suspicious people, help secure the neighbourhood, lobby for improvements (such as increased lighting), report crime to police, put out community newsletters, conduct home-security surveys, and serve as a source for crime information or tips.[95]

Although such programs are welcome additions to police services, there is little evidence that they appreciably affect the crime rate. There is also concern that their effectiveness is spottier in low-income, high-crime areas, which need the most crime-prevention assistance.[96] Block watches and neighbourhood patrols seem more successful when they are part of general-purpose or multi-issue community groups, rather than when they focus directly on crime problems.[97]

Summary

Criminologists now consider victims and victimization a major focus of study. About 7.6 million Canadians are victims of crime each year, and the social and economic costs of crime are in the billions of dollars. The discovery that victims play an important role in the crime process has prompted the scientific study of victims, or victimology. Criminologists who focus their attention on crime victims refer to themselves as victimologists.

Many of the problems experienced by victims of crime have been revealed by the General Social Survey on Victimization (GSS—V), one of the most comprehensive sources of information on victimization in Canada. These problems include economic loss including the value of the property stolen or damaged, pain and suffering, lost time at work, health-care costs, and long-term losses in earnings and occupational attainment. There are also the costs associated with the administration of justice including police, courts, and correctional services. Another problem is associated with the criminal justice system itself, with some arguing that the way victims are treated—particularly those who have been victims of sexual assault amounts—to re-victimization. Other problems include long-term stress, fear, and antisocial behaviour resulting from their experiences as victims of crime.

Research has revealed a number of risk factors associated with being a victim of crime; for example, those who engage in evening activities outside the home

(employment, socializing) have a higher risk of being victimized. Though men and woman are equally likely to be victimized, men are more likely to be victims of assault or robbery while women are more likely to be victims of sexual assault. Marital status and neighbourhood characteristics are other risk factors with singles and city dwellers at a higher risk. Like crime, victimization has stable patterns and trends. Violent crime victims tend to be young, poor, single males living in large cities, although victims come in all ages, sizes, races, and genders. Many victimizations occur in the home, and many victims are the target of relatives and loved ones.

There are a number of theories of victimization. One view, called victim precipitation, is that victims provoke criminals. More common are lifestyle theories that suggest that victims put themselves in danger by engaging in high-risk activities, such as going out late at night, living in a high-crime area, and associating with high-risk peers. Deviant place theory argues that victimization risk is related to neighbourhood crime rates. The routine activities theory maintains that a pool of motivated offenders exists and that these offenders will take advantage of unguarded, suitable targets.

Providing care for victims and helping them cope is the responsibility of all of society and there have been a number of initiatives designed with this objective in mind. Recognition of the rights of victims in the Canadian criminal justice system dates from the 1970s, when criminal injuries compensation programs were first introduced and victim–offender reconciliation programs (VORPs) began to be implemented. Legislative changes recognized the rights of victims such as Bill C-127 in 1983, which included the new offence of sexual assault with significant provisions for more equitable and humane treatment of victims. In 1988, the *Criminal Code* was amended to permit the introduction of a victim impact statement at the sentencing stage. Other recent changes to the *Criminal Code* that involve victim rights include the use of publication bans, the use of videotaped testimony for child victims, victim surcharges to fund victim assistance programs, the ordering of restitution for victims, and victim notification of "faint hope clause" hearings for offenders serving a life sentence. The *Corrections and Conditional Release Act* now contains provisions for the release of information to the victim. Finally, in 2007 the Office of the Federal Ombudsman for Victims of Crime was created to ensure the federal government meets its commitments to victims by addressing their needs, promoting their interests, and making recommendations on issues that negatively impact victims.

Numerous programs help victims by providing court services, economic compensation, public education, and crisis intervention. The federal government and the provinces and territories have endorsed a Canadian Statement of the Basic Principles of Justice for Victims of Crime that will guide the formulation of legislations, policies, and procedures for addressing the needs of victims in the future.

Victim advocates argue that crime victims have legal rights that should assure them basic services from the government. Just as the defendant has the right to counsel and a fair trial, society is also obliged to ensure basic rights for law-abiding citizens. These rights range from adequate protection from violent crimes to victim compensation and assistance from the criminal justice system. In 1988, and again in 2003, the federal, provincial, and territorial justice ministers recognized these rights in a "Canadian Statement of Basic Principles of Justice for Victims of Crime." This work laid the foundation for the creation of the Victims Bill of Rights, legislation that seeks to create clear statutory rights at the federal level for victims of crime for the first time in Canada's history. The legislation would establish statutory rights to information, protection, participation, and restitution, and ensure a complaint process is in place for breaches of these rights.

There have been a number of initiatives designed to help people avoid being victims of crime. One example is target hardening, or making one's home and business crime-proof through the use of locks, bars, alarms, and other devices. Research appears to indicate that people who protect their homes are less likely to be victimized by property crimes. Often in collaboration with police services, some communities have implemented neighbourhood patrols and block-watch programs. These programs organize local citizens in urban areas to patrol neighbourhoods, watch for suspicious people, help secure the neighbourhood, lobby for improvements (such as increased lighting), report crime to police, put out community newsletters, conduct home-security surveys, and serve as a source for crime information or tips. There is little evidence that these programs appreciably affect the crime rate and there is concern that they are not as effective in low-income, high-crime areas. Block watches and neighbourhood patrols seem more successful when they are part of general-purpose or multi-issue community groups, rather than when they focus directly on crime problems.

Discussion Questions

1. Considering what you have learned in this chapter about crime victimization, what measures can you take to better protect yourself from crime?

2. Do you agree with the assessment that for young people, a school is one of the most dangerous locations in the community? Did you find your high school to be a dangerous environment?

3. Do people bear some of the responsibility for their victimization if they maintain a lifestyle that contributes to the chances of becoming a crime victim? That is, should we "blame the victim"?

4. Have you ever experienced someone "precipitating" crime? If so, did you do anything to help the situation?

READY TO STUDY?

IN THE BOOK, YOU CAN:

✔ Check your understanding of what you've just read by reading the Summary at the end of each chapter.

✔ Rip out the Chapter in Review card at the back of the book to have the key terms and Learning Objectives handy, and complete the quizzes provided (answers are on the bottom of the back page!).

ONLINE YOU CAN:

✔ Stay organized and efficient with MindTap—a single destination with all the course material and study aids you need to succeed. Built-in apps leverage social media and the latest learning technology. For example:

✔ ReadSpeaker will read the text to you.

✔ Flashcards are pre-populated to provide you with a jump start for review—or you can create your own.

✔ You can highlight text and make notes in your MindTap Reader. Your notes will flow into Evernote, the electronic notebook app that you can access anywhere when it's time to study for the exam.

✔ Prepare for tests with quizzes.

Go to www.nelson.com/student to access these digital resources.

Choice Theory: Because They Want To

Learning Objectives

LO1 State the major principles underlying rational choice theory and contrast it with positivist theory.

LO2 Explain the concept of situational crime prevention.

LO3 Explain general deterrence and critique its effectiveness in reducing the crime rate.

LO4 Explain specific deterrence and critique its effectiveness in reducing the crime rate.

LO5 Explain the logic of incapacitation as a means of crime reduction.

LO6 Outline the policy implications of choice theory.

© Luis Pedrosa/iStockPhoto

Introduction

In a disturbing case, 28-year-old Jennifer Pan from Markham, was living at her parents' home when masked men burst through the doors and demanded cash before shooting her parents. On December 13, 2014, Pan was found guilty of the first-degree murder of her mother and the attempted murder of her father. Pan had described how her immigrant parents relentlessly demanded top grades from her and drove her to succeed in competitive figure skating, and piano lessons. To her parent's dismay they discovered that their daughter had been lying to them for nearly a decade, falsifying report cards and sharing an apartment with her high school sweetheart Daniel Wong. When her parents forced her leave Wong, the Crown alleged she hatched a plot to kill her father, 60-year-old Hann Pan. At her trail, Pan admitted scheming to kill her father but said she abandoned the plan when the man she hired absconded with her money. Months later, she came up with another plan, this time involving a fake home invasion where her parents would be killed, leaving her with a million-dollar inheritance. She enlisted Wong to help find the people to kill her parents; the cost was to be $5000 for each parent. The home invasion ensued according to plan, resulting in the death of her mother; however, her father miraculously survived with a critical head wound. In a strange twist, at her murder trial, Pan testified she called off the plot to kill her parents days before the incident when her family life began to improve. She even agreed to pay $8500 as a cancellation fee, and was gathering the money the day of the attack. However, Pan's explanation did not carry any weight with the jury who found her guilty of the first degree murder of her mother and the second degree murder of her father. Three co-accused, Lenford Crawford, David Mylvaganam and Pan's ex-boyfriend, Daniel Wong, were convicted of the same charges.[1]

The planning and actions of Jennifer Pan suggest that the decision to commit her crime was rational and detailed in her planning and decision making, designed to maximize her personal gain and avoid her capture and punishment. Some criminologists go as far as to suggest that any criminal violation—committing a theft or a robbery, selling drugs, attacking a rival, or filing a false tax return—is based on rational decision making. Such a decision may be motivated by a variety of personal reasons, including greed, revenge, need, anger, lust, jealousy, thrill seeking, or vanity. But if it is made after weighing the potential benefits and consequences, then the illegal act is a **rational choice**. This view of crime is referred to here as **choice theory**.

In this chapter, we review the philosophical underpinnings of choice theory—the view that criminals rationally choose crime. We then turn to theories of crime prevention and control that flow from the concept of choice: situational crime control, general deterrence theory, specific deterrence theory, and incapacitation. Finally, we take a brief look at how choice theory has influenced criminal justice policy.

rational choice
The view that crime is a function of a decision-making process in which the potential offender weighs the potential costs and benefits of an illegal act.

choice theory
The school of thought holding that people choose to engage in delinquent and criminal behaviour after weighing the consequences and benefits of their actions.

DID YOU KNOW?

- Choice theory can be traced to Beccaria's view that crime is rational and can be prevented by punishment that is certain, swift and severe.

- Crime is said to be offence-specific because criminals evaluate the characteristics of targets to determine their suitability.

- Crime is offender-specific because criminals evaluate their skills, motivations, and needs before committing a specific crime.

- Criminal choice involves actions such as choosing the place of crime, selecting targets, and learning criminal techniques.

At her murder trial in the fall of 2014, Jennifer Pan recounted the complicated scheme and bizarre events that led to the death of her mother at her Markham home.

Brett Gundlock/National Post

CHAPTER 4 Choice Theory: Because They Want To

LO1 The Development of Rational Choice Theory

Rational choice theory has its roots in the classical school of criminology developed by Italian social thinker Cesare Beccaria, whose utilitarian approach powerfully influenced the criminal justice system and was widely accepted throughout Europe and North America.[2] For Beccaria when punishment immediately follows a crime, then the ideas of "crime" and "punishment" will be quickly associated in a person's mind. Given the fact that the swiftness of punishment has the greatest impact on deterring others, Beccaria argues there is no justification for severe punishments; he felt it was more appropriate to let the "punishment fit the crime" than to punish criminals in a cruel and capricious manner. Beccaria's vision was influential in the move away from torture and physical punishment in the 19th century toward prison sentences geared to fit the severity of crime. These practices were the cornerstone of what is today known as classical criminology, a view that remained popular for a century.

> **classical criminology**
> The theoretical perspective suggesting that (1) people have free will to choose criminal or conventional behaviours; (2) people choose to commit crime for reasons of greed or personal need; and (3) crime can be controlled only by the fear of criminal sanctions.

By the end of the 19th century, the popularity of the classical approach began to decline, and, by the middle of the 20th century, the perspective was neglected by mainstream criminologists. During this period, positivist criminologists focused on internal and external factors that were thought to be beyond the control of the individual such as poverty, IQ, and education, rather than personal choice and decision making.

Beginning in the late 1970s, a number of criminologists began to revisit classical ideas, producing books and monographs expounding the theme that criminals are rational actors who plan their crimes, could be controlled by the fear of punishment, and deserve to be penalized for their misdeeds. In *Thinking About Crime*, political scientist James Q. Wilson observed that people who are likely to commit crime are unafraid of breaking the law because they value the excitement and thrills of crime, have a low stake in conformity, and are willing to take greater chances than the average person. If they could be convinced that their actions would bring severe punishment, only the totally irrational would be willing to engage in crime.[3]

From these roots has evolved a more contemporary version of classical theory, based on intelligent thought processes and criminal decision making; today this is referred to as the rational choice approach to crime causation.[4]

The Concept of Rational Choice

According to the rational choice approach, law-violating behaviour or "criminality" is the product of careful thought and planning. Offenders choose to engage in criminal behaviour after considering both personal needs—money, revenge, thrills, entertainment—and situational factors, such as how well a target is protected and the efficiency of the local police force. The potential offender evaluates the risk of apprehension, the seriousness of expected punishment, the potential value of the criminal enterprise, and his or her immediate need for criminal gain.

Conversely, the decision to forgo committing a crime may be based on the criminal's perception that the potential rewards of the criminal act are not worth the risk of apprehension. For example, burglars may choose not to commit a crime if they believe that a neighbourhood is well patrolled by police.[5] In fact, when police concentrate patrols in a particular area of the city, crime rates tend to increase in adjacent areas because calculating criminals view them as being safer.[6]

© BRENDAN MCDERMID/Reuters/Corbis

People choose to commit crime for reasons of greed or personal need. The former was the case with Bernie Madoff, who took billions of dollars in one of the largest Ponzi schemes in U.S. history. He is now serving a 150-year prison sentence.

© Film Fanatique/Alamy Stock Photo

Examples of rational choice theory abound in the movies. Billy Wilder's *Double Indemnity* which is viewed as one of the top 100 movies of all times contains the classic portrayal of rational choice theory. The movie commences with the film's protagonist salesman, Walter Neff declaring, "Yes, I killed him . . . I killed him for money and a woman and I didn't get the money and I didn't get the woman." Walter coldly conducted a cost benefit analysis weighing pleasure (money and woman) against the interests and life of others. In the movie, crime is depicted as the calculated choice that Walter made to determine if the benefits of committing murder outweighed the costs. According to rational choice theory, if the benefits outweigh the costs, the person will undoubtedly commit the crime.

The 2014 movie *American Sniper* is a biographical war drama starring Bradley Cooper and is based on the memoir Chris Kyle. The film follows Kyle's life as he earns the reputation as one of the deadliest marksman in U.S. military history with 255 kills from four tours during the Iraq War. While Kyle was an accomplished soldier, his time in the military took a heavy toll on his personal and family life. The film was a major success, becoming the highest-grossing film of 2014 and the highest-grossing war film of all time. Kyle died in 2013 after being shot by a former Marine who was suffering from post-traumatic stress disorder, or PTSD.

Kyle was born in Texas to a church deacon and a Sunday-school teacher who often took him hunting. He attended Tarleton State University in Texas for two years before enlisting in the Navy and undergoing SEAL training. Shortly after getting married, Kyle was deployed to Iraq and showed his skills as a sniper. His first kill was in Nasiriya, Iraq, in 2003. He shot a woman who was preparing to throw a grenade at approaching Marines.

"The first time you're killing somebody, you're not even sure you can do it," Kyle said in an interview with *Time*. "You think you can, but you never know until you're actually put in that position and you do it." In one legendary shot, later in his career, he hit an insurgent target who was 1.2 miles away. Using his scope, he spotted the insurgent on the roof of a building and took him out which he later referred to as "a lucky shot."

Kyle saw the killing he did as a necessary part of protecting American troops. "You don't think of the people you kill as people. They're just targets. You can't think of them as people with families and jobs. They rule by putting terror in the hearts of innocent people. The things they would do—beheadings, dragging Americans through the streets alive, the things they would do to little boys and women just to keep them terrified and quiet . . . That part is easy. I definitely don't have any regrets about that."

Like many veterans, Kyle had trouble adjusting to civilian life, eventually finding purpose in being a father and helping veterans and civilians. He started a defence contracting company, and in his spare time took veterans to shooting ranges as a sort of therapy. A woman who lived near Kyle called him one day to ask if he could help her son, another former soldier who was suffering from mental illness. Kyle and a friend agreed to take the 25-year-old Marine to the shooting range to blow off steam. Eddie Ray Routh shot and killed both Kyle and Littlefield. He has since been found guilty of murder and was sentenced to life in prison without parole.

Eddie Ray Routh was known to have a mental illness. How well does the rational choice theory explain Routh's actions?

Source: Excerpt from: Pamela Engel, The Incredible And Tragic Story Of The Real-Life 'American Sniper'. *Business Insider*, Jan. 20, 2015. Reprinted with permission.

Structuring Criminality

A number of personal factors condition people to choose criminality. Offenders are likely to desist from crime if they believe (1) that their future criminal earnings will be relatively low and (2) that attractive and legal opportunities to generate income are available.[7] In contrast, criminals may be motivated when they know people who have made "big scores" and are quite successful at crime. Though the prevailing wisdom is that "crime does not pay," a small but significant subset of criminals enjoy earnings of $50 000 or more per year from crime, and their success may help motivate other would-be offenders.[8] In this sense, rational choice is a function of a person's perception of conventional alternatives and opportunities.

Learning and experience may be important elements in structuring crime.[9] Career criminals may learn the limitations of their powers; they know when to take a chance and when to be cautious. Experienced criminals may turn from a life of crime when they develop a belief that the risk of crime is greater than its potential profit.[10]

> **structuring crime**
> According to the rational choice approach, the decision to commit crime, regardless of its substance, is structured by (1) where it occurs, (2) the characteristics of the target, and (3) available means.

In a study by John Carroll and Frances Weaver, experienced and novice shoplifters were asked to think aloud in stores and it was found that both were concerned with the accessibility of items and risks of being caught, suggesting that rational choice might be applicable to shoplifting.[11]

Personality and lifestyle also affect criminal choices. Criminals appear to be more impulsive and have less self-control than other people; they seem unaffected by fear of criminal punishment.[12] They are typically under stress or facing some serious personal problem or condition that forces them to choose risky behaviour.[13] (See Table 4.1.)

Choosing the Place

Criminals carefully choose where they will commit their crime. Criminologist Bruce Jacobs's interviews with 40 active crack cocaine street dealers in a Midwestern U.S. city showed that dealers carefully evaluate the desirability of their sales area before setting up shop.[14] Dealers consider the middle of a long block the best choice because they can see everything in both directions; police raids can be spotted before they occur.[15] Another tactic is to entice new buyers into spaces between apartment buildings. Although the dealers may lose the tactical edge of being on a public street, they gain a measure of protection because their colleagues can watch over the operation and come to the rescue if the buyer tries to "pull something."[16]

Choosing Targets

Evidence of rational choice may also be found in the way criminals locate their targets. Victimization data indicate that while the affluent are rarely the victims of violent crimes, high-income households are the most likely targets of break and enter.[17] Interviews

TABLE 4.1

Robbing Banks for a Living

The Motivation to Rob Banks

According to Canadian criminologist Fred Desroches, "Bank robbers need money for the same reasons we all do"—to pay debts, buy a car, take a vacation, and pay day-to-day expenses. In addition, about 15 percent of robbers need the money to support an alcohol, gambling, or drug habit, and a majority report that the initial motivation to get into the bank robbery business was to support their "partying lifestyle"—drinking, drugs, hitting the bars with friends, and living for the moment. Sometimes the motivation to rob a bank is simply for the thrill of it.

Planning the Bank Robbery

Surprisingly, little planning goes in to most bank robberies—in some cases, as little as five minutes. According to Desroches, "minimization of risk" is the primary factor in selecting a target and constructing a plan. Usually, robbers will pick times when there are likely to be only a few "civilians" present who could disrupt the robbery; choose locations based on access to a means of "getaway" (either automobile or public transit); and prefer large cities over small towns because getaway will be easier. In many cases, individuals will rob banks within or close to the neighbourhood they live, as they are most familiar with these locations and can quickly and easily construct a robbery plan.

Learning from Experience

Desroches found that a majority of bank robbers report using information gleaned from the local media about robberies, their own and those committed by others, to revise plans and techniques or determine the need to escape the community based on what the police are reported to know about them. In addition, bank robbers may search for information about the wording of notes handed to tellers, successful getaway strategies, bank policies and practices in the event of a robbery, the need to use a weapon to overcome resistance, the nature of the police response to bank robberies, and the amount of cash taken (as an indicator of potentially good targets).

A Winning Formula

Desroches reports that most bank robbers do not vary their modus operandi very much—which can greatly assist the police in their capture. Why don't they change their M.O.? Simple. If they haven't been caught yet, why tamper with a winning formula they don't believe can be improved on anyway?

Sources: Frederick J. Desroches, *Force and Fear: Robbery in Canada* (Toronto: Nelson Canada, 1995); Frederick J. Desroches, *Behind the Bars: Experiences in Crime* (Toronto: Canadian Scholars Press, 1996).

with burglars find that they check to make sure that no one is home before they enter a residence. Some call ahead, whereas others ring the doorbell, preparing to claim they had the wrong address if someone answers. Some find out which families have star high school athletes because those that do are sure to be at the weekend football game, leaving their houses unguarded.[18] Others seek unlocked doors and avoid the ones with deadbolts; houses with dogs are usually considered off-limits.[19] Burglars also report being sensitive to the activities of their victims. They note that homemakers often develop predictable behaviour patterns, which helps burglars plan their crimes.[20]

Travis Baumgartner, 21, was one of five armed guards loading a bank machine at the University of Alberta in June 2012 just after midnight when shots could be heard. In a crime that Associate Chief Justice John Rooke described as "unspeakable, outrageous, cowardly and cold-blooded," Baumgartner executed three of his fellow guards by shooting them at point blank range in the back of the head and critically injuring a fourth "all with the simple motive of robbery." In one of the harshest sentences handed down in Canada since 1962, Baumgartner was sentenced to life imprisonment with no chance of parole for 40 years.

Source (quotations): http://www.cbc.ca/news/canada/edmonton/travis-baumgartner-gets-40-years-without-parole-for-killing-co-workers-1.1706464

Burglars seem to prefer "working" between 9 A.M. and 11 A.M. and in midafternoon, when parents are either working or dropping off or picking up children at school. They also appear to monitor car and pedestrian traffic and avoid selecting targets on heavily travelled streets.[21] Yet the evidence suggests that even when well-organized communities restrict traffic and limit neighbourhood entrance and exit routes there has not been a significant decline in property crime.[22]

In sum, rational choice involves both shaping criminality and structuring crime. Personality, age,

DID YOU KNOW?

- Theft crimes appear rational because thieves and burglars typically choose targets that present little risk and they plan their attacks carefully.

- Robbers report that they select vulnerable targets who are unlikely to fight back. They avoid armed victims.

- Drug users and dealers use elaborate ploys to avoid detection. They employ businesslike practices in their commercial enterprises.

status, risk, and opportunity seem to influence the decision to become a criminal; place, target, and techniques help structure crime.[23]

Is Crime Rational?

It is relatively easy to show that some crimes are the product of rational, objective thought, especially when they involve an ongoing criminal conspiracy centred on economic gain. For example, when American stockbroker Bernard Madoff was convicted in June 2009 for criminal fraud after operating a "Ponzi" scheme that bilked thousands of clients out of billions of dollars,[24] his elaborate financial scheme not only showed signs of rationality but also exhibited brilliant, though flawed, financial expertise. Similarly, the drug dealings of organized crime bosses demonstrate a reasoned analysis of market conditions, interests, and risks. But what about crimes that are immediate rather than ongoing? Do they show signs of rationality?

Are Street Crimes Rational?

There is evidence that even seemingly "unplanned" street crimes may also be the product of careful risk assessment, including environmental, social, and structural factors. Target selection seems highly rational. Ronald Clarke and Patricia Harris found that auto thieves are very selective in their choice of targets. Vehicle selection seems to be based on attractiveness and suitability for a particular purpose; for example, German cars are selected for stripping because they usually have high-quality audio equipment that has good value on the second-hand market.[25]

There are also signs of rationality in the choices made by armed robbers. They generally choose targets close to their homes or in areas that they routinely travel. Familiarity with the area gives them ready knowledge of escape routes; this is referred to as their "awareness space."[26] Robbers may be wary of people who are watching the community for signs of trouble: research by Paul Bellair shows that robbery levels are relatively low in neighbourhoods where residents keep a watchful eye on their neighbours' property.[27] Many robbers avoid freestanding buildings because they can more easily be surrounded by police; others select targets that are known to do a primarily cash business, such as bars, supermarkets, and restaurants.[28]

Frederick Desroches found that bank robbers use specific techniques to avoid being apprehended by police. Some go as far as using police scanners to

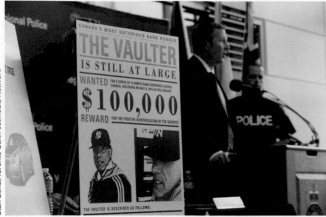

A Canada-wide warrant and a reward of $20 000 have been issued for a bank robber dubbed the "Vaulter" because he leaps over bank counters during the robberies. Referred to as Canada's most notorious bank robber, he has 18 bank heists over a three-year period to his credit. Surprisingly, according to Detective-Sergeant Fleischaker, a key to his success is that he makes little attempt to conceal his identity. It permits him to come into the bank without drawing undue attention to himself making it easy for him to just walk up on somebody. "It's obviously very ballsy."

Source (quotation): Jodee Brown, "Woman Kicked Notorious Bank Robber in the Groin During His 17th Heist, Police Say," *National Post* (11 April 2013) at http://news .nationalpost.com/2013/04/11/police-hunt-the-vaulter-suspected-of-robbing-17-banks -between-ottawa-and-calgary/ (accessed 4 January 2015)

monitor police activity in the area of the bank they plan to rob.[29] One bank robber told Desroches

> I can recall listening to the police scanner after the alarm went off. I could hear the dispatcher, "We have an alarm . . ." as they were coming out the door . . . Meanwhile my cohorts are getting into the car and one partner says, "Now it's your job." I got out onto the expressway and I could see the lights of a police cruiser coming down the road and turning into the parking lot. They were there fast! We were in the bank three minutes. [Over the scanner] I hear the police say, "The suspects left in a Chevy Nova." I can't believe my luck because this car is not even similar looking.[30]

Is Drug Use Rational?

Did actor Charlie Sheen make an objective, rational choice to abuse drugs and potentially sabotage his career? Did the "King of Pop," entertainer Michael Jackson, make a rational choice when he abused prescription drugs to the point that it killed him?[31]

Is it possible that drug users and dealers, a group not usually associated with clear thinking, make rational choices? Research does in fact show that at its onset, drug use is controlled by rational decision making. Users report that they begin taking drugs when they believe that the benefits of substance abuse outweigh its costs: They believe that drugs

will provide a fun, exciting, thrilling experience. They choose what they consider safe sites to buy and sell drugs.[32] Their entry into substance abuse is facilitated by their perception that valued friends and family members endorse and encourage drug use and abuse substances themselves.[33]

Drug dealers approach their profession in a businesslike fashion. According to criminologist George Rengert's study of drug markets, drug dealers face many of the same problems as legitimate retailers. If they are too successful in one location, rivals will be attracted to the area, and stiff competition may drive down prices and cut profits. The dealer can fight back by discounting the cost of drugs or increasing quality, as long as it doesn't reduce profit margins.[34]

Even in what appear to be senseless killings among strangers,[35] it can be argued that the underlying motives are rational—the desire of murderers to avoid retaliation from the victims they assaulted or to avoid future prosecution.[36]

Is drug use rational? If so, how can persistent abusers such as well-known celebrities Charlie Sheen, Robert Downey Jr., and Lindsay Lohan (pictured) gain from their behaviour?

Why Do People Commit Crimes?

Assuming that crime is rational, why—knowing its often-unpleasant consequences—do people choose to commit crime? English philosopher Jeremy Bentham (1748–1832) regarded as the father of utilitarianism believed in hedonism, which is a school of thought that argues that pleasure is the primary or most important intrinsic good. A hedonist strives to maximize net pleasure. Bentham further refined Beccaria's ideas with his concept of Hedonistic Calculus, the weighing of pleasure versus pain. Simply put, a rational person will commit a crime when the expected pleasure outweighs the expected pain.

Rational choice theorists believe that for many people, crime is a more attractive alternative than law-abiding behaviour. It brings rewards, excitement, prestige, or other desirable outcomes without lengthy work or effort. Whether it is violent or profit oriented, crime has an allure that some people cannot resist. Crime may produce a natural "high" and other positive sensations that are instrumental in maintaining and reinforcing criminal behaviour.[37] Some law violators describe the "adrenaline rush" that comes from successfully executing illegal activities in dangerous situations. This has been termed edgework: the "exhilarating, momentary integration of danger, risk, and skill" that motivates people to try a variety of dangerous criminal and noncriminal behaviour.[38]

According to Jack Katz, some criminals can get "high" by engaging in criminal activities.

Sociologist Jack Katz argues that there are, in fact, immediate benefits to criminality. These situational inducements, which he labels the seductions of crime,[39] directly precede the commission of crime and draw offenders into law violations. For example, someone challenges their authority or moral position, and they vanquish their opponent with a beating; or they want to do something exciting, so they break into and vandalize a school building.

According to Katz, choosing crime can help satisfy personal needs. For some people, shoplifting and vandalism are attractive because getting away with crime is a thrilling demonstration of personal competence (Katz calls this "sneaky thrills"). Even murder can have an emotional payoff: Killers behave like the avenging gods of mythology, choosing to have life-or-death control over their victims.[40]

If committing crime is a rational choice, it follows that crime can be controlled or eradicated by convincing potential offenders that crime is a poor choice—that it will bring them not rewards, but pain, hardship, and deprivation. Evidence shows that jurisdictions with relatively low incarceration rates also experience the highest crime rates.[41] As we have seen, according to rational choice theory, street-smart offenders know which areas offer the least threat and plan their crimes accordingly. A number of potential strategies flow from this premise. The following sections discuss each of these crime reduction or control strategies based on the rationality of criminal behaviour.

LO2 Situational Crime Prevention

Rational choice theory suggests that because criminal activity is offender-specific, crime prevention, or at least crime reduction, can be achieved through policies that convince potential criminals to desist from criminal activities, delay their actions, or avoid a particular target. Criminal acts will be avoided if (1) potential targets are carefully guarded, (2) the means to commit crime are controlled, and (3) potential offenders are carefully monitored. Desperate people may contemplate crime, but only the truly irrational

edgework
The excitement or exhilaration of successfully executing illegal activities in dangerous situations.

seductions of crime
The situational inducements or immediate benefits that draw offenders into law violations.

offender-specific crime
Theories of criminality that look at why people commit crime and the factors that explain criminality.

situational crime prevention
A method of crime prevention that seeks to eliminate or reduce particular crimes in narrow settings.

defensible space
The principle that crime can be prevented or displaced by modifying the physical environment to reduce the opportunity individuals have to commit crime.

will attack a well-defended, inaccessible target and risk strict punishment.

One way of preventing crime, then, is to reduce the opportunities people have to commit particular crimes. This approach is known as **situational crime prevention**. It was first popularized in the early 1970s by Oscar Newman, who coined the term **defensible space**. The idea is that crime can be prevented or displaced through the use of residential designs that reduce criminal opportunity, such as well-lit housing projects that maximize surveillance.[42] (See Table 4.2.)

Crime Prevention Strategies

Situational crime prevention involves developing tactics to reduce or eliminate a specific crime problem (such as shoplifting in an urban mall or street-level drug dealing). According to criminologists Ronald Clarke and Ross Homel, crime prevention tactics used today generally fall into one of four categories:

1. Increase the effort needed to commit crime.
2. Increase the risks of committing crime.

> Why do we kill people who kill people to show killing people is wrong?

3. Reduce the rewards for committing crime.
4. Induce guilt or shame for committing crime.

Source: CRIME PREVENTION AT THE CROSSROADS by STEVEN LAB. Copyright 1997 Reproduced with permission of ANDERSON PUBLISHING COMPANY, INC. in the format Textbook and Other Book via Copyright Clearance Center.

These basic techniques and some specific methods that can be used to achieve them are summarized in Table 4.2.

TABLE 4.2

Sixteen Techniques of Situational Prevention

Increasing Perceived Effort	Increasing Perceived Risks	Reducing Anticipated Rewards	Inducing Guilt or Shame
Target hardening	Entry/exit screening	Target removal	Rule setting
Slug rejector devices	Automatic ticket gates	Removable car radio	Harassment codes
Steering locks	Baggage screening	Women's shelters	Customs declaration
Bandit screens	Merchandise tags	Phone card	Hotel registrations
Access control	Formal surveillance	Identifying property	Strengthening moral condemnation
Parking lot barriers	Burglar alarms	Property marking	"Shoplifting is stealing"
Fenced yards	Speed cameras	Vehicle licensing	Roadside speedometers
Entry phones	Security guards	Cattle branding	"Bloody idiots drink and drive"
Deflecting offenders	Surveillance by employees	Reducing temptation	Controlling disinhibitors
Bus stop placement	Pay phone location	Gender-neutral phone lists	Drinking-age laws
Tavern location	Park attendants	Off-street parking	Ignition interlock
Street closures	Closed-circuit TV systems	Denying benefits	Server intervention
Controlling facilitators	Natural surveillance	Ink merchandise tags	Facilitating compliance
Credit card photo	Defensible space	PIN for car radios	Improved library checkout
Caller ID	Street lighting	Graffiti cleaning	Public lavatories
Gun controls	Cab driver ID		Trash bins

Source: CRIME PREVENTION AT THE CROSSROADS by STEVEN LAB. Copyright 1997 Reproduced with permission of ANDERSON PUBLISHING COMPANY, INC. via Copyright Clearance Center.

FIGURE 4.1

Crime Prevention Through Environmental Design (CPTED)

Large windows promote casual supervision of sidewalk.

Porches and sidewalk encourage interaction between neighbors.

Paving and architectural treatments define public and private zones.

Good pedestrian-scaled lighting on street.

Low landscaping and fences define property lines without creating hiding places.

Metrolinx

A design of a residential complex using "CPTED," which aims to increase safety in communities in the urban development planning stage.

Source: Melodi McGee, "'CPTED': Designing the Way to Safer Communities," *Healthy Cities & Urban Planning* (20 March 2014) at http://www.powerhousegrowers.com/cpted-designing-the-way-to-safer-communities

Some of the tactics to increase effort include target-hardening techniques such as putting unbreakable glass on storefronts, locking gates, and fencing yards. Even simple prevention measures can work. Removing signs from store windows, installing brighter lights, and instituting a pay-first policy have helped reduce thefts from gas stations and convenience stores. Many police services now offer Crime Prevention Through Environmental Design (CPTED) audits to assist individuals and businesses to identify and implement environmental changes to reduce the risk of being victimized.[43] (See Figure 4.1.)

Technological advances can also make it more difficult for would-be offenders to commit crimes; for example, having an owner's photo on credit cards should reduce the use of stolen cards. New security products such as steering locks on cars have reduced the incidence of theft.[44] Similarly, installing a locking device on cars that prevents drunk drivers from starting the vehicle significantly reduces drunk-driving rates.[45]

Target reduction strategies are designed to reduce the value of crime to the potential criminal. These include making car stereos removable so they can be kept at home at night, marking property so that it is more difficult to sell when stolen, and having gender-neutral phone listings to discourage obscene phone calls. Tracking systems can help police locate and return stolen vehicles.

Inducing guilt or shame might include techniques such as setting strict rules to embarrass offenders. For example, publishing "John lists" in the newspaper punishes those arrested for soliciting prostitutes. Facilitating compliance by providing trash bins might shame chronic litterers into using them. Widespread use of caller ID-equipped telephones has resulted in significant reductions in the number of obscene and prank phone calls, presumably because of the shame presented by the threat of exposure.[46]

THE CANADIAN PRESS IMAGES/Bayne Stanley

The RCMP introduces new bait car technology, which allows police to videotape and track thieves who steal valuables from cars rather than the vehicles themselves.

As the popularity of Facebook, Twitter, and other forms of social media increase, there are applications to, for example, Neighbourhood Watch, where homeowners could receive instantaneous messages from others in the community with warnings about suspicious persons nearby.

Displacement, Extinction, Discouragement, and Diffusion

Situational crime prevention efforts, however, may produce unforeseen and unwanted consequences. Preventing crime in one location does not address or deter criminal motivation. People who desire the benefits of crime may choose alternative targets, so that crime is not prevented but deflected or displaced.[47] For example, beefed-up police patrols in one area may shift crimes to a more vulnerable neighbourhood.[48] Although crime displacement certainly does not solve the general problem of crime, it has been shown to reduce the frequency of crime or produce less serious offence patterns.[49]

There is also the problem of extinction: Crime reduction programs may produce a short-term positive effect, but benefits dissipate as criminals adjust to new conditions. They learn to dismantle alarms or avoid patrols. They may also try new offences they had previously avoided. For example, if every residence in a neighbourhood has a foolproof burglar alarm system,

displacement
An effect of crime prevention efforts in which efforts to control crime in one area shift illegal activities to another.

extinction
The phenomenon in which a crime prevention effort has an immediate impact that then dissipates as criminals adjust to new conditions.

diffusion of benefits
An effect that occurs when efforts to prevent one crime unintentionally prevent another, or when crime-control efforts in one locale reduce crime in other nontarget areas.

discouragement
An effect that occurs when limiting access to one target reduces other types of crime as well.

motivated offenders may turn to armed robbery, a riskier and more violent crime.

Although displacement and extinction may create problems, there may also be advantages.[50] **Diffusion of benefits** occurs (1) when efforts to prevent one crime unintentionally prevent another and/or (2) when crime-control efforts in one locale reduce crime in other nontarget areas. What causes diffusion? First, crime prevention efforts may produce a generalized fear of apprehension. For example, video cameras set up in a mall to reduce shoplifting can also reduce property damage because would-be vandals fear they will be caught on camera. Or intensive police patrol efforts targeting neighbourhood drug dealers may convince prostitutes that it is too dangerous to ply their trade in that area.[51]

Situational crime prevention efforts may also produce **discouragement**: Limiting access to one target convinces would-be lawbreakers that crime no

Big Brother is watching you. Toronto police have installed closed-circuit television cameras throughout downtown Toronto; the one pictured is in the shadow of the CN Tower.

Electronic security measures have made stealing car stereos, airbags, xenon headlights, GPS, and DVD systems increasingly difficult to steal.

longer pays in general. For example, evaluations of auto protection systems that use hidden radio transmitters to track stolen cars have found that these devices help lower car theft rates. The auto protection systems not only deter auto thieves, but also seem to disrupt the operation of "chop shops," where stolen vehicles are taken apart for the resale of parts. Stolen car buyers cannot be sure if a stolen vehicle they purchase contains an auto protection system, which the police can trace to their base of operations.[52] Thus, a device designed to protect cars from theft also has the benefit of disrupting the sale of stolen car parts.

DID YOU KNOW?

- Situational crime prevention efforts are designed to reduce or redirect crime by making it more difficult to profit from illegal acts.

- General deterrence models are based on the fear of punishment that is severe, swift, and certain.

- Specific deterrence aims at reducing crime through the application of severe punishments. Once offenders experience these punishments, they will be unwilling to repeat their criminal activities

- Incapacitation strategies are designed to reduce crime by taking known criminals out of circulation, preventing them from having the opportunity to commit further offences.

LO3 General Deterrence

According to the rational choice view, motivated people will violate the law if left free and unrestricted. The concept of general deterrence is that, conversely, the decision to commit crime can be controlled by the threat of criminal punishment. If people fear being apprehended and punished, they will not risk breaking the law. An inverse relationship should exist between crime rates and the certainty, speed and severity of legal sanctions. If, for example, the punishment for a crime is increased and the effectiveness and efficiency of the criminal justice system are improved, then the number of people engaging in that crime should decline.

The factors of certainty, speed, and severity of punishment may also be interactive. For example, if a crime—say, robbery—is punished severely, but few robbers are ever caught or punished, the severity of punishment for robbery will probably not deter people from robbing. On the other hand, if the certainty of apprehension and conviction is increased by modern technology, more efficient police work, or some other factor, then even minor punishment might deter the potential robber.

Do these factors actually affect the decision to commit crime and, consequently, general crime rates?

Certainty of Punishment

According to deterrence theory, if the certainty of arrest, conviction, and sanctioning increases, crime rates should decline. Rational offenders will soon realize that the increased likelihood of punishment outweighs any benefit they perceive from committing crimes. According to this view, crime persists because most criminals believe (1) that there is only a small chance they will get arrested for committing a particular crime, (2) that police officers are sometimes reluctant to make arrests even if they are aware of crime, and (3) that even if apprehended there is a good chance of receiving a lenient punishment.[53]

Although this view seems logical enough, the relationship between certainty of punishment and crime rates is far from settled. While a few research efforts do show a direct relationship between crime rates and the certainty of punishment,[54] a great deal of contradictory evidence indicates that the likelihood of being arrested or imprisoned has little effect on crime.[55]

One reason for this ambivalent finding is that the association between certainty of punishment and crime may be time-, crime-, and group-specific. For example, research shows that when the number of arrests increases, the number of serious crimes reported to police declines soon after.[56] It is possible

general deterrence
A crime control policy that depends on the fear of criminal penalties, convincing the potential law violator that the pains associated with crime outweigh its benefits.

crackdown
The concentration of police resources on a particular problem area to eradicate or displace criminal activity.

that news of increased and aggressive police activity is rapidly diffused through the population and has an immediate impact, but that the effect erodes over time.

Research carried out in the United States also finds that the certainty of punishment may be race-specific. Arrests of blacks may influence only black offence rates, whereas arrests of whites probably affect only white offending patterns. In large cities, the threat of arrest may be communicated within neighbourhoods, some of which may be racially segregated. This threat affects residents of each racial grouping independently.[57]

Some research efforts have found a crime-specific deterrent effect. For example, using national data sets measuring crime and arrest rates in the United States, criminologist Edwin Zedlewski found that an increased probability of arrest may help lower the burglary rate, whereas theft rates remain unaffected by law enforcement efforts.[58]

Level of Police Activity

If certainty of apprehension and punishment deters criminal behaviour, then increasing the number of police officers on the street should cut the crime rate. Moreover, if these police officers are active, aggressive crime fighters, would-be criminals should be convinced that the risk of apprehension outweighs the benefits they can gain from crime. However, the evidence that adding police leads to reduced crime rates is spotty.[59] Numerous studies have failed to show that increasing the number of police officers in a community can, by itself, lower crime rates.[60]

It is possible that while adding police may not work, adding more effective police could reduce crime. Research indicates that if police could make an arrest in at least 30 percent of all reported crimes, the crime rate would decline significantly.[61] But how can that figure be achieved, considering that arrest rates today hover at 20 percent?

To lower crime rates, some police services have instituted crackdowns—sudden changes in police activity designed to increase the communicated threat or actual certainty of punishment. For example, a police task force might target street-level narcotics dealers by using undercover agents and surveillance cameras in known drug-dealing locales. However, these efforts have not proven to be successful mechanisms for lowering crime rates.[62] An analysis of 18 police crackdowns by Lawrence Sherman found that while they initially deterred crime, crime rates resumed earlier levels once the crackdown

A prison term has historically been the deterrent of choice.

ended.[63] Although these results contradict the deterrence concept, research shows that more focused efforts may reduce crime levels. Crime rates are reduced when police officers use aggressive problem-solving and community improvement techniques, such as increasing lighting and cleaning vacant lots, to fight particular crimes in selected places.[64] A good example of the effectiveness of the crackdown strategy is the success of Ontario's RIDE (Reduce Impaired Driving Everywhere) program, which has had a significant impact in reducing impaired-driving-related accidents and fatalities on Ontario highways.[65]

Severity of Punishment

The introduction or threat of severe punishment should also bring the crime rate down. Although some studies have found that increasing sanction levels can control common criminal behaviours, there is little consensus that strict punishments alone can reduce criminal activities.[66] Because the likelihood of getting caught for some crimes is relatively low, the impact of deterrent measures is negligible over the long term.[67] For example, laws that provide expanded or mandatory sentences for crimes committed with guns have received mixed reviews. While some experts believe that these laws can lower crime rates, others question their deterrent effect. In sum, there is little empirical evidence that they have worked as planned.[68]

The lack of evidence to demonstrate that severe punishment deters crime does not influence controversial Sheriff Joe Arpaio of Arizona. In 1994 he built

Sheriff Joe Arpaio, in Maricopa County, Arizona (left), erected a "tent city," in which he uses severe punishment in an attempt to deter crime (right).

Tent City using 70 surplus Korean War military tents as an outdoor jail stating, "Everything I do is geared to send a message to all the people who live in Maricopa County, that if you do something wrong you're going to end up in the tents." Of about 10 000 prisoners incarcerated in the county 800–900 of them are housed in Tent City, a figure Arpaio worries is too low; a neon sign in the corner of the jail says "vacancy." The most common crimes that will send someone to Tent City include driving under the influence, drug possession, domestic violence, and car theft. The outdoor jail has become quite a tourist attraction with visitors from around the world. Arpaio relishes the indignities he bestows upon his prisoners. For example, he eliminated meat and salt and pepper from their meals, forces them to endure 120-plus degree weather, and makes them wear pink underwear. Inmates must also perform indigent burials and work eight-hour shifts at a food factory. Television is provided but it plays only the Food Channel ("so they can see the good food they're missing on the outside," Jones said) and the Weather Channel ("Joe wants them to see how hot it's going to be").[69]

Capital Punishment

In May 2004, Cobourg Police Chief Garry Clement called for the reinstatement of the death penalty for those who kill officers of the law. Clement was reacting to the death of one of his officers, Constable Chris Garrett, slain by an 18-year-old male during the course of a robbery. Since its abolition in Canada in 1976, there have been recurring calls from members of the public and politicians to bring back the death penalty.

It seems to stand to reason that if severity of punishment can deter crime, then fear of the death penalty, the ultimate legal deterrent, should significantly reduce murder rates. Failure of the death penalty to deter violent crime jeopardizes the validity of the entire deterrence concept.

Various studies have tested the assumption that capital punishment deters violent crime. The research can be divided into three types: immediate impact studies, comparative research, and time-series analysis.

Immediate Impact

If capital punishment is a deterrent, the reasoning goes, then its impact should be greatest after a well-publicized execution. Robert Dann began testing this assumption in the United States in 1935, when he chose five highly publicized executions of convicted murderers in different years and determined the number of homicides in the 60 days before and after each execution.[70] Dann's study revealed that an average of 4.4 more homicides occurred during the 60 days following an execution than during those preceding it, suggesting that the overall impact of executions might actually be to increase the incidence of homicide.

The fact that executions may actually increase the likelihood of murders being committed is a consequence referred to as the brutalization effect. The basis of this theory is that potential criminals may begin to model their behaviour after state authorities: If the government can kill its enemies, so can they.[71] The brutalization effect means that after an execution murders may increase, causing even more deaths of innocent victims.

> **brutalization effect**
> The belief that capital punishment creates an atmosphere of brutality that enhances rather than deters the level of violence in society.

CHAPTER 4 Choice Theory: Because They Want To **89**

Although many criminologists question the utility of capital punishment, claiming that it causes more harm than it prevents, others believe that in the short run, executing criminals can bring the murder rate down.[72] Steven Stack's analysis of 16 well-publicized executions in the United States concluded that they may have saved 480 lives by immediately deterring potential murderers.[73] In sum, a number of criminologists find that executions actually increase murder rates, whereas others argue that their immediate impact is to lower murder rates.

Comparative Research

Another type of research compares the murder rates in jurisdictions that have abolished the death penalty with the rates in those that employ the death penalty.[74] Two pioneering studies, one by Thorsten Sellin (1959) and the other by Walter Reckless (1969), showed little difference in the murder rates of adjacent states, regardless of their use of the death penalty; capital punishment did not appear to influence the reported rate of homicide.[75] Similar research carried out by Canadian criminologist Ezzat Fattah in the 1970s arrived at the same conclusion.[76] More recent research gives little reason to believe that executions deter homicide[77]; more recent studies have compared murder rates in jurisdictions having a death penalty statute with those that don't and have also taken into account the number of people actually executed. These comparisons indicate that the death penalty—whether on the books or actually used—does not deter violent crime.[78]

In addition, research conducted in 14 nations around the world found little evidence that countries with a death penalty have lower violence rates than those without. In fact, homicide rates decline after capital punishment is abolished, a direct contradiction to its supposed deterrent effect.[79]

Time-Series Analysis

Statistical analysis has allowed researchers to gauge whether the murder rate changes when death penalty statutes are created or eliminated. The most widely cited study is Isaac Ehrlich's 1975 work, in which he used U.S. crime and execution data to reach the conclusion that each execution in the United States would save seven or eight people from being murdered.[80] Ehrlich's research has been widely cited by advocates of the death penalty as empirical proof of the deterrent effect of capital punishment.

informal sanctions Disapproval, stigma, or anger directed toward an offender by significant others (parents, peers, neighbours, teachers), resulting in shame, embarrassment, and loss of respect.

However, subsequent research that attempted to replicate Ehrlich's analysis showed that his approach was flawed and that capital punishment is no more effective as a deterrent than life imprisonment.[81] For example, a recent test of the deterrent effect of the death penalty during the years 1984–1997 in Texas found no association between the frequency of execution and murder rates.[82]

Why Capital Punishment Fails

In sum, studies that have attempted to show the deterrent effect of capital punishment on the murder rate indicate that executing convicted criminals has relatively little influence on behaviour.[83] Although it is still uncertain why the threat of capital punishment has failed as a deterrent, the cause may lie in the nature of homicide itself. Murder is often an expressive "crime of passion" involving people who know each other and who may be under the influence of drugs or alcohol. Murder is also a by-product of the criminal activity of people who suffer from the burdens of poverty and income inequality.[84] These factors may either prevent or inhibit rational evaluation of the long-term consequences of an immediate violent act.

The failure of the "ultimate deterrent" to deter the "ultimate crime" has been used by critics to question the validity of the general deterrence hypothesis that severe punishment will lower crime rates. In general, there is little direct evidence that severity of punishment alone can reduce or eliminate crime.

Swiftness of Punishment

A core element of general deterrence theory is that people who believe that they will be swiftly punished if they break the law will abstain from crime.[85] Again, the evidence on the association between perceived punishment risk and crime has been mixed. Some research efforts have found a relationship,[86] while others have not.[87]

The threat of swift retaliation seems to work best when would-be criminals believe they will be subjected to very harsh punishments.[88] However, even this fear may be negated or overcome by the belief that a crime gives them a significant chance for large profit. When interviewed by criminologists Alex Piquero and George Rengert, active burglars reported that fear of a quick capture was in fact a deterrent, but one that could be overcome by the promise of a "big score." In short, greed overcomes fear.[89]

Informal Sanctions

Although the threat of even the most severe punishment may not have a deterrent effect, evidence is accumulating that the fear of informal sanctions may in fact reduce crime.[90] Informal sanctions occur when significant others—such as parents, peers, neighbours, and teachers—direct their disapproval, stigma, anger, and indignation toward an offender. If this happens, law violators run the risk of feeling shame, being embarrassed, and suffering a loss of respect.[91] Can the fear of public humiliation deter crime?

Research efforts have in fact established that the threat of informal sanctions can be a more effective deterrent than the threat of formal sanctions.[92] Fear of shame and embarrassment can be a powerful deterrent to crime. Those who fear being rejected by family and peers are reluctant to engage in deviant behaviour.[93] These factors manifest themselves in two ways: (1) personal shame over violating the law and (2) the fear of public humiliation if the deviant behaviour becomes public knowledge. People who say that their involvement in crime would cause them to feel ashamed are less likely to commit theft, fraud, motor vehicular, and other offences than people who report they would not feel ashamed.[94]

Anti-crime campaigns have been designed to play on this fear of shame. They are most effective when they convince the general public that being accused of crime will make them feel ashamed or embarrassed.[95] For example, spouse abusers report they are more afraid of the social costs of crime (loss of friends and family disapproval) than they are of legal punishment (going to jail). Women are more likely to fear shame and embarrassment than men, a finding that may help explain gender differences in the crime rate.[96]

The effect of informal sanctions may vary according to the cohesiveness of community structure and the type of crime. Not surprisingly, informal sanctions may be most effective in highly unified areas where everyone knows one another and the crime cannot be hidden from public view.[97]

Christina Xu/Flickr

Critique of General Deterrence

Some experts believe that the purpose of the law and justice system is to create a "threat system."[98] The threat of legal punishment should, on the face of it, deter lawbreakers through fear. Nonetheless, the relationship between crime rates and deterrent measures is far less than choice theorists might expect. Despite efforts to punish criminals and make them fear crime, there is little evidence that the fear of apprehension and punishment alone can reduce crime rates. How can this discrepancy be explained?

Rationality

Deterrence theory assumes a rational offender who weighs the costs and benefits of a criminal act before deciding on a course of action. However, criminals may be desperate people who choose crime because they believe there is no reasonable alternative. Some may suffer from personality disorders that impair their judgment and render them incapable of making truly rational decisions. Psychologists believe that chronic offenders suffer from an emotional state that renders them both incapable of fearing punishment and less likely to appreciate the consequences of crime.[99] For example, research on repeat sex offenders finds that they suffer from an elevated emotional state that negates the deterrent effect of the law.[100]

Certainty, Severity, and Speed

As Beccaria's famous equation tells us, the threat of punishment involves not only its severity, but also its certainty and speed. The Canadian legal system is not very effective. Less than half (about 40 percent) of all crimes are reported to police, and police make arrests in only about 20 percent of reported crimes. Even when offenders are detected, police officers may choose to warn rather than arrest.[101] The odds of receiving a prison term are only about 20 per 1000 crimes committed. As a result, some offenders believe that they will not be severely punished for their acts and consequently have little regard for the law's deterrent power. Even those accused of murder are often convicted of lesser offences and spend what seem to be relatively short amounts of time behind bars.[102] In making their "rational choice," offenders may be aware that the deterrent effect of the law is minimal.

Choice

Among some groups of high-risk offenders, such as youth living in economically depressed neighbourhoods, the threat of formal sanctions is irrelevant. Young people in these areas may believe they have little to lose if arrested, because their opportunities

Kathryn Scott Osler/Getty Images

Tara Tomasi is a federal parole officer who works in Abbotsford, BC. She admits that it is a tough job and that you need to have a thick skin but says that the real key to the job is good communication and interpersonal skills. There are two classifications of parole officers in Canada. Tara is a federal parole officer and as such she is employed by Correctional Services Canada or the government of Canada. Parole officers are also hired by the respective provincial governments in Canada. Provincial parole officers have the added duties of being a probation officer. The chief difference between federal parole officers and provincial probation and parole officers is that federal officers supervise parolees who received a sentence of over two years while province officers supervise persons who received a sentence of two years less a day.

The qualifications to be either a federal parole officer or a provincial probation and parole officer include, among other things, having a social science degree. The pay ranges from $60 000 to $80 000 per year. Specialized training is required and is provided on the job. Correctional Services Canada also offers yearly training programs for parole officers to update their skills in certain areas, such as supervising Aboriginal offenders, or working with dangerous offenders. Parole and probation officers share the same government job classification as psychologists, counsellors, clergy, and social workers. The prospects for these jobs, according to Employment and Social Development Canada, are good. There are opportunities to work in both institutions and offices as a parole officer for Correctional Services Canada or probation and parole officers at the provincial level.

A parole officer, left, assisting a client.

As for Tara, she is currently stationed at a parole office. Her days and weeks are a mix of desk work and being out in the community. She's responsible for filing a lot of reports to the Parole Board of Canada, but otherwise she is out of the office making visits to offenders at their schools, homes, and workplaces. She works in a team on occasion, but also on her own. While the work can be hard, Tomasi has a very positive outlook on her job. "I love what I do," she says. "I feel blessed, I feel grateful, and I look forward to the challenges every day."

Tara has a particularly challenging case she is working on. John Z., one of her parolees, did time for armed robbery and was recently released from prison. She knows John, his wife and two children. John is a good father; however, after being injured on the job became addicted to pain killers and as a result became involved in robbing local grocery stores for money to buy drugs. Use rational choice theory to explain why John became involved in the life of crime and identify some crime prevention strategies that Tara might employ to keep John on the right course.

Source: Excerpt from: Canada's Best Jobs 2014: Probation & Parole Officer, It helps to have a thick skin. *Canadian Business*, Apr 17, 2014 CB Staff. Accessed 25 August 2015 from: http://www.canadianbusiness.com/lists-and-rankings/best-jobs/2014-probation-and-parole-officer/

---

specific deterrence
The view that criminal sanctions should be so powerful that offenders will never repeat their criminal acts.

are few and they have little attachment to social institutions such as school or family. Even if they truly fear the consequences of the law, they must commit crime to survive in a hostile environment.

To recap, studies measuring the perception of punishment agree with studies using aggregate criminal justice data that the certainty of punishment has a greater deterrent effect than its severity. Nonetheless, neither the perception nor the reality of punishment can deter most crimes.

LO4 Specific Deterrence

The theory of **specific deterrence** (also called special or particular deterrence) holds that criminal sanctions should be so powerful that known criminals will never repeat their criminal acts. According to this view, the drunk driver whose sentence is a substantial fine and a one-year licence suspension should be convinced that the price to be paid for drinking and driving is too great to consider future violations. Similarly, burglars who spend ten years in a tough, maximum-security prison should find their enthusiasm for theft dampened.[103] In principle, punishment works if a connection can be established between the planned action and memories of its consequence; if these recollections are adequately intense, the action will be unlikely to occur again.[104]

Despite the popularity of "scared straight programs" as evidenced by the popular TV program *Beyond Scared Straight*, there is little evidence to suggest that such programs act as either general or specific deterrent to youth committing crime. In fact, recent studies have shown that they may increase the likelihood of recidivism in youth. See http://ebn.bmj.com/content/6/1/12.full.

ASSOCIATED PRESS

Does Specific Deterrence Deter Crime?

At first glance, specific deterrence does not seem to work, because a majority of known criminals are not deterred by their punishment. Research on chronic offenders indicates that arrest and punishment seem to have little effect on experienced criminals and may even increase the likelihood that first-time offenders will commit new crimes.[105] Nearly two-thirds of all convicted offenders are re-arrested within three years of their release from prison, and those who have been punished in the past are the most likely to commit a new offence.[106] Incarceration may sometimes slow down or delay recidivism in the short term, but the overall probability of re-arrest does not change following incarceration.[107] On the other hand, recidivism rates are generally lower (in the 30–50 percent range) for those who have received a sentence of probation, suggesting that for some offenders, rehabilitation and ongoing integration in the community may be a more effective deterrent than punishment.[108]

Some research efforts have shown that, rather than reducing the frequency of crime, severe punishment actually increases reoffending rates.[109] Punishment may bring defiance rather than deterrence, while the stigma of apprehension may help lock offenders into a criminal career.

Stigmatization Versus Reintegrative Shaming

In his book *Crime, Shame, and Reintegration*, John Braithwaite helps explain why specific deterrence measures may be doomed to failure.[110] In most Western societies, punishment stigmatizes offenders and sets them, resentful, outside the mainstream. Law violators view themselves as victims of the justice system, punished by strangers, such as police and judges, who are being paid to act. In contrast, Braithwaite notes that countries such as Japan, in which conviction for crimes brings an inordinate amount of personal shame, have extremely low crime rates.

Braithwaite divides the concept of shame into two distinct types. In North American society, shaming typically involves stigmatization—an ongoing process of degradation in which the offender is branded as an evil person and cast out of society. Shaming can occur at a school disciplinary hearing or a criminal court trial. As a specific deterrent, stigma is doomed to failure. People who suffer humiliation at the hands of the justice system "reject their rejectors" by joining a deviant subculture of like-minded people who collectively resist social control. Despite these dangers, there has been an ongoing effort to brand offenders and make their "shame" both public and permanent. For example, most American states and some Canadian provinces have passed sex offender registry and notification laws that make public the names of those convicted of sex offences and warn neighbours of their presence in the community.[111]

Braithwaite argues that crime control can be better achieved through a policy of reintegrative shaming. In this approach, the offenders' evil deeds are condemned while, at the same time, efforts are made to reconnect them to their neighbours, friends, and family. A critical element of reintegrative shaming is an effort to help offenders understand and recognize their wrongdoing and feel ashamed of their actions. To be reintegrative, shaming must be brief and controlled and then followed by ceremonies of forgiveness, apology, and repentance.

An important part of reintegrative shaming is bringing offenders together with victims so that the offenders can learn to understand the impact of their actions. Close family members and peers are also present to help the offender reintegrate back into society. Efforts like these can humanize a system of justice that today relies on repression, rather than forgiveness, as the basis of specific deterrence.

incarceration
Confinement in jail or prison.

recidivism
Repetition of criminal behaviour.

probation
Sentence served in the community under the supervision of a probation officer and subject to certain conditions.

stigmatization
Ongoing degradation or humiliation, in which the offender is branded as an evil person and cast out of society.

reintegrative shaming
Brief and controlled shaming that is followed by forgiveness, apology, repentance, and reconnection with the community.

LO5 Incapacitation

It stands to reason that if more criminals are sent to prison, the crime rate should go down. Because most people age out of crime, the duration of a criminal career is limited. Placing offenders behind bars during their prime crime years should lessen their lifetime opportunity to commit crime. The shorter the span of opportunity, the fewer offences they can commit during their lives; hence crime is reduced. This theory, known as the incapacitation effect, seems logical, but does it work?

The past 20 years have witnessed significant growth in the number and percentage of the population held in prisons and jails. Today, on any given day, more than 32 000 Canadians are incarcerated. Advocates of incapacitation suggest that this effort has been responsible for the decade-long decline in crime rates. However, critics counter that what appears to be an incapacitation effect may actually reflect the effect of some other legal or social phenomenon. The economy has improved, the huge cohort of baby boomers is now entering their 50s and 60s and has aged out of committing many types of crime, and police may simply be more effective. Crime rates could also be dropping because potential criminals fear tough sentencing laws that provide long mandatory prison sentences for serious violent crimes. What appears to be an incapacitation effect may actually be an effect of general deterrence.[112]

Can Incapacitation Reduce Crime?

Research on the direct benefits of incapacitation has been inconclusive. A number of studies have set out to measure the precise effect of incarceration rates on crime rates, and the results have not supported a strict incarceration policy.[113] Gendreau, Goggin, Cullen, and Andrews report that, in fact, incarceration results in as much as a 3 percent increase in the likelihood that those imprisoned will reoffend when they are released, thereby increasing the crime rate.[114] On the other hand, Gendreau and colleagues report that community-based correctional programs such as probation and parole reduce the likelihood of reoffending by as much as 10 percent. Looking at the relationship from another perspective, if the prison population were reduced and community correctional programs were used more, we could reduce the crime rate by at least 3 percent and possibly more.[115]

While these findings are problematic, a few studies have found an inverse relationship between incarceration rates and crime rates. In a frequently cited study, Reuel Shinnar and Shlomo Shinnar's research on incapacitation in New York led them to conclude that mandatory prison sentences of five years for violent crime and three for property offences could reduce the reported crime rate by a factor of four or five.[116] Other research studies also claim that a strict incarceration policy can reduce the level of violent crime.[117]

The Logic Behind Incarceration

Considering that the criminals are unable to continue their illegal activities while housed in a prison or jail, incapacitation should in fact be an excellent crime control strategy. For example, a study of 201 heroin abusers in New York City found that, if given a one-year jail sentence, they would not have been able to commit their yearly haul of crimes: 1000 robberies, 4000 burglaries, 10 000 shopliftings, and more than 3000 other property crimes.[118]

Nonetheless, evaluations of incarceration strategies reveal that their impact is less than expected. For one thing, there is little evidence that incapacitating criminals will deter them from future criminality and even more reason to believe that they may be more inclined to commit crimes upon release. Prison has few specific deterrent effects: The more prior incarceration experiences inmates have, the more likely they are to reoffend (and return to prison) within 12 months of their release.[119] The short-term crime reduction effect of incapacitating criminals is negated if the prison experience has the long-term effect of escalating the frequency of criminal behaviour upon release. By its nature, the prison experience exposes young, first-time offenders to higher-risk, more experienced inmates who can influence their lifestyle and help shape their attitudes. Novice inmates also run an increased risk of becoming infected with HIV/AIDS and other health hazards, and that exposure reduces their life chances after release.[120]

Furthermore, the economics of crime suggest that if money can be made from criminal activity, there will always be someone to take the place of the incarcerated offender. New criminals will be recruited and trained, offsetting any benefit accrued by incarceration. Imprisoning established offenders may likewise open new opportunities for competitors who were suppressed by the more experienced criminals. For example, incarcerating organized crime members may open drug markets to new gangs. The flow of narcotics may actually increase after the more experienced organized crime leaders are imprisoned, because newcomers are willing to take greater risks.

incapacitation effect
The idea that keeping offenders in confinement will eliminate the risk of their committing further offences.

Though his crimes occurred over 25 years ago, the name of Allan Legere (66), the so-called "Monster of Miramichi," continues to instill fear in the residents of Miramichi, New Brunswick. While serving a sentence for murder, he escaped and while on the run he raped and beat to death 75-year-old Annie Flam and her sister. After brutally beating to death an elderly priest, he was the subject of one of the largest manhunts in Canadian history, which ended with his recapture in 1989. He is one of 90 inmates at the Special Handling Unit in Quebec, a dubious distinction he shares with the notorious child killer Clifford Olson. Should dangerous predators such as Legere ever be released from incapacitation? Is rehabilitation even a remote possibility?

Another reason that incarceration may not work is that most criminal offences are committed by teens and very young adult offenders, who are unlikely to be sent to prison for a single conviction. At the same time, many incarcerated criminals, aging behind bars, are already past the age when they are likely to commit crime. As a result, a strict incarceration policy may keep people in prison beyond the time they are a threat to society while a new cohort of high-risk adolescents is on the street. It is possible that the most serious criminals are already behind bars and that adding less dangerous offenders to the population will have little

appreciable effect while adding tremendous costs to the correctional system.[121]

An incapacitation strategy is very expensive. The prison system costs billions of dollars each year. Even if incarceration could reduce the crime rate, the costs would be enormous. Are Canadian taxpayers willing to spend millions, even billions, more on new prison construction and annual maintenance fees? A strict incarceration policy would result in a growing number of elderly inmates whose maintenance costs, estimated at as much as $80 0000–$100 000 per year, are two to three times higher than those of younger inmates. In 2000, inmates 50 years and older comprised 12 percent of the federal correctional population; 38 percent of those serving life terms will be 55 or older before they are eligible for parole, raising fears of a "geriatric overload" of the prison system and prison costs.[122]

> **three strikes and you're out**
> American policy whereby people convicted of three felony offences receive a mandatory life sentence.

Three Strikes and You're Out

Some experts maintain that incapacitation can work if it is focused on the most serious chronic offenders. For example, in the United States, the three strikes and you're out policy, giving people convicted of three felony offences a mandatory life sentence, has received widespread publicity. Many American states already employ habitual offender laws that provide long (or life) sentences for repeat offenders. In Canada, an individual can be declared a "dangerous offender" and sentenced to an indeterminate period in prison if the prosecution can show evidence of a continuing pattern of aggressive or sexual behaviour that is not likely to be deterred by a traditional sentence.[123] Criminologists retort that although such strategies are politically compelling, they will not work, for several reasons:

- Most three-time offenders are at the verge of aging out of crime anyway.
- Current sentences for violent crimes are already quite severe.
- An expanding prison population will drive up already high prison costs.
- There would be racial disparity in sentencing.
- The police would be in danger because two-time offenders would violently resist a third arrest, knowing they face a life sentence.[124]
- The prison population probably already contains the highest-frequency criminals.

Those who support a selective incapacitation strategy argue that criminals who are already in prison (high-rate offenders) commit significantly

just deserts
The principle that those who violate the rights of others deserve punishment commensurate with the seriousness of the crime, without regard for their personal characteristics or circumstances.

more crimes each year than the average criminal who is on the outside (low-rate offenders). If a broad policy of incarceration were employed, requiring mandatory prison sentences for all those convicted of crimes, more low-rate criminals would be placed behind bars.[125] It would be both costly and nonproductive to incarcerate large groups of people who commit relatively few crimes. It makes more economic sense to focus incarceration efforts on known high-rate offenders by lengthening their sentences.

LO6 Policy Implications of Choice Theory

From the origins of classical theory to the development of modern rational choice views, the belief that criminals choose to commit crime has influenced the relationship among law, punishment, and crime. Although research on the core principles of choice theory and deterrence theories has produced mixed results, these models have had an important impact on crime prevention strategies.

When police patrol in well-marked cars, it is assumed that their presence will deter would-be criminals. When the harsh realities of prison life are portrayed in movies and TV shows, the lesson is not lost on potential criminals. Nowhere is the idea that the threat of punishment can control crime more evident than in the implementation of tough mandatory criminal sentences to control violent crime and drug trafficking.

Despite its questionable deterrent effect, some advocates argue that the death penalty can effectively restrict criminality; at least it ensures that convicted criminals never again get the opportunity to kill. Many observers are dismayed because people who are convicted of murder sometimes kill again when released on parole or mandatory supervision. One study of 52 000 incarcerated murderers in the United States found that 810 had been previously convicted of murder and had killed 821 people following their previous release from prison.[126] About 9 percent of all inmates on death row in the United States have had prior convictions for homicide. Death penalty advocates argue that if these criminals had been executed for their first offences, hundreds of people would be alive today.[127]

The concept of criminal choice has also prompted the development of justice policies that treat all offenders equally, without regard for their background or personal characteristics. This is referred to as the concept of just deserts, or what has become known as the "justice model" philosophy of criminal justice. The justice model position has been most clearly spelled out by criminologist Andrew Von Hirsch in his book *Doing Justice*.[128] Von Hirsch argues that while punishment is needed to preserve the social equity disturbed by crime, it should be commensurate with the seriousness of the crime.[129] Von Hirsch's views can be summarized as follows:

1. Those who violate others' rights deserve to be punished.

2. We should not deliberately add to human suffering; punishment makes those punished suffer.

3. Punishment may prevent more misery than it inflicts, which justifies the need for desert-based punishment.

Source: Excerpt from DOING JUSTICE: THE CHOICE OF PUNISHMENTS by Andrew von Hirsch. Copyright © 1976 by Andrew von Hirsch.

The justice model is also concerned with the rights of the accused. It alleges that the rights of the person being punished should not be unduly sacrificed for the good of others (as with deterrence). The offender should not be treated as more (or less) blameworthy than is warranted by the character of his or her offence. For example, Von Hirsch asks the following question: If two crimes, A and B, are equally serious, but if severe penalties are shown to have a deterrent effect only with respect to A, would it be fair to punish the person who has committed crime A more harshly simply to deter others from committing the crime? Conversely, it is unfair for a merciful judge to impose a light sentence on a teenage criminal, because in so doing he or she arbitrarily makes the younger offender less blameworthy than an older criminal who commits the same act. All offenders must be treated the same on the basis of what they did, not who they are.

In sum, the justice model suggests that retribution justifies punishment because people deserve what they get for past deeds. Punishment based on deterrence or incapacitation is wrong because it involves an offender's future actions, which cannot be accurately predicted. Punishment should be the same for all people who commit the same crime. Criminal sentences based on individual needs or characteristics are inherently unfair because all people are equally blameworthy for their misdeeds. The influence of Von Hirsch's views can be seen in mandatory sentencing models that give the same punishment to all people who commit the same type of crime.

Summary

Choice theories assume that criminals carefully choose whether to commit criminal acts. People are influenced by their fear of the criminal penalties associated with being caught and convicted for law violations. The more severe, certain, and swift the punishment, the more likely it is to control crime. The choice approach is rooted in the classical criminology of Cesare Beccaria, who argued that punishment should be certain, swift, and severe enough to deter crime.

Today, choice theorists view crime as offence- and offender-specific. Research shows that offenders consider their targets carefully before deciding on a course of action. By implication, crime can be prevented or displaced by convincing potential criminals that the risks of violating the law exceed the benefits.

Deterrence theory holds that if criminals are indeed rational, an inverse relationship should exist between punishment and crime. However, a number of factors confound the relationship. For example, if people do not believe they will be caught, even harsh punishment may not deter crime. Deterrence theory has been criticized on the grounds that it wrongfully assumes that criminals make a rational choice before committing crimes, it ignores the intricacies of the criminal justice system, and it does not take into account the social and psychological factors that may influence criminality. Research designed to test the validity of the deterrence concept has not indicated that deterrent measures actually reduce the crime rate.

Specific deterrence theory holds that the crime rate can be reduced if known offenders are punished so severely that they never commit crimes again. However, there is little evidence that harsh punishment actually reduces the crime rate. Incapacitation theory maintains that if deterrence does not work, the best course of action is to incarcerate known offenders for long periods so that they lack criminal opportunity. Research efforts, however, have not proved that increasing the number of people in prison—and increasing prison sentences—will reduce crime rates.

Choice theory has been influential in shaping public policy. Criminal law is designed to deter potential criminals and fairly punish those who have been caught in illegal acts. Some courts have changed sentencing policies to adapt to classical principles, and the Canadian correctional system seems geared toward incapacitation and specific deterrence. The justice model view is that criminal sanctions should be geared precisely to the seriousness of the crime. People should be punished on the basis of whether they deserve to be punished for what they did, and not because punishment may affect or deter their future behaviour.

Discussion Questions

1. Are criminals rational decision makers, or are they motivated by non-controllable psychological and emotional drives?

2. Would you want to live in a society where crime rates are quite low because they are controlled by extremely harsh punishments, such as flogging for vandalism?

3. Which would you be more afraid of if you were caught by the police while shoplifting: receiving criminal punishment or having to face your friends or relatives?

4. Is it possible to create a method of capital punishment that would actually deter murder—for example, by televising executions? What might be some of the negative consequences of such a policy?

READY TO STUDY?

IN THE BOOK, YOU CAN:

✔ Check your understanding of what you've just read by reading the Summary at the end of each chapter.

✔ Rip out the Chapter in Review card at the back of the book to have the key terms and Learning Objectives handy, and complete the quizzes provided (answers are on the bottom of the back page!).

ONLINE YOU CAN:

✔ Stay organized and efficient with MindTap—a single destination with all the course material and study aids you need to succeed. Built-in apps leverage social media and the latest learning technology. For example:

✔ ReadSpeaker will read the text to you.

✔ Flashcards are pre-populated to provide you with a jump start for review—or you can create your own.

✔ You can highlight text and make notes in your MindTap Reader. Your notes will flow into Evernote, the electronic notebook app that you can access anywhere when it's time to study for the exam.

✔ Prepare for tests with quizzes.

Go to www.nelson.com/student to access these digital resources.

Aleshyn_Andrei/Shutterstock.com

Trait Theory: It's in Their Blood

Learning Objectives

LO1 Explain the basic premises of trait theory.

LO2 Describe the major perspectives of biological trait theories.

LO3 Explain how fetal alcohol spectrum disorder (FASD) and criminality may be linked.

LO4 Explain the relationship between genetics and criminality.

LO5 Describe the major varieties of psychological trait theories.

LO6 Describe the relationship between mental illness and criminality.

Introduction

For 20-year-old Adam Lanza, the morning of 14 December 2012 began with him fatally shooting his mother Nancy with a small calibre rifle. Then, armed with two semi-automatic handguns and an assault rifle, Lanza drove a short distance to Sandy Hook Elementary School, where he had attended grades 1 through 5, and where his mother had once worked as a volunteer teacher in a Grade 1 class. Though the outside doors of the school were locked, he gained entry into the school by shooting out a large window beside the main doors with the assault rifle. Once inside, Lanza encountered school principal Dawn Hochsprung, school psychologist Mary Sherlach, and lead teacher Natalie Hammond, who had come out into the hallway near the entrance to investigate the noise. He shot and killed both Hochsprung and Sherlach, and wounded Hammond as well as another staff member further down the hallway who was hit with a ricocheting bullet. The injured Hammond managed to crawl into a nearby room and use the telephone to make a 911 call, at the same time transmitting the information over the school intercom system.

After checking out the main office area at the school and finding no one there, Lanza proceeded into the classroom area of the building, entering Grade 1 classrooms 8 and 10. In classroom 8 he found Lauren Rousseau and Rachel D'Avino, two of the teaching staff, attempting to hide with their first graders in a small bathroom at the back of the classroom. Lanza killed both Rousseau and D'Avino, and 15 of the children. In classroom 10 Lanza killed staff members Victoria Soto and Anne Marie Murphy and five more children. Dropping the assault rifle, Lanza used one of the handguns to shoot himself in the head. In less than 10 minutes Adam Lanza had killed 20 children and six staff members.[1]

DID YOU KNOW?

Adam Lanza's violent shooting spree at Sandy Hook Elementary School in Newtown, Connecticut, on 14 December 2012 seemed to be the product of a deranged mind. Can people like Adam Lanza who suddenly go on murderous rampages ever be considered "normal" or "sane"?

© infukto-171/INFphoto.com/Corbis

Why did Adam Lanza kill 27 people and himself in December 2012? According to witnesses who knew Lanza and his family, he had exhibited a variety of symptoms of mental illness as a teenager and young adult, including withdrawal, anxiety, obsessive-compulsive behaviours, even characteristics of Asperger's disorder. The Connecticut medical examiner responsible for the case went so far as to order a brain dissection and DNA screening to determine if brain abnormalities or a genetic cause could be found for Lanza's sudden, violent outburst. Still, after an exhaustive investigation into the shootings, the Connecticut state's attorney concluded that there may never be a definitive answer as to what caused Adam Lanza to do what he did that day.

This chapter reviews those criminological theories that suggest that criminality is a matter of abnormal human traits. These trait theories can be subdivided into two major categories: one stressing biological makeup and the other stressing psychological functioning. Although these views often overlap (e.g., brain function may have a biological basis), each branch has unique characteristics and will be discussed separately.

LO1 The Development of Trait Theory

The view that criminals have physical or mental traits that make them different and abnormal began with Italian physician and criminologist Cesare Lombroso. The early research of Lombroso and his contemporaries is today regarded as historical curiosity, not scientific fact. The research methodology they used has since been brought into question, and many of the traits they assumed to be inherited are not really genetically determined but caused by environment and diet. As criticism of their work mounted, biological explanations of crime fell out of favour and were abandoned in the early 20th century.[2]

In the early 1970s, spurred by the publication of *Sociobiology: The New Synthesis* by Edmund O. Wilson, biological explanations of crime once again emerged.[3] Sociobiology differs from earlier theories of behaviour in that it stresses that biological and genetic conditions affect how social behaviours are learned and perceived.

Sociobiologists view biology, environment, and learning as mutually interdependent factors. These views have revived interest in finding a biological and/or psychological basis for crime and delinquency and prompted some criminologists to conclude that personal traits must separate the deviant members of society from the nondeviant. Possessing these traits may help explain why, when faced

Though in his early work Lombroso focused on born criminals and the physical characteristics or "stigmata" that identified them, Lombroso later revised his theory of the causes of criminality to include poverty, unemployment, and other environmental factors as causes of crime.

with the same life situations, one person commits crime, whereas another obeys the law. Put another way, living in a disadvantaged neighbourhood may not cause a well-adjusted person to commit crime; living in an affluent area may not stop a maladapted person from offending.[4] All people may be aware of and even fear the sanctioning power of the law, but some are unable to control their urges and passions.

trait theory
The view that criminality is a product of abnormal biological and/or psychological traits.

sociobiology
View that inherited, biological traits explain the origin and development of social behaviours, including behaviours we have classified as deviant or criminal.

Contemporary Trait Theory in Criminology

Contemporary trait theorists in criminology do not suggest that a single biological or psychological attribute adequately explains all criminality. Rather, each offender is considered physically and mentally unique; consequently, there must be different explanations for each person's behaviour. Some may have inherited poor control of their anger, resulting in violent criminal behaviour; others may be suffering from neurological problems; still others may have blood chemistry disorders that heighten their antisocial activity. Criminologists who focus on the individual and their biological and psychological traits see many explanations for crime because, in fact, there are many individual differences among criminal offenders.

Contemporary trait theorists focus on basic human behaviour and drives that are linked to antisocial behaviour patterns.

Trait theorists today recognize that having a particular physical characteristic does not, in itself, produce criminality. Crime-producing interactions involve both personal traits (such as defective intelligence, impulsive personality, and abnormal brain chemistry) and environmental factors (such as family life, educational attainment, socioeconomic status, and neighbourhood conditions). People may develop physical or mental traits at birth or soon after that affect their social functioning over the

Recent research in human genetics suggests that the worldwide decline in human male sperm counts may be a consequence of the social institution of monogamous marriage: with a stable, ongoing relationship with a female partner, a high sperm count is not required to ensure fertility, or to ensure the survival of the young child.

life course and influence their behaviour choices. For example, low-birth-weight babies have been found to suffer poor educational achievement later in life; academic deficiency, in turn, has been linked to delinquency and drug abuse.[5] A condition present at birth or soon after can thus affect behaviour across the life span. In their national longitudinal study adolescent health, Beaver, Vaughn, DeLisi, and Higgins noted that postnatal exposure to cigarette smoke, duration of breastfeeding, maternal involvement, and household income are all good predictors of adolescent and adulthood levels of neuropsychological functioning,[6] and a large body of research that has revealed that neuropsychological functioning is one of the most consistent predictors of antisocial behaviour.

Although some people may have a predisposition toward aggression, that does not mean that they will necessarily or automatically engage in violent behaviours; environmental stimuli can either suppress or trigger antisocial acts.[7]

Trait theories have gained prominence in criminology recently because of what is now known about chronic recidivism and the development of criminal careers. If only a few offenders become persistent repeaters, then what sets them apart from the rest of the criminal population may be an abnormal biochemical makeup, brain structure, genetic constitution, or some other human trait.[8] Even if crime is a choice, the fact that some people make that choice repeatedly could be linked to their physical and mental makeup. According to this view, biological makeup contributes significantly to human behaviour.

LO2 Biological Trait Theories

One branch of contemporary trait theory focuses on the biological conditions that control human behaviour. Criminologists who work in this area typically refer to themselves as biosocial criminologists, biocriminologists, or biologically oriented criminologists; the terms are used here interchangeably.

The following sections examine some important subareas within biosocial criminology (see Figure 5.1). First, we review the biochemical factors that are believed to affect how proper behaviour patterns are learned. Then we consider the relationship between brain function and crime. Next, we analyze current ideas about the association between genetic factors and crime. Finally, we evaluate evolutionary views of crime causation.

Biochemical Conditions and Crime

Some trait theorists believe that biochemical conditions, including both those that are genetically predetermined and those that are acquired through diet and environment, influence antisocial behaviour. This view of crime received widespread attention in 1979 when Dan White, who confessed to killing San Francisco Mayor George Moscone and City Councilman Harvey Milk, claimed that his behaviour was precipitated by an addiction to sugar-laden junk foods.[9]

FIGURE 5.1

Biosocial Perspectives on Criminality

Perspective	Cause
BIOCHEMICAL	• Diet • Hormones • Contaminants
NEUROPHYSIO-LOGICAL	• Brain structure • Brain damage • Brain chemicals
GENETIC	• Inherited aggressive predisposition • Inherited condition associated with crime such as impulsive personality
EVOLUTIONARY	• Aggression evolves over time • Aggressive males produce more offspring

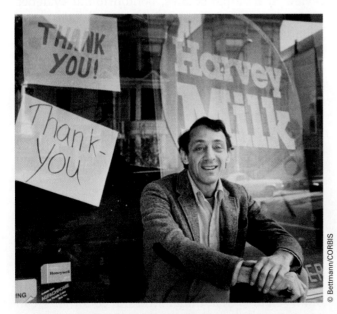

San Francisco City Councilman Harvey Milk (pictured) was murdered by Dan White, whose defence was that his actions were the result of his addiction to junk foods.

White's successful "Twinkie defence" prompted a California jury to find him guilty of the lesser offence of diminished-capacity manslaughter rather than first-degree murder. (White committed suicide after serving his prison sentence.) Some of the biochemical factors that have been linked to criminality are set out in detail here.

Chemical and Mineral Influences

Biocriminologists maintain that minimal levels of minerals and chemicals are needed for normal brain functioning and growth, especially in the early years of life.

Research conducted over the past decade shows that dietary inadequacy of certain chemicals and minerals, including sodium, potassium, calcium, amino acids, monoamines, and peptides, can lead to depression, mania, cognitive problems, memory loss, and abnormal sexual activity.[10] Research studies examining the relationship between crime and vitamin deficiency and dependency have identified a close link between antisocial behaviour and insufficient quantities of some B vitamins and vitamin C. Other studies have reported a link between low levels of vitamin D and schizophrenia in adults.[11] Children with learning and behaviour disorders have been found to have abnormal levels of vitamins B3 and B6.[12]

Another suspected nutritional influence on aggressive behaviour is a diet especially high in carbohydrates and sugar.[13] Experiments have altered children's diets so that sweet drinks were replaced with unsweetened fruit juices, table sugar was replaced with honey, and so on. Results indicate that these changes can reduce aggression levels.[14] Although these results are impressive, some recent research efforts have failed to find a link between sugar consumption and violence.[15] In one important study, a group of researchers had 25 preschool children and 23 school-age children described as sensitive to sugar follow a different diet for three consecutive three-week periods. One diet was high in sucrose, the second substituted aspartame (Nutrasweet) as a sweetener, and the third relied on saccharin. Careful measurement of the subjects found little evidence of cognitive or behavioural differences that could be linked to diet. If anything, sugar seemed to calm the children.[16] In some cases, in fact, sugar intake has been found to possibly reduce or curtail violent tendencies.[17]

While this research damages the suspected link between diet and aggression, some recent research indicates that it may be premature to dismiss the suspected association between the two factors. In a review of multiple studies, Benton found evidence in that in some adults and children, consumption of sugar and stimulation of the release of insulin can cause a rapid decline to an abnormally low blood sugar level linked to increased irritability, impulsivity, and aggression.[18]

Hormonal Influences

Biosocial theorists note that males tend to be biologically and naturally more aggressive than females, whereas women tend to be more nurturing toward the young.[19] This discrepancy has been linked to gender-based hormonal differences. Hormones cause areas of the brain to become less sensitive to environmental stimuli. Abnormally high hormone levels require people to seek excess stimulation and to be willing to tolerate pain in their quest for thrills. Hormones are linked to brain seizures that, under stressful conditions, can result in emotional volatility. Hormones also affect

Arvind Balaraman/Shutterstock.com

Reducing foods high in carbohydrates and sugars has been shown to reduce aggression levels in children.

the brain structure itself: They influence the left hemisphere of the neocortex, the part of the brain that controls sympathetic feelings toward others.[20] These effects promote violence and other serious crimes by causing people to seek greater levels of environmental stimulation and to tolerate more punishment, and by increasing impulsivity, emotional volatility, and antisocial emotions.[21]

Biosocial research has found that abnormal levels of male sex hormones (androgens) do in fact produce aggressive behaviour.[22] Other androgen-related male traits include sensation seeking, impulsivity, dominance, and reduced verbal skills; all of these androgen-related traits are also related to antisocial behaviour.[23] A growing body of evidence suggests that hormonal changes are also related to mood and behaviour. Adolescents experience more intense mood swings, anxiety, and restlessness than their elders, explaining in part the high violence rates found among teenage males.[24]

Testosterone, the most abundant androgen, which controls secondary sex characteristics such as facial hair and voice timbre, has been linked to criminality.[25] Research conducted on both human and animal subjects has found that prenatal exposure to unnaturally high levels of testosterone permanently alters behaviour. Girls who were unintentionally exposed to elevated amounts of testosterone during their fetal development display an unusually high, long-term tendency toward aggression. Conversely, boys who were prenatally exposed to steroids that decrease testosterone levels display decreased aggressiveness.[26] In *The Beast Within*, Canadian criminologist Neil Boyd argues that testosterone, and the use of aggression by males to ensure the survival of themselves and their offspring, underlies the significant gender difference in criminal behaviour.[27]

Females may be biologically protected from deviant behaviour in the same way they are immune from some diseases that strike males.[28] Hormone levels also help explain the aging-out process. Levels of testosterone decline during the life cycle, which may explain why violence rates diminish over time.[29]

Premenstrual Syndrome

The suspicion has long existed that the onset of the menstrual cycle triggers excessive amounts of the female sex hormones, which stimulate antisocial, aggressive behaviour. This condition is commonly referred to as premenstrual syndrome (PMS).[30] The link between PMS and delinquency was first popularized more than 40 years ago by Katharina Dalton, whose studies of English women indicated that

Steroids, drugs that mimic the effect of testosterone on the body, gave this German athlete, born female, masculine traits.

females are more likely to commit suicide and to be aggressive and otherwise antisocial just before or during menstruation.[31]

Although the Dalton research is often cited as evidence of the link between PMS and crime, methodological problems make it impossible to accept her findings at face value. There is still debate over any link between PMS and aggression. Some doubters argue that the relationship is spurious; it is equally likely that the psychological and physical stress of aggression brings on menstruation and not vice versa.[32] However, Diana Fishbein, a noted expert on biosocial

androgens
Male sex hormones.

testosterone
The principal male hormone.

premenstrual syndrome (PMS)
The hypothesis that several days prior to and during menstruation, excessive amounts of female sex hormones stimulate antisocial, aggressive behaviour.

theory, concludes that there is in fact an association between elevated levels of female aggression and menstruation. Research efforts, she argues, show that (1) a significant number of incarcerated females committed their crimes during the premenstrual phase and (2) at least a small percentage of women appear vulnerable to cyclical hormonal changes that make them more prone to anxiety and hostility.[33] In 2013, the American Psychiatric Association included for the first time Premenstrual Dysphoric Disorder (PDD) in its diagnostic and statistical manual the DSM-V, finding that between 2 and 5 percent of women experience severe symptoms of physical and psychological distress, including anxiety, hostility, anger, and depression.[34] Rosanna Langer observes that inclusion of PDD in the DSM-V may open the door to an increase in its use as a defence in criminal trials, at least as a mitigating mental health factor in sentencing.[35]

DID YOU KNOW?

- Brain chemistry and hormonal differences are related to aggression and violence.
- Most evidence suggests that there is no relationship between sugar intake and crime.
- The male hormone testosterone is linked to criminality.
- Neurological impairments have been linked to crime.
- Genetic theory holds that violence-producing traits can be passed on from generation to generation.
- According to evolutionary theory, instinctual drives control behaviour. The urge to procreate influences male violence.
- Biological explanations fail to account for the geographic, social, and temporal patterns in the crime rate; critics question the methodology used.

The debate is ongoing, but the overwhelming majority of females who suffer anxiety and hostility before and during menstruation do not engage in violent criminal behaviour. Thus, any link between PMS and crime is tenuous at best.[36]

Environmental Contaminants

Dangerous amounts of copper, cadmium, mercury, and inorganic gases, such as chlorine and nitrogen dioxide, are found in the ecosystem. Research indicates that these environmental contaminants can

neurophysiology
The study of brain activity.

influence behaviour. At high levels, these substances can cause severe illness or death; at more moderate levels, they have been linked to emotional and behavioural disorders.[37] Some studies have linked the ingestion of food dyes and artificial colours and flavours to hostile, impulsive, and otherwise antisocial behaviour in youths.[38] Lighting may be another important environmental influence on antisocial behaviour. Research projects have suggested that radiation from artificial light sources, such as fluorescent tubes and television sets, may produce antisocial, aggressive behaviour.[39]

A number of recent research studies have linked lead ingestion to problem behaviour. Ingestion of lead may help explain why hyperactive children manifest conduct problems and antisocial behaviour.[40] Criminologist Deborah Denno investigated the behaviour of more than 900 black youths and found that lead poisoning was one of the most significant predictors of male delinquency and persistent adult criminality.[41]

Neurophysiological Conditions and Crime

Some researchers focus their attention on neurophysiology, or the study of brain activity.[42] They believe that neurological and physical abnormalities, acquired as early as the fetal or perinatal stage, as a result of birth delivery trauma or through brain injuries later in life, control behaviour.[43]

The relationship between neurological dysfunction and crime first received a great deal of attention in 1968 following a tragic incident in Texas. Charles Whitman killed his wife and mother, and then barricaded himself in a tower at the University of Texas with a high-powered rifle; he killed 14 people and wounded 24 others before he was killed by police. An autopsy revealed that Whitman suffered from a malignant infiltrating brain tumour. He had previously experienced uncontrollable urges to kill and had gone to a psychiatrist seeking help for his problems. He kept careful notes documenting his feelings and his inability to control his homicidal urges, and he left instructions for his estate to be given to a mental health foundation to study mental problems such as his own.[44]

Since the Whitman case, a great deal of attention has been focused on the association between neurological impairment and crime. Studies have shown a significant relationship between impairment in executive brain functions (such as abstract reasoning, problem solving, and motor skills) and aggressive behaviour.[45] Research using memorization and visual awareness tests, short-term auditory memory tests, and verbal IQ tests indicates that this relationship can be detected quite early and that children who suffer measurable neurological deficits at birth or in adolescence are more likely to become criminals later in life.[46]

Studies using an electroencephalogram (EEG)— a device that records electrical impulses in the brain—have found far higher levels of abnormal EEG recordings in violent criminals than in nonviolent or one-time offenders.[47] Although about 5 percent of the general population show abnormal EEG readings, about 50 to 60 percent of adolescents with known behaviour disorders display abnormal recordings.[48] Behaviours highly correlated with abnormal EEG readings include poor impulse control, inadequate social adaptation, hostility, temper tantrums, and destructiveness.[49]

Newer brain-scanning techniques using electronic imaging, such as positron emission tomography (PET), brain electrical activity mapping (BEAM), and superconducting interference device (SQUID), have made it possible to assess which areas of the brain are directly linked to antisocial behaviour.[50] Both violent criminals and substance abusers have been found to have impairment in the prefrontal lobes, thalamus, medial temporal lobe, and superior parietal and left angular gyrus areas of the brain.[51] Chronic violent criminals have far higher levels of brain dysfunction than the general population; murderers exhibit brain pathology at a rate 32 times greater than in the general population.[52]

Minimal Brain Dysfunction (MBD)

Related to abnormal cerebral structure, minimal brain dysfunction (MBD) has been defined as an abruptly appearing, maladaptive behaviour that interrupts an individual's lifestyle and life flow. One type of minimal brain dysfunction is manifested in episodic periods of explosive rage. This form of the disorder is considered an important cause of behaviours such as spouse and child abuse, suicide, aggressiveness, and motiveless homicide. One perplexing feature of this syndrome is that people who are afflicted with it often maintain warm, pleasant personalities between episodes of violence. Studies measuring the presence of minimal brain dysfunction in offender populations have found that up to 60 percent exhibit brain dysfunction on psychological tests.[53] More sophisticated brain-scanning techniques, such as PET, have also shown that brain abnormality is linked to violent crime.[54]

Attention Deficit/Hyperactivity Disorder (ADHD)

Many parents have noticed that their children do not pay attention to them—they run around and do things in their own way. Sometimes this inattention is a function of age; in other instances it is a symptom of attention deficit/hyperactivity disorder (ADHD), in which a child shows a developmentally inappropriate lack of attention, impulsivity, and hyperactivity. About 3 percent of children, most often boys, are believed to suffer from this disorder, and it is the most common reason children are referred to mental health clinics. The condition has been associated with poor school performance, grade retention, placement in special needs classes, bullying, stubbornness, and lack of response to discipline.[55] Although the origin of ADHD is still unknown, suspected causes include neurological damage, prenatal stress, and even reactions to food additives and chemical allergies. Recent research has suggested a genetic link.[56] There are also links to family turmoil: mothers of ADHD children are more likely to be divorced or separated, and ADHD children are much more likely to move to new locales than non-ADHD children.[57] It may be possible that emotional turmoil either produces symptoms of ADHD or, if they already exist, causes them to intensify.

Research studies now link ADHD to the increased possibility of the onset and maintenance of a delinquent career.[58] Children diagnosed as having ADHD are more likely to be suspended from school and to engage in criminal behaviour as adults. This ADHD–crime association is important because symptoms of ADHD seem stable through adolescence into adulthood;[59] therefore, early diagnosis and treatment of children with ADHD may enhance their life chances. Today the most typical treatment is doses of stimulants, such as Ritalin, which ironically help control emotional and behavioural outbursts. The relationship between chronic delinquency and attention disorders may also be mediated by school performance. Children who are poor readers are the most prone to antisocial behaviour; many poor readers also have attention problems.[60] Early school-based intervention programs may thus benefit children with ADHD.

minimal brain dysfunction (MBD) An abruptly appearing, maladaptive behaviour, such as episodic periods of explosive rage.

attention deficit/ hyperactivity disorder (ADHD) A developmentally inappropriate lack of attention, along with impulsivity and hyperactivity.

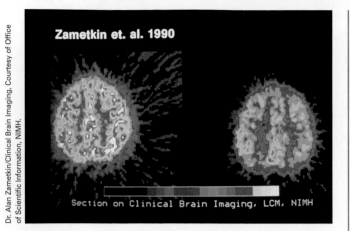

Zametkin et. al. 1990

Section on Clinical Brain Imaging, LCM, NIMH

Dr. Alan Zametkin's research utilizing brain scan images produced by positron emmision tomography (PET) show differences between an adult with attention deficit hyperactivity disorder (ADHD) (right) and an adult free of ADHD (left).

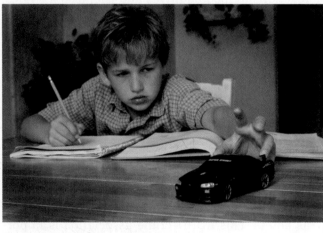

LO3 Fetal Alcohol Spectrum Disorder (FASD)

In 1970, while doing research for her thesis on infants who were hospitalized because they failed to thrive after birth, University of Washington medical student Christine Ulleland found that nearly half of the mothers of the at-risk infants she studied had a history of alcoholism. When other medical researchers began to look more closely at the link between alcohol and pre- and postnatal health problems, they began to notice a distinctive pattern of physical and behavioural characteristics in the infants and children of alcoholic mothers. In 1973, medical researchers Kenneth Lyon Jones and David Smith coined the term *fetal alcohol syndrome*. Though there are as yet no

neurotransmitters Chemical compounds that influence or activate brain functions.

firm guidelines for diagnosing FAS, scientists believe that a range or spectrum of physical characteristics (small eyes; flat face; thin, flat upper lip; poor walking coordination) and neurological problems (lower intelligence, language deficits, short attention span, lack of impulse control, problems with memory and thinking) are characteristic of individuals who have what has come to be known as fetal alcohol spectrum disorder (FASD).[61]

In recent years, increasing attention has been paid to possible links between what has come to be known as FASD and involvement in crime, in particular the link between FASD, lower intelligence, and a lack of impulse control.[62] According to Williams and Gloster, as many as half of inmates in the federal correctional system may have prenatal alcohol-related physical and neurological impairments, and as many as 300 000 Canadians currently have symptoms of FASD with a disproportionate number of these cases found among Aboriginal people.[63] According to research conducted by Streissguth and colleagues (2004), 60 percent of the individuals with FASD they studied had trouble with the law, nearly half had engaged in inappropriate sexual behaviour, 35 percent had a drug or alcohol problem, and 80 percent had not been raised by their biological parents. For individuals with FASD, lower intelligence, inability to understand and predict the consequences of their actions, and lack of impulse control are factors that make it more likely they will engage in actions that will bring them into contact with the legal system.[64] The suspected relationship between FASD and involvement in crime prompted the Department of Justice Canada in 2004 to commission a special study of the problem titled "Fetal Alcohol Syndrome and the Youth Criminal Justice System: A Discussion Paper"; websites providing information about the links between alcohol consumption, pregnancy, FASD and physical, neurological, and behavioural problems (including involvement with the justice system) have sprung up across Canada. Still, Verbrugge points out that there are many questions to be answered about the relationship between FASD and criminal behaviour, including (1) how many offenders in the youth and adult justice system have FASD, (2) what are the legal implications of having FASD (e.g., fitness to stand trial), and (3) how do we provide treatment to individuals with FASD and how effective will these treatments be in reducing the individuals' likelihood of getting in trouble with the law?[65]

Brain Chemistry

Neurotransmitters are chemical compounds that influence or activate brain functions. Those studied in relation to aggression include dopamine, norepinephrine, serotonin, monoamine oxidase (MAO-A), and GABA.[66] Numerous studies have found an association between abnormal levels of these chemicals and aggression. Studies of habitually violent Finnish criminals show that low serotonin (5-hydroxytryptamine [5-HT]) levels are associated with poor impulse control and hyperactivity. In addition, a relatively low concentration of 5-hydroxyindoleacetic acid (5-HIAA) predicts increased irritability, sensation seeking, and impaired impulse control.[67] Similarly, increased levels of dopamine have been shown to be correlated with risk-taking behaviours, impulsivity and aggression. Consumption of alcohol and other drugs interact with these neurotransmitters, and can aggravate their effects.[68]

What is the link between brain chemistry and crime? Prenatal exposure of the brain to high levels of androgens can result in a brain structure that is less sensitive to environmental inputs. Affected individuals seek more intense and varied stimulation and are willing to tolerate more adverse consequences than individuals not so affected.[69] It has

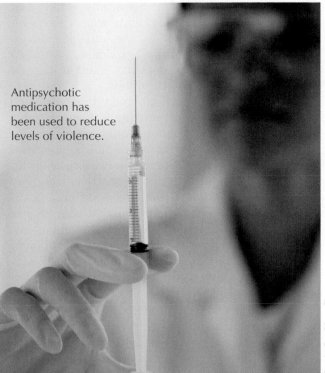

Antipsychotic medication has been used to reduce levels of violence.

© Royalty-Free/Masterfile

CRIMINOLOGY AT THE MOVIES

John Borowski, filmmaker

ALBERT FISH
IN SIN HE FOUND SALVATION

The gruesome crimes of the Depression-era psychopath Albert Fish are documented in the 2007 film *Albert Fish: In Sin He Found Salvation*. Born in Washington, DC in 1870, Fish showed an early interest in sexual perversion, including coprophilia, or human feces. By his 20s he was working as a prostitute in New York City, but was also sexually assaulting young boys. Possibly in response to his increasing bizarre sexual behaviour, his mother arranged a marriage for him, which eventually produced six children. By all accounts, Fish's children considered him to be a good father and provider—but by 1910 his violent and perverted tendencies re-emerged, when he abducted, tortured, and cut off the penis of Thomas Kedden, a young man he had befriended. In 1917 Fish's wife left him for another man. Fish's mental state spiralled out of control as he developed a taste for cannibalism, abducting young girls and boys, and torturing, dismembering, and eating their body parts. In 1928, Fish abducted and murdered 10-year-old Grace Budd, six years later, he sent young Grace's family an anonymous letter graphically recounting the details of her murder, including consuming her flesh. The letter was eventually traced back by police to Fish, who was arrested and tried for the murder. Once police began searching Fish's home and property, they found dozens and dozens of bone fragments, articles of clothing, and implements used to dismember the bodies. Fish was convicted of the murder of Grace Budd and executed at Sing Sing Prison in New York State on 16 January 1936. No one knows how many children and adults Fish actually murdered.

After he was sentenced, Fish confessed to three more murders in an attempt to have himself declared "not guilty by reason of a mental disorder" and thereby avoid the death penalty. Most of us would agree that any individual guilty of committing such horrific crimes must be suffering from a serious mental illness—but if Fish was rational, and understood the consequences of his behaviour when he committed these crimes, then according to our law he was not "not guilty by reason of a mental disorder" and was rightly convicted and sentenced to death according to New York State law at the time. What do you think—should someone like Fish be considered rational? Did he really understand what he was doing? Is he "sick," or a criminal?

also been suggested that individuals with a low supply of the enzyme monoamine oxidase (MAO-A) engage in behaviours linked with violence and property crime, including defiance of punishment, impulsivity, hyperactivity, poor academic performance, sensation seeking and risk taking, and recreational drug use. Abnormal MAO-A levels may explain both individual and group differences in the crime rate. For example, females have higher MAO-A levels than males, which may explain gender differences in the crime rate.[70] Consumption of alcohol and other drugs interact with these neurotransmitters, aggravating their effects.[71]

Because this linkage has been found, it is not uncommon for violence-prone people to be treated with antipsychotic drugs, such as Haldol, Stelazine, Prolixin, and Risperdal. These drugs, which help control levels of neurotransmitters (such as serotonin or dopamine), are sometimes referred to as chemical restraints or chemical straitjackets.

Arousal Theory

According to arousal theory, for a variety of genetic and environmental reasons, people's brains function differently in response to environmental stimuli. All of us seek to maintain a preferred or optimal level of arousal: too much stimulation leaves us anxious and stressed, whereas too little makes us feel bored and weary. However, people vary in the way their brains process sensory input. Some nearly always feel comfortable with little stimulation, whereas others require a high degree of environmental input to feel comfortable. The latter group of "sensation seekers" look for stimulating activities, which may include aggressive, violent behaviour patterns.[72]

Although the factors that determine a person's level of arousal are not fully understood, suspected sources include brain chemistry (such as serotonin levels) and brain structure. Some brains have many more nerve cells with receptor sites for neurotransmitters than others. Another view is that people with low heart rates are more likely to commit crime because they seek stimulation to increase their arousal to normal levels.[73]

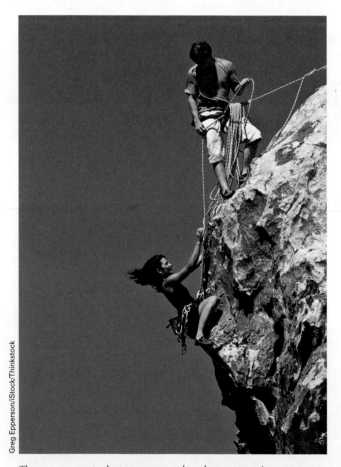

Theory suggests that some people who engage in extreme sports may have a need for stimulation to increase arousal levels.

Between 1988 and 2000, Arthur Shawcross, the "Genesee River Killer" strangled 11 prostitutes in the Rochester, NY, area. When he was finally arrested by police, records showed that his was on parole after serving 15 years for the murder of two children in the Watertown, NY, area. At his trial in Rochester, a psychiatrist testifying for the defence argued that Shawcross had a brain lesion, an injury acquired when he was a child, that caused him to behave in an erratic and aggressive manner. The court rejected the defence claims and sentenced Shawcross to 250 years in jail. He died in 2008 at the age of 63.

Acquired Brain Injury

With improvements in brain scanning technologies and testing like functional magnetic resonance imaging (fMRI) or positron emission tomography (PET), scientists are able to better identify brain injuries, and to study their link to behavioural and emotional problems. The results of these studies show that brain injuries acquired in youth increase the risk for later behavioural problems and disorders that can get worse over time.[74] Male children are at much greater risk for acquiring a brain injury (ABI), and nearly 10 percent of those with an ABI will be involved (either as the victim or offender) in a violent crime according to a study of more than 22 000 cases over a 26-year-period in Sweden.[75] Other research supports the finding that acquired brain injuries in youth are correlated with risk behaviours, including substance abuse, suicide ideation, poor academic performance, physical injuries, and aggression toward others.[76]

LO4 Genetics and Crime

Another biosocial theme is that the human traits associated with criminality have a genetic basis.[77] This line of reasoning was spotlighted in the 1970s when genetic testing of Richard Speck, the convicted killer of eight Chicago nurses, allegedly found that he had an abnormal XYY chromosomal structure (XY is normal in males). There was much public concern that all people with XYY chromosomes were potential killers and should be closely controlled. Civil libertarians expressed fear that all XYY males could be labelled dangerous and violent regardless of whether they had engaged in violent activities.[78] When it was disclosed that neither Speck nor most violent offenders actually had an extra Y chromosome, interest in the XYY theory dissipated.[79] However, the Speck case drew researchers' attention to looking for a genetic basis of crime.

Beginning in the late 1990s as an outcome of recent advances in DNA technology and genetic mapping, biosocial researchers are now actively exploring the heritability of criminal tendencies by looking at a wide range of factors. Some of the most important are described here.

Parental Deviance

If criminal tendencies are inherited, then the children of criminal parents should be more likely to become law violators than the offspring of conventional parents. A number of studies have found that parental criminality and deviance do, in fact, powerfully influence delinquent behaviour.[80] Some of the most important data on parental deviance were gathered by Donald J. West and David P. Farrington as part of the long-term Cambridge Youth Survey. These cohort data indicate that a significant number of delinquent youths have criminal fathers.[81] Although 8.4 percent of the sons of noncriminal fathers eventually became chronic offenders, about 37 percent of youths with criminal fathers were multiple offenders.[82] In another important analysis, Farrington found that one type of parental deviance, school-yard aggression or bullying, may be both inter- and intragenerational. Bullies have children who bully others, and these second-generation bullies grow up to father children who are also bullies, in a never-ending cycle.[83]

Although there is no certainty about the relationship between parental and child deviance, recent evidence indicates that at least part of the association is genetic.[84]

Twin Behaviour

If, in fact, inherited traits cause criminal behaviour, we might expect that twins would be quite similar in their antisocial activities. However, because twins are usually brought up in the same household and exposed to the same social conditions, determining whether their behaviour is a result of biological, sociological, or psychological conditions is difficult. Trait theorists have tried to overcome this dilemma by comparing identical, monozygotic (MZ) twins with fraternal, dizygotic (DZ) twins.[85] MZ twins are genetically identical, whereas DZ twins have only half their genes in common. If heredity determines criminal behaviour, we should expect that MZ twins would be much more similar in their antisocial activities than DZ twins.

The earliest studies conducted on twin behaviour detected a significant relationship between the criminal activities of MZ twins and a much lower association between those of DZ twins. A review of relevant studies found that 60 percent of MZ twins shared criminal behaviour patterns (if one twin was criminal, so was the other), whereas only 30 percent of DZ twins were similarly related.[86] These findings may be viewed as powerful evidence of a genetic basis for criminality. Similarly, criminologists David Rowe and D. Wayne Osgood analyzed the factors that influence self-reported delinquency in a sample of twin pairs and concluded that genetic influences have significant explanatory power.[87] Genetic effects significantly predict problem behaviours in children as young as three years old.[88] Although the behaviour of

monozygotic (MZ) twins
Identical twins.

dizygotic (DZ) twins
Fraternal (nonidentical) twins.

some twin pairs seems to be influenced by their environment, others display behaviour disturbances that can be explained only by their genetic similarity.[89] More recently, with data taken from a large U.S. study of adolescents in grades 7 through 12 who were interviewed about their behaviour and involvement in delinquent activity at three points in time over a 10-year period, researchers compared the findings for 692 MZ and 914 DZ twins and found that, when controlling for the social environment in which they were raised, MZ twins were significantly more likely to be highly correlated in their level of social control and association with drug-using peers compared to DZ twins.[90] However, not all research efforts have found that MZ twin pairs are more closely related in their criminal behaviour than DZ or ordinary sibling pairs, and some have found an association that is at best modest.[91] On the other hand, many experts now conclude that individuals who share genes are alike in personality regardless of how they are reared; environment, they argue, induces little or no personality resemblance in twin pairs.[92]

Adoption Studies

It seems logical that if the behaviour of adopted children is more closely aligned to that of their biological parents than to that of their adoptive parents, then the idea of a genetic basis for criminality would be supported. If, on the other hand, adoptees' behaviour is more closely aligned to the behaviour of their adoptive parents than of their biological parents, an environmental basis for crime would seem more valid.

Several studies indicate that some relationship exists between biological parents' behaviour and the behaviour of their children, even when they have had no contact.[93] In what is considered the most significant study in this area, Barry Hutchings and Sarnoff Mednick analyzed 1145 male adoptees born in Copenhagen, Denmark, between 1927 and 1941. Of these, 185 had criminal records.[94] After following up on 143 of the criminal adoptees and matching them with a control group of 143 noncriminal adoptees, Hutchings and Mednick found that the biological father's criminality strongly predicted the child's criminal behaviour. When both the biological and the adoptive fathers were criminal, the probability that the youth would engage in criminal behaviour greatly increased. Of the boys whose adoptive and biological fathers were both criminals, 24.5 percent had been convicted of a criminal law violation. Only 13.5 percent of those whose biological and adoptive fathers were not criminals had similar conviction records.[95]

The findings of the twin and adoption studies tentatively support a genetic basis for criminality. Newer, better-designed research studies continue to show a link between genetic inheritance and criminality, predicting as much as 39 percent of delinquency amount in youth, and 20 percent of later adult criminality.[96]

Evolutionary Views of Crime

Biocriminologists believe that the human traits that produce violence and aggression have been advanced by the long process of human evolution.[97] According to this evolutionary view, the competition for scarce resources has influenced and shaped the human species.[98] Over the course of human existence, people whose personal characteristics allowed them to satisfy for their basic needs for food, drink, shelter, and warmth more than others were the most likely to breed, and eventually their characteristics will be more common in the species. For example, sociobiologist Edward O. Wilson has argued that much of our success as a species comes from a long evolutionary process that rewards cooperative, social behaviour with others, while more individualistic, aggressive behaviours appear to have become less useful.[99] On the other hand, from an evolutionary perspective, impulsive, risk-taking, and aggressive males who devote little time to their female partners or family have more time to have sexual encounters with multiple partners, producing more children.[100] If sociobiologists and biocriminologists are correct, some of the problem behaviours and criminality we experience in modern society stem from genetic characteristics like impulsivity, risk-taking, and aggressiveness that once served a purpose for the human species.[101] It is therefore not surprising that human history has been marked by war, violence, and aggression.

The Evolution of Gender and Crime

Evolutionary concepts that have been linked to gender differences in violence rates are based loosely on mammalian mating patterns. To ensure survival of the gene pool (and the species), it is beneficial for a male of any species to mate with as many suitable females as possible, because each can bear his offspring. In contrast, because of the long period of gestation, females require a secure home and a single, stable, nurturing partner to ensure their survival. Because of these differences in mating patterns, the most aggressive males mate most often and have the greatest number of offspring. Therefore, over the history of the human species, aggressive males have had the greatest impact on the gene pool. The descendants of these aggressive males now account for the disproportionate amount of male aggression and violence.[102]

According to the Canadian Centre for Justice Statistics, more than two-thirds (68 percent) of victims of family violence are women; nearly half (48 percent) of all family violence victims are current or former spouses; 17 percent of incidents involved children.

Crime rate differences between the genders, then, may be less a matter of socialization than of inherent differences in behaviour patterns that have developed over time.[103] Among young men, reckless, life-threatening risk proneness is especially likely to evolve in circumstances that force them to find suitable mates to ensure their ability to reproduce. Unless they are aggressive with potential mates and potential rivals for those suitable mates, they will remain childless.[104] High rates of spouse abuse in modern society may be a function of aggressive men seeking to control and possess mates. (See Figure 5.2.) Men who feel most threatened over the potential of losing mates to rivals are the most likely to engage in sexual violence. Research shows that women in common-law marriages, especially those who are much younger than their husbands, are at greater risk of abuse than older, married women. Abusive males may fear the potential loss of their younger mates, especially if they are not bound by a marriage

contract, and may use force for purposes of control and possession.[105]

"Cheater" Theory

According to cheater theory, a subpopulation of men has evolved with genes that incline them toward extremely low parental involvement. They are sexually aggressive and use cunning to achieve sexual conquest of as many females as possible. Because females would not willingly choose them as mates, they use stealth to gain sexual access, including tactics such as mimicking the behaviour of more stable males. These deceptive reproductive tactics spill over into other endeavours, where their irresponsible, opportunistic behaviour supports their antisocial activities. Deceptive reproductive strategies, then, are linked to a deceitful lifestyle.[106]

Psychologist Byron Roth notes that cheater-type males may be especially attractive to younger, less intelligent women who begin having children at a very early age. Government-sponsored welfare, claims Roth, removes the need for

cheater theory
A theory suggesting that a subpopulation of men has evolved with genes that incline them toward extremely low parental involvement. Sexually aggressive, they use deceit for sexual conquest of as many females as possible.

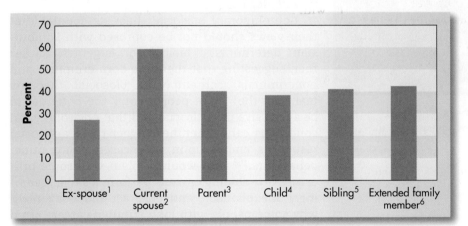

FIGURE 5.2

Victims of Family Violence in Canada

Source: http://www.statcan.gc.ca/pub/ 85-002-x/2014001/article/14114-eng.pdf

[1] Includes separated and divorced partners aged 15 years and older.
[2] Includes legally married and common-law partners aged 15 years and older.
[3] Includes a small number of victims under 18 years of age where the relationship of the accused to the victim was miscoded as "child" (including "step-child") and was therefore recoded as "parent" (including "step-parent"). Includes biological, adaptive, step, and foster parent.
[4] Includes biological, adopted, step, and foster child. Includes a small number of victims aged 65 years and older where the relationship of the accused to the victim as miscoded as "parent" (including "step-parent") and was therefore recoded as "child" (including "step-child").
[5] Includes biological, step, half, foster, or adopted brother or sister.
[6] Includes all other family members related by blood, marriage (including common-law), or adoption. Examples include uncles, aunts, cousins, and grandparents.

Note: Excludes incidents where the age or sex of the victim was unknown. Victims aged 90 years and older are excluded from the analyses due to possible instances of miscoding of unknown age within this age category. Excludes spousal victims under the age of 15 years. Excludes a small number of victims in Quebec whose age was unknown but was miscoded as 0.

potential mates to have the resources required of stable providers and family caretakers.[107] With the government meeting their financial needs, these women are drawn to men who are physically attractive and flamboyant. Their fleeting courtship produces children with low IQ scores, aggressive personalities, and little chance of proper socialization in

British scientist Francis Galton (1822–1911) coined the term *eugenics* to describe the new science of the manipulation of human breeding in order to improve the race and increase human progress. In the United States, followers of eugenics advocated for state control of the reproduction of the "unfit," including those with intellectual disabilities, the mentally ill, single women with children, alcoholics, criminals, selected racial groups, and immigrants, through the use of birth control and forced sterilization. Many prominent politicians, business leaders, and scientists, including anthropologist Ernest Hooton and psychologist Cyril Burt, were advocates of eugenics until it became apparent that scientific findings from the fields of genetics, archeology, and anthropology did not support the claims made by the followers of eugenics. The use of eugenics by the Nazi Party to justify the mass extermination of more than 6 million people in World War II put an end to the eugenics movement, although practices like enforced sterilization of the intellectually disabled and the mentally ill continued in some countries right through the 1970s.

father-absent families. According to Roth, over time, these children will grow up to be cheaters who are both antisocial and sexually aggressive.

Evaluation of the Biological Branch of Trait Theory

Biosocial perspectives on crime have raised some challenging questions. Critics find some of these theories racist, even dangerous in their implications—and point to the eugenics movement that was popular in England, the United States, Europe, and other countries in the first half of the 20th century as a stark example. If there are biological explanations for street crimes such as assault, murder, or rape, the argument goes, and if, as official crime statistics suggest, the poor and minority-group members commit a disproportionate number of such acts, then by implication biological theory says that members of these groups are biologically different, flawed, or inferior.

Biological explanations for the geographic, social, and temporal patterns in the crime rate are also problematic. Is it possible that more people are genetically predisposed to crime in the West and North than in Central and Eastern Canada? Furthermore, biological theory seems to divide people into criminals and non-criminals on the basis of their genetic and physical makeup, ignoring self-reports that indicate almost everyone has engaged in some type of illegal activity.

Contemporary biosocial theorists counter that their views should not be confused with Lombrosian, deterministic biology, or eugenics. Rather than suggesting that there are born criminals and noncriminals, contemporary biosocial theorists maintain that some people carry the potential to be aggressive or antisocial and that environmental conditions can sometimes trigger these antisocial responses, ending up in some cases with criminal behaviours.[108] This would explain why some otherwise law-abiding citizens perform a single, seemingly unexplainable antisocial act and, conversely, why some people with long criminal careers often behave conventionally. The most significant criticism of biosocial theory has been the lack of adequate empirical testing. Most research samples are relatively small and nonrepresentative. A great deal of biosocial research is conducted with samples of adjudicated offenders who have been placed in clinical treatment settings. Methodological problems make it impossible to determine whether findings apply only to offenders who have been convicted of crimes and placed in treatment or to all criminals.[109] More research is needed to clarify the relationships proposed by biosocial researchers and to silence critics.

LO5 Psychological Trait Theories

The second branch of trait theory focuses on the psychological aspects of crime, including the associations among intelligence, personality, learning, and criminal behaviour. This view has a long history, and psychologists, psychiatrists, and other mental health professionals have long played an active role in formulating criminological theory.

Among 19th-century pioneers in this area were Charles Goring (1870–1919) and Gabriel Tarde (1843–1904). Goring studied 3000 English convicts and found little difference in the physical characteristics of criminals and noncriminals. However, he uncovered a significant relationship between crime and a condition he referred to as "defective intelligence," which involved traits such as feeblemindedness, epilepsy, insanity, and defective social instinct.[110] Tarde was the forerunner of modern learning theorists, who hold that people learn from one another through imitation.[111]

In their quest to understand and treat all varieties of abnormal mental conditions, psychologists have encountered clients whose behaviour falls within the categories that society has labelled as criminal, deviant, violent, and antisocial. A number of different psychological views have been associated with criminal behaviour causation (see Figure 5.3). The most important of these perspectives are discussed in the following sections.

Sigmund Freud (1856–1939)

FIGURE 5.3

Psychological Perspectives on Criminology

Theory	Cause
PSYCHODYNAMIC (psychoanalytic)	**Intrapsychic processes** • Unconscious conflicts • Defences • Tendencies • Anger • Sexuality
BEHAVIOURAL	**Learning processes** • Past experiences • Stimulus • Rewards and punishments
COGNITIVE	**Information processing** • Thinking • Planning • Memory • Perspective • Ethical values

Trait	Cause
PERSONALITY	**Personality processes** • Antisocial personality • Sociopath/psychopath temperament • Abnormal affect, lack of emotional depth
INTELLIGENCE	**Intellectual processes** • Low IQ • Poor school performance • Bad decision making

The Psychodynamic Perspective

Psychodynamic (or psychoanalytic) psychology was originated by Viennese psychiatrist Sigmund Freud (1856–1939) and has remained a prominent segment of psychological theory ever since.[112] Freud believed that we all carry with us residue of the most significant emotional attachments of our childhood, which then guides our future interpersonal relationships.

According to Freud's version of psychodynamic theory, the human personality has a three-part structure.

> **psychodynamic (psychoanalytic)** Theory originated by Freud that the human personality is controlled by unconscious mental processes developed early in childhood, involving the interaction of id, ego, and superego.

The id is the primitive part of people's mental makeup, present at birth that represents unconscious biological drives for food, sex, and other life-sustaining necessities. The id seeks instant gratification without concern for the rights of others. The ego develops early in life, when a child begins to learn that his or her wishes cannot be instantly gratified. The ego is the part of the personality that compensates for the demands of the id by helping the individual guide his or her actions to remain within the boundaries of social convention. The superego develops as a result of incorporating within the personality the moral standards and values of parents, community, and significant others. It is the moral aspect of people's personalities; it judges their behaviour.

Psychodynamics of Abnormal Behaviour

Psychodynamic theory originally used the term neurotic to refer to people who experienced feelings of mental anguish and feared that they were losing control of their personalities. People who had completely lost control and who were dominated by their primitive id were referred to as psychotic. Today these terms have, for the most part, been replaced by the term disorder, as in *anxiety disorders, mood disorders*, and *conduct disorders*. The most serious disorder is schizophrenia, marked by hearing nonexistent voices, seeing hallucinations, and exhibiting inappropriate responses.

People with schizophrenia have illogical, incoherent thought processes and lack insight into their behaviour. They may experience delusions and hallucinate. For example, they may see

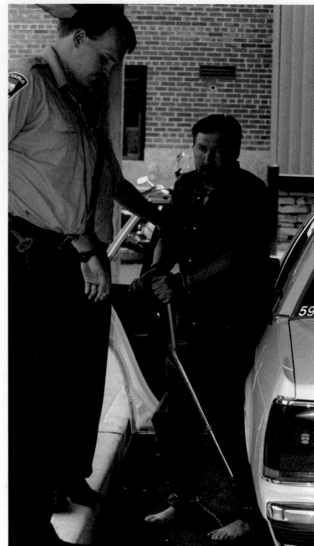

Derek Ruttan/Ottawa Sun

In 1995, Jeffrey Arenburg shot Ottawa sportscaster Brian Smith. Arenburg was found to be suffering from paranoid schizophrenia, and found not criminally responsible, After spending more than 10 years under treatment in a psychiatric hospital, Arenburg was released in 2006. One year later, Arenburg assaulted a U.S. border guard at an Ontario crossing, and was sentenced to two years in a U.S. prison. In 2009, Arenburg was released back in Canada, amid concerns that he was not receiving any psychiatric care nor taking his medication.

themselves as agents of the devil, avenging angels, or the recipients of messages from animals and plants. Serial killer David Berkowitz, dubbed "Son of Sam" or the "44-calibre killer," claimed that his 1976–1977 killing spree began after he received messages from a neighbour's dog. People with paranoid schizophrenia, such as Aaron Millar, who used a ceremonial sword to kill his mother in her Victoria, BC, home in 1997, suffer complex behavioural delusions involving wrongdoing or persecution—they think everyone is out to get them.[113]

Psychodynamics of Criminal Behaviour

Since Freud's original research, psychoanalysts have continued to view criminals as id-dominated persons who suffer from one or more disorders that render them incapable of controlling impulsive, pleasure-seeking drives.[114] The psychoanalyst whose work is most closely associated with criminality is August Aichorn.[115] After examining many delinquent youths, Aichorn concluded that societal stress, though damaging, could not in itself cause a life of crime unless a predisposition existed that psychologically prepared youths for antisocial acts. This mental state, which he labelled latent delinquency, is found in youngsters whose personality requires them to

- Seek immediate gratification (act impulsively)
- Consider satisfying their personal needs to be more important than relating to others
- Satisfy instinctual urges without considering right and wrong (i.e., they lack guilt)

The psychodynamic model of the criminal offender depicts an aggressive, frustrated person dominated by events that occurred early in childhood. Perhaps as a result of unhappy experiences in childhood or families that could not provide proper love and care, criminals suffer from weak or damaged egos that make them unable to cope with conventional society. Weak egos are associated with immaturity, poor social skills, and excessive dependence on others. People with weak egos may be easily led into crime by antisocial peers and drug abuse. Some offenders have underdeveloped superegos and consequently lack internalized representations of those behaviours that are punished in conventional society. They commit crimes because they have difficulty understanding the consequences of their actions.[116]

Offenders, then, have various mood and behaviour disorders. They may be histrionic, depressed, antisocial, or narcissistic.[117] They may exhibit conduct disorders (long histories of antisocial behaviour)

Famous writer Robert Louis Stevenson was heavily influenced by Freud's concept of the id-controlled personality as evidenced in his best-selling novel, *The Strange Case of Dr. Jekyll and Mr. Hyde.*

or mood disorders (disturbance in expressed emotions). Among the latter is bipolar disorder, in which moods alternate between periods of wild elation and deep depression.[118] Some offenders are driven by an unconscious desire to be punished for prior sins, either real or imaginary. They may violate the law to gain attention or punish their parents.

From this perspective, then, crime is a manifestation of feelings of oppression and people's inability to develop the proper psychological defences and rationales to keep these feelings under control. Criminality allows troubled people to survive by producing positive psychic results: It helps them feel free and independent, and it gives them the possibility of excitement and the chance to use their skills and imagination. In addition, it allows them to blame others for their predicament (e.g., the police), and it gives them a chance to rationalize their sense of failure ("If I hadn't gotten into trouble, I could have been a success").[119]

LO6 Crime and Mental Illness

In the early evening of 30 July 2008, a horrific scene unfolded on the side of the Trans-Canada Highway near Portage la Prairie, Manitoba. Vincent Li, 40, a passenger on a Greyhound bus travelling east from Edmonton to Thunder Bay, attacked and repeatedly stabbed fellow passenger Tim McLean, 22, as panicked passengers called out for the bus driver to stop the bus and scrambled to get off. Horrified passengers stood at the side of the highway as Li proceeded to decapitate the victim. Li was arrested at the scene by RCMP officers as he attempted to escape out a bus window. According to the court-appointed forensic psychiatrist who later examined Li, he had heard voices earlier that day telling him to use an assumed name and get on a bus. He chose to sit next to the victim, because Tim McLean had made a "friendly gesture" to him. The voices told Li that McLean was "a force of evil" who would kill him if Li did not strike first.[120] Li was deemed by the court unfit to stand trial as he was suffering from schizophrenia, and sent to Selkirk Mental Health Centre in Winnipeg, Manitoba, for further assessment and treatment. In March 2009, he was found not criminally responsible.[121] In February 2015, after Li had spent nearly seven years under treatment at the centre, psychiatrists concluded that his schizophrenia was well controlled

latent delinquency
A psychological predisposition to commit antisocial acts because of an id-dominated personality that renders an individual incapable of controlling impulsive, pleasure-seeking drives.

bipolar disorder
An emotional disturbance in which moods alternate between periods of wild elation and deep depression.

Found not criminally responsible by reason of a mental disorder in 2008 for beheading a fellow Greyhound bus passenger, Vincent Li spent the last seven years under treatment for schizophrenia at the Selkirk Mental Health Centre in Manitoba. Psychiatrists at the treatment centre have concluded that Li's schizophrenia is well controlled by medication, and he is ready to be transferred a hospital in Winnipeg where he will be released on unescorted day passes.

by medication, and that he should be transferred to a hospital in Winnipeg where he would be granted day passes out in to the community as a way of facilitating his reintegration into society.[122]

Psychodynamic theory suggests a linkage between mental illness and crime. Although the association appears clear-cut, empirical evidence has been contradictory.

Many early research efforts found that offenders who engage in serious, violent crimes suffer from some sort of mental disturbance. Studies of adolescent males accused of murder found that 75 percent could be classified as having some mental illness, including schizophrenia.[123] Abusive mothers have been found to have mood and personality disorders and a history of psychiatric diagnoses.[124] The diagnosed mentally ill appear in arrest and court statistics at a rate disproportionate to their presence in the population.[125]

Despite this evidence, questions remain as to whether the mentally ill population has a greater inclination toward criminal behaviour than the mentally sound. The mentally ill may in fact be more likely to withdraw or harm themselves or be victimized than to act aggressively toward others.[126] Research shows that after release, prisoners with prior histories of hospitalization for mental disorders are less likely to be rearrested than those who have never been hospitalized.[127] Even research that finds a mental illness–crime association indicates that the great majority of known criminals are not mentally ill and that the relationship is modest at best. And if there is a statistically significant association between mental illness and crime, the fact remains that most mentally ill people are not criminals.

There has been much recent research regarding an association between mental illness and violence. The conventional view was that there was little evidence to support a strong association between mental illness and violence. As Monahan and Steadman concluded, "… the relation between crime and mental disorder can be accounted for largely by demographic and historical characteristics that the two groups share" (p. 152).[128] As Douglas noted, by the early 1990s, a shift could be detected in the conventional view as studies began to emerge suggesting that although the majority of people with serious mental illness are not violent, the probability of committing violence was greater for people with a serious mental illness than for those in the general popula-tion.[129] According to Douglas, the strongest evidence in favour of a link comes from those investigations that have moved beyond the broad categorization of mental illness to an examination of the relationship between subcategories such as psychosis (e.g., schizophrenia) and specific symptoms (e.g., hallucinations and delusions).[130] Recently, support for the existence of a relationship between psychosis and violence has come from two **meta-analytic studies**. Investigating the association between violence and schizophrenia and other psychoses in the general population, Fazel and colleagues conducted a meta-analysis on 20 studies reporting data from 18 423 individuals with schizophrenia and other psychoses. The investigators found that the risk of violent outcomes for those having a schizophrenic disorder was 4 to 5 times greater than the general population, and between 14 and 25 times greater for homicide.[131] Also, they found that the presence of substance use disorders in addition to schizophrenia substantially increased the risk, which was estimated to be four times higher compared to individuals with schizophrenia without substance use disorders.[132] The second meta-analytic study, which was conducted by Canadian criminologist Steven

meta-analytic studies
A systematic method of evaluating statistical data based on results of several independent studies of the same problem. In effect, it is a "study of studies" on the same subject.

Douglas and colleagues, also published in 2009, examined 204 studies and found that psychosis was reliably associated with a 49 percent to 68 percent increased likelihood of violence. Like Fazel et al., Douglas et al. found that comorbid psychosis and substance-related diagnoses substantially increased the risk of violence.[133]

The Behavioural Perspective

Behaviour theory maintains that human actions are developed through learning experiences. The major premise of behaviour theory is that people alter their behaviour according to the reactions it receives from others: Behaviour is supported by rewards and extinguished by negative reactions or punishments. The behaviourist views crimes, especially violent acts, as learned responses to life situations that do not necessarily represent abnormality or moral immaturity.

Early behaviourists like Ivan Pavlov (1849–1936) and John Watson (1878–1958) showed that even basic physiological and psychological states such as salivation, anxiety and fear, or a feeling of happiness were learned reactions to the pairing of stimuli. According to the principles of classical conditioning, by pairing together one stimulus (e.g., a song) with another strong, pleasant stimulus (dancing at a club with a girlfriend or boyfriend for the first time), we can evoke that pleasant "first time" feeling each future time the song is heard, even though we may no longer be involved with that person.[134] Watson showed that the classical conditioning model can be extended to more complex learning processes, demonstrating that by pairing together a neutral stimulus (e.g., a red sweater you wore to the dance club) with

the song and dancing with a girlfriend or boyfriend for the first time, the red sweater you wore to the dance can itself act as a conditioned stimulus that can evoke the pleasant feeling associated with that first dance.[135] In this way, behaviours are learned through the pairing of stimuli, responses, and either positive (rewards) or negative (punishments) consequences to behaviours.

B.F. Skinner (1904–1990) showed that the classical conditioning model was limited in explaining how behaviours are learned in the extent to which it relied on there being a stimulus to evoke or elicit a behaviour. Skinner coined the term *operant conditioning* to explain how from birth organisms voluntarily emit a wide range of behaviours that operate on the environment around them, which results in consequences from the surrounding environment that either encourage the behaviour to be repeated (positive reinforcement) or discourage the behaviour (negative reinforcement). In contrast to the classical conditioning model of learning, which viewed the organism as passive, a responder to stimuli, Skinner emphasized the voluntary, active way in which organisms engage the environment and learn from their behaviour.[136]

Based on the principles of both classical and operant conditioning models of learning, the branch of behaviour theory most relevant to criminology is social learning theory.[137] Social learning theorists, most notably Albert Bandura, argue that people are not actually born with the ability to act violently, but that they learn to be aggressive through their life experiences. These experiences include personally observing others acting aggressively to achieve some goal or watching people being rewarded for violent acts on television or in movies. People learn to act aggressively when, as children, they model their behaviour after the violent acts of adults. Later in life, these violent behaviour patterns persist in social relationships. For example, the boy who sees his father repeatedly strike his mother with impunity is likely to become a battering parent and husband.

Although social learning theorists agree that mental or physical traits may predispose a person toward violence, they believe that a person's violent tendencies are activated by factors in the environment. The specific form of aggressive behaviour, the frequency with which it is expressed, the situations

behaviour theory
The view that all human behaviour is learned through a process of social reinforcement (rewards and punishment).

social learning theory
The view that people learn to be aggressive by observing others acting aggressively to achieve some goal or being rewarded for violent acts.

in which it is displayed, and the specific targets selected for attack are largely determined by social learning. However, people are also self-aware and engage in purposeful learning. Their interpretations of behaviour outcomes and situations influence the way they learn from experiences. One adolescent who spends a weekend in jail for drunk driving may find it the most awful experience of her life—one that teaches her never to drink and drive again. Another person, however, may find it an exciting experience about which he can brag to his friends.

Social learning theorists view violence as something learned through a process called **behaviour modelling**. In modern society, aggressive acts are usually modelled after three principal sources:

1. *Family interaction.* Studies of family life show that aggressive children have parents who use similar tactics when dealing with others.

2. *Environmental experiences.* People who reside in areas where violence occurs daily are more likely to act violently than those who dwell in low-crime areas whose norms stress conventional behaviour.

3. *Mass media.* Films and television shows commonly depict violence graphically. Moreover, violence is often portrayed as acceptable, especially for heroes who never have to face legal consequences for their actions.[138] Viewing violence is believed to influence behaviour in a number of ways:

• Media violence can provide aggressive scripts that children store in memory. Repeated exposure to these scripts can increase their retention and change attitudes.

• Children learn from what they observe. In the same way they learn cognitive and social skills from their parents and friends, children learn to be violent by watching television.

• Television violence increases the arousal levels of viewers and makes them more prone to act aggressively. Studies measuring the galvanic skin response of subjects—a physical indication of arousal based on the amount of electricity conducted across the palm of the hand—show that viewing violent television shows increases arousal levels in young children.

• Watching television violence promotes negative attitudes such as suspiciousness and the expectation that the viewer will become involved in violence. Those who watch television frequently view aggression and violence as common, socially acceptable behaviour.

• Television violence allows aggressive youths to justify their behaviour. Rather than causing violence, television may help violent youths rationalize their behaviour as socially acceptable.

• Television violence may disinhibit aggressive behaviour, which is normally controlled by other learning processes. Disinhibition takes place when adults are viewed as being rewarded for violence and when violence is seen as socially acceptable. This contradicts previous learning experiences in which violent behaviour was viewed as wrong.[139]

Dmitriy Shironosov/Shutterstock.com

Social learning theorists have tried to determine what triggers violent acts. One position is that a direct, pain-producing, physical assault will usually trigger a violent response. Yet the relationship between painful attacks and aggressive responses has been found to be inconsistent. Whether people counterattack depends, in part, on their fighting skill and their perception of the strength of their attackers. Verbal taunts and insults have also been linked to aggressive responses. People who are predisposed to aggression by their learning experiences are likely to view insults from others as a challenge to their social status and to react violently.

In summary, social learning theorists suggest that the following four factors may contribute to violent or aggressive behaviour:

1. *An event that heightens arousal*—such as a person's frustrating or provoking another through physical assault or verbal abuse.

2. *Aggressive skills*—learned aggressive responses picked up from observing others, either personally or through the media.

3. *Expected outcomes*—the belief that aggression will somehow be rewarded. Rewards can come in the form of reducing tension or anger, gaining some financial reward, building self-esteem, or gaining the praise of others.

4. *Consistency of behaviour with values*—the belief, gained from observing others, that aggression is justified and appropriate, given the circumstances of the current situation.

behaviour modelling
Process of learning behaviour (notably aggression) by observing others. Aggressive models may be parents, criminals in the neighbourhood, or characters on television or in movies.

The Cognitive Perspective

One area of psychology that has received increasing recognition in recent years is cognitive theory. Psychologists with a cognitive perspective focus on mental processes—how people perceive and mentally represent the world around them and solve problems. The pioneers of this school were Wilhelm Wundt (1832–1920), Edward Titchener (1867–1927), and William James (1842–1910). Today the cognitive area includes several subdisciplines. The moral development branch is concerned with how people morally represent and reason about the world. Humanistic psychology stresses self-awareness and getting in touch with feelings. Information-processing theory focuses on how people process, store, encode, retrieve, and manipulate information to make decisions and solve problems.

When cognitive theorists who study information processing try to explain antisocial behaviour, they do so in terms of mental perception and how people use information to understand their environment. When people make decisions, they engage in a sequence of cognitive thought processes:

1. First, they encode information so that it can be interpreted.

2. Next, they search for a proper response and decide on the most appropriate action.

3. Finally, they act on their decision.[140]

According to this cognitive approach, people who use information properly, who are better conditioned to make reasoned judgments, and who can make quick and reasoned decisions when facing emotion-laden events are best able to avoid antisocial behaviour choices.[141] In contrast, violence-prone people may use information incorrectly when they make decisions. One reason is that they may be relying on mental scripts learned in childhood that tell them how to interpret events, what to expect, how they should react, and what the outcome of the interaction should be.[142] Hostile children may have learned improper scripts by observing how others react to events; their own parents' aggressive, inappropriate behaviour would have considerable impact. Some may have had early, prolonged exposure to violence (such as child abuse), which increases their sensitivity to slights and maltreatment. Oversensitivity to rejection by their peers is a continuation of sensitivity to rejection by their parents.[143] Violence becomes a stable behaviour because the scripts that emphasize aggressive responses are repeatedly rehearsed as the child matures.

Information-processing theory has been used to explain the occurrence of date rape. Sexually violent males believe that when their dates refuse sexual advances, the women are really playing games and actually want to be taken forcefully.[144]

The Personality and Crime Perspective

Personality can be defined as the reasonably stable patterns of behaviour, including thoughts and

---

cognitive theory
Psychological perspective that focuses on mental processes—how people perceive and mentally represent the world around them and solve problems.

information-processing theory
Theory that focuses on how people process, store, encode, retrieve, and manipulate information to make decisions and solve problems.

personality
The reasonably stable patterns of behaviour, including thoughts and emotions, that distinguish one person from another.

CAREER CONNECTIONS

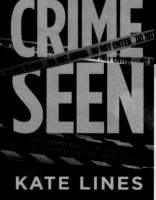

OPP Chief Superintendent Kate Lines began her career in 1977 as one of a handful of female patrol officers in what was then very much a male career, one with lots of resistance to women. Responding to an internal posting for an "unmarried, female officer" Lines later became the first woman in the history of the OPP to work undercover—working everything from drugs to biker gangs. In 1990, she was chosen to attend the FBI's criminal profiling training program, the first female police officer in Canada to do so, and only the second FBI-trained criminal profiler in Canada. Now retired, Lines describes her career in the OPP, and some of the profiling cases she was involved in, the 2015 book *Crime Seen*.

emotions, that distinguish one person from another.[145] One's personality reflects a characteristic way of adapting to life's demands and problems. The way we behave is a function of how our personality enables us to interpret life events and make appropriate behavioural choices. Can the cause of crime be linked to personality?

Several research efforts have attempted to identify criminal personality traits.[146] Suspected traits include impulsivity, hostility, and aggression.[147] For example, Hans Eysenck associates two personality traits with antisocial behaviour: extraversion-introversion and stability-instability. Extreme introverts are overaroused and avoid sources of stimulation; extreme extroverts are underaroused and seek sensation. Introverts are slow to learn and be conditioned; extroverts are impulsive individuals who lack the ability to examine their own motives and behaviours. Those who are unstable, a condition that Eysenck calls neuroticism, are anxious, tense, and emotionally unstable.[148] People who are both neurotic and extroverted lack self-insight and are impulsive and emotionally unstable; they are unlikely to have reasoned judgments of life events. Although extroverted neurotics may act self-destructively, for example, by abusing drugs, more stable people will be able to reason that such behaviour is ultimately harmful. Eysenck believes that personality is controlled by genetic factors and is heritable.

A number of other personality deficits have been identified in the criminal population. A common theme is that criminals are hyperactive, impulsive individuals with short attention spans (attention deficit disorder), conduct disorders, anxiety disorders, and depression.[149] They lack affect, cannot

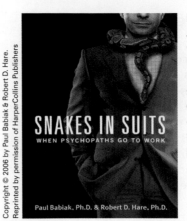

In their book *Snakes in Suits: When Psychopaths Go to Work* (2006), Paul Babiak and Robert D. Hare explain how some successful business executives exhibit traits and behaviours very similar to those of a psychopath.

empathize with others, and are shortsighted and hedonistic. These traits make them prone to problems ranging from psychopathology to drug abuse, sexual promiscuity, and violence.[150] As a group, people who share these traits are believed to have a character defect referred to as sociopathic, psychopathic, or antisocial personality. Although these terms are often used interchangeably, some psychologists distinguish between sociopaths and psychopaths by suggesting that the former are a product of a destructive home environment, whereas the latter are a product of a defect or aberration within themselves.[151]

Studies of the antisocial personality have been conducted worldwide.[152] There is evidence that offenders with an antisocial personality are crime-prone, respond to frustrating events with strong negative emotions, feel stressed and harassed, and are adversarial in their interpersonal relationships. They maintain "negative emotionality"—a tendency to experience aversive affective states such as anger, anxiety, and irritability. They also are predisposed to weak personal constraints and have difficulty controlling impulsive behaviour urges. Because they are both impulsive and aggressive, crime-prone people are quick to act against perceived threats.

Evidence that personality traits predict crime and violence suggests that the root cause of crime can be found in the forces that influence early human development. If these results are valid, rather than focus on job creation and neighbourhood improvement, crime control efforts might be better focused on helping families raise reasoned, reflective children who enjoy a safe environment.

The Intelligence and Crime Perspective

Early criminologists maintained that many delinquents and criminals have below-average intelligence and that low IQ causes their criminality. Criminals were believed to have inherently substandard intelligence and thus seemed naturally inclined to commit more crimes than more intelligent persons. Furthermore, it was thought that if authorities could determine which individuals had low IQs, they might identify potential criminals before they committed socially harmful acts. These ideas led to the nature-versus-nurture controversy that continues to rage today.

Nature Theory

Proponents of nature theory argue that intelligence is largely determined genetically, that ancestry determines IQ, and that low intelligence, as demonstrated by low IQ, is linked to criminal behaviour. When newly developed IQ tests were administered to inmates of prisons and juvenile training schools in the first decades of the 20th century, the nature position gained support because most of the inmates scored low on the tests.[153] In 1926, William Healy and Augusta Bronner tested groups of delinquent boys in Chicago and Boston and found that 37 percent were subnormal in intelligence. They concluded that delinquents were 5 to 10 times more likely to be mentally deficient than normal boys.[154] These and other early studies were embraced as proof that low IQ scores indicated potentially delinquent children and that a correlation existed between innate low intelligence and deviant behaviour. IQ tests were believed to measure the inborn genetic makeup of individuals, and many criminologists accepted the idea that individuals with substandard IQs were predisposed toward delinquency and adult criminality.

Nurture Theory

Proponents of nurture theory argue that intelligence is not inherited and that low-IQ parents do not necessarily produce low-IQ children.[155] Intelligence must be viewed as partly biological but primarily sociological. Nurture theorists discredit the notion that persons commit crimes because they have low IQs. Instead, they postulate that environmental stimulation from parents, relatives, social contacts, schools, peer groups, and innumerable others account for a child's IQ level and that low IQs may result from an environment that also encourages delinquent and criminal behaviour. Thus, if low IQ scores are recorded among criminals, these scores may reflect the criminals' cultural background, not their mental ability.

In 1931, Edwin Sutherland evaluated IQ studies of criminals and delinquents and questioned whether criminals in fact have low IQs.[156] Sutherland's research all but put an end to the belief that crime was caused by feeblemindedness; the IQ-crime link was almost forgotten in criminological literature.

IQ and Criminality

Although the alleged IQ–crime link was dismissed by mainstream criminologists, it once again became an important area of study when respected criminologists Travis Hirschi and Michael Hindelang published a widely read 1977 article linking the two variables.[157] They proposed the idea that low IQ increases the likelihood of criminal behaviour through its effect on school performance. That is, youths with low IQs do poorly in school, and school failure and academic incompetence are highly related to delinquency and later to adult criminality.

Hirschi and Hindelang's inferences have been supported by research worldwide.[158] In their influential book *Crime and Human Nature*, James Q. Wilson and Richard Herrnstein also agreed that the IQ–crime link is indirect: Low intelligence leads to poor school performance, which enhances the chances of criminality.[159] They conclude, "A child who chronically loses standing in the competition of the classroom may feel justified in settling the score outside, by violence, theft, and other forms of defiant illegality."[160]

IQ and Crime Reconsidered

In their controversial 1994 book, *The Bell Curve*, Richard Herrnstein and Charles Murray firmly advocate an IQ–crime link. Their extensive review of the available literature shows that adolescents with low IQs are more likely to commit crime, get caught, and be sent to prison. Conversely, at-risk kids with higher IQs seem to be protected from becoming criminals by their superior ability to succeed in school and in social relationships. Herrnstein and Murray conclude that criminal offenders have an average IQ of 92, about 8 points below the mean; chronic offenders score even lower than the average criminal. To those who suggest that the IQ–crime relationship can be explained by the fact that only low-IQ criminals get caught, they counter with data showing little difference in IQ scores between self-reported and official criminals.[161] This means that even criminals whose activities go undetected have lower IQs than the general public; the IQ–crime relationship cannot be explained away by the fact that slow-witted criminals are the ones most likely to be apprehended.

Although Herrnstein and Murray's review of the literature was extensive, a number

nature theory
The view that intelligence is largely determined genetically and that low intelligence is linked to criminal behaviour.

nurture theory
The view that intelligence is not inherited, but is largely a product of environment. Low IQ scores do not cause crime, but may result from the same environmental factors.

According to psychiatric experts, Leo Teskey is an "intellectually gifted man" with a tested IQ score in the top 1 percent of the population—and a dangerous psychopath. With a criminal record totalling nearly 40 convictions, Teskey, 38, was convicted for a second time in an Edmonton court in February 2008 for a brutal 2000 assault on a 63-year-old man that left the victim an invalid. With prior charges for attempted murder in the shooting of an Edmonton police officer in 1988 (reduced and convicted on lesser charges because the court ruled he did not have the capacity to understand his actions due to heavy drug use at the time), a 1992 conviction for child abuse when he severely beat and nearly tore the penis off his girlfriend's two-year-old son while supposedly toilet training the child, in 2010 Teskey was declared a dangerous offender by an Edmonton court, and is serving an indefinite sentence. However, incarceration did not end Teskey's criminal behaviour, and in 2012 he was convicted of possession and trafficking of morphine, cocaine, and amphetamines while at the Edmonton Remand Centre.

By all accounts, testimony entered at Teskey's 2010 dangerous offender hearing demonstrated that he was the product of a horribly neglectful and abusive background: his mother was a prostitute and drug user who frequently locked Teskey with his two siblings in a cold basement without food for long periods while the mother worked or went on drug binges: by age three Teskey was demonstrating violent, antisocial behaviour, attacking his father with a hammer; he was sexually abused at age four, and was skipping school beginning in Grade 1, and using

Edmonton Sun

drugs and alcohol when he was only 8 years old. By the time he was an adolescent, Teskey was well known for his outbursts of rage and increasingly uncontrollable behaviour, including arson, vandalism, and theft. When he was 16, Teskey became involved with a pedophile who supplied him with drugs and alcohol, promising a career in pornographic movies: Teskey later assaulted the man. By 1988, Teskey's antisocial behaviour was becoming increasingly violent.

According to a 2015 study by neuroscientists at the King's College London Institute of Psychiatry, Psychology and Neuroscience (IoPPN), published in *The Lancet Psychiatry*, offenders with psychopathic traits have significantly smaller amounts of brain matter in the areas responsible for reinforcement learning and decision-making, suggesting that psychopathy may be a biological, even genetically inherited disorder—paralleling other research findings suggesting that psychopaths are "untreatable," at least with conventional cognitive learning and psychotherapy approaches.

Nature or nurture? Or some combination of the two? How do you think the Leo Teskey case informs the nature or nurture debate around psychopathy?

---

of recent studies have found that IQ has negligible influence on criminal behaviour.[162] Also, a recent evaluation of research on intelligence conducted by the American Psychological Association concludes that the strength of an IQ–crime link is "very low."[163]

It is unlikely that the IQ–criminality debate will be settled soon. Measurement is beset by many methodological problems. The well-documented criticisms suggesting that IQ tests are race and class biased would certainly influence the testing of the criminal population, which is besieged with a multitude of social and economic problems. Even if it can be shown that known offenders have lower IQs than the general population, it is difficult to explain many patterns in the crime rate: Why are there more male than female criminals? Why do crime rates vary by region, time of year, and even weather patterns? Why does aging out occur? IQ does not increase with age, so why should crime rates fall?

Evaluation of Psychological Trait Theory

Psychological trait theories focus on individual differences in personality, learning, and cognition and how these affect behaviour, including problem behaviours that may lead to criminal behaviour. The findings from the research generated by psychological trait theories are the foundation for treatment programs that emphasize early identification of risk factors for problem behaviour and individualized treatment programs and cognitive behavioural therapies to train social appropriate behaviours. The *Psychology of Criminal Conduct*, by Canadian forensic psychologists Jim Bonta and Don Andrews is a leading example of the application of cognitive behavioural psychology to explaining and treating criminal behaviour.[164]

Critics of psychological trait theories of crime point out that the findings from different studies frequently contradict one another (e.g., the Twinkie defence debate), or only a small proportion of those with the psychological condition (e.g., FASD) actually engage in criminal behaviour. Skeptics argue that environmental conditions are more important in determining who, regardless of psychological disposition, will commit a crime. Critical theorists like Michel Foucault observe that the determination of what gets identified as deviant or criminal and by whom is the question that needs to be answered first before assuming that individuals who have been identified have psychological traits that are deviant or criminal. Still other critics argue that, despite the implementation of treatment programs for criminal offenders, there appears to be little success in lowering the rates of repeat offending.[165]

Psychological trait theorists counter such criticisms by observing that all behaviour, including criminal behaviour, begins with the individual and the interaction of his or her biological and psychological makeup with the surrounding environment; and a growing body of research evidence shows that psychological traits like impulsivity and lack of inhibition, low tolerance for frustration, aggressiveness, lack of emotional attachment to others, low level of intelligence, and other antisocial personality characteristics are directly linked to the early occurrence of behavioural problems in the family, at school and with peers, and a greater likelihood of involvement with the criminal justice system. Knowing the risk that these psychological traits pose, in particular in poor environments that can increase the risk, psychological trait theorists argue for early intervention and treatment so that behaviours do not develop into criminality.

Social Policy Implications

For most of the 20th century, biological and psychological views of criminality have influenced crime control and prevention policy. The result has been front-end or primary prevention programs that seek to treat personal problems before they manifest themselves as crime. To this end, thousands of family therapy organizations, substance abuse clinics, and mental health associations operate throughout North America. Teachers, employers, courts, welfare agencies, and others make referrals to these facilities. These services are based on the premise that if a person's problems can be treated before they become overwhelming, some future crimes will be prevented. Secondary prevention programs provide treatment such as psychological counselling to youths and adults after they have violated the law. Attendance at such programs may be a requirement of a probation order, part of a diversionary sentence, or aftercare at the end of a prison sentence.

Biologically oriented therapy is also being used in the criminal justice system. Programs have altered diets, changed lighting, compensated for learning disabilities, treated allergies, and so on.[166] More controversial has been the use of mood-altering chemicals, such as lithium, pemoline, imipramine, phenytoin, and benzodiazepines, to control behaviour. Another practice that has elicited concern is the use of psychosurgery (brain surgery) to control antisocial behaviour. Surgical procedures have been used to alter the brain structure of convicted sex offenders in an effort to eliminate or control their sex drives. Results are still preliminary, but some critics argue that these procedures are without scientific merit.[167]

Numerous psychologically based treatment methods range from individual counselling to behaviour modification. For example, treatment based on how people process information takes into account that people are more likely to respond aggressively to provocation if thoughts intensify the insult or otherwise stir feelings of anger. Cognitive therapists attempt to teach explosive people to control aggressive impulses by viewing social provocations as problems demanding a solution rather than retaliation. Programs are aimed at teaching problem-solving skills that may include self-disclosure, role-playing, listening, following instructions, joining in, and using self-control.[168] Therapeutic interventions designed to make people better problem solvers may involve measures that enhance[169]

- Coping and problem-solving skills
- Relationships with peers, parents, and other adults
- Conflict resolution and communication skills, and methods for resisting peer pressure related to drug use and violence
- Consequential thinking and decision-making abilities
- Prosocial behaviours, including cooperation with others, self-responsibility, respecting others, and public speaking efficacy
- Empathy*

> **primary prevention programs** Programs, such as substance abuse clinics and mental health associations, that seek to treat personal problems before they manifest themselves as crime.
>
> **secondary prevention programs** Programs that provide treatment such as psychological counselling to youths and adults after they have violated the law.

Summary

The earliest positivist criminologists were biologists. Led by Cesare Lombroso, these early researchers believed that some people manifested primitive traits that made them born criminals. Today their research is debunked because of poor methodology, testing, and logic. Biological views fell out of favour in the early 20th century. In the 1970s, spurred by the publication of Edmund O. Wilson's *Sociobiology*, criminologists again turned to study of the biological basis of criminality. For the most part, the effort has focused on the causes of violent crime. Interest has centred on several areas: (1) biochemical factors, such as diet, allergies, hormonal imbalances, and environmental contaminants (such as lead); (2) neurophysiological factors, such as brain disorders, EEG abnormalities, tumours, and head injuries; and, with new developments in biogenetics technologies, (3) genetic factors, such as the XYY syndrome and inherited traits. An evolutionary branch holds that changes in the human condition, which have taken millions of years to evolve, may help explain crime rate differences.

Psychological attempts to explain criminal behaviour have historical roots in the concept that criminals are insane or mentally damaged. This position is no longer accepted. Today there are three main psychological perspectives: the psychodynamic view, the cognitive view, and the social learning perspective. The psychodynamic view, developed by Sigmund Freud, links aggressive behaviour to personality conflicts arising from childhood. According to some psychoanalysts, psychotics are aggressive, unstable people who can easily become involved in crime. Cognitive psychology is concerned with human development and how people perceive the world. Criminality is viewed as a function of improper information processing. Behavioural and social learning theorists see criminality as a learned behaviour. Children who are exposed to violence and see it rewarded may become violent as adults.

Psychological traits such as personality and intelligence have been linked to criminality. One important area of study has been the antisocial personality, a person who lacks emotion and concern for others. The controversial issue of the relationship of IQ to criminality has been resurrected once again with the publication of research studies purporting to show that criminals have lower IQs than noncriminals.

Discussion Questions

1. If research could show that the tendency to commit crime is inherited, what should be done with the young children of violence-prone criminals?

2. Would you recommend that young children be forbidden to view films and video games with violent content?

3. Knowing what you do about trends and patterns in crime, how would you counteract the assertion that people who commit crime are physically or mentally abnormal?

4. Aside from becoming a criminal, what other career paths are open to psychopaths?

READY TO STUDY?

IN THE BOOK, YOU CAN:

✔ Check your understanding of what you've just read by reading the Summary at the end of each chapter.

✔ Rip out the Chapter in Review card at the back of the book to have the key terms and Learning Objectives handy, and complete the quizzes provided (answers are at the bottom of the back page!).

ONLINE YOU CAN:

✔ Stay organized and efficient with MindTap—a single destination with all the course material and study aids you need to succeed. Built-in apps leverage social media and the latest learning technology. For example:

  ✔ ReadSpeaker will read the text to you.

  ✔ Flashcards are pre-populated to provide you with a jump start for review—or you can create your own.

  ✔ You can highlight text and make notes in your MindTap Reader. Your notes will flow into Evernote, the electronic notebook app that you can access anywhere when it's time to study for the exam.

  ✔ Prepare for tests with quizzes.

Go to www.nelson.com/student to access these digital resources.

CHAPTER 6

Social Structure Theories

Learning Objectives

LO1 Explain why sociology has been the main orientation of criminologists.

LO2 Explain why social structure theory supports the idea that those living in poverty are more likely to commit crimes.

LO3 State the three branches of social structure theories.

LO4 Explain the concept of "collective efficacy."

LO5 Discuss how strain theories interpret crime.

LO6 Explain the concept of "differential opportunity."

LO1 Criminologists and Sociology

A 16-year-old girl was sentenced to six months jail time for aggravated assault in what the judge called the "horrendous" beating of Shawn Kurtis Jack, a homeless man in North Sydney, Nova Scotia. Jack had been living with his dog Chico in a tent in the woods behind a grocery store when the assault took place.

The court heard how the teen was present when was Jack was caught off-guard and savagely beaten with a hammer and a wrench, sustaining life-threatening injuries. According to Crown Attorney Glenn Gouthro, Jack's skull was fractured in various places and crushed, with bone fragments embedded in his brain tissue. Jack, who has had several operations since the assault, requires extensive therapy to regain his ability to speak and walk again.

As to the teen, her presentence report noted a good relationship with her mother but little to no contact with her father. She has anger issues related to two sexual assaults suffered when she was 9 and 13 at the hands of her cousin and neighbour. All who knew her agreed the girl was bright but was in need of drug and alcohol counselling and strong parenting. At her sentencing hearing, the judge warned the teen, who can't be named under provisions of the *Youth Criminal Justice Act*, to stay away from drugs and alcohol and to get new friends. Her co-accused all had prior criminal records as did she.

Criminologists are in the practice of examining crime from a sociological point of view. They believe crime cannot be fully understood without examining the surrounding social, political, and economic context. They try to understand why people commit crimes and how society should respond to it with a focus on the offender as an individual: "Why would a bright young teenager commit such a horrendous crime?" Criminologists would therefore examine factors such as her substance abuse problems, the influence of her peer group, and her mother's lack of parental skills in an effort to understand why she committed her crime. Ultimately, the aim is to use this information to assist in meeting her individual needs but also in preventing the reoccurrence of such a tragic incident.

The attack was just another in a series of assaults, robberies, and even murders of homeless people, another example of the plight of the growing number of homeless in Canadian cities.[1] Although the United Nations has ranked Canada as one of the best places on earth to live, still many Canadians—particularly

In 2014, a 16-year-old girl was convicted of aggravated assault of Shawn Jack, a homeless man who lived in the woods of Sydney, NS. Many criminologists believe that beatings such as these, of homeless people, are endemic in poor and deteriorated neighbourhoods. Understanding criminal behaviour, then, means also understanding the influences of social forces.

women, Aboriginal people, and youth—cannot afford decent housing, do not have the education or skills for employment, or are suffering from illness or addiction. As the number of homeless grows in Canadian cities, crime and victimization will increase.

The beating of a homeless man exemplifies the belief of many criminologists that crime and violence are endemic in poor, deteriorated neighbourhoods. Because these neighbourhoods have substantially higher crime rates than more affluent areas, the majority of criminologists believe it would be a mistake to ignore social and environmental factors in trying to understand the cause of criminal behaviour.[2] Most criminals are indigent and desperate, not calculating or evil. Many were raised in deteriorated parts of town and lack the social support and economic resources familiar to more affluent members of society. Understanding criminal behaviour, then, requires analyzing the influence of these destructive social forces on human behaviour.

Criminologists have long attempted to discover why certain neighbourhoods and geographic locations are more prone to criminal activity than others. Explanations of crime as an individual-level phenomenon, with its locus in either destructive personal choices or deviant traits, fail to account for these consistent crime rate patterns. If violence, as some criminologists suggest, is related to chemical or chromosome abnormality, then how can ecological differences in crime rates be explained? It is unlikely that all people with physical anomalies live in one section of town or in one area of the country. There is an ongoing public debate over the effects of violent TV shows on adolescent aggression. Yet

- Because crime rates are higher in lower-class areas, many criminologists believe that the causes of crime are rooted in socioeconomic factors.

- Despite economic headway, there are still more than 5 million indigent Canadians. Visible-minority groups and Aboriginal Canadians are more likely than the white majority to be poor.

- Some criminologists believe that destructive social forces in poor areas are responsible for high crime rates.

- The strain and frustration caused by poverty is a suspected cause of crime.

- Indigents may become involved in a deviant subculture that sustains and supports criminality.

adolescents in cities and towns with widely disparate crime rates may all watch the same shows and movies; so how can crime rate differences in these areas be explained? If violence has a biological or psychological origin, should it not be distributed more evenly throughout the social structure rather than concentrated in certain areas?

Because of these issues, many criminologists believe that understanding the dynamics of interactions between individuals and important social institutions, such as families, peers, schools, jobs, and criminal justice agencies, is important for understanding the cause of crime.[3] The relationship of one social class or group to another or to the power structure that controls a country's legal and economic system may also be closely related to criminality. It seems logical that people on the lowest rung of the economic ladder will have the greatest incentive to commit crime. They may be either enraged by their lack of economic success or simply financially desperate and disillusioned. In either case, crime, despite its inherent dangers, may be an attractive alternative to a life of indigence.

LO2 Economic Structure and Crime

All societies are characterized by some measure of social stratification. Social strata are created by unequal distribution of wealth, power, and prestige. Social classes are segments of the population whose members have a relatively similar portion of desirable things and who share attitudes, values, norms, and an identifiable lifestyle. In Canadian society, it is common to identify people as upper, middle,

working, or lower class, with a broad range of economic variations within each group. The upper-upper class consists of a small number (around 5 percent) of exceptionally well-to-do families who control enormous financial and social resources. In contrast, those in the lower class (about 20 percent of the population) have scant, if any, resources and suffer socially and economically as a result. In Canada, the most common measure of poverty is the "low income cut-offs" used by Statistics Canada. For example, in 2011, the low-income cutoff line for an individual living in a large city (over 500 000) was $23,298, and for a family of four it was around $43 292. About 10 percent of Canadians, or roughly 3.5 million people, live below these low-income cut-offs.[4]

Children are hit especially hard by poverty. While Canada is widely considered one of the best countries in which to live, one out of every ten children in Canada (about 637 000 children) were living in poverty in 2007.[5] Hundreds of studies have documented the association between family poverty and children's health, achievement, and behaviour impairments.[6] Children who grow up in low-income homes are less likely to achieve in school and are less likely to complete their schooling than children with more affluent parents.[7] Poor children are also more likely to suffer from health problems and to receive inadequate health care. Children who live in extreme poverty or who remain poor for multiple years appear to suffer the worst outcomes. The timing of poverty also seems to be relevant. Findings suggest that poverty during early childhood may have a more severe impact than poverty during adolescence.[8]

Besides their increased chance of physical illness, poor children are much more likely than wealthy children to suffer various social and physical ills, ranging from low birth weight to limited educational achievement. The social problems found in poverty-plagued neighbourhoods have been described as an "epidemic" that spreads like a contagious disease, destroying the inner workings that enable neighbourhoods to survive; they become "hollowed out."[9] As neighbourhood quality decreases, the probability that residents will develop problems sharply increases. Adolescents in the worst neighbourhoods have the greatest risks of dropping out of school and of becoming teenage parents.

Rates of child poverty vary by race and ethnicity. In Canada child poverty is

stratification
Grouping based on economic or social class and characterized by the unequal distribution of wealth, power, and prestige.

social class
Segment of the population whose members are at a relatively similar economic level and who share attitudes, values, norms, and an identifiable lifestyle.

FIGURE 6.1

Child Poverty Number and Rate, Canada

A 2014 report found a lack of progress in reducing child poverty in Canada, despite a commitment from members of Parliament more than two decades ago to eradicate child poverty by the year 2000.

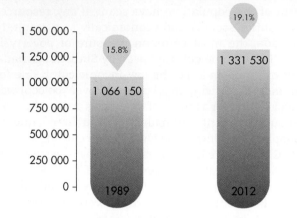

Source: 2014 Report Card on Child and Family Poverty in Canada. Copyright © Campaign 2000

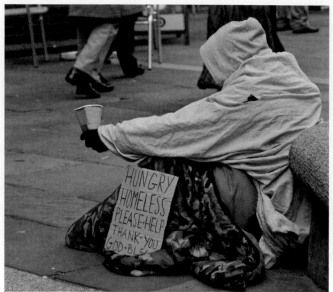

The crushing lifestyle of slum areas may create a culture of poverty that continues on to the next generation. Mistrust of social institutions, such as schools and police, prevents those from taking advantage of the meager opportunities available to them.

highest among recent immigrants, especially those who are a visible minority, and among Aboriginal people. It is estimated that more than 50 percent of Aboriginal children live in poverty.[10] (See Figure 6.1.)

Inequality and Culture

Lower-class slum areas are scenes of inadequate housing and health care, disrupted family lives, underemployment, and despair. Members of the lower class also suffer in other ways. They are more prone to depression, less likely to have achievement motivation, and less likely to put off immediate gratification for future gain. For example, they may be less willing to stay in school because the rewards for educational achievement are in the distant future. Some are driven to desperate measures to cope with their economic plight.[11]

Members of the lower class are constantly bombarded by advertisements linking material possessions to self-worth, but they are often unable to attain desired goods and services through conventional means. Although they are members of a society that extols material success above any other form, they are unable to satisfactorily compete for such success with members of the upper classes. As a result, they may turn to illegal solutions to their economic plight. They may deal drugs for profit or steal cars and sell them to chop shops; they may even commit armed robberies for desperately needed funds. They may become so depressed that they take alcohol and drugs as a form of self-tranquillization; because of their poverty, they acquire the drugs and alcohol through illegal channels.

In 1966 sociologist Oscar Lewis argued that the crushing lifestyle of slum areas produces a **culture of poverty** passed from one generation to the next.[12] Apathy, cynicism, helplessness, and mistrust of social institutions, such as schools, government agencies, and the police, mark the culture of poverty. This mistrust prevents slum dwellers from taking advantage of the meagre opportunities available to them. Lewis's work was the first of a group of studies that described the plight of at-risk children and adults. In 1970 Swedish economist Gunnar Myrdal described a worldwide **underclass** that was cut off from society, its members lacking the education and skills needed to function successfully in modern society.[13]

The burdens of underclass life are most often felt by minority group members. In Canada, this is especially true for Aboriginal people. Among persons the government officially recognize as Aboriginal, the average yearly income is less than one-half what other Canadians earn ($12 000 versus $25 000); employment rates are 60 percent

culture of poverty
A separate lower-class culture, characterized by apathy, cynicism, helplessness, and mistrust of social institutions, such as schools, government agencies, and the police, that is passed from one generation to the next.

underclass
The lowest social stratum in any country, whose members lack the education and skills needed to function successfully in modern society.

First Nation(s)
The term *First Nations* came into common usage in the 1970s to replace *band* or *Indian,* which some people found offensive. The term is distinct from *Aboriginal peoples* because it doesn't include Inuit or Métis and it applies to both Status and Non-Status Indians.

First Peoples
First peoples is a term used to describe the original peoples of Canada and their descendants. It is used less frequently than terms such as *Aboriginal peoples* and *Native peoples.*

Indian
The term *Indian* collectively describes all the *Indigenous people* in Canada who are not Inuit or Métis. Indian peoples are one of three peoples recognized as Aboriginal in the *Constitution Act* of 1982 along with Inuit and Métis. In addition, three categories apply to Indians in Canada: Status Indians, Non-Status Indians, and Treaty Indians. The term *Indian* is considered outdated by many people, and there is much debate over whether to continue using this term.

Status Indians
Status Indians are people who are entitled to have their names included on the Indian Register, an official list maintained by the federal government. Only Status Indians are recognized as Indians under the *Indian Act* and are entitled to certain rights and benefits under the law.

Non-Status Indians
Non-Status Indians are people who consider themselves Indians or members of a First Nation but whom the Government of Canada does not recognize as Indians under the *Indian Act*, either because they are unable to prove their Indian status or have lost their status rights. Non-Status Indians are not entitled to the same rights and benefits available to Status Indians.

Treaty Indians
Treaty Indians are descendants of Indians who signed treaties with Canada and who have a contemporary connection with a treaty band.

Indigenous
Indigenous means "native to the area." In this sense, Aboriginal peoples are indigenous to North America. The meaning of *Indigenous* is similar to Aboriginal peoples, Native peoples, or First peoples. Currently, the term is rarely used and, when it is, it usually refers to Aboriginal people internationally. However, the term is gaining acceptance, particularly among some Aboriginal scholars to recognize the place of Aboriginal peoples in Canada's late-colonial era and implies land tenure. The term is also used by the United Nations in its working groups and in its Decade of the World's Indigenous People.

Innu
Innu are the Naskapi and Montagnais First Nations peoples who live in Quebec and Labrador. They are not to be confused with Inuit or Inuk.

Inuit
Inuit live primarily in the Northwest Territories, Nunavut, northern parts of Quebec, and most of Labrador. They are the Aboriginal people of the Arctic. The word *Inuit* means "the people" in Inuktitut and is the term by which Inuit refer to themselves. *Inuk* is the singular form of Inuit. When referring to two people, the correct term is *Inuuk,* while three or more takes *Inuit.* Since Inuit have never lived on reserves, the terms *on-reserve* and *off-reserve* do not apply.

Métis
The word *Métis* is French for "mixed blood." The *Constitution Act* of 1982 recognizes Métis as one of the three Aboriginal peoples. Today, the term is used broadly to describe people with mixed First Nations and European ancestry who identify themselves as Métis. Métis organizations in Canada have differing criteria about who qualifies as a Métis person.

Native
Native is a word similar in meaning to *Aboriginal. Native peoples* is a collective term to describe the descendants of the original peoples of North America. The term is increasingly seen as outdated (particularly when used as a noun) and is starting to lose acceptance.

Native American
This commonly used term in the United States describes the descendants of the original peoples of North America. The term has not caught on in Canada because of the apparent reference to U.S. citizenship. However, some Aboriginal peoples in Canada have argued that because they are descendants of the original peoples of the Americas, the term *Native American* should apply to them regardless of their citizenship. *Native North American* has been used to identify the original peoples of Canada and the United States.

Source: Reprinted by permission of Office of the Provincial Advisor for Aboriginal Infant Development Programs.

lower than for non-Aboriginals; and rates of infant mortality, respiratory diseases, diabetes, and suicide are at least three times higher than for other Canadians.[14] More than half of Aboriginal people in Canada live in poverty. A 2010 study by Wilson and MacDonald confirmed that Aboriginal people are disproportionately ranked among the poorest of Canadians, and disturbing levels of income inequality continue to persist. The researchers recommend new comprehensive approaches and solutions based on Aboriginal self-determination versus the historically paternalistic administration of their communities. According to the Wilson and Macdonald, the Canadian government must abandon its long-standing colonial assumptions and acknowledge that the legacy of colonialism lies at the heart of income disparities for Aboriginal peoples.[15] Overall, First Nation peoples are almost twice as likely as nonminorities to fall below the poverty line.[16] See Figure 6.2.

FIGURE 6.2

Aboriginal Children, Visible Minority Children, and Children with Disabilities Most Likely to Be Poor

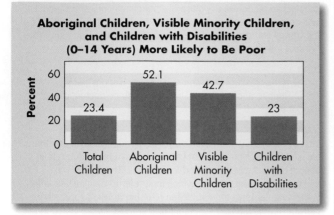

Aboriginal Children, Visible Minority Children, and Children with Disabilities (0–14 Years) More Likely to Be Poor

Source: Reprinted by permission of Canadian Council on Social Development

Economic disparity continually haunts members of the underclass and their children. Even if they value education and other middle-class norms, their desperate life circumstances (including high unemployment, crowded and dilapidated housing, poor diet, and lack of access to technology such as computers) may prevent them from developing the skills and habits that lead first to educational success and later to success in the workplace. Both of these factors have been linked to crime and drug abuse.[17]

Community effects may particularly damage children. Adolescents residing in areas of concentrated poverty are more likely to suffer in their cognitive development, sexual understanding, school attendance habits, and transition to employment.[18] Lack of education and family instability make them poor candidates for employment or for the eventual formation of their own cohesive families. These findings suggest that the poor confront obstacles far greater than the mere lack of financial resources. The social problems they face render them unprepared to take advantage of employment opportunities even in tight labour markets.[19] The fact that many of the underclass are visible minorities and Aboriginal children who can expect to spend all their lives in poverty is an important problem facing our society today.[20]

The 1998 movie *American History X*, written by David McKenna, has been described as a terrifying, violent, intense condemnation of racism and prejudice.

The movie describes the life of two brothers, Derek and Danny, who grow up in a society of racism, prejudice, and beliefs of white supremacy, and clearly demonstrates the power culture has in shaping the behaviour of its members. Sociologists use the term *deviance* to define any type of behaviour that violates social norms. Sociologists recognize that culture influences the behaviour of those persons living within it and that these behaviours, including deviant behaviours, define societal norms. The deviant behaviours exhibited by the brothers are prejudice and racism, which has more to do with the influence of family and friends than biological or psychological factors.

Derek and Danny are raised in a middle-class family with an outwardly racist father who is seen to heavily influence the boy's thinking. The unexpected death of their father at the hands of an African American gunman particularly bolsters Derek's hatred of African Americans. He becomes an active member of a white-supremacist group. On the surface, Derek, played by actor Edward Norton is an intelligent, engaging person. However, all is not what it appears to be. At one point in the movie he brutally murders two young African American thieves who were trying to steal his car, demonstrating his true vicious, impulsive character. Clearly, Derek viewed himself as a victim of society, holding minorities responsible for the problems in the world. The movie changes direction after Derek serves time for the murder of the two black men. While incarcerated, Derek is brutally gang-raped by a group of white-supremacist inmates, fundamentally changing his perception of himself and of those in the while supremacy movement. He comes to terms with his father's death and changes his beliefs about African Americans and understands the negativity and evil associated with white supremacy, racism, hate, and prejudice. He also comes to an understanding of how his views influenced his younger brother, Danny, whom he tries to discourage from following in his footsteps.

Strain theory states that when members of society do not have adequate socially acceptable means to obtain their cultural goals, they will utilize other often less desirable means to achieve them. Can Derek's behaviour be attributed to his frustration with his perceived lack of control over his environment? Did the death of his father and the cultural views instilled in him cause him to use nonconforming means to obtain change in his world? Explain.

Referring to the government's own documents, in 2015 the National Press reported that in some Manitoba First Nation communities, 80 percent of the population is on welfare, and inhabitants are more likely to grow up in poverty, drop out of school, live off social assistance in dilapidated housing, and suffer family violence. Across Canada, 25 percent of First Nation children live in poverty while 62 percent of Aboriginal children live below the poverty line. "High levels of poverty, unemployment, domestic violence and family dysfunction are prominent adverse social conditions faced by many members of First Nations, particularly those living in remote or isolated communities."

Source (quote): C. Chinta Puxley, "Grinding Poverty Faced by Manitoba First Nations Worst in Country: Aboriginal Affairs Documents," *The Canadian Press* (29 January 2015). http:// aptn.ca/news/2015/01/29/grinding-poverty-faced-manitoba-first-nations-worst-country -aboriginal-affairs-documents (accessed 8 October 2015).

LO3 Social Structure Theories

Many criminologists view disadvantaged economic-class position as a primary cause of crime. This view is referred to as **social structure theory**. As a group, social structure theories suggest that social and economic forces operating in deteriorated lower-class areas push many of their residents into criminal behaviour patterns. These theories consider the existence of unsupervised teenage gangs, high crime rates, and social disorder in slum areas as major social problems.

Lower-class crime is often the violent, destructive product of youth gangs and marginally employed or underemployed young adults. Underemployment means that many working adults earn relatively low wages and have few benefits such as vacation time, medical or dental plans, and retirement programs. Their ability to accumulate capital for home ownership is restricted and so, consequently, is their stake in society.

Although members of the middle and upper classes also engage in crime, social structure theorists view middle-class and white-collar crime as being of relatively lower frequency, seriousness, and danger to the general public. The real crime problem is essentially a lower-class phenomenon that breeds criminal behaviour, begins in youth, and continues into young adulthood. Because crime rates are higher in lower-class urban centres than in middle-class suburbs, social forces must influence or control behaviour.[21] We will examine some specific structure theories that support this perspective.

The social structure perspective encompasses three independent yet overlapping branches: social disorganization theory, strain theory, and cultural deviance theory. These three branches are summarized in Figure 6.3.

social structure theory
The view that disadvantaged economic-class position is a primary cause of crime.

FIGURE 6.3

The Three Branches of Social Structure Theory

Social disorganization theory focuses on conditions in the environment:
- Deteriorated neighbourhoods
- Inadequate social control
- Law-violating gangs and groups
- Conflicting social values

Strain theory focuses on conflict between goals and means:
- Unequal distribution of wealth and power
- Frustration
- Alternative methods of achievement

Cultural deviance theory combines the other two:
- Development of subcultures as a result of disorganization and stress
- Subcultural values in opposition to conventional values

CRIME

Glossary (margin)

social disorganization theory
Branch of social structure theory that focuses on the breakdown of institutions such as the family, school, and employment in inner-city neighbourhoods.

strain theory
Branch of social structure theory that sees crime as a function of the conflict between people's goals and the means available to obtain them.

strain
The anger, frustration, and resentment experienced by people who believe they cannot achieve their goals through legitimate means.

cultural deviance theory
Branch of social structure theory that sees strain and social disorganization together resulting in a unique lower-class culture that conflicts with conventional social norms.

subculture
A set of values, beliefs, and traditions unique to a particular social class or group within a larger society.

cultural transmission
Process whereby values, beliefs, and traditions are handed down from one generation to the next.

Social Disorganization Theory

Social disorganization theory focuses on the urban conditions that affect crime rates. A disorganized area is one in which institutions of social control, such as the family, commercial establishments, and schools, have broken down and can no longer perform their expected or stated functions. Indicators of social disorganization include high unemployment and school dropout rates, deteriorated housing, low income levels, and large numbers of single-parent households. Residents in these areas experience conflict and despair, and, as a result, antisocial behaviour flourishes.

Strain Theory

Strain theory holds that crime is a function of the conflict between people's goals and the means they can use to obtain them. Strain theorists argue that although social and economic goals are common to people in all economic strata, the ability to obtain these goals is class-dependent. Most people in Canada desire wealth, material possessions, power, prestige, and other life comforts. Members of the lower class are unable to achieve these symbols of success through conventional means. Consequently, they feel anger, frustration, and resentment, referred to collectively as strain. Lower-class citizens can either accept their condition and live as socially responsible if unrewarded citizens, or they can choose an alternative means of achieving success, such as theft, violence, or drug trafficking.

Cultural Deviance Theory

Cultural deviance theory combines elements of both strain and social disorganization theories. According to this view, because of strain and social isolation, a unique lower-class culture develops in disorganized

neighbourhoods. These independent subcultures maintain unique values and beliefs that conflict with conventional social norms. Criminal behaviour is an expression of conformity to lower-class subcultural values and traditions, not a rebellion from conventional society. Subcultural values are handed down from one generation to the next in a process called cultural transmission.

Although each of these theories is distinct in critical aspects, each approach has at its core the view that socially isolated people, living in disorganized neighbourhoods, are likely to experience crime-producing social forces. In the remainder of this chapter, each branch of social structure theory will be discussed in some detail.

Social Disorganization Theory

Social disorganization theory links crime rates to neighbourhood ecological characteristics. Crime rates are elevated in highly transient, mixed-use (where residential and commercial property exist side by side), and changing neighbourhoods in which the fabric of social life has become frayed. These localities are unable to provide essential services, such as education, health care, and proper housing, and, as a result, they experience significant levels of unemployment, single-parent families, and families on welfare.

Social disorganization theory views crime-ridden neighbourhoods as those in which residents are trying to leave at the earliest opportunity. Residents are uninterested in community matters, so the common sources of control—the family, school, business community, social service agencies—are weak and disorganized. Personal relationships are strained because neighbours are constantly moving. Constant resident turnover weakens communications and blocks attempts at solving neighbourhood problems or establishing common goals (see Figure 6.4).[22]

FIGURE 6.4

Social Disorganization Theory

Poverty
- Development of isolated slums
- Lack of conventional social opportunities
- Racial and ethnic discrimination

Social disorganization
- Breakdown of social institutions and organizations such as school and family
- Lack of informal social control

Breakdown of social control
- Development of gangs and groups
- Peer group replaces family and social institutions

Criminal areas
- Neighbourhood becomes crime-prone
- Stable pockets of delinquency develop
- Lack of external support and investment

Cultural transmission
Older youths pass norms (focal concerns) to younger generation, creating stable slum culture

Criminal careers
Most youths "age out" of delinquency, marry, and raise families, but some remain in life of crime

The Work of Shaw and McKay

Social disorganization theory was popularized by the work of two Chicago sociologists, Clifford R. Shaw and Henry McKay, who linked life in transitional slum areas to the inclination to commit crime. Shaw and McKay began their pioneering work on Chicago crime during the early 1920s while working as researchers for a state-supported social service agency.[23]

Shaw and McKay explained crime and delinquency within the context of the changing urban environment and ecological development of the city. They saw that Chicago had developed into distinct neighbourhoods (natural areas), some affluent and others wracked by extreme poverty. These poverty-ridden transitional neighbourhoods suffered high rates of population turnover and were incapable of

inducing residents to remain and defend the neighbourhoods against criminal groups.

In transitional areas, successive changes in the population composition, the disintegration of the traditional cultures, the diffusion of divergent cultural standards, and the gradual industrialization of the area dissolve neighbourhood culture and organization. The continuity of conventional neighbourhood traditions and institutions is broken, leaving children feeling displaced and without a strong or definitive set of values.

Concentric Zones

Shaw and McKay's work was influenced by Robert E. Park and Ernest W. Burgess, the creator of the *concentric zone model* which was one of the earliest theoretical explanations of urban social structures.[24] Shaw and Mckay identified the areas in Chicago that had excessive crime rates and noted that distinct ecological areas had developed in the city, forming a series of nine concentric circles, or zones, and that there were stable and significant interzone differences in crime rates (see Figure 6.5). The areas of heaviest crime concentration appeared to be the transitional inner-city zones, where large numbers of foreign-born citizens had recently settled.[25] The zones farthest from the city's centre had correspondingly lower crime rates.

Analysis of these data indicated a surprisingly stable pattern of criminal activity in the nine ecological zones over 65 years. Shaw and McKay concluded that in the transitional neighbourhoods, multiple cultures and diverse values, both conventional and deviant, coexist. Children growing up in the street culture often find that adults who have adopted a deviant lifestyle (gamblers, pimps, drug dealers) are the most financially successful people in the neighbourhood. Forced to choose between conventional and deviant lifestyles, many slum kids opt for the latter. They join other like-minded youths and form law-violating gangs and cliques. The development of teenage law-violating groups is an essential element of youthful misbehaviour in slum areas. The values that slum youths adopt often conflict with existing middle-class norms, which demand strict obedience to the legal code. Consequently, a value conflict further separates the delinquent youth and his or her peer group from conventional society; the result is a more solid embrace of deviant goals and behaviour. To further justify their choice of goals, these youths seek support for their choice by recruiting new members and passing on the delinquent tradition.

transitional neighbourhood An area undergoing a shift in population and structure, usually from middle-class residential to lower-class mixed use.

Shaw and McKay's statistical analysis confirmed that even though crime rates changed, the highest rates were always in zones I and II (the central city and a transitional area). The areas with the highest crime rates retained high rates even when their ethnic composition changed (the areas Shaw and McKay examined shifted from German and Irish to Italian and Polish).[26]

The Legacy of Shaw and McKay

Social disorganization concepts articulated by Shaw and McKay have remained prominent within criminology for more than 80 years. The most important of Shaw and McKay's findings were that crime rates

Vancouver's downtown Eastside is an example of the integrated relationship between neighbourhood disintegration and crime. After injecting almost $1 million per day in social spending, Vancouver's famous Eastside, also known as the city's gulag, the homeless count actually went up, and the social spending appeared to have little effect on the area's epidemic of drug use and on-street chaos. Known as Skid Road in the 1950s, when it was notorious for a high concentration of bars and crime, the Eastside has evolved into one of Canada's worst neighbourhoods where "hard drugs replaced booze, patients from de-institutionalized mental hospitals flooded in and police presence was pulled back and the area became dominated by social services."

Source (quote): T. Hopper, "Vancouver's 'Gulag': Canada's Poorest Neighbourhood Refuses to Get Better Despite $1M a Day in Social Spending," *National Post* (14 November 2014) http://news.nationalpost.com/2014/11/14/vancouvers-gulag-canadas-poorest-neighbourhood-refuses-to-get-better-despite-1m-a-day-in-social-spending (accessed 8 October 2015).

FIGURE 6.5

Shaw and McKay's Concentric Zones Map of Chicago

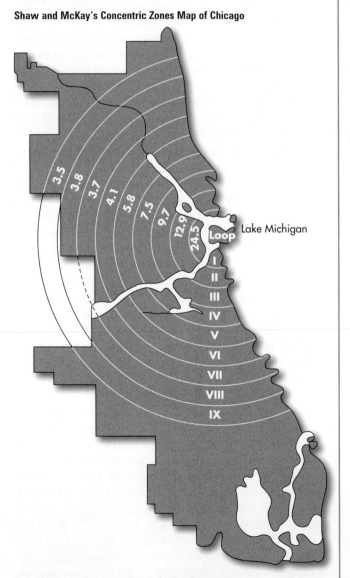

Note: Arabic numerals represent the rate of male delinquency.

Source: Clifford R. Shaw et al., *Delinquency Areas* (Chicago: University of Chicago Press, 1929), p. 99. Copyright 1929 by the University of Chicago Press. Reprinted with permission of The University of Chicago Press.

correspond to neighbourhood structure and that crime is created by the destructive ecological conditions in urban slums. They contended that criminals are not, as some criminologists of the time believed, biologically inferior, intellectually impaired, or psychologically damaged. Their research supported their belief that crime is a constant fixture in areas of poverty, regardless of residents' racial or ethnic identity. Because the basis of their theory was that neighbourhood disintegration and slum conditions are the primary causes of criminal behaviour, Shaw and McKay paved the way for many community action and treatment programs developed in the last half-century.

The Social Ecology School

During the 1970s, criminologists were influenced by several critical analyses of social disorganization theory that challenged its validity.[27] The criminological literature of the period was dominated by theories with a social–psychological orientation, stressing offender socialization within the family, school, and peer group.

In the 1980s, a group of criminologists continued studying ecological conditions, reviving concern about the effects of social disorganization.[28] These contemporary social ecologists developed a purer form of structural theory that emphasizes the association of community deterioration and economic decline with criminality but places less emphasis on value conflict. The following sections discuss some of the more recent social ecological research.

Community Disorganization

Crime rates and the need for police services are associated with community deterioration: disorder, poverty, alienation, disassociation, and fear of crime.[29] Even in rural areas, which normally have low crime rates, increased levels of crime and violence are associated with indicators of social disorganization such as residential instability (a large number of people moving in and out), family disruption, and changing ethnic composition.[30]

In larger cities, neighbourhoods with a high percentage of deserted houses and apartments experience high crime rates; abandoned buildings serve as a "magnet for crime."[31] Areas in which houses are in poor repair, boarded up, and burned out, whose owners are best described as slumlords, are also the location of the highest violence rates and gun crime.[32] These neighbourhoods, in which retail establishments often go bankrupt, are abandoned and deteriorate physically.[33]

Poverty and Unemployment

The percentage of people living in poverty and the percentage of broken homes are strongly related to neighbourhood crime rates.[34] Violent crime rates are associated with variables such as the percentage of the neighbourhood living below the poverty line, the lack of mortgage investment in a neighbourhood, the unemployment rate, and the influx of new immigrants; these factors are usually found in disorganized areas.[35] The influence of these economic disadvantages is felt by both male and female residents. Though female crime rates may be lower than male rates, women living in deteriorated areas also feel the effects of poverty.[36]

Shaw and McKay claimed that areas continually wracked by poverty also experience social disorganization.[37] Research indicates that neighbourhoods with few employment opportunities for youth and adults are the most vulnerable to predatory crime such as armed robbery and mugging.[38] Unemployment destabilizes households, and unstable families are likely to breed children who use violence and aggression to deal with limited opportunity. This lack of opportunity perpetuates higher crime rates, especially when large groups or cohorts of people of the same age compete for relatively scant resources.[39]

Community Fear

Disorganized neighbourhoods suffer social and physical incivilities—rowdy youth, trash and litter, graffiti, abandoned storefronts, burned-out buildings, littered lots, strangers, drunks, vagabonds, loiterers, prostitutes, noise, congestion, angry words, dirt, and stench. The presence of such incivilities makes residents of disorganized areas believe that their neighbourhood is dangerous and that they face a considerable chance of becoming crime victims. Therefore, when crime rates are actually high in these disorganized areas, fear levels increase dramatically.[40] Perceptions of crime and victimization produce neighbourhood fear.[41]

Fear can be contagious. People tell others when they have been victimized, thus spreading the word that the neighbourhood is getting dangerous and that the chance of future victimization is high.[42] As a result, people dread leaving their homes at night and withdraw from community life. Not surprisingly, people who have already been victimized fear the future more than those who have escaped crime.[43]

Fear is a powerful influence. When it grips a neighbourhood, business conditions begin to deteriorate, population mobility increases, and a "criminal element" begins to drift into the area.[44] In essence, the presence of fear incites more crime, increasing the chances of victimization and producing even more fear in a never-ending loop.[45]

Community Change

Communities undergoing rapid structural changes in racial and economic composition also seem to experience the greatest change in crime rates. Recent studies recognize that change, not stability, is the hallmark of many inner-city areas. A neighbourhood's residents, wealth, density, and purpose are constantly evolving. Even disorganized neighbourhoods acquire new identifying features. Some may become multiracial, while others become racially homogeneous. Some areas become stable and family-oriented, while in others, mobile, never-married people predominate.[46]

As areas decline, residents flee to safer, more stable locales. Those who cannot afford to leave for more affluent communities face an increased risk of victimization. Because of racial differences in economic well-being, those left behind are often minority citizens.[47] Those who cannot move find themselves surrounded by new residents. High population turnover can devastate community culture because it thwarts communication and information flow.[48] In response to this turnover, a culture may develop that dictates to neighbourhood youth standards of dress, language, and behaviour that are opposite to those of conventional society. All these factors are likely to increase crime rates.[49]

As communities change, neighbourhood deterioration precedes increasing rates of crime and delinquency.[50] Neighbourhoods most at risk for increased crime contain large numbers of single-parent families and unrelated people living together, have changed from owner-occupied to renter-occupied units, and have lost semiskilled and unskilled jobs (indicating a growing residue of discouraged workers who are no longer seeking employment).[51] These ecological disruptions strain existing social control mechanisms and inhibit their ability to control crime and delinquency.

Poverty Concentration

One aspect of community change may be the concentration of poverty in deteriorated neighbourhoods. William Julius Wilson describes how working- and middle-class families flee inner-city poverty areas, resulting in a concentration effect in which the most disadvantaged population is consolidated in urban ghettos. As the working and middle classes move out, they take with them their financial and institutional resources and support. Businesses are disinclined to locate in poor areas; banks become reluctant to lend

CAREER CONNECTIONS

Constable McKay is a veteran of the Peel Regional Police in Ontario. He holds a Bachelor of Commerce degree and Certificate in Law Enforcement and Administration from the University of Toronto. Since 1991, Tom has been attached to the award-winning Peel Regional Police Crime Prevention Services where he specializes in Crime Prevention Through Environmental Design (CPTED). CPTED is a proactive design philosophy built around a core set of principles that is based on the belief that the proper design and effective use of the built environment can lead to a reduction in the fear and incidence of crime as well as an improvement in the quality of life. CPTED goes well beyond conventional approaches to safeguarding the environment by exploiting natural forms of surveillance, access control, and territorial reinforcement in a deliberate attempt to present a psychological deterrent for the purpose of positively influencing human behaviour as people interact with the environment.

Tom has lectured extensively throughout the province on CPTED and is responsible for developing and teaching a basic and level II CPTED course that he has taught throughout North America and Bermuda. Tom also teaches part-time at Sheridan College, Brampton, and Humber College, Toronto, where he teaches community-based strategic policing. Tom is also responsible for developing and providing in-depth crime prevention training to the citizens of the Region of Peel through the development and co-instruction of a popular series of Crime Prevention Academy courses. Tom has frequently appeared in the local and national media as a CPTED expert. Tom holds a number of certificates from the Ontario Police College, St. Francis Xavier University, and the Canadian Securities Institute.

Tom developed a very pragmatic approach to crime prevention, which was heavily influenced by his CPTED training. This led Tom to the development of a number of insights and core beliefs that were drawn from the unprecedented amount of time he has served as a crime prevention officer. One of these insights resulted in the development of the "Know" Loitering Matrix, a tool Tom created to predict and potentially prevent the consequences that are often associated with unstructured loitering. In this way, Tom hoped to shed light on a simple, yet often pernicious activity that has a tendency to serve as an incubator for delinquent tendencies.

Tom's efforts also tended to exploit lost opportunities for natural surveillance, access control, and territorial reinforcement. In this regard, Tom recognized that there had been a general drift away from many of the conventional practices and values that helped keep our communities safe. This included the proliferation of privacy fences and computers, which fundamentally changed the nature of our environments and our desire to get to know our neighbours. This led Tom to the promotion of a "Know Your Neighbours" card based, in part, on the belief that our neighbourhood safety had been compromised by a decline in the strength of our communities.

Tom believes that as the pace of technological change continues to hasten, the advantage will naturally swing to criminals who will exploit it. Tom believes this advantage can be negated through crime prevention education and a back-to-basics approach that favours human contact over technologically inspired fixes such as surveillance cameras.

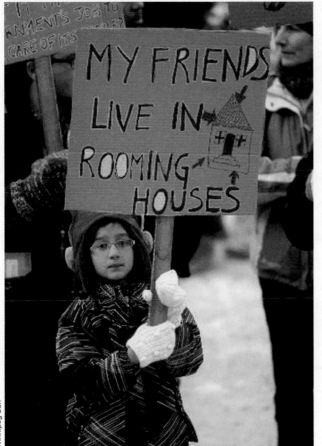

Winnipeg Sun

Areas marked by concentrated poverty, such as this in Winnipeg, become isolated and insulated from the social mainstream and more prone to criminal activity. Minority-group members living in these areas also suffer race-based inequality, including income inequality and institutional racism.

money for new housing or businesses.[52] Areas marked by concentrated poverty become isolated and insulated from the social mainstream and more prone to criminal activity. Ethnically and racially isolated areas maintain the highest crime rates.[53] Minority-group members living in these areas also suffer race-based inequality, including income inequality and institutional racism.[54] Gangs may also concentrate in these areas, bringing with them a significant increase in criminal activity.[55]

LO4 Collective Efficacy

Cohesive communities with high levels of social control develop collective efficacy: mutual trust, a willingness to intervene in the supervision of children, and the maintenance of public order.[56] In contrast, socially disorganized neighbourhoods find that efforts at social control are weak and attenuated. When community social control efforts are blunted,

crime rates increase, further weakening neighbourhood cohesiveness.

In October 2010 the Ontario Association of Chiefs of Police unveiled a new model and direction for community policing in Ontario (see Figure 6.6). The new model incorporates virtually all of the features of social disorganization theory we talked about above—including the relationship between poverty, substandard housing, addictions, and social disorder—along with the need to identify and assess the extent to which each community has the resources to demonstrate "collective efficacy" in organizing and mobilizing community resources to address crime and disorder problems.

Neighbourhoods maintain a variety of agencies and institutions of social control. Some operate on the primary or private level, involving the control placed on people by their peers and families. These sources exert informal control by either awarding or withholding approval, respect, and admiration. Informal control mechanisms include direct criticism, ridicule, ostracism, desertion, or physical punishment.[57] For example, families may exert control by corporal punishment, withholding privileges, or ridiculing lazy or disrespectful children. Communities also use internal networks and local institutions to control crime. Sources of institutional social control include businesses, schools, religious institutions, and social service and volunteer organizations.[58]

Stable neighbourhoods can arrange for external sources of social control. The level of policing, an important source of neighbourhood stability, may vary among neighbourhoods. Police officers patrolling in stable, low-crime areas may have the resources and motivation to respond vigorously to crime, preventing criminal groups from gaining a toehold in the neighbourhood.[59] Community organizations and local leaders may have sufficient political clout to get funding for additional law enforcement personnel. The presence of police sends a message that the area will not tolerate deviant behaviour. Criminals and drug dealers avoid such areas and relocate to easier and more appealing targets.[60] In more disorganized areas, police officers are less motivated, and their resources are stretched more tightly. These communities cannot mount an effective social control effort because as neighbourhood disadvantage increases, informal social control decreases.[61]

The ramifications of having adequate controls are critical. In areas where collective efficacy remains high, children are less likely to become involved with deviant peers and engage in problem behaviours.[62] In

collective efficacy
Social control exerted by cohesive communities, based on mutual trust, including intervention in the supervision of children and maintenance of public order.

FIGURE 6.6

Ontario's Mobilization & Engagement Model of Community Policing

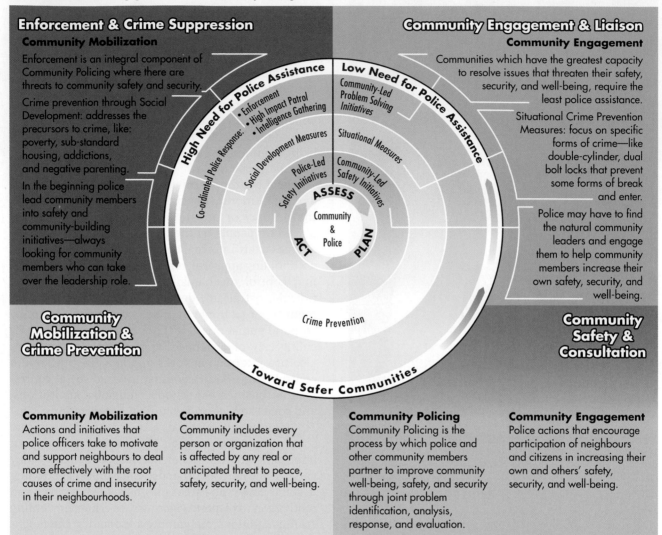

Enforcement & Crime Suppression

Community Mobilization

Enforcement is an integral component of Community Policing where there are threats to community safety and security.

Crime prevention through Social Development: addresses the precursors to crime, like: poverty, sub-standard housing, addictions, and negative parenting.

In the beginning police lead community members into safety and community-building initiatives—always looking for community members who can take over the leadership role.

Community Engagement & Liaison

Community Engagement

Communities which have the greatest capacity to resolve issues that threaten their safety, security, and well-being, require the least police assistance.

Situational Crime Prevention Measures: focus on specific forms of crime—like double-cylinder, dual bolt locks that prevent some forms of break and enter.

Police may have to find the natural community leaders and engage them to help community members increase their own safety, security, and well-being.

*(Diagram labels:)*

High Need for Police Assistance
- Enforcement
- High Impact Patrol
- Intelligence Gathering

Co-ordinated Police Response

Social Development Measures

Police-Led Safety Initiatives

Low Need for Police Assistance

Community-Led Problem Solving Initiatives

Situational Measures

Community-Led Safety Initiatives

ASSESS

Community & Police

PLAN

ACT

Crime Prevention

Toward Safer Communities

Community Mobilization & Crime Prevention

Community Safety & Consultation

Community Mobilization
Actions and initiatives that police officers take to motivate and support neighbours to deal more effectively with the root causes of crime and insecurity in their neighbourhoods.

Community
Community includes every person or organization that is affected by any real or anticipated threat to peace, safety, security, and well-being.

Community Policing
Community Policing is the process by which police and other community members partner to improve community well-being, safety, and security through joint problem identification, analysis, response, and evaluation.

Community Engagement
Police actions that encourage participation of neighbours and citizens in increasing their own and others' safety, security, and well-being.

Source: Ontario's Mobilization & Engagement Model of Community Policing, used by permission of the Ontario Association of Chiefs of Police.

---

disorganized areas, however, the population is transient, so interpersonal relationships remain superficial. Social institutions such as schools and religious institutions cannot work effectively in a climate of alienation and mistrust. In these areas, the absence of political power brokers limits access to external funding and protection; without outside money, the neighbourhood cannot get back on its feet.[63] Children who live in these neighbourhoods find that involvement with conventional social institutions, such as schools and afternoon programs, is blocked; they are instead at risk for involvement in delinquent behaviour, or recruitment into gangs.[64] These problems are stubborn and difficult to overcome. And even when an attempt is made to revitalize a disorganized neighbourhood by creating institutional

People lining up for food in downtown Winnipeg outside the Siloam Mission. It is estimated that over 130 000 Manitobans live in poverty.

Winnipeg Free Press

- Shaw and McKay first identified the concepts central to social disorganization. They found stable patterns of crime in the central city.

- Strain theories hold that economic deprivation causes frustration, which leads to crime.

- According to Merton's anomie theory, many people who desire material goods and other forms of economic success lack the means to achieve their goals. Some may turn to crime.

- Messner and Rosenfeld's institutional anomie theory argues that the goal of success at all costs has invaded every aspect of North American life.

- Agnew's general theory of strain suggests that there is more than one source of anomie.

FIGURE 6.7

The Basic Compounds of Strain Theory

Poverty
- Development of isolated lower-class culture
- Lack of conventional social opportunities
- Racial and ethnic discrimination

Maintenance of conventional rules and norms
Lower-class citizens remain loyal to conventional values and rules of dominant middle-class culture.

Strain
Lack of opportunity coupled with desire for conventional success produces strain and frustration.

Formation of gangs and groups
Youths form law-violating groups to seek alternative means of achieving success.

Crime and delinquency
Methods of groups—theft, violence, substance abuse—are defined as illegal by dominant culture.

Criminal careers
Most youthful gang members "age out" of crime, but some continue as adult criminals.

support programs such as community centres and better schools, the effort may be countered by the ongoing drain of deep-rooted economic and social deprivation.[65]

According to the social ecology school, then, social disorganization produces criminality. The quality of community life, including levels of change, fear, incivility, poverty, and deterioration, directly influences an area's crime rate. It is not some individual property or trait that causes some people to commit crime, but rather the quality and ambience of the community in which they live. Conversely, in socially altruistic areas, crime rates decrease no matter what the economic situation.

LO5 Strain Theories

Inhabitants of a disorganized inner-city area feel isolated, frustrated, ostracized from the economic mainstream, hopeless, and eventually angry. How do these feelings affect criminal activities?

Strain theorists view crime as a direct result of lower-class frustration and anger. They believe that although most people share similar values and goals, the ability to achieve personal goals is stratified by socioeconomic class. Strain is limited in affluent areas because educational and vocational opportunities are available. In disorganized areas, strain occurs because legitimate avenues for success are all but closed. To relieve strain, indigent people may achieve their goals through deviant methods, such as theft or drug trafficking, or they may reject socially accepted goals and substitute more deviant goals, such as being tough and aggressive (see Figure 6.7).

Theory of Anomie

Sociologist Robert Merton applied the sociological concepts first identified by Emile Durkheim to criminology in his theory of anomie.[66]

Merton found that two elements of culture interact to produce potentially anomic conditions: culturally defined goals and socially approved means for obtaining them. For example, modern societies stress the goals of acquiring wealth, success, and power. Socially permissible means include hard work, education, and thrift.

Merton argues that the legitimate means to acquire wealth are stratified across class and status lines. Those

> **anomie**
> According to Durkheim, anomie reflects a lack of norms or clear social standards. Because of rapidly shifting moral values, the individual has few guides to what is socially acceptable.

with little formal education and few economic resources soon find that they are denied the ability to legally acquire wealth—the preeminent success symbol. When socially mandated goals are uniform throughout society and access to legitimate means is bound by class and status, the resulting strain produces anomie among those who are locked out of the legitimate opportunity structure. Consequently, they may develop criminal or delinquent solutions to the problem of attaining goals.

Social Adaptations

Merton argues that each person has his or her own concept of society's goals and means to attain them. Some people have inadequate means of attaining success; others who have the means reject societal goals. The result is a variety of social adaptations:

1. *Conformity.* Conformity occurs when individuals embrace conventional social goals and also have the means to attain them. They remain law abiding.

2. *Innovation.* Innovation occurs when individuals accept the goals of society but are unable or unwilling to attain them through legitimate means. The resulting conflict forces them to adopt innovative solutions to their dilemma: they steal, sell drugs, or extort money. Of the five adaptations, innovation is most closely associated with criminal behaviour.

3. *Ritualism.* Ritualists gain pleasure from practising traditional ceremonies, regardless of whether they have a real purpose or a goal. The strict customs in religious orders, feudal societies, clubs, and university fraternities encourage and appeal to ritualists. Ritualists should have the lowest level of criminal behaviour because they have abandoned the success goal, which is at the root of criminal activity.

4. *Retreatism.* Retreatists reject both the goals and the means of society. They attempt to escape their lack of success by withdrawing, either mentally or physically, by taking drugs or becoming drifters.

5. *Rebellion.* Rebellion involves substituting an alternative set of goals and means for conventional ones. Revolutionaries who wish to promote radical change in the existing social structure and who call for alternative lifestyles, goals, and beliefs are engaging in rebellion. Rebellion may be a reaction against a corrupt, hated government or an effort to create alternative opportunities and lifestyles within the existing system.

Evaluation of Anomie Theory

According to anomie theory, social inequality leads to perceptions of anomie. To resolve the goals-means conflict and relieve their sense of strain, some people innovate by stealing or extorting money; others retreat into drugs and alcohol; some rebel by joining revolutionary groups; and still others get involved in ritualistic behaviour by joining a religious cult.

Merton's view of anomie has been one of the most enduring and influential sociological theories of criminality. By linking deviant behaviour to the success goals that control social behaviour, anomie theory attempts to pinpoint the cause of the conflict that produces personal frustration and consequent criminality. By acknowledging that society unfairly distributes the legitimate means to achieving success, anomie theory helps explain the existence of high-crime areas and the apparent predominance of delinquent and criminal behaviour in the lower class. By suggesting that social conditions, not individual personalities, produce crime, Merton greatly influenced the directions taken to reduce and control criminality during the latter half of the 20th century.

A number of questions are left unanswered by anomie theory.[67] Merton does not explain why people choose to commit certain types of crime. For example, why does one anomic person become a mugger while another deals drugs? Anomie may explain differences in crime rates, but it cannot explain why most young criminals desist from crime as adults. Does this mean that perceptions of anomie dwindle with age? Is anomie short lived?

Institutional Anomie Theory

Steven Messner and Richard Rosenfeld's institutional anomie theory is an updating of Merton's work.[68]

Messner and Rosenfeld agree with Merton that the success goal is pervasive in North American culture. For them, the "American Dream" refers to both a goal and a process. As a goal, it involves accumulating material goods and wealth via open individual competition. As a process, it involves both being socialized to pursue material success and believing that prosperity is achievable. Anomic conditions arise because the desire to succeed at any cost drives people apart, weakens the collective sense of community, fosters ambition, and restricts the desire to achieve anything other than material wealth. Achieving respect, for example, is not sufficient.

Why does anomie pervade modern culture? According to Messner and Rosenfeld, it is because institutions that might otherwise control the exaggerated emphasis on financial success, such as religious or charitable institutions, have been rendered powerless or obsolete. These social institutions have been undermined in three ways:

1. *Noneconomic functions and roles have been devalued.* Performance in other institutional settings—the family, school, or community—is assigned a lower priority than the goal of financial success.

2. *When conflicts emerge, noneconomic roles become subordinate to and must accommodate economic roles.* The schedules, routines, and demands of the workplace take priority over those of the home, the school, the community, and other aspects of social life.

3. *Economic language, standards, and norms penetrate into noneconomic realms.* Economic terms become part of the common vernacular: People want to get to the "bottom line." Spouses view themselves as "partners" who "manage" the household. Retired people say they want to "downsize" their household. We "outsource" home repairs instead of doing them ourselves. Corporate leaders run for public office promising to "run the country like a business."

According to Messner and Rosenfeld, the relatively high crime rates in many modern societies can be explained by the interrelationship between culture and institutions. At the cultural level, the dominance of the "Canadian Dream" mythology ensures that many people will develop desires for material goods that cannot be satisfied by legitimate means. Anomie becomes a norm, and extralegal means become a strategy for attaining material wealth. At the institutional level, the dominance of economic concerns weakens the informal social control exerted by family, religious institutions, and school. These institutions have lost their ability to regulate behaviour and have instead become a conduit for promoting material success. For example, schools are evaluated not for imparting knowledge but for their ability to train students to get high-paying jobs. Social conditions

Owning your own home is still an integral part of the Canadian dream.

reinforce each other: Culture determines institutions, and institutional change influences culture. Crime rates may rise in a healthy economy because national prosperity heightens the attractiveness of monetary rewards, encouraging people to gain financial success by any means possible, including illegal ones. In this culture of competition, self-interest prevails and generates amorality, acceptance of inequality, and disdain for the less fortunate.[69]

> **general strain theory (GST)**
> The view that multiple sources of strain interact with an individual's emotional traits and responses to produce criminality.
>
> **negative affective states**
> Anger, frustration, and adverse emotions produced by a variety of sources of strain.

General Strain Theory (GST)

Sociologist Robert Agnew's **general strain theory (GST)** helps identify the micro- or individual-level influences of strain. Whereas Merton and Messner and Rosenfeld try to explain social class differences in the crime rate, Agnew tries to explain why individuals who feel stress and strain are likely to commit crimes. Agnew also attempts to offer a more general explanation of criminal activity among all elements of society rather than restrict his views to lower-class crime.[70]

Multiple Sources of Strain

Agnew suggests that criminality is the direct result of **negative affective states**—the anger, frustration, and adverse emotions that emerge in the wake of destructive social relationships. He finds that negative affective states are produced by a variety of sources of strain (see Figure 6.8):

- *Failure to achieve positively valued goals.* This cause of strain, similar to what Merton speaks of in his theory of anomie, is a result of the disjunction between aspirations and expectations. This type of strain occurs when a youth aspires to wealth and fame but, lacking financial and educational resources, assumes that such goals are impossible to achieve; he then turns to crime and drug dealing.

- *Disjunction of expectations and achievements.* Strain can also be produced by a disjunction between expectations and achievements. When people compare themselves to peers who seem to be doing a lot better financially or socially (such as making more money or getting better grades), even those doing relatively well feel strain. For example, when a student graduating high school is accepted at a good college or university but not a prestige school, like some of her friends, she will feel strain. Perhaps she is not being treated fairly because the playing field is tilted against her: "Other kids have connections," she may say. Perceptions of inequity may result in many adverse reactions, ranging from running away from its source to lowering others' benefits through physical attacks or property vandalism.

FIGURE 6.8

Elements of General Strain Theory (GST)

Sources of strain

| Failure to achieve goals |
| Disjunction of expectations and achievements |
| Removal of positive stimuli |
| Presentation of negative stimuli |

Negative affective states

- Anger
- Frustration
- Disappointment
- Depression
- Fear

Antisocial behaviour

- Drug abuse
- Delinquency
- Violence
- Dropping out

- *Removal of positively valued stimuli.* Strain may occur because of the actual or anticipated loss of positively valued stimuli.[71] For example, the loss of a girl- or boyfriend can produce strain, as can the death of a loved one, moving to a new neighbourhood or school, or the divorce or separation of parents. The loss of positive stimuli may lead to delinquency as the adolescent tries to prevent the loss, retrieve what has been lost, obtain substitutes, or seek revenge against those responsible for the loss.

- *Presentation of negative stimuli.* Strain may also be caused by negative or noxious stimuli, such as child abuse or neglect, crime victimization, physical punishment, family or peer conflict, school failure, or stressful life events ranging from verbal threats to air pollution. For example, adolescent delinquency has been linked to maltreatment through the rage and anger it generates. Children who are abused at home may take out their rage on younger children at school or become involved in violent delinquency.[72]

Although these sources of strain are independent of one another, they may overlap. For example, if a teacher insults a student, it may be viewed as an unfair application of negative stimuli that interferes with a student's academic aspirations. The greater the intensity and frequency of strain experiences, the greater their impact and the more likely they are to cause delinquency.

According to Agnew, each type of strain increases the likelihood of experiencing negative emotions such as disappointment, depression, fear, and most important, anger. Anger increases perceptions of injury and of being wronged. It produces a desire for revenge, energizes individuals to take action, and lowers inhibitions. Violence and aggression seem justified if you have been wronged and are righteously angry. Because it produces these emotions, chronic, repetitive strain can be considered a predisposing factor for delinquency when it creates a hostile, suspicious, aggressive attitude. Individual strain episodes may trigger delinquency, such as when a particularly stressful event ignites a violent reaction.

Coping with Strain

Not all people who experience strain eventually resort to criminality. Some are able to marshal their emotional, mental, and behavioural resources to cope with the anger and frustration produced by strain. Some individuals may be able to rationalize frustrating circumstances: Getting a good job is "just not that important"; they may be poor, but the "next guy is worse off"; if things didn't work out, they "got what [they] deserved." Others seek behavioural solutions, running away from adverse conditions or seeking revenge against those who caused the strain. Some try to regain emotional equilibrium with techniques ranging from physical exercise to drug abuse.

However, some people cannot cope with strain because they have traits that make them particularly sensitive to strain. These include an explosive temperament, low tolerance for adversity, poor problem-solving skills, and being overly sensitive or emotional. Although these traits, which are linked to aggressive, antisocial behaviour, seem to be stable over the life cycle, they may peak during adolescence.[73] This is a period of social stress caused by weakening parental supervision and the development of relationships with a diverse peer group. Many adolescents going through the trauma of family breakup and frequent changes in family structure feel a high degree of strain. They may react by becoming involved in precocious sexuality or by turning to substance abuse to mask the strain.[74]

As children mature, their expectations increase. Some are unable to meet academic and social demands. Adolescents are very concerned about their standing with peers. Teenagers who are deficient in these areas may find they are social outcasts, another source of strain. In adulthood, crime rates may drop because these sources of strain are reduced. New sources of self-esteem emerge, and adults seem more likely to align their goals with reality.

Evaluating GST

Agnew's important work both clarifies the concept of strain and directs future research agendas. It also adds to the body of literature describing how social and life history events influence offending patterns. Because sources of strain vary over the life course, so too do crime rates.

There is also empirical support for GST.[75] Some research efforts have shown that indicators of strain—family breakup, unemployment, moving, feelings of dissatisfaction with friends and school, dropping out of school—are positively related to criminality.[76]

As predicted by GST, people who report feelings of stress and anger are more likely to interact with delinquent peers and to engage in criminal behaviours.[77] Lashing out at others may reduce feelings of strain, as may stealing or vandalizing property.[78] There is also evidence that, as predicted by the GST, people who fail to meet success goals are more likely to engage in criminal activities.[79]

Cultural Deviance Theory

The third branch of social structure theory combines the effects of social disorganization and strain to explain how people living in deteriorated neighbourhoods react to social isolation and economic deprivation. Because their lifestyle is draining, frustrating, and dispiriting, members of the lower class create an independent subculture with its own set of rules and values. Although middle-class culture stresses hard work, delayed gratification, formal education, and being cautious, the lower-class subculture stresses excitement, toughness, taking risks, fearlessness, immediate gratification, and street smarts.

The lower-class subculture is an attractive alternative because the urban poor find it impossible to meet the behavioural demands of middle-class society. However, subcultural norms often clash with conventional values. Urban dwellers are forced to violate the law because they obey the rules of the deviant culture with which they are in immediate contact (see Figure 6.9).

More than 40 years ago, sociologist Walter Miller identified the unique conduct norms that help define lower-class culture.[80] Miller referred to them as focal concerns, values that have evolved specifically to fit conditions in lower-class environments. The major lower-class focal concerns are set out in Table 6.1.[81]

According to Miller, clinging to lower-class focal concerns promotes illegal or violent behaviour. Toughness may mean displaying fighting prowess; street smarts may lead to drug deals; excitement may result in drinking, gambling, or drug abuse.[82] To illustrate, consider a study of violent young men in New York, conducted by sociologist Jeffrey Fagan.

FIGURE 6.9

Elements of Cultural Deviance Theory

Poverty
- Lack of opportunity
- Feeling of oppression

Socialization
Lower-class youths are socialized to value middle-class goals and ideas. However, their environment inhibits proper socialization.

Subculture
Blocked opportunities prompt formation of groups with alternative lifestyles and values.

Success goal
Gangs provide alternative methods of gaining success for some, venting anger for others.

Crime and delinquency
New methods of gaining success involve law-violating behaviour.

Criminal careers
Some gang boys can parlay their status into criminal careers; others become drug users or violent assaulters.

He found that the most compelling function that violence served was to develop status as a "tough," an identity that helps young men acquire social power while at the same time insulating them from becoming victims. Violence was also seen as a means to acquire the trappings of wealth (such as nice clothes, flashy cars, or access to clubs), control or humiliate another person, defy authority, settle drug-related disputes, attain retribution, satisfy the need for thrills or risk taking, and respond to challenges to one's manhood.[83] Lower-class focal concerns seem as relevant today as when they were first identified by Miller more than 40 years ago!

focal concerns Values, such as toughness and street smarts, that have evolved specifically to fit conditions in lower-class environments.

TABLE 6.1

Miller's Lower-Class Focal Concerns

Trouble	In lower-class communities, people are evaluated by their actual or potential involvement in making trouble. Getting into trouble includes such behaviours as fighting, drinking, and sexual misconduct. Dealing with trouble can confer prestige—for example, when a man establishes a reputation for being able to handle himself well in a fight. Not being able to handle trouble, and having to pay the consequences, can make a person look foolish and incompetent.
Toughness	Lower-class males want local recognition of their physical and spiritual toughness. They refuse to be sentimental or soft and instead value physical strength, fighting ability, and athletic skill. Those who cannot meet these standards risk getting a reputation for being weak, inept, and effeminate.
Smartness	Members of the lower-class culture want to maintain an image of being streetwise and savvy, using their street smarts, and having the ability to outfox and out-con the opponent. Although formal education is not admired, knowing essential survival techniques, such as gambling, conning, and outsmarting the law, is a requirement.
Excitement	Members of the lower class search for fun and excitement to enliven an otherwise drab existence. The search for excitement may lead to gambling, fighting, getting drunk, and sexual adventures. In between, the lower-class citizen may simply "hang out" and "be cool."
Fate	Lower-class citizens believe their lives are in the hands of strong spiritual forces that guide their destinies. Getting lucky, finding good fortune, and hitting the jackpot are all daily dreams.
Autonomy	Being independent of authority figures, such as the police, teachers, and parents, is required; losing control is an unacceptable weakness, incompatible with toughness.

Source: Walter Miller, "Lower-Class Culture as a Generating Milieu of Gang Delinquency," from *Journal of Social Issues*, v14 (1958), p. 5–19. Reprinted by permission of John Wiley and Sons via Rightslink.

Theory of Delinquent Subcultures

Albert Cohen first articulated the theory of delinquent subcultures in his classic 1955 book, *Delinquent Boys*.[84] Cohen's central position was that delinquent behaviour of lower-class youths is actually a protest against the norms and values of modern middle-class culture. Because social conditions prevent them from achieving success legitimately, lower-class youths experience a form of culture conflict that Cohen labels status frustration.[85] As a result, many of them join gangs and engage in behaviour that is "non-utilitarian, malicious, and negativistic."[86]

Cohen viewed the delinquent gang as a separate subculture, possessing a value system directly opposed to that of the larger society. He described the subculture as one that "takes its norms from the larger culture, but turns them upside down. The delinquent's conduct is right by the standards of his subculture precisely because it is wrong by the norms of the larger culture."[87]

According to Cohen, the development of the delinquent subculture is a consequence of socialization practices in lower-class environments. Here children lack the basic skills necessary to achieve social and economic success, including a proper education, which renders them incapable of developing the skills to succeed in society. Lower-class parents are incapable of teaching children the necessary techniques for entering the dominant middle-class culture. The consequences of this deprivation include developmental handicaps, poor speech and communication skills, and inability to delay gratification.

Middle-Class Measuring Rods

One significant handicap that lower-class children face is the inability to positively impress authority figures, such as teachers, employers, or supervisors. In North American society, these positions tend to be held by members of the middle class, who have difficulty relating to the lower-class youngster. Cohen calls the standards set by these authority figures middle-class measuring rods.

The conflict and frustration lower-class youths experience when they fail to meet these standards is a primary cause of delinquency. They may find themselves prejudged by others and not measuring up in the final analysis. Negative evaluations become part of a permanent file that follows an individual for the rest of his or her life. When he or she wants to improve, evidence of prior failures is used to discourage advancement.

The Formation of Deviant Subcultures

Cohen believes that lower-class boys rejected by middle-class decision makers usually join one of

delinquent subculture
A value system adopted by lower-class youths that is directly opposed to that of the larger society.

status frustration
A form of culture conflict experienced by lower-class youths because social conditions prevent them from achieving success as defined by the larger society.

middle-class measuring rods
The standards by which authority figures, such as teachers and employers, evaluate lower-class youngsters and often prejudge them negatively.

According to Cohen, the development of the delinquent subculture is a consequence of socialization practices in lower-class environments. The conflict and frustration young people experience when they fail to meet these standards is a primary cause of delinquency.

three existing subcultures: the corner boy, the college boy, or the delinquent boy.

The corner boy role is the most common response to middle-class rejection. The corner boy is not a chronic delinquent but may be a truant who engages in petty or status offences, such as precocious sex and recreational drug abuse. His main loyalty is to his peer group, on which he depends for support, motivation, and interest. His values, therefore, are those of the group with which he is in close contact. The corner boy, well aware of his failure to achieve the standards of the "Canadian Dream," retreats into the comforting world of his lower-class peers and eventually becomes a stable member of his neighbourhood, holding a menial job, marrying, and remaining in the community.

The corner boy role is the most common response to middle-class rejection. The corner boy is not a chronic delinquent but may be a truant who engages in petty or status offences. His main loyalty is to his peer group, on which he depends for support, motivation, and interest.

The college boy embraces the cultural and social values of the middle class. Rather than scorning middle-class measuring rods, he actively strives to succeed by those standards. Cohen views this type of youth as one who is embarking on an almost hopeless path because he is ill equipped academically, socially, and linguistically to achieve the rewards of middle-class life.

The delinquent boy adopts a set of norms and principles that directly oppose middle-class values. He engages in *short-run hedonism*, living for today and letting "tomorrow take care of itself."[88] Delinquent boys strive for group autonomy. They resist efforts by family, school, or other sources of authority to control their behaviour. Frustrated by their inability to succeed, these boys resort to a process Cohen calls reaction formation, including overly intense responses that seem disproportionate to the stimuli that trigger them. For the delinquent boy, this takes the form of irrational, malicious, and unaccountable hostility to the enemy, which in this case is "the norms of respectable middle-class society."[89]

Cohen's approach skillfully integrates strain and social disorganization theories and has become an enduring element of criminological literature.

LO6 Theory of Differential Opportunity

In their classic work *Delinquency and Opportunity*, written more than 40 years ago, Richard Cloward and Lloyd Ohlin combined strain and social disorganization principles to portray a gang-sustaining criminal subculture.[90]

The centrepiece of the Cloward and Ohlin theory is the concept of differential opportunity. According to this concept, people in all strata of society share the same success goals; however, those in the lower class have limited means of achieving them. People who perceive themselves as failures within conventional society will seek alternative or innovative ways to succeed. People who conclude that there is little hope for legitimate advancement may join like-minded peers to form a gang, which can provide them with emotional support. The youth who is considered a failure at school and is qualified for only a menial job at a minimum wage can earn thousands of dollars

reaction formation
Irrational hostility evidenced by young delinquents, who adopt norms directly opposed to middle-class goals and standards that seem impossible to achieve.

differential opportunity
The view that lower-class youths, whose legitimate opportunities are limited, join gangs and pursue criminal careers as alternative means to achieve universal success goals.

Recently, Winnipeg was named the most violent major city in Canada. Interestingly, in 2012, 80 of the more than 200 neighbourhoods in Winnipeg didn't report a single robbery. The Western, Eastern, and Southern portions of the city are, relatively speaking, far cleaner with little social disorder. Yet, in the highly concentrated Northern section of the city, referred to as the William Whyte neighbourhood, sexual assault, rape, and other forms of violent crime are as rampant as anywhere in Canada.

The notorious neighbourhoods that make up the North-Central portion of Winnipeg reported double the crime rate of comparable cities in the United States. The average crime rate in William Whyte is triple that of many neighbourhoods in Canada and even quadruple the rate in others. In the first nine months of 2010, there were Since January 2010, there have been ten shootings, 95 residential break and enters, and nearly 90 robberies in the small area bordered by Alfred Avenue on the north and Selkirk Avenue to the south, Salter Street on the east and McGregor Street on the west.[91]

Most of Winnipeg ranks very low on the crime index, and the city as a whole is enjoying something of a renaissance. Let's hope North-Central Winnipeg can enjoy a rebirth and a new, more peaceful beginning in the future as well.

Social structure theorists believe that social and economic forces operating in deteriorated lower-class areas such as North Winnipeg push many of their residents into criminal behaviour patterns.

You have accepted a position in Ottawa as an executive assistant to a newly formed federal–provincial task force on urban development. The chairperson of the committee informs you that he wants to initiate a demonstration project to show that governments can have an impact on reducing poverty, crime, and drug abuse.

The area he has chosen is North Winnipeg. It suffers disorganized community structure, poverty, and hopelessness. There are youth gangs operating in the neighbourhood, harassing local merchants and citizens. The school system has failed to provide opportunities and educational experiences sufficient to dampen enthusiasm for gang recruitment. Stores and homes in the area are in a dilapidated condition. Commercial enterprise has fled the area. There is an uneasy truce among the varied ethnic and racial groups that populate the area. Residents feel that little can be done to bring the neighbourhood back to life. Merchants are afraid to open stores at night for fear of being robbed, and there is little hope of outside development from major retailers or manufacturers. People who want to start their own businesses find that banks will not lend them money.

One of the biggest problems has been the large concentration of low-income dwellings, which are now overcrowded and increasingly deteriorated. Even the police are reluctant to enter some of the buildings unless they have backup. Drug dealing carries on openly outside some of the buildings, and residents are afraid to report dealers to the police for fear of reprisals.

You are asked to propose an urban redevelopment program to revitalize the area and eventually bring down the crime rate. You can bring any public or private element to bear on this overwhelming problem. You can also ask private industry to help in the struggle, promising them tax breaks for their participation. What programs would you recommend to break the cycle of urban poverty?

plus the respect of his or her peers by joining a gang and engaging in drug deals or armed robberies.

Cloward and Ohlin recognize that the opportunity for success in both conventional and criminal careers is limited. In stable areas, adolescents may be recruited by professional criminals, drug traffickers, or organized crime groups. Unstable areas, however, cannot support flourishing criminal opportunities. In these socially disorganized neighbourhoods, adult role models are absent, and young criminals have few opportunities to join established gangs or learn the fine points of professional crime. Cloward and Ohlin's most important finding, then, is that all opportunities for success, both illegal and conventional, are closed for the most disadvantaged youths.

Because of differential opportunity, young people are likely to join one of three types of gangs:

1. *Criminal gangs.* Criminal gangs exist in stable neighbourhoods where close connections among adolescent, young adult, and adult offenders create an environment for successful criminal enterprise.[92] Youths are recruited into established criminal gangs that provide training for a successful criminal career. Gang membership is a learning experience in which the knowledge and skills needed for success in crime are acquired. During this apprenticeship, older, more experienced members of the criminal subculture hold youthful trainees on tight reins, limiting activities that might jeopardize the gang's profits (e.g., engaging in nonfunctional, irrational violence).

2. *Conflict gangs.* Conflict gangs develop in communities unable to provide either legitimate or illegitimate opportunities.[93] These gangs attract tough adolescents who fight with weapons to win respect from rivals and engage in unpredictable and destructive assaults on people and property. Conflict gang members must be ready to fight to protect their own and their gang's integrity and honour. By doing so, they acquire a "rep," which gains admiration from their peers and consequently helps them develop their self-image.

3. *Retreatist gangs.* Retreatists are double failures, unable to gain success through legitimate means and unwilling to do so through illegal ones. Members of the retreatist subculture constantly search for ways of getting high—alcohol, pot, heroin, unusual sexual experiences, music. To feed their habits, retreatists develop a "hustle"—pimping, conning, selling drugs, or committing petty crimes. Personal status in the retreatist subculture is derived from peer approval.

Cloward and Ohlin's theory integrates cultural deviance and social disorganization variables and recognizes different modes of criminal adaptation. The fact that criminal cultures can be supportive, rational, and profitable seems to more realistically reflect the actual world of the delinquent than Cohen's original view of purely negativistic, destructive delinquent youths who oppose all social values.

Social Structure Theory and Social Policy

Social structure theory has significantly influenced social policy. If the cause of criminality is viewed as a schism between lower-class individuals and conventional goals, norms, and rules, it seems logical that alternatives to criminal behaviour can be provided by giving inner-city youth opportunities to share in the rewards of conventional society.

One approach is to give indigent people direct financial aid through public assistance or welfare. Although welfare has been curtailed under many provincial governments in Canada, U.S. research shows that crime rates decrease when families receive supplemental income through public assistance payments.[94]

Efforts have also been made to reduce crime by improving the community structure in high-crime neighbourhoods. Crime prevention efforts based on social structure precepts can be traced back to the Chicago Area Project supervised by Clifford R. Shaw. This program attempted to organize existing community structures to develop social stability in otherwise disorganized slums. The project sponsored recreation programs for neighbourhood children, including summer camping. It campaigned for community improvements in areas such as education, sanitation, traffic safety, resource conservation, and law enforcement. Project members also worked with police and court agencies to supervise and treat gang youth and adult offenders. Today, Shaw's legacy continues on in ambitious projects like Hamilton, Ontario's "Neighbourhood Safety Project," where police officers and community development staff work with neighbourhood associations to address the whole gamut of neighbourhood problems, including crime and public order issues.[95]

Social structure concepts, especially Cloward and Ohlin's views, were a critical ingredient in "War on Poverty" initiatives begun in the United States in the early 1960s. Similar programs in both the United States and Canada—including Head Start, Neighbourhood Legal Services, the Community Action Program, breakfast clubs for school-age children, and after-school homework and recreation programs—have continued to help people.

Summary

Sociology has been the main orientation of criminologists because they know that crime rates vary among elements of the social structure, that society goes through changes that affect crime, and that social interaction relates to criminality. Social structure theories suggest that people's places in the socioeconomic structure influence their chances of becoming a criminal. Poor people are more likely to commit crimes because they are unable to achieve monetary or social success in any other way. Social structure theory includes three schools of thought: social disorganization, strain, and cultural deviance theories.

Social disorganization theory suggests that slum dwellers violate the law because they live in areas in which social control has broken down. The origin of social disorganization theory can be traced to the work of Clifford R. Shaw and Henry D. McKay. Shaw and McKay concluded that disorganized areas, marked by divergent values and transitional populations, produce criminality. In response to contemporary criticisms of social disorganization theory, social ecology theory has developed. It looks at issues such as community fear, unemployment, and community deterioration.

Strain theories view crime as resulting from the anger people experience over their inability to achieve legitimate social and economic success. Strain theories hold that most people share common values and beliefs, but the ability to achieve them is differentiated by the social structure. The best-known strain theory is Robert Merton's theory of anomie, which describes what happens when people have inadequate means to satisfy their goals. Steven Messner and Richard Rosenfeld show that North American culture produces strain, and Robert Agnew suggests that strain has multiple sources.

Cultural deviance theories hold that a unique value system develops in lower-class areas. Lower-class values approve of behaviours such as being tough, never showing fear, and defying authority. People perceiving strain will bond together in their own groups or subcultures for support and recognition. Albert Cohen links the formation of subcultures to the failure of lower-class citizens to achieve recognition from middle-class decision makers, such as teachers, employers, and police officers. Richard Cloward and Lloyd Ohlin have argued that crime results from lower-class people's perception that their opportunity for success is limited. Consequently, youths in low-income areas may join criminal, conflict, or retreatist gangs.

Discussion Questions

1. Is there a "transitional" area in your town or city? Does the crime rate remain constant there, regardless of who moves in or out?

2. Is it possible that a distinct lower-class culture exists? Do you know anyone who has the focal concerns Miller talks about? Were there "focal concerns" in your high school, college, or university experience?

3. Have you ever perceived anomie? What causes anomie? Is there more than one cause of strain?

4. How would Merton explain middle-class crime? How would Agnew?

5. Could "relative deprivation" produce crime among university-educated white-collar workers?

READY TO STUDY?

IN THE BOOK, YOU CAN:

✔ Check your understanding of what you've just read by reading the Summary at the end of each chapter.

✔ Rip out the Chapter in Review card at the back of the book to have the key terms and Learning Objectives handy, and complete the quizzes provided (answers are at the bottom of the back page!).

ONLINE YOU CAN:

✔ Stay organized and efficient with MindTap—a single destination with all the course material and study aids you need to succeed. Built-in apps leverage social media and the latest learning technology. For example:

✔ ReadSpeaker will read the text to you.

✔ Flashcards are pre-populated to provide you with a jump start for review—or you can create your own.

✔ You can highlight text and make notes in your MindTap Reader. Your notes will flow into Evernote, the electronic notebook app that you can access anywhere when it's time to study for the exam.

✔ Prepare for tests with quizzes.

Go to www.nelson.com/student to access these digital resources.

Socialization and Crime

Learning Objectives

LO1 Describe how social process theories view criminality and explain why they have endured.

LO2 Debate the significance of family factors in predicting behaviour.

LO3 Demonstrate how the educational process and adolescent school achievement have been linked to criminality.

LO4 Evaluate the significance of peer

LO5 Differentiate between social learning theory and social control theory.

LO6 Contrast differential association theory and neutralization theory.

LO7 Describe how Travis Hirschi's contemporary social control theory explains why people obey the law.

LO8 Discuss why critics have charged that labelling theory lacks credibility.

Zikomo/SuperStock

LO1 Socialization and Crime

Some criminologists focus their attention on social–psychological processes and interactions common to people in all segments of the social structure, not just the lower class. They believe that criminality is a function of individual socialization and the interactions people have with various organizations, institutions, and processes of society. Most people are influenced by their family relationships, peer group associations, educational experiences, and interactions with authority figures, including teachers, employers, and agents of the justice system. If these relationships are positive and supportive, people can succeed within the rules of society; if these relationships are dysfunctional and destructive, conventional success may be impossible, and criminal solutions may become a feasible alternative. Taken together, this view of crime is referred to as social process theory.

Social process theories share one basic concept: All people, regardless of their race, class, or gender, have the potential to become delinquents or criminals. Although members of the lower class may have the added burdens of poverty, racism, poor schools, and disrupted family lives, these social forces can be counteracted by positive peer relations, a supportive family, and educational success. In contrast, even the most affluent members of society may turn to antisocial behaviour if their life experiences are intolerable or destructive.

Social process theories have endured because the relationship between social class and crime is still uncertain. Most residents of inner-city areas refrain from criminal activity, and few of those who commit crimes persist into adulthood. If poverty were the sole cause of crime, then indigent adults would be as criminal as indigent teenagers. But we know that, regardless of class position, most people age out of crime. The association between economic status and crime is problematic because class position alone cannot explain crime rates.[1]

Criminologists have long studied the critical elements of socialization to determine how they contribute to a burgeoning criminal career. Prominent among these elements are family, school, peer group, and church.

socialization
Process of human development and enculturation. Socialization is influenced by key social processes and institutions.

social process theory
The view that criminality is a function of people's interactions with various organizations, institutions, and processes in society.

LO2 Family Relations

Family relationships are considered a major determinant of behaviour.[2] In fact, parenting factors, such as the ability to communicate and provide proper discipline, may play a critical role in determining whether people misbehave as children and even later as adults. This is one of the most replicated findings in the criminological literature.[3]

Youths who grow up in a household characterized by conflict and tension, where parents are absent or separated, or where there is a lack of familial love and support, are susceptible to crime-promoting forces in the environment.[4]

Even children living in high-crime areas will be better able to resist the temptations of the streets if they receive fair discipline, care, and support from parents who provide them with strong, positive role models.[5] Nonetheless, living in a disadvantaged neighbourhood places terrific strain on family functioning, especially in lone-parent families that are socially isolated from relatives, friends, and neighbours. Children raised within such distressed families are at risk for delinquency.[6]

At one time, growing up in a lone-parent home was considered a primary cause of criminal behaviour. However, many criminologists today discount the association between family structure and the onset of criminality, claiming that family conflict and discord determine behaviour more than family structure.[7] Not all experts, though, discount the effects of family structure on crime. Even if lone parents can make up for the loss of a second parent, the argument goes, it is simply more difficult to do so, and the chances of failure increase.[8] Lone parents may find it difficult to provide adequate supervision, and children who live with lone parents receive less encouragement and less help with schoolwork. Poor school achievement and limited educational aspirations have been associated with delinquent behaviour. Also, because they are receiving less attention as a result of having just one parent, these children may be more prone to rebellious acts, such as running away and truancy.[9] Children in two-parent households are more likely to want to attend college or university than those raised in lone-parent homes.[10]

Other family factors that have predictive value include the following:

1. Inconsistent discipline, poor supervision, and the lack of a warm, loving, supportive parent–child relationship are all associated with delinquency.[11] Children who grow up in homes where parents use severe discipline yet lack warmth and involvement in their lives are prone to antisocial behaviour.[12]

2. Children who have affectionate ties to their parents report greater levels of self-esteem beginning in adolescence and extending into adulthood; high self-esteem is inversely related to criminal behaviour.[13] Children growing up in homes where a parent suffers mental impairment are also at risk for delinquency.[14]

3. Children as young as two whose parents are drug abusers exhibit personality defects such as excessive anger and negativity.[15] These children, as well as older children of drug abusers, are more likely to become persistent substance abusers than the children of nonabusers.[16]

4. Higher reports of delinquency are reported for children living in permanently disrupted families and, in particular, Aboriginal children[17] who were involved in the child welfare system have greater involvement in the criminal justice system as adults.[18]

szefei/Shutterstock.com

Children who have a warm, loving, and supportive relationship with their parents are less likely to be involved in criminal activity.

Monkey Business Images/Shutterstock.com

Children who grow up in homes with parents who have mental health problems, who abuse substances, or who are abusive are at risk of becoming delinquent.

5. Children who experience abuse, neglect, or sexual abuse are believed to be more crime prone.[19] Links have been found among corporal punishment, delinquency, anger, spousal abuse, depression, and adult crime.[20]

LO3 Educational Experience

The educational process and adolescent school achievement have been linked to criminality. Children who do poorly in school, lack educational motivation, and feel alienated are the most likely to engage in criminal acts.[21] Children who fail in school offend more frequently than those who succeed. These children commit more serious and violent offences and persist in crime into adulthood.[22]

Schools contribute to criminality by labelling problem youths, which sets them apart from conventional society. One way in which schools perpetuate this stigmatization is through "streaming," which identifies some students as college or university bound and others as academic underachievers or potential dropouts.[23] Streaming is a controversial practice that still occurs in many schools across the country. Young people in Canada who come from more advantaged families are more likely than those from families where neither parent had a postsecondary education and where family incomes tended to be lower, to be taking the type of math, science, and English courses that would keep all their postsecondary options open.[24] Research findings over the past two decades indicate that many school dropouts, especially those who have been expelled, face a significant chance of entering a criminal career.[25]

LO4 Peer Relations

Psychologists have long recognized that peer groups powerfully affect human conduct and can dramatically influence decision making and behaviour

Negative or inadequate peer relationships have been tied to delinquency.

choices.[26] Children who are rejected by their peers are more likely to display aggressive behaviour and disrupt group activities through bickering, bullying, or other antisocial behaviour.[27] Research shows that adolescents who report inadequate or strained peer relations, and who say they are not popular with the opposite sex, are most likely to become delinquent.[28]

Delinquent peers often exert tremendous influence on behaviour, attitudes, and beliefs.[29] In every level of the social structure, youths who fall in with a bad crowd become more susceptible to criminal behaviour patterns.[30] Deviant peers provide friendship networks that support delinquency and drug use.[31] Activities such as riding around, staying out late, and partying with deviant peers give these youths the opportunity to commit deviant acts.[32] Because delinquent friends tend to be, as criminologist Mark Warr puts it, "sticky" (once acquired, they are not easily lost), peer influence may continue through the life span.[33] The more antisocial the peer group, the more likely its members are to engage in delinquency. Nondelinquent friends help moderate delinquency.[34]

As children grow and move forward, friends influence their behaviour, and their behaviour influences their friends.[35] Antisocial friends guide delinquent careers so they withstand the aging-out process.[36] Chronic offenders surround themselves with peers who share their antisocial activities, and these relationships seem quite stable over time. People who maintain close relations with antisocial peers will sustain their own criminal behaviour into adulthood. If peer influence diminishes, so too does criminal activity.[37]

social learning theory
The view that people learn to be aggressive by observing others acting aggressively to achieve some goal or being rewarded for violent acts.

social control theory
The view that people commit crime when the forces that bind them to society are weakened or broken.

Institutional Involvement and Belief

Logic would dictate that people who hold high moral values and beliefs, who have learned to distinguish right from wrong, and who regularly attend religious services, should also eschew crime and other antisocial behaviours. Religion binds people together and forces them to confront the consequences of their behaviour. Committing crimes would violate the principles of all organized religions.

However, an often-cited study by sociologists Travis Hirschi and Rodney Stark found that, contrary to expectations, the association between religious attendance or belief and delinquent behaviour patterns was negligible.[38] However, some recent research efforts have reached an opposing conclusion: Attending religious services significantly reduces crime. Interestingly, this type of participation seems to inhibit crime more than merely having religious beliefs and values.[39] Cross-national research shows that countries with high rates of church membership and attendance have lower crime rates.[40]

LO5 Differentiate Between Social Learning Theory, Social Control Theory, and Social Reaction Theory

According to the social process view, people living in even the most deteriorated urban areas can successfully resist inducements to crime if they have a positive self-image, strong moral values, and support from their parents, peers, teachers, and neighbours. The girl with a positive self-image who is chosen for a university scholarship; has the warm, loving support of her parents; and is viewed as someone "going places" by friends and neighbours, is less likely to adopt a criminal way of life than another young woman who is abused at home, who lives with criminal parents, and whose bond to her school and peer group is shattered because she is labelled a "troublemaker." The more social problems encountered during the socialization process, the greater the likelihood that youths will encounter difficulties and obstacles as they mature, such as being unemployed or becoming teenage parents.

The social process approach has several independent branches (see Figure 7.1). The first branch, social learning theory, suggests that people learn the techniques and attitudes of crime from close relationships with criminal peers: Crime is a learned behaviour. The second branch, social control theory, maintains that everyone has the potential to become a criminal, but most people are controlled by their bonds to society.

FIGURE 7.1

The Complex Web of Social Processes That Controls Human Behaviour

Social learning theory
Criminal behaviour is learned through human interaction (e.g., Edwin H. Sutherland, Donald Cressey).

Social control theory
Human behaviour is controlled through close associations with institutions and individuals (e.g., Travis Hirschi).

Social reaction theory
Some people are labelled "criminal" by police and court authorities; people so labelled, shunned by conventional society, adopt the labelled identity (e.g., Howard Becker).

Crime occurs when the forces that bind people to society are weakened or broken. The third branch, social reaction theory (labelling theory), says that people become criminals when significant members of society label them as such and they accept those labels as a personal identity.

Put another way, social learning theories assume that people are born good and learn to be bad; social control theory assumes that people are born bad and must be controlled in order to be good; and social reaction theory assumes that whether good or bad, people are controlled by the evaluations of others. Each of these independent branches will be discussed separately.

LO6 Social Learning Theories

Social learning theorists believe that crime is a product of learning the norms, values, and behaviours associated with criminal activity. Social learning can involve the actual techniques of crime (how to hotwire a car or roll a joint) as well as the psychological aspects of criminality (how to deal with the guilt or shame associated with illegal activities). This section briefly reviews two of the most prominent forms of social learning theory: differential association theory and neutralization theory.

Differential Association Theory

One of the most prominent social learning theories is Edwin H. Sutherland's differential association theory. Often considered the preeminent U.S. criminologist, Sutherland first put forth his theory in 1939 in his text *Principles of Criminology*.[41] The final version of the theory appeared in 1947. When Sutherland died in 1950, his long-time associate Donald Cressey continued his work. Cressey was so successful in explaining and popularizing his mentor's efforts that differential association theory remains one of the most enduring explanations of criminal behaviour.

Sutherland's research on white-collar crime, professional theft, and intelligence led him to dispute the notion that crime was a function of the inadequacy of people in the lower classes.[42] He believed crime was a function of a learning process that could affect any individual in any culture. Acquiring a behaviour is a socialization process, not a political or legal process. Skills and motives conducive to crime are learned as a result of contact with pro-crime values,

social reaction theory (labelling theory)
The view that people become criminals when labelled as such and they accept the label as a personal identity.

differential association theory
The view that people commit crime when their social learning leads them to perceive more definitions favouring crime than favouring conventional behaviour.

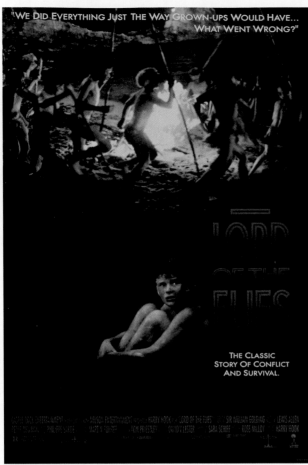

"WE DID EVERYTHING JUST THE WAY GROWN-UPS WOULD HAVE... WHAT WENT WRONG?"

THE CLASSIC
STORY OF CONFLICT
AND SURVIVAL.

The central theme of William Golding's *Lord of the Flies* reflects the concept of social control theory where young boys who are deserted on an island return to a "natural" state characterized by savagery, which highlights the need for rules of civilization to control it.

attitudes, and definitions and other patterns of criminal behaviour.

Principles of Differential Association

Sutherland and Cressey explain the basic principles of differential association as follows:[43]

1. *Criminal behaviour is learned.* This statement differentiates Sutherland's theory from prior attempts to classify criminal behaviour as an inherent characteristic of criminals. Sutherland implies that criminality is learned in the same manner as any other learned behaviour, such as writing, painting, or reading.

2. *Criminal behaviour is learned as a byproduct of interacting with others.* An individual does not start violating the law simply by living in a criminogenic environment or by manifesting personal characteristics, such as low IQ or family problems, associated with criminality. People actively learn as they are socialized and interact with other individuals who serve as teachers and guides to crime. Thus, criminality cannot occur without the aid of others.

3. *Learning criminal behaviour occurs within intimate personal groups.* People's contacts with their most intimate social companions—family, friends, peers—have the greatest influence on their deviant behaviour and attitude development. Relationships with these influential individuals colour and control the way individuals interpret everyday events. For example, children who grow up in homes where parents abuse alcohol are more likely to view drinking as socially and physically beneficial.[44]

4. *Learning criminal behaviour involves assimilating the techniques of committing crime, including motives, drives, rationalizations, and attitudes.* Young delinquents learn from their associates the proper way to pick a lock, shoplift, and obtain and use narcotics. In addition, novice criminals learn the proper terminology for their acts and acquire approved reactions to law violations. Criminals must learn how to react properly to their illegal acts, such as when to defend them, rationalize them, or show remorse for them.

5. *The specific direction of motives and drives is learned from perceptions of various aspects of the legal code as favourable or unfavourable.* Because the reaction to social rules and laws is not uniform across society, people constantly meet others who hold different views on

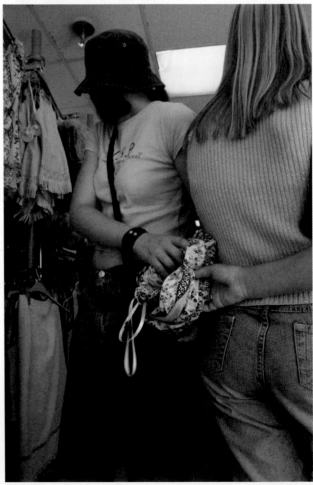

Young delinquents learn from their associates the proper way to shoplift. According to Statistics Canada, the most common type of youth crime is theft of $5,000 or under, usually shoplifting.

One of the best examples of culture conflict comes from the sporting world. Canada's Ben Johnson was disqualified after winning the 100-metre race at the Seoul Olympics when he tested positive for anabolic steroids. Some believe that it was not so much that he used them, but that he and his coach had apparently been so careless as to be detected, reflecting a cultural norm in the sporting world that still persists today.

the utility of obeying the legal code. Some people they admire may openly disdain or flout the law or ignore its substance. People experience what Sutherland calls **culture conflict** when they are exposed to opposing attitudes toward right and wrong or moral and immoral. The conflict of social attitudes and cultural norms is the basis for the concept of differential association.

6. *A person becomes a criminal when he or she perceives more favourable than unfavourable consequences to violating the law.* According to Sutherland's theory, individuals become law violators when they are in contact with persons, groups, or events that produce an excess of definitions favourable toward criminality and are isolated from counteracting forces (see Figure 7.2). A definition favourable toward criminality occurs, for example, when a person hears friends talking about the virtues of getting high on drugs. A definition unfavourable toward crime occurs when friends or parents demonstrate their disapproval of crime.

7. *Differential associations may vary in frequency, duration, priority, and intensity.* Whether a person learns to obey the law or to disregard it is influenced by the quality of social interactions. Those of lasting duration have greater influence than those that are brief. Similarly, frequent contacts have greater effect than rare, haphazard contacts. *Priority* means the age of children when they first encounter definitions of criminality. Contacts made early in life probably have more influence than those developed later on. Finally, *intensity* is generally interpreted to mean the importance and prestige attributed to the individual or groups from whom the definitions are learned. For example, the influence of a father, mother, or trusted friend far outweighs the effect of more socially distant figures.

8. *The process of learning criminal behaviour by association with criminal and anticriminal patterns involves all of the mechanisms that are involved in any other learning process.* Learning criminal behaviour

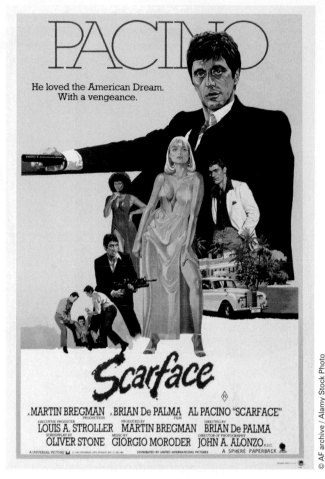

The 1983 movie *Scarface* has become a cult classic with Al Pacino's portrayal of Tony Montana named one of the most famous movie characters of all time. Montana's motto "The world is yours" exemplifies many of the principles of differential association.

patterns is similar to learning nearly all other patterns and is not a matter of mere imitation.

9. *Although criminal behaviour expresses general needs and values, it is not excused by those general needs and values because noncriminal behaviour also expresses the same needs and values.* This principle suggests that the motives for criminal behaviour cannot logically be the same as those for conventional behaviour. Sutherland rules out motives such as desire to accumulate money or social status, personal frustration, or low self-concept as causes of crime because they are just as likely to produce noncriminal behaviour, such as getting a better education or working harder on a job. Only the learning of deviant norms through contact with an excess of definitions favourable toward criminality produces illegal behaviour.

In sum, differential association theory holds that people learn criminal attitudes and behaviour during their adolescence from close,

culture conflict
Result of exposure to opposing norms, attitudes, and definitions of right and wrong, moral and immoral.

CHAPTER 7 Socialization and Crime **157**

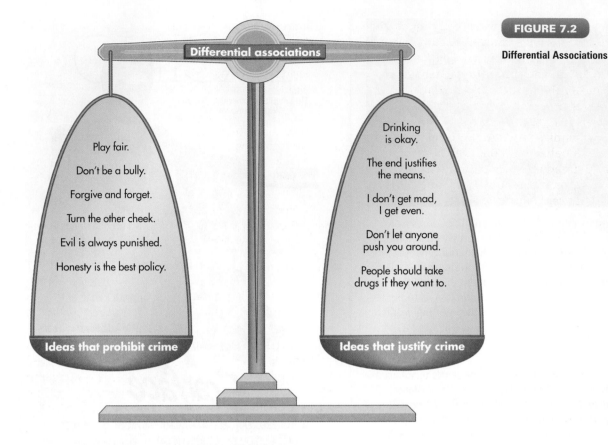

FIGURE 7.2

Differential Associations

Differential associations

Play fair.

Don't be a bully.

Forgive and forget.

Turn the other cheek.

Evil is always punished.

Honesty is the best policy.

Ideas that prohibit crime

Drinking is okay.

The end justifies the means.

I don't get mad, I get even.

Don't let anyone push you around.

People should take drugs if they want to.

Ideas that justify crime

trusted friends or relatives. A criminal career develops if learned antisocial values and behaviours are not matched or exceeded by conventional attitudes and behaviours. Criminal behaviour, then, is learned in a process that is similar to learning any other human behaviour.

Analysis of Differential Association Theory

Differential association theory is important because it does not specify that criminals come from a disorganized area or are members of the lower class. Outwardly law-abiding, middle-class parents can encourage delinquent behaviour by their own drinking, drug use, or family violence. The influence of differential associations is affected by social class; deviant learning experiences can affect youths in all classes.[45]

There are, however, a number of valid criticisms of Sutherland's work.[46] It fails to account for the origin of criminal definitions. How did the first "teacher" learn criminal attitudes and definitions in order to pass them on?

neutralization theory
The view that law violators learn to neutralize conventional values and attitudes, enabling them to drift back and forth between criminal and conventional behaviour.

Another criticism of differential association theory is that it assumes criminal and delinquent acts to be rational and systematic. This ignores spontaneous, wanton acts of violence and damage that appear to have little utility or purpose, such as many alcohol or drug-related outbursts of domestic violence, or the isolated psychopathic killing that is virtually unsolvable because of the killer's anonymity and lack of delinquent associations.

The most serious criticism of differential association theory concerns the vagueness of its terms, which makes its assumptions difficult to test. What constitutes an excess of definitions favourable toward criminality? How can we determine whether an individual actually has a crime-supporting imbalance of these deviant or antisocial definitions? Must we assume that, by definition, all criminals have experienced a majority of definitions toward crime and all noncriminals, a minority of them? Unless the theory's terms can be defined more precisely, its validity remains a matter of guesswork.

Neutralization Theory

Neutralization theory is identified with the writings of Gresham Sykes and David Matza.[47] These criminologists also view the process of becoming a criminal as a learning experience. They theorize that law violators must learn and master techniques that enable them to neutralize conventional values and attitudes, thus allowing them to drift back and forth between illegitimate and conventional behaviour.

Neutralization theory points out that even the most committed criminals and delinquents are not involved in criminality all the time; they also attend schools, family functions, and religious services. Thus, their behaviour falls along a continuum between total freedom and total restraint. This process of drift, or movement from one extreme to another, produces behaviour that is sometimes unconventional or deviant and at other times constrained and sober.[48] Learning neutralization techniques allows a person to temporarily drift away from conventional behaviour and become involved in antisocial behaviours, including crime and drug abuse.[49]

Neutralization Techniques

Individuals who engage in criminal behaviour have grown up in the same society as the rest of us—and, just like the rest of us, they know right from wrong, they have the same values and beliefs that we have, they even feel guilty over the crimes they commit—but somehow, they manage to put their conventional, law-abiding life aside and engage in criminal activities. Sykes and Matza suggest that many criminals develop a distinct set of excuses or "neutralizations" for their law violating that make it appear as though they are not really to blame for what they have done.[50]

Through their research, Sykes and Matza identified the following techniques of neutralization:

- *Denial of responsibility.* Young offenders sometimes claim that their unlawful acts are not their fault—that they result from forces beyond their control or are accidents.

- *Denial of injury.* By denying the injury caused by their acts, criminals neutralize illegal behaviour. For example, stealing is viewed as borrowing; vandalism is considered mischief that has gotten out of hand. Offenders may find that their parents and friends support their denial of injury. In fact, parents and friends may claim that the behaviour was merely a prank, helping affirm the offender's perception that crime can be socially acceptable.

- *Denial of the victim.* Criminals sometimes neutralize wrongdoing by maintaining that the crime victim "had it coming." Vandalism may be directed against a disliked teacher or neighbour, or a gang may beat up gays because their behaviour is considered offensive.

- *Condemnation of the condemners.* An offender views the world as a corrupt place with a dog-eat-dog code. Because police and judges are on the take, teachers show favouritism, and parents take out their frustrations on their children, offenders claim it is ironic and unfair for these authorities to condemn criminal misconduct. By shifting the blame to others,

criminals repress the feeling that their own acts are wrong.

- *Appeal to higher loyalties.* Novice criminals often argue that they are caught in the dilemma of being loyal to their peer group while attempting to abide by the rules of society. The needs of the group take precedence because group demands are immediate and localized (see Figure 7.3).

In sum, neutralization theory states that people neutralize conventional norms and values by using excuses that allow them to drift into crime.

Analyzing Neutralization Theory

Although the existing research findings are ambiguous,[51] the weight of the evidence shows that most adolescents generally disapprove of deviant behaviours such as violence, and that neutralizations do in fact enable youths to engage in socially disapproved behaviour.[52] And, as Matza predicted, people seem to drift in and out of antisocial behaviour rather than being committed solely to a criminal way of life.[53]

Are Learning Theories Valid?

Learning theories imply that people systematically learn techniques that allow them to be active, successful criminals. However, learning theories fail to adequately explain spontaneous, wanton acts of violence, damage, and other expressive crimes that appear to have little utility or purpose. Although principles of differential association can easily explain shoplifting, is it possible that a random shooting is caused by excessive deviant definitions? It is estimated that more than 50 percent of those who commit crimes are under the influence of drugs or alcohol when they commit the act.[54] Do "crack-heads" pause to neutralize their moral inhibitions before mugging a victim? Do drug-involved kids stop to consider what they have learned about moral values?[55]

drift
Movement in and out of delinquency, shifting between conventional and deviant values.

neutralization techniques
Methods of rationalizing deviant behaviour, such as denying responsibility or blaming the victim.

DID YOU KNOW?

- Social control theories maintain that behaviour is a function of the attachment that people feel toward society. People who have a weak commitment to conformity are free to commit crime.

- A strong self-image may insulate people from crime.

- According to Hirschi, social control is measured by a person's attachment, commitment, involvement, and belief.

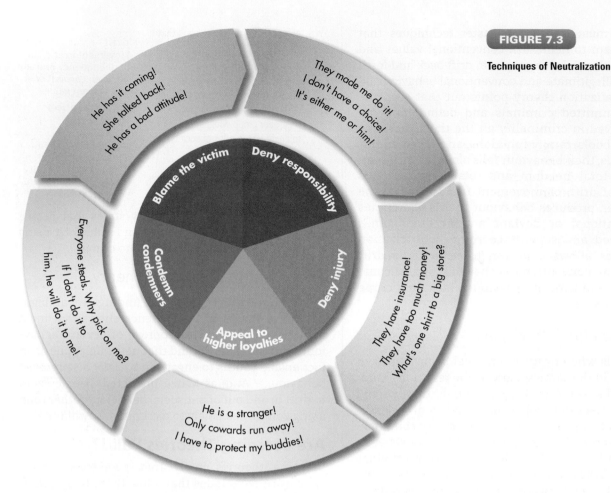

FIGURE 7.3

Techniques of Neutralization

He has it coming!
She talked back!
He has a bad attitude!

They made me do it!
I don't have a choice!
It's either me or him!

Everyone steals. Why pick on me?
If I don't do it to
him, he will do it to me!

Blame the victim

Deny responsibility

Condemn
condemners

Deny injury

Appeal to
higher loyalties

They have insurance!
They have too much money!
What's one shirt to a big store?

He is a stranger!
Only cowards run away!
I have to protect my buddies!

self-control
A strong moral sense that renders a person incapable of hurting others or violating social norms.

commitment to conformity
A strong personal investment in conventional institutions, individuals, and processes that prevents people from engaging in behaviour that might jeopardize their reputation and achievements.

Despite these criticisms, learning theories have an important place in the study of delinquent and criminal behaviour. Unlike social structure theories, these theories are not limited to explaining a single facet of antisocial activity; they explain criminality across all class structures. Even corporate executives may be exposed to pro-criminal definitions and learn to neutralize moral constraints. Learning theories can thus be applied to a wide assortment of criminal activity.

LO7 Social Control Theory

Social control theorists maintain that all people have the potential to violate the law and that modern society presents many opportunities for illegal activity. Criminal activities, such as drug abuse and

car theft, are often exciting pastimes that hold the promise of immediate reward and gratification.

Considering the attractions of crime, social control theorists question why people obey the rules of society. They argue that people obey the law because behaviour and passions are controlled by internal and external forces. Some individuals have self-control—a strong moral sense that renders them incapable of hurting others and violating social norms. Other people have been socialized to have a commitment to conformity. They have developed a real, present, and logical reason to obey the rules of society, and they instinctively avoid behaviour that will jeopardize their reputation and achievements.[56] The stronger people's commitment to conventional institutions, individuals, and processes, the less likely they are to commit crime. If that commitment is absent, there is little to lose, and people are free to violate the law.[57]

Self-Concept and Crime

Early versions of control theory speculated that criminality was a product of weak self-concept and poor self-esteem: youths who are socialized to feel good about themselves and maintain a positive attitude are able to resist the temptations of the streets.

As early as 1951, sociologist Albert Reiss described delinquents as having weak egos and lacking the self-control to produce conforming behaviour.[58] Pioneering control theorist Walter Reckless argued that a strong self-image insulates a youth from the pressures of criminogenic influences in the environment.[59] In studies conducted within the school setting, Reckless and his colleagues found that students who were able to maintain a positive self-image were insulated from delinquency.[60]

These early social control theorists suggested that people who have a weak self-image and damaged ego are crime prone. They are immune from efforts to apply social control: Why obey the rules of society when you have no stake in the future and little to lose?

Contemporary Social Control Theory

The version of control theory articulated by Travis Hirschi in his influential 1969 book *Causes of Delinquency* is today the dominant version of control theories.[61] Hirschi links the onset of criminality to the weakening of the ties that bind people to society. He assumes that all individuals are potential law violators, but most are kept under control because they fear that illegal behaviour will damage their relationships with friends, family, neighbours, teachers,

and employers. Without these social bonds or ties, a person is free to commit criminal acts. Among all ethnic, religious, racial, and social groups, people whose bond to society is weak may fall prey to criminogenic behaviour patterns.

Hirschi argues that the social bond a person maintains with society is divided into four main elements: attachment, commitment, involvement, and belief (see Figure 7.4).

1. *Attachment.* Attachment refers to a person's sensitivity to and interest in others.[62] Hirschi views parents, peers, and schools as the important social institutions with which a person should maintain ties. Attachment to parents is the most important. Even if a family is shattered by divorce or separation, a child

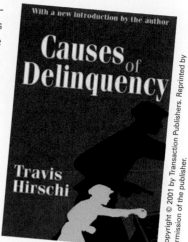

Copyright © 2001 by Transaction Publishers. Reprinted by permission of the publisher.

social bonds
The ties that bind people to society, including relationships with friends, family, neighbours, teachers, and employers. Elements of the social bond include commitment, attachment, involvement, and belief.

The familiar sight of first-year university students writing their final exams. According to Hirschi, heavy involvement in conventional activities such as schooling leaves little time for criminal activity.

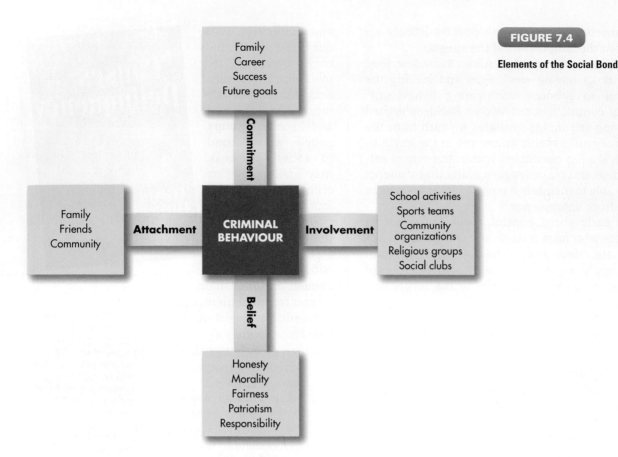

FIGURE 7.4

Elements of the Social Bond

Family
Career
Success
Future goals

Commitment

Family
Friends
Community

Attachment

CRIMINAL BEHAVIOUR

Involvement

School activities
Sports teams
Community organizations
Religious groups
Social clubs

Belief

Honesty
Morality
Fairness
Patriotism
Responsibility

must retain a strong attachment to one or both parents. Without this attachment, it is unlikely that respect for other authorities will develop.

2. *Commitment.* Commitment involves the time, energy, and effort expended in conventional actions such as getting an education and saving money for the future. If people build a strong commitment to conventional society, they will be less likely to engage in acts that jeopardize their hard-won position. Conversely, the lack of commitment to conventional values may foreshadow a condition in which risk-taking behaviour, such as crime, becomes a reasonable behaviour alternative.

3. *Involvement.* Heavy involvement in conventional activities leaves little time for illegal behaviour. Hirschi believes that involvement in school, recreation, and family insulates people from the potential lure of criminal behaviour. Idleness, on the other hand, enhances that lure.

4. *Belief.* People who live in the same social setting often share common moral beliefs; they may adhere to values such as sharing, sensitivity to the rights of others, and admiration for the legal code. If these beliefs are absent or weakened, individuals are more likely to participate in antisocial or illegal acts.

Hirschi further suggests that the interrelationship of social bond elements controls subsequent behaviour. For example, people who feel kinship and sensitivity to parents and friends should be more likely to adopt and work toward legitimate goals. On the other hand, a person who rejects such social relationships is more likely to lack commitment to conventional goals. Similarly, people who are highly committed to conventional acts and beliefs are more likely to be involved in conventional activities.

Testing Social Control Theory

One of Hirschi's most significant contributions was his attempt to test the principal hypotheses of social control theory. He administered a detailed self-report survey to a sample of more than 4000 junior and senior high school students in Contra Costa County, California.[63] In a detailed analysis of the data, Hirschi found considerable evidence to support the control theory model. Among Hirschi's more important findings are the following:

- Youths who were strongly attached to their parents were less likely to commit criminal acts.

- Youths involved in conventional activity, such as homework, were less likely to engage in criminal behaviour.

- Youths involved in unconventional behaviour, such as smoking and drinking, were more prone to delinquency.

- Youths who maintained weak, distant relationships with people tended toward delinquency.

- Those who shunned unconventional acts were attached to their peers.

- Delinquents and nondelinquents shared similar beliefs about society.

Hirschi's data gave important support to the validity of social control theory. Even when the statistical significance of his findings was less than he expected, the direction of his research data was notably consistent. Only rarely did his findings contradict the theory's most critical assumptions.

Supporting Research

Hirschi's version of social control theory has been corroborated by numerous research studies showing that delinquent youths often feel detached from society.[64] Supporting research indicates that both male and female delinquents experience attachments to the family, peer group, and school that are strained and weakened.[65] In contrast, positive attachments help control delinquency.[66] For example, youths who fail at school and are detached from the educational experience are at risk of criminality; those who do well and are committed to school are less likely to engage in delinquent acts.[67]

Opposing Views

More than 70 published attempts have been made to corroborate social control theory by replicating Hirschi's original survey techniques.[68] Though providing significant empirical support for Hirschi's work, these studies have also raised a number of questions.

- *Friendship.* One significant criticism concerns Hirschi's contention that delinquents are detached loners whose bond to family and friends has been broken. In fact, delinquents seem not to be "lone wolves" whose only personal relationships are exploitative; their friendship patterns seem quite close to those of conventional youth.[69] Some types of offenders, such as drug abusers, may maintain even more intimate relations with their peers than nonabusers.[70]

- *Failure to achieve.* Hirschi argues that commitment to career and economic advancement reduces criminal involvement. However, research indicates that people who are committed to success but fail to achieve it may be crime prone.[71]

- *Involvement negates supervision.* Adolescents who report high levels of involvement, which Hirschi suggests should reduce delinquency, actually report high levels of criminal behaviour. Perhaps adolescents who are involved in activities outside the home have less contact with parental supervision and greater opportunity to commit crime.[72]

- *Deviant peers and parents.* Hirschi's conclusion that any form of social attachment is beneficial, even to deviant peers and parents, has also been disputed. Rather than deter delinquency, attachment to deviant peers may support and nurture antisocial behaviour.[73] A number of research efforts have found that youths attached to drug-abusing parents are more likely to use drugs themselves.[74] Attachment to deviant family members, peers, and associates may help motivate youths to commit crime and facilitate their antisocial acts.[75]

Hirschi's theory proposes that a weakened bond leads to delinquency, but Robert Agnew suggests that the chain of events may flow in the opposite direction: Perhaps youngsters who break the law find that their bonds to parents, schools, and society eventually become weak. Other studies have also found that criminal behaviour weakens social bonds and not vice versa.[76]

While these criticisms are important, Hirschi's views still constitute one of the preeminent theories in criminology.[77] Many criminologists consider social control theory the most important way of understanding the onset of youthful misbehaviour.

DID YOU KNOW?

- According to labelling theory, stigma helps lock people into a deviant career.
- Labels amplify deviant behaviour rather than deter future criminality.
- Primary deviants view themselves as good people who have done a bad thing; secondary deviants accept a negative label as an identity.
- Labels are bestowed in a biased fashion. The poor and minority-group members are more likely to receive labels.

LO8 Social Reaction (Labelling) Theory

Social reaction theory, or labelling theory (the two terms are used interchangeably here), explains criminal careers in terms of destructive social interactions and stigma-producing encounters.

According to this view, people are given a variety of symbolic labels that help define not only one trait, but also the whole person. Valued labels, such as "smart," "honest," and "hard working," suggest overall competence. Sometimes the labels are symbolic, such as being named "most likely to succeed" or class valedictorian. People who hold these titles are automatically assumed to be leaders who are well on their way to success. Without meeting them, we know that they are hard working, industrious, and bright. These positive labels can improve self-image and social standing. Research shows that people who are labelled with one positive trait, such as being physically attractive, are assumed to have other positive traits, such as being intelligent and competent.[78]

In contrast, some people are given negative labels, such as "troublemaker," "mentally ill," and

HE'S OBVIOUSLY DEPRESSED, LET'S LABEL HIM AND SEE IF SEVERAL YEARS OF UNEMPLOYMENT AND POOR RELATIONSHIPS HELPS HIS CONDITION!

"stupid," that stigmatize them and reduce their self-image. For example, people labelled "insane" are also assumed to be dangerous, dishonest, unstable, violent, strange, and otherwise unsound.

Both positive and negative labels involve subjective interpretation of behaviour: A "troublemaker" is merely someone whom people label as "troublesome." There need not be any objective proof or measure indicating that the person is actually a troublemaker. Although a label may be a function of rumour, innuendo, or unfounded suspicion, its adverse impact can be immense.

If a devalued status is conferred by a significant other—teacher, police officer, parent, or valued peer—the negative label may permanently harm the target. The degree to which a person is perceived as a social deviant may affect his or her treatment at home, at work, at school, and in other social situations. Children may find that their parents consider them a bad influence on younger brothers and sisters. School officials may limit them to classes reserved for people with behavioural problems. Likewise, when adults are labelled as "criminal," "ex-con," or "drug addict," they may find their eligibility for employment severely restricted. If the label is bestowed as the result of conviction for a criminal offence, the labelled person may also be subjected to official sanctions ranging from a mild reprimand to incarceration. The simultaneous effects of labels and sanctions reinforce feelings of isolation and detachment.

stigmatize
To apply negative labelling with enduring effects on a person's self-image and social interactions.

According to labelling theory, depending on the visibility of the label and the manner and severity with which it is applied, negatively labelled individuals will become increasingly committed to a deviant career. They may be watched, suspected, and excluded more and more from legitimate opportunities.[79] Labelled persons may find themselves turning to others similarly stigmatized for support and companionship. Isolated from conventional society, they may identify themselves as members of an outcast group and become locked into deviance. Figure 7.5 illustrates this process.

Because the process of becoming stigmatized is essentially interactive, labelling theorists blame the establishment of criminal careers on the social agencies originally designed for crime control, such as police, courts, and correctional agencies. It is these institutions, labelling theorists claim, that produce the stigma that harms the people they are trying to help, treat, or correct. As a result, they actually help maintain and amplify criminal behaviour.

Crime and Labelling Theory

According to the social reaction approach, crime and deviance are defined by the social audience's reaction to people and their behaviour and the subsequent effects of that reaction; they are not defined by

FIGURE 7.5

The Labelling Process

Initial criminal act	Detection by the justice system	Decision to label	Creation of a new identity	Acceptance of labels	Deviance amplification
People commit crimes for a number of reasons.	Arrest is influenced by racial, economic, and power relations.	Some are labelled "official" criminals by police and court authorities.	Those labelled are known as troublemakers, criminals, etc., and shunned by conventional society.	Labelled people begin to see themselves as outsiders (secondary deviance, self-labelling).	Stigmatized offenders are now locked into criminal careers.

the moral content of the illegal act itself. In a famous statement, Howard Becker sums up the importance of the audience's reaction:

> Social groups create deviance by making rules whose infractions constitute deviance, and by applying those rules to particular people and labeling them as outsiders. From this point of view, deviance is not a quality of the act a person commits, but rather a consequence of the application by others of rules and sanctions to an "offender." The deviant is one to whom the label has successfully been applied; deviant behavior is behavior that people so label.[80]

In its purest form, social reaction theory argues that even crimes such as murder, sexual assault, and theft are bad or evil only because people label them as such. After all, the difference between an excusable act and a criminal one is often a matter of changing legal definition. Acts such as performing an abortion, using marijuana, possessing a handgun, and gambling have been legal at some times and places and illegal at others.

A constitutional challenge to the new law in the spring of 2015 held that it is no longer an offence to possess marijuana derivatives and also that,

- non-dried forms of marihuana could be used treatment of some serious health conditions is considered "medically reasonable"

CAREER CONNECTIONS

"Stand Up to Bullying!" was the message the founders of bullying.org were spreading during Bullying Awareness Week across Canada. Many events take place across the country to commemorate the week and to raise awareness about the harmful effects of bullying—on the people who are bullied, the bullies themselves, and anyone else involved in the problem.

Constable Lois Cormier, a community relations officer in Thompson RCMP, has taken part in Bullying Awareness Week for quite some time. She works to help address chronic substance abuse and related gang violence in the community, maintaining a strong police presence in area schools. She initiated northern restorative justice circles in schools, bicycle safety rodeos, a graffiti removal program, and an antibullying program. She's involved in the community both on duty and off, and is currently working toward establishing a skateboard park in Thompson to enhance recreational opportunities for local youth. She says that she believes bullying is an issue not only in Thompson but also throughout the province and across the country, with lasting negative effects. "What

you'll find is that when bullying has been happening in the younger years, if it's not dealt with early on, then it actually progresses into adulthood where 60 percent of bullies, by the age of 24, will end up with a criminal record." She also says that classroom bullying can translate, in adulthood, into domestic violence, spousal assaults, and bullying in the workplace.

Some of the causes of bullying, Cormier says, can result from having a bully as a parent or in your family. But she says the tables can often turn on parents and they can be bullied by their children. "There are a lot of parents that could be living in fear if their children are bullying them. And depending on what crowd they're hanging out with—a lot of parents are living in fear when their children get into gangs or gang wannabes." For her efforts in working with youth and youth issues such as bullying, Cormier was recognized with the Excellence in Law Enforcement Award.

Source: "Bullying Awareness Week goes from Nov. 15 to 21," by Miranda Healey, *Thompson Citizen*, November 18, 2009. Reprinted with permission.

In April 2014, the Canadian government banned all home growing of marijuana for medical purposes, forcing users to buy their supplies from licensed growers. However, a group of patients challenged the new regulations, arguing that licensed producers who operate businesses would inflate the price for the sake of making a profit, thereby making marijuana too expensive to purchase.

- by forcing a person to choose between a 'legal but inadequate treatment and an illegal but more effective choice', the law… contravenes the Charter of Rights

- "the criminalization of access to the treatment in question infringes liberty and security of the person"[81]

There are some lingering questions left unanswered by the Supreme Court decision and undoubtedly the new Justine Trudeau Liberal Government elected in October 2015 will attempt to remedy given their pledge to legalize marijuana in Canada.

Justice Donald Taliano found that sick people are forced to resort to crime because they cannot get access to medical marijuana through appropriate means, branding them as criminals. The judgment came in the case of a seriously ill young man, Matthew Mernagh, who used medical marijuana to help manage the symptoms from a variety of ailments including fibromyalgia, scoliosis, and seizures. Mernagh was charged by Niagara Regional Police in 2008 when police seized 70 marijuana plants in his apartment in St. Catharines, Ontario.

Even if some acts are labelled as bad or evil, those who participate in them can be spared a negative label. For example, it is possible to take another person's life but not be considered a "murderer" because the killing was considered self-defence or an accident. Acts have negative consequences for the killer only when they are labelled wrong or evil by others.

A social reaction theorist views crime as a subjective concept whose definition depends entirely on the viewing audience. An act that is considered criminal by one person may be perfectly acceptable behaviour to another. Because crime is defined by those in power, the shape of criminal law is defined by the values of those who rule, not an objective standard of moral conduct. Howard Becker refers to people who create rules as moral entrepreneurs. An example of a moral entrepreneur today might be a member of an ultra-orthodox religious group who targets gays and campaigns to prevent gays from adopting children or marrying their same-sex partners.[82]

Differential Enforcement

An important principle of social reaction theory is that the law is differentially applied, benefiting those who hold economic and social power and penalizing the powerless. The probability of being brought under the control of legal authority is a function of a person's race, wealth, gender, and social standing. A core concept of social reaction theory is that police officers are more likely to formally arrest males, minority-group members, and those in the lower class, and to use their discretionary powers to give beneficial treatment to more favoured groups.[83] Minorities and the poor are more likely to be prosecuted for criminal offences and receive harsher punishment when convicted.[84] Judges may sympathize with white defendants and help them avoid criminal labels, especially if they seem to come from "good families," whereas minority youths are not afforded that luxury.[85] This helps explain why there are significant racial and economic differences in the crime rate.

In sum, a major premise of social reaction theory is that the law is differentially constructed and applied, depending on the offender. It favours powerful members of society, who direct its content, and penalizes people whose actions threaten those in control, such as minority-group members and the poor who demand equal rights.[86]

Consequences of Labelling

Negative labels stigmatize people and alter their self-image. The labelled person is transformed into a social outcast who is prevented from enjoying higher education, well-paying jobs, and other social benefits.

Public denunciation plays an important part in the labelling process. Condemnation is often carried out in "ceremonies" in which the individual's identity is officially transformed. Examples of such re-identification ceremonies are a competency hearing in which a person is declared to be "mentally ill" or a public trial in which a person is found

moral entrepreneur
A person who creates moral rules, which thus reflect the values of those in power rather than any objective, universal standards of right and wrong.

Gordon Swanson/Hemera/Thinkstock

ROBERT DE NIRO
RAY LIOTTA   JOE PESCI

Murderers come with smiles.
Shooting people was "No big deal." We were

GoodFellas

Three Decades of Life
in the Mafia.

© Moviestore collection Ltd / Alamy Stock Photo

In the Martin Scorsese movie *Goodfellas*, the lead character, based on real-life figure Henry Hill, confidently asserts, "As far back as I can remember, I've always wanted to be a gangster." One of the most popular gangster films of the decade, *Goodfellas* chronicles Hill's life as he moves through the shady underworld of the mob. Hill, played by Ray Liotta, gets involved with the Mafia at a young age and continues his "career" throughout the film. He eventually marries and has children, but maintains his position in the organized crime family under mob boss Paulie (Paul Sorvino). His friends include Jimmy (Robert De Niro), a calm, level-headed gangster; and colourful Tommy (Joe Pesci), a wild man with serious mental problems. As Hill gets more involved in the drug trade he succumbs to drug abuse, which leads to paranoia and ultimately his downfall. Ray Liotta has been described as a perfect Henry Hill, capturing his youthful innocence yet at the same time a feeling of violence.

According to differential association theory, crime is a function of the learning process and acquiring criminal behaviour is a socialization process. Describe how this theory helps us explain Henry Hill's introduction to and acceptance of the gangster lifestyle.

---

to be a "rapist" or "child molester." During the process, a permanent record is produced, such as an arrest or conviction record, so that the denounced person is ritually separated from a place in the legitimate order and placed outside the world occupied by citizens of good standing. Harold Garfinkle has called transactions that produce irreversible, permanent labels "successful degradation ceremonies."[87]

Changing Self-Image

Successful labelling produces a re-evaluation of the self that reflects actual or perceived appraisals made by others. Children who view themselves as delinquents after being labelled as such are giving an inner voice to their perceptions of how parents, teachers, peers, and neighbours view them. When they believe that others view them as antisocial or troublemakers, they take on attitudes and roles that reflect this assumption. They expect to become suspects and then to be rejected.[88]

Tempering or enhancing the effect of this **reflective role taking** are the people and institutions with whom the labelled person comes in contact. For example, an understanding teacher can help overcome the negative label of a low-track student and encourage an adolescent to excel in school. However, when these groups are dysfunctional, such as when parents use drugs, they encourage rather than control antisocial behaviour.[89]

Joining Deviant Cliques

People who are labelled as deviant may join with similarly outcast peers who facilitate their behaviour. Eventually, antisocial behaviour becomes habitual and automatic.[90] The desire to join deviant cliques and groups may stem from self-rejecting attitudes ("At times, I think I am no good at all") that eventually weaken commitment to conventional values and behaviours. In turn, stigmatized individuals may acquire motives to deviate from social norms because they now share a common bond with similarly labelled social outcasts.[91] They may join cliques like the "Trenchcoat Mafia" whose members were involved in the 1999 Littleton, Colorado, school massacre or more recently members of "homegrown" terrorists groups Membership in a deviant subculture often involves conforming to group norms that conflict with those of conventional society, further enhancing the effects of the labelling process.

Retrospective Reading

Beyond any immediate results, labels tend to redefine the whole person. For example, the label "ex-con" may create in people's imaginations a whole series of behaviour descriptions—tough, mean, dangerous, aggressive, dishonest, sneaky—that may or may not apply to a person

reflective role taking
Assuming an identity based on the actual or perceived appraisals of others.

who has been in prison. People react to the label description and what it signifies, instead of reacting to the actual behaviour of the person who bears it. The labelled person's past is reviewed and re-evaluated to fit his or her current status—a process known as retrospective reading. For example, boyhood friends of an assassin or serial killer, interviewed by the media, report that the suspect was withdrawn, suspicious, and negativistic as a youth; they were always suspicious but never thought to report their concerns to the authorities. According to this retrospective reading, we can now understand what prompted his current behaviour; therefore, the label must be accurate.[92]

Labels, then, become the basis of personal identity. As the negative feedback of law enforcement agencies, parents, friends, teachers, and other figures amplifies the force of the original label, stigmatized offenders may begin to re-evaluate their own identities. If they are not really evil or bad, they may ask themselves, why is everyone making such a fuss? This process has been referred to as the "dramatization of evil."[93]

Primary and Secondary Deviance

One of the better-known views of the labelling process is Edwin Lemert's concept of primary deviance and secondary deviance.[94] According to Lemert, primary deviance involves norm violations or crimes that have little influence on the actor and can be quickly forgotten. For example, a university student successfully steals a textbook at the campus bookstore, gets an A in the course, graduates, is admitted to law school, and later becomes a famous judge. Because his shoplifting goes unnoticed, it is a relatively unimportant event that has little bearing on his future life.

In contrast, secondary deviance occurs when a deviant event comes to the attention of significant others or social control agents, who apply a negative label. The newly labelled offender then reorganizes his or her behaviour and personality around the

© Saed Hindash/Star Ledger/Corbis

Ex-con Andre Latallade's appearance fits the preconceived notion of an "ex-con"; however, looks can be deceiving. After spending eight years of his life locked up, Latallade turned his life around after doing time on drug and aggravated assault charges. He built a name for himself as an activist for prisoners' rights and an opponent of capital punishment. "When I was in prison, everyone forgot about me," says Latallade, a rapper whose stage name is Capital X. "I want to show inmates on death row that I won't forget about them." In July 2011, Latallade began a 2735-kilometre walk from his home in Trenton, New Jersey, to Texas, the state with the most executions and where more than 3000 prisoners are on death row.

consequences of the deviant act. The shoplifting student is caught by a security guard and expelled from university. With his law school dreams dashed and future cloudy, his options are limited; people say he lacks character, and he begins to share their opinion. He eventually becomes a drug dealer and winds up in prison (see Figure 7.6).

Secondary deviance involves resocialization into a deviant role. The labelled person is transformed into one who, according to Lemert, "employs his behaviour or a role based upon it as a means of defense, attack, or adjustment to the overt and covert problems created by the consequent social reaction to him."[95] Secondary deviance produces a deviance amplification effect: Offenders feel isolated from the mainstream

FIGURE 7.6

Primary and Secondary Deviance

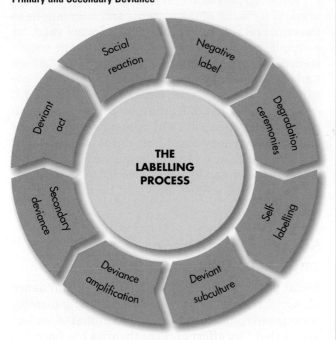

of society and become locked within their deviant role. They may seek others similarly labelled to form deviant groups. Ever more firmly enmeshed in their deviant role, they are trapped in an escalating cycle of deviance, apprehension, more powerful labels, and identity transformation. Lemert's concept of secondary deviance expresses the core of social reaction theory: Deviance is a process in which one's identity is transformed. Efforts to control offenders, whether by treatment or punishment, simply help lock them in their deviant role.

Research on Social Reaction Theory

Research on social reaction theory can be classified into two distinct categories. The first focuses on the characteristics of those offenders who are chosen for labelling. The theory predicts that they will be relatively powerless people who are unable to defend themselves against the negative labelling. The second type of research attempts to discover the effects of being labelled. Labelling theorists predict that people who are negatively labelled will view themselves as deviant and commit increasing amounts of crime.

Victims of Labelling

There is evidence that, as predicted by labelling theory, poor and powerless people are victimized by the law and justice system. Labels are not equally distributed across class and racial lines. From the police officer's decision on whom to arrest, to the prosecutor's decisions on whom to charge and how many and what kinds of charges to bring, to the court's decision on whom to release or grant bail, to the judge's decision on sentence length, discretion works to the detriment of minorities.[96] For example, in a study of the Ontario criminal justice system researchers found that blacks were more likely than other groups to be denied bail, to be convicted in court, and to receive harsher sentences.[97] Judges may also be more likely to impose prison sentences on racial minorities in borderline cases for which whites get probation.

Effects of Labelling

Empirical evidence shows that negative labels dramatically influence the self-image of offenders. Considerable evidence indicates that social sanctions lead to self-labelling and deviance amplification.[98] For example, children negatively labelled by their parents routinely suffer a variety of problems, including antisocial behaviour and school failure.[99] This process is important because once they are labelled as troublemakers, adolescents begin to reassess their self-image. Parents who label their children as troublemakers promote deviance amplification. Labelling alienates parents from their children, and negative labels reduce children's self-image and increase delinquency.[100]

As they mature, children are in danger of receiving repeated, intensive, official labelling, which has been shown to produce self-labelling and damage identities.[101] Youngsters labelled as troublemakers in school are the most likely to drop out, which has been linked to delinquent behaviour.[102] Even in adults, the labelling process can take its toll. Male drug users labelled as addicts by social control agencies eventually become self-labelled and increase their drug use.[103] People arrested in domestic violence cases, especially those with a low stake in conformity (e.g., those who are jobless and unmarried), often increase offending after being given official labels.[104]

Empirical evidence supports the view that labelling plays an important role in persistent offending.[105] Although labels may not cause adolescents to initiate criminal behaviours, experienced delinquents are significantly more likely to continue offending if they believe that their parents and peers view them in a negative light.[106] Labelling, then, may help sustain criminality over time.

Is Labelling Theory Valid?

Criminologists Raymond Paternoster and Leeann Iovanni have identified features of the labelling perspective that are important contributions to the study of criminality:[107]

- The labelling perspective identifies the role played by social control agents in crime causation. Criminal behaviour cannot be fully understood if the agencies and individuals empowered to control and treat it are neglected.

- Labelling theory recognizes that criminality is not a disease or pathological behaviour. It focuses attention on the social interactions and reactions that shape individuals and their behaviour.
- Labelling theory distinguishes between criminal acts (primary deviance) and criminal careers (secondary deviance) and shows that these concepts must be interpreted and treated differently.

Labelling theory is also important because of its focus on interaction as well as the situation surrounding the crime. Rather than viewing the criminal as a robot-like creature whose actions are predetermined, it recognizes that crime often results from complex interactions and processes. The decision to commit crime involves actions of a variety of people, including peers, victim, police, and other key characters. Labels may foster crime by guiding the actions of all parties involved in these criminal interactions. Actions deemed innocent when performed by one person are considered provocative when engaged in by someone who has been labelled as deviant. Similarly, labelled people may be quick to judge, take offence, or misinterpret others' behaviour because of past experience.

An Evaluation of Social Process Theory

The branches of social process theory—social learning, social control, and social reaction—are compatible because they all suggest that criminal behaviour is part of the socialization process. Criminals are people whose interactions with critically important social institutions and processes—the family, schools, the justice system, peer groups, employers, and neighbours—are troubled. Although some disagree about the relative importance of those influences and the form they take, there is little question that social interactions shape the behaviour, beliefs, values, and self-image of the offender. People who have learned deviant social values, who find themselves detached from conventional social relationships, or who are the subject of stigma and labels from significant others are the most likely to commit crime. These negative influences can influence anyone, beginning in youth and continuing through adulthood. The major strength of the social process view is the vast body of empirical data showing that delinquents and criminals are people who grew up in dysfunctional families, who had troubled childhoods, and who failed at school, at work, and in

marriage. Prison data show that these characteristics are typical of inmates.

Although persuasive, these theories do not always account for some of the patterns and fluctuations in the crime rate. If social process theories are valid, for example, people in Western Canada must be socialized differently from those in Central or Eastern Canada, where crime rates are generally lower. How can seasonal crime rate variations be explained if crime is a function of learning or control? How can social processes explain why criminals escalate their activity or why they desist from crime? Once a social bond is broken, how can it be reattached? Once crime is learned, how can it be unlearned? These are questions that must still be answered by social process theorists.

Social Process Theory and Social Policy

Social process theories have had a major influence on social policies since the 1950s. Learning theories have greatly influenced the way criminal offenders are treated. The effect of these theories has been felt mainly by young offenders, who are viewed as being more salvageable than hardened criminals. Advocates of the social learning approach argue that if people become criminal by learning definitions and attitudes favouring criminality, they can unlearn them by being exposed to definitions favouring conventional behaviour.

This philosophy has been used in numerous treatment facilities based in part on two early, pioneering efforts: the Highfields Project in New Jersey and the Silverlake Program in Los Angeles. These were residential treatment programs, geared toward young male offenders, that used group interaction sessions to attack criminal behaviour orientations while promoting conventional lines of behaviour.[108] It is common today for residential and nonresidential programs in both the United States and Canada to offer similar treatment, teaching children and adolescents to refuse drugs, to forgo delinquent behaviour, and to stay in school. It is even common for celebrities such as former Canadian heavyweight boxing champion George Chuvalo to publicly urge young people to stay in school and off drugs. If learning did not affect behaviour, such exercises would be futile.

Control theories have also influenced criminal justice and other social policies. Programs have been developed to increase people's commitment to conventional lines of action. Some work at creating and strengthening bonds early in life before the onset of criminality. The educational system has hosted numerous programs designed to

CP Photo by BORIS SPREMO

During the 1960s and 1970s, George Chuvalo was Canada's heavyweight boxing champion and was regularly ranked in the top ten in the world, fighting Muhammad Ali, Joe Frazier, George Foreman, and Jerry Quarry. Chuvalo was never knocked to the mat in his 93 professional fights, and is considered by many to have the toughest chin in boxing history. Chuvalo's personal life also took a beating when after retiring he lost three of his four sons and his wife to drugs. He now gives talks to high school and elementary school children about the consequences of drug abuse.

improve basic skills and create an atmosphere in which youths will develop a bond with their schools. The Head Start program in the United States is justified by both social process and social structure theory but for different reasons. According to social structure theory, the cause of criminality is the divide between lower-class individuals and conventional goals, norms, and rules. Thus, by providing children with health care services and a nutritious diet, it enables children to share in the rewards of conventional society. Further, because Head Start is an attempt to solidify social bonds, it also supported by social process theory. A Canadian example of Head Start is the Aboriginal Head Start in Urban and Northern Communities (AHSUNC) program, which began in 1995 as a community-based children's program focusing on early childhood development of First Nations, Inuit, and Métis children and their families living off-reserve. The intent of the program was to respond to general health concerns and social development of Aboriginal children. The accompanying Theoretical Applications feature discusses the Head Start program.

Control theory's focus on the family has played a key role in programs designed to strengthen the bond between parent and child. Others attempt to repair bonds that have been broken or frayed. Examples of this approach are the employment skills and educational opportunity programs that are in place in Canada's prisons. These programs are designed to help inmates maintain a stake in society so they will be less willing to resort to criminal activity after their release.

Labelling theorists caution against too much intervention. Rather than ask social agencies to attempt to rehabilitate people having problems with the law, they argue, less is better. Put another way, the more institutions try to help people, the more these people will be stigmatized and labelled. For example, a special education program designed to help problem readers may cause them to label themselves and others as slow or stupid. Similarly, a mental health rehabilitation program created with the best intentions may cause clients to be labelled as crazy or dangerous.

The influence of labelling theory can be seen in diversion and restitution programs. Diversion programs remove both juvenile and adult offenders from the normal channels of the criminal justice process by placing them in rehabilitation programs. For example, a university student whose drunken driving hurts a pedestrian may, before trial, be placed for six months in an alcohol treatment program. If he successfully completes the program, charges against him will be dismissed; thus he avoids the stigma of a criminal label. Such programs are common throughout Canada and the United States. Often they offer counselling, medical advice, and vocational, educational, and family services.

Another popular label-avoiding innovation is restitution. Rather than face the stigma of a formal trial, an offender is asked either to pay back the victim of the crime for any loss incurred or to do some useful work in the community, in lieu of receiving a court-ordered sentence.

Despite their good intentions, stigma-reducing programs have not met with great success. Critics charge that they substitute one kind of stigma for another—for instance, attending a mental health program in lieu of a criminal trial. In addition, diversion and restitution programs usually screen out violent and repeat offenders. Finally, there is little hard evidence that these alternative programs improve recidivism rates.

diversion programs
Programs of rehabilitation that remove offenders from the normal channels of the criminal justice process, thus avoiding the stigma of a criminal label.

restitution
Permitting an offender to repay the victim or do useful work in the community rather than face the stigma of a formal trial and a court-ordered sentence.

HEAD START

Head Start is probably the best-known effort to help young children achieve proper socialization and, in so doing, reduce their potential for future criminality. Head Start programs were instituted in the United States in the 1960s as part of President Lyndon Johnson's War on Poverty. In the beginning, Head Start was a two-month summer program for children who were about to enter school. Aimed at embracing the "whole child," it offered comprehensive programming designed to enhance physical health, mental processes, social and emotional development, self-image, and interpersonal relationships. Preschoolers were provided with an enriched educational environment to develop their learning and cognitive skills. They were given the opportunity to use pegs and pegboards, puzzles, toy animals, dolls, letters and numbers, and other materials that middle-class children take for granted. These opportunities provided these children a leg up in the educational process.

Head Start teachers strive to provide a variety of learning experiences appropriate to the child's age and development. These experiences allow children to read books, to understand cultural diversity, to express feelings, and to play with and relate to their peers in an appropriate fashion. Students are guided in developing gross and fine motor skills and self-confidence. Health care is also an issue, and most children enrolled in the program receive comprehensive health screenings, physical and dental examinations, and appropriate follow-up. Many programs provide meals, helping children receive proper nourishment.

Head Start programs now serve parents in addition to their preschoolers. Some programs allow parents to enroll in classes, which cover parenting, literacy, nutrition/weight loss, domestic violence prevention, and other social issues; social services, health, and education services are also available.

Considerable controversy has surrounded the success of the Head Start program. In 1970, the Westinghouse Learning Corporation issued a definitive evaluation of the Head Start effort and concluded that there was no evidence of lasting cognitive gains on the part of the participating children. Initial gains seemed to evaporate during the elementary school years, and by Grade 3, the performance of the Head Start children was no different from that of their peers. Though disappointing, this evaluation focused on IQ levels and gave short shrift to improvement in social competence and other survival skills.

More recent research has produced dramatically different results. One report found that by age five, children who had experienced the enriched daycare offered by Head Start averaged more than 10 points higher on their IQ scores than their peers who did not participate in the program. Other research that carefully compared Head Start children to similar children who did not attend the program found that the former made significant intellectual gains. Head Start children were less likely to have been retained in a grade or placed in classes for slow learners, they outperformed peers on achievement tests, and they were more likely to graduate from high school.

Head Start children have also made strides in nonacademic areas. They appear to have better health, higher immunization rates, improved nutrition, and enhanced emotional characteristics after leaving the program. Research also shows that the Head Start program can have important psychological benefits for the mothers of participants, such as decreasing depression and anxiety and increasing feelings of life satisfaction. While findings in some areas may be tentative, they are all in the same direction: Head Start enhances school readiness and has enduring effects on social competence.

If, as many experts believe, there is a close link between school performance, family life, and crime, programs such as Head Start can help some potentially criminal young people avoid problems with the law. By implication, their success indicates that programs that help socialize youngsters can be used to combat urban criminality. Although some problems have been identified in individual centres, the U.S. government has shown its faith in Head Start as a socialization agent. The current budget of more than US$4.2 billion is used to serve more than 820 000 children.

Aboriginal Head Start (AHS) in Canadian urban and northern communities is a Health Canada–funded early childhood development program for First Nations, Inuit, and Métis children and their families. Started in 1995 with an annual budget of about $23 million, and modelled on the U.S. Head Start program, AHS programs have been implemented in 114 Aboriginal communities across Canada. Evaluations of the programs show substantial gains in all areas of child development, and improved parenting skills.

CRITICAL THINKING

1. Does a program such as Head Start substitute one type of negative label (special-needs child) for another (slow starter)?

2. What do you think are some benefits that children who participate in Head Start will carry with them throughout their childhood and adolescence?

Sources: Personal contact, Head Start Program, 2000; Edward Zigler and Sally Styfco, "Head Start: Criticisms in a Constructive Context," *American Psychologist* 49 (1994): 127–132; Nancy Kassebaum, "Head Start: Only the Best for America's Children," *American Psychologist* 49 (1994): 123–126; Faith Lamb Parker, Chaya Piorkowski, and Lenore Peay, "Head Start as Social Support for Mothers: The Psychological Benefits of Involvement," *American Journal of Orthopsychiatry* 57 (1987): 220–233; Health Canada, Division of Childhood and Adolescence, "Program Overview: Aboriginal Head Start (AHS) in Urban and Northern Communities," http://www.hc-sc.gc.ca/dca-dea/programs.

Summary

Social process theories view criminality as a function of people's interaction with various organizations, institutions, and processes in society. People in all walks of life have the potential to become criminals if they maintain destructive social relationships. Social process theory has three main branches: (1) social learning theory stresses that people learn how to commit crimes; (2) social control theory analyzes the failure of society to control criminal tendencies; and (3) labelling theory maintains that negative labels produce criminal careers.

Social learning theory suggests that people learn criminal behaviours much as they learn conventional behaviours. Differential association theory, formulated by Edwin Sutherland, holds that criminality is a result of a person's perceiving an excess of definitions in favour of crime over definitions that uphold conventional values. Sykes and Matza's theory of neutralization stresses that youths learn behaviour rationalizations that enable them to overcome societal values and norms and break the law.

Control theory maintains that all people have the potential to become criminals, but their bonds to conventional society prevent them from violating the law. This view suggests that a person's self-concept aids his or her commitment to conventional action. Travis Hirschi describes the social bond as containing elements of attachment, commitment, involvement, and belief. Weakened bonds allow youths to behave antisocially.

Social reaction or labelling theory holds that criminality is promoted by becoming negatively labelled by significant others. Labels such as "criminal," "ex-con," and "junkie" isolate people from society and lock them into lives of crime. Labels create expectations that the labelled person will act in a certain way; labelled people are always watched and suspected. Eventually these people begin to accept their labels as personal identities, locking them further into lives of crime and deviance. Edwin Lemert suggests that people who accept labels are involved in secondary deviance. Unfortunately, research on labelling has not supported its major premises. Consequently, critics have charged that it lacks credibility as a description of crime causation.

Social process theories have greatly influenced social policy. They have controlled treatment orientations as well as community action policies.

Discussion Questions

1. If criminal behaviour is learned, who taught the first criminal? Are behaviours such as vandalism and bullying actually learned?

2. Children who do well in school are less likely to commit criminal acts than those who are school failures. Which element of Hirschi's theory is supported by the school failure–delinquency link?

3. Have you ever been given a negative label, and, if so, did it cause you social harm? How did you lose the label, or did it become a permanent marker that still troubles you today?

4. If negative labels are damaging, do positive ones help insulate children from crime-producing forces in their environment?

5. How would a social process theorist explain the fact that many children begin offending at an early age and then desist as they mature?

READY
TO STUDY?

IN THE BOOK, YOU CAN:

✔ Check your understanding of what you've just read by reading the Summary at the end of each chapter.

✔ Rip out the Chapter in Review card at the back of the book to have the key terms and Learning Objectives handy, and complete the quizzes provided (answers are at the bottom of the back page!).

ONLINE YOU CAN:

✔ Stay organized and efficient with MindTap —a single destination with all the course material and study aids you need to succeed. Built-in apps leverage social media and the latest learning technology. For example:

   ✔ ReadSpeaker will read the text to you.

   ✔ Flashcards are pre-populated to provide you with a jump start for review —or you can create your own.

   ✔ You can highlight text and make notes in your MindTap Reader. Your notes will flow into Evernote, the electronic notebook app that you can access anywhere when it's time to study for the exam.

   ✔ Prepare for tests with quizzes.

Go to www.nelson.com/student to access these digital resources.

8

Social Conflict Theory: Power, Privilege, and Social Justice

Learning Objectives

LO1 Discuss how social conflict theorists explain the existence of crime in a society.

LO2 Explain the purpose of the legal system according to conflict theorists.

LO3 Explain why Marxist criminologists view the justice system as an army.

LO4 Describe how Marxist criminologists explain crime.

LO5 Discuss how feminist criminologists view the role of patriarchy as a cause of both male and female criminal behaviour.

LO6 Explain how restorative justice is meant to prevent and control crime.

© NARONG SANGNAK/epa/Corbis

Shortly after 7:30 A.M. on the morning of October 17, 2013, the village of Rexton, New Brunswick, erupted in violence when a contingent of more than 50 RCMP officers moved in to enforce a court injunction preventing protesters from blockading the entrance to a compound near the village where SWN Resources Canada stored drilling and seismic equipment used to explore for shale gas, natural gas deposits trapped in underground shale rock beds. By 9:30 A.M., "all hell had broken loose," according to Robert Levi, a band councillor with Elsipogtog First Nation, as both native and non-native protestors clashed with police who had begun to use pepper-spray to disperse the growing crowd of protestors. By the end of the day, five police cruisers had been burned with Molotov cocktails, gunshots and rubber bullets had been fired, and more than 40 protesters had been arrested.

The violence that erupted in Rexton marked the culmination of growing tension between, on the one side, First Nations groups, environmentalists, and members of the public protesting the environmental destruction from the use of hydraulic fracturing ("fracking") to extract natural gas from shale beds and the trampling of native land rights to access the gas deposits, and, on the other side, Canadian and foreign-owned energy companies and the provincial conservative government of Premier David Alward. According to Alward, the extraction and sale of shale gas would have an "enormous positive impact" on the New Brunswick economy, bringing new jobs and billions in new investment to the beleaguered province. Protesters and other critics pointed out that the costs of long-term environmental damage, pollution of drinking water, and management of waste products from the fracking process could outweigh any short-term economic benefits.

The fracking controversy became a key issue in the 2014 New Brunswick provincial election in which Alward was defeated by Liberal leader Brian Gallant, who ran on a promise to put a moratorium on hydraulic fracturing in the province if elected. In March 2015, the moratorium legislation was enacted by the Liberal government, bringing a halt to fracking—at least until new regulatory safeguards can be developed. In July 2014 two of the Rexton protesters were sentenced to 15 months in jail for their part in the violence; another protester was sentenced to 200 hours of community service. Civil lawsuits and investigations in RCMP mistreatment of protesters and journalists reporting on the Rexton violence are ongoing.[1]

It would be unusual to pick up the morning paper and not see headlines loudly proclaiming renewed strife in the Middle East, between union negotiators and management lawyers, between citizens and police authorities, or between rival political parties. The world is filled with conflict. Conflict can be destructive when it leads to war, violence, and death; it can be functional when it results in positive social change.

Criminologists who view crime as a function of social conflict and economic rivalry are aligned with a number of schools of thought. These are referred to as conflict, critical, Marxist, and radical schools of criminology. Among their affiliated branches are peacemaking, left realism, feminist criminology, postmodernism (also called *deconstructionism*), and activist criminology.

Social conflict theory tries to explain crime within economic and social contexts and to express the connection between social class, crime, and social control.[2] Conflict theorists are concerned with issues such as

- Social conflict and social justice
- The view that crime is a function of class conflict and power relations; laws are created and enforced by those in power to protect their own interests
- The role that government plays in creating a criminogenic environment
- The relationship between personal or group power and the shaping of criminal law
- The prevalence of bias in justice system operations
- The relationship between a capitalist, free enterprise economy, and crime rates

DID YOU KNOW?

- Social conflict theory is aimed at identifying "real" crimes in society such as profiteering, sexism, and racism.
- It seeks to evaluate how criminal law is used as a mechanism of social control.
- It describes how power relations create inequities in society.
- The idea of the social reality of crime is that those who hold power in society define those who oppose their values as criminals.
- Racism and classism pervade the contemporary justice system and shape crime rates.
- Activist criminologists use their knowledge to work with communities and government to try to make changes that will ensure that the legal system is fair and just for all.

Conflict promotes crime by creating a social atmosphere in which the law is a mechanism for controlling dissatisfied, have-not members of society while the wealthy maintain their power. This is why crimes that are the province of the wealthy, such as illegal

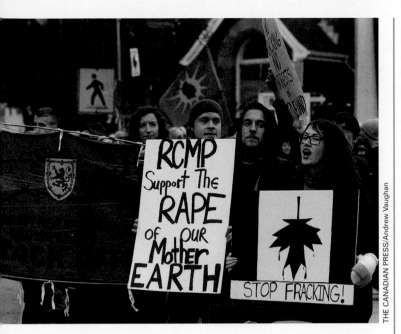

On October 17, 2013, violence erupted in Rexton, New Brunswick, as RCMP officers clashed with protesters at a blockade in front of SWN Resources Canada, a Texas-owned energy company conducting seismic tests to search for underground deposits of natural gas trapped in shale beds.

corporate activities, are sanctioned much more leniently than those such as burglary, that are considered lower-class activities. As you may recall (see Chapter 1), Karl Marx identified the economic structures in society that control all human relations. In so doing, he sowed the seeds of social conflict theory.

Those criminologists who gain their inspiration from Marx reject the notion that law is designed to maintain a tranquil, fair society and that criminals are malevolent people who wish to trample the rights of others. Conflict theorists consider acts of racism, sexism, imperialism, unsafe working conditions, inadequate child care, substandard housing, pollution of the environment, and poverty to be the most serious crimes because they create the conditions in society that lead many people to desperation, drug and alcohol abuse, and violence. The crimes of the poor and disadvantaged—drugs, break and enter, robbery, prostitution, and assault—are therefore often seen as reactions to and expressions of hopelessness or rage over unjust social conditions.[3] By focusing on how the capitalist state uses law to control the lower classes, Marxist

thought serves as the basis for all social conflict theory.

This chapter reviews criminological theories that see criminal behaviour as a function of conflict, a reaction to the unfair distribution of wealth and power in society. The social conflict perspective has several independent branches. One, generally referred to as "pure" conflict theory, maintains that intergroup conflict and rivalry cause crime in any society, regardless of its economic structure. A second branch focuses on the crime-producing traits of capitalist society; included here are critical, radical, and Marxist criminology.[4] In general, the terms radical criminology and Marxist criminology will be used interchangeably; where appropriate, distinctions will be made between the various schools of thought they contain. Finally, emerging forms of social conflict theory include feminist, new realist, peacemaking, postmodern thought, and activist criminology (see Figure 8.1).

radical criminology
The view that crime is a product of the capitalist system; also called *Marxist criminology*.

Marxist criminology
The view that crime is a product of the capitalist system; also called *radical criminology*.

FIGURE 8.1

The Branches of Social Conflict Theory

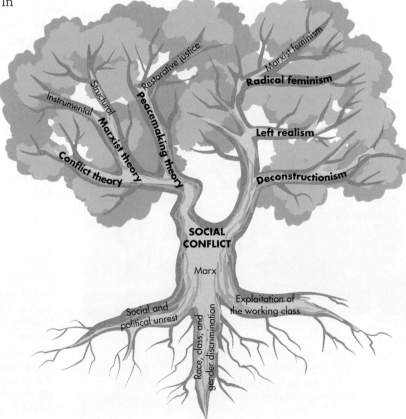

LO1 The Conflict Theory of Crime

Conflict theory came into criminological prominence during the 1960s, when self-report studies began to yield data suggesting that the class–crime correlation found in official crime data was spurious. The self-reports showed that crime and delinquency were distributed much more evenly through the social structure than indicated by official statistics, which reported more crime in lower-class environments.[5] If these self-reports were accurate, middle-class participation in crime was going unrecorded while the lower class was subjected to discriminatory law enforcement practices.[6]

The theme that dominated much of this scholarship was the contention that criminal legislation was determined by the relative power of groups determined to use criminal law to advance their own special interests or to impose their own moral preferences on others.[7] This movement was aided by the widespread social and political upheaval of the late 1960s and early 1970s. These social forces included anti–Vietnam War demonstrations, counterculture movements, and various forms of political protest, including the formation of the terrorist group the Front de Libération du Québec (FLQ), which was responsible for bombings, kidnappings, and even the murder of a provincial cabinet minister during the 1960s and 1970s.[8] Conflict theory

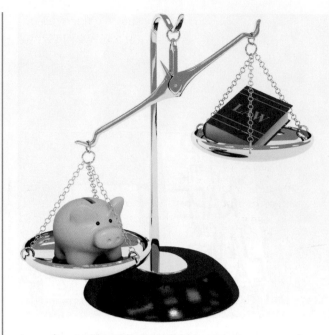

According to Chambliss and Seidman, the law serves the interests of those who can afford it.

The Front de Libération du Québec (FLQ) was responsible for a series of bombings, kidnappings, and murders in the late 1960s. The kidnapping and murder of the British Trade Commissioner in 1970 led to Prime Minister Pierre Trudeau's implementation of the *War Measures Act* and the suspension of civil liberties in Quebec.

flourished within this framework because it provided a systematic basis for challenging the legitimacy of the government's creation and application of law. Government crackdowns on political dissidents seemed designed to maintain control in the hands of the status quo.

As conflict theory began to influence criminological study, several influential scholars embraced its ideas. William Chambliss and Robert Seidman wrote the well-respected treatise *Law, Order and Power*, which documented how the justice system protects the rich and powerful. After closely observing its operations, Chambliss and Seidman concluded:

> In America, it is frequently argued that to have "freedom" is to have a system which allows one group to make a profit over another. To maintain the existing legal system requires a choice. That choice is between maintaining a legal system that serves to support the existing economic system with its power structure and developing an equitable legal system accompanied by the loss of "personal freedom." But the old question comes back to plague us: Freedom for whom? Is the black man who provides such a ready source of cases for the welfare workers, the mental hospitals, and the prisons "free"? Are the slum dwellers who are arrested night after night for "loitering," "drunkenness," or being "suspicious" free? The freedom protected by the system of law is the freedom of those who can afford it. The law serves their interests, but they are not "society"; they are one element of society. They may in some complex societies even be a majority (though this is very rare), but the myth that the law serves the interests of "society" misrepresents the facts.[9]

power
The ability of persons and groups to control the behaviour of others, to shape public opinion, and to define deviance.

Some common objectives of conflict criminology that appear in Chambliss and Seidman's writing include:

- Describing how control of the political and economic system affects the way criminal justice is administered

- Showing how definitions of crime favour those who control the justice system

- Analyzing the role of conflict in contemporary society

Their scholarship also reflects another major objective of conflict theory: to show how justice is skewed. Those who deserve the most severe sanctions (wealthy white-collar criminals whose crimes cost society millions of dollars) are actually punished the least, whereas those whose relatively minor crimes are committed out of economic necessity (petty thieves and drug dealers) receive stricter penalties.[10]

Power Relations

According to the conflict view, crime is defined by those in power. Power refers to the ability of persons and groups to determine and control the behaviour of others and to shape public opinion to meet their personal interests. Unequal distribution of power produces conflict as different groups struggle for control and dominance in society.

Nowhere is this relationship more evident than in the racism that pervades the justice process. Poor minority youths may be driven to commit crimes because they have no other way to obtain

THE CANADIAN PRESS/Graham Hughes

On Monday, February 15, 2010, Montreal investment financier Earl Jones was sentenced to 11 years in prison for defrauding 158 investors out of more than $50 million. Many of those Jones defrauded were friends, elderly couples, even his own brother. Because white-collar crime is nonviolent, and because in the opinion of the Parole Board of Canada Jones has "high potential for reintegration," he was released on parole in March 2014 after serving only four years of his sentence.

the material possessions that other "mainstream" youth have. Racial discrimination then results in discretionary decisions by law enforcement officers,

CRIMINOLOGY AT THE MOVIES

THE CANADIAN PRESS/Everett Collection

In the 2013 documentary *Snow on the Bluff*, the film makers follow Curtis Snow, a young Black man living in the "Bluff," an Atlanta neighbourhood notorious for crime. Through the eyes and words of Curtis, viewers are taken inside the frightening reality of life in the Bluff, where cocaine is supreme, gun violence and death is the norm, and all "normal rules" of life are turned upside down. Adults and children roam the streets day and night; evidently, almost no one goes to school or to work; protecting one's turf and trade in drugs are preoccupations in a life filled with danger and early death. Where are the police? Where is social order?

Conflict criminologists are critical of the way in which definitions of crime and social control reflect middle-class values, while ignoring the experience of the poor and the working class; critical race criminologists go one step further in criticizing the racialization of crime and social control—including devoting substantial resources to responding to "public disorder" crimes in upper- and middle-class neighbourhoods, while ignoring the violence, serious crime, and conflict in poor neighbourhoods. Have we abandoned the inner core of our large cities to gangs and violence?

social reality of crime
The main purpose of criminology is to promote a peaceful, just society.

who elect to charge them with indictable offences, not summary offences, and send them to criminal courts, not diversion programs. Busy duty counsel or legal aid lawyers can pressure their clients into plea bargains that ensure early criminal records. Health-care workers and teachers are quick to report suspected violent acts to the police; this results in frequent, early arrests of minority youths and adults. Police routinely search, question, and detain all black males in an area if a violent criminal has been described as "looking or sounding black"; this is called "racial profiling." By creating the image of pervasive black criminality and coupling it with unfair treatment, those in power further alienate

Though the 2015 May Day marches in Montreal started out as peaceful protests against the profits made by big banks and cuts to social programs by the Quebec government, by early evening a protest march organized by the anti-capitalism group CLAC (Convergence des Luttes Anti-Capitalistes), comprising a coalition of students, social activists, and labourers, turned violent when Montreal police declared the protest illegal. Despite the warning, protesters continued to move up McGill College Avenue in the city, and police launched canisters of teargas into the crowd. Eighty-four people were arrested in the ensuing violence, with one police car and other cars on the street damaged, and two police officers injured. According to the press release issued by the CLAC, "It's our dissent, it's our rebellion, and May 1st is our day. We don't have to ask permission, say please and thank you, or apologize for our presence disrupting the course of capitalist activity. We are in the streets because we want to be disruptive. It's a right you don't ask for, it's a right you have to claim!"[11]

© Darren Ell/Demotix/Corbis

this population from the mainstream, perpetuating a class- and race-divided society. Surveys in both the United States and Canada show that blacks are much more likely to perceive criminal injustice than whites.[12] Other research shows that Aboriginal people are both more likely to be arrested and imprisoned than other Canadians.[13]

The Social Reality of Crime

Richard Quinney, one of the more influential conflict theorists of the time, integrated these beliefs about power, society, and criminality into a theory he referred to as the social reality of crime. According to Quinney, criminal definitions (law) represent the interests of those who hold power in society. Where there is conflict between social groups—for example, the wealthy and the poor—those who hold power create laws that benefit themselves and hold their rivals in check.[14]

According to Quinney, law is not an abstract body of rules that represents an absolute moral code; rather, law is an integral part of society, a force that represents a way of life and a method of doing things. Crime is a function of power relations and an inevitable result of social conflict. Criminals are not simply social misfits, but people who have come up short in the struggle for success and are seeking alternative means of achieving wealth, status, or even survival.[15] Consequently, law violations can be viewed as political or even quasi-revolutionary acts.[16]

LO2 Research on Conflict Theory

Conflict theorists maintain that social inequality forces people to commit some crimes, such as break and enter, prostitution, and theft as a means of social and economic survival, whereas other crimes, such as assault, homicide, and drug use, are a means of expressing rage, frustration, and anger. Data show that crime rates vary according to indicators of poverty and need. For example, infant mortality rates have been associated with homicide rates, which shows that a society that cannot care for its young is also prone to social unrest and violence.[17] Crime rates seem strongly related to measures of social inequality such as income level, deteriorated living conditions, and relative economic deprivation.[18]

Another area of conflict-oriented research involves examining the criminal justice system to see if it operates as an instrument of class oppression or as a fair, even-handed social control agency. Some conflict researchers have found evidence of class bias. Legal jurisdictions with significant levels of economic disparity are also the most likely to have large numbers of people killed by police officers.

Police may act more forcefully in areas where class conflict creates the perception that extreme forms of social control are needed to maintain order.[19] It is not surprising to conflict theorists that police brutality complaints are highest in minority neighbourhoods, especially those that experience relative deprivation (minority residents earn significantly less money than the white majority).[20]

Criminal courts are also more likely to punish members of powerless, disenfranchised groups.[21] When criminals are convicted, whether white, black or Aboriginal, offenders have been found to receive stricter sentences if their personal characteristics (single, young, urban, male) show them to be members of the "dangerous classes."[22] The unemployed, especially racial minorities, may be perceived as "social dynamite" who present a real threat to society and must be controlled and incapacitated.[23]

Conflict theorists also point to studies showing that the criminal justice system is quick to act when a crime victim is wealthy, white, and male but is disinterested when the victim is poor, black or Aboriginal, and female.[24] Analysis of population trends and imprisonment rates shows that as the percentage of minority-group members increases in a population, the imprisonment rate does likewise.[25] As minority populations increase, the majority may become less tolerant or feel more threatened.

One reason for such displays of discrimination may be the overt or covert racist attitudes of decision makers. Justice professionals who express racist values (such as stating that race-based trait differences actually exist) are also more punitive, believe that courts should be stricter, and are likely to let race affect their judgments.[26] Critical theorists argue that there must be a thorough rethinking of the role and purpose of the criminal justice system, giving the powerless a greater voice to express their needs and concerns, if these inequities are to be addressed.[27]

Radical Criminology

The writings of Karl Marx and Friedrich Engels greatly influenced the development of social conflict thinking. Although Marx himself did not write much on the topic of crime, his views on the relationship between the economic structure and social behaviour deeply influenced other thinkers.

In the 1960s, theories that focused on the relationship between crime and conflict in any society began to be supplanted by more radical, Marxist-oriented theories that examined the specific role of capitalism in law and criminality.

In 1973, radical theory was given a powerful academic boost when British scholars Ian Taylor, Paul Walton, and Jock Young published *The New Criminology*.[28] This brilliant, thorough, and well-constructed critique of existing concepts in criminology called for the development of new methods of criminological analysis and critique. *The New Criminology* became the standard resource for scholars critical of both the field of criminology and the existing legal process.

During the same period, a small group of scholars in the United States and Canada also began to follow a new, radical approach to criminology. In the United States, the locus of the radical school was the criminology program at the University of California at Berkeley. The most noted Marxist scholars at that institution were Anthony Platt, Paul Takagi, Herman Schwendinger, and Julia Schwendinger. Radical scholars at other American academic institutions included Richard Quinney, William Chambliss, Steven Spitzer, and Barry Krisberg. In Canada, radical criminology took root at a number of universities across the country, and includes scholarly work by Ronald Hinch, Walter DeKeseredy, John Hagan, Thomas O'Reilly-Fleming, Brian Maclean, Neil Boyd, Christine Boyle, and others.

The North American radicals were influenced by the widespread social ferment during the late 1960s and early 1970s. The war in Vietnam, prison struggles, the Quiet Revolution in Quebec, and broad-based civil rights and feminist movements in both Canada and the United States produced a climate in which criticism of the ruling class seemed a natural byproduct. Mainstream, positivist criminology was criticized as being overtly conservative, pro-government, and antihuman. Critical criminologists scoffed when their fellow scholars used statistical analysis of computerized data to describe criminal and delinquent behaviour.

In the following years, new branches of a radical criminology developed in North America and abroad. In the early 1980s, the left realism school was started by scholars affiliated with the Middlesex Polytechnic and the University of Edinburgh in Great Britain. In the United States, scholars influenced in part by the pioneering work of Dennis Sullivan and Larry Tifft laid the foundation for what eventually became known as the peacemaking movement, which calls for a humanist vision of justice.[29] At the same time, feminist scholars began to critically analyze the relationship between gender, power, and criminality. These movements have coalesced into a rich and complex criminological tradition.

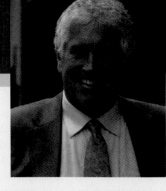

Professor Neil Boyd is director of the School of Criminology at Simon Fraser University, and one of the leading researchers and writers on criminology and criminal violence in Canada. A graduate of the University of Western Ontario, Professor Boyd worked as a probation officer in Ontario in 1974 prior to entering Osgoode Law School at York University in Toronto, Ontario. He has published more than 50 articles and reports, and 12 books on subjects ranging from drug abuse, homicide and workplace violence to Canadian law, censorship, mentally ill offenders and juvenile delinquency.

LO3 Fundamentals of Marxist Criminology

Above all, Marxism is a critique of capitalism.[30] Marx viewed the new industrial capitalist societies that developed in England and Europe in the 18th century as a result of the Industrial Revolution as societies of increasing oppression of the poor and the working class (the "proletariat") by the newly wealthy and powerful owners of the factories and commerce (the "bourgeoisie"). Marx argued that these new, capitalist societies created misery among the proletariat, who were forced to work in terrible and dangerous working conditions for low wages that barely covered the cost of their rent and food. Beaten down and angry, the proletariat turned to alcohol and drugs, prostitution, theft and violence toward one another, provoking the passage of laws and the setting up of police forces to control this underclass. Over time, as the development of capitalist societies continued on a global scale, Marx predicted that a smaller and smaller number of bourgeoisie would control most of the world's resources and wealth. In capitalist societies "wealth is power, and the bourgeoisie would call the shots when it came to determining what kinds of government economic and social policies are followed, and what kinds of criminal laws get passed and enforced.[31]

As a result of the capitalist mode of production and the economic and power divide between the bourgeoisie owners and the proletarian poor and working class, crimes of the poor tend to be "street crimes": sexual assault, murder, prostitution, drugs, theft, home invasions, and assault. Members of the middle class, what Marx called the "petit bourgeoisie" cheat on their taxes and engage in petty corporate crime (employee theft), acts that generate social disapproval but are rarely punished severely. The wealthy bourgeoisie are involved in "suite crimes," acts that should be described as crimes but are not, such as racism, sexism, stock market manipulation, destruction of the environment and profiteering.[32] Although regulatory laws control illegal business activities, these are rarely enforced, and violations are lightly punished. Laws regulating corporate crime are actually designed to impress the working class with how fair the justice system is. In reality, the justice system is the equivalent of an army that defends the owners of property in their ongoing struggle against the workers.[33]

The rich are insulated from street crimes because they live in areas far removed from crime. Those in power use the fear of crime as a tool to

"And here's when Mr. Kimbel, the company accountant, went on his extended holiday to Brazil."

maintain their control over society. The poor are controlled through incarceration, and the middle class is diverted from caring about the crimes of the powerful by their fear of the crimes of the powerless.[34] Ironically, the middle class may have more to lose from the economic crimes committed by the rich than the street crimes of the poor. Stock market swindles and price fixing cost the public billions of dollars but are typically settled with fines and probationary sentences.

Because private ownership of property is the true measure of success in capitalism (as opposed to being, say, a worthy person), the state becomes an ally of the wealthy in protecting their property interests. As a result, theft-related crimes are often punished more severely than are acts of violence because while the former may be interclass, the latter are typically intraclass.

LO4 How Marxist Criminologists Define Crime

Marxists use the conflict definition of crime: Crime is a political concept designed to protect the power and position of the upper classes at the expense of the poor. Some, but not all, Marxists would include in a list of "real" crimes acts such as violations of human rights due to racism, sexism, and imperialism, and other violations of human dignity, physical needs, and necessities. Part of the radical agenda, argues criminologist Robert Bohm, is to make the public aware that these behaviours "are crimes just as much as burglary and robbery."[35]

The nature of a society controls the direction of its criminality; criminals are not social misfits, but products of the society and its economic system. "Capitalism," claims Bohm, "as a mode of production, has always produced a relatively high level of crime and violence."[36] According to Michael Lynch and W. Byron Groves, three implications follow from this view:

1. Each society produces its own types and amounts of crime.

2. Each society has its own distinctive ways of dealing with criminal behaviour.

3. Each society gets the amount and type of crime that it deserves.[37]

This analysis tells us that criminals are not a group of outsiders who can be controlled by increased law enforcement. Criminality, instead, is a function of social and economic organization. To control crime and reduce criminality is to end the social conditions that promote crime.

Economic Structure and Surplus Value

Although no single view or theory defines Marxist criminology today, its general theme is the relationship between crime and the ownership and control of private property in a capitalist society.[38] That ownership and control is the principal basis of power in capitalist societies such as Canada and the United States.[39] Social conflict is fundamentally related to the historical and social distribution of productive private property. Destructive social conflicts inherent within the capitalist system cannot be resolved unless that system is destroyed or ended.

The CANADIAN PRESS/Graham Hughes

Social conflict is fundamentally related to the distribution of private property, a process that historically has been unfair, biased, and discriminatory. In March 2011, students in Montreal took to the streets to protest proposed tuition fee hikes. Many students from working-class and even middle-class homes are concerned that university tuition will become so expensive that only the children of the wealthy will be able to afford to go. Police responded to the student demonstration with stun grenades to disperse the crowd.

surplus value
The difference between what workers produce and what they are paid, which goes to business owners as profits.

marginalization
Displacement of workers, pushing them outside the economic and social mainstream.

One important aspect of the capitalist economic system is the effect of surplus value—the profits produced by the labouring classes that are accrued by business owners. Surplus value can be either reinvested or used to enrich the owners. To increase the rate of surplus value, workers can be made to work harder for less pay, be made more efficient, or be replaced by machines or technology. Therefore, economic growth does not benefit all elements of the population, and in the long run it may produce the same effect as a depression or recession.

As the rate of surplus value increases, more people are displaced from productive relationships, and the size of the marginal population swells. As corporations downsize to increase profits, high-paying labour and managerial jobs are lost to computer-driven machinery. Displaced workers are forced into service jobs at minimum wage. Many become temporary employees without benefits or a secure position, or enter the ranks of the permanently unemployed.

As more people are thrust outside the economic mainstream, a condition referred to as marginalization, a larger portion of the population is forced to live in areas conducive to crime. Once people are marginalized, commitment to the system declines, producing another criminogenic force: a weakened bond to society.[40] This process is illustrated in Figure 8.2.

The government may be quick to respond during periods of economic decline because those in

The homeless are often viewed as marginalized from society.

power assume that poor economic conditions breed crime and social disorder. When unemployment is increasing, public officials assume the worst and devote greater attention to the criminal justice system, perhaps building new prisons to prepare for the coming "crime wave."[41] Empirical research confirms that economic downturns are indeed linked to both crime rate increases and government activities such as passing anticrime legislation.[42] For example, as the level of surplus value increases, so too do police expenditures, most likely because of the perceived or real need for the state to control those on the economic margin.[43]

FIGURE 8.2

Surplus Value and Crime

Worker produces goods that exceed wages in value → Profit → Capitalist keeps profits → Uses profits to buy machines and replace workers → Workers are marginalized → Crime rates increase

Although these themes can be found throughout Marxist writing, a number of different schools of thought have arisen within the radical literature. Among these various approaches are instrumental Marxism and structural Marxism.

Instrumental Marxism

Instrumental Marxists view criminal law and the criminal justice system solely as instruments for controlling the poor, have-not members of society. They see the state as the tool of capitalists.

According to the instrumental view, capitalist justice serves the powerful and rich and enables them to impose their morality and standards of behaviour on the entire society. Under capitalism, those who wield economic power are able to extend their self-serving definition of illegal or criminal behaviour to encompass those who might threaten the status quo or interfere with their quest for ever-increasing profits.[44] For example, the concentration of economic assets in the nation's largest industrial firms translates into the political power needed to control tax laws to limit the firms' tax liabilities.[45] Some have the economic clout to hire top lawyers to defend themselves against antitrust actions, making them almost immune to regulation.

The poor, according to this branch of Marxist theory, may or may not commit more crimes than the rich, but they certainly are arrested and punished more often. Under the capitalist system, the poor are driven to crime because a natural frustration exists in a society in which affluence is well publicized but unattainable. When class conflict becomes unbearable, frustration can spill out in riots, such as the one that occurred in June 2010 when a large crowds of antipoverty protesters clashed with police during the G20 summit meeting in Toronto, Ontario.[46] Because of class conflict, a deep-rooted hostility is generated among members of the lower class toward a social order they are not allowed to shape and whose benefits are unobtainable.[47]

Instrumental Marxists consider it essential to **demystify** law and justice—that is, to unmask its true purpose. Criminological theories that focus on family structure, intelligence, peer relations, and school performance keep the lower classes servile by showing why they are more criminal, less intelligent, and more prone to school failure and family problems than the middle class. Demystification involves identifying the destructive intent of capitalist-inspired and capitalist-funded criminology. Instrumental Marxists' goal for criminology is to show how capitalist law preserves ruling-class power.[48]

Structural Marxism

Structural Marxists disagree with the view that the relationship between law and capitalism is unidirectional, always working for the rich and against the poor.[49] Law is not the exclusive domain of the rich, but rather is used to maintain the long-term interests of the capitalist system and control members of any class who threaten its existence. If law and justice were purely instruments of the capitalist class, why would laws controlling corporate crimes, such as price-fixing, false advertising, and illegal restraint of trade, have been created and enforced? From the perspective of structural Marxists, competition, unfairness, and exploitation of everyone is part of the very design and structure of the capitalist system, of the "way things just are"—and the criminal justice system is therefore used to defend and preserve this status quo.

To a structuralist, the law is designed to keep the capitalist system operating efficiently, and anyone, capitalist or proletarian, who rocks the boat is

instrumental Marxist
One who sees criminal law and the criminal justice system as capitalist instruments for controlling the lower class.

demystify
To unmask the true purpose of law, justice, or other social institutions.

structural Marxist
One who sees criminal law and the criminal justice system as means of defending and preserving the capitalist system.

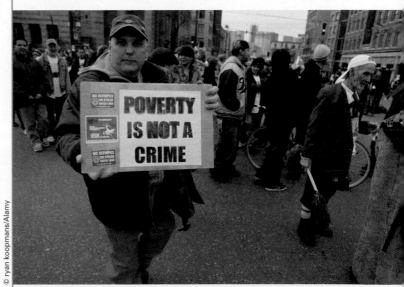

© ryan koopmans/Alamy

Antipoverty groups in Lower Mainland Vancouver demonstrated following the decision to host the 2010 Winter Olympics in the city. The groups claimed that while homelessness in Vancouver had doubled since 2003, the city introduced new bylaws making it illegal to ask for money or sleep outdoors. Also, far from being green or sustainable, the Olympic venues could cause a great deal of ecological damage.

targeted for sanction. For example, antitrust legislation is designed to prevent any single capitalist from dominating the system. If the capitalist system is to function, no single person can become too powerful at the expense of the economic system as a whole. Structuralists would regard the decision of the U.S. government to break up Microsoft, and recent efforts to regulate the dominance of Apple in the online music industry, as an example of capitalists controlling capitalists to keep the system on an even keel.

Research on Marxist Criminology

Marxist criminologists rarely use standard social science methodologies to test their views because many believe the traditional approach of measuring research subjects is antihuman and insensitive.[50] Marxists believe that the research conducted by mainstream liberal and positivist criminologists is designed to unmask weak, powerless members of society so they can be better dealt with by the legal system. Marxists are particularly offended by purely empirical studies, such as those designed to show that minority-group members have lower IQs than whites or that the inner city is the site of the most serious crime whereas middle-class areas are relatively crime-free.

Empirical research, however, is not considered totally incompatible with Marxist criminology, and there have been some important efforts to test its fundamental assumptions quantitatively.[51] For example, research has shown that the property crime rate reflects a change in the level of surplus value; the capitalist system's emphasis on excessive profits accounts for the need of the working class to commit property crime.[52] Nonetheless, Marxist research tends to be historical and analytical, not quantitative and empirical. Social trends are interpreted with regard to how capitalism has affected human interaction. Marxists investigate both macro-level issues, such as how the accumulation of wealth affects crime rates, and micro-level issues, such as the effect of criminal interactions on the lives of individuals living in a capitalist society. Of particular importance to Marxist critical thinkers is analyzing the historical development of capitalist social control institutions, such as criminal law, police agencies, courts, and prison systems.

Crime, the Individual, and the State

Marxists devote considerable attention to the relationships among crime, the victims, the criminal, and the state. Two common themes emerge: (1) crime and its control are a function of capitalism; and (2) the justice system is biased against the working class and favours upper-class interests.

Karl Marx

Marxist analysis of the criminal justice system is designed to identify the often-hidden processes that control people's lives. It takes into account how conditions, processes, and structures evolved into what they are today. One issue considered is the process by which deviant behaviour is defined as criminal or delinquent in society.[53] Another issue is the degree to which class affects the justice system's decision-making process.[54] Also subject to analysis is how power relationships help undermine any benefit the lower class receives from sentencing reforms.[55] In general, Marxist research efforts have yielded evidence linking operations of the justice system to class bias.[56] In addition, some researchers have attempted to show how capitalism intervenes across the entire spectrum of crime-related phenomena.

Historical Analysis

Another type of Marxist research focuses on the historical background of commonly held institutional beliefs and practices. One goal is to show how changes in criminal law correspond to the development of the capitalist economy. The second goal is to investigate the development of modern police agencies.

To examine the changes in criminal law, historian Michael Rustigan analyzed historical records to show that law reform in 19th-century England was largely a response to pressure from the business community to increase punishment for property law violations in order to protect business owners' rapidly increasing wealth.[57] Other research has focused on topics such as how the relationship between convict work and capitalism evolved during the 19th century. During this period, prisons became a profitable method of centralized state control over lower-class criminals, whose labour was exploited by commercial concerns. These criminals were forced to labour in order to pay off wardens and correctional administrators.[58]

Critique of Marxist Criminology

Marxist criminology has been sharply criticized by some members of the criminological mainstream, who charge that its contribution has been "hot air, heat, but no real light."[59] In turn, radicals have accused mainstream criminologists of being culprits in developing state control over individual lives and selling out their ideals for the chance to receive government funding.

Mainstream criminologists have also attacked the substance of Marxist thought. Some argue that Marxist theory simply rehashes the old tradition of helping the underdog, in which the poor steal from the rich to survive.[60] In reality, most theft is for luxury, not survival. While the wealthy do commit their share of illegal acts, these are nonviolent and leave no permanent injuries.[61] People do not live in fear of corrupt businessmen and stock traders; they fear muggers and rapists.

Other critics suggest that Marxists unfairly neglect the capitalist system's efforts to regulate itself—for example, by instituting antitrust regulations and putting violators in jail. Similarly, they ignore efforts to institute social reforms aimed at helping the poor.[62] There seems to be no logic in condemning a system that helps the poor and empowers them to take on corporate interests in a court of law. Some argue that Marxists refuse to address the problems and conflicts that exist in socialist countries, such as the gulags and purges of the Soviet Union under Stalin. Similarly, Marxists fail to explain why some highly capitalist countries, such as Japan, have extremely low crime rates. Marxists are too quick to blame capitalism for every human vice without adequate explanation or regard for other

social and environmental factors.[63] In so doing, they ignore objective reality and refuse to acknowledge that members of the lower classes tend to victimize one another. They ignore the plight of the lower classes, who must live in crime-ridden neighbourhoods, while condemning the capitalist system from the security of the "ivory tower."

Marxist scholars criticize their critics for relying on "traditional" variables, such as class and poverty, in their analysis of radical thought. Although important, these do not reflect the key issues in the structural and economic process. In fact, like crime, they too may be the outcome of the capitalist system.[64] Marxists also point out that although other capitalist nations may have lower crime rates, this does not mean they are crime-free. Even Japan has significant problems with teen prostitution and organized crime.

DID YOU KNOW?

- Marxist criminology tries to explain how the workings of the capitalist system produce inequality and crime.

- In this view, the state serves the interests of the ruling capitalist class. Criminal law is an instrument of economic oppression. Capitalism demands that the subordinate classes remain oppressed.

- Instrumental Marxists believe that the legal system supports the owners at the expense of the workers.

- Structural Marxists believe that the law also ensures that no capitalist becomes too powerful. The law is used to maintain the long-term interests of the capitalist system.

- Marxist research is designed to show how capitalism creates the people who turn to crime for survival.

Emerging Forms of Social Conflict Theory

Although radical criminologists dispute criticisms, they have also responded by creating new theoretical models that innovatively incorporate Marxist ideas. The following sections discuss in detail some recent forms of radical theory.

Left Realism

Some radical scholars are now addressing the need for the left wing to respond to the increasing power of right-wing conservatives. They are troubled by the emergence of a strict "law and order" philosophy, which has as its centrepiece a policy of punishing juveniles severely in adult court. At the same time, they find the focus of most left-wing scholarship—the abuse of power by the ruling elite—too narrow. It is wrong, they argue, to ignore inner-city gang crime and violence, which often target indigent people.[65] The approach of scholars who share these concerns is referred to as left realism.[66]

Left realism is most often connected to the writings of British scholars John Lea and Jock Young. In their well-respected 1984 work, *What Is to Be Done About Law and Order?* they reject the utopian views of "idealistic" Marxists who portray street criminals as revolutionaries.[67] They take the more "realistic" approach that street criminals prey on the poor and disenfranchised, thus making the poor doubly abused, first by the capitalist system and then by members of their own class.

Lea and Young's view of crime causation borrows from conventional sociological theory and closely resembles the relative deprivation approach, which posits that experiencing poverty in the midst of plenty creates discontent and breeds crime. As they put it, "The equation is simple: relative deprivation equals discontent; discontent plus lack of political solution equals crime."[68]

Left realists argue that crime victims in all classes need and deserve protection; crime control reflects community needs. Left realists do not view police and the courts as inherently evil tools of capitalism whose tough tactics alienate the lower classes. In fact, they recognize that these institutions offer life-saving public services. The left realists wish, however, that police would reduce their use of force and increase their sensitivity to the public.[69]

Preemptive deterrence is an approach in which community organization efforts eliminate or reduce crime before police involvement becomes necessary. The reasoning behind this approach is that if the number of marginalized youths (those who feel they are not part of society and have nothing to lose by committing crime) could be reduced, then delinquency rates would decline.[70]

Although implementing a socialist economy might help eliminate the crime problem, left realists recognize that something must be done to control crime under the existing capitalist system. To develop crime control policies, left realists not only welcome radical ideas but also build on the work of strain theorists, social ecologists, and other mainstream views. Community-based efforts seem to hold the greatest promise of crime control.

Left realism has been criticized by radical thinkers as legitimizing the existing power structure: By supporting existing definitions of law and justice, it suggests that the "deviant" and not the capitalist system causes society's problems. Critics question whether left realists advocate the very institutions that "currently imprison us and our patterns of thought and action."[71] In rebuttal, left realists would say that it is unrealistic to speak of a socialist state lacking a police force or a system of laws and justice. They believe that the *Criminal Code* does, in fact, represent public opinion.

LO5 Feminist Criminologists' View of the Role of Patriarchy as a Cause of Criminal Behaviour

Beginning in the 1970s, feminist researchers began to question traditional criminological theories that by and large ignored women in the criminal justice system.[72] Like Marxists, feminist theorists are interested in inequality and power, but point out that many of the most significant differences in these are based on gender. In most societies, men hold the privileged positions of power in the economy, politics, law and even the family, while women are relegated to giving up their jobs and careers to have children and care for the family home, resulting in lower pay and less career advancement, and ultimately greater vulnerability than men. Feminists point out that the inequality between men and women is not based on biological or psychological differences but rather is socially constructed, a set of ideas and customs about what is acceptable behaviour for males and females. Feminist criminologists therefore consider gender a key variable in explaining the causes of crime, criminal behaviour, victimization, and the functioning of the criminal justice system. Marxist feminism views gender inequality as stemming from the unequal power of men and women in a capitalist society, which leads to the exploitation of women by fathers and husbands. Under this system, women are considered a commodity worth possessing, like land or money.[73]

The origin of gender differences can be traced to the development of private property and male domination of the laws of inheritance, which led to male control over property and power.[74] A patriarchal system developed in which men's work was valued and women's work was devalued. As capitalism prevailed, the division of labour by gender made women responsible for the unpaid maintenance and reproduction of the current and future labour force, which was derisively called "domestic work." Although this unpaid work done by women is crucial and profitable for capitalists, who reap these free benefits, such labour is exploitative and oppressive for women.[75] Even when women gained the right to work for pay, they were exploited as cheap labour. The dual exploitation of women within the household and in the labour market means that women produce far greater surplus value for capitalists than men.

Patriarchy, or male supremacy, has been and continues to be supported by capitalists. This system sustains female oppression at home and in the workplace.[76] Although the number of traditional patriarchal families is in steep decline, in those that still exist, a wife's economic dependence ties men more securely to wage-earning jobs, further serving the interests of capitalists by undermining potential rebellion against the system.

Patriarchy and Crime

Marxist feminists link criminal behaviour patterns to the gender conflict created by the economic and social struggles common in postindustrial societies. In his book *Capitalism, Patriarchy, and Crime*, James Messerschmidt argues that capitalist society is marked by both class conflict and patriarchy. Capitalists control the labour of workers, while men control women both economically and biologically.[77] This "double marginality" explains why females in a capitalist society commit fewer crimes than males. Because they are isolated in the family, they have fewer opportunities to engage in elite deviance (white-collar and economic crimes). Although powerful females as well as males will commit white-collar crimes, the female crime rate is restricted because of the patriarchal nature of the capitalist system.[78] Women are also denied access to male-dominated street crimes. Because capitalism renders lower-class women powerless, they are forced to commit less serious, nonviolent, self-destructive crimes, such as abusing drugs.

Powerlessness also increases the likelihood that women will become targets of violent acts.[79] When lower-class males are shut out of the economic opportunity structure, they try to build their self-image through acts of machismo; such acts may involve violent abuse of women. This type of reaction accounts for a significant percentage of female victims who are attacked by a spouse or intimate partner.

In *Masculinities and Crime*, Messerschmidt expands on these themes.[80] He suggests that in every culture, males try to emulate "ideal" masculine behaviours. In Western culture, this means being authoritative, in charge, combative, and controlling. Failure to adopt these roles leaves men feeling effeminate and unmanly. Their struggle to dominate women in order to prove their manliness is called "doing gender." Crime is a vehicle for men to "do gender" because it separates them from the weak and allows them to demonstrate physical bravery. Violence directed toward women is an especially economical way to demonstrate manhood. Would a weak, effeminate male ever attack a woman?

patriarchal
Male-dominated.

Exploitation and Criminality

Radical feminists also focus on the social forces that shape women's lives and experiences to explain female criminality, but focus in particular on the role that patriarchy, regardless of the type of economic system, plays in the domination, exploitation, and victimization of women around the world.[81] For example, radical feminists point out that even in many traditional hunting and gathering and agricultural societies, social and even religious practices reinforce the dominance of males over females.[82] Radical feminist criminologists attempt to show how the sexual victimization of girls is a function of male socialization because so many young males learn to be aggressive and to exploit women. Males seek out same-sex peer groups for social support; these groups encourage members to exploit and sexually abuse women. On college and university campuses, peers encourage sexual violence against women who are considered "teasers," "bar pickups," or "loose women." These derogatory labels allow the males to justify their actions; a code of secrecy then protects the aggressors from retribution.[83]

According to the radical feminist view, patriarchal exploitation explains much about onset of female delinquent and deviant behaviour. When female victims run away and abuse substances, they may be reacting to abuse they have suffered at home or at school. Their attempts at survival are labelled as deviant or delinquent behaviour.[84] In a sense, the female criminal is herself a victim.

Research shows that a significant number of girls who are sent to hospital emergency rooms to be treated for sexual abuse later report engaging in physical fighting as a teen or as an adult. Many of these abused girls later form romantic attachments with abusive partners. Clearly, many girls involved in delinquency, crime, and violence have themselves been the victims of violence in their youth and later as adults.[85]

Radical feminist opinions differ on certain issues. For example, some feminist scholars charge that the movement focuses on the problems and viewpoints of white, middle-class, heterosexual women without taking into account the special interests of lesbians and visible-minority women.[86]

How the Justice System Penalizes Women

Radical feminists have indicted the justice system and its patriarchal hierarchy as contributing to the onset of female delinquency. Some have studied the early history of the justice system and uncovered an enduring pattern of discrimination. From its inception, the juvenile justice system has viewed most female delinquents as sexually precocious girls who have to be brought under control. Writing about the "girl problem," Ruth Alexander has described how working-class young women desiring autonomy and freedom in the 1920s were considered delinquents and placed in reformatories. Lacking the ability to protect themselves from the authorities, these young girls were considered outlaws in a male-dominated society because they flouted the very narrow rules of appropriate behaviour that were applied to females. Girls who rebelled against parental authority or who engaged in sexual behaviour deemed inappropriate were incarcerated in order to protect them from a career in prostitution.[87]

Using court records, training school files, government documents, and other publications, Joan Sangster investigated the "social construction" of female delinquency in Ontario from 1940 to 1960, and found that sexual activity, real or presumed, was often the "lightning rod" that resulted in girls being incarcerated in a training school. Young girls were routinely subjected to gynecological exams to obtain evidence of wrongdoing. Sometimes, girls were even incarcerated in training school as a preventive measure, to avert contact with boys. In some cases, if officials deemed a girl's family "immoral," that was enough to prompt her removal from the home and incarceration. Sangster concludes that in the 1940–1960 period, the criminal justice system was one designed to "punish, rather than to aid, working-class girls" who were somehow perceived as threats to middle-class notions of proper upbringing and behaviour.[88]

Meda Chesney-Lind has written extensively about the victimization of female delinquents by agents of the juvenile justice system.[89] She suggests that because female adolescents have a much narrower range of acceptable behaviour than male adolescents, any sign of misbehaviour in girls is seen

as a substantial challenge to authority and to the viability of the double standard of sexual inequality. Female delinquency is viewed as relatively more serious than male delinquency and therefore is more likely to be severely sanctioned.

Power–Control Theory

Canadian criminologist John Hagan and his associates have created a radical feminist model that uses gender differences to explain the onset of criminality.[90] Hagan's view is that crime and delinquency rates are a function of two factors: (1) class position (power) and (2) family functions (control).[91] The link between these two variables is that, within the family, parents reproduce the power relationships they hold in the workplace; a position of dominance at work is equated with control in the household. As a result, parents' work experiences and class position influence the criminality of children.

In paternalistic families, fathers assume the traditional role of breadwinners, while mothers tend to have menial jobs or remain at home to supervise domestic matters. Within the paternalistic home, mothers are expected to control the behaviour of their daughters while granting greater freedom to sons. In such a home, the parent–daughter relationship can be viewed as a preparation for the "cult of domesticity," which makes girls' involvement in delinquency unlikely, whereas boys are freer to deviate because they are not subject to maternal control. Girls growing up in patriarchal families are socialized to fear legal sanctions more than are males; consequently, boys in these families exhibit more delinquent behaviour than their sisters.

In egalitarian families—those in which the husband and wife share similar positions of power at home and in the workplace—daughters gain a kind of freedom that reflects reduced parental control. These families produce daughters whose law-violating behaviour mirrors their brothers'. Ironically, these relationships also occur in female-headed households with absent fathers. Hagan and his associates found that when fathers and mothers hold equally valued managerial positions, the similarity between the rates of their daughters' and sons' delinquency is greatest. By implication, middle-class girls are the most likely to violate the law because they are less closely controlled than their lower-class counterparts. In homes in which both parents hold positions of power, girls are more likely to have the same expectations of career success as their brothers. Consequently, siblings of both sexes will be socialized to take risks and engage in other behaviour related to delinquency.

This power–control theory has received a great deal of attention in the criminological community because it encourages a new approach to the study of criminality, one that includes gender differences, class position, and the structure of the family. Empirical analysis of its premises has generally been supportive. For example, Brenda Sims Blackwell's research supports a key element of power–control theory: Females in paternalistic households have learned to fear legal sanctions more than have their brothers.[92]

Postmodern Theory

A number of radical thinkers, referred to as postmodernist or deconstructionist thinkers, have embraced semiotics as a method of understanding all human relations, including criminal behaviour. Semiotics refers to the use of language elements as signs or symbols beyond their literal meaning. Thus, deconstructionists critically analyze communication and language in legal codes to determine whether they contain language and content that institutionalizes racism or sexism.[93]

Postmodernists rely on semiotics to conduct their research efforts. For example, the term *special-needs children* is designed to describe these youngsters' learning needs, but it may also characterize the children themselves as mentally challenged, dangerous, or uncontrollable. Similarly, application of the term *young offender* to a young person carries with it much more than a legal consequence; in the public mind, the term has been constructed to be associated with threat, unpredictability, violence, and the need for strong control. Though the youth crime rate in Canada has been in decline for more than ten years, and though only a very small number of youth commit serious violent crimes (usually against other youth) still, as postmodernist criminologists such as Moore and Padavic observe, we continue to use language to "demonize" young persons who come into conflict with the law, including using subtle notions of race and "good girl/bad girl" stereotypes in judges' sentencing decisions.[94]

Postmodernists believe that value-laden language can promote inequities. Truth, identity, justice, and power are all concepts whose meaning is derived from the language dictated by those in power.[95] Laws, legal skill, and justice are commodities that can be bought and sold like any other service or product.[96] For example, the O.J. Simpson case is vivid proof that the affluent can purchase a different brand of justice than the indigent.[97]

Postmodernists go further to assert that there are different languages and ways of knowing, depending on time and position from which one is looking at the issue. For example, prior to the implementation of the new legislation on sexual assault implemented in 1986, many male Canadians (including politicians) could not conceive of a sexual assault being committed by a husband against his wife—though women had long pointed to this problem.

Those in power can use their own language to define crime and law while excluding or dismissing those who oppose their control, such as prisoners and the poor. By dismissing these oppositional languages, certain versions of how to think, feel,

Postmodernists rely on semiotics, or the study of signs and symbols, to conduct their research efforts.

deezign/Shutterstock.com

According to Elizabeth Watkinson, a social work professor at the University of Regina and board member of the Elizabeth Fry Society of Saskatchewan, 80 percent of women in prison are there for committing nonviolent, "income-generating" crimes (e.g., sex trade work, theft and fraud, trafficking). Why? Because almost all female offenders were living in poverty at the time of their arrest, and three-quarters of them are mothers of young children under the age of 18—and usually are lone parents. Unlike their male counterparts, female offenders are more likely to have mental health and addiction problems but are at low risk for violence.

Critics, including feminist criminologists, ask what is the purpose behind incarcerating female offenders, most of whom are at low risk for violence and commit their crimes out of a need for money to support themselves and their children. According to the Correctional Investigator of Canada, one of the best ways to help female offenders to reintegrate into society and refrain from reoffending is to maintain and support the relationships between women and their children but prisons are not set up to do this.

When mothers are sentenced to prison, their children are sentenced to separation, often with profound consequences. Current research has found a detrimental impact on the behavioural and developmental outcomes for children deprived of a parent due to the adult's imprisonment, and more so when the imprisoned parent is the mother. Children are reported to be five times more likely to enter foster care when it's their mother who is incarcerated.

With all of the evidence we have pointing to fundamental differences between male and female offenders with respect to the motivations, types, level of violence, and potential for rehabilitation, feminist criminologists ask whether it is not time to re-examine how we address the legal and social response to female offending—perhaps community sentences that allow women to maintain family contact with their children, and educational supports that allow women to find decent-paying jobs to support their families are better (and cheaper) alternatives.

Source: Kristen McEwen, "Cruel, Unusual, and Inhumane," *The Carillon* (28 March 2013) at http://www.carillonregina.com/cruel-unusual-and-inhumane (accessed 21 October 2015).

Photo courtesy of Correctional Service of Canada

The Fraser Valley Institution for Women in Abbotsford, B.C. opened in 2004, and houses 112 female federal inmates. It is a multi-level (minimum, medium, maximum) security facility.

or act are devalued and excluded. This exclusion is seen as the source of conflict in society.

Allen studied the narratives of women survivors of abuse in an attempt to explore how women's resistance develops and unfolds as a survival mechanism

and, perhaps, as a movement toward exit from the abusive situation—in contrast to "official" or "governmental" theories, laws, and treatment approaches to domestic violence. For postmodernist criminologists, research such as Allen's challenges, and ultimately improves upon and makes more relevant, current approaches to addressing domestic violence.[98]

One of the newer movements in radical theory is **peacemaking** criminology. To members of the peacemaking movement, the main purpose of criminology is to promote a peaceful, just society. Rather than standing on empirical analysis of data, peacemaking draws its inspiration from religious and philosophical teachings ranging from traditional North American Aboriginal to Zen.

Peacemakers view the efforts of the state to punish and control as crime encouraging rather than crime discouraging. These views were first articulated in a series of books with an anarchist theme written by criminologists Larry Tifft and Dennis Sullivan in 1980.[99] Tifft argues, "The violent punishing acts of the state and its controlling professions are of the same genre as the violent acts of individuals. In each instance these acts reflect an attempt to monopolize human interaction."[100]

Sullivan stresses the futility of correcting and punishing criminals in the context of our conflict-ridden society: "The reality we must grasp is that we live in a culture of severed relationships, where every available institution provides a form of banishment but no place or means for people to become connected, to be responsible to and for each other."[101] Sullivan suggests that mutual aid rather than coercive punishment is the key to a harmonious society.

Today, advocates of the peacemaking movement, such as Harold Pepinsky and Richard Quinney (who has shifted his theoretical orientation from conflict theory to Marxism and now to peacemaking), try to find humanist solutions to crime and other social problems.[102] Rather than punishment and prison, they advocate policies such as mediation and conflict resolution.

LO6 Restorative Justice

There has been an ongoing effort to reduce the conflict created by the criminal justice system when it harshly punishes offenders, many of whom are powerless social outcasts. Rather than cast them aside, peacemakers have found a way to bring them back into the community. This peacemaking movement has applied nonviolent methods through what is known as **restorative justice**. Springing from both academia and justice system personnel, and based on methods of conflict resolution used in traditional societies, the restorative approach relies on nonpunitive strategies to prevent and control crime.[103] The principles of restorative justice are outlined in Table 8.1.

TABLE 8.1

Principles of Restorative Justice

1. Crime is fundamentally a violation of people and interpersonal relationships.
   a. Victims and the community have been harmed and need restoration. Victims include the target of the offence, family members, witnesses, and the community at large.
   b. Victims, offenders, and the affected communities are the key stakeholders in justice. The state must investigate crime and ensure safety, but it is not the centre of the justice process. Victims are the key, and they must help in the search for restoration, healing, responsibility, and prevention.

2. Violations create obligations and liabilities.
   a. Offenders have the obligation to make things right as much as possible. They must understand the harm they have caused. Their participation should be as voluntary as possible; coercion is to be minimized.
   b. The community's obligations are to victims, to offenders, and to the general welfare of its members. This includes the obligation to reintegrate offenders back into the community and to ensure them the opportunity to make amends.

3. Restorative justice seeks to heal and put right the wrongs.
   a. Victims' needs are the focal concern of the justice process. Safety is a top priority, and victims should be empowered to participate in determining their needs and case outcomes.
   b. The exchange of information between victim and offender should be encouraged; when possible, face-to-face meetings might be undertaken. There should be mutual agreement over imposed outcomes.
   c. Offenders' needs and competencies need to be addressed. Healing and reintegration are emphasized; isolation and removal from the community are restricted.
   d. The justice process belongs to the community; members are encouraged to "do justice." The justice process should be sensitive to community needs and geared toward preventing similar harm in the future. Early interventions are encouraged.
   e. Justice is mindful of the outcomes, intended and unintended, of its responses to crime and victimization. It should monitor case outcome and provide necessary support and opportunity to all involved. The least restrictive intervention should be used, and overt social control should be avoided.

Source: 'Fundamentals Concepts of Restorative Justice' by Howard Zehr and Harry Mika, *Contemporary Justice Review* (1998) vol. 1 pp. 47–55. Reprinted by permisison of Taylor & Francis Ltd, http://www.tandf.co.uk/journals

---

Restoration turns the justice system into a healing process rather than a distributor of retribution and revenge. Most people involved in offender–victim relationships know one another or were related in some way before the crime took place. According to restorative justice advocates, instead of treating one involved party as a victim deserving sympathy and the other as a criminal deserving punishment, it is more productive to address the issues that produced conflict between these people. Rather than take sides and choose whom to isolate

peacemaking
Approach that considers punitive crime control strategies to be counterproductive and favours the use of humanistic conflict resolution to prevent and control crime.

restorative justice
Using humanistic, nonpunitive strategies to right wrongs and restore social harmony.

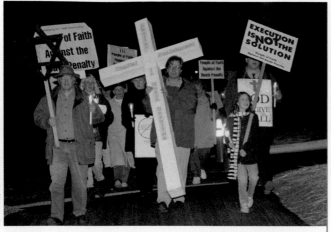

AP Photo/Karen Tam

Restorative justice advocates argue that if the goal of the criminal justice system is to create long-term peace in communities, then we need to identify strategies that focus less on punishment of offenders, and more on bringing together victims, offenders, and the community to agree on solutions. But is it possible to reintegrate all offenders back into their communities, even those who have taken another's life?

and punish, society should try to reconcile the parties involved in conflict.[104] The goal is to restore the relationships in the community, for all affected by the conflict, to the peaceful state they were in before the conflict crime took place.[105]

There are now more than 100 different restorative justice programs operating in Canada. In 1996 the *Criminal Code* was amended to recognize restorative justice principles in sentencing, and in 1999 the Law Commission of Canada formally endorsed restorative justice as a practice. In line with the principles on which they are based, restorative justice programs have a built-in flexibility to allow them to deal with different circumstances. Referrals to make use of restorative programs may come from the police, Crown attorneys, offenders themselves, or correctional services. The point at which referrals are made can be precharge, postcharge, presentence, or postsentence. Recommended solutions for restoring peace can range from victim–offender mediation and restitution, through public apologies and community service, to incarceration or community probation. Most programs offer training for volunteers and local justice personnel who are involved in the programs, and a national website (http://www.csc-scc.gc.ca/restorative-justice/003005 -0002-eng.shtml) has been established to provide information about the operations of the different programs.

sentencing circle
A peacemaking technique in which offenders, victims, and other community members are brought together in an effort to formulate a sanction that addresses the needs of all.

Services offered by restorative justice include facilitating dispute resolution/mediation between offenders and victims; family/community group conferencing to provide opportunities for victims, offenders, and the community to express their feelings and to renew their faith in the community; and sentencing circles, where all come together to agree on appropriate measures to address the behaviour of the offender in a way that will restore peace in the community.

Restorative justice programs can be found operating in large cities, towns, rural areas, and on First Nations reserves across Canada. Programs typically serve both adults and youth but, with the *Youth Criminal Justice Act*'s emphasis on alternative measures for young offenders, programs for youth are growing much more rapidly. Programs deal with a wide variety of criminal offences from simple shoplifting through physical assault and domestic abuse.

Because traditional Aboriginal justice systems were based on the same principles, restorative justice programs are a natural fit in Aboriginal communities. In fact, peacemaking circles have been held in Aboriginal communities in Yukon since the late 1980s.

Restorative programs typically divert cases away from the formal court process. Instead, these programs encourage reconciling the conflicts between offenders and victims through victim advocacy, mediation programs, and sentencing circles, in which crime victims and their families are brought together with offenders and their families in an effort to formulate a sanction that addresses the needs of each party.[106]

Negotiation, mediation, consensus building, and peacemaking have been part of the dispute resolution process in European and Asian communities for centuries.[107] North American Aboriginal people have long used the type of community participation in the adjudication process (e.g., sentencing circles, sentencing panels, and elders panels) that restorative justice advocates now embrace.[108] In some First Nations communities, people accused of breaking the law will meet with community members, victims, village elders, and agents of the justice system in a sentencing circle. Each member of the circle expresses his or her feelings about the act that was committed and raises questions or concerns. The accused can express regret about his or her actions and a desire to change the harmful behaviour. People may suggest ways the offender can make things up to the community and those he or she has harmed. A treatment program such as Alcoholics Anonymous may be suggested, if appropriate. The purpose of this process is to reduce the conflict and harm and restore rather than punish.[109] The accompanying Policy and

ABORIGINAL EXPERIENCE, SOCIAL JUSTICE, AND THE *GLADUE* DECISION

In September 1996, as part of a comprehensive set of amendments to the *Criminal Code*, the government enacted Section 718.2(e), which required that in imposing a sentence judges take into consideration that all available sanctions other than imprisonment that are reasonable in the circumstances should be considered for all offenders, with particular attention to the circumstances of aboriginal offenders.

Section 718.2(e) directs judges to adopt a restorative approach when levying a sentence on an Aboriginal offender, taking into account unique individual circumstances as well as historical and systemic factors. Judges were also directed to investigate all alternatives to a sentence of incarceration.

Due to a lack of community corrections services and treatment programs in most remote Aboriginal communities, incarceration was often the only sentence considered. Among those living in cities, judges were often unaware of Aboriginal community programs and services that could represent an alternative to incarceration. The new sentencing guidelines represented by Section 718.2(e) provided judges with greater flexibility in considering sentences that better reflected the unique past and current circumstances of Aboriginal offenders.

In June 1996, Jamie Tanis Gladue, 19, was charged with second degree murder in the death of her boyfriend, Reuben Beaver, 20. The charge stemmed from the police investigation into events of September 16, 1995. On that evening Jamie Gladue was celebrating her 19th birthday and drinking beer with family and friends at a townhouse she shared Reuben Beaver and their young daughter. Gladue was five months pregnant with their second child. Gladue's father, Lloyd, and two of her sisters, Tara and Bianca Chalifoux, lived nearby in another townhouse in the complex, and were in attendance at the party.

During the course of the evening Gladue became increasingly angry and vocal about her suspicions that Beaver was having an affair with her sister Tara, even telling friends, "The next time he fools around on me, I'll kill him." At some point in the evening Gladue became aware that both Beaver and her sister Tara were no longer at the party, and she went searching for the two, finding them at Tara's townhouse. Gladue accused Beaver and Tara of engaging in sexual activity, shouting at her sister Tara, "How could you do this to me?"

Gladue fled back to her own townhouse, and Beaver returned soon after. Neighbours reported hearing a loud quarrel between the two, including noises suggesting a physical altercation. One neighbour, Mr. Gretchin, decided to go to the house to tell the couple to settle down, but as he opened his front door he saw Gladue come running out of her front door in pursuit of Beaver, who was banging on Tara's front door yelling, "Let me in, let me in." Gladue ran up to Beaver and stabbed him in the chest, piercing his heart. As she left Beaver dying at her sister's front door, Mitchin heard Gladue say, "I got you, you fucking bastard." When arrested later the same evening by police, Gladue had a blood alcohol level of between 155 and 165 milligrams, twice the legally impaired limit.

In February 1997 Jamie Gladue pled guilty to manslaughter in the death of Reuben Beaver. Evidence presented at trial showed that Gladue had in fact stabbed Beaver twice on the evening of September 16, 1995; once in the arm with a small paring knife during their loud quarrel in their townhouse, and a second time, fatally, on the steps of her sister Tara's townhouse. Though other evidence presented at court showed that Reuben Beaver had been convicted of physically assaulting Gladue in June 1994 while she was pregnant with their first child, and while there was evidence of bruising on her arms and collarbone at the time of her arrest by police, the trial judge rejected the defence that Gladue was a "battered or fearful wife" and found her guilty of manslaughter.

Though evidence presented at her sentencing hearing showed that in the 17 months since the stabbing Gladue had enrolled in an alcohol and drug treatment program and had also been diagnosed with a hyperthyroid condition that could cause uncontrolled emotional outbursts, Gladue was sentenced to three years in federal prison, along with a ten-year weapons prohibition order. Despite the provisions of Section 718.2(e) of the *Criminal Code*, Gladue's Aboriginal status as a Cree was not considered as a factor by the trial judge nor in the sentencing hearing. When defence counsel had been asked by the trial judge whether the town of McLennan, Alberta where Gladue grew up was an Aboriginal community, defence counsel responded that it was "just a regular community." No other consideration was given at trial or in sentencing to Gladue's status as an Aboriginal person.

Jamie Gladue appealed her sentence on the grounds that the trial judge had failed to give adequate consideration to her status as an Aboriginal person, as per Section 718.2(e) of the *Criminal Code*. In October 1997 the B.C. Court of Appeal found that Section 718.2(e) did not apply because Gladue was not currently living on a reserve but in an urban setting, and there did not appear to be any special circumstances to be taken into consideration when considering the seriousness of the offence and sentencing.

Gladue appealed the B.C. Court of Appeal decision to the Supreme Court of Canada, and in April 1999 the court rendered its decision, finding that although both the trial court and the appeal court had failed to adequately consider evidence relevant to the accused's Aboriginal status, and in particular had failed to understand the application of Section 718.2(e) to all Aboriginal persons regardless of residence, the sentence handed down to Gladue was not unreasonable given the seriousness of the crime, even when her Aboriginal status was considered. Consequently, the Supreme Court of Canada rejected the appeal and upheld the sentence of the trail court.

The Supreme Court of Canada ruling in the *Gladue* case represented a significant step forward in the recognition of the unique position of Aboriginal persons in the criminal justice system, despite the rejection of the appeal. Most important, among the findings that the Supreme Court recognized in its decision are that

Section 718.2(e) is not simply a codification of existing jurisprudence. It is remedial in nature. Its purpose is to ameliorate the serious problem of overrepresentation of aboriginal people in prisons, and to encourage sentencing judges to have recourse to a restorative approach to sentencing. There is a judicial duty to give the provision's remedial purpose real force.

'and,

Section 718.2 (e) directs sentencing judges to undertake the sentencing of aboriginal offenders individually, but also differently, because the circumstances of aboriginal people are unique. In sentencing an aboriginal offender, the judge must consider:

(A) The unique systemic or background factors which may have played a part in bringing the particular aboriginal offender before the courts; and (B) The types of sentencing procedures and sanctions which may be appropriate in the circumstances for the offender because of his or her particular aboriginal heritage or connection. …

Section 718.2 (e) applies to all aboriginal persons wherever they reside, whether on- or off-reserve, in a large city or a rural area. In defining the relevant aboriginal community for the purpose of achieving an effective sentence, the term "community" must be defined broadly so as to include any network of support and interaction that might be available, including in an urban centre. At the same time, the residence of the aboriginal offender in an urban centre that lacks any network of support does not relieve the sentencing judge of the obligation to try to find an alternative to imprisonment."

Based on the foregoing, the jail term for an aboriginal offender may in some circumstances be less than the term imposed on a non-aboriginal offender for the same offence.

In effect, the *Gladue* decision for the first time recognized the restorative role that the law should play in addressing the sentencing of persons of Aboriginal heritage who come into conflict with the law, via a comprehensive understanding and interpretation of Section 718.2(e). Significantly, the *Gladue* decision has now set the stage for judges to take a more active restorative approach in considering sentences for all offenders, Aboriginal, non-Aboriginal, and youth.[110]

CRITICAL THINKING

1. Restorative justice may be the model that best serves alternative sanctions. How can this essentially humanistic approach be sold to the general public, which now supports more punitive sanctions? For example, would it be feasible to argue that using restoration with nonviolent offenders frees up resources for the relatively few dangerous people in the criminal population?

Sources: Canadian Restorative Justice, Department of Justice Restorative Justice in Canada, 2003 (http://www.csc-scc.gc.ca/restorative-justice/003005-0002-eng.shtml)

Practice in Criminology feature reviews restorative justice programs now being used in Canada.

LO6 Critical Theory and Social Justice in Canada

In their 2011 book *Critical Criminology in Canada*, Aaron Doyle and Dawn Moore bring together research from a growing number of critical criminologists in Canada, broadly defined as those who study "crime and social and governmental reactions to it."[111] There are more criminologists and many more students in Canada studying criminology than ever before, and more questions being raised and researched about how we understand what a crime is—is it just what is written in the *Criminal Code*?—or do we need to understand crime as something much more, as violations of basic human rights and freedoms—as a broader question about social justice? Critical criminologists in Canada have questioned the impact of conservative government policies in restricting social welfare payments, child-care subsidies and cut-backs to social services on the increasing number of women being incarcerated in Canada jails and prisons;[112] the negative clinical and public health outcomes of criminalizing HIV non-disclosure;[113] and government censorship and restriction of access to data in the study of offender treatment and the study of dangerous offenders.[114] For this new generation of Canadian critical criminologists, the goal of criminological theory and research is to challenge what we think we know about crime and its causes in the search for a system of justice that is fair and just for all.

Summary

Social conflict theorists view crime as a function of the conflict that exists in society. Conflict theorists suggest that crime in any society is caused by class conflict. Laws are created by those in power to protect their rights and interests.

All criminal acts have political undertones; Richard Quinney has called this the social reality of crime. Unfortunately, research efforts to validate the conflict approach have not produced significant findings. One of conflict theory's most important premises is that the justice system is biased and designed to protect the wealthy. Research has not been unanimous in supporting this point.

Marxist criminology views the competitive nature of the capitalist system as a major cause of crime. The poor commit crimes because of their frustration, anger, and need. The wealthy engage in illegal acts because they are used to competition and because they must do so to keep their positions in society. Marxist scholars have attempted to show that the law is designed to protect the wealthy and powerful and to control the poor, have-not members of society. Branches of radical theory include instrumental Marxism and structural Marxism.

During the 1990s, new forms of conflict theory emerged. Left realism takes a centrist position on crime by showing its rational, destructive nature. Feminist writers draw attention to the influence of patriarchal society on crime, as an important underlying cause of both male and female criminal behaviour. Deconstructionism looks at the symbolic meaning of law and culture. Peacemaking criminology calls for humanism in criminology. Based on methods of conflict resolution used in traditional societies like Canada's First Nations, the restorative approach relies on nonpunitive strategies to prevent and control crime.

Discussion Questions

1. How would a conservative reply to a call for more restorative justice? How would a restorative justice advocate respond to a conservative call for more prisons?

2. Considering the changes that have occurred in women's role in Canadian society beginning in the 1960s, how would a power–control theorist explain recent increases in the violent crime rate among females? What are the three main principles of restorative justice? How might this approach positively (or negatively) impact society?

3. Is conflict inevitable in all cultures? If not, what can be done to reduce the level of conflict in our own society?

4. If Marx were alive today, what would he think about the prosperity enjoyed by the working class in industrial societies? Might he alter his vision of the capitalist system?

READY TO STUDY?

IN THE BOOK, YOU CAN:

✔ Check your understanding of what you've just read by reading the Summary at the end of each chapter.

✔ Rip out the Chapter in Review card at the back of the book to have the key terms and Learning Objectives handy, and complete the quizzes provided (answers are at the bottom of the back page!).

ONLINE YOU CAN:

✔ Stay organized and efficient with MindTap—a single destination with all the course material and study aids you need to succeed. Built-in apps leverage social media and the latest learning technology. For example:

✔ ReadSpeaker will read the text to you.

✔ Flashcards are pre-populated to provide you with a jump start for review—or you can create your own.

✔ You can highlight text and make notes in your MindTap Reader. Your notes will flow into Evernote, the electronic notebook app that you can access anywhere when it's time to study for the exam.

✔ Prepare for tests with quizzes.

Go to www.nelson.com/student to access these digital resources.

Integrated Theories

Learning Objectives

LO1 Describe how latent trait theorists explain criminality.

LO2 Explain what makes people commit crime according to Gottfredson and Hirschi.

LO3 Describe the two distinct elements of control according to Tittle's control balance theory and what happens when there is an imbalance.

LO4 Describe important developmental concepts of problem behaviour syndrome (PBS), pathways to crime, criminal trajectories, and continuity of crime, and explain how they help us understand how criminal careers evolve.

LO5 Describe briefly how the major theories of criminal development account for the onset, continuance, and desistance of crime.

To derive more powerful explanations of crime, some criminologists have begun integrating individual factors into complex multifactor theories. These integrated theories attempt to blend seemingly independent concepts into coherent explanations of criminality.

Integrated theories seek to avoid the shortcomings of single-factor theories, which focus on the onset of crime and tend to divide the world into criminals and noncriminals—those who have a crime-producing condition and those who do not. For example, people with high testosterone levels are violent; people with low levels are not.

DID YOU KNOW?

- Latent trait theories assume a physical or psychological trait makes some people crime-prone.

- Opportunity to commit crime varies; latent traits remain stable.

- The general theory of crime says an impulsive personality is key.

- Impulsive people have low self-control, and a weak bond to society.

- Impulsive people often cannot resist criminal opportunities.

- According to Tittle, crime may be a function of efforts to maintain control and avoid restraint.

The view that people can be classified as either criminals or noncriminals, with this status being stable for life, is now being challenged. Criminologists today are concerned not only with the onset of criminality but also with its termination. Why do people age out of crime? If, for example, criminality is a function of lower intelligence, as some criminologists claim, why do most delinquents fail to become adult criminals? It seems unlikely that intelligence increases as young offenders mature. If the onset of criminality can be explained by low intelligence, then some other factor must explain its termination.

It has also become important to chart the natural history of a criminal career. Why do some offenders escalate their criminal activities while others decrease or limit their law violations? Why do some offenders specialize in a particular crime while others become generalists? Why do some criminals reduce criminal activity and then resume it once again? Research now shows that some offenders begin their criminal careers at a very early age, whereas others begin later. How can early- and late-onset criminality

be explained?[1] This view of the nature of crime is referred to as developmental criminology.

Integrated theories focus attention on the explanation of crime and criminal behaviour as a process in which individual characteristics and situational factors combine over the life course to either promote ongoing criminal behaviour (e.g., the "chronic" offender), to put an end to the behaviour at some point later in the individual's life ("desistance"), or to prevent the criminal behaviour altogether. Criminologists are still struggling to understand why, when faced with a similar set of life circumstances, such as poverty and family dysfunction, one youth becomes a chronic offender while another may commit an occasional illegal act but later desists from crime. Single-factor theories, such as social structure and social process theories, have trouble explaining why only a relatively few of the many individuals exposed to criminogenic influences in the environment actually become chronic offenders.

By integrating a variety of ecological, social, psychological, biological, and economic factors into a coherent structure, criminologists are attempting to answer the complex questions listed above.

integrated theory
A complex, multifactor theory that attempts to blend seemingly independent concepts into a coherent explanation of criminality.

developmental criminology
A branch of criminology that examines changes in criminal careers over the life course.

desistance
The process through which an individual's criminal behaviour subsides, or abruptly stops.

raluca teodorescu/Shutterstock.com

Do violent men have higher levels of testosterone? The latest research indicates that there's only a weak connection between the two; and when aggression is defined as simple physical violence, the connection all but disappears. Castration experiments demonstrate that testosterone is necessary for violence, but other research has shown that testosterone by itself is not sufficient.

Trailer Park Boys was a popular Canadian television series focusing on the misadventures of a group of career criminals living in the fictional Sunnyvale Trailer Park, located near Cole Harbour, Nova Scotia. The show became a hit with audiences worldwide. The original series ran from April 2001 to December 2008, and spawned three feature-length films, *The Big Dirty*, 2006, *Countdown to Liquor Day,* 2009, and *Don't Legalize It,* 2014. Since 2014, Netflix has continued the series with Season 10 scheduled to be released in 2016.

Recent attempts at creating integrated theories can be divided into two distinct groups. **Latent trait theories** hold that criminal behaviour is controlled by a "master trait," present at birth or soon after, that remains stable and unchanging throughout a person's lifetime. Latent trait theorists believe that "people don't change, opportunities do." **Developmental theories** view criminality as a dynamic process, influenced by individual characteristics

latent trait theories
The view that criminal behaviour is controlled by a "master trait," present at birth or soon after, that remains stable and unchanging throughout a person's lifetime.

FIGURE 9.1

Latent Trait versus Developmental Theories

Latent trait theory
- Master trait
  - Personality
  - Intelligence
  - Genetic makeup
- People do not change, criminal opportunities change; maturity brings fewer opportunities
- Early social control and proper parenting can reduce criminal propensity
- Criminal careers are a passage
- Personal and structural factors influence crime
- Change affects crime
- Personal versus situational

Developmental theory
- Multiple traits: social, psychological, economic
- People change over the life course
- Family, job, peers influence behaviour

as well as social experiences. Thus, developmental theorists hope for personal change and growth. These two positions are summarized in Figure 9.1 and discussed in detail in the following sections.

LO1 Latent Trait Theories

In a popular 1985 book, *Crime and Human Nature*, two prominent social scientists, James Q. Wilson and Richard Herrnstein, argued that personal traits, such as genetic makeup, intelligence, and body build, operate in tandem with social variables such as poverty and family function. Together these factors influence people to "choose crime" over noncriminal behavioural alternatives.[2]

Following their lead, David Rowe, D. Wayne Osgood, and W. Alan Nicewander proposed the concept of **latent traits**. Their model assumes that a number of people in the population have a personal attribute or characteristic that controls their inclination or propensity to commit crimes.[3] This disposition, or latent trait, is either present at birth or established early in life, and it remains stable over time. Suspected latent traits include defective intelligence, impulsive personality, genetic abnormalities, the physical–chemical functioning of the brain, and environmental influences on brain function such as drugs, chemicals, and injuries.[4] Those who carry one of these latent traits are in danger of becoming career criminals; those who lack the traits have a much lower risk. Latent traits should affect the behavioural choices of

David Tadevosian/Shutterstock.com

all people equally, regardless of their gender or personal characteristics.[5]

According to this emerging latent trait view, the *propensity* to commit crime is stable, but the *opportunity* to commit crime fluctuates over time. People age out of crime because, as they mature, there are simply fewer opportunities to commit crime and greater inducements to remain "straight." They may marry, have children, and obtain jobs. The former delinquents' newfound adult responsibilities leave them little time to hang with their friends, abuse substances, and get into scrapes with the law.

Assume, for example, that a stable latent trait such as low IQ causes some people to commit crime. Teenagers have more opportunity to commit crime than adults, so at every level of intelligence, adolescent crime rates will be higher. As they mature, however, teens with both high and low IQs will commit less crime because their adult responsibilities provide them with fewer criminal opportunities. Thus, latent trait theories integrate concepts usually associated with trait theories (such as personality and temperament) and concepts associated with rational choice theories (such as criminal opportunity and suitable targets).

LO2 General Theory of Crime

Michael Gottfredson and Travis Hirschi's **general theory of crime (GTC)** modifies and redefines some of the principles articulated in Hirschi's social control theory (Chapter 7) by integrating the concepts of control with those of biosocial, psychological, routine activities, and rational choice theories.[6]

The Act and the Offender

In their general theory of crime, Gottfredson and Hirschi consider the criminal offender and the criminal act as separate concepts.

Criminal acts, such as robberies or break and enter, are illegal events or deeds that people engage in when they perceive them to be advantageous. For example, break and enter is typically committed by young

males looking for cash, liquor, and entertainment; the crime provides "easy, short-term gratification."[7] Crime is rational and predictable: People commit crime when it promises rewards with minimal threat of pain. The threat of punishment can deter crime: If targets are well guarded, crime rates diminish.

Criminal offenders are individuals predisposed to commit crimes. They are not robots who commit crime without restraint; their days are also filled with conventional behaviours, such as going to school, parties, concerts, and places of worship. But given the same set of criminal opportunities, such as having a lot of free time for mischief and living in a neighbourhood with unguarded homes containing valuable merchandise, crime-prone people have a much higher probability of violating the law than do noncriminals. The propensity to commit crimes remains stable throughout a person's life. Change in the frequency of criminal activity is purely a function of change in criminal opportunity.

developmental theories
The view that criminality is a dynamic process, influenced by social experiences as well as individual characteristics.

latent trait
A stable feature, characteristic, property, or condition, such as defective intelligence or impulsive personality, that makes some people crime-prone over the life course.

general theory of crime (GTC)
A latent trait theory that modifies social control theory by integrating concepts from biosocial, psychological, routine activities, and rational choice theories.

© Prisma Bildagentur AG/Alamy

The "smash and grab" provides easy short-term gratification for young males in need of money.

FIGURE 9.2

The General Theory of Crime

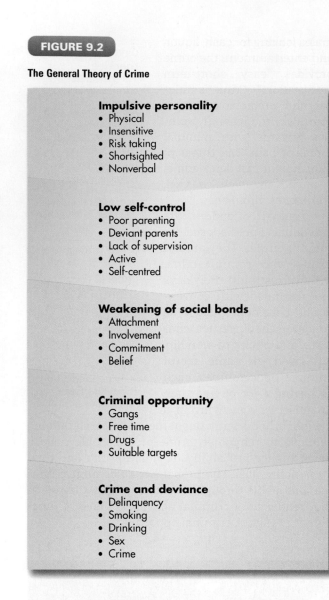

Impulsive personality
- Physical
- Insensitive
- Risk taking
- Shortsighted
- Nonverbal

Low self-control
- Poor parenting
- Deviant parents
- Lack of supervision
- Active
- Self-centred

Weakening of social bonds
- Attachment
- Involvement
- Commitment
- Belief

Criminal opportunity
- Gangs
- Free time
- Drugs
- Suitable targets

Crime and deviance
- Delinquency
- Smoking
- Drinking
- Sex
- Crime

By recognizing that there are stable differences in people's propensity to commit crime, the GTC adds a biosocial element to the concept of social control. The biological and psychological factors that make people impulsive and crime-prone may be inherited or may develop through incompetent or absent parenting. (See Figure 9.2.)

What Makes People Crime-Prone?

What, then, causes people to become excessively crime-prone? Gottfredson and Hirschi attribute the tendency to commit crimes to a person's level of self-control. People with limited self-control tend to be impulsive; they are insensitive to other people's feelings, physical (rather than mental), risk takers, short-sighted, and nonverbal.[8] They have a "here and now" orientation and refuse to work for distant goals; they lack diligence, tenacity, and persistence. People lacking self-control tend to be adventuresome, active, physical, and self-centred. As they mature, they often have unstable marriages, jobs, and friendships.[9] People lacking self-control are less likely to feel shame if they engage in deviant acts and are more likely to find them pleasurable.[10] They are also more likely to engage in dangerous behaviours such as drinking, smoking, and reckless driving; all of these behaviours are associated with criminality.[11] (See Figure 9.2.)

Because those with low self-control enjoy risky, exciting, or thrilling behaviours with immediate gratification, they are more likely to enjoy criminal acts, which require stealth, agility, speed, and power, than conventional acts, which demand long-term study and cognitive and verbal skills. Because they enjoy taking risks, they are more likely to get involved in accidents and suffer injuries than people who maintain self-control.[12] As Gottfredson and Hirschi put it, they derive satisfaction from "money without work, sex without courtship, revenge without court delays."[13] Many of these individuals who have a propensity for committing crime also engage in other behaviours such as smoking, drinking, gambling, and illicit sexuality.[14] Although these acts are not illegal, they too provide immediate, short-term gratification. Figure 9.3 lists the elements of impulsivity, or low self-control.

Gottfredson and Hirschi trace the root cause of poor self-control to inadequate childrearing practices (Figure 9.3). Parents who are unwilling or unable to monitor a child's behaviour, to recognize deviant behaviour when it occurs, and to punish that behaviour, will produce children who lack self-control. Children who are not attached to their parents, who are poorly supervised, and whose parents are criminal or deviant themselves are the most likely to develop poor self-control. In a sense, lack of self-control occurs naturally when steps are not taken to stop its

"I fell in with a bad crowd when I was young — my parents."

FIGURE 9.3

The Elements of Impulsivity: Signs that a Person Has Low Self-Control

- Insensitive

- Physical

- Shortsighted

- Nonverbal

- Here-and-now orientation

- Unstable social relations

- Enjoys deviant behaviours

- Risk taker

- Refuses to work for distant goals

- Lacks diligence

- Lacks tenacity

- Adventuresome

- Self-centred

- Shameless

- Imprudent

- Lacks cognitive and verbal skills

- Enjoys danger and excitement

development.[15] Low self-control develops early in life and remains stable into and through adulthood.[16]

Self-Control and Crime

Gottfredson and Hirschi claim that the principles of self-control theory can explain all varieties of criminal behaviour and all the social and behavioural correlates of crime. That is, such widely disparate crimes as break and enter, robbery, embezzlement, drug dealing, murder, sexual assault, and insider trading all stem from a deficiency of self-control. Likewise, gender, racial, and ecological differences in crime rates can be explained by discrepancies in self-control. Put another way, the male crime rate is higher than the female crime rate because males have lower levels of self-control.

Unlike other theoretical models that explain only narrow segments of criminal behaviour (such as theories of teenage gang formation), Gottfredson and Hirschi argue that self-control applies equally to all crimes, ranging from murder to corporate theft. For example, Gottfredson and Hirschi maintain that white-collar crime rates remain low because people who lack self-control rarely attain the positions necessary to commit those crimes. However, the relatively few white-collar criminals lack self-control to the same degree and in the same manner as criminals such as rapists and burglars. Although the criminal activity of individuals with low self-control also declines as those individuals mature, they maintain

Photo by Rex Features/CP Photo

According to the general theory of crime, people who have low self-control are crime-prone even if they are born into affluent families. One example is Hollywood actress and celebrity Lindsay Lohan, 28, who has a string of convictions for impaired driving, possession of cocaine, and breach of probation dating back to 2007, including a May 2011 conviction and sentence of 120 days in jail for stealing a $2500 necklace from a jewellery store in Venice, California. The young actress has a history of low self-control and impulsivity.

an offence rate that remains consistently higher than for those with strong self-control.

Supporting Evidence for the GTC

Following the publication of *A General Theory of Crime*, dozens of research efforts tested the validity of Gottfredson and Hirschi's theoretical views. One approach involved identifying indicators of impulsiveness and self-control to determine whether scales measuring these factors correlate with measures of criminal activity. A number of studies have successfully shown this type of association.[17] Some of the most important findings are summarized in Figure 9.4.

Analyzing the GTC

By integrating the concepts of socialization and criminality, Gottfredson and Hirschi help explain why some people who lack self-control can escape criminality,

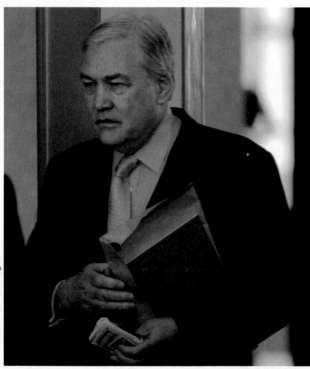

In November 2005, Conrad Black, media mogul, member of the British House of Lords, and (former) Canadian citizen was charged by U.S. authorities with more than a dozen counts of fraud related to the operations of his media company, Hollinger International. Convicted in 2007 on four counts and sentenced to serve six and one-half years in U.S. federal prison, Black appealed the sentence, and was ultimately convicted in June 2011 of one count of fraud and one count of obstruction of justice, and sentenced to 42 months in a minimum-security federal correctional facility in Miami, Florida. Credited with time already served, in May 2012 Black was released from prison. Since his release he has returned to public life and the newspaper and publishing world, even hosting a television interview show.

FIGURE 9.4

Empirical Evidence Supporting the General Theory of Crime

- Novice offenders, lacking in self-control, commit a garden variety of criminal acts.[18]

- More mature and experienced criminals become more specialized in their choice of crime (e.g., robbers, burglars, drug dealers).[19]

- Male and female drunk drivers are impulsive individuals who manifest low self-control.[20]

- Repeat violent offenders are more impulsive than their less violent peers.[21]

- Incarcerated youth enjoy risk-taking behaviour and hold values and attitudes that suggest impulsivity.[22]

- Kids who take drugs and commit crime are impulsive and enjoy engaging in risky behaviours.[23]

- Measures of self-control can predict deviant and antisocial behaviour across age groups ranging from teens to adults age 50.[24]

- People who commit white-collar and workplace crime have lower levels of self-control than nonoffenders.[25]

- Gang members have lower levels of self-control than the general population; gang members report lower levels of parental management, a factor associated with lower self-control.[26]

- Low self-control shapes perceptions of criminal opportunity and consequently conditions the decision to commit crimes.[27]

- People who lack self-control expect to commit crime in the future.[28]

- Kids whose problems develop early in life are the most resistant to change in treatment and rehabilitation programs.[29]

- Gender differences in self-control are responsible for crime rate differences. Females who lack self-control are as crime-prone as males with similar personalities.[30]

- Parents who manage their children's behaviour increase their self-control, which helps reduce their delinquent activities.[31]

- Having parents (or stepparents) available to control behaviour may reduce the opportunity to commit crime.[32]

- Victims have lower self-control than nonvictims. Impulsivity predicts both the likelihood that a person will engage in criminal behaviour and the likelihood that the person will become a victim of crime.[33]

and, conversely, why some people who have self-control might not escape criminality. People who are at risk because they have impulsive personalities may forgo criminal careers because there are no criminal opportunities that satisfy their impulsive needs; instead they may find other outlets for their impulsive personalities. In contrast, if the opportunity is strong enough, even people with relatively strong self-control may be tempted to violate the law; the incentives to commit crime may overwhelm self-control.

Integrating criminal propensity and criminal opportunity can explain why some children enter into chronic offending while others living in similar environments are able to resist criminal activity. It can also help us understand why the corporate executive with a spotless record gets caught up in business fraud. Even a successful executive may find self-control inadequate if the potential for illegal gain is large. The driven executive, used to both academic and financial success, may find that the fear of failure can overwhelm self-control. During tough economic times, the impulsive manager who fears dismissal may be tempted to circumvent the law to improve the bottom line.[34]

Although the general theory seems persuasive, several questions and criticisms remain unanswered. Among the most important are the following:

1. *Tautological*. Sme critics argue that the theory is tautological—that is, it involves circular reasoning. How do we know when people are impulsive? When they commit crimes. Are all criminals impulsive? Of course, or else they would not have broken the law![35]

2. *Personality disorder*. Saying someone lacks self-control implies a personality defect that makes him or her impulsive and rash. There is still no conclusive proof that criminals can be distinguished from noncriminals on the basis of personality alone.

3. *Ecological/individual differences*. The GTC also fails to address individual and ecological patterns in the crime rate. For example, if crime rates are higher in Hamilton, Ontario, than in Edmonton, Alberta, can it be assumed that residents of Hamilton are more impulsive than residents of Edmonton?

4. *Racial and gender differences*. Although distinct gender differences in the crime rate exist, there is little evidence that males are more impulsive than females (although females and males differ in many other personality traits).[36] Similarly, Gottfredson and Hirschi explain racial differences in the crime rate as a failure of childrearing practices in the black community.[37] In so doing, they overlook issues of institutional racism, poverty, and relative deprivation, which have been shown to have a significant impact on crime rate differentials.

5. *People change*. The general theory assumes that criminal propensity does not change; opportunities change. A number of research efforts show that factors that help control criminal behaviour, such as peer relations and school performance, vary over time. Social influences, which are dominant in early adolescence, may fade and be replaced by others in adulthood.[38] This finding contradicts the GTC, which suggests that the influence of friends should be stable and unchanging.

Gottfredson and Hirschi assume that low self-control varies little with age and that low self-control is almost exclusively a product of early childhood rearing; however, research shows that self-control may vary with age. As people mature, they may be better able to control their impulsive behaviour.[39] These findings contradict the GTC, which assumes that levels of self-control and therefore criminal propensity are constant and independent of personal relationships. However, it is uncertain whether life changes affect the propensity to commit crime or merely the opportunity, as Gottfredson and Hirschi suggest.

6. *Modest relationship*. Some research results support the proposition that self-control is a causal factor in criminal and other forms of deviant behaviour, but that the association is quite modest.[40] This would indicate that other forces influence criminal behaviour and that low self-control alone cannot predict the onset of a criminal or deviant career.

7. *Cross-cultural differences*. Evidence shows that criminals in other parts of the world do not lack self-control, indicating that the GTC may be culturally limited.[41] Behaviour that may be considered imprudent in one culture may be socially acceptable in another and therefore cannot be viewed as "lack of self-control."[42]

Although questions like these remain, the strength of the general theory lies in its scope and breadth; it attempts to explain all forms of crime and deviance, from lower-class gang delinquency to sexual harassment in the business community.[43] By integrating concepts of criminal choice, criminal opportunity, socialization, and personality, Gottfredson and Hirschi make a plausible argument that all deviant behaviours may originate at the same source. Continued efforts are needed to test the GTC and establish the validity of its core concepts. It remains one of the key developments of modern criminological theory.

LO3 Control Balance Theory

Charles Tittle's control balance theory expands on the concept of personal control as a predisposing element for criminality.[44] According to Tittle, the concept of control has two distinct elements: the amount of control one is subject to by others and the amount of control one can exercise over others. Conformity results when these two elements are in balance; control imbalances produce deviant and criminal behaviours.

Tittle envisions control as a continuous variable (see Figure 9.5), ranging from a control deficit, which occurs when a person's desires or impulses are limited by other people's ability to regulate or punish their behaviour, to a control surplus, which occurs when the amount of control one can exercise over

control balance theory
A latent trait theory that attributes deviant and criminal behaviours to imbalances between the amount of control that the individual has over others and that others have over him or her.

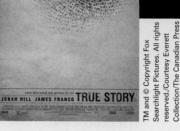

Actor James Franco plays Christian Longo, a man who murders his family and later impersonates journalist Michael Finkel (played by Jonah Hill) in the 2015 film *True Story*. The film chronicles the increasingly disturbed behaviour and criminal trajectory of Longo beginning with his marriage at 17 and the beginning of a series of thefts from his employers and, after he started his own business, from his customers and even his own father. He, wife MaryJane, and their three young children flee to Oregon to avoid the law. Next, in a bizarre plan to restart his life, Longo moves the family to an expensive condominium development in Yacquina Bay, Oregon, where in 2001 police found the bodies of the Longo's two oldest children, Zachary and Sadie, floating in Yacquina Bay; later, police found two suitcases in the bay containing the bodies of his wife MaryJane and two-year-old daughter Madison. Longo fled to Mexico, where he masqueraded as journalist Michael Finkel, a former *New York Times* reporter who had been fired years earlier for falsifying a story. Eventually, Longo is recognized in Mexico and deported back to the United States to face multiple charges of murder.

The real Michael Finkel contacted Longo in prison to find out why he chose him to impersonate, and so began a series of telephone calls and letters between the two men that forms the basis of Finkel's 2005 book, *True Story: Murder, Memoir, Mea Culpa*, upon which the 2015 movie is based.

Developmental or life course theorists would point out that Longo's criminal career follows a classic trajectory for a late onset, "life course persister" beginning with "pseudomaturity" in his marriage at 17 that masked his lack of self-control and sociopathic tendencies. As Longo matures, and as the pressure mounts when his thefts and frauds are revealed to police, his criminal behaviour and impulsive, self-centred decision making takes a violent turn, culminating in the murder of his wife and children.

others exceeds the ability others have to control or modify one's own behaviour.

People who sense a deficit of control turn to three types of behaviour to restore balance: *predation*, *defiance*, and *submission*. Predation involves direct forms of physical violence, such as robbery or sexual assault. Defiance is designed to challenge control mechanisms but stops short of physical harm, such as vandalism, curfew violations, or unconventional sex. Submission involves passive obedience to the demands of others, such as submitting to physical or sexual abuse without response.

According to Tittle, an excess of control can also lead to deviance and crime—a contention that contradicts Hirschi and Gottfredson's view that only low control leads to crime. Those who have an excess of control engage in three types of behaviour: exploitation, plunder, and decadence. Exploitation involves using others to commit crime—for example, as contract killers or drug runners. Plunder involves using power without regard for others, such as committing a hate crime or polluting the environment. Decadence involves spur-of-the-moment, irrational acts such as child molesting.

Control imbalance represents a potential to commit crime and deviance. That is, possessing deficient or excessive control increases the likelihood that when presented with situational motivations a person will react in an antisocial manner. Deviant motivations emerge when a person suffering from control imbalance believes that engaging in some antisocial act will alter his or her control ratio in a favourable

FIGURE 9.5

Tittle's Control Balance Theory

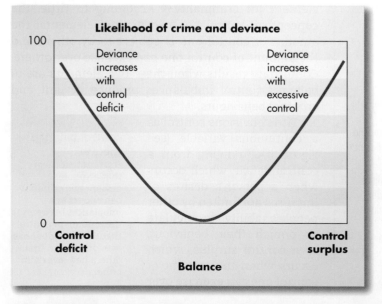

way. For example, when a person who has a surplus of control is insulted, he may tell his friends to attack the instigator; a student with a control deficit may vandalize a school after getting a bad grade on her report card.

Even if people are motivated to commit crime, they may be constrained by their perceptions of external forces of control. Even highly motivated individuals may be constrained if they believe that their deviant behaviour is very serious and likely to be discovered by those who can exert control, such as the police. Tittle also recognizes that opportunity shapes antisocial behaviour. No matter how great the motivation or how little the restraint, the actual likelihood of a crime occurring depends on the opportunity.

Tittle's view is essentially integrated because, like Hirschi and Gottfredson before him, he incorporates external or social concepts such as opportunity and restraint with internal or individual variables such as degree of control.

LO4 Developmental Theory

The second integrated approach that has emerged is developmental theory. According to this view, even as toddlers, people begin relationships and behaviours that will determine their adult life course. At first they must learn to conform to social rules and function effectively in society. Later they are expected to begin thinking about careers, leave their parental homes, find permanent relationships, and eventually marry and begin their own families.[45] These transitions are expected to take place in order, beginning with finishing school, entering the workforce, getting married, and having children.

Some individuals, however, are incapable of maturing in a reasonable and timely fashion because of family, environmental, or personal problems. In some cases transitions can occur too early—for example, when adolescents engage in precocious sex. In other cases transitions may occur too late, as when a student fails to graduate on time because of bad grades or too many incomplete classes. Sometimes disruption of one trajectory can harm another. For example, teenage childbirth will most likely disrupt educational and career development. Because developmental theories focus on the associations between life events and deviant behaviours, they are sometimes referred to as life-course theories.

Disruptions in life's major transitions can be destructive and ultimately can promote criminality. Those who are already at risk because of socioeconomic problems or family dysfunction are the most susceptible to these awkward transitions. The cumulative impact of these disruptions sustains criminality from childhood into adulthood.

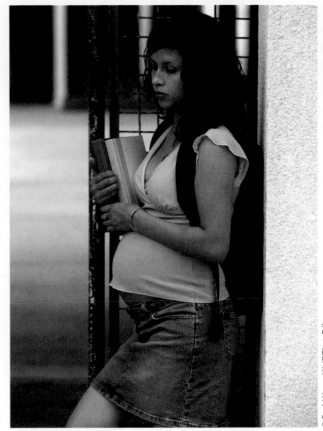

Teenage childbirth has been known to disrupt educational and career development.

Because a transition from one stage of life to another can be a bumpy ride, the propensity to commit crimes is neither stable nor constant; it is a developmental process. A positive life experience may help some criminals desist from crime for a while, whereas a negative one may cause them to resume their activities. Criminal careers are also said to be interactional because people are influenced by the behaviour of those around them and, in turn, influence others' behaviour. For example, a youth's antisocial behaviour may turn his or her more conventional friends against him; their rejection solidifies and escalates the antisocial behaviour.

Developmental theories also recognize that as people mature, the factors that influence their behaviour change.[46] At first, family relations may be most influential; in later adolescence, school and peer relations predominate; in adulthood, vocational achievement and marital relations may be the most critical influences. For example, some antisocial children who are in trouble throughout their adolescence may manage to find stable work and maintain intact marriages as adults;

life-course theory
Theory that focuses on changes in criminality over the life course; developmental theory.

these life events help them desist from crime. In contrast, the less fortunate adolescents who develop arrest records and get involved with the wrong crowd may find themselves limited to menial jobs and at risk for criminal careers.

Developmental theories are inherently multidimensional, suggesting that criminality has multiple roots, including maladaptive personality traits, educational failure, and dysfunctional family relations. Criminality, according to this view, cannot be attributed to a single cause, nor does it represent a single underlying tendency.[47] People are influenced by different factors as they mature. Consequently, a factor that may have an important influence at one stage of life (such as delinquent peers) may have little influence later on.[48]

The Glueck Research

One of the cornerstones of recent developmental theories has been a renewed interest in the research efforts of Sheldon and Eleanor Glueck. While at Harvard University in the 1930s, the Gluecks popularized research on the life cycle of delinquent careers. In a series of longitudinal research studies, they followed the careers of known delinquents to determine the factors that predicted persistent offending.[49] The Gluecks made extensive use of interviews and records in their elaborate comparisons of delinquents and nondelinquents.[50]

The Gluecks' research focused on early onset of delinquency as a harbinger of a criminal career: "The deeper the roots of childhood maladjustment, the smaller the chance of adult adjustment."[51] They also noted the stability of offending careers: Children who are antisocial early in life are the most likely to continue their offending careers into adulthood.

The Gluecks identified a number of personal and social factors related to persistent offending. The most important of these factors was family relations, considered in terms of quality of discipline and emotional ties with parents. The adolescent raised in a large, single-parent family of limited economic means and educational achievement was the most vulnerable to delinquency.

The Gluecks did not restrict their analysis to social variables. When they measured biological and psychological traits such as body type, intelligence, and personality, they found that physical and mental factors also played a role in determining behaviour.

Children with low intelligence, a background of mental disease, and a powerful (mesomorph) physique were the most likely to become persistent offenders.

Developmental Concepts

A 1990 review paper (revised in 1998) by Rolf Loeber and Marc LeBlanc was an important event in popularizing developmental theory.[52] In their landmark work, Loeber and LeBlanc proposed that criminologists should devote time and effort to understanding some basic questions about the evolution of criminal careers: Why do people begin committing antisocial acts? Why do some stop while others continue? Why do some escalate the severity of their criminality (e.g., go from shoplifting to drug dealing to armed robbery) while others de-escalate and commit less serious crimes as they mature? If some terminate their criminal activity, what, if anything, causes them to begin again? Why do some criminals specialize in certain types of crime, whereas others are generalists engaging in a variety of antisocial behaviours? According to Loeber and LeBlanc's developmental view, criminologists must pay attention to how a criminal career unfolds.

Consequently, a view of crime has emerged that both incorporates personal change and growth and recognizes that the factors that produce crime and delinquency at one point in the life cycle may not be relevant at another.[53] People may show a propensity to offend early in their lives, but the nature and frequency of their activities are affected by outside forces beyond their control, such as the likelihood of getting arrested and being punished for crime.[54]

In this section, we review some of the more important concepts associated with the developmental perspective. In the remainder of the chapter, we discuss some prominent developmental theories.

Problem Behaviour Syndrome

The developmental view is that criminality can best be understood as one of many social problems faced by at-risk youth. Crime is just one among a group of antisocial behaviours that cluster together, referred to collectively as problem behaviour syndrome (PBS). PBS typically involves family dysfunction, substance abuse, smoking, precocious sexuality and early pregnancy, educational underachievement, suicide attempts, sensation seeking, and unemployment as well as crime (see Figure 9.6).[55] People who exhibit one of these conditions typically exhibit many of the others.[56] All varieties of criminal behaviour, including violence, theft, and drug offences, may be part of a generalized PBS, indicating that all forms of antisocial behaviour have similar developmental patterns.[57]

Social
- Family dysfunction
- Unemployment
- Educational underachievement
- School misconduct

Personal
- Substance abuse
- Suicide attempts
- Early sexuality
- Sensation seeking
- Early parenthood
- Accident-proneness
- Medical problems
- Mental disease
- Anxiety
- Eating disorders (bulimia, anorexia)

Environmental
- High-crime area
- Disorganized area
- Racism
- Exposure to poverty

Those who exhibit PBS are prone to more difficulties than the general population.[58] They face a range of personal dilemmas ranging from drug abuse, to being accident-prone, to requiring more health care and hospitalization, to becoming teenage parents. PBS has been linked to personality problems (such as rebelliousness and low ego), family problems (such as intrafamily conflict and parental mental disorder), and educational failure.[59] Multisite research has shown that PBS is not unique to any single geographical area, and that children who exhibit PBS, including drug use, delinquency, and precocious sexuality, display symptoms at an early age.[60]

LO5 Pathways to Crime

Developmental theorists recognize that career criminals may travel more than a single road. Some may specialize in violence and extortion; some may be involved in theft and fraud; others may engage in a variety of criminal acts. Some offenders may begin their careers early in life, whereas others are late bloomers who begin committing crime when most people desist.

Are there different pathways to crime? Using data from a longitudinal cohort study conducted in Pittsburgh, Pennsylvania, Rolf Loeber and his associates have identified three distinct paths to a criminal career (see Figure 9.7):[61]

1. The **authority conflict pathway** begins at an early age with stubborn behaviour. This leads to defiance (doing things one's own way, disobedience) and then to authority avoidance (staying out late, truancy, running away).

authority conflict pathway
Pathway to criminal deviance that begins at an early age with stubborn behaviour and leads to defiance and then to authority avoidance.

Photo courtesy of Danisha Bhaloo

SJDhanji Photography 2015

Danisha Bhaloo graduated from the University of Alberta in 2007 with a Bachelor's degree in Criminology. She made history in 2007 becoming the youngest probation officer in the history of Alberta Correctional Services. In 2009 she obtained a position as a caseworker with Big Brothers Big Sisters in Montreal, but returned to Edmonton in 2012 to take up the position of Manager, Fund Development for Boys and Girls Clubs/Big Brothers Big Sisters Edmonton. In 2014 she was appointed as senator at the University of Alberta.

Bhaloo's father died when she was 12, leaving her mother to raise her and a sister on a very meagre income. Both of the young girls were registered with Big Brothers Big Sisters Edmonton, a relationship Bhaloo maintained until to this day. A strong believer in 'giving back', she is a very active member of the Edmonton community, serves as a National Member of the Aga Khan Youth and Sports Board of Canada, sits as Vice-Chair of Edmonton John Howard Society, A Board Member with the Edmonton Opera, and a Trustee for the Big Brothers Big Sisters of Canada Foundation.

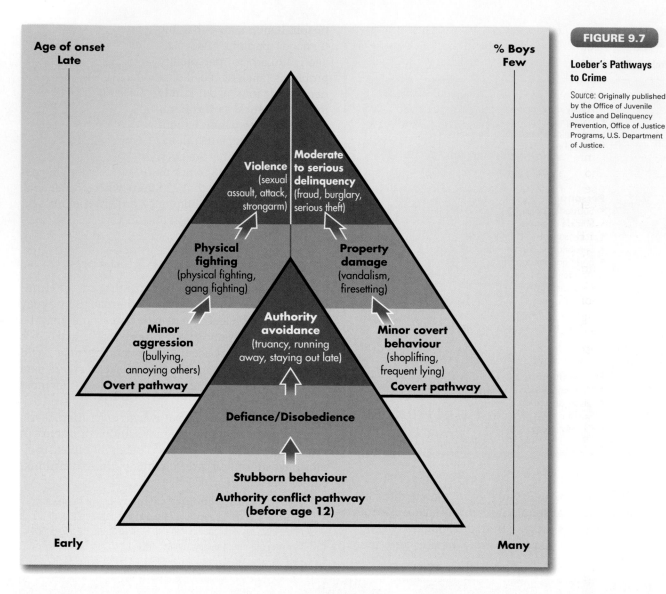

Age of onset
Late

% Boys
Few

Violence (sexual assault, attack, strongarm)

Moderate to serious delinquency (fraud, burglary, serious theft)

Physical fighting (physical fighting, gang fighting)

Property damage (vandalism, firesetting)

Minor aggression (bullying, annoying others)

Authority avoidance (truancy, running away, staying out late)

Minor covert behaviour (shoplifting, frequent lying)

Overt pathway

Covert pathway

Defiance/Disobedience

Stubborn behaviour

Authority conflict pathway (before age 12)

Early

Many

FIGURE 9.7

Loeber's Pathways to Crime

Source: Originally published by the Office of Juvenile Justice and Delinquency Prevention, Office of Justice Programs, U.S. Department of Justice.

2. The **covert pathway** begins with minor, underhanded behaviour (lying, shoplifting) that leads to property damage (setting nuisance fires, damaging property). This behaviour eventually escalates to more serious forms of criminality, ranging from joyriding, pocket picking, larceny, and fencing to passing bad cheques, using stolen credit cards, stealing cars, dealing drugs, and breaking and entering.

3. The **overt pathway** escalates to aggressive acts beginning with aggression (annoying others, bullying), leading to physical (and gang) fighting and then to violence (attacking someone, forced theft).

The Loeber research indicates that each of these paths may lead to a sustained deviant career. Some people enter two or even three paths simultaneously: They are stubborn, lie to teachers and parents, are bullies, and commit petty thefts. These adolescents are the most likely to become persistent offenders as they mature. Although some persistent offenders may specialize in one type of behaviour, others engage in varied criminal acts and antisocial behaviours as they mature. For example, they cheat on tests, bully others in the schoolyard, take drugs, commit burglary, steal a car, and shoplift from a store.

Criminal Trajectories

In addition to taking different paths to criminality, people may begin their journey at different times. Some are precocious, beginning their criminal careers early; others stay out of trouble until their teenage years. Some offenders may peak at an early age, whereas others persist into adulthood.

Research indicates a number of different classes of criminal careers that seem to reflect changes in the

covert pathway
Pathway to a criminal career that begins with minor underhanded behaviour, leads to property damage, and eventually escalates to more serious forms of theft and fraud.

overt pathway
Pathway to a criminal career that begins with minor aggression, leads to physical fighting, and eventually escalates to violent crime.

life course. Some adolescents maximize their offending rate at a relatively early age and then reduce their criminal activity; others persist into their 20s. Some are high-rate offenders, whereas others offend at relatively low rates.[62] According to psychologist Terrie Moffitt, although the prevalence and frequency of antisocial behaviour peak in adolescence and then diminish for most offenders (she labels these adolescent-limiteds), a small group of life-course persisters who offends well into adulthood.[63]

Life-course persisters combine family dysfunction with severe neurological problems that predispose them to antisocial behaviour patterns. These problems can be the result of maternal drug abuse, poor nutrition, or exposure to toxic agents such as lead. Life-course persisters may have lower verbal ability, which inhibits reasoning skills, learning ability, and school achievement. They seem to mature faster and engage in early sexuality and drug use, referred to as pseudomaturity.[64] There may be more than one subset of life-course persisters. One group

Joe Seer/Shutterstock.com

Actor Mark Wahlburg grew up in Dorchester, a tough area of Boston, and had already dropped out of school at 14. A cocaine addiction coupled with a growing history of violence and petty crime culminated in a two-year sentence for robbery and assault at age 16. His brother Donnie, of the boy band *New Kids on the Block,* helped Mark reinvent himself as hip-hop rapper "Marky Mark"—from which developed aspirations for an acting career. According to Wahlberg, "I think I was better off growing up in the world I did. If people are able to survive that, then they can survive anything. Coping skills are big on the résumé, in my book."

begins acting out during the preschool years; these children show signs of ADHD and do not outgrow the levels of disobedience typical of the preschool years. The second group shows few symptoms of ADHD but, from an early age, is aggressive, underhanded, and in constant opposition to authority.[65]

Adolescent-limited delinquents mimic the behaviour of these more troubled teens, but reduce the frequency of their offending as they mature to around age 18.[66] They are deeply influenced by the misbehaviour of their friends and peers up to around age 16, when peer group influence begins to decline. Peer influence, then, has a significant influence on their law-violating behaviour.[67] This group tends to focus on a specific type of misbehaviour such as drug abuse.

Why do some people enter a "path to crime" later rather than sooner? Early starters, who begin offending before age 14, follow a path from (1) poor parenting to (2) deviant behaviours and then to (3) involvement with delinquent groups. Late starters, who begin offending after age 14, follow a somewhat different path: (1) Poor parenting leads to (2) identification with delinquent groups and then to (3) deviant behaviours. By implication, adolescents who suffer poor parenting and are at risk for deviant careers can avoid criminality if they can bypass involvement with delinquent peers.[68]

Continuity of Crime

Another aspect of developmental theory is the continuity of crime: The best predictor of future criminality is past criminality. Children who are repeatedly in trouble during early adolescence generally will still be antisocial in their middle and late teens and as adults.[69] Early criminal activity is likely to be sustained because these offenders seem to lack the social survival skills necessary to find work or to develop the interpersonal relationships needed to allow them to drop out of crime.[70]

One explanation for this phenomenon suggests that criminal propensity may be "contagious." Children at risk to commit crime may be located in families and neighbourhoods in which they are constantly exposed to deviant behaviour. As they mature, having brothers, fathers, neighbours, and friends who engage in and support their activities reinforces their deviance.[71]

The discovery that people begin their criminal careers at different ages and follow different criminal paths and trajectories provides strong support for developmental theory. If all criminals possessed a singular latent trait that made them crime-prone, it would be unlikely that these variations in criminal careers would be observed. It is difficult to explain concepts such as late-onset and adolescent-limited behaviour from the perspective of latent trait theory.

DID YOU KNOW?

- Pioneering criminologists Sheldon and Eleanor Glueck tracked the onset and termination of criminal careers.

- Developmental theories look at issues such as the onset of crime, escalation of offences, continuity of crime, and desistance from crime.

- The concept of a problem behaviour syndrome suggests that criminality may be just one of a cluster of social, psychological, and physical problems.

- There is more than one pathway to crime.

- Adolescent-limited offenders begin offending late and age out of crime. Life-course persisters exhibit early onset of crime that persists into adulthood.

Theories of Criminal Development

An ongoing effort has been made to track persistent offenders over their life course.[72] The early data seem to support what is already known about delinquent and criminal career patterns: Juvenile offenders are likely to become adult criminals; early onset predicts more lasting crime; and chronic offenders commit a significant portion of all crimes.[73] Based on these findings, criminologists have formulated a number of systematic theories that account for the onset, continuance, and desistance from crime.

social development model (SDM)
A developmental theory that attributes criminal behaviour patterns to childhood socialization and proor antisocial attachments over the life course.

prosocial bonds
Socialized attachment to conventional institutions, activities, and beliefs.

The Social Development Model

In their social development model (SDM), Joseph Weis, Richard Catalano, J. David Hawkins, and their associates show how different factors affecting a child's social development over the life course influence criminal

behaviour patterns.[74] As children mature within their environment, elements of socialization control their developmental process. Children are socialized and develop bonds to their families through four distinct interactions and processes:

1. Perceived opportunities for involvement in activities and interactions with others

2. The degree of involvement and interaction with parents

3. The children's ability to participate in these interactions

4. The reinforcement (such as feedback) they perceive for their participation

To control the risk of antisocial behaviour, a child must maintain prosocial bonds. These are developed within the context of family life, which not only provides prosocial opportunities but also reinforces them by consistent, positive feedback. Parental attachment affects a child's behaviour for life, determining both school experiences and personal beliefs and values. For those with strong family relationships, school will be a meaningful experience marked by academic success and commitment to education. Young people in this category are likely to develop conventional beliefs and

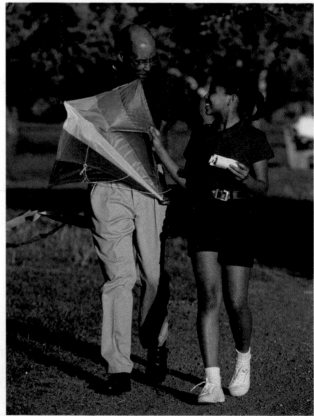

According to the social development model, children must develop prosocial bonds in order to control the risk of antisocial behaviour. These bonds are usually formed within the context of the family.

values, become committed to conventional activities, and form attachments to conventional others.

Children's antisocial behaviour also depends on the quality of their attachments to parents and other influential relations. If they remain unattached or develop attachments to deviant others, their behaviour may become deviant as well. Unlike Hirschi's control theory, which assumes that all attachments are beneficial, the SDM suggests that interaction with antisocial peers and adults promotes participation in delinquency and substance abuse.[75]

Interactional Theory

Terence Thornberry has proposed an age-graded view of crime that he calls interactional theory (see Figure 9.8).[76] He too finds that the onset of crime can be traced to a deterioration of the social bond during adolescence, marked by weakened attachment to parents, commitment to school, and belief in conventional values.

Interactional theory holds that seriously delinquent youths form belief systems that are consistent with their deviant lifestyle. They seek out the company of other adolescents who share their interests and who are likely to reinforce their beliefs about the world and support their delinquent behaviour. According to interactional theory, delinquents find a criminal peer group in the same way that chess buffs look for others who share their passion for the game; hanging out with other chess players helps improve their game. Similarly, deviant peers do not turn an otherwise innocent boy into a delinquent; they support and amplify the behaviour of those who have already accepted a delinquent way of life.[77]

Thornberry suggests that criminality is a developmental process that takes on different meanings and forms as a person matures. According to Thornberry, the causal process is a dynamic one and develops over a person's life.[78] During early adolescence, attachment to the family is the single most important determinant of whether a youth will adjust to conventional society and be shielded from delinquency. By mid-adolescence, the influence of the family is replaced by the "world of friends, school and youth culture."[79] In adulthood, a person's behavioural choices are shaped by his or her place in conventional society and his or her own nuclear family.

In sum, interactional theory suggests that criminality is part of a dynamic social process and not just an outcome of that process. Although crime is influenced by social forces, it also influences these processes and associations to create behavioural trajectories toward increasing law violations for some people.[80] Interactional theory integrates elements of social disorganization, social control, social learning, and cognitive theories into a powerful model of the development of a criminal career.

Sampson and Laub: Age-Graded Theory

If there are various pathways to crime and delinquency, are there trails back to conformity? In an important 1993 work, *Crime in the Making*, Robert Sampson and John Laub identify turning points in a criminal career.[81] Reanalyzing the original Glueck data, they found that the stability of delinquent behaviour can be affected by events that occur later in life, even after a chronic delinquent career has been established. They agree with Hirschi and Gottfredson that formal and informal social controls restrict criminality and that crime begins early in life and continues over the life course; they disagree that once this course is set, nothing can impede its progress.

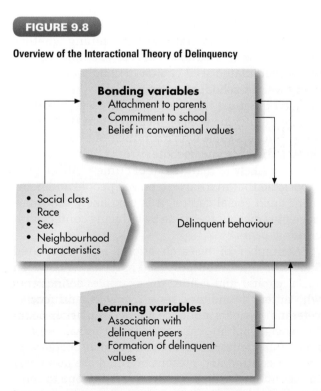

FIGURE 9.8

Overview of the Interactional Theory of Delinquency

Bonding variables
- Attachment to parents
- Commitment to school
- Belief in conventional values

- Social class
- Race
- Sex
- Neighbourhood characteristics

Delinquent behaviour

Learning variables
- Association with delinquent peers
- Formation of delinquent values

Source: Reprinted by permission of the Hindelang Criminal Justice Research Center.

interactional theory
A developmental theory that attributes criminal trajectories to mutual reinforcement between delinquents and significant others over the life course—family in early adolescence, school and friends in mid-adolescence, and social peers and one's own nuclear family in adulthood.

turning points
Critical life events, such as career and marriage, that may enable adult offenders to desist from crime.

Turning Points

Sampson and Laub's most important contribution is identifying the life events that enable adult offenders to desist from crime. Two critical turning points are career and marriage.

Adolescents who are at risk for crime can live conventional lives if they can find good jobs or achieve successful careers. Their success may hinge on a lucky break. Even those who have been in trouble with the law may turn from crime if employers are willing to give them a chance despite their records.

Adolescents who have had significant problems with the law are also able to desist from crime if, as adults, they become attached to a spouse who supports and sustains them even when the spouse knows they have been in trouble in the past. Happy marriages are life sustaining, and marital quality improves over time (as people work less and have fewer parental responsibilities).[82] Spending time in marital and family activities also reduces exposure to deviant peers, which in turn reduces the opportunity to become involved in delinquent activities.[83] People who cannot sustain secure marital relations are less likely to desist from crime.

Sampson and Laub's age-graded theory is supported by research that shows that children who grow up in two-parent families are more likely to have happier marriages than children whose parents were divorced or never married.[84] This finding suggests that the marriage–crime association may be intergenerational: If people with marital problems are more crime-prone, their children will also suffer a greater long-term risk of marital failure and antisocial activity.

Social Capital

Social scientists recognize that people build **social capital**—positive relations with individuals and institutions that are life sustaining. In the same manner that building financial capital improves the chances for economic success, building social capital supports conventional behaviour and inhibits deviant behaviour. A successful marriage creates social capital when it improves a person's stature, creates feelings of self-worth, and encourages others to trust the person. A successful career inhibits crime by creating a stake in conformity: Why commit crime when you are doing well at your job? The relationship is reciprocal. If people are chosen to be employees, they return the favour by doing the best job possible; if they are chosen as spouses, they blossom into devoted partners. In contrast, moving to a new city reduces social capital by closing people off from long-term relationships.[85]

Sampson and Laub's research indicates that building social capital and strong social bonds reduces the likelihood of long-term deviance. This finding suggests that, in contrast to latent trait theories, events that occur in later adolescence and adulthood do, in fact, influence the direction of delinquent and criminal careers. Life events can help either terminate or sustain deviant careers. For example, getting arrested and punished may have little direct effect on future criminality. It can however, help sustain a criminal career because it reduces the chances of employment and job stability, two factors that are directly related to crime (see Figure 9.9).[86]

Testing Age-Graded Theory

Several indicators support the validity of age-graded theory.[87] Evidence now shows that once begun, criminal career trajectories can be reversed if life conditions improve, an outcome predicted by age-graded theory.[88] For example, employment status affects behaviour. Men who are unemployed or underemployed report higher criminal participation rates than employed men. Similarly, men released from prison on parole who obtain jobs are less likely to reoffend than those who lack or lose employment.[89]

Research has been directed at identifying the sources of social capital and determining whether and how it is related to crime. For example, youths who accumulate social capital in childhood (e.g., by doing well in school or having a tightly knit family) are also the most likely to maintain steady work as adults; employment may help insulate them from crime.[90] Also, people who maintain a successful marriage in their 20s and become parents themselves are the most likely to mature out of crime.[91] Although it is possible that marriage stabilizes people and helps them build social capital, it is also likely that marriage may discourage crime by reducing contact with criminal peers.[92]

A number of research efforts have supported Sampson and Laub's proposed association between social capital and crime. For example, delinquents who enter the military, serve overseas, and receive veterans' benefits enhance their occupational status (social capital) while reducing criminal involvement.[93] In contrast, research shows that people who are self-centred and present oriented are less likely to accumulate social capital and more prone to commit criminal acts.[94]

> **social capital**
> Positive relations with individuals and institutions, as in a successful marriage or a successful career, that support conventional behaviour and inhibit deviant behaviour.

FIGURE 9.9

Sampson and Laub's Age-Graded Theory

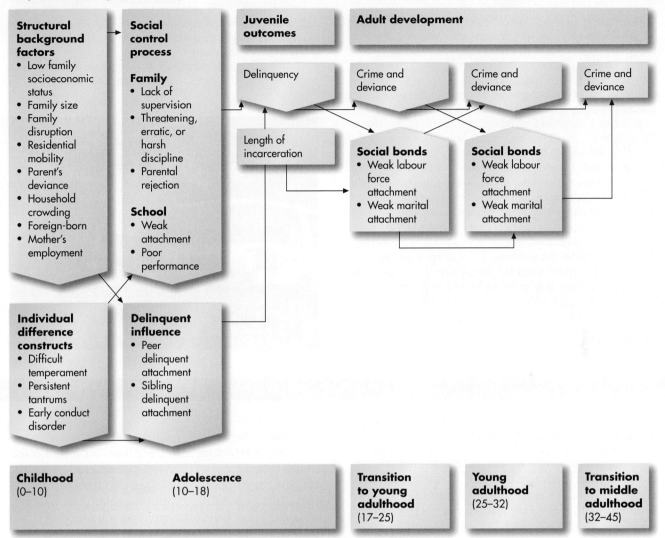

Finding the Glueck Delinquents

John Laub and Robert Sampson conducted an important follow-up to their original research: They located and interviewed the survivors from the original Glueck research, the oldest subject being 70 years old and the youngest 62.[95]

Their findings suggest that delinquency and other forms of antisocial conduct in childhood are strongly related to adult crime and drug and alcohol abuse. Former delinquents also suffer consequences in other areas of social life, such as school, work, and family life. For example, delinquents are far less likely to finish high school than nondelinquents and subsequently are more likely to be unemployed, receive welfare, and experience separation or divorce as adults.[96]

Laub and Sampson addressed one of the key questions posed by developmental theories: Is it possible for former delinquents to rehabilitate themselves as adults? They found that most antisocial children do not remain antisocial as adults. Of those men who survived to age 50, 24 percent had no arrests for crimes of violence and property after age 17 (6 percent had no arrests for any crime); 48 percent had no arrests for these predatory crimes after age 25 (19 percent for total crime); 60 percent had no arrests for predatory crimes after age 31 (33 percent for total crime); and 79 percent had no arrests for predatory crimes after age 40 (57 percent for total crime). They concluded that desistance from crime is the norm and that most, if not all, serious delinquents later desist from crime.[97]

Tagged "Canada's youngest multiple murderer," 12-year-old Medicine Hat, Alberta, "tweeny" J.R. was convicted along with her 23-year-old boyfriend Jeremy Allan Steinke of killing her parents and eight-year-old brother in April 2006. At her trial in 2007, the court heard from psychiatric experts that J.R. was "seriously disturbed" and showed an immature capacity for problem solving and dependency on others—and appeared to show no remorse or acceptance of her own role in the murders.

In August 2015, Justice Scott Brooker lifted the curfew restriction on J.R., allowing the now 21-year-old to live on her own in Calgary without any curfew dictating the hours when she must be at home. Under the terms of her 2007 sentence, J.R. will continue to live under conditional supervision in the community for another nine months until the end of her sentence, which also included a four-year stay in a psychiatric institution. According to J.R.'s lawyer, the young woman is now enrolled in university, is described as a "model offender," and is at very low risk to reoffend—and has expressed what the court was told is real and deep remorse for the crimes she committed. If J.R does not break the law for five years after her sentence ends, her criminal record will be wiped clean. Steinke remains in federal prison serving three life sentences.

According to the general theory of crime, "novice offenders" commit a wide variety of different types of crimes that reflect a lack of self-control learned in early childhood—and GTC theorists maintain that such lack of self-control is maintained throughout the life course. However, given the right social circumstances and daily structure, poor self-control can be managed very successfully, giving hope for nearly complete rehabilitation and reintegration into society.

What do you think—can an individual ever fully be rehabilitated and reintegrated into society after committing such horrific crimes?

Calgary Herald

Why Do Delinquents Desist?

Laub and Sampson's earlier research had already indicated that marriage and job, as means of building social capital, were key components of desistance from crime. In this new round of research, Laub and Sampson were able to find out more about long-term desistance by interviewing 52 men as they approached age 70. Drawing on the men's own words, they found that one important element for "going straight" is the "knifing off" of individuals from their immediate environment, offering them a new "script" for the future. Joining the military can provide this "knifing-off" effect, as does marriage and changing one's residence. One former delinquent (age 69) told them:

> I'd say the turning point was, number one, the Army. You get into an outfit, you had a sense of belonging, you made your friends. I think I became a pretty good judge of character. In the Army, you met some good ones, you met some foul balls. Then I met the wife. I'd say probably that would be the turning point. Got married, then naturally, kids come. So now you got to get a better job, you got to make more money. And that's how I got to the Navy Yard and tried to improve myself.*

---

*John Laub, "Crime Over the Life Course," *Poverty Research News*, Newsletter of the Northwestern University/University of Chicago Joint Center for Poverty Research, vol. 4, no. 3 (May–June 2000). Reprinted with permission.

Former delinquents who "went straight" were able to put structure into their lives. Structure often led the men to disassociate from delinquent peers, reducing the opportunity to get into trouble. Getting married, for example, may limit the number of nights men can "hang with the guys." As one wife of a former delinquent said, "It is not how many beers you have, it's who you drink with." Even multiple offenders who had done time in prison were able to desist with the help of a stabilizing marriage.

The former delinquents who were able to turn their lives around, who had acquired a degree of maturity by taking on family and work responsibilities, and who had forged new commitments were the ones most likely to make a fresh start and find new direction and meaning in life. It seems that men who desisted changed their identity as well, and this, in turn, affected their outlook and sense of maturity and responsibility. The ability to change did not reflect crime "specialty"; violent offenders followed the same path as property offenders.

Policy Implications

Laub and Sampson found that youth problems— delinquency, substance abuse, violence, dropping out, teen pregnancy—often share common risk characteristics. Intervention strategies, therefore, should consider a broad array of antisocial, criminal, and deviant behaviours, and not limit their focus to one subgroup or crime type. Because delinquency and other social problems are linked (problem behaviour syndrome), early prevention efforts that reduce crime will probably also reduce alcohol abuse, drunk driving, drug abuse, sexual promiscuity, and family violence, as well as school failure, unemployment, marital disharmony, and divorce.

The best way to achieve these goals is through four significant life-changing events: marriage, joining the military, getting a job, and changing one's environment or neighbourhood. What appears to be important about these processes is that they all involve, to varying degrees, the following items: a "knifing off" of the past from the present, new situations that provide supervision and monitoring as well as new opportunities for social support and growth, and new situations that provide the opportunity for transforming identity. Prevention of crime must therefore be a policy at all times and at all stages of life.

DID YOU KNOW?

- The social development model (SDM) integrates social control, social learning, and structural models.

- According to interactional theory, the causes of crime are bidirectional. Weak bonds lead to deviant peer relations and delinquency; delinquency weakens conventional bonds and strengthens relations with deviant peers.

- According to age-graded theory, building social capital and strong social bonds reduces the likelihood of long-term deviance.

- Many delinquents desist as adults. Building social capital helps people desist.

The Future of Criminological Theory

In his 2010 address to the American Society of Criminology, Francis T. Cullen, the Edwin H. Sutherland Award Winner for outstanding contributions to theory or research in criminology, argued that for more than half a century the field of criminology has been dominated by what he called the "adolescent limited theory" paradigm: a focus on the study of adolescents using self-report surveys to test theories of crime that focus almost exclusively on the social environment and government policies as the causes of crime. Cullen goes further to argue in his address (p. 304) that the "adolescent limited theory" paradigm is "bankrupt and should be discarded," as this approach has nothing more to add to our understanding of crime and, in fact, did little to tell us how to design interventions or treatments to reduce crime or criminal behaviour.[98]

Instead, Cullen called for a new approach in criminology, one that integrates the knowledge we have from biology, genetics, psychology, sociology, and other fields to design a comprehensive theory of crime according to the following eight steps:[*]

1. *Accept life course criminology is criminology.* The study of the causes and correlated of criminal behaviour over the life course should be the "organizing framework" for the field of criminology.

2. *Embrace biosocial theory.* Criminology cannot ignore the mounting evidence of the impact of genetics and biology on human behaviour and, therefore, criminal behaviour.

3. *Explore how individuals travel through contexts.* Individuals move through different social contexts throughout their life course that represent shared beliefs (culture) and shared actions (social constraints) in interaction with individual genetics and biological and psychological characteristics.

4. *Understand criminal decision making.* New neuropsychological research on risk-taking behaviour, combined with other studies of situational factors and the role of emotions in decision making, will help explain how individual and contextual factors work together as decisions to engage in criminal behaviour are made.

5. *Know something about the crime event.* Criminologists know little about what actually happens during the commission of a crime, and how individual offender characteristics and the motivation to commit crime are enhanced, modified, and deterred by different situational factors.

6. *Talk to offenders, not to high school students.* To understand crime, talk to actual criminals.

7. *Revolutionize the organization of knowledge.* The discipline of criminology needs to organize completed research in a way that tells us what we know and do not know about crime and criminals, so that we know where to focus our research efforts.

8. *Take doing good seriously.* Use criminological theory and research to do good, with a focus on identifying what works to intervene in the lives of offenders to reduce or eliminate their involvement in criminal behaviour.[99]

Already, we can see this new paradigm in criminological theory, in the work of Barnes and his colleagues on the significance of new finding in genetics for understanding criminal behaviour; on the link between personality disorder and criminal behaviour in the work of Falk and his colleagues; in

*Cullen, Frances T. (2011). "Beyond Adolescence-limited criminology: Choosing our future – the American Society of Criminology 2010 Sutherland address," *Criminology*, 49(2), 287–330. © 2011 American Society of Criminology the integative theorizing by Wiebe, bringing together biological and sociological perspectives on adaptive decision making as a means of understanding criminal behaviour choices; in the work encompassed by Farrington's integrated cognitive antisocial potential theory; and other efforts to integrate new findings from the fields of biology, genetics, psychology, and sociology.[100]

Summary

Integrated theories seek to avoid the shortcomings of single-factor theories and attempt to blend seemingly independent concepts into coherent explanations of criminality.

Latent trait theories hold that some underlying condition present at birth or soon after controls behaviour. Suspect traits include low IQ, impulsivity, and personality structure. This underlying trait explains the continuity of offending because, once present, it remains with a person throughout his or her life.

In their general theory of crime, Gottfredson and Hirschi integrate concepts from biosocial, psychological, routine activities, and rational choice theories with social control theory to come up with an overall theory of crime. According to Gottfredson and Hirschi, criminal offenders are individuals predisposed to commit crimes. The biological and psychological factors that make people impulsive and crime-prone may be inherited or may develop through incompetent or absent parenting. However, crime-prone individuals are not robots who commit crime without restraint; their days are also filled with conventional behaviours, such as going to school, parties, concerts, and religious institutions. But given the same set of criminal opportunities, such as having a lot of free time for mischief and living in a neighbourhood with unguarded homes containing valuable merchandise, crime-prone people have a much higher probability of violating the law than do noncriminals.

Developmental theories look at multiple factors derived from a number of different structural and process theories, and seek to explain how criminal careers develop and change over the life course. Examples include the social development model, interactional theory, and age-graded theory. The cause of crime constantly changes as people mature.

Early family and childhood experiences are important factors that can set the stage for later criminal behaviour. Crime can be thought of as just one among a group of antisocial behaviours that can cluster together, referred to collectively as problem behaviour syndrome (PBS).

Depending on their individual biological and psychological makeup, the environment the individual grows up in, the opportunities available to them, and the choices they make, the pathway (or trajectory) individuals will follow may be criminal or noncriminal. Different transitions and events in life can change the course of the trajectory; for example, an influential teacher, a satisfying relationship, or a good job could turn the trajectory of someone with PBS from being potentially negative and criminal to positive and law abiding. Even as the individual matures and ages, the likelihood of his or her involvement in criminal behaviour will change. Research shows that marriage and a job, and aging itself, are important reasons behind desistance, the decision to end a criminal trajectory.

According to criminologist Francis T. Cullen, the future development of criminological theories rests on eight important requirements:

1. Accept life course criminology is criminology.

2. Embrace biosocial theory.

3. Explore how individuals travel through contexts.

4. Understand criminal decision making.

5. Know something about the crime event.

6. Talk to offenders, not to high school students.

7. Revolutionize the organization of knowledge.

8. Take doing good seriously.

Discussion Questions

1. Do you consider yourself the holder of "social capital"? If so, what form does it take?

2. A person maintains a 4.0 GPA throughout university. Without knowing this person, what personal, family, and social characteristics must he or she have? Another person becomes a serial killer. Without knowing this person, what personal, family, and social characteristics must he or she have? If "bad behaviour" is explained by multiple problems, is "good behaviour" explained by multiple strengths?

3. Do you believe there is a "latent trait" that makes a person crime-prone, or is crime a function of environment and socialization?

4. Do you agree with Loeber's multiple pathway model? Do you know people who have travelled down those paths?

READY
TO STUDY?

IN THE BOOK, YOU CAN:

✔ Check your understanding of what you've just read by reading the Summary at the end of each chapter.

✔ Rip out the Chapter in Review card at the back of the book to have the key terms and Learning Objectives handy, and complete the quizzes provided (answers are at the bottom of the back page!).

ONLINE YOU CAN:

✔ Stay organized and efficient with MindTap—a single destination with all the course material and study aids you need to succeed. Built-in apps leverage social media and the latest learning technology. For example:

✔ ReadSpeaker will read the text to you.

✔ Flashcards are pre-populated to provide you with a jump start for review—or you can create your own.

✔ You can highlight text and make notes in your MindTap Reader. Your notes will flow into Evernote, the electronic notebook app that you can access anywhere when it's time to study for the exam.

✔ Prepare for tests with quizzes.

Go to www.nelson.com/student to access these digital resources.

10

Violent Crime

Learning Objectives

LO1 Describe the different types of interpersonal violent crime.

LO2 Contrast the various explanations for violent crimes.

LO3 Evaluate the significance of the changes in Canadian law in regard to rape.

LO4 Identify the different degrees of murder.

LO5 Explain the prevalence of assault that occurs in the family home.

LO6 Discuss why robbery is considered a violent crime.

LO7 Define and describe contemporary forms of interpersonal violent crime.

LO1 Introduction

In 2010, 47-year-old career criminal John Steele concealed his face with a hoodie, walked into a Winnipeg drugstore, and told the clerk, "Give me the money. It's a robbery. I have a gun." After being convicted of robbery, wearing a disguise, and two counts of breaching a probation order in relation to the robbery, the Crown wanted to proceed with a dangerous offender application. If successful, Steele would receive an indefinite prison sentence, to be released only when corrections officials are satisfied he no longer poses a danger to the community. The problem faced by the Crown was that Steele lied about having a weapon. The clerk was not harmed, although he testified that he was "real scared" and another staff member went into shock. But is a robbery where no physical violence was used still a violent offence? The Manitoba Court of Appeal ruled that "implied threat of violence" was not enough to have Steele declared a dangerous offender, since the drugstore clerks were not injured or put in "imminent danger." However, in a 2014 landmark decision, the Supreme Court of Canada overturned the decision, declaring that merely telling someone you have a gun, that is, the simple act of threatening a drugstore clerk, was in effect the commission of a violent act against another person. The consequences of this decision mean that Steele could spend the remainder of his life behind bars. Previously, the case law on whether a threat of violence constituted actual violence was unclear. By interpreting all threats of violence as actual violence, the ruling is expected to have wide-ranging implications on how Canada defines violent behaviour.[1]

The robbery committed by Steele and the Supreme Court of Canada ruling that it provoked will certainly expand the definition of violence in Canada. According to social historian, David Courtwright, violence is a "primal problem," "… the dark reverse of its coin of freedom and abundance."[2] Although the violent crime rate has recently declined, people are continually bombarded with news stories featuring grisly accounts of mass murder, child sexual abuse, and serial rape. Many people have personally experienced violence and almost everyone knows someone who has been robbed, beaten, or killed. Riots and mass disturbances have ravaged urban areas; racial attacks

DID YOU KNOW?

- There are a number of suspected causes of violence.
- Some violent criminals have personal traits, including mental impairment and intellectual dysfunction, that make them violence-prone.
- Victims of severe child abuse and neglect may become violence-prone adults.
- Violence may have its roots in human evolution, being almost instinctual in some instances.
- Drug and alcohol abuse has been linked to violence, through either a psychopharmacological relationship, an economic compulsive behaviour, or a systemic link.
- Although guns do not cause violence, their presence can escalate its severity.

plague schools and university and college campuses; and assassination has claimed the lives of political, religious, and social leaders all over the world.[3]

When violence is designed to improve the financial or social position of the criminal, as in an armed robbery, it is referred to as instrumental violence. Crimes that vent rage, anger, or frustration are known as expressive violence. An extreme example of expressive violence occurred when Corporal Nathan Cirillo, 24, of Hamilton, Ontario, was killed in October 2014 while standing guard at the National War Museum in Ottawa. Described by family and

> **instrumental violence**
> Violence designed to improve the financial or social position of the criminal.
>
> **expressive violence**
> Violence that vents rage, anger, or frustration.

Corporal Nathan Cirillo guarded the Tomb of the Unknown Soldier at the National Memorial in Ottawa. In October 2014, he was fatally shot in the abdomen by a man who later attacked the Parliament buildings.

friends as a doting father who was planning to serve Canada full-time as a member of the armed services, he left behind a six-year-old son. His attacker, Michael Zehaf-Bibeau was a recent convert to Islam described by the RCMP as a lone-wolf gunman, driven by crazed religious beliefs. After killing Cirillo, Zehaf-Bibeau stormed the Parliament Buildings and was eventually stopped by the heroic efforts of security guards. Thousands of people lined Hamilton's downtown streets as Cirillo's casket passed, accompanied by the sound of pipers and drummers.[4]

This chapter surveys the nature and extent of violent crime. First, it briefly reviews some possible causes of violence. Then, it focuses on specific types of interpersonal violence—rape, homicide, assault (including domestic violence), and robbery. Finally, it briefly examines political violence, including terrorism.

LO2 The Roots of Violence

What causes people to behave violently? A number of competing explanations have been offered for violent behaviour. A few of the most prominent are discussed here.

Personal Traits

On December 6, 1989, Marc Lepine burst into a classroom at l'École Polytechnique Montréal with an automatic gun in his hand. First, he ordered the male students to leave the room; then, shouting a few incoherent curses against feminists, Lepine opened fire into the crowd of terrified women students. Lepine claimed 14 lives before turning the gun on himself. This horrific crime shocked Canadians into implementing strict controls on all guns in the form of Bill C-68, which was proclaimed on December 5, 1995, in time for the sixth anniversary of the Montreal murders.[5]

Bizarre outbursts such as Lepine's support a link between violence and personal traits and personality disorders. Violent offenders often display abnormal personality structures marked by psychopathic tendencies such as impulsivity, aggression, dishonesty, pathological lying, and lack of remorse.[6]

American psychologist Dorothy Otnow Lewis and her associates found that murderous youths often show signs of major neurological impairment, such as abnormal EEGs, multiple psychomotor impairment, and severe seizures; low intelligence as measured on standard IQ tests; close relatives diagnosed with psychosis; and psychotic symptoms such as paranoia, illogical thinking, and hallucinations.[7] In her 1998 book *Guilty by Reason of Insanity*, Lewis reports that American death-row inmates often have a history of mental impairment and intellectual dysfunction.[8] Many murderers kill themselves shortly after committing their crime and there are documented cases of people who commit murder with the expectation that they will be executed for their crimes, a form of "suicide-murder."[9]

Abnormal personality structure, including depression, borderline personality syndrome, and psychopathology, have been associated with various forms of spousal and family abuse.[10] A high proportion of serial rapists and repeat sexual offenders exhibit psychopathic personality structures.[11] Although this evidence indicates that violent offenders may be more prone to psychological disorders than other people, no single clinical diagnosis can characterize their behaviour.[12]

Ineffective Families

Much research traces violence to rejecting, ineffective, or abusive parenting.[13] Absent or deviant parents, inconsistent discipline, and lack of supervision have all been linked to persistent violent offending.[14]

A number of research studies have found that children who are clinically diagnosed as abused later engage in delinquent behaviours, including violence, at a rate significantly greater than that of unabused children.[15] Samples of convicted murderers reveal a high percentage of seriously abused youth.[16] The abuse–violence association has been established in many cases in which parents have been killed by their children; sexual abuse is also a constant factor in father (patricide) and mother (matricide) killings.[17] Dorothy Otnow Lewis found in her study of juvenile death row inmates that all had long histories of intense child abuse.[18]

Evolutionary Factors/Human Instinct

Perhaps violent responses and emotions are actually inherent in all humans, easily triggered by the right spark. Sigmund Freud believed that human aggression and violence are produced by two instinctual drives: *eros*, the life instinct, which drives people toward self-fulfillment and enjoyment; and *thanatos*, the death instinct, which produces self-destruction. Thanatos can be expressed externally (as violence and sadism) or internally (as suicide, alcoholism, or other self-destructive behaviours). Because aggression is instinctual, Freud saw little hope for its treatment.[19] A number of biologists and anthropologists have also speculated that instinctual violence-promoting traits may be common in the human species. One view is that aggression and violence are the results of instincts inborn in all animals, including human beings.[20]

Exposure to Violence

People who are constantly exposed to violence at home, at school, or in the environment may adopt violent methods themselves.[21] In a study of Chicago youth, social scientist Felton Earls found that between 30 and 40 percent of the children who reported exposure to violence also displayed significant violent behaviour themselves.[22] Exposure to violence may also have an effect on adults, even police officers. Research indicates that police officers' use of deadly force is much higher in areas with high violence and murder rates. The perception of danger may contribute to the use of violent means for self-protection, even among people trained in the use of force.[23]

Cultural Values

The various sources of crime statistics tell us that interpersonal violence is more common in urban areas than in rural areas.[24] It is unlikely that violent crime rates would be so high in these socially disorganized areas, however, unless other social forces encouraged violent crime.[25]

Criminologists Marvin Wolfgang and Franco Ferracuti have attributed these disproportionately high violence rates in urban areas to a subculture of violence.[26] The norms of this subculture are separate from society's central, dominant value system. In this subculture, a potent theme of violence influences lifestyles, the socialization process, and interpersonal relationships. Its members expect that violence

subculture of violence
Norms and customs that, in contrast to society's dominant value system, legitimize and expect the use of violence to resolve social conflicts.

CRIMINO

WARNER BROS/HAWK FILMS / THE KOBAL COLLECTION

Stanley Kubrick's controversial 1971 film A *Clockwork Orange* is still considered one of the most violent movies of all times. With reference to psychiatry, juvenile delinquency, youth gangs, and other social, political, and economic subjects, it tells the story of Alex (Malcolm McDowell), the main character, who is a charismatic, sociopathic delinquent. Alex leads a gang of thugs who engage in a horrific crime spree that involves beating an elderly vagrant, fighting a rival gang, stealing a car, beating a man to the point of crippling him for life then raping his wife while singing "Singin' in the Rain." On a subsequent occasion, Alex breaks into a wealth woman's home and bludgeons her to death with a phallic statue. For this act, he is sentenced to 14 years in prison.

Two years into his sentence, he is offered the opportunity to shorten his sentence if he participates in an experiment involving the Ludovico technique, a form of aversion therapy thought to be useful for rehabilitating criminals. The process involves drugging the subject, strapping him to a chair, propping his eyelids open, and forcing him to watch images of violence. Alex becomes conditioned to get sick as the sight of a naked woman. After two weeks of treatment he is deemed cured. He is incapable of fighting back against an actor who insults and attacks him, and becomes violently ill at the sight of a topless woman. The prison chaplain protests at the results, feeling that Alex has been robbed of his God-given free will, proclaiming, "He ceases also to be a creature capable of moral choice." Alex is released and soon finds himself homeless. After being attacked by elderly vagrants, he is saved by two policemen who turn out to be former members of his gang. They proceed to beat and nearly drown him until he escapes to the countryside where he encounters the man he crippled and whose wife he had raped. The man does not recognize

Alex until he hears Alex singing "Singin' in the Rain" in the bath after which he drugs Alex and locks him in a upstairs bedroom. Alex tries to commit suicide by jumping out the window and is knocked unconscious by the fall. He wakes up in a hospital with broken bones. After a series of psychological tests, Alex finds that he no longer has an aversion to violence or sex, and has vivid thoughts of himself raping a women in the snow in front of an approving crowd: "I was cured, all right!"

The author of the book upon which A *Clockwork Orange* was based clearly intended to criticize classical conditioning as reflected in the Ludovico technique, which he believed was a danger to mankind. Some believe that Alex represents man in his natural state and the Ludovico technique was intended to "civilize" him. Kubrick had stated he believed Alex "makes no attempt to deceive himself or the audience as to his total corruption or wickedness. He is the very personification of evil. On the other hand, he has winning qualities: his total candour, his wit, his intelligence and his energy; these are attractive qualities and ones, which I might add, which he shares with Richard III."

Does the film provide support for those who believe that evolutionary, biological factors explain why man is violent and capable of rape and murder? What about the concept of hypermasculinity? Alex was certainly impulsive and did indeed brag about his sexual conquests. Are all men capable of engaging in such behaviours or is this an oversimplification of the true nature of men? Explain.

will be used to solve social conflicts and dilemmas, and violence is legitimized by custom and norms. It is considered appropriate behaviour within culturally defined conflict situations, in which an individual who has been offended by a negative outcome in a dispute seeks reparations through violent means.[27]

Substance Abuse

It has become common to link violence to substance abuse. In fact, substance abuse, particularly of alcohol, influences violence in three ways:[28]

1. *Psychopharmacological relationship.* Violence may be a direct consequence of ingesting mood-altering substances. Experimental evidence shows that high doses of drugs such as PCP and amphetamines may produce violent, aggressive behaviour.[29] Alcohol abuse has long been associated with all forms of violence. A direct alcohol–violence link may occur because drinking reduces cognitive ability, making miscommunication more likely, while at the same time limiting the capacity for rational dialogue and compromise.[30]

2. *Economic compulsive behaviour.* Drug users may resort to violence to support their habit.

3. *Systemic link.* Violence may be a function of rival gangs' battling over drug markets and territories. Drug trafficking activities can lead to personal vendettas and a perceived need for violent self-protection.[31]

Canadian crime statistics show that in about half of all cases of homicide, the accused had consumed drugs or alcohol at the time of the murder.[32] Surveys of prison inmates show that a significant majority report being under the influence of drugs or alcohol when they committed their last criminal offence.[33] Drug testing of arrestees in major American cities consistently shows that criminals are also drug abusers; almost three-quarters of all people incarcerated in American jails and prisons have a substance abuse or substance dependency problem.[34]

Georgii Shipin/Shutterstock.com

The link between acts of violence and substance abuse, particularly alcohol, has been clearly established.

Firearm Availability

Although firearm availability does not cause violence, it is certainly a facilitating factor. A petty argument can escalate into a fatal encounter if one party has a handgun. In Canada, handguns account for over half of all homicides involving a firearm. In 2012 shootings and stabbings were the most common methods used to commit homicide accounting for 33 percent and 31 percent respectively.[35] It may not be a coincidence that the United States, which has a huge surplus of guns and in which most firearms (80 percent) used in crimes are stolen or obtained through illegal or unregulated transactions, also has one of the world's highest violence rates.[36] Figure 10.1 lists some facts about weapons and violent crime.

FIGURE 10.1

Quick Facts about Weapons and Violent Crime in Canada

- Physical force or threats are the methods used in 75% of violent crimes.[37]

- Weapons are used against victims of violent crime only 19% of the time.[38]

- Knives are the most common weapon used to commit violent crime.[39]

- Homicide and attempted murder are the violent crimes most likely to involve the use of a weapon.[40]

- Shooting was the cause of death in about one-quarter (27%) of homicides.[41]

- Stabbings accounted for 40% of all homicides in Canada in 2013.[42]

- Almost 9 in 10 (87%) solved homicides in 2013 involved a victim being killed by someone he or she knew, compared with 13% of victims who were killed by a stranger.[43]

- In 2013, the police-reported crime rate was at its lowest point since 1969.[44]

- In Canada, about 80% of firearm-related deaths are suicides.[45]

Source: Tracey Lee, "Weapons and Violent Crime." Adapted from the Statistics Canada publication "Juristat," Catalogue 85-002, "Weapons and violent crimes," Vol. 17, No. 7, June 23, 1997; Statistics Canada, CCJS, "Family Violence in Canada: A Statistical profile" Minister of Industry, January 2011, Catalogue no. 85-224-X. Table 102-05401,2,3,4,5; Deaths, by cause, Chapter XX: External causes of morbidity and mortality (V01 to Y89), age group and sex, Canada, annual (number); Statistics Canada catalogue no. 85-002-X, Juristat; Knives and violent crime in Canada, 2008 by Mia Dauvergne, Spring 2010 Vol. 30, no. 1; Statistics Canada Catalogue85-002-X "Juristat" Volume 28, number 2, 2009; Firearms and Violent Crime by Mia Dauvergne and Leonardo De Socio

Each of these factors is believed to influence violent crimes, including both traditional common-law crimes, such as sexual assault, murder, assault, and robbery, and more recently recognized problems, such as workplace violence, hate crimes, and biker gangs. Each of these forms of violent behaviour is discussed in some detail later in this chapter.

LO3 Rape and Sexual Assault

Rape (from the Latin *rapere*, to take by force) is defined in common law as "the carnal knowledge of a female forcibly and against her will."[46] It is one of the most loathed, misunderstood, and frightening of crimes. Under traditional common-law definitions, rape involves nonconsensual sexual intercourse that a male performs against a female whom he is neither married to nor cohabitating with. Before the 1980s, husbands were immune from prosecution for raping their wives. However, in 1983 the government of Canada reformed the laws pertaining to rape and this immunity was removed. Further, because rape is viewed as a violent, coercive act of aggression, the term *rape*

was replaced with *sexual assault*, which refers to any form of sexual contact that is without voluntary consent.

> **sexual assault**
> Anything from unwanted touching to rape.

There have been various national campaigns to alert the public to the seriousness of sexual assault and, in particular, the impact it has on victims. Such efforts have made significant progress in revising rape laws and developing a vast social service network to aid victims.

Rape Versus Sexual Assault

As previously noted, the term *rape* is no longer used in a legal sense in Canada. After the 1983 revisions to the *Criminal Code* of Canada, *rape* was replaced with *sexual assault*. Part of the rationale underlying the change was to recognize the violent, aggressive nature of the act. **Sexual assault** can be anything from unwanted touching to rape. The *Criminal Code* identifies numerous types of sexual assault, some of which include descriptions of specific acts (e.g., using a weapon, causing bodily harm) as well as types of relationships (e.g., where the aggressor is in a position of authority). Further, there are three levels of sexual assault:

- Level I—simple sexual assault
- Level II—sexual assault with a weapon or resulting in bodily harm
- Level III—aggravated sexual assault

For the purposes of the present text, the term *rape* will be used in a colloquial sense, whereas *sexual assault* will refer to the *Criminal Code* definition.

History of Rape and Sexual Assault

Rape has been a recognized crime throughout history. It has been the subject of art, literature, film, and theatre. Paintings such as the *Rape of the Sabine Women* by Nicolas Poussin, novels such as *Clarissa* by Samuel Richardson, poems such as *The Rape of*

All photos: Sexual Assault Voices of Edmonton

"Don't Be That Guy," an edgy anti-rape campaign released in Edmonton targets young men aged 18–24. While anti-rape ads have commonly focused on the victims of the crime, this new focus puts the spotlight on potential perpetrators.

Nation-wide protests were sparked by the brutal gang-rape of a 23-year-old woman in Delhi, India, in 2012. The victim's ordeal began when six men lured her and her boyfriend onto a bus and repeatedly raped and sexually assaulted her with an iron bar after which she was thrown off the bus. She later succumbed to intestinal injuries. One of the accused sparked outrage when he declared from his jail cell, "A decent girl won't roam around at 9 o'clock at night. A girl is far more responsible for rape than a boy. Boy and girl are not equal. Housework and housekeeping is for girls, not roaming in discos and bars at night doing wrong things, wearing wrong clothes. About 20 percent of girls are good."

Four of the six men charged with her rape and murder have since been sentenced to death. Her killing garnered international attention to the plight of victims of rape in India and prompted government promises to implement changes to outdated laws in the country.

Source (quote): Ryan Barrell, "India Gang Rape Convict Blames Victim Jyoti Singh for Her Own Rape and Death," Huffington Post (3 March 2015) http://www.huffingtonpost.co.uk/2015/03/03/delhi-bus-rapist-interview-bbc_n_6789994.html (accessed 16 October 2015).

Lucrece by William Shakespeare, and films such as *Rape Nation* based on the gang rape in India, have sexual violence as their central theme.

In early civilization, rape was common. Men staked a claim of ownership on women by forcibly abducting and raping them. This practice led to males' solidification of power and their historical domination of women.[47] During the Middle Ages, it was common for ambitious men to abduct and rape wealthy women in an effort to force them into marriage. The practice of "heiress stealing" illustrates how feudal law gave little thought or protection to women and equated them with property.[48] Only in the late 15th century was forcible sex outlawed, and then only if the victim was of the nobility. Peasant women and married women were not considered rape victims until well into the 16th century.

Sexual Assault and War

The link between military conflicts and sexual assault is inescapable. Throughout recorded history, sexual assault has been associated with armies and warfare. Soldiers of conquering armies have considered sexual possession of their enemies' women one of the spoils of war. Among the ancient Greeks, rape was socially acceptable within the rules of warfare. During the Crusades, even knights and pilgrims, ostensibly bound by vows of chivalry and Christian piety, took time to rape as they marched toward Constantinople.

The belief that women are part of the spoils of war has continued. During World War II, the Japanese army forced as many as 200 000 Korean women into frontline brothels, where they were repeatedly assaulted. In a 1998 Japanese ruling, the surviving Korean women were awarded the equivalent of US$2300 each in compensation.[49] The systematic rape of Bosnian and Kosovar women by Serbian army officers during the civil war in the former Yugoslavia horrified the world during the 1990s. These crimes seemed particularly atrocious because they were part of an official policy of genocide: rape was deliberately used to impregnate Bosnian women with Serbian children.[50] Human rights groups have estimated that more than 30 000 women and young girls were sexually abused in the Balkan fighting. In Congo, where a decades-long war rages, it is estimated that in the population of 70 million more than 1000 women are raped every day.[51]

Incidence of Sexual Assault

According to the Canadian Centre for Justice Statistics, between 1993 and 2007 the rate of police-reported sexual assaults in Canada declined from a historical high of 136 per 100 000, to 73 per 100 000. Police-reported statistics show that females are more than five times more likely to be a victim of a sexual assault.[52]

These data must be interpreted with caution, because many cases of sexual assault go unreported. For example, it is estimated that only 10 percent of sexual assaults are reported to police.[53] Many people fail to report sexual assaults because they are embarrassed, believe nothing can be done, or blame themselves. Because other victim surveys indicate that at least 20 percent of women, 15 percent of university and college-age women, and 12 percent of adolescent girls have experienced sexual abuse or assault sometime during their lives, it is evident that both official and victimization statistics significantly undercount the incidence of sexual assault.[54]

Population density influences the sexual assault rate. Metropolitan areas today have sexual assault rates significantly higher than rural areas; nonetheless, urban areas have experienced a much greater drop in sexual assault reports than rural areas. Sexual assault is also a warm-weather crime. Most incidents occur during July and August, with the lowest rates reported for December, January, and February.[55]

Types of Sexual Assault

Some rapes are planned; others are spontaneous. Some focus on a particular victim, while in others the victim appears to be chosen at random.[56] Some sexual assaults involve a single offender; others, called gang rapes, involve multiple attackers. Compared to individual assaults, gang rapes are more likely to involve alcohol and drugs, to occur at night, and to include other types of sexual assault such as penetration with objects.[57]

Although some sexual assaults involve strangers, others involve people who are acquainted with one another. Acquaintance rape is a subcategory of date rape, which involves a sexual attack during a courting relationship. More than 50 percent of all rapes involve acquaintances.[58] According to the Canadian Centre for Justice Statistics, only 19 percent of police-reported sexual assaults are committed by a stranger.[59]

Some rapists are one-time offenders, but others engage in multiple or serial rapes. Some serial rapists constantly increase their use of force; others do not.[60] Some rapists commit "blitz" rapes, in which they attack their victims without warning; others try to "capture" their victims by striking up a conversation or offering them a ride; still others use personal relationships to gain access to their targets.[61]

One of the best-known attempts to classify the personalities of rapists was made by psychologist A. Nicholas Groth, an expert on classifying and treating sex offenders. According to Groth, every sexual assault contains three elements: anger, power, and sexuality.[62] Consequently, rapists can be classified according to one of the dimensions described in Table 10.1. In treating rape offenders, Groth found that about 55 percent were of the power type; about 40 percent, the anger type; and about 5 percent, the sadistic type. Groth's major contribution has been his recognition that rape is generally a crime of violence, not a sexual act. In all of these circumstances, sexual assault involves a violent criminal offence in which a predatory criminal chooses to attack a victim.[63]

Date Rape

One disturbing trend is the increase in sexual assault involving people who are in some form of courting relationship. There is no single form of date rape. Some sexual assaults occur on first dates; others after a relationship has been developing; still others after the couple has been involved for some time. In long-term or close relationships, the male partner may feel he has invested so much time and money in his partner that he is "owed" sexual relations or that sexual intimacy is an expression that the involvement is progressing. He may make comparisons to other couples who have dated as long and are sexually active.[64] Males who use force in

> **gang rape**
> Forcible sex involving multiple attackers.
>
> **acquaintance rape**
> Forcible sex in which offender and victim are acquainted with one another.
>
> **date rape**
> Forcible sex during a courting relationship.

TABLE 10.1

Varieties of Sexual Assault

Anger rape	occurs when sexuality becomes a means of expressing and discharging pent-up anger and rage. The rapist uses far more brutality than would have been necessary if his real objective had been simply to have sex with his victim. His aim is to hurt his victim as much as possible; the sexual aspect of rape may be an afterthought. Often the anger rapist acts on the spur of the moment after an upsetting incident has caused him conflict, irritation, or aggravation. ... Because a woman is usually physically beaten during an anger rape, she is more likely to receive sympathy from her peers, relatives, and the justice system and consequently be immune from any suggestion that she complied with the attack.
Power rape	involves an attacker who does not want to harm his victim as much as he wants to possess her sexually. His goal is sexual conquest, and he uses only the amount of force necessary to achieve his objective. The power rapist wants to be in control, to be able to dominate women and have them at his mercy. Yet it is not sexual gratification that drives the power rapist; in fact, he often has a consenting relationship with his wife or girlfriend. Sexual assault is instead a way of putting personal insecurities to rest, asserting heterosexuality, and preserving a sense of manhood. The power rapist's victim usually is a woman equal in age to or younger than the rapist. The lack of physical violence may reduce the support given the victim by family and friends. Therefore, the victim's personal guilt over her rape experience is increased—perhaps, she thinks, she could have done something to get away.
Sadistic rape	involves both sexuality and aggression. The sadistic rapist is bound up in ritual—he may torment his victim, bind her, or torture her. Victims are usually related, in the rapist's view, to a personal characteristic that he wants to harm or destroy. The rape experience is intensely exciting to the sadist; he gets satisfaction from abusing, degrading, or humiliating his captive. This type of rape is particularly traumatic for the victim. Victims of such crimes need psychiatric care long after their physical wounds have healed.

Source: From *Men Who Rape* by A. Nicholas Groth and Jean Birnbaum. Copyright © 2001 A. Nicholas Groth. Reprinted by permission of Basic Books, a member of the Perseus Books Group.

their dating relationships are more likely to be angry, jealous, and stressed; have poor communication skills; act irrationally; use alcohol; and report more efforts to control their partners than those men who never use force in dating relationships.[65]

Date rape is believed to be frequent on university and college campuses. It has been estimated that 15 to 20 percent of all college women are victims of rape or attempted rape.[66] The incidence of date rape may be even higher than surveys indicate because many victims blame themselves and do not recognize the incident as a sexual assault, saying, for example, "I should have fought back harder" or "I shouldn't have gotten drunk."[67] Thus, despite their seriousness and prevalence, fewer than one in ten date rapes may be reported to police.[68] Another disturbing issue is the increasing use of date rape drugs such as rohypnol, gamma hydroxybutyrate (GHB), ecstasy (MDMA), and ketamine hydrochloride ("K"). In response to calls from victims, police, and the public, in September 2011 the Canadian government tabled new legislation introducing tough new penalties for trafficking in date rape drugs, which was made into law in 2012 and implements higher maximum penalties for date-rape drugs and amphetamines.[69]

Knowing that young women on college and university campuses are at a high risk for date rapes involving the use of drugs or alcohol, four enterprising university students have developed a nail polish that changes color when exposed to date rape drugs.

Marital Rape

In 1978, Greta Rideout filed rape charges against her husband John. This Oregon case grabbed headlines because it was one of the first in which a husband was prosecuted for raping his wife while sharing a residence with her. John was acquitted, and the couple briefly reconciled; later, continued violent episodes culminated in divorce and a jail term for John.[70]

Traditionally, in Canada a legally married husband could not be charged with raping his wife; this legal doctrine was referred to as the **marital exemption**. The origin of this doctrine can be traced to the 16th-century pronouncement of Matthew Hale, England's chief justice, who wrote:

> But the husband cannot be guilty of rape committed by himself upon his lawful wife, for by their mutual matrimonial consent and contract the wife hath given up herself in this kind unto the husband which she cannot retract.[71]

However, research indicates that many women are raped each year by their husbands as part of an overall pattern of spousal abuse. Many **marital rapes** are accompanied by brutal, sadistic beatings and have little to do with normal sexual interests.[72] The marital exemption was removed from the Canadian *Criminal Code* in 1983 and has been abolished in many American states, in Australia, Belgium, Denmark, Israel, Scotland, New Zealand and in more than 60 other countries around the world.[73]

Sexual Assault and Persons Under the Age of Consent

In Canada, traditional statutory rape laws were replaced in 1988 with laws against a variety of sexual offences, including sexual interference, invitation to sexual touching, and sexual exploitation. Anyone who for sexual purposes touches any part of the body of someone under the age of 16 is guilty of the offence of **sexual interference**. Consent by the minor or mistake concerning the age of the victim cannot be used as a defence. However, there is no crime if the accused person is between the ages of 12 and 14 and the victim is less than two years younger than the accused and consented to the activity. Anyone who invites a person under the age of 16 years to touch them or another person for a sexual purpose is guilty of the crime of **invitation to sexual touching**. Similarly, consent by the minor or mistake concerning the age of the victim cannot be used as a defence. However, there is no crime if the accused person is between the ages of 12 and 14 and the victim is less than two years younger than the accused and consented to the activity; or, if the victim is between the ages of 14 and 16, and the accused is less than five years older than the complainant, or is married to the complainant.

Sexual exploitation also makes it an offence for an adult to have any sexual contact with boys and girls between 16 and 18, where a relationship of trust or authority exists between the adult and the child.

The Causes of Sexual Assault

What factors predispose some men to commit sexual assault? Criminologists' responses to this question are almost as varied as the crime itself. However, most explanations can be grouped into a few consistent categories.

Evolutionary/Biological Factors

One explanation for sexual assault focuses on the evolutionary, biological aspects of the male sexual drive. This perspective suggests that sexual assault may be instinctual, developed over the ages as a means of perpetuating the species. In more primitive times, forcible sexual contact may have helped spread genes and maximize offspring. Some believe that these prehistoric drives remain: Males still have a natural sexual drive that encourages them to have intimate relations with as many women as possible.[74] The evolutionary view is that the sexual urge corresponds to the unconscious need to preserve the species by spreading one's genes as widely as possible. Men who are sexually aggressive will have a reproductive edge over their more passive peers.[75]

Male Socialization

In contrast to the evolutionary biological view, some researchers argue that sexual assault is a function of modern male socialization.[76] According to this view, from an early age, boys are taught to be aggressive, forceful, tough, and dominating, and are led to believe that women want to be dominated. This "virility mystique" dictates that males must separate their sexual feelings from needs for love, respect, and affection. Men are socialized to be the aggressors and expect to be sexually active with many women; consequently, male virginity and sexual inexperience are shameful. Conversely, sexually aggressive women frighten some men and cause them to doubt their own masculinity. Sexual insecurity may lead some men to commit sexual assault to bolster their self-image and masculine identity.

Hypermasculinity

If rape is an expression of male anger and devaluation of women and not an act motivated by sexual desire, it follows that men who hold so-called macho attitudes will be more likely to engage in sexual violence. Hypermasculine men typically have a callous sexual attitude and believe that violence is manly. They perceive danger as exciting and are overly sensitive to insult and ridicule. They are also impulsive, more apt to brag about sexual conquests, and more likely to lose control, especially when using alcohol.[77] These men are quicker to anger and more likely to be sexually aggressive. In fact, the sexually aggressive male may view almost any female as a likely victim for sexual violence.

sexual exploitation
Sexual contact, even if consensual, between a person aged 16 to 18 and someone in a position of trust or authority, such as a minister, coach, employer, or teacher.

Violent Experiences

Another view is that men learn to commit sexual assaults much as they learn any other behaviour. Groth found that 40 percent of the rapists he studied had been sexually victimized as adolescents.[78] A growing body of literature links personal sexual trauma with the desire to inflict sexual trauma on others.[79] Watching violent or pornographic films featuring women who are beaten, raped, or tortured has been linked to sexually aggressive behaviour in men.[80] A 2011 Bartol and Bartol study found that men who are highly aggressive toward women tend to drink, watch porn, and believe men should overpower women sexually.[81]

Sexual Motivation

Studies have revealed that sexual assault victims tend to be young and that rapists prefer younger, presumably more attractive victims. Data show an association between the ages of rapists and their victims, indicating that men choose sexual assault targets of approximately the same age as consensual sex partners. And, despite the fact that younger criminals are usually the most violent, older rapists tend to harm their victims more than younger rapists. This pattern suggests that older criminals may rape for motives of power and control, whereas younger offenders may be seeking sexual gratification and may therefore be less likely to harm their victims.[82]

In sum, criminologists are still at odds over the precise cause of sexual assault, but there is evidence that it is the product of a number of social, cultural, and psychological forces.[83] Although some experts view it as a normal response to an abnormal environment, others view it as the product of a disturbed mind and deviant life experiences.

Sexual Assault and the Law

Of all violent crimes, none has created such conflict in the legal system as rape. Even if women choose to report a sexual assault to police, they may be initially reluctant because of the discriminatory provisions built into many rape laws. Historically, the sexist fashion in which rape victims are treated by police, prosecutors, and court personnel, and the legal technicalities that can authorize invasion of women's privacy when a sexual assault case is tried in court, can devastate the victim.

While the prosecution of sexual assault cases has always been a problem, police and courts are now more sensitive to the plight of victims. High-profile cases, such as the Jane Doe sexual assault case in Toronto and several well-publicized coroner's inquests, have forced the justice system to take sexual assault cases more seriously.[84]

Law Reform

In 1983, the Canadian government introduced Bill C-127 containing a series of sweeping amendments to the *Criminal Code*, which completely eliminated the term *rape*, introducing instead a three-step ladder of sexual assault offences. The goal of the amendments was to eliminate long-standing misconceptions and biases in the way in which the public and even criminal justice officials themselves viewed the crime of rape; namely, as an act of forced vaginal penetration only; as an act committed only against women; and an act protected by "spousal immunity." Instead, pushed by women's rights lobby groups such as the Women's Legal Education and Action Fund, the National Action Committee on the Status of Women, the National Association of Women and the Law, along with women's shelter and rape crisis centre organizations, the 1983 amendments introduced the legal position that unwanted touching or grabbing, or the use of threats or force to get any form of sexual gratification (ranging from unwanted kissing or touching through to forced penetration) is an assault, and should be treated as such in law. A sexual assault can occur against a male as well as a female and a spousal or partner relationship does not mean that threats or force can be used to obtain sexual gratification—there is no spousal immunity from sexual assault. In addition, Bill C-127 abolished the provisions that a complaint of a sexual assault must have been recent, that there must be corroboration of the assault by a witness, and that the previous "reputation" of the victim can be taken into account as a factor in determining the "degree of guilt" of the accused.[85]

In 1992, Bill C-49 introduced additional amendments to the *Criminal Code* clarifying in law the meaning of "consent" with respect to sexual acts, eliminating the defence of "mistaken belief," placing the onus on both of the partners to ensure that consent to a sexual act is freely given; and further clarifying the legal parameters under which evidence about a victim's sexual past can be introduced as evidence in court.[86]

Still, with nearly half a million police-recorded sexual assaults against women each year (males account for about 85 000 each year), representing possibly only 10 percent of actual cases, it is clear that much more needs to be done to deal with the crime of sexual assault.[87] Critics observe that, beyond any ongoing changes in law, education in contemporary knowledge about male and female sexuality and gender roles and confronting male use of aggression in relationships will go much further in addressing the problem of sexual assault.[88]

LO4 Murder and Homicide

Murder is defined in common law as "the unlawful killing of a human being with malice aforethought."[89] It is the most serious of all common-law crimes and although the death penalty was abolished in Canada in 1976, it is still law in some American states. The last two people to be executed in Canada were Arthur Lucas and Ronald Turpin, who were hanged on 10 December 1962. Before capital punishment was abolished in Canada, 1481 people were sentenced to death, and 710 of these were executed, of whom 697 were men and 13 were women.

Murder is divided into first-degree murder and second-degree murder. First-degree murder is the killing of another person that is planned and deliberate, the killing of a law enforcement agent, or a killing that is related to committing or attempting to commit other crimes that are particularly offensive to society (e.g., hostage taking, sexual assault, hijacking an airplane, etc.). Second-degree murder is intentional homicide that does not fit under the definition of first-degree murder. Western society's abhorrence of murderers is illustrated by the fact that there is no statute of limitations in murder cases. Accused killers can be brought to justice at any time after their crimes were committed.

A homicide may be either culpable or nonculpable. Culpable homicide is where the person who caused the death is blameworthy, accountable, and

murder
Intentional killing of another person; recognized as having two classes: first- and second-degree murder.

first-degree murder
The killing of another person that is planned and deliberate, the killing of a law enforcement agent, or killing that is related to committing or attempting other crimes that are particularly offensive to society (e.g., hostage taking, sexual assault, hijacking an airplane, etc.).

second-degree murder
Intentional killing of another person that is not first-degree murder.

homicide
First-degree murder, second-degree murder, manslaughter, or infanticide. Deaths caused by criminal negligence, suicide, and accidental or justifiable homicide are not included.

responsible for the death, which includes murder, manslaughter, and infanticide. It is a wrongful act, but does not involve malice. Nonculpable homicide is not an offence because no one is held responsible. Culpable homicide that does not qualify as murder is, by definition, manslaughter. The punishment for murder is life imprisonment with no parole eligibility for periods that range from 10 to 25 years. The punishment for manslaughter ranges from a suspended sentence to life imprisonment.

One issue that has received national attention is whether a fetus can be a murder victim. In some instances, fetal harm involves a mother whose behaviour endangers an unborn child; in other cases, feticide results from the harmful action of a third party. Canada adheres to the traditional common-law rule that only persons have rights and that the fetus, whatever its stage of gestation, is not a person. According to section 223(1) of the *Criminal Code of Canada*, "A child becomes a human being within the meaning of this Act when it has completely proceeded, in a living state, from the body of its mother whether or not (a) it has breathed, (b) it has an independent circulation, or (c) the navel string is severed."

The Nature and Extent of Murder

It is possible to track murder rate trends with the aid of Uniform Crime Report (UCR) data. For example, the Canadian homicide rate decreased by 42 percent between 1975 and 1998, and since 1999 the homicide rate in Canada has hovered around 1.8 per 100 000. There were 505 homicides in Canada in 2013, 38 fewer than the previous year.[90] (See Figure 10.2.)

In 2013, homicide was a relatively rare event in Canada, representing less than 1 percent of all violent crime with 505 police reported homicides, 38 fewer than the previous year. The national homicide rate declined to 1.44 per 100 000 population in 2013, the lowest homicide rate recorded since 1966.

What else do official crime statistics tell us about murder today? Murder victims tend to be males over 18 years of age. Most victims of homicide knew their killer. In Canada in 2013, about one-third of all solved homicides were committed by a family member, one-half by an acquaintance, and the remaining 18 percent by a stranger, an increase of 17 percent over 2008 figures. Stabbings accounted for 40 percent of all homicides in 2013. There were 131 firearm-related homicides in 2013, down 41 from 2012. This resulted in the lowest rate of firearm-related homicide since comparable data became available in 1974. Despite the decline, shooting was the cause of death in about one-quarter (27 percent) of homicides. The majority (68 percent) of firearm-related homicides were committed with the use of a handgun, a trend that has held over the last 20 years.[91]

According to Statistics Canada, the country's homicide rate in 2013 fell to its lowest level since 1966 with the overall number of homicides dropping from 610 in 2009 to 505 in 2013. In 45 percent of the cases the victim knew the accused person as an acquaintance

manslaughter
Homicide, or the killing of another person, by committing an unlawful act with only a general intent (e.g., speeding and killing a pedestrian, giving a lethal punch in a sudden, provoked brawl).

infanticide
The killing of an infant shortly after birth by the mother because she is not fully recovered from the effects of giving birth (e.g., in the case of postpartum depression) and her mind is disturbed.

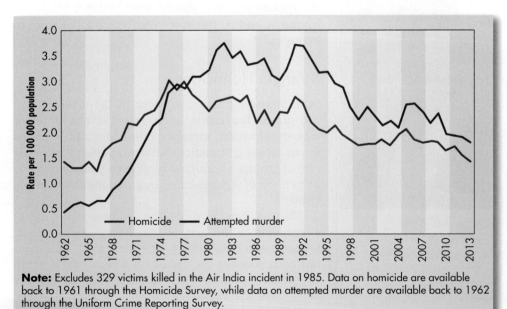

FIGURE 10.2

Homicides and Attempted Murders in Canada, 1962–2013

Source: Statistics Canada, "Canada's crime rate: Two decades of decline," The Daily, 2015. http://www.statcan.gc.ca/pub/11–630-x/11-630-x2015001-eng.htm

Note: Excludes 329 victims killed in the Air India incident in 1985. Data on homicide are available back to 1961 through the Homicide Survey, while data on attempted murder are available back to 1962 through the Uniform Crime Reporting Survey.

thrill killing
Impulsive slaying of a stranger as an act of daring or recklessness.

a family member (33 percent) or through a criminal relationship (9 percent). While the number of homicides involving strangers decreased 25 percent in 2013, those involving acquaintances or non-spousal family members were relatively stable.[92] There were 85 gang-related homicides in 2013 compared to 96 reported in the previous year and this was the lowest level since 2004.[93] Historically, homicide rates are higher in Western and Northern Canada. In 2013, Manitoba reported the highest homicide rate (3.87 per 100 000 population), followed by Saskatchewan (2.71), Alberta (2.04) and British Columbia (1.66). Nunavut (11.24) and the Northwest Territories (4.59) reported homicide rates higher than any province, while there were no homicides in Yukon for the third consecutive year.[94] Overall, the Canadian homicide rate continues to remain at a low level compared to the peak levels in the 1960s and 1970s, and is only one-third the rate found in the United States.[95]

Murderous Relations

One factor that has received a great deal of attention from criminologists is the relationship between the murderer and the victim.[96] Most criminologists agree that murders can generally be separated into those involving strangers, typically involving an indictable offence such as a robbery or a crime involving drugs, and acquaintance homicides involving disputes between family members, friends, and acquaintances.[97] The quality of relationships and interpersonal interactions, then, may influence murder.

The last two people to receive the death penalty in Canada after its abolition in 1962 were Ronald Turpin, 29, (left) and Arthur Lucas, 54, (right). Both considered small-time criminals, Turpin was a thief who shot a Toronto police officer after robbing a restaurant and Lucas had killed an FBI informant who some believed had an intellectual disability.

Acquaintance Homicide

Killing someone you know or interact with is actually the most common form of murder. Social change has influenced this phenomenon. For example, the rate of homicide among married couples has declined significantly during the past two decades, a finding that can be attributed to the shift away from marriage in modern society. There are, however, significant gender differences in spousal homicide. Women are more likely to be murdered by a legally married spouse, while men are at greater risk for homicide from a common-law partner. Females are at a much greater risk of being murdered by a former spouse or intimate partner, with 28 percent of spousal homicides of females committed by a separated or divorced ex-partner. Research indicates that females who kill their mates most often do so after suffering repeated violent attacks.[98] Perhaps the number of males killed by their partners has declined because alternatives to abusive relationships, such as women's shelters, are becoming more prevalent. Regions that provide greater social support for physically abused women and that have passed legislation to protect abuse victims also have lower rates of homicide committed by females.[99]

It is possible that men kill their spouses or partners because they fear losing control and power. Some people kill their mates because they find themselves involved in a love triangle.[100] Interestingly, women who kill out of jealousy aim their aggression at their partners; in contrast, men are more likely to kill their mates' suitors. Love triangles tend to become lethal when the offenders believe they have been lied to or betrayed. Lethal violence is more common when (1) the rival initiated the affair, (2) the killer knew the spouse was in a steady relationship outside the marriage, and (3) the killer was repeatedly lied to or betrayed.[101]

Stranger Homicides

Most stranger homicides occur in the aftermath of a common-law crime, such as break and enter or robbery. However, stranger homicides take various forms. In 2013, Statistics Canada reported the lowest rate of stranger homicide in over 40 years with only 13 percent of victims killed by someone they did not know.[102]

Thrill killing involves the deliberate slaying of a stranger as an act of daring or recklessness. Sometimes a thrill killing is performed by a stranger but such was not the case in the 2012 brutal death of Jun Lin, 33 who died at the hands of his gay lover Luka Magnotta, 32. Court-appointed psychiatrist Dr. Gilles Chamberland described Magnotta, an ex–gay porn actor, as a sexual sadist who progressed from killing kittens online to killing a human being, after which he dismembered his body and sent one of Lin's feet to the Conservative Party in May 2012.[103] Lin's torso was discovered in a suitcase in the garbage outside Magnotta's apartment building in Montreal and a week later a foot and hand were mailed to two schools in Vancouver. "If this was a strong thrill" for Mr. Magnotta, Dr. Chamberland said, "eventually ... to get the same satisfaction or power, you have to move on."[104] After eight days of deliberation, Magnotta was found guilty of first-degree murder and sentenced to life in prison with no chance of parole for 25 years.

Paul Bernardo, Russell Williams, and Robert Pickton are three of Canada's most infamous killers.

Gang-related homicides decreased across most regions in Canada in 2013, with Quebec (–8), and Ontario (–7) leading the way. British Columbia (+7) and Manitoba (+3) reported the highest rates of gang-related homicide.[105] Most gang-related homicides involved young adults. The average age of those accused of committing a gang-related homicide was 23 years; the age of victims was 28 years.[106]

Serial Murder

In 2014, the RCMP released a report on murdered and missing Aboriginal women. It covered the period between 1980 and 2012.[107] According to the report there were

- 1181 investigations of Aboriginal females murdered or missing during the period, including 1017 homicide victims and 164 missing

- 225 unsolved cases of either missing or murdered Aboriginal females: 105 missing for more than 30 days as of 4 November 2013, whose cause of disappearance was "unknown" or "foul play suspected" and 120 unsolved homicides

- 20 313 homicides across Canada. Of these, 6551, or 32 percent, were women

- 1017 Aboriginal female homicide victims in the period, representing 16 percent of all female victims, even though they make up only about 4.3 percent of the total female population.[108]

The 164 Aboriginal females who were missing as of 4 November 2013 made up 11.3 percent of the 1,455 females listed as missing.[109]

Almost half of the murders of Aboriginal women remain unsolved, compared to an 84 percent clearance rate for murders of non-Aboriginal women. Most of the Aboriginal women who go missing or are murdered are under the age of 31, and more than two-thirds were living in cities; Aboriginal women were more likely than non-Aboriginal women to be murdered by a stranger.[110] Most **serial killers** operate over an extended period of months and even years, and can be distinguished from **mass murderers**, who kill many victims in a single, violent outburst. While most serial killers are males, an estimated 10 to 15 percent of serial killers are women. (See Table 10.2.)

Paul Bernardo remains one of Canada's most famous serial killers. He was charged and convicted for three murders that occurred between December 1990 and April 1992.

In contrast, Mattew de Grood of Calgary may become one of Canada's most famous mass murderers. De Grood, 23, son of a Calgary police inspector, had recently graduated from the University of Calgary and was ready to begin studying to become a lawyer when something went terribly wrong. After being invited to an end-of-term house party, without warning de Grood commenced stabbing other guests. Five people were stabbed to death in what Calgary police chief called the worst mass murder in Calgary's history. The motivation for the attacks remains unclear. No one had any previous contact with police, from all accounts the party was not out of control, and de Grood was not under the influence of alcohol or drugs. De Grood has since been charged with murder and, according to his lawyer, a not criminally responsible defence has not been ruled out.[111]

Criminologists Belea Keeney and Kathleen Heide, who investigated the characteristics of a sample of 14 female serial killers, found some striking differences between the way male and female killers carried out their crimes.[112] Males were much more likely than

serial killer
One who kills a series of victims, usually over an extended period of time.

mass murderer
One who kills many victims in a single, violent outburst.

TABLE 10.2

Explanation for Multiple Murder

Motivation for Multiple Murder	Type of Multiple Murder	
	Serial Murder	**Mass Murder**
Power	Inspired by sadistic fantasies, a man tortures and kills a series of strangers to satisfy his need for control and dominance.	A pseudo-commando, dressed in battle fatigues and armed with a semiautomatic, turns a shopping mall into a "war zone."
Revenge	Grossly mistreated as a child, a man avenges his past by slaying women who remind him of his mother.	After being fired from his job, a gunman returns to the worksite and opens fire on his former boss and co-workers.
Loyalty	A team of killers turn murder into a ritual for proving their dedication and commitment to one another.	A depressed husband/father kills his entire family and himself to remove them from their miserable existence to a better life in the hereafter.
Profit	A woman poisons to death a series of husbands in order to collect on their life insurance.	A band of armed robbers executes the employees of a store to eliminate all witnesses to their crime.
Terror	A profoundly paranoid man commits a series of bombings to warn the world of impending doom.	A group of antigovernment extremists blows up a train to send a political message.

Sources: James Alan Fox and Jack Levin, "Multiple Homicide: Patterns of Serial and Mass Murder," *Crime and Justice: An Annual Edition*, vol. 23, ed. Michael Tonry (Chicago: University of Chicago Press,1998): 407–455, Table A, p. 444; James Alan Fox and Jack Levin, *Overkill: Mass Murder and Serial Killing Exposed* (New York: Plenum,1994); James Alan Fox and Jack Levin, "A Psycho-Social Analysis of Mass Murder," in *Serial and Mass Murder: Theory, Policy, and Research*, ed. Thomas O'Reilly-Fleming and Steven Egger (Toronto: University of Toronto Press,1993); James Alan Fox and Jack Levin, "Serial Murder: A Survey," in *Serial and Mass Murder: Theory, Policy and Research*, ed. Thomas O'Reilly-Fleming and Steven Egger (Toronto: University of Toronto Press,1993); Jack Levin and James Alan Fox, *Mass Murder* (New York: Plenum, 1985).

assault level 1
Applying, attempting to apply, or threatening to apply force, with intent and without consent, against another person, or openly wearing a weapon (or an imitation) and accosting or impeding another person.

females to use extreme violence and torture including beating, bludgeoning, and strangling their victims, while females were more likely to poison or smother their victims. Also, men were more likely to track or stalk their victims, but women tended to lure victims to their death.

To date, law enforcement officials have been at a loss to control random killers who leave few clues, constantly move, and have little connection to their victims. Serial killers come from diverse backgrounds, and catching them is often a matter of luck. In Canada, the RCMP coordinates the Violent Crime Linkage Analysis System (ViCLAS) for all police agencies across the country. It links crimes to determine if they appear to be the work of a single culprit. In addition, the RCMP makes available the services of trained criminal profilers to all police agencies. Other large police services, such as the Ontario Provincial Police, have now added trained criminal profilers to their agencies.

LO5 Assault

The word *assault* is used to describe different kinds of incidents with different levels of seriousness. Contrary to popular belief, assault does not necessarily have to involve a physical act; however, it must involve more than words alone. That is, there must be a gesture or some other act that leads to harm or the threat of harm. According to the *Criminal Code* of Canada, an assault is the intentional application of force, directly or indirectly, to another person without that person's consent. There are three levels of assault. Assault level 1, or common assault, can include situations when there is intentional application of force without consent, when there is an attempt or threatening to apply force to another person, or openly wearing a weapon (or an imitation) and accosting or

Matthew de Grood, 23, is charged with the stabbing deaths of five young persons who attended an end-of-term house party in what has been described as one of Calgary's worst mass murders.

impeding another person. Assault with a weapon or causing bodily harm is known as assault level 2. It comprises assault with a weapon, threats to use a weapon (or an imitation), or assault causing bodily harm. Aggravated assault level 3 involves wounding, maiming, disfiguring, or endangering the life of another person.[113]

In addition, each of the Level 1, 2, 3 categories of assault committed against a peace officer (including police officers, correctional officers, and others as defined in the *Criminal Code*), along with "disarming a peace officer," are outlined as distinct categories of crime in the *Criminal Code*.

The Nature and Patterns of Assault

The pattern of criminal assault is quite similar to that of homicide; one could say that the only difference between the two is that the victim survives.[114]

In 2013, Statistics Canada reported that the traditional crime rate had declined from that of 2012, falling 8 percent and reaching its lowest level since 1969. In the same year, Canadian police services reported just over 1.8 million *Criminal Code* of Canada offences, down approximately 132 000 from the previous year.[115] Physical assaults (i.e. all levels of assault) continued to be the most frequent type of police-reported violent crime in Canada accounting for 6 in 10 (57 percent) violent offences reported by police. The majority of the 219 400 police-reported assaults (72 percent) were classified as common assaults (level 1), which have been declining over the previous 10 years. All other forms of assault have also been on the decline to the lowest major assault rate recorded since 1999.[116]

Assault in the Home

Among the most frightening types of assault are violent attacks within the home. Criminologists recognize that intrafamily violence is an enduring social problem in our society.

Child Abuse

One area of intrafamily violence that has received a great deal of media attention is child abuse. This term describes any physical, sexual, or emotional trauma or neglect to a child for which no reasonable explanation, such as an accident or ordinary parental or disciplinary practices, can be found.[117] Abuse may take place anywhere and may occur, for example, within the child's home or that of someone known to the child.

Child abuse can result from physical beatings administered to a child by hands, feet, weapons, belts, sticks, burning, and so on. Another form of abuse results from child neglect—not providing a child with the care and shelter to which he or she is entitled. For example, neglect includes failing to provide a child with food, clothing, shelter, cleanliness, medical care, or protection from harm. Emotional neglect includes failing to provide a child with love, safety, and a sense of worth.

A third form is sexual abuse—the exploitation of a child through rape, incest, or molestation by a parent or other adult. Examples of child sexual abuse include fondling, inviting a child to touch or be touched sexually, intercourse, sodomy, exhibitionism, or involving a child in prostitution or pornography.

In a recent study from the University of Manitoba, investigators reported that a third of Canadians (32 percent) have experienced some form of child abuse (physical abuse, sexual abuse, and exposure to intimate partner violence) with the highest rates in Western provinces. (See Figure 10.3.) Further, all types of child abuse were associated with mental conditions, including suicidal ideation and suicide attempts. Finding a robust association between child abuse and mental conditions suggests that preventing child abuse could lead to reductions in the prevalence of mental disorders, suicidal ideation, and suicide attempts.[118]

There were over 58 000 police-reported incidents of child and youth victims of violence in 2013. This was slightly lower than those of the adult population except for sexual offences, which were more likely to occur among children and youth than among those 18 years of age and over. There were 16 700 child and youth victims of family-related violence in 2013 and, similar to police-reported violent crime in general, the majority of violence against children and youth was committed by someone known to the victim (81 percent).[119]

assault level 2
Assault with a weapon, threatening to use a weapon (or an imitation), or assault causing bodily harm.

assault level 3
Aggravated assault involving wounding, maiming, disfiguring, or endangering the life of another person.

disarming a peace officer
Taking or attempting to take a weapon without consent from a peace officer engaged in the execution of his or her duties.

child abuse
Physical, sexual, or emotional maltreatment or neglect that a child or adolescent may experience while in the care of someone he or she either trusts or depends on, such as a parent, sibling, other relative, caregiver, or guardian.

child neglect
Failing to provide what a child needs for his or her physical, psychological, or emotional development and well-being.

sexual abuse
The exploitation of a child through rape, incest, or molestation by a parent or other adult.

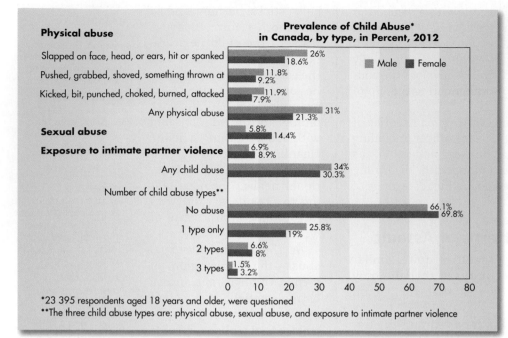

FIGURE 10.3

Prevalence of Child Abuse in Canada, 2012

Source: Sarah Boesveld, "One-third of Canadians have suffered child abuse, highest rates in the western provinces, study says." *National Post*, April 22, 2014. Material reprinted with the express permission of: National Post, a division of Postmedia Network Inc.

Prevalence of Child Abuse* in Canada, by type, in Percent, 2012

■ Male ■ Female

Physical abuse

Slapped on face, head, or ears, hit or spanked — 26% / 18.6%
Pushed, grabbed, shoved, something thrown at — 11.8% / 9.2%
Kicked, bit, punched, choked, burned, attacked — 11.9% / 7.9%
Any physical abuse — 31% / 21.3%

Sexual abuse — 5.8% / 14.4%

Exposure to intimate partner violence — 6.9% / 8.9%

Any child abuse — 34% / 30.3%

Number of child abuse types**

No abuse — 66.1% / 69.8%
1 type only — 25.8% / 19%
2 types — 6.6% / 8%
3 types — 1.5% / 3.2%

*23 395 respondents aged 18 years and older, were questioned
**The three child abuse types are: physical abuse, sexual abuse, and exposure to intimate partner violence

Why do parents physically assault their children? Such maltreatment is a highly complex problem with neither a single cause nor a readily available solution. It cuts across ethnic, religious, and socioeconomic lines. Abusive parents cannot be categorized by sex, age, or educational level; they come from all walks of life.[120]

Three factors have been linked to abuse and neglect. First, a pattern of family violence seems to be perpetuated from one generation to the next within families. Evidence indicates that many abused and neglected children grow into adolescence and adulthood with a tendency to engage in violent behaviour. The behaviour of abusive parents can often be traced to negative experiences in their own childhood—physical abuse, lack of love, emotional neglect, incest, and so on. These parents become unable to separate their own childhood traumas from their relationships with their children; they also often have unrealistic perceptions of the appropriate stages of childhood development.[121]

Second, blended families, in which children live with an unrelated adult such as a stepparent or another unrelated co-resident, have also been linked to abuse. For example, children who live with a mother's boyfriend are at much greater risk for abuse than children living with two genetic parents. According to sociologists Martin Daly and Margo Wilson, some stepparents do not have strong emotional ties to their nongenetic children, nor do they reap emotional benefits from the parent–child relationship.[122]

Third, parents may become abusive if they are isolated from friends, neighbours, or relatives who can help in times of crisis.[123] Many abusive and neglectful parents describe themselves as highly alienated from their families and lacking close relationships with people who could provide support in stressful situations. These people are unable to cope effectively with life crises such as divorce, financial problems, alcohol and drug abuse, or poor housing conditions, and excessive stress leads them to maltreat their children.[124]

Spouse Abuse

Spouse abuse has occurred throughout recorded history. Roman men had the legal right to beat their wives for attending public games without permission, drinking wine, or walking outdoors with their faces uncovered.[125] More serious transgressions, such as adultery, were punishable by death.[126] During the early Middle Ages, a husband was expected to beat his wife for "misbehaviours" and might himself be punished by neighbours if he failed to do so.[127] Between 1400 and 1900, there was little community objection to a man's using force against his wife as long as the assaults did not exceed certain limits, usually construed as death or disfigurement. By the mid-19th century, severe wife beating fell into disfavour, and accused wife beaters were subject to public ridicule. Yet the long history of husbands' domination of their wives has made physical coercion hard to control.

There is still some debate over the cause of spouse abuse. One view is that people who physically abuse their spouses are damaged individuals who suffer a variety of neuropsychological disorders and cognitive deficits; many suffered brain injuries in youth.[128] Psychologists Neil Jacobson and John Mordechai Gottman studied 200 couples and found that batterers tend to fall into one of two categories, which they call "Pit Bulls" and "Cobras."[129] Pit Bulls, whose emotions are quick to erupt, are driven by deep insecurity and a dependence on the wives and partners they abuse. They tend to become stalkers, unable to let go of relationships once they have ended. In contrast, Cobras coolly and methodically inflict pain and humiliation on their spouses. Many Cobras were physically or sexually abused in childhood and, as a consequence, see violence as an unavoidable part of life.

Some experts view spousal abuse from an evolutionary standpoint: Males are aggressive toward their mates because they have evolved with a high degree of sexual proprietariness. Men fear both losing a valued reproductive resource to a rival and making a paternal investment in a child that is not their own. Violence serves as a coercive social tool to dissuade interest in other males and to lash out in jealousy if threats are not taken seriously (i.e., if the woman leaves). This explains why men often kill or injure their ex-wives; threats lose their effectiveness if they are merely a bluff.[130]

Both women and men experience spousal abuse. According to GSS data from 2013, 6 percent of Canadian women experienced spousal violence in the previous five years, which is similar to the rate for men; however, women experienced more severe forms of spousal violence. In 2009, over half of female victims reported multiple victimizations, compared to just over a third of male victims. Police-reported data reveal that 73 percent of women were physically assaulted by their intimate partners and 11 percent experienced aggravated assault or assault with a weapon. The rates were higher for dating partners. In 2011,

the violence rate of unmarried females was 60 percent higher than the spousal violence rate.[131]

Women in common-law relationships seem to be at much greater risk of domestic violence than legally married or single women. A possible cause may be that domestic relationships among unmarried people tend to be less stable and more short lived.[132] Nonetheless, the rate of domestic violence appears to be declining among both married couples and single cohabitants. One reason is that females now find it easier to get high-paying jobs, to obtain legal divorces, and to receive domestic violence counselling. Financial independence and emotional support allow women to leave a bad relationship before interspousal conflict leads to violence and death. And even if partners stay together in troubled relationships, newly emerging social interventions empower women to end male partner violence.[133]

8 out of 10 adult victims of intimate partner violence were female	9 out of 10 adult victims of sexual violence were female	7 out of 10 adult victims of criminal harassment were female

A 2014 RCMP report estimated that a total of 1017 Aboriginal women and girls were murdered between 1980 and 2012 in Canada. There were 164 Aboriginal women and girls missing in Canada on November 4, 2013 for a period exceeding 30 days[1]. There have been repeated calls for a national public inquiry into this devastating Canadian crisis.

[1]Royal Canadian Mounted Police, "Missing and Murdered Aboriginal Women: A National Operational Overview" (2014), pp. 19 & 20 at http://www.rcmp-grc.gc.ca/pubs/mmaw-faapd-eng.pdf (accessed 5 November 2015).

Source: Statistics Canada, 2013, Juristat Article (ISSN 1209-6393), Measuring Violence Against Women: Statistical Trends, pp. 20, 29, 32: http://www.statcan.gc.ca/pub/85-002-x/2013001/article/11766-eng, Infographic reproduced by permission of VAW Learning Network.

LO6 Robbery

The common-law definition of robbery is "taking or attempting to take anything of value from the care, custody or control of a person or persons by force or threat of force or violence and/or by putting the victim in fear."[134] A robbery is considered a violent crime because it involves the use of force to obtain money or goods. Robbery is punished severely because the victim's life is put in jeopardy. In fact, the severity of punishment is based on the amount of force used during the crime, not the value of the items taken.

A large decrease in robbery was the main reason for the overall decline in the violent Crime Severity Index (CSI) between 2012 and 2013, which represents one of the largest decreases in robbery rates ever recorded. In 2013, the robbery rate fell 17 percent to 66 robberies per 100 000 population and, according to police data, there were over 23 200 robberies in 2013, approximately 4500 fewer than the year before.[135]

Robberies are much more likely than all other violent crimes to involve youths aged 12 to 17. By 2013, the severity of police-reported crime involving youth accused, as measured by the youth CSI, was down 16 percent from the previous year and was primarily due to considerable declines in the number of youth accused of robbery, breaking and entering, and theft of $5000 or under.[136]

Robbery rates are almost three times higher in the United States than in Canada. Further, a larger proportion of robberies in the United States involve firearms. Firearm robbery rates in the United States are four times higher than in Canada. In the United States the average firearm robbery rate is 60 per 100 000 population, compared to 14 per 100 000 population in Canada. Both the American and Canadian robbery rates have declined in recent years.[137]

Robbery is most often a street crime; that is, fewer robberies occur in the home than in public places, such as parks, streets, and alleys. The U.S. Bureau of Justice Statistics analyzed more than 14 million robbery victimizations to provide a more complete picture of the nature and extent of robbery. It found that about two-thirds of victims had property stolen, one-third were injured in the crime, and one-quarter suffered both personal injury and property loss.[138]

While most robberies involve strangers, about one-third involve acquaintances. Richard Felson and his associates found that when robbers target someone they know, they choose victims who are least likely to call police. Targets may be people with whom the robber has a pre-existing grievance, so that the robbery is a form of "payback." Robbers may also have "inside information" that the victims are carrying valuables, making them a hard target to resist.[139]

Attempts have been made to classify and explain the nature and dynamics of robbery. One approach is to characterize robberies (see Table 10.3); another is to characterize types of robbers based on their specialties.

As these typologies indicate, the typical armed robber is unlikely to be a professional who carefully studies targets while planning a crime. Convenience stores, gas stations, and people walking along the street are much more likely robbery targets than banks or other highly secure environments. Robbers seem to be diverted by modest defensive measures, such as having more than one clerk in a store or locating stores in strip malls; they are more likely to try an isolated store.[140]

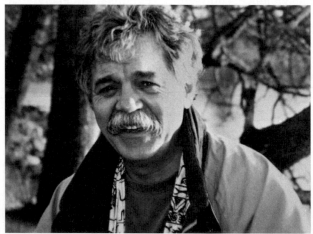

Stephen Reid was one member of the infamous "Stopwatch Gang." Known as the gentleman bandits, they stole an estimated $15 million from banks across North America. They never fired a shot during a holdup and no bank employees or customers were ever harmed. Mitchell died while still in custody while Reid became a best-selling author while behind bars. In 2013, he was awarded the 2013 City of Victoria Butler Book Prize for his collection of essays, *A Crowbar in the Buddhist Garden: Writing from Prison*.

TABLE 10.3

Types of Robberies

Robbery of persons who, as part of their employment, are in charge of money or goods	This category includes robberies in jewellery stores, banks, offices, and other places in which money changes hands.
Robbery in an open area	These robberies include street muggings, purse snatchings, and other attacks. Street robberies are the most common type, especially in urban areas, where this type of robbery constitutes about 60 percent of reported totals. Street robbery is most closely associated with mugging or yoking, which refers to grabbing victims from behind and threatening them with a weapon. Street muggers often target unsavory characters such as drug dealers or pimps who carry large amounts of cash, because these victims would find it awkward to report the crime to the police. Most robbers commit their robberies within a short distance of their homes.
Commercial robbery	This type of robbery occurs in businesses ranging from banks to liquor stores. Banks are among the most difficult targets to rob, usually because they have more personnel and a higher level of security.
Robbery on private premises	In Canada, there were 865 residential robberies recorded, a rate of 5 per 100 000 population.
Robbery after a short, preliminary association	This type of robbery comes after a chance meeting—in a bar, at a party, or after a sexual encounter.
Robbery after a longer association between the victim and offender	An example of this type of robbery would be an intimate acquaintance robbing his paramour and then fleeing the jurisdiction.
Carjacking	Carjacking is a completed or attempted theft of a motor vehicle by force or threat of force. Carjacking is a relatively rare event in Canada; however, in the United States there are on average about 49 000 completed or attempted carjackings each year.

Sources: Patsy Klaus, National Crime Victimization Survey, Carjacking, 1993–2002, U.S. Department of Justice, Bureau of Justice Statistics, July 2004; Peter J. van Koppen and Robert Jansen, "The Road to the Robbery: Travel Patterns in Commercial Robberies," *British Journal of Criminology* 38 (1998): 230–247; F H. McClintock and Evelyn Gibson, *Robbery in London* (London: Macmillan, 1961), p. 15; Orest Fedorowycz, *Breaking and Entering in Canada—2002*, Canadian Centre for Justice Statistics, Statistics Canada, Cat. 85-002-XPE, vol. 24, no. 5; Marnie Wallace, *Motor Vehicle Theft in Canada—2007*, Statistics Canada, Canadian Centre for Justice Statistics, 85-002-X, *Juristat*, December 2008; Jillian Boyce, Adam Cotter and Samuel Perreault, Police-reported crime statistics in Canada, 2013, Statistics Canada, *Juristat*, 85-002-x, 2014.

While most robbers may be opportunistic rather than professional, the patterns of robbery suggest that it is not merely a random act committed by an alcoholic or drug abuser. Though most crime rates are higher in the summer, robberies seem to peak during the winter months. One reason may be that the cold weather allows for greater disguise. Another is that robbers may be attracted to the large amounts of cash people and merchants carry during the holiday shopping season.[141] Robbers may also be more active during the winter because the days are shorter, affording them greater concealment in the dark.

LO7 Contemporary Forms of Interpersonal Violent Crime

Assault, sexual assault, robbery, and murder are traditional forms of interpersonal violence. As more data become available, criminologists have recognized relatively new subcategories within these crime types, such as serial murder and date rape. Additional categories of interpersonal violence are now receiving attention in criminological literature; the following sections describe some of these newer forms of violent crime.

Stalking

In 2012, one of the most bizarre cases of celebrity stalking came to light. Dana Martin, who was serving a sentence for the rape and murder of a 15-year-old girl, hired two hit-men to strangle Canadian pop star Justin Bieber and then to cut off his testicles. Martin described how he was obsessed with thoughts of having sex with the singer. However, the plot was foiled when the two would-be assassins took a wrong turn and ended up in Canada. When stopped by police, they readily admitted to their nefarious plans.[142]

Convicted killer Dana Martin (left) was obsessed with Canadian pop star Justin Bieber (right).

Stalking is defined in the *Criminal Code* under a general heading of "Criminal Harassment," which prohibits the following conduct:

(a) repeatedly following from place to place the other person or anyone known to them;

(b) repeatedly communicating with, either directly or indirectly, the other person or anyone known to them;

(c) besetting or watching the dwelling-house, or place where the other person, or anyone known to them, resides, works, carries on business or happens to be; or

(d) engaging in threatening conduct directed at the other person or any member of their family.[143]

Prior to 1993, stalking was not against the law in Canada. The *Criminal Code* was amended to include section 264, which deals with criminal harassment. In it are sections prohibiting trespassing on another's property at night, uttering threats, indecent or harassing phone calls, intimidation, and mischief to another person's property. It is possible to get a restraining order or a peace bond against a person to prevent contact.

A key requirement of Section 264 of the *Criminal Code* is that the "following" or "communicating" be "repeated," which means that it must happen more than once for it to be criminal harassment. However, if the behaviour is severe enough and is threatening, one incident may be sufficient to get a conviction. Some facts about stalking include the following:

- In 2013 there were 21 555 police-reported criminal harassment (stalking) incidents in Canada, representing about 5 percent of all violent crimes.[144] Nearly 70 percent of stalking incidents occur at the victim's home.[145]

- Seventy-six percent of the stalking victims in Canada were women. One-half of the female victims were criminally harassed (stalked) by a current or former intimate partner.[146]

- Eighty-six percent of persons accused of stalking in these cases were male.[147]

- Male victims of stalking are more likely (37 percent) to be criminally harassed by a casual acquaintance.[148]

In a 2015 report casts doubt on whether the *Criminal Code* definition of criminal harassment adequately protects women victims in Canada. Professor Isabel Grant from the University of British Columbia compared case law in Canada to other jurisdictions. She found that Canadian courts overly focus attention on the victim's response to harassment, which she believes creates the same disincentives for women to report incidents to police that have traditionally existed for sexual assault.[149] Under the current law, the onus is on the victim to communicate to the accused that she is feeling harassed. "They are put in a "Catch-22" situation—she has to speak to him because he has to know he is harassing her, but if she does speak to him, courts may be less likely to believe that she was really afraid of him." Also, the current law emphasizes that a woman must be afraid for her safety and ignores other ways that criminal harassment negatively impacts on a victim's life such as undue stress, increased risk of becoming depressed, and elevated risk of self-harm. Grant suggests that Canadian lawmakers look to England where they have enacted a new law that defines criminal harassment in terms of whether it has a significant impact on the daily life of the complainant such as moving, changing routes to and from work, installing home security systems, and indicators of mental health concerns.[150]

stalking
An offence of criminal harassment, which is behaviour that causes another person to fear for his or her safety or for another person's safety: for example, repeatedly following a person, repeatedly communicating with a person, or watching a person's workplace or home.

Home Invasions

Although home invasions are not a major source of crime in Canada, when they do occur they are horrifying to victims. The term *home invasion* is used to describe a robbery or break and enter of a private residence where someone uses force to enter another's home, and uses or threatens to use violence against the occupants. In 2002 the *Criminal Code* was amended (through Bill C-15A) to make home invasion an aggravating circumstance that a judge must take into consideration at the time of sentencing. The amendment makes it clear that home invasion is viewed as a serious crime that should be met with significant penalties. Under Part IX, "Offences Against Rights of Property—Breaking and Entering," it states:

Aggravating circumstance—home invasion
348.1. If a person is convicted of an offence under any of subsection 279(2) or sections 343, 346 and 348 in relation to a dwelling-house, the court imposing the sentence on the person shall consider as an aggravating circumstance the fact that the dwelling-house was occupied at the time of the commission of the offence and that the person, in committing the offence,

(a) knew that or was reckless as to whether the dwelling-house was occupied; and

(b) used violence or threats of violence to a person or property.[151]

According to Statistics Canada, home invasion can be defined in two ways: a narrow definition that would include all robberies occurring in a residential dwelling, and a broader definition that would include robberies occurring in a residential dwelling as well as break and enters with an associated violent offence. Using the first definition, the rate of police-reported home invasions rose by 38 percent between 1999 and 2005 and has remained stable through to 2008 when approximately 2700 such incidents came to the attention of police.[152] Other examples of incidents that could be considered as "home invasions" include:

- A homeowner returns home unexpectedly while a break and enter is in progress and there is a confrontation.

- A person breaks into a home believing that no one is home and someone is, or believing that the occupants are all asleep and they wake up, and there is a confrontation.

- Someone forcibly enters the home of a person known to him or her to "settle a score."[153]

- Since 1998, the rate of "home invasions" of this sort has increased by 24 percent, to a total of 865 in Canada in 2002, or 5 per 100 000 population.[154]

Studies have shown that older adults (65 years and older) tend to be at greater risk for home invasion than for other types of robbery. In 2008, 6 percent of victims involved in a home invasion were 65 years or older, compared to 3 percent who were robbed on the street or other outdoor public location. About 2 percent of victims of total violent crime in 2008 were 65 years or older. Information on robberies that have been solved by police shows that home invasions tend to involve strangers less often than those that occur in commercial locations or on the street.[155]

Three general categories of home invasions have been identified: residential robberies, those committed by criminals against other criminals, and those targeting the elderly. Home invasions account for a very small proportion of robberies, but they have prompted public concern and fear because of the unique predatory nature of these crimes and the often-devastating psychological effect that they have on their victims.[156]

Hate Crimes

A hate crime is a violent act directed toward a particular person or group because of a discernible colour, race, religion, or ethnic origin. References to "hate" can be found in sections 318 and 319 of the *Criminal Code* of Canada. Section 318 describes the criminal act of "advocating genocide" by supporting or arguing for the killing of members of an "identifiable group"— persons distinguished by their colour, race, religion, or ethnic origin. The intention or motivation would be the destruction of members of the targeted group. Any person who promotes genocide is guilty of an indictable offence, and liable to imprisonment for a term not exceeding five years. To obtain a conviction, there must be factual proof that it occurred, but also that it was a deliberate act with intent and motivation. Amendments to the *Criminal Code*, made under the *Anti-Terrorism Act* in December 2001, identify offences in relation to Internet hate crimes.

Section 319(1) refers to the crime of "publicly inciting hatred," which involves four elements:

- Communicating (by telephone, broadcasting, or other audible or visible means) statements (spoken, written, or recorded) or gestures, and signs or other visible representations

- Doing so in a public place (one to which the public has access by right or invitation)

- Inciting hatred against an identifiable group

- Doing so in such a way that there will likely be a breach of the peace

All the above elements must be proven for a court to find an accused guilty of either an indictable offence, for which the punishment is imprisonment for a term not exceeding two years; or an offence punishable on summary conviction. Section 320 permits the seizure and forfeiture of physical hate propaganda material kept on any premises for distribution or sale. Section 320.1 was added under the *Anti-Terrorism Bill* in 2001; it allows hate propaganda to be deleted from computer systems and websites.

If hate, bias, or prejudice was involved while committing other offences such as assault, damage to property, threatening, or harassment, the courts may view them as aggravating circumstances, which could result in a more severe punishment.

The Roots of Hate

Why do people commit hate crimes? Research by sociologist Jack McDevitt shows that hate crimes are generally spontaneous incidents motivated by the victims' walking, driving, shopping, or socializing in an area in which their attackers believe they "do not belong."[157] Other factors that motivate bias attacks include a victim's moving into an ethnically distinct neighbourhood or dating a member of a different race or ethnic group. Although hate crimes are

> **hate crime**
> A violent act directed toward a particular person or group because of a discernible colour, race, religion, or ethnic origin.

often unplanned, McDevitt finds that most of these crimes are serious incidents that involve assaults and robberies.[158] In their book *Hate Crimes*, McDevitt and Jack Levin note that hate crimes are typically one of three types that reflect different motives:

1. *Thrill-seeking hate crimes*. In the same way some kids like to get together to shoot hoops, hate-mongers join forces to have fun by assaulting minorities or destroying property. Inflicting pain on others gives them a sadistic thrill.

2. *Reactive hate crimes*. Perpetrators of these crimes rationalize their behaviour as a defensive stand taken against outsiders who they believe are threatening their community or way of life. A gang of teens who attacks a new family in the neighbourhood because they are the "wrong" race is committing a reactive hate crime.

3. *Mission hate crimes*. Some disturbed individuals see it as their duty to rid the world of evil. Those on a "mission"—skinheads, the Ku Klux Klan (KKK), white supremacist groups—may seek to eliminate people who threaten their religious beliefs because they are members of a different faith or threaten "racial purity" because they are of a different race.[159]

Extent of Hate Crime

In 2012, there were 1414 criminal incidents motivated by hate in Canada representing 4.1 incidents per 100 000 population. Just over 50 percent (704) of all hate crimes were motivated by hatred toward a race or ethnicity, 30 percent (419) were motivated by hatred toward a particular religion, 13 percent (185) were motivated by sexual orientation, and the remaining 6 percent (106) were motivated by language, mental or physical disability, sex, age or some other characteristic (incidents) such as occupation or political beliefs (see Figure 10.4). The highest incidents of hate crimes in Canada occurred in Hamilton, Thunder Bay, and Peterborough, Ontario.[160]

Compared to the previous four years leading up to 2012:

- The overall level of hate crimes remained stable (about 1400 per year).
- Mischief continues to be the most common hate crime.
- Race and ethnicity continue to account for around 50 percent.
- Black victims consistently account for about 40 percent.
- Jewish victims range from 53 to 71 percent.
- Muslim victims range between 9 and 15 percent.
- Those accused of hate crimes are overwhelmingly young.[161]

Workplace Violence

On 6 April 1999, a former employee of OC Transpo in Ottawa stunned the country when he went on a shooting rampage that left four employees dead, before turning the gun on himself. The subsequent coroner's inquest identified the killer as being a victim of workplace harassment. Among the inquest recommendations was that the definition of workplace violence include both physical and psychological violence such as bullying, mobbing, teasing, ridicule, or any other act or words that could psychologically hurt or isolate a person in the workplace.[162] Another significant inquest came about after the 2005 workplace murder of nurse Lori Dupont by her ex-boyfriend Dr. Marc Daniel. Dupont was stabbed to death with a scalpel by Daniel, who then took his own life. Both worked at the Hôtel-Dieu Grace Hospital in Windsor, Ontario. The coroner's inquest recommendations included a call for amendments to Ontario's health and safety legislation (OHS) to protect workers from workplace violence.[163]

Workplace violence continues to be in the news today because of such high-profile cases. According to Statistics Canada there are over 365 000 violent incidents of workplace violence per year in Canadian.[164] The majority of such incidents are committed by someone known to the victim, and both men and women are equally likely to report being victimized. People who work in the healthcare or social services employment sectors are at highest risk, with

FIGURE 10.4

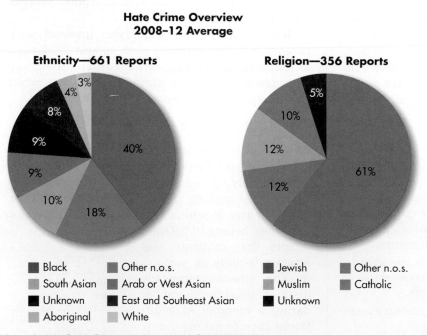

Hate Crime Overview
2008–12 Average

Ethnicity—661 Reports

40%, 18%, 10%, 9%, 9%, 8%, 4%, 3%

Religion—356 Reports

61%, 12%, 12%, 10%, 5%

Legend (Ethnicity):
- Black
- South Asian
- Unknown
- Aboriginal
- Other n.o.s.
- Arab or West Asian
- East and Southeast Asian
- White

Legend (Religion):
- Jewish
- Muslim
- Unknown
- Other n.o.s.
- Catholic

Source: Statistics Canada, Police-reported hate crimes in Canada (2008–12)

33 percent of workplace violence taking place there. Fourteen percent of workplace violence incidents took place in the hotel and food services sector, and 11 percent in educational services. Most incidents took place inside a building such as a store, office, hospital, or school, and in two-thirds of cases the perpetrator was known to the victim.[165]

Most workplace violent incidents are physical assaults (71 percent), followed by sexual assault (24 percent). Alcohol or drugs were believed to be involved in almost half of the incidents (46 percent), and males were identified as the perpetrator in more than 90 percent of the incidents. Who engages in workplace violence? The typical offender is a middle-aged white male who faces termination in a worsening economy. The fear of economic ruin is especially strong in many traditional workplaces, where long-term employees fear job loss because of automation and reorganization. Repeated incidents have generated the term *going postal* as a synonym for a violent workplace incident. The U.S. Postal Service, stung by this bad publicity, was forced to issue a statement claiming that there is far less on-the-job homicide in the postal service than at other workplaces, and that the term *going postal* is unjustified and unfair.[166]

A number of factors precipitate workplace violence. One may simply be the conflict caused by economic restructuring. As corporations cut their staffs due to recent trends such as office automation and company buyouts, long-term employees who had never thought of themselves losing a job are suddenly unemployed. There is often a correlation between sudden, unexpected layoffs and violent reactions.[167] Another trigger may be leadership styles. Some companies have authoritarian management styles that demand performance, above all else, from employees. Unsympathetic, unsupportive managers may help trigger workplace violence.

Not all workplace violence is triggered by management-induced injustice. In some incidents, co-workers have been killed because they refused romantic relationships with the assailants or reported them for sexual harassment. Others have been killed because they got a job the assailant coveted. Irate clients and customers have also killed because of poor service or perceived slights. For example, in one Los Angeles incident, a former patient shot and critically wounded three doctors because his demands for painkillers had gone unheeded.[168]

There is a variety of responses to workplace provocations. Some people take out their anger and aggression by attacking their supervisors in an effort to punish the company that dismissed them; this is a form of murder by proxy.[169] Disgruntled employees may also attack family members or friends, misdirecting the rage and frustration caused by their work situation. Others are content with sabotaging company equipment; computer data banks are particularly vulnerable to tampering. The aggrieved party may do nothing to rectify the situation; this inaction is referred to as sufferance. Over time, the unresolved conflict may be compounded by other events that cause an eventual eruption.

A number of efforts have been made to control workplace violence. One approach is to use third parties to mediate disputes before they escalate into violence. Another idea involves a human resources approach, with aggressive job retraining and extended medical coverage after layoffs. It is also important to hold objective, fair hearings to thwart unfair or biased terminations. Perhaps rigorous screening tests can help identify violence-prone workers so that they can be given anger management training.

Workplace violence is a complex problem for employers with potential liabilities. In some cases, employers could find that they are subject to litigation from both the accused and the victim. For example, in most Canadian jurisdictions, human rights legislation requires employers to protect workers from harassment and discrimination; if employers fail to do, so they may face civil liability. If victims of workplace violence or harassment resign they may choose to initiate legal action against former employers for not adequately protecting them. Conversely, the accused also has the option of initiating legal action on the grounds of wrongful dismissal. Further, many workplace safety and insurance plans recognize that workers may be entitled to compensation due to loss of earnings as a result of mental stress associated with such incidents. Thus, employers must be prepared to respond to incidents of workplace violence to avoid costly litigation—not to mention the negative media attention that it will undoubtedly attract.[170]

In response to heightened concerns regarding workplace violence, Canada's Occupational Health & Safety Regulations and similar provincial and territorial legislative frameworks have been amended to include obligations for employers to protect workers from workplace violence. This legislation also includes obligations to develop policies on workplace violence, conduct workplace violence risk assessments, and provide training to educate employers and employees as to their rights and responsibilities.

To recognize the importance of workplace mental health across the country, the Mental Health

Improving Mental Health in the MHCC Workplace
Our Experience Implementing The Standard

Mental Health Commission of Canada

Commission de la santé mentale du Canada

KEY STEPS

1. Information gathering. (Review existing data and collect new data)
2. Leadership commitment. (Including board-endorsed policy.)
3. Establish a Physical and PH&S Committee.
4. Develop wellness and operational indicators.
5. Risk identification, assessment and action plan.
6. Set objectives and priorities.
7. Develop wellness and work plans aligned with fiscal year.
8. Integration of physical and psychological health and safety, within policies and procedures.
9. Training and competency development. (Including Mental Health First Aid.)
0. Employee wellness surveys and focus groups.
1. Regular internal and external audits and management review.

Mental Health Commission of Canada (MHCC) is an independent, not-for-profit organization funded by Health Canada with a 10-year mandate (2007-2017) to act as a catalyst in Canada for improving the mental health system and changing the attitudes and behaviours of Canadians around mental health issues.

ABOUT MHCC
- Approximately 80 employees
- Two offices, with several remote locations
- Three employees in Human Resources

GUIDING PRINCIPLE
Integrating physical and psychological health and safety (PH&S) in a comprehensive wellness plan methodology

ISSUE
CANADIAN DISABILITY COSTS
70% Attributed to Mental Illness

PRELIMINARY OUTCOMES

CULTURAL
Increased collaboration, engagement, and shared responsibility for organizational success.

RECOGNITION
Increased awareness of the employer-employee role in maintaining a healthy and safe work environment.

REPORTING
Utilizing established metrics as measures toward continuous improvement and benchmarks against established standards (such as those found in the Standard).

CONTINUOUS IMPROVEMENT
Measuring key indicators that reflect health and safety and business outcomes in the workplace.

OUR CRITICAL TOOL
National Standard of Canda on Psychological Health and Safety in the Workplace (the Standard) was used by MHCC to guide its efforts to address mental health at work and provided us with the framework, tools and resources to design our approach.

Download for free at: www.csa.ca/z1003

RESOURCES
Visit www.mentalhealthcommission.ca to:
- Join our free monthly webinars | Hear from employers and experts about implementing the Standard
- Share your story | We want to hear from those who are using the Standard
- Learn about Mental Health First Aid | Train management and employees to recognize signs and provide initial help
- Learn about the ground-breaking Case Study research project | Follow more than 20 organizations as they adopt the Standard
- Watch video testimonials | Learn how champion organizations are promoting psychological health & safety in their workplace

For more on Mental Health First Aid visit www.mentalhealthfirstaid.ca

THREE PILLARS FOR SUCCESS

Leadership Commitment

Employee Engagement and Collaboration

Effective and Continuous Communication

For more information please contact Sapna Mahajan at smahajan@mentalhealthcommission.ca

Source: Reprinted by permission of Mental Health Commission of Canada

---

Commission of Canada has developed a national standard to help employers promote good mental health and prevent psychological harm for all employees. The aim is to develop and implement processes and policies to ensure the psychological well-being of employees in their workplace. The commission now offers Mental Health First Aid training at no cost and has established/revised policies to include psychological health and safety such as policies covering accessibility, accommodation, disability/health management, anti-harassment, and discrimination and workplace violence prevention.[171]

Summary

Among the various explanations for violent crimes are human traits, ineffective parenting, evolutionary factors, exposure to violence, a subculture of violence that stresses violent solutions to interpersonal problems, and the availability of firearms.

There are many types of interpersonal violent crime. Rape has been known throughout history; however, the view of rape has evolved. Rape was an extremely difficult charge to prove in court; however, with the amendments to the *Criminal Code* in 1983, many more people have been charged and convicted. The term *rape* has been replaced with *sexual assault* in Canadian law and there are three levels that pertain to anything from unwanted touching to forced intercourse. Among the various types of sexual assault are date rape, marital rape, and sexual assault with persons under the age of consent. Victims' rights are now also solidly established in Canadian law.

Murder is defined in common law as killing a human being with malice aforethought. There are different degrees of murder, and punishments vary accordingly. One important characteristic of murder is that the victim and criminal often know each other.

THEORETICAL APPLICATIONS

PUBLISHED: THURSDAY,
MARCH 28, 2013

CTV News has learned a man known as the Motorcycle Rapist will soon be out of prison.

In 1989, John O'Brien was convicted of raping eight women in Nova Scotia. He was sentenced to 37 years in prison, and now qualifies for statutory release. According to the Parole Board of Canada, O'Brien is set to be released on April 3, which means he would have served two-thirds of his 37-year sentence.

Parole board documents indicate O'Brien is now in his early 50s. His criminal record dates back to the mid 1970s.

In the late 1980s, he was convicted of a number of offences including five counts of sexual assault with a weapon, two counts of sexual assault, and two counts of using a firearm while committing an offence.

O'Brien was dubbed the Motorcycle Rapist because he was wearing a helmet and riding a motorcycle in many of the cases, most of which occurred in rural and secluded areas in and around the Halifax area.

The documents also indicate O'Brien's case-management team reports there is little evidence to suggest his risk levels have been reduced, and that he has a pattern of persistent violent behaviour. They say O'Brien has, in their view, "the potential to be very dangerous" and that his most recent psychological assessment shows his "risk of sexually offending is in the high end of the moderate range" and his "risk for general violence is in the moderate range." O'Brien has had a number of private family visits without incident, and he has participated in a number of programs, including the sex offender maintenance program, where he was described as open and engaged in the process.

There are conditions tied to his statutory release; he is to have no contact with his victims or with members of their families. O'Brien must reside in a halfway house, but there is no indication where he is being released to. According to parole documents, he will be closely monitored and supervised. (Source: CTV News Atlantic)

As it turned out, O'Brien never made it to the streets. He was found dead in his cell just prior to being released after what authorities referred to as a violent altercation with other inmates.

O'Brien's case is not unique in Canada. Presuming O'Brien had lived and you were the parole officer assigned to the case, how would you have monitored and supervised the case? You have always believed in the choice theory. That is, O'Brien chose to engage in sexual assaults after weighing the consequences and benefits of his behaviour. As to why he rapes women, you believe that in O'Brien's case his motivation stems more from an expression of male anger and devaluation of women as opposed to sexual desire. How will your beliefs impact on your proposed supervision plan? Will you be able to prevent O'Brien from reoffending? Will you be able to protect the women in your community?

Source: "Serial rapist to be released from prison next week," *CTV Atlantic*, published Thursday, March 28, 2013. Used with permission of CTV News, a division of Bell Media Inc.

Assault, another serious interpersonal violent crime, often occurs in the home and includes child abuse and spouse abuse.

There were over 58 000 police-reported incidents of child and youth victims of violence in 2013. This was slightly lower than those of the adult population except for sexual offences, which were more likely to occur among children and youth than among those 18 years of age and over. There were 16 700 child and youth victims of family-related violence in 2013 and, similar to police-reported violent crime in general, the majority of violence against children and youth was committed by someone known to the victim (81 percent). Both women and men experience spousal abuse. However, women experience more severe forms of violence, and are more than twice as likely as men to report being physically injured.[172]

Robbery involves theft by force, usually in a public place. Types of offenders include professional, opportunist, addict, and alcoholic robbers. Robbery is considered a violent crime because it can and often does involve violence.

Emerging forms of interpersonal violence include stalking, home invasions, hate crimes, workplace violence and political violence.

Discussion Questions

1. If robbers are in fact rational decision makers, what can potential victims do to reduce their chances of becoming targets?

2. What cultural values present in contemporary society promote violence? For example, is there a link between materialism and violence?

3. "It is my conviction that killing under the cloak of war is nothing but an act of murder" (Albert Einstein). What do you think?

READY TO STUDY?

IN THE BOOK, YOU CAN:

✔ Check your understanding of what you've just read by reading the Summary at the end of each chapter.

✔ Rip out the Chapter in Review card at the back of the book to have the key terms and Learning Objectives handy, and complete the quizzes provided (answers are at the bottom of the back page!).

ONLINE YOU CAN:

✔ Stay organized and efficient with MindTap—a single destination with all the course material and study aids you need to succeed. Built-in apps leverage social media and the latest learning technology. For example:

✔ ReadSpeaker will read the text to you.

✔ Flashcards are pre-populated to provide you with a jump start for review—or you can create your own.

✔ You can highlight text and make notes in your MindTap Reader. Your notes will flow into Evernote, the electronic notebook app that you can access anywhere when it's time to study for the exam.

✔ Prepare for tests with quizzes.

Go to www.nelson.com/student to access these digital resources.

Property Crimes

Learning Objectives

LO1 List the major types of theft and fraud.

LO2 Identify the role "target hardening" strategies can play in reducing the incidence of shoplifting.

LO3 Identify the difference between "false pretences" and "fraud."

LO4 Define "break and enter" and explain why victims are likely to be revictimized.

LO5 List the motives for the crime of arson.

As a group, economic crimes can be defined as acts that violate criminal law and are designed to bring financial reward to an offender. The range and scope of Canadian criminal activity motivated by financial gain are tremendous. Self-report studies show that committing property crime is widespread among the young in every social class. According to the General Social Survey—Victimization Survey (GSS—VS), in 2009 about 3.6 million Canadians were victims of theft of personal property, and nearly 8.0 million households were victimized; corporate and other white-collar crimes are accepted as commonplace; and political scandals, including an ongoing RCMP investigation beginning in 2013 into fraudulent expense claims by members of Canada's Senate that has already resulted in criminal charges against three senators, indicate that even high government officials engage in criminal acts.

- Theft offences have been common throughout recorded history.

- During the Middle Ages, poachers stole game, smugglers avoided taxes, and thieves worked as pickpockets and forgers.

- Occasional thieves are opportunistic amateurs who steal because of situational inducements.

- Professional thieves learn their trade and develop skills that help them avoid capture.

This chapter is the first of two that review the nature and extent of economic crime in Canada. This chapter begins with some background information on the history and nature of theft as a crime. It then discusses theft and related offences, including shoplifting, credit card theft, motor vehicle theft, fraud, confidence games, and embezzlement. Next the discussion turns to a more serious form of theft, "burglary" or break and enter, which involves forcible entry into a person's home or workplace for the purpose of theft. Finally, the crime of arson is discussed briefly. The next chapter is devoted to white-collar

crimes and economic crimes that involve criminal organizations.

History of Theft

Theft is not unique to modern times; the theft of personal property has been known throughout recorded history. The Crusades of the 11th century inspired peasants and downtrodden noblemen to leave the shelter of their estates to prey upon passing pilgrims.[1] Crusaders felt it within their rights to appropriate the possessions of any infidels—Greeks, Jews, or Muslims—they happened to encounter during their travels. By the 13th century, returning pilgrims, not content to live as serfs on feudal estates, gathered in the forests of England and the European continent to poach game that was the rightful property of their lord or king and, when possible, to steal from passing strangers. By the 14th century, many such highwaymen and poachers were full-time livestock thieves, stealing great numbers of cattle and sheep.[2]

The 15th and 16th centuries brought hostilities between England and France in the Hundred Years' War. Foreign mercenary troops fighting for both sides roamed the countryside; loot and pillage were viewed as a rightful part of their pay. In Canada, the arrival of Europeans in the 15th century in search of gold and other valuables resulted in conflict with and forced colonization of Aboriginal peoples, and widespread theft of land and resources, fraudulent treaties, and corrupt trading practices.[3]

With the advent of the Industrial Revolution in Europe in the 18th century, cities developed and a permanent class of propertyless urban poor[4] was established, and theft became a more professional enterprise. By the 18th century, three separate groups of property criminals were active:

- Skilled thieves typically worked in the larger cities, such as London and Paris. This group included pickpockets, forgers, and counterfeiters, who operated freely. They congregated in flash houses—public meeting places, often taverns, that served as headquarters for gangs. Here, deals were made, crimes were plotted, and the sale of stolen goods was negotiated.[5]

- Smugglers moved freely in sparsely populated areas and transported goods, such as spirits, gems, gold, and spices, without paying tax or duty.

- Poachers typically lived in the country and supplemented their diet and income with game that belonged to a landlord.

At the same time, professional thieves in the larger cities had banded together into gangs to protect themselves, increase the scope of their

An Exact Representation of MACLAINE the Highwayman Robbing LORD EGLINGTON on Hounflow Heath on the 26th of June 1750.

(From a Contemporary Engraving.)

Early in the 18th century, there are well-documented cases of gentlemen who engaged in highway robbery and other violent property crimes.

Contemporary Thieves

Of the millions of property and theft-related crimes that occur each year, most are committed by occasional criminals who do not define themselves by a criminal role or view themselves as committed career criminals. Other thefts are committed by skilled professional criminals.

Criminologists suspect that most economic crimes are the work of amateur occasional criminals, whose decision to steal is spontaneous and whose acts are unskilled, unplanned, and haphazard. Millions of thefts occur each year, and most are not reported to police agencies. Many of these theft offences are committed by school-age youths who are unlikely to enter criminal careers and who drift between conventional and criminal behaviour. Added to the pool of amateur thieves are the millions of adults whose behaviour may occasionally violate the law—shoplifters, pilferers, tax cheats—but whose main source of income is conventional and whose self-identity is noncriminal. Added together, their behaviours form the bulk of theft crimes.

Occasional property crime occurs when there is an opportunity or situational inducement to commit crime.[7] Members of the upper class have the opportunity to engage in lucrative business-related crimes such as price-fixing, bribery, and embezzlement; lower-class individuals, lacking such opportunities, are overrepresented in street crime. Situational inducements are short-term influences on a person's behaviour that increase risk taking. They include psychological factors, such as financial problems, and social factors, such as peer pressure.

activities, and help dispose of stolen goods. Jonathan Wild, perhaps London's most famous thief, perfected the process of buying and selling stolen goods and gave himself the title of "Thief-Taker General of Great Britain & Ireland." Before he was hanged, Wild controlled numerous gangs and dealt harshly with any thief who violated his strict code of conduct.[6]

During this period, individual theft-related crimes began to be defined by common law. The most important of these categories are still used today.

Jonathan Wild

Occasional criminals may deny their criminality and instead view their transgressions as out of character. For example, they were only "borrowing" the car the police caught them with; they were going to pay—eventually—for the merchandise they stole from the store. Because of their lack of commitment to a criminal lifestyle, occasional offenders may be the most likely to respond to the general deterrent effect of the law.

occasional criminals
Offenders who do not define themselves by a criminal role or view themselves as committed career criminals.

situational inducement
Short-term influence on a person's behaviour, such as financial problems or peer pressure, that increases risk-taking.

CRIMINOLOGY AND THE MOVIES

The YouTube documentary *The Great Train Robbery* documents the events of one of the most famous robberies in history. In August 1963 a gang of 15 men robbed the Royal Mail Train at Bridego Railway Bridge in Buckinghamshire, England, making off with £2.6 million (about $8 million Canadian in today's dollars). Amazingly, no guns were used in the heist—though the train engineer was injured when hit over the head with a metal bar.

It took Scotland Yard's "Flying Squad" and other police agencies more than five years to track down and arrest the 15 men involved in the robbery. Others involved, including a mysterious insider known as "The Ulsterman," were never caught, and most of the money was never recovered. Once sentenced, five of the robbers escaped from prison, one of them living in an upscale neighbourhood in Montreal for nearly five years before being caught by police. Another member of the gang, Ronnie Biggs, escaped from prison in 1965, and spent 36 years on the run in Australia and Brazil, where he openly flaunted his part in the robbery, recording a song with the punk rock band the Sex Pistols, and publishing an autobiography *Odd Man Out*. Biggs returned to England in 2001 to reunite with his family, but was quickly arrested by British police. He spent the next eight years in prison, and died in 2013 at the age of 84.

Crime-prevention strategies have made "target hardening" techniques common, often built into the very physical design and technologies we use, making crimes like the Great Train Robbery much harder to pull off. However, criminologists fear that our reliance on technology, in particular the Internet, has opened other doors of opportunity for enterprising criminals.

The August 1963 robbery of Royal Mail Train is one of the most famous crimes in history. Target hardening strategies, including surveillance technologies, make such a crime nearly impossible now.

In contrast to occasional criminals, **professional criminals** make a significant portion of their income from crime. Professionals do not delude themselves with the belief that their acts are impulsive, one-time efforts, nor do they use elaborate rationalizations to excuse the harmfulness of their actions (e.g., "shoplifting doesn't really hurt anyone"). Consequently, professionals pursue their craft with vigour, attempting to learn from older, experienced criminals the techniques that will earn the most money with the least risk. Although their numbers are relatively few, professionals engage in crimes that produce the greater losses to society and perhaps cause the more significant social harm.

Professional theft traditionally refers to nonviolent forms of criminal behaviour that are undertaken with a high degree of skill for monetary gain and that maximize financial opportunities and minimize the possibilities of apprehension. The most typical forms include pocket-picking, break and enter, shoplifting, forgery, counterfeiting, extortion, sneak theft, and confidence swindling (see Figure 11.1).[8]

professional criminals
Offenders who make a significant portion of their income from crime.

FIGURE 11.1

Categories of Professional Theft

- Pickpocket (cannon)
- Sneak thief from stores, banks, and offices (heel)
- Shoplifter (booster)
- Jewel thief who substitutes fake gems for real ones (pennyweighter)
- Thief who steals from hotel rooms (hotel prowl)
- Confidence game artist (con artist)
- Thief in rackets related to confidence games
- Forger
- Extortionist from those engaging in illegal acts (shakedown artist)

Source: Edwin Sutherland and Chic Conwell, *The Professional Thief* (Chicago: University of Chicago Press, 1937). Copyright 1937 by the University of Chicago. Reprinted with permission of The University of Chicago Press.

Michael Fresco/Getty Images

Theft is probably the most common of all crimes.

The following sections discuss some of the more important contemporary theft categories in some detail.

LO1 Theft

Theft was one of the earliest common-law crimes created by English judges to define acts in which one person took for his or her own use the property of another.[9] According to common law, theft was defined as "the trespassory taking and carrying away of the personal property of another with intent to steal."[10] Contemporary definitions of theft often include familiar acts such as shoplifting, passing bad cheques, and other theft offences that do not involve using force or threats on the victim or forcibly breaking into a person's home or workplace. (The former is robbery; the latter, break and enter.)

As originally construed, theft involved taking property that was in the possession of the rightful owner. For example, it would have been considered theft for someone to sneak into a farmer's field and steal a cow. Thus, the original common-law

definition required a "trespass in the taking"; that is, for an act to be considered theft, goods must have been taken from the physical possession of the rightful owner. In creating this definition of theft, English judges were more concerned with disturbance of the peace than with theft itself. They reasoned that if someone tried to steal property from another's possession, the act could eventually lead to a physical confrontation and possibly the death of one party or the other. Consequently, the original definition of theft did not include crimes in which the thief had taken the property by trickery or deceit. For example, if someone entrusted with another person's property decided to keep it, it was not considered theft.

The growth of manufacturing and the development of the free enterprise system required greater protection for private property. The pursuit of commercial enterprise often required that one person's legal property be entrusted to a second party; therefore, larceny evolved to include the theft of goods that had come into the thief's possession through legitimate means.

To get around the element of "trespass in the taking," English judges created the concept of constructive possession. This legal fiction applies to situations in which persons voluntarily, temporarily give up custody of their property, but still believe that the property is legally theirs. For example, if a person gives a jeweller her watch for repair, she still believes she owns the watch, although she has handed it over to the jeweller. Similarly, when a person misplaces his wallet and someone else finds it and keeps it (although identification of the owner can be plainly seen), the concept of constructive possession makes the person who has kept the wallet guilty of theft.

The *Criminal Code* separates theft into two categories—theft under $5000 and theft over $5000—for the purposes of trial and sentencing. Theft under $5000 is treated as a "hybrid offence" for which the Crown attorney can choose to proceed by way of a summary

theft
Taking for one's own use the property of another, by means other than force or threats on the victim or forcibly breaking into a person's home or workplace.

constructive possession
A legal fiction that applies to situations in which persons voluntarily give up physical custody of their property but still retain legal ownership.

theft under $5000
Theft where the value of the property stolen does not exceed $5000; treated as a hybrid offence for which the Crown can proceed by way of summary conviction or indictment.

theft over $5000
Theft where the value of property stolen exceeds $5000; treated as an indictable offence.

conviction offence (maximum penalty six months in jail and $2000 fine) or by way of indictment (maximum two years' imprisonment). Theft over $5000 is automatically treated as an indictable offence, and carries with it a maximum sentence of ten years' imprisonment.

Theft is probably the most common of all crimes. Self-report studies indicate that a significant number of youths have engaged in theft. Based on police-reported UCR data, the Canadian Centre for Justice Statistics recorded 486 263 thefts in 2013, a rate of approximately 1383 per 100 000 persons. Theft rates declined more than 30 percent between 2003 and 2013.[11]

There are many different varieties of theft. Some involve small items of little value. Many of these go unreported, especially if the victims are business owners who do not want to take the time to get involved with police; they simply write off losses as a cost of doing business. For example, according to a 2013 survey, about 30 percent of English-speaking Canadians admitted to stealing an item from a hotel they stayed in, compared to thirty-four percent of Americans and just 19 percent of French-speaking Canadians: hotel owners in the United States estimate that each year guests filch more than US$100 million worth of towels, bathrobes, ashtrays, bedspreads, showerheads, flatware, and even television sets and wall paintings.[12]

shoplifting
The taking of goods from retail stores.

Other thefts can involve complex schemes involving many different people. For example, in 144 break-ins at convenience stores and gas bars, a gang of ten thieves operating in the Port Hope–Cobourg area northeast of Toronto netted more than $1 million in cigarettes.[13] Satellite service providers claim to lose millions every year in lost revenues due to the sale of "pirated" decoder chips produced illegally by "homebrew" operations. Every year, employees steal more than $2 billion from Canadian employers in the retail section, half of it out of the cash register.[14]

In September 2014, in one of the largest computer security breaches in history, Home Depot confirm that thieves hacked into its customer payment information system in Canada and the United States, stealing more than 56 million customer credit and debit card numbers, along with customer email addresses. Thieves used a password stolen from one of the company's suppliers to access the Home Depot system and install a malware program that downloaded information electronically to the hackers' computer. Once the company discovered the security breach, customers were made aware and offered free identity-protection services, a year of free credit monitoring, even gift cards as compensation. So far, the theft has cost Home Depot more than $62 million in investigation fees, to develop and implement new computer security measures, to pay for the cost of credit monitoring and identity-protection services and gift cards offered to customers, increased call-centre staffing, and legal and professional fees.[15] Earlier in 2003, theft of four computers from a Canada Revenue Agency office in Laval, Quebec, resulted in the names, dates of birth, home addresses, and social insurance numbers of thousands of Canadians possibly being sold on the black market and used to construct new identities for criminals or terrorists.[16]

Identity theft is one of the fastest-growing crimes in North America. The Canadian Anti-Fraud Centre, an antifraud call centre jointly operated by the RCMP Ontario Provincial Police and the Competition Bureau Canada, reported that in 2013, 19 473 people were victims of identity fraud, with losses totalling more than $11 million.[17]

There is growing evidence that identity theft is being used by organized crime and to further the aims of other crimes such as terrorism.[18]

LO2 Shoplifting

Shoplifting is a common form of theft involving the taking of goods from retail stores. Usually shoplifters try to snatch goods—such as jewellery, clothes, CDs, and appliances—when store personnel are otherwise occupied and hide the goods on their bodies. The "five-finger discount" is an extremely common

In Canada and the United States, about one-third of hotel guests admit to stealing an item from the hotel they stayed in, from ashtrays to television sets.

crime, and the Retail Council of Canada estimates that Canadian retailers lose as much as $8 million a day to retail theft, most of it due to shoplifting.[19] Retail security measures add to the already high cost of this crime, all of which is passed on to the consumer, with Canadian consumers paying as much as 20 percent more for goods as a result of retail theft.[20] Some studies estimate that about one in every nine shoppers steals from department stores. Moreover, the increasingly popular discount stores, such as Walmart and Costco, have minimal sales help and depend on highly visible merchandise displays to attract purchasers, all of which makes them particularly vulnerable to shoplifters.

DID YOU KNOW?

- Theft is the taking and carrying away of the constructive possessions of another.

- Shoplifting involves theft from a retail establishment by stealth and deception. Some shoplifters are impulsive; others are professionals who use elaborate means and devices.

- Passing bad cheques without adequate funds is a crime of fraud.

- The use of stolen credit cards and account numbers results in annual losses of more than $200 million.

- Auto theft adds up to more than $1 billion each year.

- Embezzlement or criminal breach of trust occurs when trusted persons or employees take someone else's property for their own use.

Criminologists view shoplifters as people who are likely to reform if apprehended.

© Pinto/Corbis

The Shoplifter

In the early 1960s, Mary Owen Cameron conducted a classic study of shoplifting.[21] In her pioneering effort, Cameron found that about 10 percent of all shoplifters were professionals who derived the majority of their income from shoplifting. Sometimes called boosters, or heels, professional shoplifters steal with the intention of reselling stolen merchandise to pawnshops or fences (people who buy stolen property), usually at half the original price.[22]

Cameron found that the majority of shoplifters are amateur pilferers, called snitches in thieves' argot. Snitches are otherwise respectable persons who do not conceive of themselves as thieves but systematically steal merchandise for their own use. They are not simply taken by an uncontrollable urge to snatch something that attracts them; they come equipped to steal. Usually snitches who are arrested have never been apprehended before. For the most part, they lack the kinds of criminal experience that suggest extensive association with a criminal subculture.

Criminologists view shoplifters as people who are likely to reform if apprehended. Cameron reasoned that because snitches are not part of a criminal subculture and do not think of themselves as criminals, they are deterred by initial contact with the law. Getting arrested traumatizes them, and they will not risk a second offence.[23] Although this argument seems plausible, some criminologists suggest that apprehension may in fact have a labelling effect that inhibits deterrence and results in repeated offending.[24]

booster
Professional shoplifter who steals with the intention of reselling stolen merchandise.

fence
A receiver of stolen goods.

snitch
Amateur shoplifter who does not self-identify as a thief but who systematically steals merchandise for personal use.

In October 2010, Toronto grocery store owner David Chen was acquitted on charges of assault and forcible confinement stemming from an incident in May 2010 when Chen chased down and tied up a man who had stolen a plant from his store. The same day that Chen learned of his acquittal he was again victimized by a shoplifter: this time he called police and let them handle it.[25]

"Target hardening" involves making a home or business more resistant to burglars. For example, when thieves try to smash glass where "security film" has been applied, the glass will break but the transparent film will hold the shards in place, making entry very difficult.

Controlling Shoplifting

Fewer than 10 percent of shoplifting incidents are detected by store employees; customers who notice boosters are unwilling to report even serious cases to managers.[26]

Section 494(2) of the *Criminal Code* allows for arrest by owner of property—that is, business owners and their employees are permitted by law to arrest without a warrant anyone found committing an offence on or in relation to the owner's property. The law requires that arrests be made on reasonable and probable grounds, that detention be short, and that store employees or security guards conduct themselves reasonably and in accordance with the law.

Retail stores are now initiating a number of strategies designed to reduce or eliminate shoplifting. Target removal strategies involve displaying dummy or disabled goods while the real merchandise is locked up. For example, audio equipment is displayed with parts missing, and only after items are purchased are the necessary components installed. Some stores sell from catalogues, keeping the merchandise in stockrooms.

Target hardening strategies involve locking goods into place or having them monitored by electronic systems. Clothing stores may use racks designed to prevent large quantities of garments from being slipped off easily. Store owners also rely on electronic article surveillance (EAS) systems, featuring tags with small electronic sensors that trip alarms if not removed by employees before the item leaves the store. Security systems now feature source tagging, a process by which manufacturers embed the tag in the packaging or in the product itself. Thieves have trouble removing or defeating such tags, and retailers save on the time and labour needed to attach the tags at the store.

Here are some of the steps retail insurers recommend to reduce the incidence of shoplifting:*

- Train employees to watch for suspicious behaviour such as a shopper loitering over a trivial item. Have employees keep an eye out for shoppers wearing baggy clothes, carrying their own bag, or using some other method to conceal products taken from the shelf.

- Develop a call code. When employees suspect that a customer is shoplifting, they can use the call to bring store management or security to the area.

- Because products on lower floors face the greatest risk, relocate the most tempting targets to upper floors.

---

*Marcus Felson, "Preventing Retail Theft: An Application of Environmental Criminology," *Security Journal* 7 (1996): 71–75; Marc Brandeberry, "$15 Billion Lost to Shoplifting," *Today's Coverage*, a newsletter of the Grocers Insurance Group, Portland, Oregon, 1997.

- Use smaller exits, and avoid placing the most expensive merchandise near these exits.

- Design routes within stores to make theft less tempting and funnel customers toward cashiers.

- Place service departments (credit and packaging) near areas where shoplifters are likely to stash goods. Extra supervision reduces the problem.

- Avoid creating corners where there are no supervision sight lines in areas of stores favoured by young males. Restrict and supervise areas where electronic tags can be removed.[27]

Credit and Debit Card Theft

The use of stolen credit cards is a major problem in North America. Most credit card abuse is the work of amateurs who acquire stolen cards through theft or mugging and then use them for two or three days. However, professional credit card rings have gotten into the act. In January 2007 Montreal police arrested five men in raids on two high-tech fake credit card operations, seizing sophisticated colour printers, hologram-producing machines, computers, credit card blanks, and a $30 000 embossing machine to imprint the fake cards. "Obviously with that kind of equipment, you're able to produce cards a lot quicker than you were with older equipment," said a Montreal police spokesperson.[28]

It is a criminal offence to steal, forge, or falsify a credit card, or to knowingly use a credit card that has been revoked or cancelled. According to the RCMP, credit and bank card fraud losses topped $360 million in 2010.[29]

Debit card fraud is a growing problem that alone resulted in losses of nearly $120 million in 2010 according to RCMP statistics.[30] "Skimming" involves swiping a debit card without the owner's knowledge—most often when the owner is making a purchase and hands the debit card to the cashier, who then "double swipes" the card—once to send the information legitimately to the owner's bank, the second time to record that information on a hidden device. Close observation of the owner entering her PIN number, or use of an overhead camera, gives the thief all the information needed to make a duplicate of the debit card for use with the owner's stolen PIN number.[31] In a February 2010 case, Windsor, Ontario, police discovered a bogus debit card reader used in a local fast food restaurant equipped with a Bluetooth device that allowed thieves to collect both the owner's card and PIN number wirelessly. The information collected by the thieves was then used to withdraw hundreds of thousands of dollars from ATMs in the Montreal area. Thieves have even been known to place false fronts and fake PIN pads on ATM's in order to steal the owner's debit card information.[32]

In October 2009 the Canadian government introduced amendments to the *Criminal Code* to address specifically the theft of personal information to be employed to make use of or produce bogus credit or debit cards, with conviction punishable by up to ten years in prison.[33] Coupled with the introduction of new embedded computer chip technology in both credit and debit cards, and the use of PIN numbers for both cards, total losses from the fraudulent use of credit and debit cards in Canada fell in 2014.[34]

Motor Vehicle Theft

Under Section 355(1) of the *Criminal Code*, auto theft is defined as "Taking [a] motor vehicle or vessel or [being] found therein without consent." There were 78 068 vehicles reported stolen in Canada in 2013, down 8 percent from the previous year, and a 62 percent decrease since 2003.[35] The Insurance Bureau of Canada estimates that motor vehicle thefts cost Canadians $1 billion annually.[36] (See Table 11.1.)

Though almost all motor vehicle thefts are reported to police (as every province requires owners to insure their vehicles), 2007 Statistics Canada data show that fully 40 percent of all vehicles stolen are never recovered. Canada ranks in the top one-third of industrialized countries for car thefts, and our theft rate is higher than the American rate.[37]

Types of Motor Vehicle Theft

A number of attempts have been made to categorize the various forms of motor vehicle theft. Typically, distinctions are made between theft for temporary personal use, for resale, and for chopping or stripping cars for parts. One of the most detailed of these typologies was developed by Charles McCaghy and his associates after examining data from police and court files in several American states.[38]

The researchers uncovered five categories of auto theft transactions:

1. *Joyriding.* Many motor vehicle thefts are motivated by teenagers' desire to acquire the power, prestige, sexual potency, and recognition associated with an automobile. Joyriders steal cars not for profit or gain but to experience, even briefly, the benefits associated with owning an automobile.

2. *Short-term transportation.* Motor vehicle theft for short-term transportation is similar to joyriding. It involves the theft of a car, an SUV, or other motor vehicle simply to go from one place to another. In more serious cases, the thief may drive to another city and then steal another vehicle to continue the journey.

Myths About Car Theft

Automobile theft is often thought of as a minor crime but in reality it's a serious problem in our society. Let's dispel some of the more common myths around this growing problem.

Myth 1: Only sports cars or deluxe models are stolen. Who would want a two- or three-year-old ordinary car?

Authorities report that the most popular makes are the most likely stolen and the least likely to be recovered. Ordinary sedans are the backbone of the lucrative stolen used-parts market and therefore are the least frequently recovered.

Myth 2: Car theft is not really a big issue and everything is usually covered under insurance anyway.

In Canada, thieves steal a vehicle every 5 1/4 minutes and a vehicle is broken into every 30 seconds. Auto theft is a crime that everyone pays for. Car theft costs Canadian consumers about $470 million a year in insurance premiums for unrecovered vehicles, damage to vehicles that are stolen and later recovered, and items stolen from vehicles.

Myth 3: Canada has a much lower auto theft rate than the United States.

When it comes to theft of insured cars, the Canadian rate exceeds the American rate. There is no doubt that organized crime rings are involved in the auto theft market, which presents very low risks for thieves and generates spectacular profits.

Myth 4: Cars are mostly stolen for joy rides and are usually found intact very quickly.

Statistics show that 60 percent of the time authorities find the stolen vehicles within two–ten days. The state of the recovered cars depends on what the thieves used them for. They are rarely abandoned intact. While automobile theft is an urban phenomenon, what happens to your car depends on where you live in Canada. For example, a car stolen in Quebec is quite likely to end up in pieces in a "chop shop." The vehicles are dismantled and the parts sold, often for much more than the whole car may have been worth. A car stolen in Alberta would more likely be taken on a joy ride and recovered.

Myth 5: I don't park in dark alleys or unsupervised parking lots so I'm not at risk for having my car stolen.

Your place of residence ranks as the number-one spot where thieves are most likely to strike, followed by shopping centre parking lots. Most people are not as sympathetic to automobile theft victims as they are to victims of burglary. Because they are viewed as nonviolent crimes, automobile thefts hardly cause a ripple. Usually the victim is not injured and if they are insured, they will be reimbursed and everything will soon be back to normal. But the reality includes the emotional upset of victims and the loss of irreplaceable personal belongings.

Source: Reprinted with permission of The Co-operators.

3. *Long-term transportation.* Thieves who steal motor vehicles for long-term transportation intend to keep the cars for their personal use. Usually older than joyriders and from a lower-class background, these thieves may repaint and otherwise disguise vehicles to avoid detection.

4. *Profit.* Motor vehicle theft for profit is motivated by the hope of monetary gain. At one extreme are highly organized professionals who resell expensive cars after altering their identification numbers and falsifying their registration papers. At the other end of the scale are amateur auto strippers who steal batteries, tires, and wheel covers to sell them or re-equip their own cars.

5. *Commission of another crime.* A few motor vehicle thieves steal vehicles to use in other crimes, such as robberies and thefts. This type of thief desires both mobility and anonymity.

According to police, joyriding remains a primary motive for motor vehicle theft. Youth aged 12–17 account for 28 percent of vehicle thefts. However, the clearance rate for motor vehicle theft continues to decline, with police identifying an accused in only 12.5 percent of incidents. The low clearance rate, coupled with declining recovery rates for stolen vehicles, suggests to many that there may be increased involvement by professional car thieves linked to chop shops, export rings, or both. More than 30 percent of vehicles stolen in Canada are now exported to foreign countries. Exporting stolen vehicles has become a global problem, and the emergence of capitalism in Eastern Europe and rapid economic growth in Africa, the Middle East, and China has increased the demand for North American–made cars.[39]

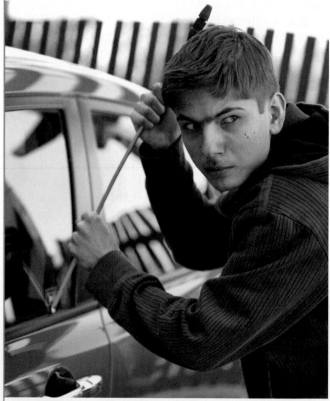

Each year millions of thefts from cars, homes, and schools are reported to police. Some are the work of professionals, while others are the spontaneous acts of occasional or amateur thieves.

Tips for Preventing Theft

Automobile manufacturers have introduced features designed to reduce the incidence of vehicle theft (e.g., alarms and ultrasonic devices, the etching of parts and accessories, fuel cutoff systems, vehicle immobilizers, etc.). Ask your local police and motorists' associations for advice on which vehicles are the most difficult for thieves to steal. Here are some tips on how to discourage car thieves:

- Don't leave your car unlocked or with the key in the ignition. Always pocket the keys.

- Keep your house keys separate from your car keys.

- Park your car in a busy, well-lit area.

- Do not leave valuable items or packages in sight in your car.

- Keep your vehicle registration in your wallet or purse.

- Etch or mark some of the more expensive parts on your car in an inconspicuous place with an engraving tool, using your car's Vehicle Identification Number (VIN). On metal parts, cover the number with rust-inhibitor.

- Install safety door-lock buttons.

- Always keep your car trunk locked.

Source: Reprinted with permission of The Co-operators.

Combating Motor Vehicle Theft

Motor vehicle theft is a significant target of situational crime prevention efforts. One approach to theft deterrence has been to increase the risks of apprehension. Information hotlines offer rewards for information leading to the arrest of car thieves. A British Columbia-based antitheft strategy known as IMPACT (Integrated Municipal Provincial Auto Crime Team) brings together police investigators from seven different police services in the Greater Vancouver Area, and is credited with a decline of 75 percent in motor vehicle thefts in B.C. since 2003 when the team was formed. One especially successful component of the IMPACT strategy is the "Bait Car" program, where a vehicle equipped with "Boomerang" GPS tracking technology and onboard audio-video surveillance technology is left locked on a street, in a mall or another public place known to be frequented by auto thieves. Police are notified by the Boomerang GPS system the moment the vehicle is entered, and can use a remote control system to lock the vehicle doors and prevent the engine from starting—effectively locking the thief in the vehicle until police arrive.[40] Alternatively, police can follow the thief and the stolen vehicle to a chop shop where the car will be taken apart and sold for parts or prepared for export out of Canada. Other antitheft measures include manufacturer-marking of VIN numbers on vehicle engine and body panel parts and etching of the VIN number into vehicle glass, along with electronic vehicle keys equipped with voice recognition or coded engine immobilizer technology that prevent anyone except the owner starting the vehicle.[41] Other prevention approaches involve public education campaigns reminding drivers to lock their vehicles, equipping parking lots with theft-deterring closed-circuit TV cameras and barriers, and tightening requirements and surveillance of used car sales. However, a study by the Highway Loss Data Institute (HLDI) in the United States found that most car-theft prevention methods, especially alarms, have little effect on theft rates. The most effective methods appear to be devices that immobilize a vehicle by cutting off the electrical power needed to start the engine when a theft is detected.[42]

LO3 False Pretences and Fraud

Unlike theft, the crime of false pretences involves deliberate misrepresentation of facts to obtain money or property. In 1757, the English Parliament defined false pretences in order to cover an area of law left untouched by theft statutes. The first false pretences law punished people who "knowingly and designedly by false pretence or pretences, [obtained] from any person or persons, money, goods, wares or merchandise with intent to cheat or defraud any person or persons of the same."[43]

False pretence differs from traditional theft because the victims willingly give their possessions to the offender, and the crime does not, as does theft, involve a "trespass in the taking." Examples of false pretences would be an unscrupulous merchant selling someone a chair by claiming it was an antique, knowing that it was a cheap copy, or a phony healer selling coloured sugar water as an "elixir" that would cure a disease.

Fraud is a broader offence than false pretences that involves the use of deceit or falsehood, whether or not it is a false pretence, to obtain property, money, or other valuables from a person or the public. An example of a fraud is using the mail or the Internet to distribute information about get-rich-quick

false pretences
Misrepresenting a fact in a way that causes a deceived victim to give money or property to the offender.

fraud
Use of deceit or falsehood, whether or not it is a false pretence, to obtain property, money, or other valuables from a person or the public.

schemes that require an initial down payment by investors, money that is then pocketed by the fraud artist. Another example would be defrauding someone of his or her money by convincing the person that you are in contact with the spirit world, and a payment must be made to appease the spirits. So-called confidence games are another common type of fraud.

Bad Cheques

Despite the growth and convenience of electronic banking, Canadian banks still process more than half a billion paper cheques every year, and writing bad cheques remains a common example of the crime of fraud.[44] The cheques are intentionally drawn on a nonexistent or underfunded bank account. In general, for a person to be guilty of passing a bad cheque, the bank the cheque is drawn on must refuse payment and the cheque casher must fail to make the cheque good within ten days after finding out the cheque was not honoured.

Edwin Lemert conducted the best-known study of cheque forgers more than 50 years ago.[45] Lemert found that the majority of cheque forgers—he calls them naïve cheque forgers—are amateurs who do not believe their actions will hurt anyone.

Most naïve cheque forgers come from middle-class backgrounds and have little identification with a criminal subculture. They cash bad cheques because of a financial crisis that demands an immediate resolution—perhaps they have lost money at the horse track and have some pressing bills to pay. Naïve cheque forgers are often socially isolated people who have been unsuccessful in their personal relationships. They are risk-prone when faced with a situation that is unusually stressful for them. The willingness of stores and other commercial establishments to cash cheques with a minimum of fuss to promote business encourages the cheque forger to risk committing a criminal act.

Lemert found that a few professionals, whom he calls systematic forgers, make a substantial living by passing bad cheques. It is difficult to estimate the number of such forgeries committed each year or the amounts involved. Stores and banks may choose not to press charges because the effort to collect the money due them is often not worth their while. It is also difficult to separate the true cheque forger from the neglectful shopper.

With the development of smartphone applications to scan and deposit cheques, fears are being raised about a new form of cheque fraud using electronic means to alter account numbers or dollar amounts, or to duplicate and double-process cheques.[46]

Confidence Games

Confidence games are a good example of the crime of fraud, run by swindlers who aspire to separate a victim from his or her hard-earned money. These con games usually involve getting a mark (target) interested in some get-rich-quick scheme, which may have illegal overtones. The criminal's hope is that when victims lose their money, they will be either too embarrassed or too afraid to call the police. There are hundreds of varieties of con games.

Contemporary confidence games have gone high tech. Corrupt telemarketers contact people, typically elderly victims, over the phone in order to bilk them out of their savings. The Canadian Anti-Fraud Centre received complaint calls from nearly 43 000 Canadians in 2013, and nearly 12 000 persons were confirmed victims of mass marketing fraud. The Anti-Fraud Centre estimates the losses due to mass marketing fraud in 2013 at almost $60 million. One recent scam is known as the "Anti-Virus" scam, where a phone caller claiming to represent Microsoft Corporation or the "Canadian Cyber Incident Response Centre" tells the homeowner that their computer is being used by hackers and they will be held responsible if they do not allow the caller to access their computer and "disinfect" it. The homeowner is asked to log their computer on to the Internet, and to provide their user ID and password to the caller so that the computer can be repaired. The scam involves the caller installing keyloggers and other malware designed to retrieve personal banking information that could be used to steal money from accounts—and even involves charging the homeowner a fee for the service, payable by credit card.

Fotoline/Shutterstock.com

The movie *American Hustle* (2013) depicts the exploits of two professional con artists who are forced by an FBI agent to engage in an elaborate scam to trap a corrupt politician.

Since 2010 more than 15 000 Canadian have logged a complaint about the scam with the Canadian Anti-Fraud Centre, and nearly 5000 victims have recorded losses totalling more than $1 million.[47]

In June 2007, the *Toronto Star* reported that the "Wish Kids Foundation," a charitable foundation claiming to be raising money to give dying children their final wish, was in fact using the funds raised to buy an airplane; in another scam, the executive director of "Canadians Against Child Abuse" was accused of using the funds raised to pay for his own home and vacations.[48]

Embezzlement/Breach of Trust

Embezzlement (breach of trust) goes back at least to ancient Greece; the writings of Aristotle allude to theft by road commissioners and other government officials.[49]

The crime of embezzlement was first codified into law by the English Parliament during the 16th century.[50] Until then, to be guilty of theft, a person had to take goods from the physical possession of another (trespass in the taking). However, as explained earlier, this definition did not cover instances in which one person trusted another and willingly gave that person temporary custody of his or her property. For example, in everyday commerce, store clerks, bank tellers, brokers, and merchants gain lawful possession but not legal ownership of other people's money. Embezzlement occurs when someone who is trusted with property fraudulently converts it—that is, keeps it for his or her own use or for the use of others. In Canada, embezzlement is defined in Section 336 of the *Criminal Code* as the offence of "criminal breach of trust," which carries with it a penalty of up to 14 years' imprisonment. An example of criminal breach of trust is collecting funds from the sale of raffle tickets and "converting" them to one's own use, perhaps to buy a car or pay a debt.

Due to their relatively small number, the Canadian Centre for Justice Statistics does not report arrests for criminal breach of trust as a separate category. In the United States, the FBI found that only 17 000 people were arrested for embezzlement in 1999—probably an extremely small percentage of all embezzlers. However, the number of people arrested for embezzlement has increased in the past two decades, indicating that (1) more employees are willing to steal from their employers, (2) more employers are willing to report instances of embezzlement, or (3) law enforcement officials are more willing to prosecute embezzlers.

> **embezzlement (breach of trust)** Taking and keeping the property of others, such as clients or employers, with which one has been entrusted.

DID YOU KNOW?

- Burglary/break and enter is the breaking into and entering of a structure in order to commit an indictable offence, typically theft.

- Some burglars specialize in residential theft; others steal from commercial establishments.

- Some burglars repeatedly attack the same target, mainly because they are familiar with the layout and protective measures.

- Professional burglars have careers in which they learn the tricks of the trade from older, more experienced pros.

LO4 Burglary/Break and Enter

Common law defines the crime of burglary (break and enter) as "the breaking and entering of a dwelling house of another in the nighttime with the intent to commit an indictable offence within."[51] Burglary is considered a much more serious crime than theft because it involves entering another's home, which threatens occupants. Even though the home may be unoccupied at the time of the break and enter, the potential for harm to the occupants is so significant that break and enter is punished as an indictable offence.

burglary (break and enter)
Breaking into and entering a place with the intent to commit an indictable offence.

The legal definition of burglary has undergone considerable change since its common-law origins. When first created by English judges during the late Middle Ages, laws against burglary were designed to protect people whose home might be set upon by wandering criminals. Including the phrase "breaking and entering" in the definition protected people from unwarranted intrusions; if an invited guest stole something, it would not be considered a burglary. Similarly, the requirement that the crime be committed at nighttime was added because evening was considered the time when honest people might fall prey to criminals.[52]

Recent Canadian criminal laws do not require forced entry. Entry through deceit (e.g., by posing as a delivery person), through threat, or through conspiracy with others such as guests or servants is deemed legally equivalent to breaking and entering and is called "constructive breaking." Similarly, there is no longer a requirement that the crime be committed during nighttime, and all structures, whether or not a private dwelling, are covered by the law. However, breaking into and entering a private home is considered a much more serious invasion of privacy and security than entry into other types of structures, and carries with it a maximum penalty of life imprisonment (compared to ten years for other types of structures).

The Nature and Extent of Break and Enter

The *Criminal Code* definition of break and enter includes three different categories of the offence: (1) break and enter with intent to commit an indictable offence; (2) break and enter and committing an indictable offence; and (3) break out of a place and intending or actually committing an indictable offence.

The need to get money to buy drugs is a common motive for break and enter crimes. One example is that of Richard Seguin, the Ottawa-area burglar

Burglary is considered a much more serious crime than theft because it involves entering another's home, which threatens occupants.

According to the GSS—PRVS, those most likely to be victims of break and enter live in cities and in rented or multiple family dwellings.

© Dave Henrys/Alamy

DavidEwingPhotography/Shutterstock.com

According to an August 2015 article in *Maclean's* magazine, the reason the crime rate is falling so fast in Canada is that the number of crimes committed by the 18- to 24-year-old population—usually the group responsible for most of the crime—have plummeted 30 percent since 2009. Other Western countries have seen a similar surprising drop in crime rates among young people. A number of criminologists are now theorizing that the reason the 18- to 24-year-old group is committing fewer crimes is simply that they have other, more interesting things to do with their time—that is, texting, social media, video games, online movies and television shows—that consume more and more of that age group's time, and also offer cyberspace outlets for attitudes and behaviour that once translated into criminal behaviours.

According to Hirshi's social control theory, as the level of involvement and commitment to conventional activities increases, the probability of engagement in nonconventional (e.g., criminal) activities decreases—so goes the logic of involving young children and teens in sports, the arts, clubs, and other structured activities, keeping them busy, encouraging involvement and commitment to conventional activities, and, ideally, socializing them to have both attachment to and belief in conventional values learned as part of their activities. Though Hirschi could not have predicted it when he wrote *Causes of Delinquency* in 1969, the growth of technology, the Internet and smartphone use may be achieving what four decades of social programming could not—mass socialization of the adolescent and young adult population through digital media.

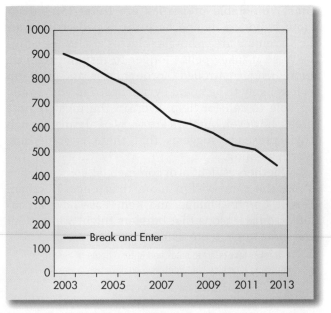

called "Spiderman" because of his heroin-induced spider-like powers to scale tall buildings and break into apartments in search of money and valuables. Once arrested, he pled guilty to 20 counts of break and enter.

According to Statistics Canada, 156 357 police-reported break and enters were recorded in 2013. The break and enter rate has dropped by 51 percent since 2003 (see Figure 11.2).

Overall, the average loss for a burglary is about $1500 per victim, for a total of about $3 billion.[53] On the other hand, self-reported data collected as part of the 2009 GSS—VS reveals that about 630 000 residential break and enters were either attempted or completed in 2009, a 20 percent increase from 2004. Only slightly more than 50 percent of these were reported to police.[54]

According to the GSS—VS, those most likely to be victims of break and enter live in cities and in households earning over $60 000 per year. Owner-occupied and single-family residences had lower break and enter rates than renter-occupied and multiple-family dwellings.

Types of Break and Enter

Though some burglars are crude thieves who smash a window and enter a vacant home or structure with minimal preparation, others plan a strategy. Because it involves planning, risk, and skill, break and enter has long been associated with professional thieves who carefully learn their craft.[55]

FIGURE 11.2

Break and Enter Rate, 2003–2013

Source: Adapted from Statistics Canada CANSIM Database (http://www5.statcan.gc.ca/cansim/home-accueil?lang=eng, Table 252-0051

Burglars must master the skills of their trade, learning to spot environmental cues that nonprofessionals fail to notice.[56] In an important book called *Burglars on the Job*, Richard Wright and Scott Decker describe the working conditions of active burglars.[57] Most are motivated by the need for cash in order to get high; they want to enjoy the good life, "keep the party going," without having to work. They approach their job in a rational, businesslike fashion; still, their lives are controlled by their culture and environment. Unskilled and uneducated, urban burglars choose crime because they have few conventional opportunities for success. (See Figure 11.3.)

Some burglars prefer to victimize commercial property rather than private homes. Of all business establishments, retail stores are the favourite target. Because they display merchandise, burglars know exactly what to look for, where it can be found, and, because the prices are also displayed, how much they can hope to gain from resale to a fence. Burglars can legitimately enter a retail store during business hours and see what the store contains and where it is stored; they can also check for security alarms and devices. Commercial burglars perceive retail establishments as ready sources of merchandise that can be easily sold.[58]

Other commercial establishments, such as service centres, warehouses, and factories, are less attractive targets because it is more difficult to gain legitimate access to plan the theft. The burglar must use guile to scope out these places, perhaps posing as a delivery person. In addition, the merchandise is more likely to be used or more difficult to fence at a premium price. If burglars choose to attack factories, warehouses, or service centres, the most vulnerable properties are those located far from major roads and away from pedestrian traffic. In remote areas, burglar alarms are less effective because it takes police longer to respond than on more heavily patrolled thoroughfares, and an alarm is less likely to be heard by a pedestrian who would be able to call for help. Even in the most remote areas, however, burglars are wary of alarms, though their presence suggests that there is something worth stealing.

Whether residential or commercial, some burglars strike the same victim more than once.[59] Graham Farrell, Coretta Phillips, and Ken Pease have articulated some reasons that burglars might want to hit the same target more than once:

- It takes less effort to break and enter a home or apartment known to be a suitable target than an unknown or unsuitable one.
- The burglar is already aware of the target's layout.
- The ease of entry of the target has probably not changed, and escape routes are known.

How Burglars Approach Their "Job"

- Targets are often acquaintances.

- Drug dealers are a favoured target because they have lots of cash and drugs, and victims aren't going to call police.

- Tipsters help the burglars select attractive targets.

- Some stake out residences to learn the occupants' routine.

- Many burglars approach a target masquerading as workers, such as carpenters or housepainters.

- Most avoid occupied residences, considering them high-risk targets.

- Alarms and elaborate locks do not deter burglars but tell them there is something inside worth stealing.

- Some call the occupants from a pay phone; if the phone is still ringing when they arrive, they know no one is home.

- After entering a residence, their anxiety turns to calm as they first turn to the master bedroom for money and drugs. They also search kitchens, believing that some people keep money in the mayonnaise jar!

- Most work in groups, one serving as a lookout while the other(s) ransack the place.

- Some dispose of goods through a professional fence; others try to pawn the goods, exchange the goods for drugs, or sell them to friends and relatives. A few keep the stolen items for themselves, especially guns and jewellery.

Source: Richard Wright and Scott Decker, *Burglars on the Job: Streetlife and Residential Break-ins* (Boston: Northeastern University Press, 1994). Manne Laukkanen, Pekka Santtila, Patrick Jern and Kenneth Sandnabba, "Predicting offender home location in urban burglary series," *Forensic Science International* Volume 176, Issues 2–3, 7 April 2008, Pages 224–235.

- The lack of protective measures and the absence of nosy neighbours, which made the first burglary a success, have probably not changed.

- Goods have been observed that could not be taken out the first time.[60]

Careers in Break and Enter

Some criminals make break and enter their career and continually develop new specialized skills. Neal Shover has studied the careers of professional burglars and uncovered the existence of a particularly successful type—the "good burglar."[61] Characteristics of the good burglar include technical competence, personal integrity, specialization in burglary, financial success, and the ability to avoid prison sentences. Shover found that to receive recognition as good burglars, novices must develop four key requirements of the trade:

1. *They must learn the many skills needed to commit lucrative break and enters.* These skills may include gaining entry into homes and apartments; selecting targets with high potential payoffs; choosing items with a high resale value; opening safes properly without damaging their contents; and using the proper equipment, including cutting torches, electric saws, explosives, and metal bars.

2. *The good burglar must be able to team up to form a criminal gang.* Choosing trustworthy companions is essential if the obstacles to completing a successful job— police, alarms, secure safes—are to be overcome.

3. *The good burglar must have inside information.* Without knowledge of what awaits them inside, burglars can spend a tremendous amount of time and effort on empty safes and jewellery boxes.

4. *The good burglar must cultivate fences or buyers for stolen wares.* Once the burglar gains access to people who buy and sell stolen goods, he or she must also learn how to successfully sell these goods for a reasonable profit.

According to Shover, a person becomes a good burglar by learning the techniques of the trade from older, more experienced burglars. During this process, the older burglar teaches the novice how to handle requirements of the trade such as dealing with defence lawyers, bail bond agents, and other agents of the justice system. Apprentices must be known to have the appropriate character before they are accepted for training. Usually the opportunity to learn burglary comes as a reward for being a highly respected juvenile gang member; from knowing someone in the neighbourhood who has made a living at burglary; or, more often, from having built a reputation for being solid while serving time in prison. Consequently, the opportunity to become a good burglar is not open to everyone.

The "good burglar" concept is supported by the interviews Paul Cromwell, James Olson, and D'Aunn Wester Avary conducted with 30 active burglars in Texas. They found that burglars go through stages of career development, beginning as young novices who learn the trade from older, more experienced burglars, frequently siblings or relatives. Novices continue to get this tutoring as long as they can develop their own markets (fences) for stolen goods. After their education is over, novices enter the journeyman stage, characterized by forays in search of lucrative targets and by careful planning. At this point they develop reputations as experienced, reliable criminals. They become professional burglars when they have developed advanced skills and organizational abilities that give them the highest esteem among their peers.[62] Cromwell, Olson, and Avary also found that many

CAREER CONNECTIONS

Glenn T. Gibson is CEO of Crawford & Company Consulting (Canada). Crawford is the world's largest independent provider of insurance claims management, including property and casualty claims adjustment services and risk management. A graduate of Mohawk College (1973), Gibson began his career in the insurance industry as a frontline "road adjuster" with Fireman's Insurance Company in 1973, joining Adjuster's Canada in 1980, which was purchased by Crawford in 1998. An internationally recognized expert in arson and explosives investigation, he is an adjunct professor at the US Federal Law Enforcement Training Centre with the Bureau of Alcohol, Tobacco, Firearms and Explosives (ATF), and has published more than 180 articles on various topics related to claims adjustment, investigation, risk management, and organizational planning. Gibson is a much-in-demand speaker around the world, and has also spoken at various universities to students interested in careers in insurance investigations.

burglars had serious drug habits and that their criminal activity was, in part, aimed at supporting their substance abuse.

LO5 Arson

Arson is the intentional or reckless damage by fire or explosion to property, and includes damage to one's own property, bodily harm to another as a consequence of the arson, possession of incendiary devices, negligence, and fraudulent burning of property.

About 45 percent of those charged with arson in Canada are youth 12 to 17 years of age. Canadian Centre for Justice Statistics data show that juveniles are arrested for a greater share of this crime than any other.[63]

There are several motives for arson. Adult arsonists may be motivated by severe emotional turmoil. Some psychologists view fire starting as a function of a disturbed personality and claim that arson should be viewed as a mental health problem, not a criminal act.[64] It is alleged that arsonists often experience sexual pleasure from starting fires and then observing their destructive effects. Although some arsonists may be aroused sexually by their activities, there is little evidence that most arsonists are psychosexually motivated.[65] It is equally likely that fires are started by angry people looking for revenge against property owners or by teenagers out to vandalize property.

Juveniles, who are the most prolific fire starters, may get involved in arson for a variety of reasons as they mature. Other fires are set by professionals, who engage in arson for profit. People looking to collect insurance money, but who are afraid or unable to set the fires themselves, hire professional arsonists who know how to set fires yet make the cause seem accidental (such as an electrical short). Another form is arson fraud, which involves a business owner burning his or her property, or hiring someone to do it, to escape financial problems.[66] Over the years, investigators have found that businesspeople are willing to become involved in arson to collect fire insurance or for various other reasons, such as

- Obtaining money during a period of financial crisis
- Getting rid of outdated or slow-moving inventory
- Destroying outmoded machines and technology
- Paying off legal and illegal debts
- Relocating or remodelling a business—for example, a theme restaurant that has not been accepted by customers

arson
The intentional or reckless damage by fire or explosion to property.

- Taking advantage of government funds available for redevelopment
- Applying for government-funded energy conservation or retrofitting construction grants, pocketing the money without making any repairs, and then claiming that fire destroyed the "rehabilitated" building
- Planning bankruptcies to eliminate debts after the merchandise supposedly destroyed was secretly sold before the fire
- Eliminating business competition by burning out rivals
- Employing extortion schemes that demand that victims pay up or the rest of their holdings will be burned
- Solving labour–management problems (this type of arson may be committed by a disgruntled employee)
- Concealing another crime, such as embezzlement

During the past decade, a variety of programs across Canada have been established to address the growing concern about juvenile fire setting. Housed

© Oleksiy Maksymenko/Alamy

About 45 percent of those charged with arson in Canada are youth 12 to 17 years of age. Canadian Centre for Justice Statistics data show that juveniles are arrested for a greater share of this crime than any other.

primarily within the fire service, these programs are designed to identify, evaluate, and treat juvenile fire setters to prevent the recurrence of fire-setting behaviours.

Summary

Economic crimes are designed to financially reward the offender. Opportunistic amateurs commit the majority of economic crimes. However, economic crime has also attracted professional criminals. Professionals earn most of their income from crime, view themselves as criminals, and possess skills that aid them in their law-breaking behaviour. A good example of the professional criminal is the fence who buys and sells stolen merchandise.

Common theft-type offences include theft, fraud, and embezzlement (breach of trust). These are common-law crimes, defined by English judges, to meet social needs. Theft involves taking the legal possession of another. The crime of false pretences is similar to theft in that it involves the theft of goods or money; it differs in that the criminal makes a false claim or statement to get victims to voluntarily give up their money or possessions. Embezzlement (breach of trust) involves people taking something that was temporarily entrusted to them, such as bank tellers taking money out of the cash drawer and keeping it for themselves. These common-law crimes have been codified into legal codes.

Shoplifting is a common form of theft involving the taking of goods from retail stores. Usually shoplifters try to snatch goods—such as jewellery, clothes, CDs, and appliances—when store personnel are otherwise occupied and hide the goods on their bodies. Retail stores are now initiating a number of strategies designed to reduce or eliminate shoplifting. Target removal strategies involve displaying dummy or disabled goods while the real merchandise is locked up. Target hardening strategies involve locking goods into place or having them monitored by electronic systems.

The Internet has become a significant factor in the commission of property crimes, including theft (e.g., identity theft) and fraud (e.g., credit card fraud).

Break and enter, a serious theft offence, was defined in common law as the "breaking and entering of a dwelling house of another in the nighttime with the intent to commit a felony within." This definition has evolved over time; today, break and enter includes theft from any structure, at any time of the day. Because break and enter involves planning and risk, it attracts professional thieves. The most competent have technical competence, specialize in burglary, are financially successful, and avoid prison sentences.

Arson is another serious property crime. Although many arsonists are teenage vandals, there are professional arsonists who specialize in burning commercial buildings for profit.

Discussion Questions

1. Differentiate between an occasional and professional criminal. Which one would be more likely to resort to violence?

2. What crime occurs when a person who owns an antique store sells a client an "original" Tiffany lamp that he or she knows is a fake? Would it still be a crime if the seller was not aware that the lamp was a copy? Should antique dealers have a duty to determine the authenticity of the products they sell?

3. What is the difference between a booster and a snitch? If caught, should each receive different punishments? What about naïve and systematic cheque forgers?

4. What are the characteristics of the "good burglar"? Can you compare them to any other professionals?

READY TO STUDY?

IN THE BOOK, YOU CAN:

✔ Check your understanding of what you've just read by reading the Summary at the end of each chapter.

✔ Rip out the Chapter in Review card at the back of the book to have the key terms and Learning Objectives handy, and complete the quizzes provided (answers are at the bottom of the back page!).

ONLINE YOU CAN:

✔ Stay organized and efficient with MindTap—a single destination with all the course material and study aids you need to succeed. Built-in apps leverage social media and the latest learning technology. For example:

✔ ReadSpeaker will read the text to you.

✔ Flashcards are pre-populated to provide you with a jump start for review—or you can create your own.

✔ You can highlight text and make notes in your MindTap Reader. Your notes will flow into Evernote, the electronic notebook app that you can access anywhere when it's time to study for the exam.

✔ Prepare for tests with quizzes.

Go to www.nelson.com/student to access these digital resources.

White-Collar Crime and Organized Crime

Learning Objectives

LO1 Differentiate between white-collar crime and organized crime and demonstrate how they are similar and how they are different.

LO2 Identify the various types of white-collar crime.

LO3 Describe some of the law enforcement strategies that government is using to combat white-collar crime.

LO4 Describe major characteristics of organized crime and the groups involved in this criminal activity.

LO5 Interpret the debate about what is organized about organized crime.

LO1 Introduction

To say that 26-year-old Montrealer John Babikian has a taste for the good life would be considered by many to be a gross understatement. His U.S. assets that have been frozen include two houses, one in Los Angeles estimated at $2.2 million, and farm land property in Oregon. He also owns shares in a private airplane, and a luxury car collection that includes a million-dollar Bugatti Veyron sports car capable of accelerating from zero to 96.6 km/h in 2.5 seconds, a Lamborghini and a Bentley.[1]

According to allegations by Canadian and American authorities, Babikian was involved in what is known in the stock promotion field as "pumping and dumping," a term given to a stock promoter who aggressively hypes a company. In effect, the promoter is conning investors into thinking a mediocre stock is actually a superstar moneymaker. Typically, investors are unaware that the promoter secretly owns shares in the company and when the price of the stock rises, the promoter sells his shares leaving the stock to plummet in value. Babikian was behind two stock promotion websites— AwesomePennyStocks.com and PennyStocksUniverse.com. He used these websites to send out 700 000 emails to potential investors hyping an obscure mining company known as America West. The electronic promotion triggered a trading frenzy. Babikian, who owned 1.4 million worth of shares in the company, sold them within 90 minutes pocketing $1.9 million in profit. Of course, he failed to disclose to investors that not only was he behind the stock promotion companies but also that he owned a sizable number of shares in the company. Babikian fled Canada in 2012 and his current whereabouts are unknown; however, it is believed that he possesses passports from Guatemala, Lebanon and Nevis. He was last reported to be in Monaco.[2]

A PricewaterhouseCoopers survey reported that a third of Canadian organizations acknowledged that they have been victims of white-collar crime.[3] Although cases like that of Babikian attract considerable media attention, investment fraud has also had a wide-ranging impact on average Canadians. Unfortunately, not only do these cases not make national news, but also few victims of smaller securities fraud cases will ever get the help they deserve. Victims and advocates have complained that the reason is because Canada remains soft on white collar crime.[4] They note that although laws and regulations governing white-collar criminals have been strengthened in recent years, smaller securities fraud cases often do not lead to criminal charges and jail sentences.[5]

white-collar crime
Illegal acts that may include theft, embezzlement, fraud, market manipulation, restraint of trade, and false advertising; also known as commercial/business crime or economic offences.

organized crime
Illegal activities of people and organizations whose acknowledged purpose is profit through illegitimate business enterprise.

enterprise
Taking risks for profit in the marketplace.

DID YOU KNOW?

- White-collar crime involves the illegal distribution of legal material.
- Organized crime involves the illegal distribution of illegal material.
- White-collar and organized crime are linked together because they involve entrepreneurship.
- The definition of white-collar crime has expanded to include all forms of corrupt business practices by individuals as well as corporations.
- Losses from white-collar crime may far outstrip any other type of crime.

Typically, business-related crimes involve efforts to bend the rules of enterprise and commerce in order to make a profit or gain an illegal advantage over competitors. In this chapter, we divide these crimes of illicit entrepreneurship into two distinct categories: white-collar crime and organized crime. White-collar crime involves illegal activities of people and institutions whose acknowledged purpose is profit through legitimate business transactions. Organized crime involves illegal activities of people and organizations whose acknowledged purpose is profit through illegitimate business enterprise. Organized crime and white-collar crime are linked here because enterprise, the goal of making money through criminal means, is the governing characteristic of both phenomena.[6]

According to criminologist Dwight Smith, business enterprise can be viewed as flowing through a spectrum of acts ranging from the most "saintly" to the most "sinful."[7] Although "sinful" organizational practices may be desirable to many consumers (such as the sale of narcotics) or an efficient way of doing business (such as the dumping of hazardous wastes), society has regulated or outlawed these behaviours. Organized crime and business crimes are the results of a process by which "political, value-based constraints are based on economic activity."[8]

White-collar crime and organized crime share some striking similarities. Mark Haller has coined the phrase "illegal enterprise crimes" to signify the sale of illegal goods and services to customers who know they are illegal. Haller's analysis also shows the overlap between criminal and business enterprise. For example, he compares the Mafia crime family to a chamber of commerce, as an association of businesspeople who join to further their business careers. Joining a crime syndicate allows one to cultivate contacts and be in a position to take advantage of good deals offered by more experienced players. The criminal group settles disputes between members, who, after all, cannot take their problems to court.[9]

Both organized crime and white-collar crime taint and corrupt the free market system; they involve all phases of illegal entrepreneurial activity. Organized crime involves individuals or groups whose marketing techniques (threat, extortion, smuggling) and product lines (drugs, prostitution, gambling, loan-sharking) have been outlawed. White-collar crimes include the use of illegal business practices (theft, embezzlement, price-fixing, bribery) to merchandise what are ordinarily legitimate commercial products.

Surprisingly to some, both forms of crime can involve violence. Although the use of force and coercion by organized crime members has been popularized in the media and therefore comes as no shock, that white-collar crimes may inflict pain and suffering seems more astonishing. Yet experts claim that the number of occupational deaths that occur each year is on the rise and that "corporate violence" annually kills and injures more people than all street crimes combined.[10]

It is also possible to link organized crime and white-collar crime because some criminal enterprises involve both forms of activity. Organized criminals may seek legitimate enterprises to launder money, diversify their source of income, increase their power and influence, and gain and enhance respectability.[11] Otherwise legitimate businesspeople may turn to organized criminals to help them with economic problems (such as breaking up a strike or dumping hazardous waste products), stifle or threaten competition, and increase their influence. The distinction between organized crime and white-collar criminals may often become blurred.[12]

Some forms of white-collar crime may be more like organized crime than others.[13] Although some corporate executives cheat to improve their company's position in the business world, others are motivated purely for personal gain. It is this latter group, people who engage in ongoing criminal conspiracies

for their own profit, that most resembles organized crime.[14]

LO2 White-Collar Crime

In the late 1930s, distinguished criminologist Edwin Sutherland first used the phrase "white-collar crime" to describe the criminal activities of the rich and powerful. He defined white-collar crime as "a crime committed by a person of respectability and high social status in the course of his occupation."[15] As Sutherland saw it, white-collar crime involved conspiracies by members of the wealthy classes to use their position in commerce and industry for personal gain without regard to the law. Often these actions were handled by civil courts, because injured parties were more concerned with recovering their losses than seeing the offenders punished criminally. Yet the cost of white-collar crime is probably several times greater than all the crimes that are customarily regarded as the "crime problem." And, in contrast to street crimes, white-collar offences breed distrust in economic and social institutions, lowering public morale and undermining faith in business and government.[16]

Although Sutherland's work is considered a milestone in criminological history, his focus was on corporate criminality, including the crimes of the rich and powerful. Contemporary definitions of white-collar crime are typically much broader, including

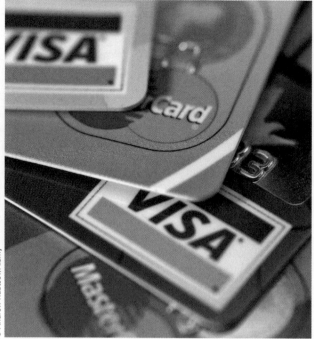

Double-charging customers for a purchase they have made with their credit card is a common credit card scam. It is up to credit card holders to check their statements to make sure they are accurate.

both middle-income earners and corporate executives who use the marketplace for their criminal activity.[17] Included within recent views of white-collar crime are middle-class acts such as income tax evasion, credit card fraud, and mortgage fraud. Other white-collar criminals use their positions of trust in business or government to commit crimes. Their activities might include pilfering, soliciting bribes or kickbacks, and embezzlement. Some white-collar criminals set up business for the sole purpose of victimizing the general public.

In addition to acting as individuals, some white-collar criminals become involved in criminal conspiracies designed to improve the market share or profitability of their corporations. This type of white-collar crime, which includes antitrust violations, price-fixing, and false advertising, is known as corporate crime.[18]

It is difficult to estimate the extent and influence of white-collar crime on victims because all too often those who suffer the consequences of white-collar crime are ignored by victimologists.[19] According to the PricewaterhouseCoopers' 2009 Global Economic Crime Survey, which was based on over 3000 respondents from 54 countries, 30 percent of

corporate crime
A legal offence, such as price-fixing, restraint of trade, or hazardous waste dumping, committed by a corporate entity to improve its market share or profitability.

companies worldwide reported being a victim of an economic crime in the previous 12 months. More than 50 percent of Canadian companies were victims of economic crime, and in more than half of cases the losses were reported to be in excess of $500 000.[20] According to a 2012 survey by the British Columbia Securities Commission, 17 percent of Canadians over 50 believe they have already been the victim of an investment fraud and almost 30 percent of active investors have the same belief.[21]

Beyond their monetary cost, white-collar crimes often damage property and kill people. Violations of safety standards, pollution of the environment, and industrial accidents due to negligence can be classified as corporate violence. White-collar crime also destroys confidence, saps the integrity of commercial life, and has the potential for devastating destruction. Think of the possible results if nuclear regulatory rules are flouted or if toxic wastes are dumped into a community's drinking water supply.[22]

Nor is white-collar crime a uniquely Western phenomenon. It occurs in other parts of the world as well, often in the form of corruption by government agents. In China, corruption by public officials accounts for a high percentage of all cases of economic crime, despite the fact that the penalty for corruption is death.[23] China is not alone in experiencing organizational crimes. In Thailand, crime and corruption are skyrocketing; top executives of the Bangkok Bank of Commerce are believed to have

"In a further effort to increase profits, control costs and satisfy shareholders, we've decided to steal stuff."

absconded with billions of dollars worth of depositors' money.[24] Western companies are also the targets of white-collar criminals. Agents have been inserted into North American companies abroad to steal trade secrets and confidential procedures, including intellectual property such as computer programs and technology. The cost is somewhere between a conservative US$50 billion and an astounding US$240 billion a year.[25]

Types of White-Collar Crime

White-collar crimes today represent a range of behaviours involving individuals acting alone and within the context of a business structure. The victims of white-collar crime can be the general public, the organization that employs the offender, or a competing organization. Numerous attempts have been made to create subcategories or typologies of white-collar criminality.[26]

This text adopts a typology created by criminologist Mark Moore to organize the analysis of white-collar crime.[27] Moore's typology contains seven elements, ranging from an individual's using a business enterprise to commit theft-related crimes, to an individual's using his or her place within a business enterprise for illegal gain, to business enterprises collectively engaging in illegitimate activity. Because no single typology of white-collar crime may sufficiently encompass the complex array of acts that the term usually denotes, Moore's typology has been expanded to include newly emerging high-tech crimes such as Internet fraud (see Figure 12.1).[28]

Stings and Swindles

The first category of white-collar crime involves stealing through deception by individuals who use their institutional or business position to bilk people out of their money. Although the terms *swindles* and *stings* can be used interchangeably, the former generally means to defraud a person through some scheme or plan while the latter is to deliberately set up a situation to entice someone to take part with a view to swindle them. Offences in this category range from selling faulty merchandise over the Internet to passing millions of dollars in counterfeit stock certificates to an established brokerage firm. If caught, white-collar swindlers are usually charged with theft or fraud.

Another case involves Albert Walker, a small-town Ontario businessman who specialized in financial services. Walker, his wife, and their four children were regular churchgoers and respected members of their community. Partly because of his solid standing in the community, Walker gained the trust of many in his congregation, including seniors, and convinced them to invest heavily in his company. In 1990, his congregation was stunned after it was revealed that both Walker and his daughter Sheena mysteriously disappeared while on a trip to London, England, along with much of his clients' money. Subsequent investigations revealed that Walker had deposited millions in various European banks.

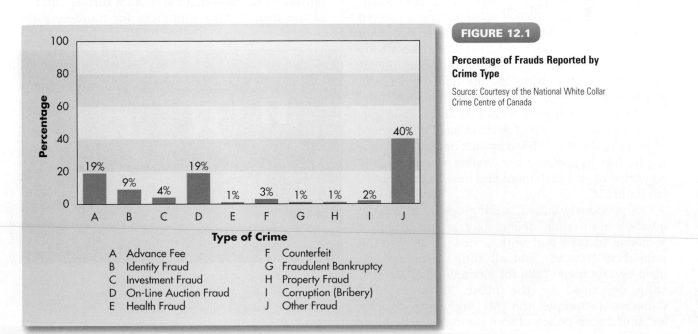

FIGURE 12.1

Percentage of Frauds Reported by Crime Type

Source: Courtesy of the National White Collar Crime Centre of Canada

WARNING: EXPOSING THE TRUTH MAY BE HAZARDOUS

AL PACINO RUSSELL CROWE

"TOTALLY ENGROSSING, EXCITING & EMOTIONALLY POWERFUL"

© AF archive/Alamy Stock Photo

The movie *The Insider* (1999) is roughly based on the real-life events surrounding obscure scientist Jeffrey Wigand, the man who blew the whistle on the tobacco industry. Although the emphasis of the movie is on painting a damning picture of corporate-media culture, it also reveals how the tobacco industry was able to manipulate the evidence pertaining to the harmful effects of smoking. Wigand was intent on revealing the deception by participating in a segment of the popular TV show *60 Minutes*; however, it turned into a nightmare when the show was edited down to little more than a sound bite because the station's then-owner was also the head of a tobacco company. After much pressure, the segment eventually aired in its entirety three months later and only after Wigand and his family had already lost everything and the full story had appeared in the newspapers.

For years the tobacco industry had been hiding the harmful effects of smoking while at the same time engaging in efforts to increase the nicotine content of tobacco to ensure people remained addicted to the product. How was the tobacco industry able to continue to deceive the public for such a long time? Given the size of the industry, why was Wigand the only one to attempt to expose the wrongdoing of the companies? Is the film a good example of what happens to people who work in companies whose cultural values stress profit over fail play? Does the "corporate culture view" of white collar crime accurately explain the actions of tobacco companies?

In an attempt to change their identities, Walker befriended Englishman Ronald Platt, who had a keen interest in visiting Canada. He convinced Platt to give him his birth certificate and driver's licence in exchange for a plane ticket to Canada. With new identities, Walker and his daughter, the new "Mrs. Platt," moved to southeast England, where they lived for the next six years and where Sheena had two children.

Unfortunately, Platt decided to return to England and look up his old friend, Albert Walker. The investigation revealed that Walker subsequently murdered Platt and dumped his weighted, battered body into the sea. Shortly afterward, fishermen pulled a body out of the water that was identified as that of Platt through a serial number on the Rolex watch still strapped to his wrist. When apprehended by police, Walker and his daughter were planning a quick getaway with over £67 000 of gold bullion. In the bizarre aftermath, Sheena testified against her father, claiming he had hypnotized her. Walker was eventually convicted of embezzlement and murder and sent to jail for life.[29]

As previously stated, a sting operation usually involves a situation deliberately set up to entice someone to take part with a view to deceive the individual. However, not all sting operations are used by criminals. Take for example, the "Mr. Big" sting developed by the RCMP. Known as the Canadian technique, the "Mr. Big" sting involves an undercover police officer posing as a member of a fictitious gang. A personal relationship is built between the undercover agent and the suspect, who is invited to become a member of the gang. But first the suspect must participate in criminal activities that have been faked by police. Eventually, the suspect is introduced to the gang leader, Mr. Big, who explains that in order to join the gang the suspect must confess to a previous crime. The sting was revealed in 2005 after the shooting deaths of four officers in Edmonton, Alberta. As it turned out, two of the men serving sentences for murdering the

REUTERS/Andy Clark

Memorial service held in Edmonton, Alberta, in 2005 for four RCMP officers slain by men who had previously made confessions to undercover officers involved in a "Mr. Big" sting.

officers had previously made confessions to Mr. Big operatives. While the controversial technique has resulted in hundreds of convictions, in 2012 the Supreme Court of Canada argued that it can entail "powerful inducements" and "veiled threats," and therefore requires monitoring to ensure that it is not used inappropriately.[30]

Chiselling

Chiselling, the second category of white-collar crime, involves regularly cheating an organization, its customers, or both. Chisellers may be individuals looking to make quick profits in their own businesses or employees of large organizations who decide to cheat on obligations to their own company or its clients by doing something contrary to either the law or company policy.

Chiselling may involve charging for bogus auto repairs, cheating customers on home repairs, or short-weighting (intentionally tampering with the accuracy of scales used to weigh products) in supermarkets or dairies. Chiselling may even involve illegal use of information about company policies that have not been disclosed to the public. The secret information can be sold to speculators or used to make money in the stock market. Use of the information violates the obligation to keep company policy secret.

Professional Chiselling

It is not uncommon for professionals to use their positions to chisel clients. Pharmacists have been known to alter prescriptions or substitute low-cost generic drugs for more expensive name brands. One study found that pharmacists who were business oriented—those who stressed merchandising, inventory turnover, and the pursuit of profit at the expense of professional ethics—were the ones most inclined to chisel customers.[31]

The legal profession has also come under fire because of the unscrupulous behaviour of some of its members. Many people believed that Toronto lawyer Alan Eagleson, executive director of the NHL Players' Association from 1967 to 1990, had done more for the game of hockey and hockey players than anyone else. He had helped Bobby Orr and other big-name players obtain lucrative contracts. He organized the famous 1972 Canada Cup series that many believe represented a defining moment in Canadian history and nationalism. Truly, Eagleson was one of the most prominent lawyers in Canada. That was until the 1990s, when he was charged with racketeering and defrauding the NHL Players' Association. Eventually, Eagleson pleaded guilty to fraud and served six months of an 18-month sentence. To add to his

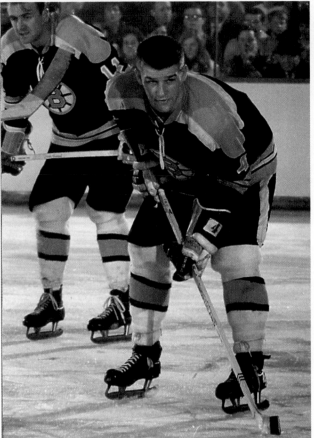

Some of the greatest names in hockey including Bobby Orr (pictured) were clients of Alan Eagleson, executive director of the NHL Players' Association, who had helped organize the famous 1972 Canada Cup series. Eagleson received an 18-month sentence for defrauding the NHL Players' Association.

woes, he was fined $1 million, disbarred, forced to resign from the Hockey Hall of Fame, and stripped of his Order of Canada.[32]

Investment and Securities Fraud

A great deal of chiselling takes place on the commodity and stock markets, where individuals engage in deceptive practices that are prohibited by law. Securities fraud, also known as stock fraud and investment fraud, involves deceiving investors with false information about stocks or commodities intended to induce the investors into making purchases or sales that frequently result in investor losses. Some brokers will use their positions to cheat individual clients, for example, by churning the client's account through repeated, excessive,

> **chiselling**
> Regularly cheating an organization, its customers, or both.
>
> **churning**
> A form of stockbroker chiselling involving repeated, excessive, and unnecessary buying and selling of stock.

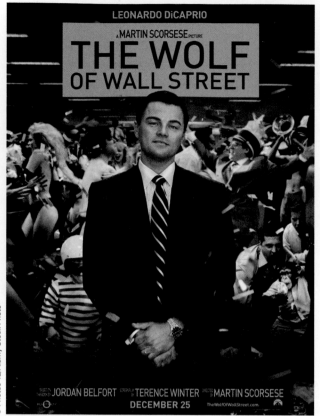

In the movie *The Wolf of Wall Street,* Leonardo DiCaprio portrayed Jordan Belfort, a 1990s penny stock broker, who went to prison on charges of fraud and stock market manipulation for orchestrating a massive "pump and dump" scheme. The real-life Belfort has since been released from jail and continues to be active on the speaking and seminar circuit while attempting to pay down the US$110 million fine he received from the U.S. government after being indicted in 1998 for securities fraud.

front running
A form of stockbroker chiselling in which brokers place personal orders ahead of a large customer's order to profit from the market effects of the trade.

bucketing
A form of stockbroker chiselling in which brokers skim customer trading profits by falsifying trade information.

insider trading
Buying and selling securities based on business information derived from a position of trust and not available to the general public.

and unnecessary buying and selling of stock.[33] Other broker fraud includes front running, in which brokers place personal orders ahead of a large customer's order to profit from the market effects of the trade, and bucketing, which is skimming customer trading profits by falsifying trade information.[34]

Securities chiselling can also involve using one's position of trust to profit from inside business information, referred to as insider trading. The information can then be used to buy and sell securities, giving the trader an

unfair advantage over the general public, which lacks this inside information. A good example of insider trading was provided by Canadian lawyer Stanko J. Grmovsek, who made an estimated US$9 million over 14 years based on illegal insider tips. After a joint investigation by the Ontario Securities Commission, the U.S. Securities and Exchange Commission, and the RCMP Integrated Market Enforcement Team, Grmovsek and his accomplice Gil Cornblum were charged with insider trading. The two had met and began trading in stocks while still in law school, by investing their student loans in the stock market. While working at various law firms, first as an articling student then lawyer, Cornblum covertly gained access to his company's computer database, and during off-hours he searched photocopy rooms, fax machines, and other employee's files to obtain information about pending corporate transactions. Then, using pay phones and calling cards, he would transmit the information to Grmovsek. While Grmovsek received a sentence of 39 months and was disbarred, Cornblum committed suicide. Referring to his illegal actions, Grmovsek, told the judge that it was "the worst decision in my life."[35]

Traders and even company executives can use insider information about what will happen to a company to buy or sell stock shares, and make huge profits. The big losers are honest citizens who can lose thousands of dollars.

Insider trading violations can occur in a variety of situations. In its most basic form, it is illegal for corporate employees with direct knowledge of market-sensitive information to use that information for their own benefit—for example, by buying stock in a company that they learn will be taken over by the larger organization for which they work. In recent years, the definition of insider trading has been expanded to include employees of financial institutions, such as law or banking firms, who misappropriate confidential information on pending corporate actions to purchase stock or give the information to a third party so that party may buy shares in the company. Courts have ruled that such actions are deceptive and violate security trading codes.

One interesting Canadian case concerns Bre-X, a small Calgary mining company. The company's investors were made overnight millionaires as the stock skyrocketed from pennies in 1994 to $240 in less than a year. Bre-X had reportedly discovered one of the world's largest deposits of gold in Indonesia. But all was not as it appeared. After further tests, it was reported that the original core samples had been "salted" in order to increase the gold content. Shortly thereafter, the geologist employed by Bre-X, Michael de Guzman, died after jumping from a helicopter, in what many believe was a suicide. Trading in the company's stock on the Toronto Stock Exchange came to a halt, and the price of the stock dropped from $15.80 to $2.50. An estimated 40 000 investors in Canada lost over $3 billion.[36] In 2014, after 17 years in which victims of the massive fraud attempted to obtain restitution, the Bre-X saga came to an anticlimactic ending when an Ontario judge dismissed the last lawsuits against Bre-X Minerals Ltd. Though investors lost hundreds of millions of dollars and despite investigations by police and regulators in Canada and the United States, those behind the swindle were never caught. According to one Toronto lawyer, "This was one of the great frauds perpetrated in North America," "And nobody was convicted of it, and nobody paid any money."[37]

Investor confidence was seriously undermined by such well-publicized scandals as that involving Bre-X in Canada, and Enron, WorldCom, and ImClone in the United States. The Canadian government responded to these scandals when Bill C-13 was passed in 2004, establishing the criminal offences of insider trading, tipping, and whistleblowing retaliation. Maximum sentences for corporate criminal offences were increased and judges were given the discretion to impose harsher penalties in cases where there were aggravating factors, such as where a crime had eroded the confidence of the public. Integrated market enforcement teams (comprising RCMP investigators, lawyers, and forensic accountants) were also established to respond quickly to major capital markets fraud and other market-related crimes.

Individual Exploitation of Institutional Position

Another type of white-collar crime involves individuals' exploiting their power or position in an organization by extorting money from people who do business with that organization by threatening to withhold services that the victim has a clear right to expect. For example, a fire inspector who threatens to cause trouble or find phantom fire code violations unless a business owner pays him is abusing his institutional position. Here the victim is the person who is being extorted.

Influence Peddling and Bribery

Sometimes individuals holding important institutional positions will sell power, influence, and information to outsiders who hold no legitimate interest in the institution or who hope to gain a favourable position by influencing the activities of the institution. Offences within this category include government employees' taking of kickbacks from contractors in return for awarding them contracts they could not have won on merit or outsiders' bribing of government officials who might sell information about future government activities.

One major difference distinguishes influence peddling from the previously discussed exploitation of an institutional position. Exploitation involves forcing victims to pay for services to which they have a clear right. In contrast, influence peddlers and bribe takers use their institutional positions to grant favours and sell information to which their coconspirators are not entitled. In sum, in crimes of institutional exploitation, the victim is the person forced to pay for services he or she deserves, whereas the victim of influence peddling is the organization compromised by its employees for their own interests.

Influence Peddling in Government

In March 2011, Prime Minister Stephen Harper called in the RCMP to investigate one of his own former top advisers, Bruce Carson, for allegedly promising privileged access to Conservative government ministers in return for money. The Aboriginal Peoples Television Network (APTN) first uncovered the alleged influence peddling when investigating complaints that Carson had used his connections in the Conservative government to illegally lobby Indian Affairs Minister John Duncan on behalf of a company seeking to sell water filtration systems to remote First Nations communities. APTN claimed to have in its possession an email written to the water filtration company in which Carson boasted about having insider knowledge that Duncan was about to be appointed Minister of Indian Affairs, his insider connections

CHAPTER 12 White-Collar Crime and Organized Crime **275**

to the newly appointed minister, and that he would be "calling the new Minister this morning—so it is full steam ahead." Carson responded to the allegations and the RCMP investigation by announcing that he was taking a leave of absence from his professional activities with the government, effective immediately. Carson, a long-time Conservative party insider, had been disbarred in the 1980s for defrauding his clients.[38] He was subsequently charged with influence peddling and the case is ongoing. Critics have pointed out that this was the first time in living memory than an adviser to a prime minister has been charged with influence-peddling.[39]

Corruption in the Criminal Justice System

Agents of the criminal justice system have also been involved in official corruption, a circumstance that is particularly disturbing because society expects a higher standard of moral integrity from people empowered to uphold the law and judge their fellow citizens. Police officers have been particularly vulnerable to charges of corruption.

One of the largest police corruption investigations in Canadian history was sparked by a 2003 RCMP wiretap in a Toronto bar, where names of Toronto police officers were overheard in connection to loans and organized crime. A special RCMP-led task force was established to investigate organized crime and the Toronto Police Force. The investigation identified three major areas of concern: (1) the Toronto drug squad was accused of physically assaulting informants, stealing from drug dealers, falsifying documents, and conducting illegal searches; (2) the 52 Division plainclothes unit was alleged to have been engaged in a protection racket with bar owners in the entertainment area of the city; and (3) there were allegations over an inappropriate relationship between some officers and a car-leasing salesman who reportedly had connections with organized crime.[40]

After three years of investigation and a cost of millions of dollars, over 20 Toronto officers were charged with 135 criminal and *Police Services Act* charges. Then–Toronto Police Chief Julian Fantino stated, "I will not tolerate any unprofessional behaviour, corrupt practices, compromises to the moral and ethical code of conduct demanded of the policing profession, abuses of power and authority, racial intolerance or discriminating conduct on or off the job."[41] Later, other allegations were made against a second police narcotics squad by Milos Markovic, a suspected drug dealer, who claimed that officers had stolen money from his safety deposit boxes during an investigation. Markovic's lawyer, Julian Falconer, alleged that Toronto police chose to ignore his client's

Toronto Mayor Rob Ford admitted to Toronto reporters on 5 November 2013 that he has smoked crack cocaine.

claims in their investigation in an attempt to mask the full extent of the corruption.[42]

Corruption in Government

As one of many newspaper headlines declared in 2013, "The scandals keep on coming" referring to the actions of the mayors of some of Canada's largest cities.[43] Toronto mayor Rob Ford had been involved in several conflict-of-interest complaints but his actions caught on video made him a household name on the U.S. talk show circuit.[44] Ford could be seen on video smoking crack cocaine and, after initially denying his drug use, he finally admitted using crack "probably in one of my drunken stupors."[45] Refusing to step down as mayor, it was not until the following year when a second video emerged again showing the him smoking crack that he took a leave of absence to enter drug rehabilitation.[46] The photos placed Ford in the company of one person who had been murdered and others who had been swept up in a massive police raid that resulted in charges of murder, murder, attempted murder, and operating a sophisticated gun- and drug-smuggling ring. Although Ford lost the 2014 mayoral race, he still sits on Toronto council with many loyal supporters referred to as "Ford Nation."[47] Meanwhile, in the same year, Montreal interim mayor Michael Applebaum, who took over from the previous mayor who had resigned over allegations of corruption, was himself arrested and charged with 14 counts of corruption. Including Applebaum, to date six mayors and former mayors in Quebec have faced charges of corruption, fraud or gangersterism.[48]

Influence Peddling in Business

Politicians and government officials are not the only ones accused of bribery; business has had its share of scandals. The 1970s witnessed revelations that multinational corporations regularly made payoffs to foreign officials and businesspeople to secure business contracts. Gulf Oil executives admitted paying US$4 million to the South Korean ruling party; Burroughs Corporation admitted paying US$1.5 million to foreign officials; and Lockheed Aircraft admitted paying US$202 million to Japanese politicians in return for an agreement to buy new aircraft. McDonnell–Douglas Aircraft Corporation was indicted for paying US$1 million in bribes to officials of Pakistani International Airlines to secure orders.[49]

Theft and Employee Fraud

The fifth type of white-collar crime involves individuals' use of their positions to embezzle or steal company funds or appropriate company property for themselves. Here the company or organization that employs the criminal, rather than an outsider, is the victim of white-collar crime. Employee theft can reach all levels of the organizational structure.

Blue-collar employees have been involved in systematic theft of company property, commonly called pilferage.[50] Employee theft is most accurately explained by factors relevant to the work setting, such as job dissatisfaction and the workers' belief that they are being exploited by employers or supervisors; economic problems play a relatively small role in the decision to pilfer. Although employers attribute employee fraud to economic conditions and declining personal values, workers themselves say they steal because of strain and conflict. It is difficult to determine the value of goods taken by employees, but it has been estimated that pilferage accounts for 30 to 75 percent of all shrinkage.[51]

> **pilferage**
> Employee theft of company property.

Blue-collar workers are not the only employees who commit corporate theft. Management-level fraud is also quite common. Such acts include (1) converting company assets for personal benefit; (2) fraudulently receiving increases in compensation (such as raises or bonuses); (3) fraudulently increasing personal holdings of company stock; (4) retaining one's present position within the company by manipulating accounts to show success; and (5) concealing unacceptable performance from stockholders.[52]

Client Fraud

A sixth component of white-collar crime is theft from an organization that advances credit to its clients or reimburses them for services rendered. These offences are linked because they involve cheating an organization (such as a government agency or insurance company) with many individual clients that the organization supports financially (such as welfare clients), reimburses for services provided (such as health-care providers), covers losses of (such as insurance policyholders), or extends credit to (such as bank clients or taxpayers). Included in this category are insurance fraud, credit card fraud, fraud related to the health-care system, and tax evasion.

Health Care Fraud

According to the National Health Care Anti-Fraud Association, "health care fraud is an intentional deception or misrepresentation that the individual or entity makes knowing that the misrepresentation could result in some unauthorized benefit to the individual, or the entity or to some other party."[53] Ten common types of health care fraud are

1. Billing for services not rendered
2. Billing for a non-covered service as a covered service
3. Misrepresenting dates of service
4. Misrepresenting locations of service
5. Misrepresenting provider of service
6. Waiving of deductibles and/or co-payments
7. Incorrect reporting of diagnoses or procedures (includes unbundling)
8. Overutilization of services
9. Corruption (kickbacks and bribery)
10. False or unnecessary issuance of prescription drugs[54]

Between 2010 and 2013 Canadian doctors were forced to pay back nearly $25 million in improper medical insurance billings. According to the

The scandal in the Canadian Senate over inappropriate expenses has captured the media over the past few years and shows no signs of letting up. Senator Mike Duffy has been charged by the RCMP with bribery, fraud, and 29 other charges related to Senate expenses.

Canadian Health Care Anti-Fraud Association, money was sometimes inappropriately billed due to human error but there were also cases of health-care fraud. Surprisingly, although millions of dollars were recovered between 2009 and 2013, only seven doctors were charged, six from Ontario and one from Alberta. A major reason for not pursuing legal action against doctors is the costs involved in prosecution.[55]

In 1998, Ontario established a health-care fraud squad run by Ontario Provincial Police officers to crack down on fraud in relation to the Ontario Health Insurance Plan (OHIP). Since the establishment of the unit, more than 500 cases have been investigated, the majority of which involved people attempting to defraud OHIP. Some of the cases investigated by the unit have included that of 62-year-old Stephen Kai Yiu Chung of Hamilton, who posed as a

bank fraud
To obtain money or property from a financial institution by false pretences, as by forgery or misrepresentation.

physician for 15 years and allegedly defrauded OHIP of $4.5 million; Dr. Alexander Scott of Kingston, who received 30 months in a penitentiary after defrauding OHIP of $600 000; and Dr. Donald MacDiarmid of Ajax, who received an 18-month conditional sentence and was fined $100 000 for defrauding OHIP of $150 000. One of the most complex cases to date involves 12 doctors at a Mississauga walk-in clinic who were charged with defrauding OHIP of about $2 million.[57]

Bank Fraud

Bank fraud can encompass diverse schemes as such as cheque kiting, cheque forgery, false statements on loan applications, sale of stolen cheques, bank credit card fraud, unauthorized use of automated teller machines (ATMs), auto title fraud, and illegal transactions with offshore banks. To be found guilty of **bank fraud**, one must knowingly execute or attempt to execute a scheme to fraudulently obtain money or property from a financial institution. For example,

Alex Tavshunsky

In 2009, Dr. Lorne Sokol, a Toronto doctor, was found guilty of fraud and money laundering and agreed to repay $3.5 million he fraudulently billed the Ontario Health Insurance Plan (OHIP). Between March 2003 and February 2007, Sokol, a pain specialist, submitted billings for services that were never provided. In 2011, Dr. Sokol admitted professional misconduct, in that he was found guilty of an offence relevant to his suitability to practise medicine. In return, Ontario's College of Physicians and Surgeons dropped charges of conduct unbecoming a physician and disgraceful, dishonourable, or unprofessional conduct, and he was suspended for three months. He was also ordered to take a course on ethics, have his practice monitored, and pay legal costs of $3650 to the College of Physicians and Surgeons of Ontario.[56]

Edmonton Sun/Walter Tychnowicz

Bank employees who steal from their employers commit bank fraud. In 2002, Nick Lysyk of Edmonton pleaded guilty to 63 counts of fraud over $5000 in what was the largest bank fraud case to date in Canadian history. By falsifying a steady stream of loans dating back to the late 1990s, he defrauded his employer, the Bank of Montreal, out of an estimated $16 million, $10 million of which still remains unaccounted for. Lysyk used the money to bankroll a lavish lifestyle that included 40 vehicles, expensive jewellery, 17 homes, and home furnishings, not to mention a family and two girlfriends. For his crime, Lysyk was sentenced to just over seven years in prison.[58]

a car dealer would commit bank fraud by securing loans on titles to cars it no longer owned. A real estate owner would be guilty of bank fraud if he or she obtained a false appraisal on a piece of property with the intention of obtaining a bank loan in excess of the property's real worth.

In 2003, two Toronto women, Marina Kachin and Ioulia Rovenskaya, were found guilty and sentenced to 20 months in jail for their role in one of the most significant attacks on the ATM network in Canada. The investigation revealed that ten people from Vancouver to Sudbury were involved in a scam using independent ATMs set up in stores. The machines were equipped to record user card information and personal identification numbers that were later used to make counterfeit cards. Approximately $1.2 million has been recovered from funds illegally withdrawn from customers' accounts.[59] In a similar case in November 2010, Winnipeg police arrested a health centre employee for fraudulently withdrawing over $1 million over a ten-year period from an ATM at the site.[60]

Tax Evasion

Another important aspect of client fraud is tax evasion. Here the victim, the government, is cheated by one of its clients, the errant taxpayer to whom it has extended credit by allowing the taxpayer to delay paying taxes on money he or she has already earned. Tax fraud is a particularly challenging area for criminological study because (1) so many citizens regularly underreport their income, and (2) it is often difficult to separate honest error from deliberate tax evasion.[61]

The Canada Revenue Agency (CRA) regularly reviews taxes submitted by businesses and individuals. When fraudulent activity is discovered, the CRA is responsible for enforcement through its Special Investigations Section. If it is determined that reasonable and probable grounds exist, then the investigators apply for a search warrant and prepare the case for prosecution in the courts under section 239 of the *Income Tax Act*. Convictions are made public in the hope of deterring others from evading taxes and can be found on CRA website. Unfortunately, however in terms of the severity of the penalty for failing to pay taxes, Canada is again lax compared to our U.S. counterparts. Take for example, Beanie Baby creator and billionaire H. Ty Warner, 69, who was charged with tax evasion in the United States and could face up to 5 years in jail for his crime.[62]

Corporate Crime

Yet another component of white-collar crime involves situations in which powerful institutions or their representatives wilfully violate the laws that restrain these institutions from doing social harm or that require them to do social good. This is also known as corporate crime.

Corporate crimes are socially injurious acts committed by people who control companies to further their business interests. The target of their crimes can be the general public, the environment, or even their companies' workers. What makes these crimes unique is that the perpetrator is a legal fiction—a corporation—and not an individual. In reality, it is company employees or owners who commit corporate crimes and who ultimately benefit through career advancement or greater profits.

Some of the acts included within corporate crime are price-fixing and illegal restraint of trade, false advertising, and the use of company practices that violate environmental protection statutes. The variety of crimes contained within this category is great, and they cause vast damage. The following subsections examine some of the most important offences.

Illegal Restraint of Trade and Price-Fixing

A restraint of trade involves a contract or conspiracy designed to stifle competition, create a monopoly, artificially maintain prices, or otherwise interfere with free market competition.

Price-fixing is an example of restraint of trade, and it has several variations. In one variation, large companies agree among themselves to sell their product at a price below

restraint of trade
A contract or conspiracy designed to stifle competition, create a monopoly, artificially maintain prices, or otherwise interfere with free market competition.

price-fixing
A conspiracy to set and control the price of a necessary commodity.

© Kevin Horan/Corbis

Beanie Baby creator and billionaire H. Ty Warner, 69.

market value, so weaker companies are then pushed out of business. In another type of price-fixing, companies agree beforehand to submit identical inflated bids for a contract. Rotational bidding, a third variation, occurs when companies decide beforehand who will put in a low bid. Of course, the other bids are inflated, making the "low bid" not necessarily as low as it would have been if the companies had not conspired.[63]

Deceptive Pricing

Even the largest corporations commonly use deceptive pricing schemes when they respond to contract solicitations. Deceptive pricing occurs when contractors provide the government or other corporations with incomplete or misleading information on how much it will actually cost to fulfill the contracts they are bidding on or use mischarges once the contracts are signed.[64] For example, defence contractors have been prosecuted for charging the government for costs incurred on work they are doing for private firms or shifting the costs on fixed-price contracts to ones in which the government reimburses the contractor for all expenses ("cost-plus" contracts).

False Claims and Advertising

Executives in even the largest corporations sometimes face stockholders' expectations of ever-increasing company profits, which seem to demand that sales be increased at any cost. Executives sometimes respond to this challenge by making claims about their products that cannot be justified by actual performance. However, the line between clever, aggressive sales techniques and fraudulent claims is a fine one. It is traditional to show a product in its best light, even if that involves resorting to fantasy. It is not fraudulent to show a delivery service vehicle taking off into outer space or to imply that taking one sip of iced tea will make people feel they have just jumped into a swimming pool. However, it is illegal to knowingly and purposely advertise a product as possessing qualities that the manufacturer realizes it does not have.

Environmental Crimes

Much attention has been paid to intentional or negligent environmental pollution caused by many large corporations. The numerous allegations in this area involve almost every aspect of business.

There are many different types of environmental crimes. Some corporations have endangered the lives of their own workers by maintaining unsafe conditions in their plants and mines. According to one report of fatal on-the-job accidents occurring annually in Canada, more than half were the result of unsafe working conditions. It was estimated that annual workplace deaths approximate those for street homicides, without including the number of "lingering deaths." Studies conducted in Ontario indicate that over 100 000 employees were often needlessly exposed to dangerous pollutants found in the workplace.[65]

Global warming caused by the continued emission of greenhouse gases will inevitably lead to serious harmful effects on the earth's climate, not to mention social, economic and political harms to the human race. Many view the actions or inactions of major energy corporations and governments as constituting a criminal offence. Unfortunately, there are currently no laws, domestic or international, to bring such offenders to justice. There are, however, efforts underway to change this situation. British lawyer Polly Higgins proposed that "ecocide," which is defined as the extensive destruction of ecosystems should be recognized by the United Nations as an international crime in a similar category as genocide, crimes against humanity, war crimes, and crimes of aggression.

Examples of ecocide include

- Large-scale land use that causes the direct destruction of habitats—as is the case with deforestation in most tropical rainforests

- Significant pollution—for example, excess greenhouse gases from the industrial activities, and dangerous industrial activity where entire landscapes are destroyed—such as unconventional oil extraction.

If adopted by the United Nations, ecocide global warming and climate change would become not only an environmental problem, but also an international crime. By criminalizing ecocide at an international level, a global duty of care is created. Unfortunately, such efforts to criminalize ecocide may be doomed to failure given that the United Nations is dominated by carbon-dependent and carbon-profiting nations of the world.[66]

Joel Bakan's award-winning documentary film, entitled *The Corporation,* is a scathing attack on one of capitalism's most prominent institutions. The film examines the nature of the modern corporation and asks the question, "If a corporation were a person, what kind of person would it be?" The film suggests that the modern corporation has all the traits of a psychopath, because of its pathological pursuit of profit.

The Cause of White-Collar Crime

When Wall Street financial whiz Ivan Boesky pleaded guilty to one count of securities fraud, he agreed to pay a civil fine of US$100 million, the largest at that time in the history of the U.S. Securities and Exchange Commission. Boesky's fine was later surpassed by financier Michael Milken's fine of more than US$1 billion. In June 2009, Wall Street financier Bernard Madoff was sentenced by a U.S. court to 150 years in prison. Madoff was accused of running the world's biggest "Ponzi scheme," a fake investment scam that bilked his investment clients, many of them members of high society or Hollywood celebrities, out of more than $13 billion.[67] How, people asked, can people with so much disposable wealth get involved in a risky scheme to produce even more? (For other examples of scams, see Table 12.1.)

There probably are as many explanations for white-collar crime as there are white-collar crimes. Many offenders feel free to engage in business crime because they can easily rationalize its effects: they are convinced that their actions are not really crimes because the acts involved do not resemble street crimes. For example, a banker who uses his position of trust to lend his institution's assets to a company he secretly controls may see himself as a shrewd businessman, not as a criminal. Some businesspeople feel justified in committing white-collar crime because they believe that government regulators do not really understand the business world or the problems of competing in the free enterprise system. Even when caught, many white-collar criminals cannot see the error of their ways. For example, one offender convicted in a major electrical industry price-fixing conspiracy categorically denied the illegality of his actions. "We did not fix prices," he said; "I am telling you that all we did was recover costs."[68] Some white-collar criminals believe that everyone violates business laws, so it is not so bad if they do so themselves. Rationalizing greed is a common trait of white-collar criminals.

Greed is not the only motivation for white-collar crime; need also plays an important role. Executives may tamper with company books because they feel the need to keep or improve their jobs, satisfy their egos, or support their children. Blue-collar workers may pilfer because they want to keep pace with inflation or buy a new car.[69]

A well-known study of embezzlers by Donald Cressey illustrates the important role need plays in white-collar crime.[70] According to Cressey, embezzlement is caused by what he calls a "nonshareable financial problem." This condition may be the result of offenders' living beyond their means, perhaps piling up gambling debts; offenders feel they cannot let anyone know about such financial problems without ruining their reputations. Cressey claims that the door to solving personal financial problems through criminal means is opened by the rationalizations society has developed for white-collar crime: "Some of our most respectable citizens got their start in life by using other people's money temporarily"; "in the real estate business, there is nothing wrong about using deposits before the deal is closed"; "all people steal when they get in a tight spot."[72] Offenders use these and other rationalizations to resolve the conflict they experience over engaging in illegal

TABLE 12.1

High-Tech Frauds and Scams

The number and complexity of frauds and scams now operating means that enforcement agencies are always playing catch-up. Below are examples of some frauds and scams now being used:

Advanced fee loans	A company guarantees you a loan even if you have bad credit or no credit and requests an up-front fee.
Travel scams	These can take the form of filling out a ballot to win a dream vacation. Later someone calls by phone requesting your credit card number and other personal information in order to hold the vacation for you.
False charities	Fraudulent charities often use names that are very close to legitimate charities.
Pyramid schemes	These are based on recruiting more and more investors with those at the peak of the pyramid, those who got in early, making the most profit. Sooner or later, the number of investors dries up and those at the bottom stand to lose the most.
900 scams	These scams usually start with an offer in the mail to call a 1-900 number in order to collect a prize. When the number is dialed, the caller is charged by the minute and a voice-response system is used so that the call cannot be speeded up. The cost of the call is inevitably more than the prize.
Advance fee fraud	This fraud requires that you make a payment up-front before you receive an item or a service; however, you will not receive either.
Identity theft	A very prevalent crime usually involving the illegal acquisition and use of personal information such as credit card numbers or a social insurance number to commit fraud.
"Phishing"	Using email lures to "fish" for passwords and financial data from the sea of Internet users.
Auto-dial programs	These programs use your modem to dial long-distance telephone numbers and bill your phone account.
Telephone fraud	Selling fraudulent services or products over the telephone.
Counterfeit	Frauds associated with counterfeit currency or debit or credit cards.[71]

Source: Reprinted with the permission of the RCMP

behaviour. Rationalizations allow offenders' financial needs to be met without compromising their values.

There are a number of more formal theories of white-collar crime. The corporate culture view is that some business organizations promote white-collar criminality in the same way that lower-class culture encourages the development of juvenile gangs and street crime. According to this view, some business enterprises cause crime by placing excessive demands on employees while at the same time maintaining a business climate tolerant of employee deviance. New employees acquire the attitudes and techniques needed to commit white-collar crime from their business peers through a learning process. Those holding the corporate culture view would see the savings and loan and insider trading scandals as prime examples of what happens when people work in organizations whose cultural values stress profit over fair play, in which government scrutiny is limited and regulators are viewed as the enemy, and in which senior members encourage newcomers to believe that "greed is good."

According to the self-control view, the motives that produce white-collar crimes are the same as those that produce any other criminal behaviours: "the desire for relatively quick, relatively certain benefit, with minimal effort."[73] According to this view, white-collar criminals have low self-control and are inclined to follow momentary impulses without considering the long-term costs of such behaviour.[74] White-collar crime is relatively rare because, as a matter of course, business executives tend to hire people with self-control, thereby limiting the number of potential white-collar criminals.

CAREER CONNECTIONS BEING UNCLE CHARLIE

As an undercover police officer, Bob Deasy hung out with drug kingpins, made friends in the Russian mafia, and infiltrated some of Canada's most notorious crime groups. He wrote a book about his experiences called *Being Uncle Charlie: A Life Undercover with Killers, Kingpins, Bikers and Druglords*.

When he first joined the Ontario Provincial Police, he had not intended to work undercover. However, his first assignment was to join an undercover operation already in progress that was aimed at drug dealers. Initially, I really did not fit the gang mould: "I was right out of uniform and really clean-cut, so there was no sense trying to camouflage me with jewelry and leather jackets," he said. "They just put me into what they called the pretty bars." He kept his undercover identity close to his real one, as someone who had been to university and played sports. His job was to "to identify who was dealing drugs and make drug buys from them," Deasy said. I quickly realized there was "a market for clean-cut university people wanting drugs."

In the course of that assignment, Deasy met a major drug dealer who prided himself on never being caught for drug-dealing. After getting himself invited to the drug dealer's house, in a remote area gang members took his car keys and bolted the door shut after him. There were six people in the Kingston police's drugs unit and the gang had managed to obtain five of those names. Deasy was actually the sixth, but he was new to the team and his name was not known to the gang. "So that sixth spot was me, they just didn't know what I was yet." Luckily, the gang leader vouched for Deasy, but it was "harrowing."

Another assignment, near the end of his undercover career, involved infiltrating the Russian mob. "It turned out to be the hardest and the longest project of all of them," he said. "I'm not sure if it was the Russians themselves, or if I was just so tired of being somebody else at this point." Deasy was based in Toronto, set up to operate an import/export business which was a front to move a variety of stolen goods for the Russians. "Most organized crime groups, it doesn't matter what the commodity is, only that you can make money on it," he said, adding that at one point, he was "getting tractor trailers of jeans and faucets and taps." Deasy's lifestyle at the time involved "flashy cars and expensive jewelry and clothing. It was a money-is-no-object atmosphere," he said. "The operation ended with a takedown of people all over the world, Italy, Austria, the United States, and Canada."

Deasy was careful to keep his real life and his undercover life separate. And once a job was finished, "you just simply don't put yourself back in that atmosphere," he said. "If you know that group of bikers is in Bar X, because you spent a year in there with him, after it's over there's no reason to go back in Bar X."

Source: CBC Licensing

LO3 Controlling White-Collar Crime

The prevailing wisdom is that unlike lower-class street criminals, white-collar criminals are rarely prosecuted and, when convicted, receive relatively light sentences. In years past, it was rare for a corporate or white-collar criminal to receive a serious criminal penalty.[75]

What efforts have been made to bring violators of the public trust to justice? White-collar criminal enforcement typically involves two strategies designed to control organizational deviance: compliance and deterrence.[76]

Compliance Strategies

Compliance strategies aim for law conformity without the necessity of detecting, processing, or penalizing individual violators. At a minimum, they ask for cooperation and self-policing from the business community. Compliance systems attempt to create conformity by giving companies economic incentives to obey the law. They rely on administrative efforts to prevent unwanted conditions before they occur. Compliance systems depend on the threat of economic sanctions or civil penalties to control corporate violators.

Deterrence Strategies

Deterrence strategies involve detecting criminal violations, determining who is responsible, and penalizing the offenders to deter future violations.[77] Deterrence systems are oriented toward apprehending violators and punishing them rather than creating conditions that induce conformity to the law.

Deterrence strategies should work—and they have in the past—because white-collar crime by its nature is a rational act whose perpetrators are extremely sensitive to the threat of criminal sanctions. Perceptions of detection and punishment for white-collar crimes should be a powerful deterrent to future law violations.[78] However, the recent evidence about the effectiveness of deterrence strategies is mixed—too often, the crimes go undetected or the laws are poorly enforced.[79] At the same time, courts have traditionally been reluctant to sentence corporate executives to jail. As mentioned earlier, amendments to the *Criminal Code* brought about by Bill C-13 created the criminal offences of insider trading, tipping, and whistle-blowing retaliation. The bill increased maximum sentences and provides some guidance to judges on sentencing for corporate criminal offences, even allowing for harsher penalties where there are aggravating

factors. Senior executives should no longer be able to avoid a jail term by using their status, reputation, or good standing in the community to mitigate the sentence. Bill C-13 is viewed as a step in the right direction, with Canadian corporations increasingly becoming the subjects of criminal investigation and prosecution in the courts.[80] In November 2009, Toronto lawyer Stan Grmovsek pled guilty to illegal insider trading, marking Canada's first conviction under the new law.[81]

Because white-collar crime is rarely a one-time event, the identification of white-collar criminals is certainly less difficult than it is for street criminals.[82] Deterrence strategies have gone so far as charging business executives with murder in incidents where employees have died because of business-related injuries or illness. This issue is discussed in the accompanying Policy and Practice in Criminology feature.

compliance strategies
Fostering law conformity, cooperation, and self-policing in the business community through the use of economic incentives and administrative agencies.

deterrence strategies
Detecting criminal violations, determining who is responsible, and penalizing the offenders to deter future violations.

LO4 Organized Crime

The second branch of organizational criminality involves organized crime—the ongoing criminal enterprise groups whose ultimate purpose is personal economic gain through illegitimate means. Here, a structured enterprise system is set up to supply consumers with merchandise and services banned by criminal law but for which a ready market exists: prostitution, pornography, gambling, and narcotics. The system may resemble a legitimate business run by an ambitious chief executive officer, his or her assistants, staff lawyers, and accountants, with thorough, efficient accounts receivable and complaint departments.[83]

Because of its secrecy, power, and fabulous wealth, organized crime has a great mystique. Its legendary leaders—Al Capone, Meyer Lansky, Lucky Luciano—have been the subjects of books and films. The famous *Godfather* films popularized and humanized organized crime figures; the media often glamorize organized crime figures.[84] Most citizens believe that organized criminals are capable of taking over legitimate business enterprises if given the opportunity. Almost everyone is familiar with terms such as *mob, underworld, Mafia, wise guys, syndicate,* or *La Cosa Nostra,* all of which refer to

CAN CORPORATIONS COMMIT MURDER?

One of the most controversial issues surrounding the punishment of white-collar criminals involves prosecuting corporate executives who work for companies that manufacture products believed to have killed workers or consumers. Are the executives guilty of manslaughter, or even murder? This issue is especially relevant when we consider the number of deaths caused by the negligence of some corporations. How should corporate executives whose products or services cause death or whose business practices result in fatal harm to their employees be treated?

CONSUMER SAFETY

An infamous example of how a corporation could be found negligent for causing the needless death of consumers involves the Ford Motor Company's Pinto. Ford executives knew that due to the design of the vehicle, there was a serious fire hazard when struck from the rear, even in low-speed collisions. Instead of redesigning the defective fuel tanks, they decided to proceed with the production of the subcompact despite the risk it represented to consumers. The reasoning was clearly profit motivated. Ford executives ruthlessly calculated the costs of redesigning the

Time Magazine included the Ford Pinto in its list of "The 50 Worst Cars of All Time."

car ($121 million) versus the potential payout to victims ($50 million) through and cost/benefit formula and decided that human life took a back seat to profits.[85]

Between 1971 and 1978, approximately 50 lawsuits were brought against Ford in connection with the Pinto's defective fuel tanks. In one case, the jury awarded $3 million in compensatory damages to the victims of a Pinto crash, as well as a landmark $125 million in punitive damages. Though punitive damages were later reduced to $3.5 million, a clear message was sent to corporate leaders that it is wrong to make decisions that may sacrifice the lives of its consumers in order to reduce the company's cost or increase its profits, and those found guilty of such wrongdoing will be severely punished.[86] Given the number of vehicle "recalls" in recent years for defective vehicle parts, it would appear that large automobile companies are listening.

EMPLOYEE SAFETY

About 800 000 Canadians are hurt on the job each year, but successful prosecution of corporations for wrongdoing has been rare. Criminal negligence used to be something that mainly applied to accidents involving vehicles, but in 2003 legislation was enacted in Canada, making it easier to convict a corporation or individual of criminal negligence due to a workplace accident.

The new legislation had much to with a mining accident that occurred in 1992 in Plymouth, Nova Scotia, where 26 coal miners lost their lives following an explosion caused by a buildup of methane gas and coal dust at the Westray mine. Charges were laid against the company, Curragh Inc., and two managers under provincial health and safety regulations and under the *Criminal Code*. When all charges were eventually dropped, a public inquiry was called that resulted in 74 recommendations, including one that would make corporate executives and directors responsible for workplace safety.

In the fall of 2003, almost 11 years after the Westray accident, the federal government passed Bill C-45, which was designed to improve workplace safety and to modernize the *Criminal Code* regarding the criminal liability of corporations. Bill C-45 complemented recent changes to the Canada Labour Code, which gave new rights to workers—for example, the right to be informed about hazards in the workplace, the

---

organized crime. Although most of us have neither met nor seen members of organized crime families, we feel sure that they exist, and we fear them. This section briefly defines organized crime, reviews its activities, and discusses its economic effect and control.

Stephen Schneider from the Department of Sociology and Criminology at St. Mary's University, Nova Scotia, authored a book on organized crime in Canada, appropriately titled *Iced: The Story of Organized Crime*

in Canada. For the past 20 years he has specialized in organized crime and innovations in organized crime enforcement. According to Schneider, Canada has a unique history of organized crime commencing with 16th-century pirates who robbed fishing vessels off the Grand Banks, to British Columbia's role as one of the world's largest producers of smokeable opium in the early 20th century. During American prohibition, Canada was America's biggest source of contraband liquor, employing thousands of Canadians who

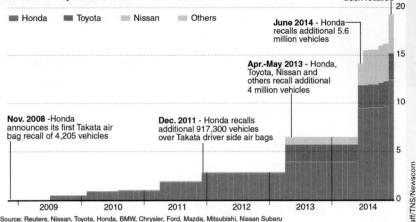

Takata recalls

Cumulative vehicles recalled over Takata air bag and inflator problems

Global recalls by manufacturers - in million units

■ Honda ■ Toyota ■ Nissan ■ Others

Dec. 2014
To date, more than 19 million vehicles have been recalled

June 2014 - Honda recalls additional 5.6 million vehicles

Apr.-May 2013 - Honda, Toyota, Nissan and others recall additional 4 million vehicles

Nov. 2008 -Honda announces its first Takata air bag recall of 4,205 vehicles

Dec. 2011 - Honda recalls additional 917,300 vehicles over Takata driver side air bags

2009　2010　2011　2012　2013　2014

Staff/TNS/Newscom

Source: Reuters, Nissan, Toyota, Honda, BMW, Chrysler, Ford, Mazda, Mitsubishi, Nissan Subaru
Graphic: Tribune News Service

In May 2015, the Takata Corporation declared 33.8 million air bags defective, ordering the largest recall in U.S. history. Millions of Canadian cars may also be included in the recall. The chemical that inflates the air bags can explode with too much force, blowing apart a metal inflator and sending shrapnel into the passenger compartment. The faulty inflators are responsible for six deaths and more than 100 injuries worldwide.

right to participate in correcting those hazards, and the right to refuse dangerous work. Fines of up to $1 000 000 are provided for breach of the Canada Labour Code.

Under Bill C-45, not only is proving negligence made easier but also the consequences of being found guilty are more substantial. There is now a legal duty on employers and those who direct work to take reasonable measures to protect employee and public safety. If it is demonstrated that this duty is wantonly or recklessly disregarded and bodily harm or death results, an organization could be charged with criminal negligence.

The penalty for individuals convicted of criminal negligence is ten years of jail time for an accident resulting in injury; if someone dies, those responsible could face life imprisonment. The organization could also receive an unlimited fine and be placed on probation, which could include publicly acknowledging the conviction, the sentence, and any health and safety reforms imposed.

Whether Bill C-45 has been effective in improving workplace safety has been questioned. Since the passing of the bill, corporations have indeed been found guilty and fined but no one to date has received a jail sentence. Some have questioned if fines are a sufficient punishment. Further, the prosecution rate has been very low at about 10 prosecutions, one per year since the law was created, which is concerning given that the number of fatalities has remained the same at about 990 per year. It has been argued that inadequate training provided to police and Crown attorneys and confusion over their roles may be factors that help explain the low prosecution rate. Regardless, until police and Crown attorneys enhance the enforcement of Bill C-45, it is doubtful that it will make a significant impact in improving the health and safety of workers in Canada.[87]

CRITICAL THINKING

1. Should corporate executives be found guilty of murder if they fail to take reasonable measures to protect their staff and an employee subsequently dies?

2. Is it fair to blame a single executive for the activities of a company that has thousands of employees?

Sources: H. Glasbeek, "Westray Bill Doesn't Make Shareholders Accountable," *Daily News* (Halifax, NS), November 28, 2004, p.17. Reprinted by permission of the *Daily News*, Halifax; Andrew Sharpe and Jill Hardt, *Five Deaths a Day: Workplace Fatalities in Canada*, 1993–2005, CSLS Research Paper 2006-04, December 2006, http://odin.pragmatic-solutions.com/drupal/sites/default/files/images/pdf/Five%20Deaths%20a%20Day%20Workplace%20Fatalities%20in%20Canada.pdf (accessed August 3, 2011).

interacted with some of Americas most infamous gangsters. During the mid-20th century, Canadian organized criminals were key players in smuggling heroin from Europe to lucrative markets in North America. In the 1970s Canada was a major producer of synthetic drugs, and by the 1990s, a major supplier of marijuana, methamphetamines, and ecstasy. As Schneider noted, in the world of biker gangs, almost one in four Hell's Angels worldwide reside in Canada.[88]

Scope of Organized Crime in Canada

The *Criminal Code* of Canada defines a criminal organization as a group that

(a) is composed of three or more persons in or outside Canada; and,

(b) has as one of its main purposes or main activities the facilitation or commission of one or more serious offences that, if committed, would likely result in the direct or indirect receipt of a material benefit, including a financial benefit, by the group or by any of the persons who constitute the group.[89]

Famous American mobster Al Capone (left), with the assistance of his Canadian counterpart, Rocco Perri (right), made a fortune bootlegging liquor from Canada during prohibition. Capone denied any involvement in his operations in Canada, demonstrating his ignorance of the country with his famous statement, "I don't even know what street Canada is on."[90] Perri specialized in exporting liquor from old Canadian distilleries, such as Seagram's and Gooderham's to the United States. When Prohibition ended, he expanded into gambling, extortion, and prostitution. Last seen in 1944, he is believed to be at the bottom of the bay area of the city of Hamilton wearing "cement shoes."[91]

While the traditional concept of organized crime is based on notorious mafia figures such as Al Capone and his Canadian equivalent, Rocco Perri, by the 1990s, organized crime was characterized predominantly by outlaw motorcycle gangs such as the Hell's Angels and the Outlaws.

Today, organized crime activities are known to include diverse activities such as migrant smuggling, trafficking in humans and firearms, marijuana grow

The popular TV series *Sons of Anarchy* ran for seven seasons, and depict biker lifestyle including members' involvement in illegal activities.

operations, identity theft, sexual exploitation of children on the Internet, the production and smuggling of counterfeit goods and money, motor vehicle theft, and more. In 2013, 672 organized crime groups were reported in Canada, many of them concentrated in major metropolitan areas. Illegal activities such as drug trafficking, cybercrime, and financial crime form the main activities of organized crime groups in Canada.[92]

Characteristics of Organized Crime

A precise description of the characteristics of organized crime is difficult to formulate, but here are some of its general traits:[93]*

- Organized crime is a conspiratorial activity, involving the coordination of numerous persons in the planning and execution of illegal acts or in the pursuit of a legitimate objective by unlawful means (e.g., threatening a legitimate business to get a stake in it). Organized crime involves continuous commitment by primary members, although individuals with specialized skills may be brought in as needed. Organized crime is usually structured along hierarchical lines—a chieftain supported by close advisers, several ranks of subordinates, and so on.

- Organized crime has economic gain as its primary goal, although power and status may also be motivating factors. Economic gain is achieved through maintenance of a near-monopoly on illegal goods and services, including drugs, gambling, pornography, and prostitution.

- Organized crime activities are not limited to providing illicit services. They include sophisticated activities such as laundering illegal money through legitimate businesses, land fraud, and computer crimes.

- Organized crime employs predatory tactics, such as intimidation, violence, and corruption. It appeals to greed to accomplish its objectives and preserve its gains.

- By experience, custom, and practice, organized crime's conspiratorial groups are usually very quick and effective in controlling and disciplining their members, associates, and victims. The individuals involved know that any deviation from the rules of the organization will evoke a prompt response from the other participants. This response may range from a reduction in rank and responsibility to a death sentence.

- Organized crime is not synonymous with the Mafia—the most experienced, most diversified, and possibly best-disciplined of these groups. The Mafia is actually a common stereotype of organized crime. Although several families in the organization called the Mafia are important components of organized crime activities, they do not hold a monopoly on underworld activities.

- Organized crime does not include terrorists dedicated to political change. Although violent acts are a major tactic of organized crime, the use of violence does not mean that a group is part of a confederacy of organized criminals.

---

*Organized Time Today, 2006

READY TO STUDY?

IN THE BOOK, YOU CAN:

✔ Check your understanding of what you've just read by reading the Summary at the end of each chapter.

✔ Rip out the Chapter in Review card at the back of the book to have the key terms and Learning Objectives handy, and complete the quizzes provided (answers are on the bottom of the back page!).

ONLINE YOU CAN:

✔ Stay organized and efficient with MindTap—a single destination with all the course material and study aids you need to succeed. Built-in apps leverage social media and the latest learning technology. For example:

✔ ReadSpeaker will read the text to you.

✔ Flashcards are pre-populated to provide you with a jump start for review—or you can create your own.

✔ You can highlight text and make notes in your MindTap Reader. Your notes will flow into Evernote, the electronic notebook app that you can access anywhere when it's time to study for the exam.

✔ Prepare for tests with quizzes.

Go to www.nelson.com/student to access these digital resources.

Public Order Crimes

Learning Objectives

LO1 Define a public order crime.

LO2 Describe the consequences of the implementation of Bill C-36 for the control of prostitution and sex work in Canada; should we consider legalizing sex work in Canada?

LO3 Evaluate how we decide what is pornographic and understand how the law has changed to support police in dealing with child pornography.

LO4 Know the impact, the good and the bad, of legal gambling in Canada.

LO5 Understand the role that substance abuse plays in criminal behaviour.

LO6 Think critically about whether Canada should legalize the possession of cannabis for personal use.

Introduction

In March 1998, Montreal police raided l'Orage Club, a "swingers club" in the downtown area, after conducting an undercover operation at the club. The owner, Jean-Paul Labaye, was charged under s.210(1) of the *Criminal Code* with keeping a common bawdy house for the "practice of acts of indecency."[1] According to undercover police officers, adult men and women were observed engaged in a variety of sexual acts with multiple partners while on public view at the club. In addition to Labaye, 44 people found inside the club were arrested and charged with being found in a common bawdy house.[2]

At his trial in Montreal, Labaye's lawyers argued that l'Orage Club is an adult members-only club where consenting adults engaged in legal consensual sexual acts in a locked room on the private third floor of the club, and hence the activities taking place there did not meet the definition of a common bawdy house. The Montreal municipal court judge rejected Labaye's argument, ruling that the club was in fact a "public place" where sexual acts were performed in the open, and that the behaviour at the club was "degrading" and "dehumanizing" and so met the requirements of s.210(1), and fined the club owner $2500.[3]

On appeal to the Quebec Court of Appeal in 2004, Labaye's conviction was upheld, though another Montreal swingers club owner, James Kouri had his conviction quashed by the appeal court. Labaye's lawyers sought leave to appeal the decision against him to the Supreme Court of Canada based on the contradictory proceedings of the Quebec court.

In December 2005 the Supreme Court ruled that Labaye's swingers club was not illegal, and that the trial judge's application of subjective, undefined "community standards" could not be used as the criterion to determine whether an act was indecent. Instead, the Court ruled that a more objective test of indecency must be employed, one that establishes that (1) the behaviour represents a harmful threat to the Constitution of other fundamental laws by promoting behaviour that interferes with autonomy and liberty, or promotes antisocial behaviour in others, or causes those engaged in the behaviour physical or psychological harm, and (2) that the risk of harm is "incompatible with the proper functioning of society."[4] The Court determined that the behaviours witnessed at the swingers club did not meet

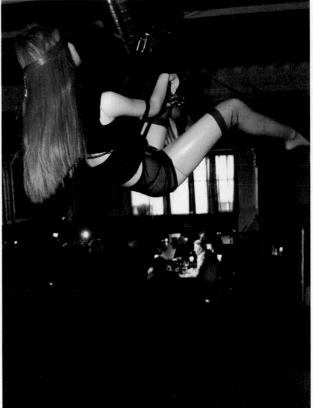

A mannequin hangs over the dance floor of the Club L'Orage as owner Jean-Paul Labaye speaks to reporters at a news coference in 2000. The club was eventually cleared of charges of a common bawdy house, and a 2006 Supreme Court decision cleared the way for so-called "swingers" clubs. Should politicians and the courts have the right to determine what kinds of sexual behaviours are morally acceptable for consenting adults to engage in?

an objective test of indecency, as the Crown failed to show that they represented a risk of harm to the Constitution or fundamental laws, or were incompatible with the proper functioning of society and, consequently, Labaye's conviction was set aside.[5]

DID YOU KNOW?

- Societies can ban behaviours that lawmakers consider offensive. Critics question whether this amounts to censorship.

- The line between behaviours that are merely immoral and those that are criminal is often blurred. What is considered deviant or criminal at one time may later be thought of as normal and legal at another time.

- People who seek to control or criminalize deviant behaviours are called moral entrepreneurs.

Should politicians and the courts have the right to determine what kinds of sexual behaviours are morally acceptable for consenting adults to engage in?

public order crime
Behaviour that is outlawed because it threatens the general well-being of society and challenges its accepted moral principles.

victimless crime
Public order crime that violates the moral order but has no specific victim other than society as a whole.

Should a politician be able to ban a piece of artwork like Michelangelo's *David*, one of the world's most famous sculptures, because he or she considers the nude statue pornographic? Societies have long banned or limited behaviours that are believed to run contrary to social norms, customs, and values. These behaviours are often referred to as public order crimes or victimless crimes, although the latter term can be misleading.[6] Public order crimes involve acts that interfere with the operations of society and the ability of people to function efficiently. Put another way, whereas common law crimes such as sexual assault or robbery are considered inherently wrong and damaging, other behaviours are outlawed because they conflict with social policy, prevailing moral standards, and current public opinion.

Statutes designed to uphold public order usually prohibit the manufacture and distribution of morally questionable goods and services such as erotic material, commercial sex, and mood-altering drugs. Such statutes are controversial in part because millions of otherwise law-abiding citizens often engage in these outlawed activities and consequently become criminal. These statutes are also controversial because they selectively prohibit desired goods, services, and behaviours; in other words, they outlaw sin and vice.

This chapter covers these public order crimes. It first briefly discusses the relationship between law and morality. Next, it addresses public order crimes of a sexual nature: pornography and prostitution. Gambling is discussed as another example of a public order crime, and the chapter concludes by focusing on the abuse of drugs and alcohol.

LO1 Law and Morality

Legislation of moral values has continually frustrated lawmakers. There is little debate that the purpose of criminal law is to protect society and reduce social harm. When a store is robbed or a child assaulted, it is relatively easy to see and condemn the harm done to the victim. It is, however, more difficult to sympathize with or even identify the victims of immoral acts, such as pornography or prostitution, where the parties involved may be willing participants. If there is no victim, can there be a crime? Should acts be made illegal merely because they violate prevailing moral standards? If so, who defines morality?

To answer these questions, we might first consider whether there is actually a victim in so-called victimless crimes. Some participants may have been coerced into their acts; if so, then they are victims. Opponents of pornography, such as Andrea Dworkin, charge that women involved in adult films, far from being highly paid stars, are "dehumanized—turned into objects and commodities."[7] Research on prostitution shows that many young runaways and abandoned children are coerced into prostitution where they are cruelly treated and held as virtual captives.[8]

Some scholars argue that pornography, prostitution, and drug use erode the moral fabric of society

Photo by Susan Watts/NY Daily News Archive via Getty Images

The Holy Virgin Mary, a painting by Chris Ofili, a British artist of Nigerian descent, at the Brooklyn Museum in New York City. Declaring the work "sick stuff," in 1999 New York's mayor threatened to withhold the museum's funding and evict it from its city-owned building. Should a politician's moral values dictate what can be shown at a metropolitan museum? Who is to say what is offensive and what is "art"?

Proliferation of Internet porn may have far-reaching effects, particularly on the young.

and therefore should be prohibited and punished. They are crimes, according to the great legal scholar Morris Cohen, because "it is one of the functions of the criminal law to give expression to the collective feeling of revulsion toward certain acts, even when they are not very dangerous."[9]

According to this view, so-called victimless crimes are prohibited because one of the functions of criminal law is to express a shared sense of public morality.[10] However, basing criminal definitions on moral beliefs is often an impossible task. Who defines morality? Are we not punishing differences rather than social harm? As U.S. Supreme Court Justice William O. Douglas so succinctly put it, "What may be trash to me may be prized by others."[11] Would not any attempt to control or limit "objectionable" material eventually lead to the suppression of free speech and political dissent? Is this not a veiled form of censorship? Not so, according to social commentator Irving Kristol:

> If we start censoring pornography and obscenity, shall we not inevitably end up censoring political opinion? A lot of people seem to think this would be the case—which only shows the power of doctrinaire thinking over reality. We had censorship of pornography and obscenity for 150 years, until almost yesterday, and I am not aware that freedom of opinion in this country was in any way diminished as a consequence of this fact.[12]

Criminal or Immoral?

Acts that most of us deem highly immoral are not criminal. There is no law against lust, gluttony, avarice, spite, or envy, although they are considered some of the "seven deadly sins." Nor is it a crime in most jurisdictions to ignore the pleas of a drowning person, even though such callous behaviour is surely immoral.

Some acts that seem both well intentioned and moral are nonetheless considered criminal. It is a crime (euthanasia) to kill a loved one who is suffering from an incurable disease to spare him or her further pain. Stealing a rich person's money to feed a poor family is considered theft. Marrying more than one person is considered a crime (bigamy), even though multiple marriage may conform to religious beliefs.[13]

As legal experts Wayne LaFave and Austin Scott, Jr., state, "A good motive will not normally prevent what is otherwise criminal from being a crime."[14]

Generally, immoral acts can be distinguished from crimes on the basis of the social harm they cause: Acts that harm the public are usually outlawed. Yet this perspective does not always hold sway. Some acts that cause enormous amounts of social harm are perfectly legal. All of us are aware of the illness and death associated with the consumption of tobacco and alcohol, but they remain legal to produce and sell. Governments, charities, and sports organizations run lotteries and charity casinos. Manufacturers continue to sell sports cars and motorcycles that can accelerate to more

In November 2011, the B.C. Supreme Court upheld Canada's laws prohibiting polygamy, the union of a husband or wife with multiple spouses. Male members of a fundamentalist Mormon sect located in Bountiful, B.C., such as religious leader Winston Blackmore (above), have pursued the practice of having more than one wife since the 1940s. Though a 2009 charge was quashed by the B.C. Supreme Court, Blackmore was charged by police again in August 2014 with one count of polygamy.[15]

than 200 km/hour, although the legal speed limit on major Canadian highways is usually 100 km/hour. More people die each year from alcohol-, tobacco-, and auto-related deaths than from all illegal drugs combined. Should drugs be legalized and fast cars outlawed?

Moral Crusaders

Public order crimes often trace their origin to moral crusaders who seek to shape the law toward their own way of thinking; Howard Becker calls them moral entrepreneurs. These rule creators, argues Becker, operate with an absolute certainty that their way is right and that any means are justified to get their way; "the crusader is fervent and righteous, often self-righteous."[16] Today's moral crusaders take on issues such as the right to legal abortions, Internet pornography, polygamous marriage and the elimination of the long-gun registry.

Vince Talotta/GetStock.com

Marc Emery, the Canadian "Prince of Pot," was arrested in July 2005 by Canadian police, at the request of the United States Drug Enforcement Agency (DEA). Emery operated a Vancouver-based business that sold marijuana seeds over the Internet, including to buyers in the United States. In May 2010, Emery was extradited to Seattle, Washington, to stand trial in a U.S. court for manufacturing and distributing marijuana seeds, and for conspiracy to engage in money laundering. Convicted and sentenced to serve five years in prison, Emery was released in July 2014. During the period Emery operated his Vancouver marijuana seed business, he paid $578 000 in income taxes to the Canada Revenue Agency, clearly identifying his business as "seed selling." U.S. states Washington and Colorado legalized recreational use of marijuana in 2012, followed by Alaska and Oregon in 2014.[17]

Moral crusades are often directed against people clearly defined as evil by one segment of the population, even though they may be admired by others. For example, antismut campaigns may attempt to ban the books of a popular author from the school library or prevent a controversial figure from speaking at the local university. One way for moral crusaders to accomplish their goal is to prove to all who will listen that some unseen or hidden trait makes their target truly evil and unworthy of a public audience—for example, the Bible condemns the behaviour. This polarization of good and evil creates a climate where those categorized as "good" are deified while the "bad" are demonized and become objects suitable for control.

Moral crusaders seek to rid society of people whose behaviour falls outside their personal standards of right and wrong.

The public order crimes discussed in this chapter are divided into two broad areas. The first relates to what conventional society considers deviant sexual practices: pornography and prostitution. The second area concerns practices that have been outlawed or controlled because of the alleged harm they cause: gambling, drugs, and alcohol.

DID YOU KNOW?

- Sex work, including prostitution, erotic massage, exotic dancing, escort services, and professional dominance and submission among other activities, has been common throughout recorded history.

- Many of those involved in sex work come from troubled backgrounds, and substance abuse is common.

- Sex work is a billion-dollar industry that is growing through technological advances such as the Internet.

- There is great debate whether obscene materials are harmful and are related to violence.

- The Supreme Court of Canada has ruled that material is obscene if it links sex with undue exploitation, violence, or degrading or dehumanizing treatment, and has no redeeming social value.

LO2 Prostitution

Prostitution has been known for thousands of years. The term derives from the Latin *prostituere*, which means "to cause to stand in front of." The prostitute is viewed as publicly offering his or her body for sale. The earliest record of prostitution appears in ancient

Mesopotamia, where priests engaged in sex to promote fertility in the community. All women were required to do temple duty, and passing strangers were expected to make donations to the temple after enjoying its services.[18]

Modern commercial sex appears to have its roots in ancient Greece, where Solon established licensed brothels in 500 b.c. The earnings of Greek prostitutes helped pay for the temple of Aphrodite. Famous men openly went to prostitutes to enjoy intellectual, aesthetic, and sexual stimulation; prostitutes, however, were prevented from marrying.[19]

The act of prostitution can be defined as the consensual exchange of sex for money, established by mutual agreement of the prostitutes, their clients, and their employers. In September 2010, sex trade workers Terri-Jean Bedford, Amy Lebovitch, and Valerie Scott petitioned an Ontario court to strike down sections 210 "keeping a common bawdy house," 212(1) "living on the avails of prostitution," and 213(1) "communicating in public for the purposes of prostitution" of the Criminal Code as violating their rights under Section 7 of the Charter of Rights and Freedoms, "Everyone has the right to life, liberty and security of the person and the right not to be deprived thereof except in accordance with the principles of fundamental justice." Their lawyer, Alan Young, argued that the Criminal Code provisions put sex trade workers, including prostitutes, at risk of serious personal harm or even death by preventing them from operating indoors and making use of security staff to screen clients and monitor their safety.[20] The Ontario Superior Court agreed with their argument, and struck down each of the identified Criminal Code provisions. The decision was first appealed to by the

Attorney General of Canada to the Ontario Court of Appeal, and then to the Supreme Court of Canada.

In its December 2013 judgment, the Supreme Court struck down each of sections 210, 212(1), 213(1) as being inconsistent with the Charter, but upheld the earlier Ontario appeal court decision to suspend the invalidity of the sections for one year in order to give the Government of Canada sufficient time to seek a remedy.[21]

In November 2014, the Attorney General of Canada's response to the Supreme Court of Canada decision, Bill C-36, "An Act to amend the Criminal Code in response to the Supreme Court of Canada decision in Attorney General of Canada v. Bedford and to make consequential amendments to other Acts" received Royal Assent. Under the provisions introduced under Bill C-36, the word prostitute was removed from s.197(1) in accordance with the Supreme Court ruling, such that a "common bawdy house" is now defined solely as a place occupied for the practice of "acts of indecency." Under the title of "Commodification of Sexual Activity," s.286(1) makes it an offence to either obtain sexual services, or to communicate for the purpose of providing sexual services, with more serious penalties imposed if the offence takes place in a public place or in a place open to public view close to a school, a religious place, or where persons under the age of 18 are present; s.286(2) makes it an offence to receive financial or any other material benefit from the provision of sexual services; s.286(3) imposes stiff penalties for procuring a person to engage in providing sexual services, while s.286(4) makes it an offence to advertise sexual services. Though not defined in Bill C-36, "sexual services for consideration" include genital, oral and anal sex, as well as lap-dancing, masturbation of a massage parlour client, and sado-masochistic activities.[22]

Critics of Bill C-36 argue that the law will push sex work further into the shadows, making it even more dangerous because those purchasing sexual services can now be charged criminally—possibly increasing the risk to sex workers, and making it less likely that the purchasers will come forward to assist police when sex workers are assaulted or even murdered. Others point out that Bill C-36 will end up criminalizing a greater number of individuals who provide sex services, and will end up also criminalizing persons who live or work with them as possibly receiving "financial or any other material benefit" from sexual services. Still others point out that individuals who engage in sex work, mostly women, will be as vulnerable as ever.[23]

In Canada, the act of prostitution is not illegal; rather, the illegal act is the means used to practise it, such as "soliciting" for the purpose of prostitution. This photo shows sex-trade workers Terri-Jean Bedford, Amy Lebovitch and Valerie Scott and their lawyer, Alan Young, outside the Supreme Court of Canada.

prostitution
The consensual exchange of sex for money.

Incidence of Prostitution in Canada

In 2013, a total of 1203 individuals were charged with prostitution-related offences, down from 2448 in 2009, a 51 percent decline. Most recorded offences are for so-called street prostitution— little is known about other forms of prostitution such as "call girl" operations and escort services, or other forms of sex work like massage parlours, professional dominance and submission, or fetish services.[24]

Even less is known about the customers, almost exclusively male, who use prostitutes. One study conducted in British Columbia found the average age of men frequenting prostitutes was 34, most (53 percent) were white, and "blue collar" (36 percent) was the most common occupational group.[25] In a 2015 report by the B.C. Centre for Addictions Research, the researchers found that nearly half of the men who frequented prostitutes were married, living common-law, divorced or widowed; were employed full time; and made incomes about the average. Loneliness, sexual insecurity, an unsatisfactory relationship with a current partner, adventure, and sex/gender exploration were common reasons for seeking out prostitutes.[26]

Men may be less likely to use prostitutes now than in the past because legitimate alternatives for sexuality are more open to them. In addition, the prevalence of sexually transmitted diseases has caused many men to avoid visiting prostitutes for fear of irreversible health hazards.[27]

Sex Work

In 1978 prostitution rights activist Carol Leigh coined the term **sex work** to better reflect that prostitution and the sale of a broad range of other sex services has much in common with other types of service work, but its criminalization makes sex workers vulnerable to exploitation and abuse.[28] In their 2013 book *Selling Sex; Experience, Advocacy and research on Sex Work in Canada*, van derMeulen, Durisin, and Love note that the terms *sex work* and *sex worker* are now commonly used by workers and rights advocates in the field, which encompasses a broad range of sexual services including phone sex work, exotic dancing, massage, street-based sex work, escort services, Web shows, prostitution, professional dominance and submission, pornography acting and performing, fetish services, and others.[29]

sex work
The consensual exchange of sexual services for money.

Estimates of the global dollar value of the sex work industry range from $10 billion to as much as $57 billion annually. Prostitution has become the economic mainstay of many countries including regardless of whether it has been legalized. For example, in Netherlands prostitution accounts for 5 percent of the Gross Domestic Product (GDP) and 14 percent in Thailand. Taking into account the ongoing growth of the Internet, it is a safe bet that the sex work industry will continue to be among the most profitable business ventures in the global economy.[30]

According to van derMeulen, Durisin and Love, three different perspectives are taken in understanding why individuals engage in sex work: (1) as a form of sexual slavery, (2) as a necessary evil, or (3) as labour. Each perspective leads to different assumptions and strategies about how best to address the place of sex work in society.[31]

Those who view sex work as a form of sexual slavery, among whom van derMeulen, Durisin and Love include prohibitionists, abolitionists and radical feminists, argue for strong measures to criminalize the actions of pimps, customers, and others who control or coerce sex workers into selling themselves for the profit of others. Consequently, those who view sex work as sexual slavery support laws line bill C-36 which is aimed at punishing the buyers of sexual services or profit from providing such services. Although politically appealing, law enforcement crusades dedicated to controlling the sex business rarely obtain the desired effect. Get-tough policies make sex-related goods and services scarce, driving up prices and making their sale even more desirable and profitable.

Followers of the sex-work-as-a-necessary-evil perspective accept that sex work cannot be prohibited or abolished and instead support policies that regulate and control sex work in an attempt to limit its negative impact on society, including implementing strong laws to punish human traffickers and others who coerce individuals into sex work, while allowing those who choose to voluntarily engage in sex work. One example of the necessary-evil perspective is the operation of legalized, health-inspected brothels in Nevada; another is Germany. In Canada, Winnipeg and Edmonton have each implemented municipal bylaws in an attempt to regulate the prostitution trade, and many Canadian cities now license and regulate adult entertainment establishments such as sex shops, adult video stores, and "body rub" parlours.[32] In April 2010, the Fort Nelson, B.C. municipal council voted six to one in favour of licensing sex-related businesses, including an escort service, in specific, designated areas of the community.[33]

The third and more recent perspective, held by feminists, rights advocates and others, advocates for the decriminalization of sex work, and the establishment of employment rights, protections and safeguards for sex workers that are the same as other workers have. Those who view sex work as work like any other argue that taking such a position will ensure that sex workers are safe, free from exploitation by others, and protected by the law. In Australia and the Netherlands, sex workers are given many of the same rights and protections as other workers.[34]

Sex Workers

In their 2015 report commissioned by the B.C. Centre for Addictions, Benoit and Shumka found that sex work continues to be highly gendered, with the majority of workers being women. Other studies have found that sex workers in Canada are highly racialized, with a disproportionate number of Aboriginal girls and women involved, especially in street-level work. Most sex work takes place in private places, like hotel rooms, massage parlours, private homes, or escort agencies.[35]

A 2014 study of female sex workers in London, Ontario, found that many of the women studied reported having grown up in difficult "non-normative" family circumstances, characterized by having to take on adult responsibilities for care of the household when they were as young as eight or nine years old; being removed from the home and spending time in foster care; and experiencing physical abuse by parents and sexual abuse by their father. Mental health problems and alcoholism and drug abuse were common among the parents of the women in the study.[36] In another study comparing the characteristics of both male and female sex workers in the United States and Canada with workers in servicing and hairstyling occupations, research showed that both early experiences of childhood poverty and abuse and family instability, and later lack of education and employment skills along with substance abuse, were much more common among sex workers. Compared to servers and hairstylists, sex workers were significantly more likely to be members of a minority group; to be victims of emotional, sexual, or physical abuse as children; to have been a victim of a crime; and to have been homeless as a child. A significantly higher proportion of sex workers were involved in illegal substance use.[37]

Though as adults they may voluntarily choose to engage in sex work, research shows that most individuals engaged in sex work come from disadvantaged childhood backgrounds and minority-status groups that are barriers to acquiring the education

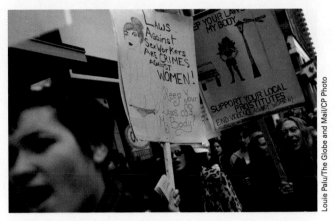

In Canada, the purchase, advertisement, or profit from the sale of sexual services is a criminal offence. Sex workers argue that the current law continues to make them vulnerable to exploitation and abuse, and they continue to lobby for recognition of sex work as legitimate work, with all of the usual rights and protections.

and job skills necessary to achieving obtain a good job, and a stable, normative lifestyle: instead, as children and as adults, sex workers remain vulnerable to exploitation, even under the most liberal laws. It is a commonly held belief that making available social services, including counselling, education and employment, especially to youth at high risk for exploitation and involvement in sex work, is an important step in addressing the often negative consequences of engaging in sex work.[38]

> **pornography**
> Books, magazines, films, tapes, pictures, or videos that graphically exploit sex or depict sex in combination with crime, horror, cruelty, or violence; includes any and all sexual exploitation of children.

LO3 Pornography

The term **pornography** derives from the Greek *porne*, meaning "prostitute," and *graphein*, meaning "to write." As many as 4 percent of all websites on the public internet are devoted to pornography, and as many as 14 percent of public Internet searches are for pornography. There is no way to estimate how much Internet activity in search of pornography, including illegal child pornography, bestiality, and "snuff" videos takes place on the "darknet" where users can search anonymously in little-known corners of the Internet, though observers suspect that a high proportion of the activity is for this purpose.[39]

Though some materials depicting nudity and sex are legal in Canada, the *Criminal Code* prohibits

In March 2015, Benjamin Levin pleaded guilty to three child pornography offences, and received a sentence of three years in prison. The former deputy minister of Education for both Manitoba and Ontario and University of Toronto professor was arrested in July 2013 after he contacted an Internet chat room and, posing as a couple, posted images depicting pornographic images of young girls, and stories and comments promoting sexual relationships between mothers and daughters. Police officers posing as single mothers with a sexual interest in their own children engaged in chat room exchanges with Levin beginning in August 2012.[40]

the production, display, and sale of material that is deemed "obscene" as per section 163(8), which states that "For the purpose of this Act, any publication a dominant characteristic of which is the undue exploitation of sex, or of sex and any one or more of the following subjects, namely, crime, horror, cruelty and violence, shall be deemed to be obscene." Additional provisions under s.163(1) and s.164(1) address the making, distribution, accessing, and possession of child pornography, that is, any written, audio or visual material that advocates, describes, or depicts sexual activity with a person under the age of 18 years.[41]

Obscenity, derived from the Latin *caenum* for "filth," is defined by Webster's dictionary as "deeply offensive to morality or decency … designed to incite to lust or depravity."[42] The problem of controlling pornography centres on this definition of obscenity. Police and law enforcement officials can legally seize only material that is judged obscene, "But who," critics ask, "is to judge what is obscene?" At one time, novels such as *Tropic of Cancer* by Henry Miller, *Ulysses* by James Joyce, *Lady Chatterley's Lover* by D. H. Lawrence, and even Margaret Laurence's *Stone Angel* were prohibited because they were considered

obscenity
Material that links sex with undue exploitation, violence, or degrading or dehumanizing treatment, and has no redeeming social value.

obscene; today they are considered works of great literary value. In the past, the definition of what was obscene usually relied almost exclusively on the "community standards" test; what "crosses the line" or is intolerable to members of a community at the time defines obscenity. However, such an approach to defining obscenity opens the door to all sorts of different interpretations of community standards. Consequently, the Supreme Court of Canada has ruled that what is "obscene" and therefore harmful to society is any media that link sex with undue exploitation, violence, or degrading or dehumanizing treatment, and have no redeeming social value.[43]

Is Pornography Harmful?

Opponents of pornography argue that it degrades both the people who are photographed and those who view obscene material. Though some studies report that pornographers exploit the poor and disadvantaged to serve as models and actors, more recent research shows that there are no significant differences in the backgrounds or psychological characteristics of actors in pornography compared to other comparable groups of men and women, though the pornography actors did report greater fears about contracting a sexually transmitted disease (STD), and reported more use of drugs.[44]

A growing body of research reports that excessive use of pornography, in particular Internet pornography, can lead to psychological distress, sexual dysfunction, problems at work, family dysfunction, and social isolation. Excessive viewing of Internet pornography has also been linked to the formation of unrealistic sexual attitudes and expectations, the pursuit of ever-more titillating stories and images, and possibly gradual involvement in illegal pornography-related activities. Other research has found a link between excessive viewing of Internet pornography and depression, anxiety, frustration and aggression.[45]

An uncontested danger of pornography is "kiddie porn." ECPAT International, a child welfare and children's rights group, estimates that on any given day there are more than 1 million child pornographic images cycling through the Internet, and somewhere between 50 000 and 100 000 individuals, mostly white males living in Western countries, involved in swapping and sharing child pornographic images and videos.[46] Ann Wolbert Burgess studied 55 child pornography rings and found that they typically contain between 3 and 11 children, predominantly males, some of nursery-school age. The adults who control the ring use positions of trust to recruit the children and then continue to exploit them through a combination of material and psychological rewards. Burgess found different types of child pornography rings. Solo sex rings involve several children and a single adult, usually male, who uses a position of trust (counsellor, teacher, Boy Scout leader) to recruit children into sexual activity. Transition rings are impromptu groups set up to sell and trade photos and sex. Syndicated rings are well-structured organizations that recruit children and create extensive networks of customers who desire sexual services.[47] Sexual exploitation by these rings can devastate the child victims. Exploited children are prone to acting-out behaviour such as setting fires and becoming sexually focused in the use of language, dress, and mannerisms. In cases of extreme, prolonged victimization, children may lock onto the sex group's behaviour and become prone to further victimization or even become victimizers themselves.

In 2013, Canadian police recorded 2668 incidents of child pornography, an 85 percent increase since 2009, and a 38 percent increase in the number of persons charged, from 442 to 622. The increase reflects changes in legislation, better police enforcement both nationally and internationally, and changes in public attitudes toward the crime.[48]

Does Pornography Cause Violence?

An issue critical to the debate over pornography is whether viewing it produces sexual violence or assaultive behaviour. This debate was given added interest when serial killer Ted Bundy claimed his murderous rampage was fuelled by reading pornography.

Though early studies of the relationship between viewing pornography and sexual violence failed to find a link between the two, more recent research has found a consistent relationship between frequent viewing of pornography and sexually aggressive attitudes and behaviours, especially for males already at high risk for antisocial attitudes and aggressiveness.[49] In a 2009 review of research on the subject, Kingston, Malamuth, Federoff, and Marshall found that both experimental and non-experimental studies consistently reported a positive correlation between frequency of viewing pornography and antisocial attitudes, sexual arousal, and sexual aggressiveness, in both noncriminal and criminal subjects.[50] A 2012 review of research on the effects of adolescents viewing Internet pornography found that frequent exposure to Internet pornography leads to the development of unrealistic sexual values and beliefs among both male and female adolescents, along with a negative impact on self-image for both boys and girls who are made to feel inadequate in comparison to the body image and sexual

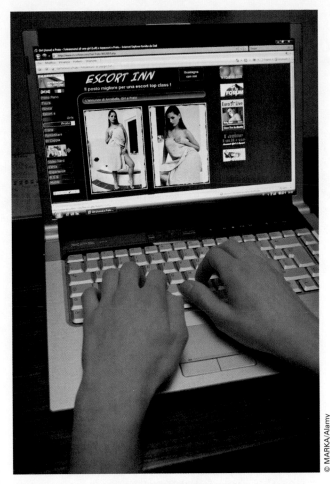

The technology revolution represented by the Internet poses a major obstacle for people who want to control or limit sex-related entertainment. Should such activities be criminalized? Or are they legitimate and harmless business transactions between consenting adults?

behaviours depicted in Internet pornography. In addition, studies showed that for male adolescents, early exposure to violent pornography was positively correlated with sexually aggressive attitudes and behaviours.[51] In the 2013 book *The Social Net*, Malamuth, Linz, and Weber conclude that the anonymity and uncontrolled nature of the Internet and the lack of an emotional connection to the people and acts being depicted, coupled with the social support that can be received from others with similar inclinations, sets the stage for the development of impersonal, aggressive attitudes among those attracted to viewing pornography, especially violent pornography.[52]

Pornography and the Law

Section 2(b) of the Canadian *Charter of Rights and Freedoms* protects free speech and prohibits police agencies from limiting the public's right of free expression. However, the Supreme Court held in *R. v.*

Butler (1992)[53] that although section 2(b) protects the right to "freedom of thought, belief, opinion and expression, including freedom of the press and other media communication," such freedom is subject to interpretation under section 1 of the *Charter*, which states that rights and freedoms will be subject to "reasonable limits prescribed by law as can be demonstrably justified in a free and democratic society." In the *Butler* case, the Supreme Court ruled that the distribution of obscene material is sufficiently harmful to society as to restrict its freedom of expression.[54]

The Supreme Court went one step further and ruled that any media that link sex with undue exploitation, violence, or degrading or dehumanizing treatment will almost always be considered obscene and potentially harmful to society, unless, based on an argument of artistic merit, the larger benefit to the community of viewing the material outweighs the potential harm. In effect, the Court shifted the emphasis in deciding what is obscene away from simply considering what the community finds offensive to a more comprehensive consideration of "harm" to Canadian society as a whole, as in promoting antisocial behaviour:[55]

> Harm in this context means that it predisposes people to act in an antisocial manner as, for example, the physical or mental mistreatment of women by men, or possibly the reverse. Antisocial conduct for this purpose is conduct that society formally recognizes as incompatible with its proper functioning.[56]

In other words, to convict a person of obscenity, courts must now refer both to what the community has defined as intolerable or "incompatible with its proper functioning," along with the potential harm of the material to Canadian society as a whole.[57]

In response in part to public outcry over the deaths of Amanda Todd and Rehtaeh Parsons, teenage girls bullied by others distributing sexual images over the Internet, in 2014 the government Bill C-13, *Protecting Canadians from Online Crime Act*. The amended s.162(1) of the *Criminal Code* now makes it an offence to observe or record and distribute by any means a visual recording of another individual secretly taken without their consent. Child pornography offences are also covered under s.163(1), which makes it an offence to make, print, publish, or access any written, audio, or visual material in which a person who is or is depicted to be under the age of 18 is engaged in any form of sexual activity.[58]

A March 2005 *Dr. Phil** show provided an update to the problem, when Kiza and Chris, a young couple about to be married, discussed Chris's addiction to Internet pornography on the show. "My fiancé's addiction to porn is out of control. I don't want to marry someone who has this problem. Can you help us?" asked young bride-to-be, Kiza. "Are you worried about marrying this guy?" Dr. Phil asked. "If he's not going to stop, yeah. Definitely," she said. "Porno is a normal guy thing," claimed Chris. "Every guy should have the right to look at porn." Chris said he'd never had any of his past girlfriends complain about it.

By the end of the discussion, Dr. Phil advised young Kiza that "You're not ready to get married to him in a few weeks. If you do, you are asking for trouble. You will absolutely break your heart if you are married to a porn addict."

LO4 Gambling

Legalized gambling is a relatively new phenomenon in Canada. A little over 100 years ago, gambling in any form was illegal everywhere in the country. However, beginning in 1892, the restrictions on gambling-type activities began to be lifted, first to allow religious organizations to operate raffles,

In January 2015, the Ontario government joined British Columbia, Manitoba, Quebec, and the Atlantic provinces in launching an online gaming site. The province hopes the online site will generate $375 million in profits annually to add to the $1.8 billion in revenue already generated from casinos, lottery tickets, and bingo. Critics argue the easy access and anonymity of online gambling will lead to an increase in the number of problem gamblers.

*From transcript: http://drphil.com/slideshows/slideshow/2385/?id=2385&showID=473

FIGURE 13.1

Net Revenue from Government-Run Gambling

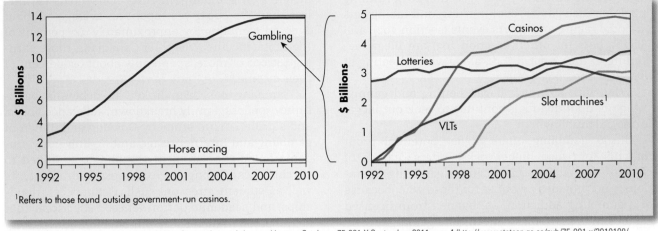

¹Refers to those found outside government-run casinos.

Source: Adapted from Statistics Canada publication *Perspectives on Labour and Income*, Catalogue 75-001-X September, 2011 page 4 (http://www.statcan.gc.ca/pub/75-001-x/2010108/pdf/11297-eng. pdf).

bazaars, and bingos, and later to allow racetrack betting. (See Figure 13.1.)

Though Irish Sweepstakes tickets were a popular, though illegal, lottery operating in Canada through the 1930s and into the 1960s, it was not until 1969 that the Canadian *Criminal Code* was amended to allow the provinces and the federal government to operate lotteries and casinos on a charitable basis to fund "worthwhile" activities, such as the 1976 Montreal Olympics, various other recreation and sports projects, and a host of religious and charitable activities.

Today, lotteries are operated exclusively by provincial governments, in the form of "commissions" that regulate lottery activities and distribute revenues. In 1985, an amendment to the *Criminal Code* gave provincial governments exclusive control over gambling, including administration of computer and video-gaming devices. On the heels of the amendment, a number of provinces introduced video lottery terminals (VLTs) into bars and corner stores, along with allowing racetracks to install computerized slot machines. In the late 1980s, in recognition of the sovereignty of their lands and government, First Nations people were granted the right to run permanent casinos in order to support band activities, provide funds for infrastructure development, and create employment.

According to Statistics Canada, government-run lotteries, video lottery terminals, casinos, and slot machines generated $13.74 billion in net revenues in 2010. Betting on horse races generated another $315 million in revenues. In Canada, gambling is big business—in 2010–11, 78 percent of Canadian households engaged in at least one gambling activity in the year, spending an average of $495 over the course of the year. Gambling is now included as a component of Canadian gross domestic product, with profits from gambling now accounting for 2.3 percent of total provincial revenues. Critics claim that provincial governments, charities, sports organizations, and others have now become dependent on gambling profits to make ends meet.[59]

DID YOU KNOW?

- Legalized gambling is a relatively new phenomenon in Canada.

- Provincial governments have exclusive control over gambling, generating an estimated $7.0 billion in net profits in Canada every year.

- Illegal gambling offers higher potential profit margins, and is especially attractive to chronic, addicted gamblers who have been banned from legal establishments.

- An estimated 3–5 percent of the adult Canadian population has a gambling problem.

- Gambling has been linked to debt and bankruptcy, job loss, family breakdown, substance abuse, crime, and suicide.

The Law on Gambling

Section 207 of the *Criminal Code* gives provincial governments the exclusive right to operate or grant others the licence to operate lotteries and other games of chance, including casinos (see Figure 13.1 for revenues). Anyone else operating lotteries or games of chance without the permission of the provincial government is breaking the law. Similarly, operating a gaming or betting house (section 201); running "pools" or dice games, book-making, and taking bets on horse racing and sports events (section 202); and placing bets for others (section 203) are illegal according to the *Criminal Code*, along with "cheating at play" (section 209).

Why, with so much "legal" betting and gaming going on, do individuals continue to seek out illegal forms of gambling?

Illegal gambling offers higher potential profit margins (but also higher risks); offers "games of chance" not available in licensed gambling operations; and provides an outlet for those who, because of a gambling addiction, are banned from licensed establishments.[60] Police officials and gaming regulators agree that while legal gambling formats are well regulated, illegal gambling enforcement is severely deficient. According to Statistics Canada, only 68 illegal gambling and betting-related incidents were recorded by police in 2013, a 37 percent decline since 2009.[61]

The Social Costs of Gambling

In a nationwide study of gambling problems in Canada, Cox, Yu, Afifi, and Ladouceur found that the proportion of Canadians estimated to have a "moderate" or "severe" gambling problem ranged from a low of 1.5 percent of the population in New Brunswick to a high of 2.9 percent in Manitoba and Saskatchewan. The average for Canada as a whole was 2 percent.[62]

Gambling is likely to be a problem in families that can least afford it. According to Statistics Canada, poorer Canadians spend a greater percentage of their incomes on gambling. In 2010, households earning less than $20 000 a year spent an average of about $390 on gambling, or approximately 2.7 percent of their total income. Wealthier Canadians, those earning $80 000 or more, spend only about 0.5 percent of their income.[63]

Gambling has been linked to debt and bankruptcy, job loss, family breakdown, substance abuse, and suicide. A 2010 study by Dowling and Brown of gambling and Internet usage among university students found that problem gambling was linked to psychological feelings of loneliness and anxiety as well as student stressors such as finances, friendships, and academic performance.[64] Police fear that as the problem increases, crime related to "feeding" the gambling habit will increase as well. According to a 2014 study conducted in Alberta, approximately 7.0 percent of problem gamblers engage in crimes, largely theft, fraud, domestic violence, and suicide. Overall, gambling-related crime accounted for only 0.6 percent of crime in Alberta; and since the introduction of legalized gambling in the province, charges for illegal gambling have fallen dramatically.[65]

LO5 Substance Abuse

Substance abuse is a problem found in all areas of the world. Large urban inner-city areas are beset by drug-dealing gangs, drug users who engage in crime to support their habits, and alcohol-related violence. Rural areas are important staging centres for the shipment of drugs all over the world, and are often the production sites for synthetic drugs and marijuana farming.[66] In Canada, 33 percent of young people between the ages 15 and 24 have used illegal drugs at some point in their lives.[67] According to the Health Canada 2011 Canadian Alcohol and Drug Use Monitoring Survey, nearly 40 percent of the Canadian population (about 13.4 million people) has used cannabis in their lifetime, with an average age of first-time use of 15.6 years. One percent of the Canadian population (more than 300 000 people) used cocaine or crack in the previous year, and nearly 10 percent of Canadians used at least one of six illegal drugs including cannabis, cocaine or crack, speed, ecstasy, or hallucinogens in the previous year.[68] According to Public Safety Canada, three out of every four offenders entering a federal correctional facility has a substance abuse problem.[69]

Possibly of even greater concern to police and treatment professionals now is the rapid increase in the illegal use of prescription drugs. According to the

DID YOU KNOW?

- Substance abuse is an ancient practice dating back more than 4000 years.

- There is a wide variety of drugs in use today; alcohol continues to be major problem.

- Police report that drug offences have been on the increase since 1999.

- More than half of drug crimes are for simple cannabis possession.

- There is no single cause of substance abuse. Some people may use drugs because they are predisposed to abuse.

- There is a strong link between drug abuse and crime. People who become addicts may increase their illegal activities to support their habits. Others engage in violence as part of their drug-dealing activities.

Canadian Centre on Substance Abuse, young people are most likely to be first exposed to prescription drugs through an illegal, recreational use, in most cases (67 percent) with prescription drugs taken from home.[70] Canada is now second only to the United States in the use of prescription opioids, powerful narcotics used to relieve severe pain. Between 1999 and 2007, prescriptions for oxycodone, one of the most powerful opioids, increased by 850 percent in Canada; across Canada, prescription opioid-related deaths now account for 50 percent of drug deaths annually.[71] In 2011, there were 102 overdose deaths in Ontario from fentanyl, an opioid said to be 100 times more powerful than morphine. In 2013, Alberta recorded more than 100 fatalities attributed to illegal, non-medical use of fentanyl.[72]

Despite the crimes, addiction, and deaths that flow from the use of drugs, including alcohol, many still view substance abuse as another type of victimless public order crime. There is great debate over the decriminalization or even legalization of drugs along with measures for the control of alcohol. Some consider drug use a private matter and drug control another example of government intrusion into people's private lives. Others see these substances as dangerous, believing that the criminal activity of users, and the death and destruction flowing from illegal drug use, makes the term *victimless* nonsensical. Still another position is that the possession of cannabis should be decriminalized; those found by police to have marijuana in their possession would be issued a ticket and fined for the offence, rather than receiving a criminal conviction. In the United States, recreational and medical use of marijuana is completely legal in Colorado, Oregon, Washington, and Alaska, and other states are already moving to full legalization. Others go even further to call for the end of the criminalization of all drug use and possession, arguing that substance abuse is better dealt with as a public health problem, making use of government control, education, and harm reduction strategies to reduce use and the harmful effects on individuals and society.[73] Alternatively, critics like Kevin Sabet, director of the Drug Policy Institute at the University of Florida, warn that legalization, even of marijuana, will lead to increases in drug use and addiction, especially among children, and points to research that shows poor educational outcomes for youth who smoke marijuana; others note the serious problems associated with alcohol and tobacco, and argue that the last thing society needs is another legalized drug problem. Police have expressed concerns that legalization of drugs will mean more impaired drivers on the road, and note that except for alcohol they lack the means to test for impairment.[74]

The Origins of Drug Use?

The use of chemical substances to change reality and provide stimulation, relief, or relaxation has gone on for thousands of years. Mesopotamian writings indicate that opium was used 4000 years ago—it was known as the "plant of joy."[75] The ancient Greeks knew and understood the problem of drug use. At the time of the Crusades, the Arabs were using marijuana. In the Western Hemisphere, natives of Mexico and South America chewed coca leaves and used "magic mushrooms" in their religious ceremonies.[76] Drug use was also accepted in Europe well into the 20th century. Recently uncovered pharmacy records circa 1900 to 1920 showed sales of cocaine and heroin solutions to members of the British royal family; records from 1912 show that Winston Churchill, then a member of Parliament, was sold a cocaine solution while staying in Scotland.[77]

In Canada, opium and its derivatives were easily obtained. Opium-based drugs were used in various patent medicine cure-alls, and recreational use of the drug was not uncommon, particularly in British Columbia, where a large population of Chinese immigrant labourers had been brought in to build the national railway. In fact, beginning in the 1820s, the British forced the Chinese government to accept opium as payment for trade goods, even going to war with China to force the issue.[78]

Alcohol and Its Prohibition

The history of alcohol and the law in Canada and the United States has also been controversial and dramatic. At the turn of the last century, a drive was mustered to prohibit the sale of alcohol. This temperance movement was fuelled by the belief that the purity of North American agrarian culture was being destroyed by the growth of cities and a lifestyle that included the consumption of alcohol. Urbanism was viewed as a threat to the traditional values and lifestyle of those living on farms and in villages.

The forces behind the temperance movement in Canada were lobbying groups such as the Woman's Christian Temperance Union and the Dominion Alliance for the Total Suppression of Liquor Traffic, a coalition of English Protestant groups.[79] They viewed the growing city, filled with newly arriving Irish, Italian, and Eastern European immigrants, most of them Catholics, as centres of drunkenness, degradation, and wickedness. In 1878, the *Canada Temperance Act* was passed, giving local

temperance movement The drive to prohibit the sale of alcohol in the United States and Canada, led by the Woman's Christian Temperance Union.

governments the right to restrict the sale of alcohol in their jurisdiction, with the result that some rural areas, towns, and cities were by law "dry," while others were "wet." During World War I, a total ban on the sale of alcohol in Canada was promoted by the Woman's Christian Temperance Union as a gesture of patriotism, and all provinces except Quebec had by 1916 imposed a ban on the retail sale of alcohol.[80] Though the province of Quebec did follow with its own ban in 1919, by the early 1920s support for Prohibition in Canada was on the wane, and most legislation was repealed by the end of the decade.

The situation in the United States was very different. The Eighteenth Amendment to the U.S. Constitution ushered in Prohibition in 1919. Legislation, in the form of the *Volstead Act*, restricted the sale of intoxicating beverages, defined as those containing one-half of 1 percent, or more, alcohol.[81] One consequence of Prohibition was the funding and growth of organized crime groups to supply illegal alcohol to a thirsty American population. Much of the alcohol was purchased from Canadian sources, which by 1925 could openly produce and sell beer, wine, and spirits.[82] Despite the exploits of Elliot Ness and his "Untouchables," American law enforcement agencies were inadequate, and officials were likely to be corrupted by wealthy bootleggers.[83] In 1933, the Twenty-First Amendment to the U.S. Constitution repealed Prohibition.

The Extent of Substance Abuse

Despite continuing efforts at control, the use of mood-altering substances, including alcohol, continues to grow in Canada. What is the extent of the substance abuse problem today? What should Canadians do about substance abuse?

Despite the media attention devoted to drug abuse, there is actually significant controversy over its nature and extent. Most illegal drug use by Canadians involves the possession of small amounts of marijuana. In May 2001, a federal parliamentary committee was struck to investigate drug use in Canada, and reported back that Canada should consider decriminalizing the "possession and cultivation of not more than thirty grams of cannabis for personal use." An April 2010 Angus Reid poll reported that 53 percent of Canadians believe that marijuana should be legalized.[84] In October 2014, the Toronto-based Centre for Addiction and Mental Health, one of Canada's largest substance abuse treatment providers, called for the

legalization of marijuana, arguing that Canada's current approach does more harm than good.[85]

In 2003, Vancouver opened the first "safe injection site" for heroin and other injection drug users to combat the spread of HIV/AIDS and other blood-borne infections. In response to claims made by the federal government that the program fosters addiction and runs counter to the government's "get tough on crime" policies, the case was brought before the Supreme Court of Canada in May 2011.[86] In September of the same year, in a 9–0 decision, the court ruled in favour of the continued operation of the site, stating that the risk of death and disease to injection drug users outweighed any benefit that might be derived from maintaining an absolute prohibition of possession of illegal drugs at the injection site.[87]

In 2013, Canadian police charged 61 367 persons with drug offences. As is clear in Figure 13.2, the majority of charges (56 percent) were cannabis-related, primarily possession, followed by cocaine-related offences (22 percent). Between 1999 and 2013, total drug-related criminal offences increased by 36 percent. Though still accounting for a small proportion of the total number of offences, offences related to the possession or trafficking of crystal meth increased by 400 percent between 2009 and 2013.[88]

How can the trends in drug use be explained? The increasing trend in drug crimes is similar to a pattern previously recorded in the late 1970s and early 1980s, when the baby boomers reached the prime ages for illegal drug use; some have argued their children, the "baby boom echo," are now passing through the same

FIGURE 13.2

Drug Offences in Canada, 1999–2013

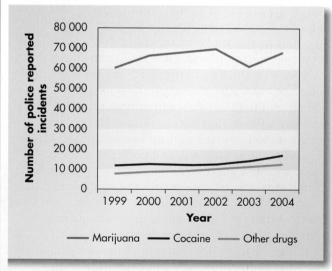

Source: CANSIM TABLE Table 252-0051 1, 2, 3, 54 Incident-based crime statistics, by detailed violations annual (number unless otherwise noted)

phase. But why has drug use remained a major social problem? When drug use declined in the 1980s, some believed that changing perceptions about the harmfulness of drugs such as cocaine and marijuana had had an impact, reducing the likelihood that youth would try them. Others believed that widespread publicity linking drug use, needle sharing, and the AIDS virus was leading people to see drug taking as dangerous and risky. Still, statistics show that illegal drug use among Canadians is on the rise, in particular for cannabis and other drugs, including ecstasy, amphetamines, barbiturates, hallucinogens such as LSD and PCP, and anabolic steroids. For example, in December 2010, Canada Border Services Agency and the RCMP made the biggest seizure of the date rape hallucinogenic drug ketamine in Canadian history. Five men were arrested and charged with importing a controlled substance and possession for the purposes of trafficking after police discovered more than 1000 kilograms of the drug, worth more than $15 million, hidden in a shipment of coffee mugs imported into the Vancouver port from Hong Kong.[89]

It also appears that it is easier to obtain drugs, especially for younger adolescents. For example, a U.S. survey found that in 1992 about 42 percent of Grade 8 students said it was easy to obtain pot; today about 47 percent say that it is easy to get that drug. In addition, parents may now be unwilling or reluctant to educate their children about the dangers of substance abuse because as baby boomers they were likely drug abusers themselves in the 1960s and 1970s.

The Causes of Substance Abuse

What causes people to abuse substances? Although there are many different views on the cause of drug use, most can be characterized as seeing the onset of an addictive career as either an environmental or a personal matter.

Subcultural View

Those who view drug abuse as having an environmental basis concentrate on lower-class addiction. Because a disproportionate number of drug abusers are poor, the onset of drug use can be tied to factors such as racial prejudice, devalued identities, low self-esteem, poor socioeconomic status, and the high level of mistrust, negativism, and defiance found in impoverished areas.

Residing in a deteriorated inner-city slum area is often correlated with entry into a drug subculture. Youths living in these depressed areas, where feelings of alienation and hopelessness run high, often meet established drug users, who teach them that narcotics provide an answer to their feelings of personal inadequacy and stress.[90] The youths may join peers to learn the techniques of drug use and receive social support for their habit. Research shows that peer influence is a significant predictor of drug careers that actually grows stronger as people mature.[91] Shared feelings and a sense of intimacy lead the youths to become fully enmeshed in what has been described as the "drug-use subculture."[92] Some join gangs and enter into a career of using and distributing illegal substances while also committing property and violent crimes.[93]

Psychodynamic View

Not all drug abusers reside in lower-class slum areas; the problem of middle-class substance abuse is very real. Consequently, some experts have linked substance abuse to personality disturbance and emotional problems that can strike people in any economic class. Psychodynamic explanations of substance abuse suggest that drugs help youths control or express unconscious needs and impulses. Drinking alcohol may be an indication of depression or other forms of mental illness.[94] A young teen may resort to drug abuse to reduce the emotional turmoil of adolescence, or to cope with troubling impulses.[95]

Personality testing of known users suggests that a significant percentage suffer from psychotic disorders, including various levels of schizophrenia. Surveys show that youngsters with serious behavioural problems were more than seven times more likely than those with less serious problems to report that they were dependent on alcohol or illicit drugs. Youths with serious emotional problems were nearly four times more likely to report dependence on drugs than those without such issues.[96]

These views have been substantiated by research involving a sample of 20 291 people in five large American cities. The results of this first large-scale study on the personality characteristics of abusers indicate a significant association between mental illness and drug abuse: About 53 percent of drug abusers and 37 percent of alcohol abusers have at least one serious mental illness. Conversely, 29 percent of the diagnosed mentally ill people in the survey have substance abuse problems.[97]

Genetic Factors

It is also possible that substance abuse may have a genetic basis. For example, the biological children of alcoholics reared by nonalcoholic adoptive parents develop alcohol problems more often than the biological children of the adoptive parents.[98] In a similar vein, a number of studies comparing alcoholism among identical twins and fraternal twins have found that the degree of concordance (both siblings behaving identically) is twice as high among the identical twin groups. These inferences are still inconclusive because identical twins are more likely to be treated similarly than fraternal twins and are therefore more likely to be influenced by environmental conditions. Nonetheless, most children of abusing parents do not become drug dependent themselves, suggesting that even if drug abuse is heritable, environment and socialization must play some role in the onset of abuse.[99]

In a recent study from McGill University, researchers have identified a "faulty gene" (known as CYP2A6) that may help to explain how some teenagers become more addicted to tobacco than others. The research suggests that there is no safe level and that those teens with the gene may be more susceptible to nicotine addiction even if they smoke fewer cigarettes per week.[100]

Social Learning

Social psychologists suggest that drug abuse may also result from observing parental drug use. Parental drug abuse begins to have a damaging effect on children as young as two years old, especially when parents manifest drug-related personality problems such as depression or poor impulse control.[101] Children whose parents abuse drugs are more likely to have persistent abuse problems than the children of nonabusers.[102]

People who learn that drugs provide pleasurable sensations may be the most likely to experiment with illegal substances; a habit may develop if the user experiences lower anxiety, fear, and tension levels.[103] Having a history of family drug and alcohol abuse has been found to be a characteristic of violent teenage sexual abusers.[104] Heroin abusers report an unhappy childhood that included harsh physical punishment and parental neglect and rejection.[105]

According to the social learning view, drug involvement begins with using tobacco and drinking alcohol at an early age, which progresses to experimentation with marijuana and hashish and finally to cocaine and even heroin. Although most recreational users do not progress to "hard stuff," few addicts begin their involvement with narcotics without first experimenting with recreational drugs. By implication, if teen smoking and drinking could be reduced, the gateway to hard drugs would be narrowed.

Problem Behaviour Syndrome (PBS)

For many people, substance abuse is just one of many problem behaviours. Longitudinal studies show that drug abusers are maladjusted, alienated, and emotionally distressed, and that their drug use is one among many social problems.[106] Having a deviant lifestyle begins early in life and is punctuated with criminal relationships, family history of substance abuse, educational failure, and alienation. People who abuse drugs lack commitment to religious values, disdain education, and spend most of their time in peer activities. An analysis of PBS by sociologist John Donovan found robust support for the interconnection of problem drinking and drug abuse, delinquency, precocious sexual behaviour, school failure, family conflict, and other similar social problems.[107]

Rational Choice

Not all people who abuse drugs do so because of personal pathology. Some may use drugs and alcohol because they want to enjoy their effects: get high, relax, improve creativity, escape reality, and increase sexual responsiveness. Research indicates that adolescent alcohol abusers believe that getting high will make them powerful, increase their sexual performance, and facilitate their social behaviour; they care little about negative future consequences.[108]

Substance abuse, then, may be a function of the rational but mistaken belief that drugs can benefit the user. The decision to use drugs involves evaluations of personal consequences (such as addiction, disease, and legal punishment) and the expected benefits of drug use (such as peer approval, positive affective states, heightened

© David J. Green - lifestyle themes/Alamy

awareness, and relaxation). Adolescents may begin using drugs because they believe their peers expect them to do so.[109]

Is There a Single "Cause" of Drug Abuse?

There are many different views of why people take drugs, and no one theory has proved adequate to explain all forms of substance abuse. Recent research efforts show that drug users suffer a variety of family and socialization difficulties, have addiction-prone personalities, and are generally at risk for many other social problems.[110] And although it is popular to believe that addicts progress along a continuum from using so-called gateway drugs to using ever more potent substances, that view may also be misleading. Research by Andrew Golub and Bruce Johnson shows that many hard-core drug abusers have never smoked or used alcohol. Examining a sample of more than 130 000 hard drug–using arrestees, Golub and Johnson found that the proportion who used marijuana before trying heroin and cocaine shifted significantly over time. The pathways may be different at various times and in different locales.[111]

In sum, there may be no single cause of substance abuse. People may try and continue to use illegal substances for a variety of reasons. As sociologist James Inciardi points out:

> There are as many reasons people use drugs as there are individuals who use drugs. For some, it may be a function of family disorganization, or cultural learning, or maladjusted personality, or an "addiction-prone" personality. ... For others, heroin use may be no more than a normal response to the world in which they live.[112]

An RCMP officer stands guard over fake bags filled with drugs representing one of the largest joint busts in Canadian history during a press conference in Toronto.

Drugs and Crime

One of the main reasons for the criminalization of particular substances is the significant association believed to exist between drug abuse and crime. Research suggests that many criminal offenders have extensive experience with alcohol and drug use and that abusers commit an enormous amount of crime.[113] Statistics Canada estimates that 11 percent of homicides are related to drug trafficking,[114] and more than two-thirds of those accused of homicide had consumed drugs or alcohol at the time of the offence.[115]

Substance abuse appears to be an important precipitating factor in domestic assault. Women (and men) whose partners are "heavy drinkers" are three times more likely to be victims of spousal abuse than if their partners drank only moderately, or not at all.[116]

Although the drug–crime connection is powerful, the relationship is still uncertain because many users had a history of criminal activity before the onset of their substance abuse.[117] Nonetheless, if drug use does not turn otherwise law-abiding citizens into criminals, it certainly amplifies the extent of their criminal activities.[118] And as addiction levels increase, so do the frequency and seriousness of criminality.[119]

It is of course possible that most criminals are not actually drug users but that police are more likely to apprehend muddle-headed substance abusers than clear-thinking abstainers. A second, and probably more plausible, interpretation is that most criminals are in fact substance abusers. Drug use interferes with maturation and socialization. Drug abusers are more likely to drop out of school, be underemployed, engage in premarital sex, and become unmarried parents. These factors have been linked to a weakening of the social bond that leads to antisocial behaviours.[120] Typically, as Table 13.1 shows, the drug–crime relationship may be explained in one of three possible ways.

Despite drug seizures like the one staged for the media in the accompanying photo, the importation and trafficking of illegal drugs remains a major source of income for organized crime.

In sum, research testing both the criminality of known narcotics users and the narcotics use of known criminals produces a very strong association between drug use and crime. Even if the crime rate of drug users were actually half that reported in the research literature, users would be responsible for a significant portion of total criminal activity.

Drugs and the Law

The federal government first initiated legal action to curtail the use of some drugs in 1908, with the

TABLE 13.1

Summary of Drug–Crime Relationship

Drugs and Crime Relationship	Definition	Examples
Drug-defined offences	Violation of laws prohibiting or regulating the possession, use, distribution, or manufacture of illegal drugs.	Drug possession or use; cultivation, methamphetamine production; cocaine, heroin, or marijuana sales.
Drug-related offences	Offences in which a drug's pharmacologic effects contribute; offences motivated by the user's need for money to support continued use, and offences connected to drug distribution itself.	Violent behaviour resulting from drug effects, stealing to get money to buy drugs; violence against rival drug dealers.
Drug-using lifestyle	Drug use and crime are common aspects of a deviant lifestyle. The likelihood and frequency of involvement in illegal activity is increased because drug users may not participate in the legitimate economy and are exposed to situations that encourage crime.	A life orientation with an emphasis on short-term goals supported by illegal activities; opportunities to offend resulting from contacts with offenders and illegal markets; criminal skills learned from other offenders.

Source: White House Office of National Drug Control Policy, *Fact Sheet: Drug-Related Crime* (Washington, DC, 1997).

passage of *An Act to Prohibit the Importation, Manufacture and Sale of Opium for Other than Medicinal Purposes*. Criminologist Neil Boyd observes that the original impetus for the act really had very little to do with an "opium use problem." Instead, racist, anti-Chinese sentiments in the Vancouver area had blossomed into full-scale rioting over fears that Chinese labourers were taking jobs away from white workers, and action to deal with the conflict was called for. Mackenzie King, the federal minister of labour at the time, intervened and, based on complaints from citizens about opium use in the Vancouver area, resolved that some good would come from the conflict, at least in the passage of an act to restrict opium use, which King found personally distasteful.[121]

In 1911, a revised statute, the *Opium and Drug Act*, was introduced, which now included cocaine as a prohibited drug. In addition, the 1911 act provided for a term of imprisonment for possession of either smoking-opium or cocaine. Additional amendments in 1922 introduced the new *Opium and Narcotic Drug Act*, which provided for a minimum six months' term for possession, deportation of immigrants convicted

of possession, and whipping of the convicted offender if so directed by the judge.[122] In 1923, marijuana was added to the act as a prohibited drug. In 1929, the penalty for possession of a prohibited drug was increased to a maximum of seven years' imprisonment.

In later years, other laws were passed to clarify existing drug statutes and revise penalties. For example, in 1961 the *Narcotic Control Act* was passed, which included the penalty of life imprisonment for importing or trafficking in narcotics. However, with growing drug use among the baby boomer youth population, increasing pressure was put on the federal government by parents and others to soften penalties for simple possession. Consequently, in 1969 the act was amended to provide for lesser "summary conviction" offences for possession.[123]

Throughout the 1970s, youth continued to challenge the law on drugs, and public sentiments about the use of drugs, particularly cannabis, continued to soften. Gerald Ledain, dean of the Osgoode Hall Law School, was commissioned by the federal government to review the laws on drug use, and bring forth recommendations to more effectively manage the growing problem of illegal drug use. Based on the Ledain Commission reports, in 1973 the *Narcotic Control Act* was amended to provide for absolute and conditional discharges as decisions of the court in drug crimes cases.[124]

The *Narcotics Control Act* was repealed in 1996, and replaced with the *Controlled Drugs and Substances Act*, which continues to govern illegal drug use in Canada today, along with the *Food and Drug Act*, which governs the use of legal drugs, including prescription drugs and other restricted substances. In March 2012, in the form of Bill C-10, the *Safe Streets and Communities Act*, the government of Canada introduced new mandatory minimum penalties for serious drug offences, including the production of marijuana, which now carries a minimum sentence of six months if committed for the purpose of trafficking or if the offender has a previous conviction, a maximum sentence of 14 years; and a minimum sentence of two years if the offence is committed near a school, in prison, or used the services of a person under the age of 18.[125] A relatively new initiative in Canada is the emergence of drug courts. Currently there are ten such courts in operation in major centres in Canada, including Toronto, Ottawa, Winnipeg, Calgary, and Vancouver, where court-monitored treatment and recovery is emphasized over incarceration for drug-addicted offenders. The Canadian government has committed funding additional funding for more drug treatment courts throughout Canada. The federal government has also acted to control alcohol-related

In June 2014, George Jung was released after spending 20 years behind bars in a federal U.S. prison. By all accounts, during the 1970s and 1980s Jung was personally responsible for smuggling more than 80 percent of the cocaine entering the United States, working with Columbian suppliers. Some credit him with responsibility for kick-starting the cocaine epidemic in the United States.

Jung's unlikely rise to cocaine kingpin is chronicled in the 2001 film *Blow* starring Johnny Depp as Jung. Dropping out of university and leaving his home in Boston for California, Jung soon realized the business potential of importing easily accessible and relatively cheap pot from California back to New England, and begins his smuggling activities. Caught by police and imprisoned, Jung meets a member of the notorious Columbian Medellín Cartel in prison, and so begins a partnership between Jung as the smuggling genius and the Cartel as the supplier of cocaine. The film portrays the wild, outrageous wealth and excess of Jung's world, driven by the growing demand for cocaine in the United States.

crimes. Spurred by groups such as Mothers Against Drunk Driving, impaired-driving laws in Canada are now among the toughest in the Western world. Under section 253 of the *Criminal Code*, an operator of a motor vehicle is "impaired" when the concentration of alcohol in his or her blood exceeds 80 milligrams per 100 millilitres of blood.[126] The penalties for being impaired when operating a motor vehicle range from a fine of $600 and prohibition from driving for at least one year for a first-time offence to 90 days in jail and as much as a lifetime ban from driving for a third offence.[127]

Drug Control Strategies

Substance abuse remains a major social problem in North America and in other countries throughout the world. Politicians looking for a safe campaign issue can take advantage of the public's fear of drug addiction by calling for a war on drugs. These wars have been declared even when drug usage is stable or in decline.[128] Can these efforts pay off? Can illegal drug use be eliminated or controlled?

A number of different drug control strategies have been tried, with varying degrees of success. Some aim to deter drug use by stopping the flow of drugs into the country, apprehending and punishing dealers, and cracking down on street-level drug deals. Others focus on preventing drug use by educating potential users to the dangers of substance abuse (convincing them to "say no to drugs") and by organizing community groups to work with the at-risk population in their area. Still another approach is to treat known users so they can control their addictions. Some of these efforts are discussed here.

Source Control

One approach to drug control is to deter the sale and importation of drugs through the systematic apprehension of large-volume drug dealers, coupled with the enforcement of strict drug laws that carry heavy penalties. This approach is designed to capture and punish known international drug dealers and deter those who are considering entering the drug trade. A major effort has been made to cut off supplies of drugs by destroying overseas crops and arresting members of drug cartels in Central and South America, Asia, and the Middle East, where many drugs are grown and manufactured. Canadian police and other drug enforcement officials work closely with their counterparts in the United States in an attempt to stem the flow across their mutual border. Three South American nations, Peru, Bolivia, and Colombia, have agreed to coordinate control efforts. However, translating words into deeds is a formidable task. Drug lords are willing and able to fight back through intimidation, violence, and corruption when necessary. The Colombian drug cartels do not hesitate to use violence and assassination to protect their interests.

The amount of narcotics grown each year is so vast that even if three-quarters of the opium crop were destroyed, the North American market would still require only 10 percent of the remainder to sustain the drug trade.

Adding to control problems is the fact that the drug trade is an important source of foreign revenue for developing nations, and destroying the drug trade undermines their economies. More than 1 million people in Peru, Bolivia, Colombia, Thailand, Laos, and other developing nations depend on the cultivating and processing of illegal substances. The U.S. government estimates that North Americans spend more than US$40 billion annually on illegal drugs, and much of this money is funnelled overseas. Even if the government of one nation were willing to cooperate in vigorous drug suppression efforts, suppliers in other nations, eager to cash in on the seller's market, would be encouraged to turn more acreage over to coca or poppy production. For example, between 1994 and 1999, enforcement efforts in Peru and Bolivia were so successful that they altered cocaine cultivation patterns. As a consequence, Colombia became the premier coca-cultivating country because the local drug cartels encouraged local growers to cultivate coca plants. When the Colombian government mounted an effective eradication campaign in the traditional growing areas, the cartels linked up with rebel groups in remote parts of the country for their drug supply.[129] Neighbours expressed fear when, in August 2000, the United States announced US$1.3 billion in military aid to fight Columbia's rural drug dealers/rebels. Ecuador's foreign minister, Heinz Moeller, told reporters, "Our worry is that the removal of this cancerous tumor will cause it to metastasize into Ecuador."[130] With increasing pressure applied by the United States during the 1990s for countries in South America to deal with the cultivation and distribution of cocaine, by 2005 Mexico had assumed a leadership role in the cocaine distribution market. Struggles between rival drug gangs caused violence and murders in the country to spiral, with more than a dozen Canadians murdered in the country since 2000, and in 2011 alone six Canadians were murdered.[131]

Interdiction Strategies

Law enforcement efforts have also been directed at intercepting drug supplies as they enter the country. Border patrols and military personnel using sophisticated hardware have been involved in massive interdiction efforts; many impressive multimillion-dollar seizures have been made. Yet the American and Canadian borders are so vast and unprotected that meaningful interdiction is impossible. And even if all importation were shut down, home-grown marijuana and laboratory-made drugs such as "ice," LSD, PCP, and crystal meth could become the drugs of choice.

Law Enforcement Strategies

It has proven easier for the police to infiltrate and prosecute known traditional organized crime groups than to take on the relatively unorganized drug-dealing gangs. Police also target, intimidate, and arrest street-level dealers and users in an effort to make drug use so much of a hassle that consumption is cut back and the crime rate reduced. Approaches that have been tried include reverse stings, in which undercover agents pose as dealers to arrest users who approach them for a buy. Police have attacked fortified crack houses with heavy equipment to breach their defences. They have used racketeering laws to seize the assets of known dealers. Special police task forces have used undercover operations and drug sweeps to discourage both dealers and users.[132]

Although some street-level enforcement efforts have succeeded, others are considered failures. Drug sweeps have clogged courts and correctional facilities with petty offenders while draining police resources. There are also suspicions that a displacement effect occurs: Stepped-up efforts to curb drug dealing in one area or city simply encourage dealers to seek out friendlier territory.[133]

Punishment Strategies

Even if law enforcement efforts cannot produce a general deterrent effect, the courts may achieve the required result by severely punishing known drug dealers and traffickers. In the United States, courts have taken a strong stand against possession and trafficking, imposing long, sometimes life sentences that have led to overflow of the prison system.[134] Many drug offenders sent to prison do not serve their entire sentences because they are released in an effort to relieve prison overcrowding.[135]

In contrast, Canada's federal Parliament introduced a bill in May 2003 to decriminalize marijuana possession, imposing instead a small fine. Significantly, although the proposed bill did not pass, drug arrests, the majority of which are for cannabis possession, dropped the same year.[136] A March 2010 EKOS poll found that 50 percent of Canadians agreed with the statement "Possession of small amounts of marijuana for personal use should not be a crime," an increase of 5 percent over a June 2000 poll.[137]

Community Strategies

Another type of drug control effort relies on the involvement of local community groups to lead the fight against drugs. Representatives of various local government agencies, churches, civic organizations, and similar institutions are being brought together to create drug prevention and awareness programs.

Citizen-sponsored programs attempt to restore a sense of community in drug-infested areas, reduce fear, and promote conventional norms and values.[138] These efforts can be classified into one of four distinct categories.[139] The first involves law enforcement–type efforts, which may include block watches, cooperative police–community efforts, and citizen patrols. Some of these citizen groups are non-confrontational: they simply observe or photograph dealers, write down their licence plate numbers, and then notify police.

A second tactic is to use the civil justice system to harass offenders. Landlords have been sued for owning properties that house drug dealers; neighbourhood groups have scrutinized drug houses for building code violations. Information acquired from these various sources is turned over to local authorities, such as police and housing agencies, for more formal action.

A third approach is through community-based treatment efforts in which citizen volunteers participate in self-help support programs, such as Narcotics Anonymous or Cocaine Anonymous. Other programs provide youths with martial arts training, dancing, and social events as alternatives to the drug life.

A fourth type of community-level drug prevention effort is designed to enhance the quality of life, improve interpersonal relationships, and upgrade the neighbourhood's physical environment. Activities might include the creation of drug-free school zones (which encourage police to keep drug dealers away from the vicinity of schools). Consciousness-raising efforts include demonstrations and marches to publicize the drug problem and build solidarity among participants.

Drug Education and Prevention Strategies

Prevention strategies are aimed at convincing youths not to get involved in drug abuse; heavy reliance is placed on educational programs that teach kids to say no to drugs. The most widely used program is Drug Abuse Resistance Education (DARE), an elementary and high school course designed to give students the skills for resisting peer pressure to experiment with tobacco, drugs, and alcohol. It is unique in that it employs uniformed police officers to carry the antidrug message to the students before they enter junior high school. The program has five major focus areas:

- Providing accurate information about tobacco, alcohol, and drugs
- Teaching students techniques to resist peer pressure
- Teaching students respect for the law and law enforcers
- Giving students ideas for alternatives to drug use
- Building the self-esteem of students

DARE is based on the concept that young students need specific analytical and social skills to resist peer pressure and refuse drugs.[140] However, evaluations show that the program does little to reduce drug use or convince abusers that drugs are harmful.[141] Although there are indications that DARE may be effective with some subsets of the population, such as children in junior grades, females, and Hispanic students, overall success appears problematic at best.[142]

Drug-Testing Programs

Some believe that drug testing of private employees, government workers, and criminal offenders helps deter substance abuse. In the United States, employees are tested to enhance on-the-job safety and productivity. In some industries, such as mining and transportation, drug testing is considered essential because abuse can pose a threat to the public.[143] Business leaders have been enlisted in the fight against drugs. Mandatory drug-testing programs in government and industry are common; more than 40 percent of the largest companies in the United States, including IBM and AT&T, have drug-testing programs. The American government requires employee testing in regulated industries such as nuclear energy and defence contracting.

In Canada, drug testing of employees is severely limited, and generally applies only where individuals are employed in "safety-sensitive" occupations (e.g., airline pilots) or where testing is a required condition attached to an alcohol or drug treatment program (e.g., probation or parole).[144]

Criminal defendants are now routinely tested at all stages of the justice system, from arrest to parole. The goal is to reduce criminal behaviour by detecting current users and curbing their abuse. Can such programs reduce criminal activity? At this point, the results of research evaluations of pretrial drug-testing programs are split in terms whether the programs reduce criminal behaviour.[145]

Treatment Strategies

A number of approaches are taken to treat known users, getting them clean of drugs and alcohol and thereby reducing the at-risk population. One approach rests on the assumption that users have low self-esteem and treatment efforts must focus on building a sense of self. For example, users have been placed in programs of outdoor activities and wilderness training to create self-reliance and a sense of accomplishment.[146] More intensive efforts use group therapy approaches, relying on group leaders who have been substance abusers; through such sessions, users get the skills and support to help them reject social pressure to use drugs. These programs are based on the Alcoholics Anonymous approach, which holds that users must find within themselves the strength to stay clean and that peer support from those who understand their experiences can help them achieve a drug-free life.

There are also residential programs for the more heavily involved, and a large network of drug treatment centres has been developed. Some detoxification units use medical procedures to wean patients from the more addicting drugs to others, such as methadone, that can be more easily regulated. Methadone is a drug similar to heroin, and addicts can be treated at clinics where they receive methadone under controlled conditions. However, methadone programs have been undermined because some users sell their methadone in the black market, and others supplement their dosages with illegally obtained heroin.

Other therapeutic programs attempt to deal with the psychological causes of drug use. Hypnosis, aversion therapy (getting users to associate drugs with unpleasant sensations, such as nausea), counselling, biofeedback, and other techniques are often used.

The long-term effects of treatment on drug abuse are still uncertain. Critics charge that a stay in a residential program can help stigmatize people as addicts even if they never used hard drugs; and in treatment they may be introduced to hard-core users with whom they will associate after release. Users do not often enter these programs voluntarily and have little motivation to change.[147] Supporters of treatment argue that many addicts are helped by intensive inpatient and outpatient treatment, and the cost saving is considerable.[148] Moreover, it is estimated that fewer than half of those who need drug treatment actually get it, so treatment strategies have not been given a fair trial.

Employment Programs

Research indicates that drug abusers who obtain and keep employment will end or reduce the incidence of their substance abuse.[149] Not surprisingly, then, there have been a number of efforts to provide vocational rehabilitation for drug abusers. One approach is the supported work program, which typically involves job-site training, ongoing assessment, and job-site intervention. Rather than teach work skills in a classroom, support programs rely on helping drug abusers deal with real work settings. Other programs provide training to overcome barriers to employment, including help with motivation, education, experience, the job market, job-seeking skills, and personal issues. For example, female abusers may be unaware of child-care resources that would enable them to seek employment opportunities while caring for their children. Another approach is to help addicts improve their interviewing skills so that once a job opportunity can be identified, they are equipped to convince potential employers of their commitment and reliability.

LO6 Decriminalization and Legalization

Considering these problems, some commentators have called for the legalization or decriminalization of restricted drugs. Drug enforcement costs Canadians more than $500 million each year, money that could be spent on health care or education.[150] One-half of Canadians support decriminalization of marijuana,[151] while others argue that "harm reduction" strategies, including public education and prevention, are a better means to address the drug problem than "prohibitionist" criminalizing approaches.[152] Certainly, the effectiveness of law

More than half of Canadians now support legalization of marijuana for personal use. At 4:20 sharp on April 20, 2012, thousands across Canada flooded the streets to call for the legalization of pot.

In July 2014 the U.S. state of Washington legalized the personal recreational use of small amount of marijuana. According to *The Province*, a Vancouver newspaper, as of July 2015 there were 171 licensed marijuana retail stores operating in Washington state. Across the border in B.C. at the same time there were 135 "medical marijuana dispensaries" in operation, despite the fact that they all operate in illegally in contravention of the *Controlled Drug and Substances Act*. In June 2015, in defiance of Ottawa, the city of Vancouver began licensing the illegal dispensaries, at a cost of $30 000 for a retail store, and $1000 for cooperative, nonprofit compassionate "clubs." As more U.S. states move toward legalization, and as public acceptance of pot smoking as a noncriminal activity grows, local governments are struggling to come to terms with the proliferation of illegal pot sales outlets—to accept license, and control them—or to continue to spend resources on shutting them down and prosecuting owners and customers.

Criminologist John Hagan notes that "conflict crimes" like pot smoking, gambling, and prostitution are difficult for the criminal justice system to deal with, simply because members of the public are unsure about whether such activities should be treated as crimes, and many members of the normally "law-abiding" public regularly engage in these activities. According to Hagan's schema, as more and more members of the public begin to question the illegality of these activities, as the "normative definition" of activities begins to change from illegal to legal, conflict crimes devolve into public accepted forms of social deviance, or even social diversions perhaps not completely acceptable, but still harmless.

Charlie Smith/The Georgia Straight

enforcement to stem the flow of illegal drugs must be questioned.

Drug expert Ethan Nadelmann argues that legalization is warranted because the use of mood-altering substances is customary in almost all human societies; people have always wanted, and will find ways of obtaining, psychoactive drugs.[153] Banning drugs creates networks of manufacturers and distributors, many of whom use violence as part of their standard operating procedures. Although some believe that drug use is immoral, Nadelmann questions whether it is any worse than the unrestricted use of alcohol and cigarettes, both of which are addicting and unhealthful. Far more people die each year because they abuse these legal substances than are killed in drug wars or from abusing illegal substances.[154]

Nadelmann also states that just as Prohibition failed to stop the flow of alcohol in the United States and Canada in the 1920s while it increased the power of organized crime, the policy of prohibiting drugs is similarly doomed to failure. When drugs were legal and freely available early in the 20th century, the proportion of North Americans using drugs was not much greater than today. Most users led normal lives, most likely because of the legal status of their drug use.[155]

If drugs were legalized, the argument goes, price and distribution could be controlled by the government. This would reduce addicts' cash requirements, so crime rates would drop, because users would no longer need the same cash flow to support their habits. Drug-related deaths would decline because government control would reduce needle sharing and the spread of HIV/AIDS. Legalization would also destroy the drug-importing cartels and gangs. Because drugs would be bought and sold openly, the government would reap a tax windfall both from taxes on the sale of drugs and from income taxes paid by drug dealers on profits that have been part of the hidden economy. Of course, as with alcohol, drug distribution would be regulated, keeping drugs away from adolescents, public servants such as police and airline pilots, and known felons. Those who favour legalization point to Portugal and the Netherlands as a countries that have legalized drugs and remain relatively crime-free.[156]

This approach might have the short-term effect of reducing the association between drug use and crime, but also might have grave social consequences. Legalization might increase the rate of drug usage, creating an even larger group of nonproductive, drug-dependent people who must be cared for by the rest of society.[157] In countries such as Iran and Thailand, where drugs are cheap and readily available, the rate of narcotics use is quite high. Historically, the availability of cheap narcotics has preceded drug-use epidemics, as was the case when British and American merchants sold opium in 19th-century China.

If juveniles, criminals, and members of other at-risk groups were forbidden to buy drugs, who would be the customers? Noncriminal, nonabusing middle-aged adults? And would not those prohibited from legally buying drugs create an underground market almost as vast as the current one? If the government tried to raise money by taxing legal drugs, as it now does with liquor and cigarettes, that might encourage drug smuggling to avoid tax payments; these "illegal" drugs might then fall into the hands of adolescents.

Full-scale legalization of controlled substances is unlikely in the near term, but further study is warranted. On the other hand, what effect would the Canadian government's policy of partial decriminalization (e.g., legalizing small amounts of marijuana) have on drug use rates? Would a get-tough policy help "widen the net" of the justice system and actually deepen some youths' involvement in substance abuse? Can society provide alternatives to drugs that will reduce teenage drug dependency?[158] The answers to these questions have proven elusive.

Summary

Public order crimes are acts considered illegal because they conflict with social policy, accepted moral rules, and public opinion. There is usually great debate over public order crimes. Some charge that they are not really crimes at all and that it is foolish to legislate morality. Others view morally tinged acts such as prostitution, gambling, and drug abuse as harmful and therefore subject to public control.

Some public order crimes are sex related, such as prostitution and pornography. In December 2013 the Supreme Court of Canada struck down the prostitution-related offences described in sections 210, 212(1), and 213(1) of the *Criminal Code* as being inconsistent with the *Charter of Rights and Freedoms*, in particular as they violated the right to safety and security of the person. In response to the Supreme Court ruling, in November 2014 new legislation was introduced by the Government of Canada, removing the word *prostitute* from the *Criminal Code*, but making the obtaining of, sale, advertising, and profits from the sale of sexual services illegal.

Studies indicate that most prostitutes come from poor, troubled families and have abusive parents. However, there is little evidence that prostitutes are emotionally disturbed, addicted to drugs, or sexually abnormal. Although prostitution is illegal, some cities have set up adult entertainment areas where commercial sex is tolerated by law enforcement agents.

Pornography involves the sale of sexually explicit material intended to sexually excite paying customers. The depiction of sex and nudity is not illegal, but it does violate the law when it is judged obscene. Obscenity is a legal term that today is defined as material offensive to community standards. Thus, each local jurisdiction must decide what pornographic material is obscene. A growing problem is the exploitation of children in obscene materials (kiddie porn). There is no hard evidence that pornography is related to crime or aggression, but data suggest that sexual material with a violent theme is related to sexual violence by those who view it.

Though gambling (in the form of lotteries, VLTs, casinos, bingos, and horseracing) is legal in Canada, it is not without its problems. Gambling operations net $5.4 billion in profits every year, and it is estimated that between 3 and 5 percent of Canadians now have a gambling problem. Gambling is especially likely to be a problem in families that can least afford it, and it has been linked to debt and bankruptcy, job loss, family breakdown, substance abuse, suicide, and a host of crimes.

Substance abuse is another type of public order crime. Most countries outlaw a wide variety of drugs they consider harmful, including narcotics, amphetamines, barbiturates, cocaine, hallucinogens, and marijuana. One of the main reasons for the continued ban on drugs is their relationship to crime. Numerous studies have found that drug addicts commit enormous amounts of property crime.

Alcohol is another commonly abused substance. Although alcohol is legal to possess, it too has been linked to crime. Drunk driving and deaths caused by drunk drivers are national problems.

There are many different strategies to control substance abuse, ranging from source control to treatment. So far, no single method seems effective. Although decriminalization of the possession of marijuana for personal use has been considered, the fact that so many people already take drugs and the association of drug abuse with crime make decriminalization or legalization unlikely in the near term.

Discussion Questions

1. Why do you think people take drugs? Do you know anyone with an addiction-prone personality, or do you believe that is a myth?

2. What policy might be the best strategy to reduce teenage drug use? Source control? Reliance on

treatment? National education efforts? Community-level enforcement?

3. Under what circumstances, if any, might the legalization or decriminalization of restricted drugs be beneficial to society?

4. Do you consider alcohol a drug? Should greater control be placed on the sale of alcohol?

5. Is prostitution really a crime? Should men or women have the right to sell sexual favours if they so choose?

READY TO STUDY?

IN THE BOOK, YOU CAN:

✔ Check your understanding of what you've just read by reading the Summary at the end of each chapter.

✔ Rip out the Chapter in Review card at the back of the book to have the key terms and Learning Objectives handy, and complete the quizzes provided (answers are at the bottom of the back page!).

ONLINE YOU CAN:

✔ Stay organized and efficient with MindTap—a single destination with all the course material and study aids you need to succeed. Built-in apps leverage social media and the latest learning technology. For example:

✔ ReadSpeaker will read the text to you.

✔ Flashcards are pre-populated to provide you with a jump start for review—or you can create your own.

✔ You can highlight text and make notes in your MindTap Reader. Your notes will flow into Evernote, the electronic notebook app that you can access anywhere when it's time to study for the exam.

✔ Prepare for tests with quizzes.

Go to www.nelson.com/student to access these digital resources.

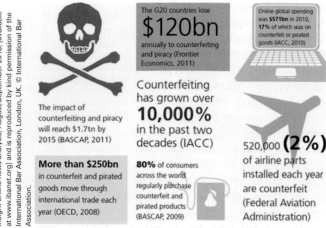

The impact of counterfeiting and piracy will reach $1.7tn by 2015 (BASCAP, 2011)

More than $250bn in counterfeit and pirated goods move through international trade each year (OECD, 2008)

The G20 countries lose **$120bn** annually to counterfeiting and piracy (Frontier Economics, 2011)

Counterfeiting has grown over **10,000%** in the past two decades (IACC)

80% of consumers across the world regularly purchase counterfeit and pirated products (BASCAP, 2009)

Online global spending was $571bn in 2010, **17%** of which was on counterfeit or pirated goods (IACC, 2010)

520,000 **(2%)** of airline parts installed each year are counterfeit (Federal Aviation Administration)

88% of high income Russians claim to have purchased counterfeit products (BASCAP, 2009)

2% of all world trade is in counterfeit goods (World Trade Organisation)

In 2011, over 114 million articles worth over **€1.2bn** suspected of infringing IP rights were stopped by customs at the EU border (EU Taxation and Customs Union)

LO5 Human Trafficking

Although human trafficking is today an offence under the *Criminal Code* of Canada and the *Immigration and Refugee Protection Act*,[55] the issue of the "trade" or "trafficking" in human beings is a relatively new issue that emerged only in the latter part of the 1980s.[56] The United Nations defines human trafficking as the recruitment, transportation, transfer, harboring, or receipt of persons by improper means (such as force, abduction, fraud, or coercion) for an improper purpose including forced labour or sexual exploitation, and refers to it as one of the world's most shameful crimes that robs people of their dignity and basic rights.[57]

the least policed form of global crime, even while it represents an increasingly important source of profits for organized crime and terrorist groups.[47] For example, recent research by Italian cyber-security experts Andrea Stroppa and Agostino Specchiarello shows that one out of every four (25 percent) of Facebook advertisements for cut-rate designer goods such as Ray-Ban sunglasses or Louis Vuitton handbags are in reality cheap counterfeit knockoffs.[48] Sales of counterfeit malaria drugs in Asia and Africa, which contain no active ingredients to combat the disease, may be responsible for as many as 200 000 deaths a year.[49]

According to the RCMP, organized crime groups have even entered the counterfeit children's clothing market, selling infant and children clothing that does not contain the fire-retardant fibres required by Canadian law—and that could burst into flames when exposed to heat or an electrical spark.[50] According to Lorne Lipkus, a Toronto lawyer who specializes in defending companies who are victims of IP theft and goods counterfeiting, "The Internet is on fire" with the proliferation of websites selling counterfeits. "It's giving them the ability to access the marketplace in a much easier way than if you just have a sign on a store."[51] A June 2012 report by the Canadian Chamber of Commerce reported that 80 percent of the counterfeit goods seized by Canadian authorities are manufactured in China;[52] the Alibaba.com website was identified as a major source of counterfeit goods, and governments and police agencies around the world have put increasing pressure on the Chinese government to regulate the goods sold on the website.[53] The Canadian Chamber of Commerce report concludes that Canadian laws and enforcement resources are inadequate to deal with the tide of counterfeit goods entering Canada, and their potentially deadly consequences.[54]

The UNODC maintains a human trafficking case law database that provides examples of human trafficking from almost every country in the world.[58] Human trafficking is a form of global crime affecting millions of victims and, while organized crime has a firm stakehold in human trafficking as seen in Figure 14.1, it is not the only perpetrator of such crimes. Furthermore, human trafficking comes in many forms and occurs in many locations from the sex trade to domestic servitude and forced labour in restaurants.

The true extent of human trafficking, in Canada and internationally, is difficult to determine because of the veiled nature of the crime and the difficulty identifying victims; however, it is known that in Canada women represent the majority of victims.[59] According to the Canadian government, those most at-risk are socially or economically disadvantaged, and include Aboriginal women, youth and children, migrants and new immigrants, teenaged runaways, children who are in protection, as well as girls and women, who may be lured to large urban centres.[60]

Canada was among the first countries to ratify the United Nations Protocol to Prevent, Suppress and Punish Trafficking in Persons through the creation of a National Action Plan to Combat Human Trafficking and the implementation of a four-pillar approach: prevention, protection, prosecution, and partnerships. A Human Trafficking Taskforce, led by Public Safety Canada and comprising key departments, is responsible for overseeing the implementation of the National Action Plan commitments and for coordinating the federal anti-human trafficking response and reporting annually on progress to the public.

In 2013 a new dedicated integrated enforcement team was created led by the RCMP and, since

FIGURE 14.1

Human Trafficking: Types and Locations

There are many subtypes of human trafficking, and it can take place almost anywhere. Though not a comprehensive list, each of the following forms of sex and labour trafficking can occur in any community in the Canada or the United States under the conditions of force, fraud, or coercion. Typical locations where sex trafficking cases are found include beauty salons, massage parlors and spas, bus stations or truck stops, casinos, hotels/motels, private and residential group homes, restaurants, bars, cantinas, streets, and strip clubs. Many sex trafficking cases are facilitated through Internet-initiated transactions. Some examples of sex trafficking cases include:

Massage Parlors
- "Former Chicago Massage Parlor Operator Sentenced to Life in Prison for Human Trafficking of Four Women" (US Department of Justice, http://www.justice.gov/opa/pr/former-chicago-massage-parlor-operator-sentenced-life-prison-human-trafficking-four-women (26 November 2012)).

Escort Services
- "Chicago Man Sentenced to 5 years in Prison for Sex Trafficking of Teenage Girl" (Cook County State's Attorney's Office, http://www.statesattorney.org/press_5YearsPrisonSexTraffickingTeenager.html (2 October 2014)).

Street Prostitution
- "Milwaukee Man Pleads Guilty to Sex Trafficking Offenses," (United States Department of Justice, http://www.justice.gov/opa/pr/milwaukee-man-pleads-guilty-sex-trafficking-offenses (6 November 2013)).

Child Sex Tourism
- "Pennsylvania Priest Indicted for Traveling to Honduras and Sexually Abusing Minor Boys" (US Immigration and Customs Enforcement http://www.ice.gov/news/releases/pennsylvania-priest-indicted-child-sexual-tourism-charges (6 October 2014)).

Typical locations where labour trafficking is found include agricultural fields, retail businesses, private and residential group homes, construction sites, manufacturing plants or factories, restaurants, bars, or cantinas, and fairs and other community events. Some examples of labour trafficking cases are listed below. Please note, some cases were resolved as discrimination or immigration cases, though they involved forced labour or individuals exploited and vulnerable to forced labour.

Agricultural Work
- "Federal Judge Finds Global Horizons Liable for Discriminating, Harassing, and Retaliating Against Hundreds of Thai Farm Workers in EEOC Suit" (US EEOC Press Release, http://www.eeoc.gov/eeoc/newsroom/release/3-24-14.cfm (24 March 2014)).

Construction Labour
- "Federal Agency Says 48 Thai Welders Forced to Work Without Pay in Squalid Conditions" (US Equal Opportunity Commission, http://www.eeoc.gov/eeoc/newsroom/release/archive/12-8-06.html (8 December 2006)).

Custodial Work (Hotels, Schools, Public, and Private Buildings)
- "Five Brothers Charged in Human Trafficking Scheme that Smuggled Young Ukrainian Migrants to Work as Cleaning Crews in Retail Stores, Private Homes, and Office Buildings" (US Department of Justice, http://www.justice.gov/opa/pr/five-brothers-charged-human-trafficking-scheme-smuggled-young-ukrainian-migrants (30 June 2010)).
- "Eight Uzbekistan Nationals Among 12 Charged With Racketeering, Human Trafficking, and Immigration Violations in Scheme to Employ Illegal Aliens in 14 States" (US Department of Justice, http://www.justice.gov/opa/pr/eight-uzbekistan-nationals-among-12-charged-racketeering-human-trafficking-immigration (27 May 2009)).

Elder Care
- "Highlands Ranch Man Found Guilty of Human Trafficking and Other Offenses" (US Department of Justice, http://www.justice.gov/usao-co/pr/highlands-ranch-man-found-guilty-human-trafficking-and-other-offenses (1 July 2013)).

Exotic Dancing
- "Lebanon Man Sentenced to 20 Years for Coercing a Minor to Become a Sex Slave" (FBI, https://www.fbi.gov/kansascity/press-releases/2013/lebanon-man-sentenced-to-20-years-for-coercing-a-minor-to-become-a-sex-slave (11 September 2013)).

Domestic Servitude (Housekeepers, Nannies, Home Care Providers)
- "Alexandria, Virginia, Couple Arrested on Immigration Charges for Harbouring Domestic Servant in Their Home" (US Department of Justice, http://www.justice.gov/opa/pr/alexandria-va-couple-arrested-immigration-charges-harboring-domestic-servant-their-home (5 March 2014)).

Food Industry
- "Jury Awards $240 Million for Long-Term Abuse of Workers With Intellectual Disabilities at Henry's Turkeys" (US EOCC, http://www.eeoc.gov/eeoc/newsroom/release/5-1-13b.cfm (1 May 2014)).

Public Begging/Street Peddling
- "Deaf Mexicans Forced to Peddle the Streets of New York and Sell Trinkets on Subways" (*The New York Sun*, http://www.nysun.com/new-york/deaf-mexicans-recount-enslavement-in-the-city/40556 (28 September 2006)).

Salons
- "Togolese Woman Sentenced to 27 Years in Prison for Forcing Young West African Women to Work Without Pay at Hair Braiding Salons" (US Immigration and Customs Enforcement (20 September 2010)).

Travelling Sales Crews
- "Two Men Arrested in Case of Orlando Kids Selling Items Door-To-Door in Palm Bay, Florida" (Florida Today, http://www.floridatoday.com/article/20131029/NEWS01/310290024/children-human-trafficking (29 October 2013)).

Restaurant Work
- "Mankato, Minnesota Woman Sentenced in Forced Labour Case" (FBI, https://www.fbi.gov/minneapolis/press-releases/2014/mankato-minnesota-woman-sentenced-in-forced-labor-case (16 December 2014)).

Source: Accessed August 16, 2015 from: https://www.ovcttac.gov/taskforceguide/eguide/1-understanding-human-trafficking/11-forms-of-human-trafficking/

UNITED NATIONS
VOLUNTARY TRUST FUND
FOR VICTIMS OF
HUMAN TRAFFICKING

Have a heart

for victims of human trafficking.

UNODC
United Nations Office on Drugs and Crime

www.unodc.org/humantraffickingfund

Donate now: United Nations Office on Drugs and Crime; Bank Austria; Bank code: Austrian BLZ Code 12000; Account no. 52515 025 025; BIC/Swift code: BKAUATWW; IBAN: AT62 1200 0525 1502 5025; Vienna International Center, Wagramerstrasse 5, 1400 Vienna, Austria

the beginning of 2014, the RCMP Human Trafficking Enforcement Team has launched investigations into 14 suspected cases of human trafficking involving foreign nationals. Of these cases, six have been closed, six are currently still under investigation, one has become a project considered among national and divisional RCMP priorities, and one ended with arrests, charges, and guilty pleas.[61]

Cybercrime

Cybercrime is any crime where the Internet and information technologies, such as computers, tablets, personal digital assistants, or mobile devices have a major role in the commission of a criminal offence. Public Safety and Emergency Preparedness Canada classifies high-tech crime as falling into two broad categories: (1) "traditional crimes" that are committed with the aid of a computer where the technology is the instrument used to commit crimes, such as fraud, identity theft, intellectual property infringements, money laundering, drug trafficking, human trafficking, organized crime activities, child sexual exploitation or cyberbullying, money laundering, distributing child pornography, illegal gambling,

virus
A computer program that disrupts or destroys existing programs and networks.

Internet fraud, and hate propaganda; and (2) "technically advanced crimes" that exploit vulnerabilities found in digital technologies. In these "pure" high-tech crimes, the technology is the target and activities are directed against a computer or a computer network such as "hacking" (unauthorized use of computer systems) and spreading viruses. Another form of global crime, cybercrimes can be launched from anywhere in the world against virtually any person or organization that uses a computer or other type of digital communications technology. (See Figure 14.2.)

A different type of computer crime involves installing a virus in a computer system. A virus is a program that disrupts or destroys existing programs and networks.[62] All too often, this high-tech vandalism is the work of hackers, who consider their efforts to be pranks. Many of these crimes are motivated more by malice than by profit. When computers themselves are the target, criminals are typically motivated by revenge for some perceived wrong, a need to exhibit their technical prowess and superiority, a wish to highlight the vulnerability of computer security systems, a desire to spy on other peoples' private financial and personal information ("computer voyeurism"), or a philosophy of open access to all systems and programs.[63] It has been estimated that these types of crimes cost the world

Back in 1993, Ontario Provincial Police Detective Sgt. Barry Elliott was working in the Anti-Rackets Branch in North Bay when he realized that telemarketing fraud was a rapidly growing, very lucrative form of crime that police were ill-prepared to deal with. In that year Det. Sgt. Elliott started Phonebusters, a call centre in North Bay designed to handle and track complaints about telemarketing scams—from fake charities, phoney prizes, computer repair scams and fake long-lost relatives needing financial help, to home repair scams, investment opportunities, phoney invoices and "special offer" deals requiring a credit card number. It soon became clear that telemarketing fraud was more than a North Bay, Ontario problem—and soon, the call centre was handling complaints from all around the world, and working with police agencies internationally to conduct investigations. By 2010, Phonebusters was handling telemarketing and computer scam complaints and mass marketing fraud and counterfeit good sales, and more and more companies and banks were approaching the unit with requests for assistance. In that year the Royal Canadian Mounted Police committed to providing long-term financial and operational support, along with renaming the unit the Canadian Anti-Fraud Centre (CAFC). Now retired from the OPP, Elliott continues to lead the CAFC's Criminal Intelligence Analytic Unit.

Elliott has received many national and international awards for his leadership in fighting mass marketing fraud and cybercrime. It's a long way from his start as a front-line OPP constable in Whitby, Ontario.

SANS Institute, poster is based on the original work of Brian Krebs.

YOU ARE A TARGET

Username & Passwords

Once hacked, cyber criminals can install programs on your computer that capture all your keystrokes, including your username and password. That information is used to log into your online accounts, such as:

- Your bank or financial accounts, where they can steal or transfer your money.
- Your iCloud, Google Drive, or Dropbox account where they can access all your sensitive data.
- Your Amazon, Walmart or other online shopping accounts where they can purchase goods in your name.
- Your UPS or Fedex accounts, where they ship stolen goods in your name

Email Harvesting

Once hacked, cyber criminals can read your email for information they can sell to others, such as:

- All the names, email addresses and phone numbers from your contact list.
- All of your personal or work email.

Virtual Goods

Once hacked, cyber criminals can copy and steal any virtual goods you have and sell them to others, such as:

- Your online gaming characters, gaming goods or gaming currencies.
- Any software licenses, operating system license keys, or gaming licenses.

Botnet

Once hacked, your computer can be connected to an entire network of hacked computers controlled by the cyber criminal. This network, called a botnet, can then be used for activities such as:

- Sending out spam to millions of people.
- Launching Denial of Service attacks.

You may not realize it, but you are a target for cyber criminals. Your computer, your mobile devices, your accounts and your information all have tremendous value. This poster demonstrates the many different ways cyber criminals can make money by hacking you. Fortunately, by taking some simple steps, you can help protect yourself and your family. To learn more, subscribe to OUCH!: a security newsletter designed to help people just like you.

www.securingthehuman.org/ouch

Identity Hijacking

Once hacked, cyber criminals can steal your online identity to commit fraud or sell your identity to others, such as:

- Your Facebook, Twitter or LinkedIn account.
- Your email accounts
- Your Skype or other IM accounts

Web Server

Once hacked, cyber criminals can turn your computer into a web server, which they can use for the following:

- Hosting phishing websites to steal other people's usernames and passwords.
- Hosting attacking tools that will hack people's computers
- Distributing child pornography, pirated videos or stolen music

Financial

Once hacked, cyber criminals can scan your system looking for valuable information, such as:

- Your credit card information.
- Your tax records and past filings.
- Your financial investments and retirement plans.

Extortion

Once hacked, cyber criminals can take over your computer and demand money. They do this by:

- Taking pictures of you with your computer camera and demanding payment to destroy or not release the pictures
- Encrypting all the data on your computer and demanding payment to decrypt it
- Tracking all websites you visit and threatening to publish them

This poster is based on the original work of Brian Krebs. You can learn more about cyber criminals at his blog at http://krebsonsecurity.com

As the above image details, computer crime encompasses a broad range of activities and in many cases we are all the target of cybercriminals.

Two Types of Cybercrime as Defined by RCMP

Source: Reprinted with the permission of the RCMP

economy over US$1 trillion per year in damaged computer systems and lost business.

In 2014, the RCMP released its first report on cybercrime in Canada and concluded with three general observations. (1) The Internet and related technologies have reshaped Canada's society and economy and created new opportunities for serious and organized criminal networks. Criminals are expanding their reach to create new crimes, and commit old crimes in new ways. (2) Cybercrime is expanding beyond the domain of criminals with specialized skills. Knowledge and tools to commit these crimes are more accessible, providing criminals with simplified ways to steal personal information and cause havoc to Canadian businesses and citizens. With the emergence of cyber technologies there has been a troubling rise in online child sexual exploitation and cyberbullying. (3) Cybercrime requires new ways of policing.

> The criminal exploitation of new and emerging technologies— such as cloud computing and social media platforms, anonymous online networks and virtual currency schemes—requires new policing measures to keep pace in a digital era. Criminal activities in cyberspace are complex and often transnational in character, where potential evidence is transient and spread across multiple jurisdictions. Addressing these challenges requires broad-based domestic and international law enforcement cooperation, engagement with public and private sector organizations, and integrating new technical skills and tools with traditional policing measures.[64]

Computer Theft Techniques

Computer theft has become so common that experts have created their own jargon to describe theft styles and methods:

- *The Trojan horse.* One computer is used to reprogram another for illicit purposes. In one incident, two high school–age computer users reprogrammed the computer at DePaul University, preventing that institution from using its own processing facilities.

- *The salami slice.* An employee sets up a dummy account in the company's computerized records. A small amount—even a few pennies—is subtracted from each customer's account and added to the thief's account. Even if they detect the loss, the

customers don't complain, because a few cents is an insignificant amount to them. The pennies picked up here and there eventually amount to thousands of dollars in losses.

- *"Super-zapping."* Most computer programs used in business have built-in antitheft safeguards. However, employees can use a repair or maintenance program to supersede the antitheft program. Some tinkering with the program is required, but the "super-zapper" is soon able to order the system to issue cheques to the thief's private account.

- *The logic bomb.* A program is secretly attached to the company's computer system. The new program monitors the company's work and waits for a sign of error to appear, some illogic that was designed for the computer to follow. Illogic causes the logic bomb to kick into action and exploit the weakness. The way the thief exploits the situation depends on his or her original intent—theft of money or defence secrets, sabotage, or whatever.

- *Impersonation.* An unauthorized person uses the identity of an authorized computer user to access the computer system.

- *Data leakage.* A person illegally obtains data from a computer system by leaking it out in small amounts.

An accurate accounting of computer crime will probably never be made because so many offences go unreported. Sometimes company managers refuse to report the crime to police lest they display their incompetence and vulnerability to stockholders and competitors.[65] In other instances, computer crimes go unreported because they involve low-visibility acts such as copying computer software in violation of copyright laws.[66]

Cybercrime is of utmost concern for the future, given society's increasing reliance on vital computerized services and the threat to national security that a disruption in these services might entail. Hackers pose one type of problem, but a disruption caused by organized criminal groups or political extremists might pose yet-unforeseen consequences.[67]

LO6 Cyberbullying

Cyberbullying has received much attention in recent years primarily due to high-profile incidents such as that involving Amada Todd. Cyberbullying is a type of harassment using social media (Facebook, Twitter,

Instagram, Snapchat, and YouTube), blogs, texting, and instant messaging. Cyberbullying is not always criminal harassment but if social media is used to engage in deliberate, repeated, and hostile conduct intended to harm, embarrass, or slander someone it may be classified as such. In March 2015, the *Criminal Code* of Canada was further amended to include the illegal distribution of intimate images of a person if the person distributing know that the person in the image did not consent to that image being distributed—or if the person distributing it is reckless about whether the person in the image gave his or her consent to that image being distributed. "Reckless" means knowing the person may not have consented to the image being distributed, but disregarding that fact.[68]

Cyberbullying may also be defamation. The *Criminal Code* (section 300) outlaws publishing a defamatory libel—material published, without lawful justification or excuse, likely to injure the reputation of any person by exposing them to hatred, contempt or ridicule, or designed to insult the person. But criminal defamation is rare; more common is civil defamation where communication about a person tends to hurt their reputation.

Whether cyberbullying is criminal harassment depends on the facts of a case. Cyberbullies use social media, blogs, texting, instant messaging, and other Internet avenues to engage in deliberate, repeated, and hostile conduct intended to harm, embarrass, or slander someone. Although their work is public, cyberbullies are often anonymous and it is often harder to identify and stop them.

Criminal Harassment

If a person is charged with criminal harassment or distributing an intimate image without consent,

Crown Counsel (the prosecutor) makes the case against (or prosecutes) him or her. The prosecutor may proceed by indictment for serious cases, and then the maximum penalty is 10 years in jail for harassment and five years in jail for distributing an intimate image without consent. Or the prosecutor may proceed by summary conviction for less serious cases, and then the maximum penalty is either a fine or six months in jail, or both.

The first stage of any criminal proceeding is generally an application by the accused person for judicial interim release, also known as bail. If the court grants bail to a person, it will usually order him or her not to contact the victim directly or through another person, or go anywhere near the victim's home, school, or place of work. It may also ban the accused from using the Internet, depending on the details of the crime he or she is charged with.

If the accused disobeys those terms, the court may revoke, or cancel, his or her bail. Then he or she may be charged with a separate offence of breaching bail conditions. If the accused is denied bail and sent to jail until a trial or a guilty plea, the prosecutor may ask the court to order that the person have no contact with the victim from jail. Again, if the accused disobeys this order, he or she may be charged with a separate offence.

If a court finds the accused guilty of criminal harassment or distributing an intimate image without consent, it can impose many different sentences. The court will choose a sentence based on the convicted person's criminal record and the severity of the crime. If the convicted person is not sent to jail, he or she will usually be ordered to obey certain conditions similar to the conditions imposed at the bail stage. For example, a court will normally order a person convicted

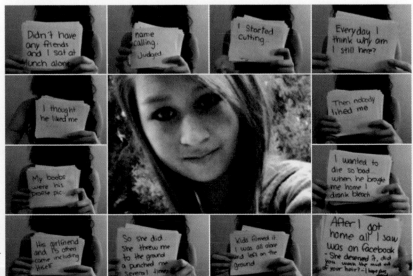

Courtesy of Carol Todd.

The Amanda Todd story made international headlines in 2012. After a topless video chat photo of the 15-year-old from British Columbia circulated to her Facebook friends, she endured a life of torment from classmates and strangers. In the wake of two failed attempts at suicide, hurtful, vicious comments appeared on Facebook suggesting that she try harder to kill herself: "I hope she dies this time and isn't so stupid." After posting a now famous cry-for-help YouTube video using note cards to detail her torturous life, she killed herself.

In March 2013 Jennifer Pawluck was charged with criminal harassment after posting anti-police graffiti on Instagram. The photo depicted senior Montreal police officer Commander Ian Lafreniere with a bullet in his head. The officer testified that the disturbing photo frightened shook him up, frightened his children, and caused his wife to stop working for a few months. Though Pawluck stated she was unaware of who the officer was in the photo, after considerable debate in the media about whether a charge should be laid in such circumstances, she was found guilty and received a suspended sentence.

of criminal harassment to have no contact with the victim directly or indirectly, to stay away from the victim's home and workplace, and to not own or carry any weapons. A court may also ban a convicted person from using the Internet. And a court may order a convicted person to take counseling, if it might help.

WHAT CAN YOU DO IF SOMEONE IS STALKING, HARASSING, OR CYBERBULLYING YOU?

1. First, if the harassment is attempted communication with you, tell the person to stop. Otherwise, they may not know that they are harassing you. Never reply to harassing messages—except to tell the person to stop.

2. Call the police to report the problem. Record the details of every incident, including time, date, place, who was involved, and what was said and done. Keep letters, notes, voicemail messages, emails, texts, instant messages, and social media and Internet posts. Give them to the police.

3. If the harassment happens at school, report it to school authorities, as well as to the police. If it happens at work, report it to your boss (or a co-worker, especially if the boss is the one harassing you), plus the police.

4. Report cyberbullying or other harassing communication to your Internet or cell phone company. Most companies have policies on acceptable use of their services, and can cancel the service of a customer who violates those policies. The company can also help police find a cyberbully who is using their network.

5. If you get a harassing phone call on a landline, dial *57 immediately when the call ends. The phone company will record the phone number that made the call, so the police can get it. If you receive harassing calls on your cell phone, call the phone company for help in tracking the calls.

6. You can seek a civil protection order in court. To do this, you need legal help. Links to more information on these orders are listed at the start of this script.

More information

- The **Cyberbullying** resource page. http://www.cyberbullying.ca
- **Web Aware**. Click on "cyberbullying" at http://www.bewebaware.ca
- The **Canada Safety Council**. Search for "cyber bullying" at http://www.safety-council.org
- **VictimsInfo.ca** http://www.victimsinfo.ca
- **Domestic Violence** http://www.domesticviolencebc.ca/dvbc/index.page

Source: Dial-A-Law © Canadian Bar Association BC Branch

Internet Scams

In the first six months of 2012 the Canadian Anti-Fraud Centre received almost 21 000 complaints of mass marketing fraud with losses of over $30 million and another 11 500 claims related to identity fraud/identity theft, costing cost victims $7.5 million. "These calls represent only about 5 percent of the people who have been duped," says Detective Con. John Schultz who is part of the CAFC team.[69]

The BBB has compiled its lists of the biggest scams of the year, showing that something that seems good may not live up to its promises.

1. *Top advertising scam:* If you place an ad on a free site such as Craigslist to sell your car, you may receive a call from unlicensed telemarketers offering to help sell your car. If you accept their offer, you will pay a fee of about $500 for posting to online classifieds you can post yourself at no charge.

2. *Top love scam:* You meet someone through a social networking or dating site who turns out to be from a faraway place. They fall in love with you in a very short time. The person gains your trust and asks for money to travel or help with a family emergency. Victims usually send money through wire transfer.

3. *Top financial scam:* Here the person earns the trust of an influential member of a group, family, or workplace to use this connection to get their hands on their money. The investment is a fraud; you lose your money and your relationships could be irreparably harmed.

4. *Top online scam:* Online financial fraudsters send email spam or they approach you on a social media website or a web forum. The target is consumers who go online for financial advice. Some spam will lead to an Internet ad, designed to gather your personal information. A fraudster will later approach you directly about the phony investment.

5. *Top sales scam:* "Curbers," buy old or damaged cars and sell them from parking lots or curbsides, advertising in newspapers and online ads. The buyer is out-of-pocket after realizing the vehicle has a long history of damages, a lien against it or the odometer has been rolled back. In some cases the vehicle may be stolen.

6. *Top youth scam:* You receive a text message that invites you to participate in a contest for a great prize. The target is smartphone users with web-browsing capabilities. You are asked to enter the PIN and later an email address with a link to another site to apply for a credit card. In the end you never receive a credit card and have given out personal information.

7. *Top computer scam:* Consumers receive a call with a warning that your computer has been infected with a virus. Then an offer is made to clean your computer for a fee. The target is homeowners who have a computer with an Internet connection. The result is that the scammer gets remote access to your computer and will also ask for credit card information for payment.

8. *Top business scam:* The business receives an invoice that appears to be past due, when in reality the company has had no dealings with the business listed on the invoice. The target is business owners and busy employees handling accounts payable. The result is that businesses pay a fake invoice or receive more threatening letters about the credit consequences of non-payment.

9. *Top home improvement scam:* Rogue door-to-door contractors will come to your home to seal or repave your driveway or fix your roof with product left over from another job. In some cases they offer a furnace repair that wasn't requested or a free "inspection." Targeted home owners are then out-of-pocket for unnecessary work or a poor job that has to be redone.

10. *Scam of the year:* An email that mentions the Better Business Bureau and says something like "Complaint against your business." You are asked to either click on a link or open an attachment. If you click on the attachment, you may download a malware virus.[70]

How Can You Recognize a Scam?

The CAFC says if it sounds too good to be true, it probably is. For example, you've won a big prize in a contest that you don't recall entering. You are offered a once-in-a-lifetime investment that offers a huge return. You are told that you can buy into a lottery ticket pool that cannot lose.

Controlling Internet Crime

The Canadian government recognized the threat posed by cybercrime in a 2007 report entitled *Overview of the National Agenda to Combat Organized Crime 2000–2006* that recommended that the government pay particular attention to high-tech crime. In the same year, the federal government passed the *Personal Information Protection and Electronic Documents Act* to protect e-commerce transactions in Canada. The legislation was designed to protect and ensure the safety of Internet-based commerce both nationally and internationally.[71]

Other legislation has been aimed at particular aspects of high-tech crime; for example, Bill C-15A, passed in 2002, created the offence of "luring" or exploiting children through the Internet. It is now an offence to transmit, make available, export, and access child pornography on the Internet. Tougher penalties for other related crimes have also been included.

Also in 2002, the Office of Critical Infrastructure Protection and Emergency Preparedness (OCIPEP) was established to provide national leadership in protecting Canada's infrastructure, both from external physical threats and those emanating from cybercrime. A comprehensive website (http://www.psepc.gc.ca) was created that includes information on subjects ranging from cybercrime to emergency procedures in the advent of natural catastrophes.[72]

A number of agencies have been created to deal with telemarketing fraud and cybercrime. For example, since 1993, the Canadian Anti-Fraud Centre has been operated jointly by the RCMP and the Ontario Provincial Police as a national anti-fraud call centre that collects information on organized telemarketing crime throughout Canada and disseminates the information to the appropriate enforcement agencies. A toll-free telephone number provides an avenue for complaints to be registered and, more importantly, to be used for prosecution and education purposes. In 1997, SeniorBusters was established to educate seniors about telemarketing fraud, to provide support for victims, and to collect information on the latest scams.[73] In December 2010, the Government of Canada passed the *Canadian Anti-Spam Law* (CASL) making it illegal to send unsolicited commercial electronic messages to non-consenting recipients, and a national anti-spam investigation and enforcement centre will be established in 2012.[74]

RECOL (Reporting Economic Crime On-Line), another national Web-based crime-reporting centre, was established in 2000 by the RCMP. Complaints can be made by phone, fax, or Internet concerning any frauds (traditional or Internet based), and clients will be referred to the appropriate agency for possible

In the 2015 movie *Blackhat* actor Chris Hemsworth plays a convicted computer-hacker Nick Hathaway who is released from prison to help a joint U.S.–Chinese task force that is racing against time to catch a cyber-terrorist responsible for sabotaging a nuclear reaction in Hong Kong, and causing a stock market crash on the New York Stock Exchange. Led by Nick's former MIT roommate, Chinese agent Chen Dawai (Wang Leehom), his network engineer sister Lien (Tang Wei), and FBI agent Carol Barrett (Viola Davis), the group pursues the cyberterrorist across the globe in a frantic, sometime violent attempt to identify and stop him before worldwide disaster strikes. With the murders of both Dawai and Barrett, Hathaway and Lien are left to pursue the cyberterrorist, now known as the deadly paramilitary leader Kassar, to Jakarta, where they hack into his computer and discover that his motive is to make billions in profits by destabilizing world markets. By stealing his ill-gotten profits, Hathaway and Lien provoke a violent confrontation with the cyberterrorist and his gang, ending with Hathaway killing Kassar, and escaping with Lien and the cyberterrorist's money.

© Photos 12/Alamy Stock Photo

investigation and follow-up. RECOL is also involved with consumer education. The RECOL Centre links the RCMP, the Ontario Provincial Police, the U.S. Federal Bureau of Investigation, and other international police agencies. The RCMP is working with the Law Enforcement Working Group of the G8 nations to establish similar complaint-distribution systems in each country. Canadian Eagle is yet another joint law enforcement effort between the RCMP and the FBI that investigates organized crime where fraudulent cross-border telemarketing activity is involved.[75]

LO8 Terrorism

In addition to interpersonal violence and street crime, another category of violence is politically motivated acts, including terrorism. Political crime has been with us throughout history. It is virtually impossible to find a society without political criminals, who have been described as "those craftsmen of dreams who possess a gigantic reservoir of creative energy as well as destructive force."[76] One aspect of political violence that greatly concerns criminologists is terrorism.[77] Because of its complexity, an all-encompassing definition of terrorism is difficult to formulate. However, most experts agree that it generally involves the illegal use of force against innocent people to achieve a political objective.[78]

terrorism
The illegal use of force against innocent people to achieve a political objective.

One U.S. commission defined terrorism as "a tactic or technique by means of which a violent act or the threat thereof is used for the prime purpose of creating overwhelming fear for coercive purposes."[79] In Canada, "terrorism" is defined in law by Section 83.01 of the *Criminal Code*. Terrorism is generally defined as a type of political crime that emphasizes violence as a mechanism to promote change. Although some political criminals may demonstrate, counterfeit, sell secrets, or spy, terrorists systematically murder and destroy or threaten such violence to terrorize individuals, groups, communities, or governments into conceding to the terrorists' political demands.[80] However, it may be erroneous to equate terrorism with political goals because not all terrorist actions are aimed at political change; some terrorists may try to bring about economic or social reform, for example, by attacking women wearing fur coats or sabotaging property during a labour dispute. Terrorism must also be distinguished from conventional warfare because it requires secrecy and clandestine operations to exert social control over large populations.[81]

Forms of Terrorism

Today the term *terrorism* describes many different behaviours and goals. Some of the more common forms are briefly described here.[82]

Revolutionary Terrorists

Revolutionary terrorists use violence against a regime that they consider to have unjustly taken control of their land either by force or coercion. In the Middle East, terrorist activities were first linked to Jewish groups such as the Irgun and Stern Gang, which were successful in driving the British out of Palestine in the 1940s, leading to the creation of Israel and today to Muslim groups such as Hamas and Hezbollah, which seek to do the same to Israel.

Political Terrorists

Political terrorism is directed at people or institutions who oppose the terrorists' political ideology. North American political terrorists tend to be heavily armed groups organized around themes such as white supremacy, militant tax resistance, and religious revisionism. Identified groups have included the Aryan Nation, the Posse Comitatus, and the Ku Klux Klan.

Recently, right-wing political extremists have engaged in a pattern of uncoordinated violence motivated by hate, rage, and the inability of more coordinated groups to either bring down the U.S. government or gain public support.[83] Although unlikely to topple the government, these individualistic acts of terror are difficult to predict or control. On 19 April 1995, 168 people were killed during the Oklahoma City bombing, and on 11 September 2001, over 3000 people perished in the World Trade Center towers in New York City and the Pentagon in Washington, D.C. These were the most extreme examples of political terrorism in North America.

Nationalist Terrorism

Nationalist terrorism promotes the interests of a minority ethnic or religious group that believes it has been persecuted under majority rule in an effort to secure a homeland within the country. In Spain, Basque terrorists have assassinated Spanish officials in order to convince the government to create a separate Basque homeland in Northern Spain. In December 2006, Pakistani political leader Benazir Bhutto was assassinated in front of thousands of supporters while attending a rally in a public park. Bhutto died in an explosion that also killed those responsible for detonating the bomb. It is believed that Islamist terrorists, or perhaps even Pakistan's own secret intelligence service, may have been behind the assassination, with the goal of destabilizing the Pakistan People's Party (PPP) that Bhutto led, and that was poised to return the popular leader to power.[84]

Cause-Based Terrorism

When the U.S. embassies in Kenya and Tanzania were bombed in 1998, killing more than 250 people,

Osama bin Laden's Al Qaeda movement was quickly identified as the culprit. In a 1997 interview with CNN, bin Laden said his *jihad*, or holy war, against the United States was started because American forces were still operating in Saudi Arabia. He demanded that the United States end its "aggressive intervention against Muslims in the whole world."[85] On 11 September 2001, bin Laden continued the *jihad* by bringing the holy war onto American soil, with attacks on the World Trade Center and the Pentagon. Thus began a ten-year-long search by U.S. authorities for the terrorist, which ended in the early morning hours of 1 May 2011, when U.S. Navy Seals shot and killed bin Laden at a residential compound in Pakistan, where he had been living in hiding for some months.

Osama bin Laden's brand of terrorist activity is one of many conducted by groups that espouse a particular social or religious cause and use violence to address their grievances.[86] For example, anti-abortion groups have demonstrated at abortion clinics, and some members have attacked clients, bombed offices, and killed doctors who perform abortions. On 31 May 2009, Dr. George Tiller was shot and killed while serving as an usher for Sunday services at the Reformation Lutheran Church in Wichita,

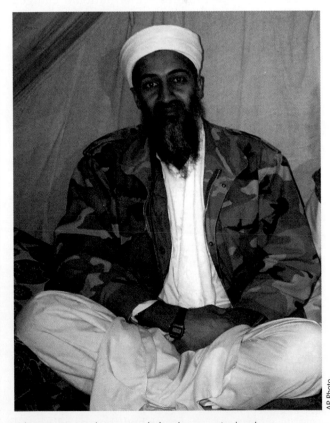

After a 10-year-long search for the terrorist leader, U.S. Navy Seals shot and killed Osama bin Laden at a residential compound in Pakistan.

CHAPTER 14 The Challenge of Crime in the 21st Century: A Global Criminology **333**

Kansas. He was one of a growing number of abortion providers believed to be the victims of terrorists who ironically claim to be "pro-life."[87]

State-Sponsored Terrorism

State-sponsored terrorism occurs when a repressive governmental regime forces its citizens into obedience, oppresses minorities, and stifles political dissent.[88]

Much of what we know about state-sponsored terrorism comes from the efforts of human rights groups. London-based Amnesty International maintains that tens of thousands of people continue to become victims of security operations that result in disappearances and executions.[89] Political prisoners are now being tortured in about 100 countries; people have disappeared or are being held in secret detention in about 20; and government-sponsored death squads have been operating in more than 35. Countries known for encouraging violent control of dissidents include Brazil, Colombia, Guatemala, Honduras, Peru, Sudan, Libya, and, most notably, Iraq, where the United States waged an all-out war against Saddam Hussein's state-sponsored terrorism. When Tupac Amaru rebels seized and held hostages at the Japanese ambassador's villa in Peru on 17 December 1996, Amnesty International charged that the action came in response to a decade-long campaign of human rights violations by national security forces and extensive abuses against opposition groups.[90]

The most extreme form of state-sponsored terrorism occurs when a government seeks to wipe out a minority group within its jurisdiction. This atrocity is referred to as genocide. The Holocaust is the most extreme example of genocide to date, but more recent occurrences have taken place in Cambodia, Rwanda, Sudan, the Democratic Republic of the Congo, Bosnia, and Somalia, among others.

Cyberterrorism

FBI director James Comey is steadfast in his belief that the North Korean government was responsible for the mammoth computer hack on Sony pictures following the release of the movie, *The Interview*. He said that the hackers "got sloppy" and allowed their location to be identified on a number of occasions and that this belief is shared by the entire intelligence community.

genocide
The attempt by a government to wipe out a minority group within its jurisdiction.

In December 2015 the FBI stated that an analysis of the malware used in the attack had shown coding and encryption similarities to previous malignant software

The release of the controversial movie *The Interview* (2014) was originally delayed because of a series of terrorist threats aimed at the theatre chain planning to screen the film connected to Sony's computer hacking scandal. The media attaction no doubt contributed to making it Sony's most successful digital release ever.

used in known North Korean attacks. The director of national intelligence, James Clapper, described the attack as "the most serious cyber-attack ever made against US interests."[91] He said that North Korean government officials will not tolerate criticism or affronts to their supreme leader, whom they consider to be a deity. "I watched *The Interview* over the weekend and it's obvious to me that North Koreans don't have a sense of humour."[92] Sony pictures has been left reeling from the November attack after thousands of documents were published online including personal email correspondence, employees' personal data, executive pay information, and unreleased films and scripts. *The Interview*, which stars James Franco and Seth Rogen, was initially pulled from theatrical release but subsequently made available online and has become Sony's highest-grossing digital release.

North Korea is not the only country to engage in cyberattacks. The United States is involved in efforts to hamper Iran's uranium enrichment program, which Western powers and the International Atomic Energy Agency say it is not authorized to develop. The Stuxnet virus, which first emerged in 2010, has been referred to as the world's first cyberweapon.[93] Jointly developed by the United States and Israel, it was designed to shut down the development of Iran's nuclear program. The work on the Stuxnet virus can be traced to the 2006 Olympic Games when the Iranians restarted their uranium enrichment program. Initially, US president Bush considered military action, but his intelligence advisors suggested cyberattacks. Teaming up with a secret Israeli unit, the Americans had workers at the facility where the uranium enrichment program was housed unwittingly infect Iran's computer system with the virus, which was loaded on thumb drives.

A Russian computer security expert identified some of the biggest cyberthreats to world security, the first being the type of cyber warfare exemplified by Stuxnet and the malware attack on Iranian computer systems.[94] This type of attack could be replicated on a world-wide scale and one of the most sensitive and damaging targets is hydroelectric plants. Most hydro plants in the world are similar in design and a calculated cyberattack has the potential to plunge the world into darkness.

The potential manipulation of social media poses a significant cyberthreat to world security. The Arab Spring was a revolutionary wave of demonstrations, protests, riots, and civil wars in the Arab world that began in December 2010 and quickly spread throughout the Arab world. By the end of February 2012, rulers had been forced from power in Tunisia, Egypt, Libya, and Yemen, with civil uprisings erupting in more than a dozen other countries that make up the Arab League of Nations. Though the uprisings used traditional techniques of civil resistance such as strikes, demonstrations, marches, and rallies, it was one of the first times that social media was used to organize and communicate, even when Arab governments attempted to shut down the Internet. It is argued that social media could be manipulated by using false information that could lead to mass panic and disobedience.[95]

Another threat to world security is the threat to personal privacy. With the advent of Google street view, drones taking pictures from the air, the proliferation of closed circuit television cameras, and web-based companies collecting so much personal information, personal privacy may be a thing of the past. Even world leaders are affected by this lack of privacy as evidenced by the recent incident where it was discovered that Chancellor Angela Merkel's cell phone was being monitored not by China or Russia but by U.S. intelligence services. The scandal caused Merkel to send a stern admonition to the U.S. president.[96] Another incident causing considerable

On 14 August 2003, it took only three minutes to shut down 21 power plants in the Eastern United States and Canada, knocking out power to 50 million people and stopping trains and disrupting cell phone service, water service, traffic lights, airports, and hospitals. Though this event was caused by overworked power grids due to hot weather, experts warn that a well-planned cyberattack could plunge the entire world into a blackout with catastrophic consequences.

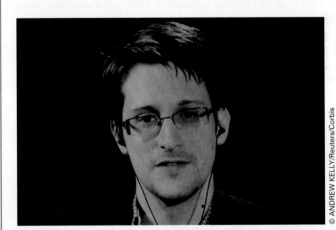

Former contractor for the National Security Agency (NSA) operated by the United States, Edward Snowden was charged with theft of government property, unauthorized communication of national defence information, and willful communication of classified communications intelligence after disclosing classified information. Allegations of NSA phone-tapping came out in the secrets leaked by the whistleblower in 2013. After revealing extensive, global Internet and phone surveillance, Snowden fled to Russia where he lives today.

In June 2013, the Calgary Police Service's Cybercrime Support Team was called into action to deal with a threat of a mass shooting at the Calgary Stampede. Why the Cybercime Support Team and not the SWAT Team? Because cybercrime, including the use of digital technology to threaten others, is the new reality in 21st-century policing. According to Calgary Mayor Naheed Nenshi "It's a new world out there, in terms of the law and how we imagine crime." The Cybercrime Support Team officers quickly traced the threatening email to a Calgary man who was found in possession of multiple weapons. He was later sentenced to two years in prison, along with mandatory psychiatric counselling. According to Staff Sergeant Ryan Jepson, who supervises the Cybercrime Support Team, there has been a dramatic increase in cybercrime complaints, and the Calgary team is "on the leading edge" in investigating and prosecuting cybercrimes.

The Calgary Police Service Cybercrime Support team is a good example of the changing nature of crime confronting police officers in the 21st century, and points to what many criminologists now advocate for in terms of a "global criminology." Cybercrimes can be committed by perpetrators from anywhere in the world, which points to the need for international cooperation between law enforcement agencies, private organizations, and government to devise new crime prevention strategies to deter cybercriminals.

Source: Dylan Robertson, "Cybercrime Unit Tackles Digital Crime at the 'Leading Edge' of policing," *Calgary Herald* (14 May 2014), p. A12.

---

anxiety among some world leaders, not to mention much of the general public, was the 2015 hack into the Ashley Madison website, which offers an extra-marital dating service. Close to 40 million customer profiles from the service were published online leading in some instances to extortion, phishing attempts and even suicide. Two Canadian law firms have filed a $578 million class-action lawsuit against the companies that run the website.[97]

Home-Grown Terrorism

In a recent speech, Canadian Defence Minister Jason Kenney warned Canadians that homegrown terrorism in this country is now a "reality" and that the threat of terrorism has never been greater.[98] Kenney said "brutal attacks" including that in Quebec in 2014 of 53-year-old Warrant Officer Patrice Vincent; the fatal 2014 shooting of Corporal Nathan Cirillo in Ottawa; the "Toronto 18" terrorist cell caught in 2006; the plot to bomb the B.C. legislature in 2013; and the plot to bomb Via Rail in 2012 all involved home-grown terrorists. According to Kenney, *jihadism* is a global movement with terrorist attacks occurring in Paris, West Africa, the Middle East, the Philippines and Indonesia. In an attempt to thwart future terrorist attacks, the conservative government introduced Bill C-51 aimed at giving additional powers to the Canadian Security and Intelligence Service (CSIS) and the RCMP. Some believe the bill threatens civil liberties and lacks sufficient independent oversight. The bill redefines threats to national security to include interference with critical infrastructure, including cybersystems, and to the "economic and financial stability" of Canada. The bill also gives police-like powers to Canadian spies to enable them to disrupt suspected threats to the nation, often without judicial warrants. A new category of crime will be created, making it illegal to promote terrorism and lowering the legal threshold required for police to arrest and detain suspected extremists. Bill C-50 is a clear indication of the impact terrorism and, particularly home-grown terrorism, is having on Canada and other nations of the world.[99] Whether the bill will ultimately become law will be determined by the 2015 Canadian federal election.

Responses to Terrorism

Governments have tried numerous responses to terrorism. The attacks on 11 September 2001, changed these responses from being largely passive to more active steps. Across the world, governments have implemented tough new security measures at border checkpoints and in airports and at seaports. In Canada, the *Anti-Terrorism Act* was implemented in 2001 to give the government more powers to investigate and arrest suspected terrorists and sympathizers providing support and financial resources to terrorist groups, along with other measures designed to strengthen Canada's border security. In the United States, the Department of Homeland Security was created to coordinate all efforts to protect citizens at home in the United States. In addition, the U.S. government went to war with Iraq to end Saddam Hussein's campaign of state-sponsored terrorism. Law enforcement agencies have infiltrated terrorist groups and turned members over to police.[100] Rewards are often offered for information leading to the arrest of terrorists. "Democratic" elections have been held to discredit terrorists' complaints that the state is oppressive. Counterterrorism laws have increased penalties and decreased political rights afforded known terrorists.

Summary

Internet sites that can be accessed using only specialized software like TOR make up what is known as the Dark Web, where anonymous users can use untraceable Bitcoin currency to sell and purchase almost any contraband or illegal product or service, including drugs, child pornography, weapons, even murder for hire. Today, the motives for committing crimes, such as greed, jealousy, control, anger, revenge, and excitement remain the same, but the means to commit these crimes have become more technological and more anonymous, and require a new level of sophistication in the techniques used by the criminal justice system to detect, investigate, and prosecute those involved.

A growing number of criminologists and criminal justice professionals recognize the need for a more encompassing "global theory of criminology," one that appreciates the extent to which the causes, techniques, and consequences of crime are connected across societies. Among the crimes pointed to as examples of the transnational nature of crime by global criminologists are state crime, international finance crime, transnational goods counterfeiting, human trafficking, cybercrime, and terrorism. In the 21st century, Canadian police and other criminal justice professionals will need to draw on the resources and expertise of their international partners if the security and social order we enjoy now is to be maintained in the future.

State crime is a significant form of harm carried out on behalf of the state or its agencies. State crime can involve the government acting against its own citizens illegally. An example is the Canadian government's past funding and promotion of the residential school system for Aboriginal children, referred to as "cultural genocide" by the government-appointed Truth and Reconciliation Commission. Acts of state crime range from the promotion of racism and denial of human rights through destruction or seizure of property and acts of violence against targeted groups, to acts of genocide and war crimes.

Finance crime refers to illegal and unethical financial practices employed by large transnational financial institutions, such as major banks, stock trading exchanges, and international financial organizations. Either directly or indirectly, the financial policies and practices of large IFIs (international financial institutions) are often the cause of political and financial corruption, conflict, violence and poverty in many developing countries

Goods counterfeiting is the practice of manufacturing goods, often of inferior quality, and selling them under a brand name without the brand owner's authorization. The sale of counterfeit goods, including clothing, cosmetics, and pharmaceuticals such as Oxycontin through fraudulent "name brand" Internet sites is a growing source of concern to law enforcement because counterfeit goods are an increasingly important source of profits for organized crime and terrorist groups.

Human trafficking is the recruitment, transportation, transfer, harbouring, or receipt of persons by improper means (such as force, abduction, fraud, or coercion) for an improper purpose including forced labour or sexual exploitation. Human trafficking is a global crime affecting millions of victims and organized crime has a firm stakehold in human trafficking.

Cybercrime is any crime where the Internet and information technologies, such as computers, tablets, personal digital assistants, or mobile devices have a major role in the commission of a criminal offence. Computer theft, or taking control of another person's computer by means of infecting it with a virus or malware, cyberbullying, and Internet scams are forms of cybercrime.

Terrorism involves the illegal use of force against innocent people to achieve a political objective. In Canada, "terrorism" is defined in law by Section 83.01 of the *Criminal Code*. Terrorism is generally defined as a type of political crime that emphasizes violence as a mechanism to promote change. Different forms of terrorism include revolutionary terrorism, political terrorism, nationalist terrorism, cause-based terrorism, state-sponsored terrorism, cyberterrorism, and homegrown terrorism.

Discussion Questions

1. What is terrorism? How serious a threat does it pose, and to whom?

2. List the six computer theft techniques listed in this chapter. Why might a company not report this type of criminal activity to the police?

3. Incidents of cyberbullying are increasingly in the news headlines and more schools are incorporating antibullying courses into their curriculum. What is cyberbullying and what, if anything, do you believe will stop it?

4. In Canada, there is currently no legal requirement for companies to report incidents of computer hacking, making the true number difficult to determine, but according to security company Websense in August 2014, 36 percent of Canadian businesses had observed a breach in their IT security in the previous 12 months. Should a law be passed requiring companies to post such information?

READY TO STUDY?

IN THE BOOK, YOU CAN:

✔ Check your understanding of what you've just read by reading the Summary at the end of each chapter.

✔ Rip out the Chapter in Review card at the back of the book to have the key terms and Learning Objectives handy, and complete the quizzes provided (answers are at the bottom of the back page!).

ONLINE YOU CAN:

✔ Stay organized and efficient with MindTap—a single destination with all the course material and study aids you need to succeed. Built-in apps leverage social media and the latest learning technology. For example:

✔ ReadSpeaker will read the text to you.

✔ Flashcards are pre-populated to provide you with a jump start for review—or you can create your own.

✔ You can highlight text and make notes in your MindTap Reader. Your notes will flow into Evernote, the electronic notebook app that you can access anywhere when it's time to study for the exam.

✔ Prepare for tests with quizzes.

Go to www.nelson.com/student to access these digital resources.

Notes

Chapter 1

1. Michael Friscolanti, "Investigating the Unthinkable," *Maclean's* (428/2014), vol. 127, iss. 16: 20–21; Matthew Coutts, "Who Are Matthew de Grood and the Five Calgary Stabbing Victims?," Daily Brew (16 April 2014) https://ca.news.yahoo.com/blogs/dailybrew/matthew-grood-five-calgary-stabbing-victims-151612726.html (accessed 1 October 2015).

2. Michael Friscolanti, "No Ordinary Call of Duty," *Maclean's*, vol. 127, iss. 17 (5 May 2014): 28–30; "De Grood Family Speaks: RAW" CBC News (17 April 2014) at http://www.macleans.ca/news/canada/for-a-veteran-calgary-cop-it-was-no-ordinary-call-of-duty/.

3. John Hagan and Alberto Palloni, "Sociological Criminology and the Mythology of Hispanic Immigration and Crime," *Social Problems* 46 (1999): 617–632.

4. Eugene Weber, *A Modern History of Europe* (New York: W.W. Norton, 1971), p. 398.

5. Anne Llewellyn Barstow, *Witchcraze: A New History of the European Witch Hunts* (Toronto: HarperCollins Canada, 1995).

6. Cesare Beccaria, *Essay on Crimes and Punishments*, [1764]. Trans. H. Paolucci (New York: Macmillan, 1985).

7. Cesare Bonesana Marchese Beccaria, *Of Crimes and Punishments* [1764] in *On Crimes and Punishments and Other Writings* (University of Toronto Press: Toronto, 2008).

8. Described in David Lykken, "Psychopathy, Sociopathy, and Crime," *Society* 34 (1996): 29–38.

9. See Peter Scott, "Henry Maudsley" in *Pioneers in Criminology*, ed. Hermann Mannheim (Montclair, NJ: Prentice Hall, 1991).

10. Cesare Lombroso, *Crime: Its Causes and Remedies* [1918], trans. Henry Pomeroy Horton (Boston: Little, Brown, 1911).

11. Nicole Hahn Rafter, "Criminal Anthropology in the United States," *Criminology* 30 (1992): 525–547.

12. See, generally, Robert Nisbet, *The Sociology of Emile Durkheim* (New York: Oxford University Press, 1974).

13. L. A. J. Quetelet, *A Treatise on Man and the Development of His Faculties* (Gainsville, FL: Scholars' Facsimiles and Reprints, 1969), pp. 82–96.

14. Ibid, p. 85.

15. Emile Durkheim, *The Rules of Sociological Method*, reprint ed., trans. W.D. Halls (New York: Free Press, 1982).

16. Emile Durkheim, *The Division of Labor in Society*, reprint ed. (New York: Free Press, 1997).

17. Robert Park and Ernest Burgess, *The City* (Chicago: University of Chicago Press, 1925).

18. Karl Marx and Friedrich Engels, *Capital: A Critique of Political Economy*, trans. E. Aveling (Chicago: Charles Kern, 1906); Karl Marx, *Selected Writings in Sociology and Social Philosophy*, trans. P. B. Bottomore (New York: McGraw-Hill, 1956). For a general discussion of Marxist thought, see Michael Lynch and W. Byron Groves, A Primer in Radical Criminology (New York: Harrow and Heston, 1986), pp. 6–26.19.

19. Parliament of Canada. Bill C-13 *Competition Act and the Mutual Legal Assistance in Criminal Matters Act: Protecting Canadians from Online Crime Act.* Reprinted as amended by the standing committee on justice and human rights as a working copy for the use of the House of Commons at report stage and as reported to the House on 13 June 2014.

20. Stephen Maher, "Ottawa Slyly Expands Power to Intrude; Tories Link C-13's Child Protections to a Massive Invasion of Privacy," *Edmonton Journal* (17 May 2014), p. A14; Justin Ling, "Cyberbullying Law Would Let Police 'Remotely Hack into Computers, Mobile Devices, or Cars," *Special to National Post*, 10 June 2014. Justin Ling, "Cyberbullying Law Would Let Police 'Remotely Hack into Computers, Mobile Devices, or Cars," *Special to National Post* (10 June 2014) at http://news.nationalpost.com/news/canada/canadian-politics/proposed-cyberbullying-law-would-let-police-remotely-hack-into-computers-mobile-devices-or-cars (accessed 16 October 2015).

21. Karen Seidman, "Harsh Laws Not Solution," *The Gazette* [Montreal] (21 November 2013) at http://sciencessociales.uottawa.ca/5496 (accessed 16 October 2015).

22. Evidence presented by Mr. Michael Spratt (Member and Criminal Defence Counsel, Criminal Lawyers' Association) to the House of Commons Standing Committee on Justice and Human Rights (27 May 2014) at http://www.parl.gc.ca/content/sen/committee/412/LCJC/21EV-51748-E.HTM (accessed 16 October 2015).

23. L. Culbert and M. Hager, "Dutch Man Charged in Amanda Todd Online Blackmail Case," *Vancouver Sun* (27 June 2014) at http://www.vancouversun.com/life/Dutch+charged+Amanda+Todd+online+blackmail+case/9749151/story.html (accessed 16 October 2015).

24. Sarah Petrescu, "New Law Adds Risk, Sex Workers Say; Criminalizing Clients Makes It Difficult to Safely Screen Them and Negotiate," *The Vancouver Sun* (14 July 2014), p. A6 at http://www.realwomenofcanada.ca/tag/prostitution (accessed 16 October 2015).

25. "Prostitution Law Canada: Should Bill C-36 Debate Hear from Johns?" at http://www.huffingtonpost.ca/2014/06/17/prostitution-law-canada-bill-c-36_n_5502229.html (accessed 1 October 2015).

26. Marvin Wolfgang, *Patterns in Criminal Homicide* (Philadelphia: University of Pennsylvania Press, 1958).

27. Hans von Hentig, *The Criminal and His Victim* (New Haven: Yale University Press, 1948); Stephen Schafer, *The Victim and His Criminal* (New York: Random House, 1968); Ezzat Fattah, *Understanding Criminal Victimization: An Introduction to Theoretical Criminology* (Scarborough, ON: Prentice Hall, 1991); Rob Mawby and Sanda Walklate, *Critical Victimology: International Perspectives* (London, England: Sage Publications, 1994).

28. Paul Rock, "The Public Faces of Public Criminology," *Criminology and Criminal Justice September*, vol. 14 no. 4 (2014): 412–433, doi: 10.1177/1748895813509638; Elliott Currie, "Against Marginality: Arguments for a Public Criminology," *Theoretical Criminology*, vol. 11(2) (May 2007): 175–190.

29. Charles McCaghy, *Deviant Behavior* (New York: Macmillan, 1976), pp. 2–3.

30. John Hagan, "Crime and Deviance," in Robert Hagedorn, ed., *Sociology*, 4th ed. (Toronto: Holt, Rinehart and Winston of Canada, 1990), chap. 6.

31. Alexandra Posadzki, "Canadian Pot Tourists Head South," *The Globe and Mail* (9 July 2014), p. S1; Heather Perlberg, "Legal Pot Makes for High Times; Colorado Has Seen Business Boom in Many Sectors Since It Legalized Marijuana, But Commercial Real Estate Has Been the Star," *The Ottawa Citizen* (6 May 2014), p. D1; Mark Kennedy, "Federal Poll Shows Canadians Want Marijuana Laws Changed," *The Ottawa Citizen* (31 July 2014), p. A1.

32. Edwin Sutherland and Donald Cressey, *Criminology*, 8th ed. (Philadelphia: J. B. Lippincott, 1960), p. 8.

33. Eugene Doleschal and Nora Klapmuts, "Toward a New Criminology," *Crime and Delinquency* 5 (1973): 607.

34. Michael Lynch and W. Byron Groves, *A Primer in Radical Criminology* (Albany, NY: Harrow and Heston, 1989).

35. Howard Becker, *Outsiders: Studies in the Sociology of Deviance* (New York: Free Press, 1963), p. 9.

36. Ibid.

37. Consolidation Criminal Code, R.S.C., 1985, c. C-46, Current to 12 June 2014, Last amended on 1 June 2014 at http://laws-lois.justice.gc.ca; *Controlled Drugs and Substances Act* S.C. 1996, c. 19, Current to 12 June 2014; Last amended on 6 November 2012, at http://laws-lois.justice.gc.ca

38. Criminal Code (R.S. 1985), S. 319.

39. R. v. White [2009] B.C.J. no. 2276, 2009 BCCA 513248 C.C.C. (3d) 499, 278 B.C.A.C. 177 71 C.R. (6th) 266, 2009 at http://www.lexisnexis.com.roxy.nipissingu.ca/ca/legal/auth/bridge.do?rand=0.9419169015728337; Supreme Court of Canada, R. v. White, 2011 SCC13 [2011] 1 S.C.R. 433; "Killer Offers Tearful Apology to Victim's Family, Friends Court Hears from Parents of Murdered Vancouver Artist Lee Matasi," CBC News (25 January 2008) at http://www.cbc.ca/news/canada/british-columbia/killer-offers-tearful-apology-to-victim-s-family-friends-1.703317 (accessed 1 October 2015).

40. Christie Blatchford, "Boston Displays Grace and Toughness; President Obama Captures City's Mood with a Speech Emphasizing America's Resilience in the Face of Terrorism," The Vancouver Sun (19 April 2013), p. B1.

41. Richard Barnhorst and Sherrie Barnhorst, Criminal Law and the Canadian Criminal Code, 6th ed. (Toronto: McGraw-Hill Ryerson, 2013).

42. Sandra Martin, "Shot 6 Times by His Wife, Tycoon Pleaded with Her to Call 911 and He'd Say Nothing," The Globe and Mail (1 December 2006) at http://www.theglobeandmail.com/news/national/shot-6-times-by-his-wife-tycoon-pleaded-with-her-to-call-911-and-hed-say-nothing/article4113116/ (accessed 16 October 2015).

43. R. v. Ruzic, at http://www.lexum.umontreal.ca/csc-scc/en/pub/2001/vol1/html/2001scr1_0687.html

44. Criminal Code of Canada (R.S. 1985, c. C-46) S. 83—Part II, 1 Terrorism.

45. Ontario Women's Justice Network, Arlene May—Coroner's Inquest, at http://www.owjn.org/archive/arlene.htm (accessed 20 February 2004); Criminal Code (R.S.C., 1985), S. 264 (1) (2) (3).

46. "Christopher's Law: A Bold Measure in Community Safety," Ontario Ministry of Community Safety and Correctional Services at http://www.mpss.jus.gov.on.ca (accessed 20 February 2004).

47. See, for example, Michael Hindelang and Travis Hirschi, "Intelligence and Delinquency: A Revisionist Review," American Sociological Review 42 (1977): 471–486; Jean Marie McGloin, Travis C. Pratt, and Jeff Maahs, "Rethinking the IQ-Delinquency Relationship: A Longitudinal Analysis of Multiple Theoretical Models," Justice Quarterly, vol. 21, iss. 3 (September 2004): 603–635.

48. Richard Herrnstein and Charles Murray, The Bell Curve (New York: Free Press, 1994).

49. Danylo Hawaleshka, "Most Aboriginal Children Are Healthy and Well-Adjusted," Maclean's (4 August 2003): 41; Kent Roach, "Blaming the Victim: Canadian Law, Causation, and Residential Schools," vol. 64, iss. 4 (Fall 2014): 566–595 doi: 10.3138/utlj.2419.

50. Anthony Petrosino, Carolyn Turpin-Petrosino, and James Finckenauer, "Well-Meaning Programs Can Have Harmful Effects! Lessons from Experiments of Programs Such as Scared Straight," Crime and Delinquency 46 (2000): 354–379.

51. Victor Boruch, Timothy Victor, and Joe Cecil, "Resolving Ethical and Legal Problems in Randomized Experiments," Crime and Delinquency 46 (2000): 330–353.

Chapter 2

1. Kevin Rollason, "Arrests Made in Brutal Assault," Winnipeg Free Press (13 November 2014), p. A3; "Police Identify Rinelle Harper, 16, as Victim in Midtown Bridge Attack—Winnipeg Police Hope Taking Rare Step of Naming Teen Will Help Investigators Find Her Attacker," CBC News (10 November 2014) at http://www.cbc.ca/news/canada/manitoba/police-identify-rinelle-harper-16-as-victim-in-midtown-bridge-attack-1.2830371 (accessed 1 October 2015); Kathryn Blaze Carlson, "Rinelle Harper's Rescuer Marvels at Her 'Will to Live,'" The Globe and Mail (20 November 2014), p. A1; Kathryn Blaze Carlson, "Rare Police Move, Help of Community Yield Arrests in Brutal Attack," The Globe and Mail (13 November 2014): A1.

2. Uniform Crime Reporting Survey (Ottawa: Canadian Centre for Justice Statistics, 2004).

3. Statistics Canada, Uniform Crime Reporting Survey (UCR): Detailed Information for 2013, at http://www23.statcan.gc.ca/imdb/p2SV.pl?Function=getSurvey&SDDS=3302 (accessed 1 October 2015).

4. Samuel Perreault, "Police-reported Crime Statistics in Canada," 2012 Juristat (July 2013) Statistics Canada cat. no. 85-002-X.

5. Samuel Perreault and Shannon Brennan, Criminal Victimization in Canada, 2009, Canadian Centre for Justice Statistics, vol. 30, no. 2 (Summer, 2010).

6. James D. Unnever, Michael L. Benson, and Francis T. Cullen, "Public Support for Getting Tough on Corporate Crime: Racial and Political Divides," Journal of Research in Crime and Delinquency, vol. 45, 2 (May 2008): 163–190; Susan Will, Stephen Handelman, and David C. Brotherton (eds.), "How They Got Away with It: White Collar Criminals and the Financial Meltdown," (New York: Columbia University Press, 2012); Yingyi Situ and David Emmons, Environmental Crime: The Criminal Justice System's Role in Protecting the Environment (Thousand Oaks, CA: Sage, 2000).

7. Rémi Boivin and Gilbert Cordeau, "Measuring the Impact of Police Discretion on Official Crime Statistics: A Research Note," Police Quarterly, vol. 14, iss. 2 (June 2011): 186–203.

8. David Seidman and Michael Couzens, "Getting the Crime Rate Down: Political Pressure and Crime Reporting," Law and Society Review 8 (1974): 457.

9. Jennifer L. Schulenberg, Joanna C. Jacob, and Peter J. Carrington, "Ecological Analysis of Crime Rates and Police Discretion with Young Persons: A Replication," Canadian Journal of Criminology & Criminal Justice, vol. 49, iss. 2 (April 2007): 261–277.

10. M. Wallace, J. Turner, A. Matarazzo, and C. Babyak, Measuring Crime in Canada: Introducing the Crime Severity Index and Improvements to the Uniform Crime Reporting Survey, 2009, at http://www.statcan.gc.ca/pub/85-004-x/2009001/part-partie4-eng.htm (accessed 21 July 2011).

11. Ibid.

12. Biderman, A. D. & Reiss, A. J. (1967). On exploring the "dark figure" of crime. The Annals of the American Academy of Political and Social Science, 374(1), 1-15.

13. Statistics Canada, "The General Social Survey: An Overview" (October 2013) at http://www.statcan.gc.ca/pub/89f0115x/89f0115x2013001-eng.htm (accessed 1 October 2015); Statistics Canada, "Summary of Changes over Time—General Social Survey—Victimization (GSS)" (January 2014) at http://www23.statcan.gc.ca/imdb/p2SV.pl?Function=getMainChange&SurvId=4504&SurvVer=4&InstaId=16857&SDDS=4504&lang=en&db=imdb&adm=8&dis=2 (accessed 1 October 2015).

14. Statistics Canada, "General Social Survey: Victimization," The Daily (28 September 2010) http://www.statcan.gc.ca/daily-quotidien/100928/dq100928a/eng.htm (accessed 1 October 2015).

15. S. Perreault and S. Brennan, Criminal Victimization in Canada, 2009: An Overview of Findings (Ottawa: Statistics Canada, 2009), at http://www.statcan.gc.ca/pub/85-002-x/2010002/article/11340-eng.htm#a3 (accessed 1 October 2015).

16. Ibid.

17. Ibid.

18. Samuel Perreault, "Self-reported Internet victimization in Canada, 2009" (Juristat, September 2011). Statistics Canada cat. no. 85-002-X.

19. Rebecca Kong, "Canadian Crime Statistics," in Robert A. Silverman, James J. Teevan, and Vincent F. Sacco, eds., Crime in Canadian Society (Toronto: Harcourt Brace, 2000) chap. 5, pp. 63–95.

20. A pioneering effort in self-report research is A. L. Porterfield, Youth in Trouble (Fort Worth, TX: Leo Potishman Foundation, 1946); for a review, see Robert Hardt and George Bodine, Development of Self-Report Instruments in Delinquency Research: A Conference Report (Syracuse, NY: Syracuse University Youth Development Center, 1965); Sonia Lucia, Leslie Herrmann, and Martin Killias, "How Important Are Interview Methods and Questionnaire Designs in Research on Self-Reported Juvenile Delinquency? An Experimental Comparison of Internet vs Paper-and-Pencil Questionnaires and Different Definitions of the Reference Period," Journal of Experimental Criminology, vol. 3, iss. 1 (March 2007): 39–64; for a critical perspective, see Francis T. Cullen, "Beyond Adolescence-Limited Criminology: Choosing Our Future—The American Society of Criminology 2010 Sutherland Address," Criminology, vol. 49, iss. 2 (May 2011): 287–330; and see Janne Kivivuori, Discovery of Hidden Crime: Self-Report Delinquency Surveys in Criminal Policy Context (Oxford, UK: Oxford University Press, 2011)

21. Allison Ann Payne and Steven Salotti, "A Comparative Analysis of Social Learning and

Social Control Theories in the Prediction of College Crime," *Deviant Behavior*, vol. 28, iss. 6 (November/December 2007): 553–573; Andrew Welsh and Jennifer A. A. Lavoie, "Risky eBusiness: An Examination of Risk-taking, Online Disclosiveness, and Cyberstalking Victimization," *Cyberpsychology*, vol. 6, iss. 1 (2012): 1–12. doi: 10.5817/CP2012-1-4.

22. John Hagan and Bill McCarthy, "Streetlife and Delinquency," *British Journal of Criminology* 43 (1992): 533–561. See also Brian P. Gendron, Kirk R. Williams, and Nancy G. Guerra, "An Analysis of Bullying Among Students Within Schools: Estimating the Effects of Individual Normative Beliefs, Self-Esteem, and School Climate," *Journal of School Violence*, vol. 10, iss. 2 (April–June 2011): 150–164.

23. For example, the following studies have noted the discrepancy between official statistics and self-report studies: Martin Gold, "Undetected Delinquent Behavior," *Journal of Research in Crime and Delinquency* 3 (1966): 27–46; Michael Hindelang, "Causes of Delinquency: A Partial Replication and Extension," *Social Problems* 20 (1973): 471–487; Julian Roberts and William Wells, "The Validity of Criminal Justice Contacts Reported by Inmates: A Comparison of Self-Reported Data with Official Prison Records," *Journal of Criminal Justice*, vol. 38, no. 5 (2010): 1031–037; Alex R. Piquero, Carol A. Schubert, and Robert Brame, "Comparing Official and Self-report Records of Offending across Gender and Race/Ethnicity in a Longitudinal Study of Serious Youthful Offenders," *Journal of Research in Crime and Delinquency*, vol. 51, 4 (July 2014): 526–556.

24. D. Wayne Osgood, Lloyd Johnston, Patrick O'Malley, and Jerald Bachman, "The Generality of Deviance in Late Adolescence and Early Adulthood," *American Sociological Review* 53 (1988): 81–93.

25. Jane B. Sprott, Anthony N. Doob, and Jennifer M. Jenkins, *Problem Behaviour and Delinquency in Children and Youth* (Ottawa: Statistics Canada, 2001), cat. no. 85-002-XPE.

26. Leonore Simon, "Validity and Reliability of Violent Juveniles: A Comparison of Juvenile Self-Reports with Adult Self-Reports Incarcerated in Adult Prisons," paper presented at the annual meeting of the American Society of Criminology, Boston, November 1995, p. 26; J. Hagan and B. McCarthy B, *Mean Streets: Youth Crime and Homelessness* (Cambridge: Cambridge University Press, 1997); David Shannon, "Chronic Offenders or Socially Disadvantaged Youth? Institutionalized Males as Missing Cases in School based Delinquency Research," *Journal of Scandinavian Studies in Criminology & Crime Prevention*, vol. 7, iss. 1 (2006): 78–100 doi: 10.1080/14043850500512205.

27. Stephen Cernkovich, Peggy Giordano, and Meredith Pugh, "Chronic Offenders: The Missing Cases in Self-Report Delinquency Research," *Journal of Criminal Law and Criminology* 76 (1985): 705–732; David Shannon, "Chronic Offenders or Socially Disadvantaged Youth? Institutionalized Males as Missing Cases in

School based Delinquency Research," *Journal of Scandinavian Studies in Criminology & Crime Prevention*, vol. 7, iss. 1 (2006): 78–100 doi: 10.1080/14043850500512205.

28. Terence Thornberry, Beth Bjerregaard, and William Miles, "The Consequences of Respondent Attrition in Panel Studies: A Simulation Based on the Rochester Youth Development Study," *Journal of Quantitative Criminology* 9 (1993): 127–158; David Shannon, "Chronic Offenders or Socially Disadvantaged Youth? Institutionalized Males as Missing Cases in School based Delinquency Research," *Journal of Scandinavian Studies in Criminology & Crime Prevention*, vol. 7, iss. 1 (2006): 78–100 doi: 10.1080/14043850500512205.

29. See also Michael Hindelang, Travis Hirschi, and Joseph Weis, *Measuring Delinquency* (Beverly Hills, CA: Sage, 1981); Callie Marie Rennison and Chris Melde, "Exploring the Use of Victim Surveys to Study Gang Crime: Prospects and Possibilities," *Criminal Justice Review* (December 2009) 34 (4): 489–514. Alex R. Piquero, Carol A. Schubert, and Robert Brame, Comparing Official and Self-report Records of Offending across Gender and Race/Ethnicity in a Longitudinal Study of Serious Youthful Offenders, *Journal of Research in Crime and Delinquency*, vol. 51, 4 (July 2014): 526–556.

30. Frank J. Leacy (ed.), *Historical Statistics of Canada* (Ottawa: Statistics Canada, 1983), cat. no. 11-516-X1E.

31. Samuel Perreault, "Police-reported Crime Statistics in Canada," 2012 *Juristat* (July 2013) Statistics Canada cat. no. 85-002-X.

32. Ibid.

33. Ibid.

34. Jillian Boyce and Adam Cotter, "Homicide in Canada, 2012," *Juristat* Canadian Centre for Justice Statistics (19 December 2013) Statistics Canada cat. no. 85-002-X.

35. Statistics Canada, "Study: Firearms and Violent Crime," *The Daily*, 20 February 2008.

36. Samuel Perreault, "Police-reported Crime Statistics in Canada," 2012 *Juristat* (July 2013) Statistics Canada cat. no. 85-002-X.

37. Statistics Canada, "Criminal Victimization in Canada, 2009," *Juristat* (Summer 2010).

38. Marc Ouimet, "Crime in Canada and in the United States: A Comparison," *Canadian Review of Sociology and Anthropology* (1999) 36(3): 389–408.

39. Peter Carrington, "Population Aging and Crime in Canada, 2000–2041," *Canadian Journal of Criminology* (2001) 43(3): 331–356.

40. Susan Oh, "The Hidden Horror," *Maclean's* (19 July 1999): 46; Eileen Kinsella, "Seniors, Prey of Con Artists and Brokers, Are Mad as Heck, Won't Take It Anymore," *Wall Street Journal* (Eastern Edition) (20 February 1997): C1; Government of Canada, Department of Justice, "Crime and Abuse Against Seniors: A Review of the Research Literature with Special Reference to the Canadian Situation," at http://www.justice.gc.ca/eng/rp-pr/cj-jp/fv-vf/

crim/sum-som.html (accessed 17 December 2014).

41. Ralph Weisheit and L. Edward Wells, "The Future of Crime in Rural America," *Journal of Crime and Justice* 22 (1999): 1–22; Meghan G. McDowell, "Becoming a Waste Land Where Nothing Can Survive: Resisting State-Corporate Environmental Crime in a 'Forgotten' Place, *Contemporary Justice Review*, vol. 16, iss. 4 (December 2013): 394–411 doi: 10.1080/10282580.2013.857094.

42. Peter Van Koppen and Robert Jansen, "The Time to Rob: Variations in Time of Number of Commercial Robberies," *Journal of Research in Crime and Delinquency* 36 (1999): 7–29; Alex Sagovsky, and Shane D. Johnson, "When Does Repeat Burglary Victimisation Occur?" *Australian & New Zealand Journal of Criminology*, vol. 40 iss. 1 (April 2007):1–26 doi: 10.1375/acri.40.1.1.

43. Alex Sagovsky and Shane D. Johnson, "When Does Repeat Burglary Victimisation Occur?" *Australian & New Zealand Journal of Criminology* , vol. 40, iss. 1 (April 2007): 1–26; Lisa Tompson and Michael Townsley, "(Looking) Back to the Future: Using Space–Time Patterns to Better Predict the Location of Street Crime," *International Journal of Police Science & Management*, vol. 12 iss. 1 (Spring 2010): 23–40 doi: 10.1350/ijps.2010.12.1.148.

44. Ellen Cohn, "The Effect of Weather and Temporal Variations on Calls for Police Service," *American Journal of Police* 15 (1996): 23–43; James Rotton and Ellen G. Cohn, "Outdoor Temperature, Climate Control, and Criminal Assault: The Spatial and Temporal Ecology of Violence," *Environment and Behavior*, vol. 36, 2 (March 2004): 276–306.

45. R. A. Baron, "Aggression as a Function of Ambient Temperature and Prior Anger Arousal," *Journal of Personality and Social Psychology* 21 (1972): 183–189; Christine Gockel, Peter M. Kolb, and Lioba Werth, "Murder or Not? Cold Temperature Makes Criminals Appear to Be Cold-Blooded and Warm Temperature to Be Hot-Headed," *PLoS ONE*, vol. 9, iss. 4 (April 2014): 1–6 doi: 10.1371/journal.pone.0096231.

46. Ellen Cohn, "The Prediction of Police Calls for Service: The Influence of Weather and Temporal Variables on Rape and Domestic Violence," *Journal of Environmental Psychology* 13 (1993): 71–83; James Rotton and Ellen G. Cohn, "Outdoor Temperature, Climate Control, and Criminal Assault: The Spatial and Temporal Ecology of Violence," *Environment and Behavior*, vol. 36, 2 (March 2004): 276–306.

47. See, generally, Franklin Zimring and Gordon Hawkins, *Crime Is Not the Problem: Lethal Violence in America* (New York: Oxford University Press, 1997).

48. Canada Firearms Centre, *History of Gun Control in Canada*, at http://www.cfc-ccaf.gc.ca; Firearms Act and Regulations: Canadian Firearms Program—*Firearms Act* at http://www.rcmp-grc.gc.ca/cfp-pcaf/pol-leg/act-loi-eng.htm (accessed 1 October 2015).

49. Library of Congress, Firearms-Control Legislation and Policy: Canada at http://www.loc.gov/law/help/firearms-control/canada.php (accessed 1 October 2015).

50. Adam Cotter, "Firearms and Violent Crime in Canada," 2012, *Juristat* (23 April 2014) Canadian Centre for Justice Statistics, Statistics Canada cat. no. 85-002-X.

51. Michael O. Maume and Matthew R. Lee, "Social Institutions and Violence: A Sub-National Test of Institutional Anomie Theory," *Criminology* 41 (2003): 1137; John K. Cochran and Beth Bjerregaard, "Structural Anomie and Crime: A Cross-National Test," *International Journal of Offender Therapy and Comparative Criminology*, vol. 56, 2 (April 2012): 203–217.

52. Victoria Brewer and M. Dwayne Smith, "Gender Inequality and Rates of Female Homicide Victimization across U.S. Cities," *Journal of Research in Crime and Delinquency* 32 (1995): 175–190; Andromachi Tseloni and Ken Pease, "Area and Individual Differences in Personal Crime Victimization Incidence: The Role of Individual, Lifestyle/Routine Activities and Contextual Predictors," *International Review of Victimology*, vol. 21, 1 (January 2015): 3–29.

53. Michelle Mann, "Corporate Criminals," *Canadian Business*, vol. 77, iss. 2 (19 January 2004): 29; John Hagan, *Structural Criminology* (New Brunswick, NJ: Rutgers University Press, 1989); John Hagan and P. Parker, "White Collar Crime and Punishment: The Sentencing of White Collar Criminals in the Southern District of New York," *American Criminal Law Review*, 20 (1985): 259–301; C. Goff and C.E. Reasons, *Corporate Crime in Canada* (Scarborough, ON: Prentice Hall, 1978).

54. R. Gregory Dunaway, Francis Cullen, Velmer Burton, and T. David Evans, "The Myth of Social Class and Crime Revisited: An Examination of Class and Adult Criminality," *Criminology* 38 (2000): 589–632; Jukka Savolainen, Lorine A. Hughes, Thoroddur Bjarnason, "Cross-National Variation in Socioeconomic Status and Delinquency: A Comparative Study of Adolescents from 26 European Countries," *Comparative Sociology*, vol. 12, iss. 5 (2013): 677–704 doi: 10.1163/15691330-12341280.

55. Andrea Dottolo and Abigail Stewart, "'Don't Ever Forget Now, You're a Black Man in America': Intersections of Race, Class and Gender in Encounters with the Police," *Sex Roles*, vol. 59, iss. 5/6 (September 2008): 350–364; Ivan Nye, James Short, and Virgil Olsen, "Socioeconomic Status and Delinquent Behavior," *American Journal of Sociology* 63 (1958): 381–389; Robert Dentler and Lawrence Monroe, "Social Correlates of Early Adolescent Theft," *American Sociological Review* 63 (1961): 733–743; see also Terence Thornberry and Margaret Farnworth, "Social Correlates of Criminal Involvement: Further Evidence of the Relationship Between Social Status and Criminal Behavior," *American Sociological Review* 47 (1982): 505–518.

56. Charles Tittle, Wayne Villemez, and Douglas Smith, "The Myth of Social Class and Criminality: An Empirical Assessment of the Empirical Evidence," *American Sociological Review* 43 (1978): 643–656; see also Charles Tittle and Robert Meier, "Specifying the SES/Delinquency Relationship," *Criminology* 28 (1990): 271–301; Rolf Becker and Guido Mehlkop Social Class and Delinquency: An Empirical Utilization of Rational Choice Theory with Cross-Sectional Data of the 1990 and 2000 German General Population Surveys (ALLBUS) *Rationality and Society*, vol. 18, 2 (May 2006): 193–235.

57. Delbert Elliott and Suzanne Ageton, "Reconciling Race and Class Differences in Self-Reported and Official Estimates of Delinquency," *American Sociological Review* 45 (1980): 95–110; Jukka Savolainen, Lorine A. Hughes, and Thoroddur Bjarnason, "Cross-National Variation in Socioeconomic Status and Delinquency: A Comparative Study of Adolescents from 26 European Countries," *Comparative Sociology*, vol. 12, iss. 5 (2013): 677–704 doi: 10.1163/15691330-12341280.

58. Filomin C. Gutierrez, and Donald J. Shoemaker, "Self-Reported Delinquency of High School Students in Metro Manila: Gender and Social Class," *Youth & Society*, vol. 40, iss. 1 (September 2008): 55–85; see also Delbert Elliott and David Huizinga, "Social Class and Delinquent Behavior in a National Youth Panel: 1976–1980," *Criminology* 21 (1983): 149–177; for a similar view, see John Braithwaite, "The Myth of Social Class and Criminality Reconsidered," *American Sociological Review* 46 (1981): 35–58; Hindelang, Hirschi, and Weis, *Measuring Delinquency*, p. 196; Rolf Becker and Guido Mehlkop, "Social Class and Delinquency: An Empirical Utilization of Rational Choice Theory with Cross-Sectional Data of the 1990 *and* 2000 German General Population Surveys (ALLBUS)" *Rationality and Society*, vol. 18, 2 (May 2006): 193–235.

59. Judith Blau and Peter Blau, "The Cost of Inequality: Metropolitan Structure and Violent Crime," *American Sociological Review* 147 (1982): 114–129; Richard Block, "Community Environment and Violent Crime," *Criminology* 17 (1979): 46–57; Robert Sampson, "Structural Sources of Variation in Race-Age-Specific Rates of Offending Across Major U.S. Cities," *Criminology* 23 (1985): 647–673; Mogens Nygaard Christoffersen, Keith Soothill, and Brian Francis, "Violent Life Events and Social Disadvantage: A Systematic Study of the Social Background of Various Kinds of Lethal Violence, Other Violent Crime, Suicide, and Suicide Attempts," *Journal of Scandinavian Studies in Criminology & Crime Prevention*, vol. 8, iss. 2 (2007): 157–184 doi: 10.1080/14043850701498469.

60. Chin-Chi Hsieh and M. D. Pugh, "Poverty, Income Inequality, and Violent Crime: A Meta-Analysis of Recent Aggregate Data Studies," *Criminal Justice Review* 18 (1993): 182–199. Mogens Nygaard Christoffersen, Keith Soothill, and Brian Francis, "Violent Life Events and Social Disadvantage: A Systematic Study of the Social Background of Various Kinds of Lethal Violence, Other Violent Crime, Suicide, and Suicide Attempts," *Journal of Scandinavian Studies in Criminology & Crime Prevention*, vol. 8, iss. 2 (2007): 157–184 doi: 10.1080/14043850701498469.

61. Robert Agnew, "A General Strain Theory of Community Differences in Crime Rates," *Journal of Research in Crime and Delinquency* 36 (1999): 123–155.

62. Wouter Steenbeek and John R. Hipp, "A Longitudinal Test of Social Disorganization Theory: Feedback Effects Among Cohesion, Social Control, and Disorder," *Criminology*, vol. 49, iss. 3 (August 2011): 833–871; see also Bonita Veysey and Steven Messner, "Further Testing of Social Disorganization Theory: An Elaboration of Sampson and Groves's "Community Structure and Crime," *Journal of Research in Crime and Delinquency* 36 (1999): 156–174.

63. Lance Hannon and James Defronzo, "Welfare and Property Crime," *Justice Quarterly* 15 (1998): 273–288; Kerstin Johansson, "Crime Prevention Cooperation in Sweden: A Regional Case Study," *Journal of Scandinavian Studies in Criminology & Crime Prevention*, vol. 15, iss. 2 (2014): 143–158 doi: 0.1080/14043858.2014.954830.

64. David T. Lykken, "The Causes and Costs of Crime and a Controversial Cure," *Journal of Personality*, vol. 68, iss. 3 (June 2000): 559–605; Alan Lizotte, Terence Thornberry, Marvin Krohn, Deborah Chard-Wierschem, and David McDowall, "Neighborhood Context and Delinquency: A Longitudinal Analysis," in *Cross National Longitudinal Research on Human Development and Criminal Behavior*, ed. E. M. Weitekamp and H. J. Kerner (Stavernstr, Netherlands: Kluwer, 1994), pp. 217–227.

65. Travis Hirschi and Michael Gottfredson, "Age and the Explanation of Crime," *American Journal of Sociology* 89 (1983): 552–584, p. 581; Gary Sweeten, Alex Piquero, and Laurence Steinberg, "Age and the Explanation of Crime, Revisited," *Journal of Youth & Adolescence*, vol. 42, iss. 6 (June 2013): 921–938 doi: 10.1007/s10964-013-9926-4.

66. Darrell Steffensmeier and Cathy Streifel, "Age, Gender, and Crime Across Three Historical Periods: 1935, 1960 and 1985," *Social Forces* 69 (1991): 869–894.

67. Mia Dauvergne, "Motor Vehicle Theft in Canada, 2007," *Juristat*, vol. 28, no. 10 (December 2008); Marnie Wallace, "Motor Vehicle Theft in Canada—2001" *Juristat* 23 (2003).

68. Shannon Brennan, "Police-reported Crime Statistics in Canada, 2011" *Juristat* (24 July 2012), Statistics Canada cat. no. 85-002-X, p. 20.

69. Gregory P. Brown and Kari Brozowski, "Golden Years? The Incarceration of the Older Offender," *Geriatrics Today* 6 (2003): 32–35.

70. Doreen Higgins and Margaret E. Severson, "Community Reentry and Older Adult Offenders: Redefining Social Work Roles," *Journal of Gerontological Social Work*, vol. 52, iss. 8 (November/December 2009): 784–802. See also Julius H. E. Uzoaba, *Managing Older Offenders: Where Do We Stand?* (Ottawa: Correctional Services of Canada, 1998).

71. Margo Wilson and Martin Daly, "Life Expectancy, Economic Inequality, Homicide, and Reproductive

Timing in Chicago Neighbourhoods," *British Journal of Medicine* 314 (1997): 1271–1274; Michael Rocque, "The Lost Concept: The (Re)emerging Link between Maturation and Desistance from Crime," *Criminology and Criminal Justice* (3 September 2014) doi 10.1177/1748895814547710.

72. Ray Paternoster and Shawn Bushway, "Desistance and the "Feared Self": Toward An Identity Theory of Criminal Desistance," *Journal of Criminal Law & Criminology*, vol. 99, iss. 4 (Fall 2009): 1103–1156.

73. Michael Rocque, "The Lost Concept: The (Re)emerging Link between Maturation and Desistance from Crime," *Criminology and Criminal Justice* (3 September 2014) doi 10.1177/1748895814547710; Walter Forrest and Carter Hay, "Life-course Transitions, Self-Control and Desistance from Crime," *Criminology and Criminal Justice*, vol. 11, (November 2011): 487–513.

74. James Q. Wilson and Richard Herrnstein, *Crime and Human Nature* (New York: Simon and Schuster, 1985), pp. 126–147.

75. Wilson and Herrnstein, *Crime and Human Nature*, p. 219.

76. Monica Barry, "Youth Transitions: From Offending to Desistance," *Journal of Youth Studies*, vol. 13, iss. 1 (February 2010): 121–136; and also Ralph C. Serin, and Caleb D. Lloyd," Examining the Process of Offender Change: The Transition to Crime Desistance," *Psychology, Crime & Law*, vol. 15, iss. 4 (May 2009): 347–364.

77. Walter Gove, "The Effect of Age and Gender on Deviant Behavior: A Biopsychosocial Perspective," in *Gender and the Life Course*, ed. A. Ross (Chicago: Aldine, 1985), p. 131; Lila Kazemian Desistance From Crime: Theoretical, Empirical, Methodological, and Policy Considerations, *Journal of Contemporary Criminal Justice*, vol. 23, 1 (February 2007): 5–27.

78. Jillian Boyce, "Adult Criminal Court Statistics in Canada, 2011/2012" (Juristat, June 13, 2013) Canadian Centre for Justice Statistics, Statistics Canada cat. no. 85-002-X.

79. Cesare Lombroso, *The Female Offender* (New York: Appleton Publishers, 1920), p. 122.

80. Ibid.

81. Lee Ellis, Shyamal Das, and Hasan Buker, "Androgen-promoted Physiological Traits and Criminality: A Test of the Evolutionary Neuroandrogenic Theory," *Personality & Individual Differences*, vol. 44, iss. 3 (February 2008): 699–709; Alan Booth and D. Wayne Osgood, "The Influence of Testosterone on Deviance in Adulthood: Assessing and Explaining the Relationship," *Criminology* 31 (1993): 93–118.

82. Gisela Konopka, *The Adolescent Girl in Conflict* (Englewood Cliffs, NJ: Prentice Hall, 1966); Clyde Vedder and Dora Somerville, *The Delinquent Girl* (Springfield, IL: Charles C. Thomas, 1970).

83. Leslie D. Leve and Patricia Chamberlain, "Female Juvenile Offenders: Defining an Early-Onset Pathway for Delinquency," *Journal of Child & Family Studies*, vol. 13, iss. 4 (December 2004): 439–452; Robert Hoge, D. A. Andrews,

and Alan Leschied, "Tests of Three Hypotheses Regarding the Predictors of Delinquency," *Journal of Abnormal Child Psychology* 22 (1994): 547–559.

84. Rita James Simon, *The Contemporary Woman and Crime* (Washington, DC: U.S. Government Printing Office, 1975).

85. David Rowe, Alexander Vazsonyi, and Daniel Flannery, "Sex Differences in Crime: Do Mean and Within-Sex Variation Have Similar Causes?" *Journal of Research in Crime and Delinquency* 32 (1995): 84–100; Michael Hindelang, "Age, Sex, and the Versatility of Delinquency Involvements," *Social Forces* 14 (1971): 525–534; Martin Gold, *Delinquent Behavior in an American City* (Belmont, CA: Brooks/Cole, 1970); Gary Jensen and Raymond Eve, "Sex Differences in Delinquency: An Examination of Popular Sociological Explanations," *Criminology* 13 (1976): 427–448. Jyh-Yaw Joseph Chen and David E. A. Giles, "Gender Convergence in Crime: Evidence from Canadian Adult Offence Charge Data," Econometrics Working Paper, Department of Economics, University of Victoria B.C., Canada (April 2003) at http://web.uvic.ca/econ/research/papers/pdfs/ewp0303.pdf.

86. Marie Drolet, "Why Has the Gender Wage Gap Narrowed?" Statistics Canada (Spring 2011) at http://www.statcan.gc.ca/pub/75-001-x/2011001/pdf/11394-eng.pdf.

87. Samuel Perreault, "Police-reported Crime Statistics in Canada," 2012 *Juristat* (July 2013) Statistics Canada cat. no. 85-002-X.

88. Ibid.

89. Ibid.

90. Peter J. Carrington and Jennifer L. Schulenberg, "Introduction: The Youth Criminal Justice Act—A New Era in Canadian Juvenile Justice?" *Canadian Journal of Criminology & Criminal Justice*, vol. 46, iss. 3 (April 2004): 219–223.

91. Bernard Schissel, *Social Dimensions of Canadian Youth Justice* (Toronto: Oxford University Press, 1993); Bernard Schissel, *Blaming Children: Youth Crime, Moral Panics and the Politics of Hate* (Halifax, Fernwood Publishing, 1997).

92. Nicholas Bala, Peter J. Carrington, and Julian V. Roberts, "Evaluating the Youth Criminal Justice Act after Five Years: A Qualified Success," *Canadian Journal of Criminology & Criminal Justice*, vol. 51, iss. 2 (April 2009): 131–167 doi: 10.3138/cjccj.51.2.131.

93 Shannon Brennan, "Police-reported Crime Statistics in Canada," 2011 *Juristat* (July 24, 2012) Statistics Canada cat. no. 85-002-X.

94. Statistics Canada, Table 252-0029, "Youth Court Survey, Number of Cases by Sex of the Accused, Annual, 1994–2002"; Eileen Poe-Yamagata and Jeffrey A. Butts, "Female Offenders in the Juvenile Justice System, 1996," https://www.ncjrs.gov/txtfiles/femof.txt; Katherine Stevenson, Jennifer Tufts, Diane Hendrick, and Melanie Kowalski, "Youth and Crime," *Canadian Social Trends* (Summer 1999).

95. Scot Wortley, "A Northern Taboo: Research on Race, Crime, and Criminal Justice in Canada," *Canadian Journal of Criminology* 41 (1999): 261–275.

96. Ann Finn, Shelley Trevethan, Gisele Carriere, and Melanie Kowalski, "Female Inmates, Aboriginal Inmates, and Inmates Serving Life Sentences: A One Day Snapshot," *Juristat* 19 (April 1999); Statistics Canada, "Incarceration of Aboriginal People in Adult Correctional Services," *The Daily* (21 July 2009).

97. Robert D. Crutchfield, April Fernandes, and Jorge Martinez, "Racial and Ethnic Disparity and Criminal Justice: How Much Is Too Much?" *Journal of Criminal Law & Criminology*, vol. 100, iss. 3 (Summer 2010): 903–932.

98. "Singled Out: Star Analysis of Police Crime Data Shows Justice Is Different for Blacks and Whites," *Toronto Star* (19 October 2002) p. A1.

99. Scot Wortley and Lysandra Marshall, *Race and Police Stops in Kingston, Ontario: Results of a Pilot Project* (Kingston: Kingston Police Services Board, 2005).

100. Scot Wortley and Akwasi Owusu-Bempah, "The Usual Suspects: Police Stop and Search Practices in Canada," *Policing & Society*, vol. 21, iss. 4 (December 2011): 395-407 doi: 10.1080/10439463.2011.610198

101. Graham C. Ousey, and Matthew R. Lee, "Racial Disparity in Formal Social Control: An Investigation of Alternative Explanations of Arrest Rate Inequality," *Journal of Research in Crime & Delinquency*, vol. 45, iss. 3 (August 2008): 322–355.

102. Robert D. Crutchfield, April Fernandes, and Jorge Martinez, "Racial and Ethnic Disparity and Criminal Justice: How Much Is Too Much?" *Journal of Criminal Law & Criminology*, vol. 100, iss. 3 (Summer 2010): 903–932.

103. Carol La Prairie, *Seen but Not Heard: Native People in the Inner City*, Aboriginal Justice Directorate (Ottawa: Department of Justice, 1994).

104. Ibid.

105. Ibid.

106. Gary LaFree, Eric P. Baumer, and Robert O'Brien, "Still Separate and Unequal? A City-Level Analysis of the Black-White Gap in Homicide Arrests since 1960," *American Sociological Review*, vol. 75, iss. 1 (February 2010): 75–100.

107. Ravi de Costa, "Aboriginal Self-Government in Canada: Current Trends and Issues," *Native Studies Review*, vol. 19, iss. 1 (2010); 139–143.

108. G. L. Kelling, T. Pate, D. Dieckman, and C. E. Brown, *The Kansas City Preventive Patrol Experiment: Summary Report* (Washington, DC: Police Foundation, 1974).

109. W. Spelman and D. K. Brown, *Calling the Police: Citizen Reporting of Serious Crime*. Washington, DC: United States Government Printing Office, 1984).

110. David Weisburd and Cynthia Lum, "The Diffusion of Computerized Crime Mapping in Policing: Linking Research and Practice," *Police Practice and Research*, vol. 6, no. 5 (December 2005): 419–434 doi 10.1080/15614260500433004.

Chapter 3

1. Amanda Hess, "Rehtaeh Parsons Was the Most Famous Victim in Canada. Now, Journalists

Can't Even Say Her Name, Slate (September 29 2014), at http://www.slate.com/blogs/ xx_factor/2014/09/29/rehtaeh_parsons _canadian_journalists_can_t_print_her _name_as_a_suspect_pleads.html (accessed 5 October 2015).

2. Ibid.

3. S. Derene, S. Walker, and J. Stein, "History of the Crime Victims' Movement in the United States," 2007 National Victim Assistance Academy, Track 1, at http://ualr.edu/avaa/ uploads/2010/07/History%20of%20Crime.pdf (accessed 5 October 2015).

4. Canadian Resource Centre for Victims of Crime, "History of Victims' Rights in Canada" (January 2006), at http://www.crcvc.ca/docs/vicrights .pdf (accessed 5 October 2015).

5. Rosie DiManno, "The Day Tori Stafford was Murdered," *The Guelph Mercury* (10 December 2010), p. A9.

6. "The General Social Survey: An Overview" (August 2013), Statistics Canada, at http://www.statcan .gc.ca/pub/89f0115x/89f0115x2013001-eng .htm. (accessed 5 October 2015).

7. "Criminal Victimization in Canada 2009," vol. 30, no. 2 (Summer 2010), Statistics Canada cat. 85-002-X.

8. Department of Justice Canada, Research and Statistics Division, "Costs of Crime in Canada: An Update," at http://www.justice.gc.ca/ eng/pi/rs/rep-rap/jr/jr12/p7.html (accessed 5 October 2015).

9. Ibid.

10. Ibid.

11. Ibid.

12. Ross Macmillan, "Adolescent Victimization and Income Deficits in Adulthood: Rethinking the Costs of Criminal Violence from a Life-Course Perspective," *Criminology* 38 (2000): 553–588.

13. Rebecca Campbell and Sheela Raja, "Secondary Victimization of Rape Victims: Insights from Mental Health Professionals Who Treat Survivors of Violence," *Violence and Victims* 14 (1999): 261–274.

14. Peter Finn, *Victims* (Washington, DC: Bureau of Justice Statistics, 1988), p. 1.

15. Michael Wiederman, Randy Sansone, and Lori Sansone, "History of Trauma and Attempted Suicide Among Women in a Primary Care Setting," *Violence and Victims* 13 (1998): 3–11; Susan Leslie Bryant and Lillian Range, "Suicidality in College Women Who Were Sexually and Physically Abused and Physically Punished by Parents," *Violence and Victims* 10 (1995): 195–215; William Downs and Brenda Miller, "Relationships Between Experiences of Parental Violence During Childhood and Women's Self-Esteem," *Violence and Victims* 13 (1998): 63–78; Sally Davies-Netley, Michael Hurlburt, and Richard Hough, "Childhood Abuse as a Precursor to Homelessness for Homeless Women with Severe Mental Illness," *Violence and Victims* 11 (1996): 129–142.

16. Jeanne Kaufman and Cathy Spatz Widom, "Childhood Victimization, Running Away, and Delinquency," *Journal of Research in Crime and Delinquency* 36 (1999): 347–370.

17. Dina Vivian and Jean Malone, "Relationship Factors and Depressive Symptomology Associated with Mild and Severe Husband-to-Wife Physical Aggression," *Violence and Victims* 12 (1997): 19–37; Walter Gleason, "Mental Disorders in Battered Women," *Violence and Victims* 8 (1993): 53–66; Daniel Saunders, "Posttraumatic Stress Symptom Profiles of Battered Women: A Comparison of Survivors in Two Settings," *Violence and Victims* 9 (1994): 31–43.

18. K. Daniel O'Leary, "Psychological Abuse: A Variable Deserving Critical Attention in Domestic Violence," *Violence and Victims* 14 (1999): 1–21.

19. James Anderson, Terry Grandison, and Laronistine Dyson, "Victims of Random Violence and the Public Health Implication: A Health Care of Criminal Justice Issue," *Journal of Criminal Justice* 24 (1996): 379–393.

20. "Most Homicides by Rejected Men, Judge Says During Stalking Case," *Guelph Mercury*, 9 November 2004, p. A2.

21. Pamela Wilcox Rountree, "A Reexamination of the Crime–Fear Linkage," *Journal of Research in Crime and Delinquency* 35 (1998): 341–372.

22. Robert Davis, Bruce Taylor, and Arthur Lurigio, "Adjusting to Criminal Victimization: The Correlates of Postcrime Distress," *Violence and Victimization* 11 (1996): 21–34.

23. Martin Patriquin et al., "The Secret Life of Colonel Russell Williams" *Maclean's* (22 February 2010), 123 (6): 20–23; and Chris Cobb, "Ex-Colonel's Lawyers Call Lurid Courtroom Tweets 'Unnecessary'" *Calgary Herald* (24 January 2011), p. A2.

24. Timothy Ireland and Cathy Spatz Widom, *Childhood Victimization and Risk for Alcohol and Drug Arrests* (Washington, DC: National Institute of Justice, 1995).

25. Brigette Erwin, Elana Newman, Robert McMackin, Carlo Morrissey, and Danny Kaloupek, "PTSD, Malevolent Environment, and Criminality Among Criminally Involved Male Adolescents," *Criminal Justice and Behavior* 27 (2000): 196–215.

26. Cathy Spatz Widom, *The Cycle of Violence* (Washington, DC: National Institute of Justice, 1992), p. 1.

27. Steve Spaccarelli, J. Douglas Coatsworth, and Blake Sperry Bowden, "Exposure to Serious Family Violence Among Incarcerated Boys: Its Association with Violent Offending and Potential Mediating Variables," *Violence and Victims* 10 (1995): 163–180; Jerome Kolbo, "Risk and Resilience Among Children Exposed to Family Violence," *Violence and Victims* 11 (1996): 113–127.

28. Ibid.

29. Ibid.

30. Jerry K. Daday, Lisa M. Broidy, Cameron S. Crandall, and David P. Sklar, "Individual, Neighborhood, and Situational Factors Associated with Violent Victimization and Offending," *Criminal Justice Studies* (2005) 18 (2): 215–235.

31. "Canada's Population Estimates: Age and Sex, 2014," *The Daily* (26 September 2014), at http:// www.statcan.gc.ca/daily-quotidien/140926/ dq140926b-eng.htm?HPA (accessed 5 October 2015).

32. Steve Spaccarelli, J. Douglas Coatsworth, and Blake Sperry Bowden, "Exposure to Serious Family Violence Among Incarcerated Boys: Its Association with Violent Offending and Potential Mediating Variables; Jerome Kolbo, "Risk and Resilience Among Children Exposed to Family Violence."

33. Benjamin Bowling, *Violent Racism: Victimization, Policing and Social Context* (Oxford: Clarendon Press); James Jacobs and Kimberely Potter, *Hate Crimes: Criminal Law and Identity Politics* (New York: Oxford University Press).

34. Morton Beiser, Samuel Noh, Feng Hou, Vilet Kaspar, and Joanna Rummens, "Southeast Asian Refugees' Perceptions of Racial Discrimination in Canada," *Canadian Ethnic Studies* 33 (January 2001): 46–55.

35. Karin Wittebrood and Paul Nieuwbeerta, "Criminal Victimization During One's Life Course: The Effects of Previous Victimization and Patterns of Routine Activities," *Journal of Research in Crime and Delinquency* 37 (2000): 91–122; Janet Lauritsen and Kenna Davis Quinet, "Repeat Victimizations Among Adolescents and Young Adults," *Journal of Quantitative Criminology* 11 (1995): 143–163.

36. Denise Osborn, Dan Ellingworth, Tim Hope, and Alan Trickett, "Are Repeatedly Victimized Households Different?" *Journal of Quantitative Criminology* 12 (1996): 223–245.

37. Graham Farrell, "Predicting and Preventing Revictimization," in *Crime and Justice: An Annual Review of Research*, Michael Tonry and David Farrington, eds., vol. 20 (Chicago: University of Chicago Press, 1995): pp. 61–126.

38. Ibid., p. 61.

39. David Finkelhor and Nancy Asigian, "Risk Factors for Youth Victimization: Beyond a Lifestyles/ Routine Activities Theory Approach," *Violence and Victimization* 11 (1996): 3–19.

40. Graham Farrell, Coretta Phillips, and Ken Pease, "Like Taking Candy: Why Does Repeat Victimization Occur?" *British Journal of Criminology* 35 (1995): 384–399.

41. Chris Purdy, "Man Charged with Attempted Murder of Six-Year-Old on Alberta Reserve," *The Globe and Mail* (22 December 2015), at http:// www.theglobeandmail.com/news/alberta/ alberta-girl-6-in-critical-condition-after -weekend-assault/article22176420/ (accessed 5 October 2015).

42. Besserer and Trainor, "Criminal Victimization in Canada."

43. Hans Von Hentig, *The Criminal and His Victim: Studies in the Sociobiology of Crime* (New Haven, CT: Yale University Press, 1948), p. 384.

44. Marvin Wolfgang, *Patterns of Criminal Homicide* (Philadelphia: University of Pennsylvania Press, 1958).

45. Ibid.

46. Menachem Amir, *Patterns in Forcible Rape* (Chicago: University of Chicago Press, 1971).

47. Susan Estrich, *Real Rape* (Cambridge, MA: Harvard University Press, 1987).

48. B. S. Fisher and S. P. Lab (Eds.), *Encyclopedia of Victimology and Crime Prevention*, Thousand Oaks, CA: Sage Publications.

49. Dean Scoville. "Suicide by Cop," *Police Magazine* (30 April 2010), at http://www.policemag.com/channel/patrol/articles/2010/04/suicide-by-cop.aspx (accessed 5 October 2015).

50. Edem Avakame, "Female's Labor Force Participation and Intimate Femicide: An Empirical Assessment of the Backlash Hypothesis," *Violence and Victims* 14 (1999): 277–283.

51. Martin Daly and Margo Wilson, *Homicide* (New York: Aldine de Gruyter, 1988).

52. Rosemary Gartner and Bill McCarthy, "The Social Distribution of Femicide in Urban

53. M. J. Hindelang, M. R. Gottfredson, and J. Garofalo (1978). *Victims of Personal Crime: An Empirical Foundation for a Theory of Personal Victimization* (Cambridge, MA: Ballinger, 1978). Susan Estrich, Real Rape (Cambridge, MA: Harvard University Press, 1987).

54. Dan Hoyt, Kimberly Ryan, and Mari Cauce, "Personal Victimization in a High-Risk Environment: Homeless and Runaway Adolescents," *Journal of Research in Crime and Delinquency* 36 (1999): 371–392.

55. See, generally, Gary Gottfredson and Denise Gottfredson, *Victimization in Schools* (New York: Plenum Press, 1985).

56. Gary Jensen and David Brownfield, "Gender, Lifestyles, and Victimization: Beyond Routine Activity Theory," *Violence and Victims* 1 (1986): 85–99.

57. Rolf Loeber, Mary DeLamatre, George Tita, Jacqueline Cohen, Magda Stouthamer-Loeber, and David Farrington, "Gun Injury and Mortality: The Delinquent Backgrounds of Juvenile Offenders," *Violence and Victims* 14 (1999): 339–351.

58. Bonnie Fisher, John Sloan, Francis Cullen, and Chunmeng Lu, "Crime in the Ivory Tower: The Level and Sources of Student Victimization," *Criminology* 36 (1998): 671–710.

59. James Garofalo, "Reassessing the Lifestyle Model of Criminal Victimization," in *Positive Criminology*, ed. Michael Gottfredson and Travis Hirschi (Newbury Park, CA: Sage, 1987), pp. 23–42.

60. Terance Miethe and David McDowall, "Contextual Effects in Models of Criminal Victimization," *Social Forces* 71 (1993): 741–759.

61. Rodney Stark, "Deviant Places: A Theory of the Ecology of Crime," *Criminology* 25 (1987): 893–911.

62. Ibid., p. 902.

63. Pamela Wilcox Rountree, Kenneth Land, and Terance Miethe, "Macro–Micro Integration in the Study of Victimization: A Hierarchical Logistic Model Analysis Across Seattle Neighborhoods," paper presented at the annual meeting of the American Society of Criminology, Phoenix, Arizona, November 1993.

64. Lawrence Cohen and Marcus Felson, "Social Change and Crime Rate Trends: A Routine Activities Approach," *American Sociological Review* 44 (1979): 588–608.

65. For a review, see James LeBeau and Thomas Castellano, "The Routine Activities Approach: An Inventory and Critique," unpublished paper, Center for the Studies of Crime, Delinquency, and Corrections, Southern Illinois University, Carbondale, 1987.

66. Teresa LaGrange, "The Impact of Neighborhoods, Schools, and Malls on the Spatial Distribution of Property Damage," *Journal of Research in Crime and Delinquency* 36 (1999): 393–422.

67. Lawrence Cohen, Marcus Felson, and Kenneth Land, "Property Crime Rates in the United States: A Macrodynamic Analysis, 1947–1977, with Ex-ante Forecasts for the Mid-1980s," *American Journal of Sociology* 86 (1980): 90–118.

68. Terence Miethe and Robert Meier, *Crime and Its Social Context: Toward an Integrated Theory of Offenders, Victims, and Situations* (Albany: State University of New York Press, 1994).

69. Richard Felson, "Routine Activities and Involvement in Violence as Actor, Witness, or Target," *Violence and Victimization* 12 (1997): 209–223.

70. Georgina Hammock and Deborah Richardson, "Perceptions of Rape: The Influence of Closeness of Relationship, Intoxication, and Sex of Participant," *Violence and Victimization* 12 (1997): 237–247.

71. Karin Wittebrood and Paul Nieuwbeerta, "Criminal Victimization During One's Life Course," pp. 112–113.

72. Patricia Resnick, "Psychological Effects of Victimization: Implications for the Criminal Justice System," *Crime and Delinquency* 33 (1987): 468–478.

73. Dean Kilpatrick, Benjamin Saunders, Lois Veronen, Connie Best, and Judith Von, "Criminal Victimization: Lifetime Prevalence, Reporting to Police, and Psychological Impact," *Crime and Delinquency* 33 (1987): 479–489.

74. Michelle Grossman and Catherine Kane, "Victims of Crime and the Justice System," in *Criminal Justice in Canada*, ed. Julian V. Roberts and Michelle G. Grossman (Toronto: Thomson Nelson, 2004), pp. 106–119.

75. Ibid.

76. Ibid.

77. Ibid.

78. Ibid.

79. "Working for Victims: Canada's New Federal Ombudsman for Victims of Crime," Sue O'Sullivan, Begins Term" (16 August 2010), *Market Wired*, at http://www.marketwired.com/press-release/working-victims-canadas-new-federal-ombudsman-victims-crime-sue-osullivan-begins-term-1304815.htm (accessed 5 October 2015).

80. This section leans heavily on Albert Roberts, "Delivery of Services to Crime Victims: A National Survey," *American Journal of Orthopsychiatry* 6 (1991): 128–137; see also Albert Roberts, *Helping Crime Victims: Research, Policy, and Practice* (Newbury Park, CA: Sage, 1990).

81. Randall Schmidt, "Crime Victim Compensation Legislation: A Comparative Study," *Victimology* 5 (1980): 428–437.

82. Ibid.

83. Ontario Ministry of the Attorney General, "Victim/Witness Assistance Program (VWAP)," at http://www.attorneygeneral.jus.gov.on.ca.

84. Peter Jaffe, Marlies Sudermann, Deborah Reitzel, and Steve Killip, "An Evaluation of a Secondary School Primary Prevention Program on Violence in Intimate Relationships," *Violence and Victims* 7 (1992): 129–145.

85. Andrew Karmen, "Victim–Offender Reconciliation Programs: Pro and Con," *Perspectives of the American Probation and Parole Association* 20 (1996): 11–14.

86. United States Department of Justice, "Growth of Victim-Offender Mediation—National Survey of Victim Offender Mediation Programs in the United States," at http://www.ojp.usdoj.gov.

87. See Frank Carrington, "Victim's Rights Litigation: A Wave of the Future," in *Perspectives on Crime Victims*, ed. Burt Galaway and Joe Hudson (St. Louis: Mosby, 1981).

88. A Cornerstone for Change: A Response to Bill C-32, the *Victims Bill of Rights Act*, from the Federal Ombudsman for Victims of Crime, *Office of the Federal Ombudsman for Victims of Crime* (13 December 2013), at http://www.victimsfirst.gc.ca/vv/vbra-cdv.html (accessed 5 October 2015).

89. Sara Flaherty and Austin Flaherty, *Victims and Victims' Risk* (New York: Chelsea House, 1998).

90. Pamela Wilcox Rountree and Kenneth Land, "Burglary Victimization, Perceptions of Crime Risk, and Routine Activities: A Multilevel Analysis Across Seattle Neighborhoods and Census Tracts," *Journal of Research in Crime and Delinquency* 33 (1996): 1147–1180.

91. Leslie Kennedy, "Going It Alone: Unreported Crime and Individual Self-Help," *Journal of Criminal Justice* 16 (1988): 403–413.

92. Ronald Clarke, "Situational Crime Prevention: Its Theoretical Basis and Practical Scope," in *Annual Review of Criminal Justice Research*, ed. Michael Tonry and Norval Morris (Chicago: University of Chicago Press, 1983).

93. See, generally, Dennis P. Rosenbaum, Arthur J. Lurigio, and Robert C. Davis, *The Prevention of Crime: Social and Situational Strategies* (Belmont, CA: Wadsworth, 1998).

94. Andrew Buck, Simon Hakim, and George Rengert, "Burglar Alarms and the Choice Behavior of Burglars," *Journal of Criminal Justice* 21 (1993): 497–507; for an opposing view, see James Lynch and David Cantor, "Ecological and Behavioral Influences on Property Victimization at Home: Implications for Opportunity Theory," *Journal of Research in Crime and Delinquency* 29 (1992): 335–362.

95. James Garofalo and Maureen McLeod, *Improving the Use and Effectiveness of Neighborhood Watch Programs* (Washington, DC: National Institute of Justice, 1988).

96. Peter Finn, *Block Watches Help Crime Victims in Philadelphia* (Washington, DC: National Institute of Justice, 1986).

97. Ibid.

Chapter 4

1. Will Campbell, "Jennifer Pan Found Guilty of First-Degree Murder and Attempted Murder," *The Canadian Press* (December 13, 2014) at http://www.cp24.com/news/jennifer-pan-found-guilty-of-first-degree-murder-and-attempted-murder-1.2146501#ixzz3NU6pVNsH (accessed 5 October 2015).

2. Bob Roshier, *Controlling Crime* (Chicago: Lyceum Books, 1989), p. 10.

3. James Q. Wilson, *Thinking About Crime*, rev. ed. (New York: Vintage Books, 1983), p. 260.

4. See, generally, Derek Cornish and Ronald Clarke, eds. *The Reasoning Criminal: Rational Choice Perspectives on Offending* (New York: Springer Verlag, 1986); Philip Cook, "The Demand and Supply of Criminal Opportunities," in *Crime and Justice*, vol. 7, eds. Michael Tonry and Norval Morris (Chicago: University of Chicago Press, 1986), pp. 1–28; Ronald Clarke and Derek Cornish, "Modeling Offenders' Decisions: A Framework for Research and Policy," in *Crime and Justice*, vol. 6, eds. Michael Tonry and Norval Morris (Chicago: University of Chicago Press, 1985), pp. 147–187; Morgan Reynolds, *Crime by Choice: An Economic Analysis* (Dallas: Fisher Institute, 1985).

5. George Rengert and John Wasilchick, *Suburban Burglary: A Time and Place for Everything* (Springfield, IL: Charles Thomas, 1985).

6. John McIver, "Criminal Mobility: A Review of Empirical Studies," in *Crime Spillover*, ed. Simon Hakim and George Rengert (Beverly Hills, CA: Sage, 1981), pp. 110–121; Carol Kohfeld and John Sprague, "Demography, Police Behavior, and Deterrence," *Criminology* 28 (1990): 111–136.

7. Liliana Pezzin, "Earnings Prospects, Matching Effects, and the Decision to Terminate a Criminal Career," *Journal of Quantitative Criminology* 11 (1995): 29–50.

8. Pierre Tremblay and Carlo Morselli, "Patterns in Criminal Achievement: Wilson and Abrahmse Revisited," *Criminology* 38 (2000): 633–660.

9. Ronald Akers, "Rational Choice, Deterrence and Social Learning Theory in Criminology: The Path Not Taken," *Journal of Criminal Law and Criminology* 81 (1990): 653–676.

10. Neal Shover, *Aging Criminals* (Beverly Hills, CA: Sage, 1985).

11. J. Carroll, and F. Weaver, "Shoplifters' Perceptions of Crime Opportunities: A Process-Tracing Study, in *The Reasoning Criminal: Rational Choice Perspectives on Offending*, eds. Derek Cornish and Ronald Clarke, eds. (New York: Springer Verlag, 1986).

12. Robert Agnew, "Determinism, Indeterminism, and Crime: An Empirical Exploration," *Criminology* 33 (1995): 83–109.

13. Ibid., pp. 103–104.

14. Bruce Jacobs, "Crack Dealers' Apprehension Avoidance Techniques: A Case of Restrictive Deterrence," *Justice Quarterly* 13 (1996): 359–381.

15. Ibid., p. 367.

16. Ibid., p. 372.

17. Michael Rand, *Crime and the Nation's Households, 1989* (Washington, DC: Bureau of Justice Statistics, 1990), p. 4.

18. Paul Cromwell, James Olson, and D'Aunn Wester Avary, *Breaking and Entering: An Ethnographic Analysis of Burglary* (Newbury Park, CA: Sage, 1989), p. 24.

19. Ibid., pp. 30–32.

20. George Rengert and John Wasilchick, *Space, Time, and Crime: Ethnographic Insights into Residential Burglary* (Washington, DC: National Institute of Justice, 1989); see also Rengert and Wasilchick, *Suburban Burglary*.

21. Matthew Robinson, "Lifestyles, Routine Activities, and Residential Burglary Victimization," *Journal of Criminal Justice* 22 (1999): 27–52.

22. Patrick Donnelly and Charles Kimble, "Community Organizing, Environmental Change, and Neighborhood Crime," *Crime and Delinquency* 43 (1997): 493–511.

23. Ronald Clarke and Marcus Felson, "Introduction: Criminology, Routine Activity and Rational Choice," in *Routine Activity and Rational Choice* (New Brunswick, NJ: Transaction Publishers, 1993), pp. 1–14.

24. Jonathan Stempel, "Madoff Says Banks Had to Know of Ponzi Scheme—Report" *National Post*, 16 February 2011, p. A3.

25. Ronald Clarke and Patricia Harris, "Auto Theft and Its Prevention," in *Crime and Justice: An Annual Edition*, ed. Michael Tonry and Norval Morris (Chicago: University of Chicago Press, 1992), pp. 1–54, at pp. 20–21; see also Marnie Wallace, "Motor Vehicle Theft in Canada—2001," *Juristat* 23 (January 2003) 5.

26. William Smith, Sharon Glave Frazee, and Elizabeth Davison, "Furthering the Integration of Routine Activity and Social Disorganization Theories: Small Units of Analysis and the Study of Street Robbery as a Diffusion Process," *Criminology* 38 (2000): 489–521.

27. Paul Bellair, "Informal Surveillance and Street Crime: A Complex Relationship," *Criminology* 38 (2000): 137–167.

28. John Gibbs and Peggy Shelly, "Life in the Fast Lane: A Retrospective View by Commercial Thieves," *Journal of Research in Crime and Delinquency* 19 (1982): 229–230.

29. Frederick J. Desroches, *Behind the Bars: Experiences in Crime* (Toronto: Canadian Scholars Press, 1996).

30. Ibid., p. 34.

31. Linda Deutsch, "No Plea Bargain in Jackson MD's Case," *Winnipeg Free Press*, 17 April 2010, at http://www.highbeam.com/doc/1P3-2013076541.html (accessed 6 October 2015).

32. Gordon Knowles, "Deception, Detection, and Evasion: A Trade Craft Analysis of Honolulu, Hawaii's Street Crack Cocaine Traffickers," *Journal of Criminal Justice* 27 (1999): 443–455.

33. John Petraitis, Brian Flay, and Todd Miller, "Reviewing Theories of Adolescent Substance Use: Organizing Pieces in the Puzzle," *Psychological Bulletin* 117 (1995): 67–86.

34. George Rengert, *The Geography of Illegal Drugs* (Boulder, CO: Westview Press, 1996).

35. Scott Decker, "Deviant Homicide: A New Look at the Role of Motives and Victim–Offender Relationships," *Journal of Research in Crime and Delinquency* 33 (1996): 427–449.

36. Felson and Messner, "To Kill or Not to Kill?"

37. Peter Wood, Walter Gove, James Wilson, and John Cochran, "Nonsocial Reinforcement and Habitual Criminal Conduct: An Extension of Learning," *Criminology* 35 (1997): 335–366.

38. Jeff Ferrell, "Criminological Verstehen: Inside the Immediacy of Crime," *Justice Quarterly* 14 (1997): 3–23, p. 12.

39. Jack Katz, *Seductions of Crime* (New York: Basic Books, 1988).

40. Bill McCarthy, "Not Just 'For the Thrill of It': An Instrumentalist Elaboration of Katz's Explanation of Sneaky Thrill Property Crime," *Criminology* 33 (1995): 519–539.

41. George Rengert, "Spatial Justice and Criminal Victimization," *Justice Quarterly* 6 (1989): 543–564.

42. Ronald Clarke, *Situational Crime Prevention: Successful Case Studies* (Albany, NY: Harrow and Heston, 1992).

43. Brian Dexter, "How to Make Your Home Safe," *Toronto Star*, 19 September 2002, p. J5.

44. Barry Webb, "Steering Column Locks and Motor Vehicle Theft: Evaluations for Three Countries," in *Crime Prevention Studies*, vol. 2, ed. Ronald Clarke (Monsey, NY: Criminal Justice Press, 1994), pp. 71–89.

45. Barbara Morse and Delbert Elliott, "Effects of Ignition Interlock Devices on DUI Recidivism: Findings from a Longitudinal Study in Hamilton County, Ohio," *Crime and Delinquency* 38 (1992): 131–157.

46. Ronald Clarke, "Deterring Obscene Phone Callers: The New Jersey Experience," in *Situational Crime Prevention*, ed. Ronald Clarke (Albany, NY: Harrow and Heston, 1992), pp. 124–132.

47. Robert Barr and Ken Pease, "Crime Placement, Displacement, and Deflection," in *Crime and Justice, A Review of Research*, vol. 12, eds. Michael Tonry and Norval Morris (Chicago: University of Chicago Press, 1990): 277–319.

48. Clarke, *Situational Crime Prevention*, p. 27.

49. Ibid., p. 35.

50. Ronald Clarke and David Weisburd, "Diffusion of Crime Control Benefits: Observations of the Reverse of Displacement," in *Crime Prevention Studies*, vol. 2, ed. Ronald Clarke (New York: Criminal Justice Press, 1994).

51. David Weisburd and Lorraine Green, "Policing Drug Hot Spots: The Jersey City Drug Market Analysis Experiment," *Justice Quarterly* 12 (1995): 711–734.

52. Ian Ayres and Steven D. Levitt, "Measuring Positive Externalities from Unobservable Victim Precaution: An Empirical Analysis of Lojack," *Quarterly Journal of Economics* 113 (1998): 43–78.

53. R. Steven Daniels, Lorin Baumhover, William Formby, and Carolyn Clark-Daniels, "Police Discretion and Elder Mistreatment: A Nested Model of Observation, Reporting, and Satisfaction," *Journal of Criminal Justice* 27 (1999): 209–225.

54. R. Yeaman, *The Deterrent Effectiveness of Criminal Justice Sanction Strategies: Summary Report* (Washington, DC: U.S. Government Printing Office, 1972). See, generally, Jack Gibbs, "Crime Punishment and Deterrence," *Social Science Quarterly* 48 (1968): 515–530.

55. Robert Bursik, Harold Grasmick, and Mitchell Chamlin, "The Effect of Longitudinal Arrest Patterns on the Development of Robbery Trends at the Neighborhood Level," *Criminology* 28 (1990): 431–450; Theodore Chiricos and Gordon Waldo, "Punishment and Crime: An Examination of Some Empirical Evidence," *Social Problems* 18 (1970): 200–217.

56. Stewart D'Alessio and Lisa Stolzenberg, "Crime, Arrests, and Pretrial Jail Incarceration: An Examination of the Deterrence Thesis," paper presented at the annual meeting of the American Society of Criminology, San Diego, November 1997.

57. Jiang Wu and Allen Liska, "The Certainty of Punishment: A Reference Group Effect and Its Functional Form," *Criminology* 31 (1993): 447–464.

58. Edwin Zedlewski, "Deterrence Findings and Data Sources: A Comparison of the Uniform Crime Rates and the National Crime Surveys," *Journal of Research in Crime and Delinquency* 20 (1983): 262–276.

59. David Bayley, *Policing for the Future* (New York: Oxford, 1994).

60. For a review, see Thomas Marvell and Carlisle Moody, "Specification Problems, Police Levels, and Crime Rates," *Criminology* 34 (1996): 609–646.

61. Charles Tittle and Alan Rowe, "Certainty of Arrest and Crime Rates: A Further Test of the Deterrence Hypothesis," *Social Forces* 52 (1974): 455–462.

62. Kenneth Novak, Jennifer Hartman, Alexander Holsinger, and Michael Turner, "The Effects of Aggressive Policing of Disorder on Serious Crime," *Policing* 22 (1999): 171–190.

63. Lawrence Sherman, "Police Crackdowns," *NIJ Reports* (March/April 1990): 2–6, p. 2.

64. Anthony Braga, David Weisburd, Elin Waring, Lorraine Green Mazerolle, William Spelman, and Francis Gajewski, "Problem-Oriented Policing in Violent Crime Places: A Randomized Controlled Experiment," *Criminology* 37 (1999): 541–580.

65. Ontario Provincial Police, *2003 Report* (Toronto: Ministry of Community Safety and Correctional Service, 2004).

66. Ed Stevens and Brian Payne, "Applying Deterrence Theory in the Context of Corporate Wrongdoing: Limitations on Punitive Damages," *Journal of Criminal Justice* 27 (1999): 195–209; Jeffrey Roth, *Firearms and Violence* (Washington, DC: National Institute of Justice, 1994); Thomas Marvell and Carlisle Moody, "The Impact of Enhanced Prison Terms for Felonies Committed with Guns," *Criminology* 33 (1995): 247–281; Gary Green, "General Deterrence and Television Cable Crime: A Field Experiment in Social Crime," *Criminology* 23 (1986): 629–645.

67. H. Laurence Ross, "Implications of Drinking-and-Driving Law Studies for Deterrence Research," in *Critique and Explanation: Essays in Honor of Gwynne Nettler*, ed. Timothy Hartnagel and Robert Silverman (New Brunswick, NJ: Transaction Books, 1986), pp. 159–171; H. Laurence Ross, Richard McCleary, and Gary LaFree, "Can Mandatory Jail Laws Deter Drunk Driving? The Arizona Case," *Journal of Criminal Law and Criminology* 81 (1990): 156–167.

68. For a review, see Jeffrey Roth, *Firearms and Violence* (Washington, DC: National Institute of Justice, 1994); and Thomas Marvell and Carlisle Moody, "The Impact of Enhanced Prison Terms for Felonies Committed with Guns," *Criminology* 33 (1995): 247–281.

69. T. Mak, "Arizona's Tent City Jail: Where Prisoners Wear Pink Underwear, Eat Meatless Meals and Swelter in the 120-Degree Heat," *Washington Examiner* (8 April 2014), at http://www.washingtonexaminer.com/tent-city-jail-where-prisoners-wear-pink-and-swelter-in-120-degree-heat/article/2546924 (accessed 6 October 2015).

70. Robert Dann, "The Deterrent Effect of Capital Punishment," *Friends Social Service Series* 29 (1935).

71. William Bowers and Glenn Pierce, "Deterrence or Brutalization: What Is the Effect of Executions?" *Crime and Delinquency* 26 (1980): 453–484.

72. John Cochran, Mitchell Chamlin, and Mark Seth, "Deterrence or Brutalization? An Impact Assessment of Oklahoma's Return to Capital Punishment," *Criminology* 32 (1994): 107–134. David Phillips, "The Deterrent Effect of Capital Punishment," *American Journal of Sociology* 86 (1980): 139–148; Hans Zeisel, "A Comment on 'The Deterrent Effect of Capital Punishment' by Phillips," *American Journal of Sociology* 88 (1982): 167–169; see also Sam McFarland, "Is Capital Punishment a Short-Term Deterrent to Homicide? A Study of the Effects of Four Recent American Executions," *Journal of Criminal Law and Criminology* 74 (1984): 1014–1032.

73. Steven Stack, "Publicized Executions and Homicide, 1950–1980," *American Sociological Review* 52 (1987): 532–540; for a study challenging Stack's methods, see William Bailey and Ruth Peterson, "Murder and Capital Punishment: A Monthly Time-Series Analysis of Execution Publicity," *American Sociological Review* 54 (1989): 722–743.

74. Karl Schuessler, "The Deterrent Influence of the Death Penalty," *Annals of the Academy of Political and Social Sciences* 284 (1952): 54–62.

75. Thorsten Sellin, *The Death Penalty* (Philadelphia: American Law Institute, 1959); Walter Reckless, "Use of the Death Penalty," *Crime and Delinquency*, 15 (1969): 43–51.

76. Ezzat Fattah, *Understanding Criminal Victimization: An Introduction to Theoretical Criminology* (Scarborough, ON: Prentice Hall, 1991).

77. Richard Lempert, "The Effect of Executions on Homicides: A New Look in an Old Light," *Crime and Delinquency* 29 (1983): 88–115.

78. Derral Cheatwood, "Capital Punishment and the Deterrence of Violent Crime in Comparable Counties," *Criminal Justice Review* 18 (1993): 165–181.

79. Dane Archer, Rosemary Gartner, and Marc Beittel, "Homicide and the Death Penalty: A Cross-National Test of a Deterrence Hypothesis," *Journal of Criminal Law and Criminology* 74 (1983): 991–1014.

80. Isaac Ehrlich, "The Deterrent Effect of Capital Punishment: A Question of Life and Death," *American Economic Review* 65 (1975): 397–417.

81. James Fox and Michael Radelet, "Persistent Flaws in Econometric Studies of the Deterrent Effect of the Death Penalty," *Loyola of Los Angeles Law Review* 23 (1987): 29–44; William B. Bowers and Glenn Pierce, "The Illusion of Deterrence in Isaac Ehrlich's Research on Capital Punishment," *Yale Law Journal* 85 (1975): 187–208.

82. Jon Sorenson, Robert Wrinkle, Victoria Brewer, and James Marquart, "Capital Punishment and Deterrence: Examining the Effect of Executions on Murder in Texas," *Crime and Delinquency* 45 (1999): 481–493.

83. William Bailey, "Disaggregation in Deterrence and Death Penalty Research: The Case of Murder in Chicago," *Journal of Criminal Law and Criminology* 74 (1986): 827–859.

84. Steven Messner and Kenneth Tardiff, "Economic Inequality and Level of Homicide: An Analysis of Urban Neighborhoods," *Criminology* 24 (1986): 297–317.

85. Donald Green, "Past Behavior as a Measure of Actual Future Behavior: An Unresolved Issue in Perceptual Deterrence Research," *Journal of Criminal Law and Criminology* 80 (1989): 781–804.

86. Donna Bishop, "Deterrence: A Panel Analysis," *Justice Quarterly* 1 (1984): 311–328; Julie Horney and Ineke Haen Marshall, "Risk Perceptions Among Serious Offenders: The Role of Crime and Punishment," *Criminology* 30 (1992): 575–594.

87. Wanda Foglia, "Perceptual Deterrence and the Mediating Effect of Internalized Norms Among Inner-City Teenagers," *Journal of Research in Crime and Delinquency* 34 (1997): 414–442; Raymond Paternoster, "Decisions to Participate in and Desist from Four Types of Common Delinquency: Deterrence and the Rational Choice Perspective," *Law and Society Review* 23 (1989): 7–29; Raymond Paternoster, "Examining Three-Wave Deterrence Models: A Question of Temporal Order and Specification," *Journal of Criminal Law and Criminology* 79 (1988): 135–163; Raymond Paternoster, Linda Saltzman, Gordon Waldo, and Theodore Chiricos, "Estimating Perceptual Stability and Deterrent Effects: The Role of Perceived Legal Punishment in the Inhibition of Criminal Involvement," *Journal of Criminal Law and Criminology* 74 (1983): 270–297; M. William Minor and Joseph Harry, "Deterrent and Experiential Effects in Perceptual Deterrence Research: A Replication and Extension," *Journal of Research in Crime and Delinquency* 19 (1982): 190–203; Lonn Lanza-Kaduce, "Perceptual Deterrence and Drinking and Driving Among College Students," *Criminology* 26 (1988): 321–341.

88. Steven Klepper and Daniel Nagin, "The Deterrent Effect of Perceived Certainty and Severity of Punishment Revisited," *Criminology* 27 (1989):

721–746; Scott Decker, Richard Wright, and Robert Logie, "Perceptual Deterrence Among Active Residential Burglars: A Research Note," *Criminology* 31 (1993): 135–147.

89. Alex Piquero and George Rengert, "Studying Deterrence with Active Residential Burglars," *Justice Quarterly* 16 (1999): 451–462.

90. Foglia, "Perceptual Deterrence and the Mediating Effect of Internalized Norms Among Inner-City Teenagers," pp. 414–442.

91. Harold Grasmick, Robert Bursik, and Karyl Kinsey, "Shame and Embarrassment as Deterrents to Noncompliance with the Law: The Case of an Anti-Littering Campaign," paper presented at the annual meeting of the American Society of Criminology, Baltimore, November 1990, p. 3.

92. Charles Tittle, *Sanctions and Social Deviance* (New York: Praeger, 1980).

93. Green, "Past Behavior as a Measure of Actual Future Behavior," p. 803; Matthew Silberman, "Toward a Theory of Criminal Deterrence," *American Sociological Review* 41 (1976): 442–461; Linda Anderson, Theodore Chiricos, and Gordon Waldo, "Formal and Informal Sanctions: A Comparison of Deterrent Effects," *Social Problems* 25 (1977): 103–114. See also Maynard Erickson and Jack Gibbs, "Objective and Perceptual Properties of Legal Punishment and Deterrence Doctrine," *Social Problems* 25 (1978): 253–264; Daniel Nagin and Raymond Paternoster, "Enduring Individual Differences and Rational Choice Theories of Crime," *Law and Society Review* 27 (1993): 467–485.

94. Harold Grasmick and Robert Bursik, "Conscience, Significant Others, and Rational Choice: Extending the Deterrence Model," *Law and Society Review* 24 (1900): 837–861, at p. 854.

95. Grasmick, Bursik, and Kinsey, "Shame and Embarrassment as Deterrents to Noncompliance with the Law"; Harold Grasmick, Robert Bursik, and Bruce Arneklev, "Reduction in Drunk Driving as a Response to Increased Threats of Shame, Embarrassment, and Legal Sanctions," *Criminology* 31 (1993): 41–69.

96. Harold Grasmick, Brenda Sims Blackwell, and Robert Bursik, "Changes in the Sex Patterning of Perceived Threats of Sanctions," *Law and Society Review* 27 (1993): 679–699.

97. Thomas Peete, Trudie Milner, and Michael Welch, "Levels of Social Integration in Group Contexts and the Effects of Informal Sanction Threat on Deviance," *Criminology* 32 (1994): 85–105.

98. Ernest Van Den Haag, "The Criminal Law as a Threat System," *Journal of Criminal Law and Criminology* 73 (1982): 709–785.

99. David Lykken, "Psychopathy, Sociopathy, and Crime," *Society* 34 (1996): 30–38.

100. George Lowenstein, Daniel Nagin, and Raymond Paternoster, "The Effect of Sexual Arousal on Expectations of Sexual Forcefulness," *Journal of Research in Crime and Delinquency* 34 (1997): 443–473.

101. David Klinger, "Policing Spousal Assault," *Journal of Research in Crime and Delinquency* 32 (1995): 308–324.

102. James Williams and Daniel Rodeheaver, "Processing of Criminal Homicide Cases in a Large Southern City," *Sociology and Social Research* 75 (1991): 80–88.

103. James Q. Wilson, *Thinking About Crime* (New York: Basic Books, 1975).

104. James Q. Wilson and Richard Herrnstein, *Crime and Human Nature* (New York: Simon and Schuster, 1985), p. 494.

105. Christina Dejong, "Survival Analysis and Specific Deterrence: Integrating Theoretical and Empirical Models of Recidivism," *Criminology* 35 (1997): 561–576; Paul Tracy and Kimberly Kempf-Leonard, *Continuity and Discontinuity in Criminal Careers* (New York: Plenum Press, 1996).

106. Allen Beck and Bernard Shipley, *Recidivism of Prisoners Released in 1983* (Washington, DC: Bureau of Justice Statistics, 1989).

107. Dejong, "Survival Analysis and Specific Deterrence," p. 573.

108. Paul Gendreau, Claire Goggin, Francis T. Cullen and Donald A. Andrews, "The Effects of Community Sanctions and Incarceration on Recidivism," *Forum on Corrections Research* 12 (May 2000): 10.

109. Dejong, "Survival Analysis and Specific Deterrence"; Raymond Paternoster and Alex Piquero, "Reconceptualizing Deterrence: An Empirical Test of Personal and Vicarious Experiences," *Journal of Research in Crime and Delinquency* 32 (1995): 251–258.

110. John Braithwaite, *Crime, Shame, and Reintegration* (Melbourne, Australia: Cambridge University Press, 1989).

111. Anthony Petrosino and Carolyn Petrosino, "The Public Safety Potential of Megan's Law in Massachusetts: An Assessment from a Sample of Criminal Sexual Psychopaths," *Crime and Delinquency* 45 (1999): 140–158; Owen Wood, "Sex Offender Registry," *CBC News Online*, 15 May 2003 (updated 20 June 2003), at http://www.cbc.ca/news.

112. See, generally, Raymond Paternoster, "Absolute and Restrictive Deterrence in a Panel of Youth: Explaining the Onset, Persistence/Desistance, and Frequency of Delinquent Offending," *Social Problems* 36 (1989): 289–307; Raymond Paternoster, "The Deterrent Effect of Perceived Severity of Punishment: A Review of the Evidence and Issues," *Justice Quarterly* 42 (1987): 173–217.

113. Isaac Ehrlich, "Participation in Illegitimate Activities: An Economic Analysis," *Journal of Political Economy* 81 (1973): 521–567; Lee Bowker, "Crime and the Use of Prisons in the United States: A Time Series Analysis," *Crime and Delinquency* 27 (1981): 206–212.

114. Paul Gendreau, Claire Goggin, Francis T. Cullen, and Donald A. Andrews, "The Effects of Community Sanctions and Incarceration on Recidivism," *Forum on Corrections Research* 12 (May 2000) 12.

115. Ibid.

116. Reuel Shinnar and Shlomo Shinnar, "The Effects of the Criminal Justice System on the Control of Crime: A Quantitative Approach," *Law and Society Review* 9 (1975): 581–611.

117. Thomas Marvell and Carlisle Moody, "The Impact of Out-of-State Prison Population on State Homicide Rates: Displacement and Free-Rider Effects," *Criminology* 36 (1998): 513–538; Thomas Marvell and Carlisle Moody, "The Impact of Prison Growth on Homicide," *Homicide Studies* 1 (1997): 205–233.

118. David Greenberg and Nancy Larkin, "The Incapacitation of Criminal Opiate Users," *Crime and Delinquency* 44 (1998): 205–228.

119. John Wallerstedt, *Returning to Prison: Bureau of Justice Statistics Special Report* (Washington, DC: U.S. Department of Justice, 1984).

120. James Marquart, Victoria Brewer, Janet Mullings, and Ben Crouch, "The Implications of Crime Control Policy on HIV/AIDS-Related Risk Among Women Prisoners," *Crime and Delinquency* 45 (1999): 82–98.

121. José Canela-Cacho, Alfred Blumstein, and Jacqueline Cohen, "Relationship Between the Offending Frequency of Imprisoned and Free Offenders," *Criminology* 35 (1997): 133–171.

122. Dennis Findlay, "Getting by with a Little Help from Their Friends," *Let's Talk* 2 (2000): 1–5; Gregory P. Brown and Kari Brozowski, "Golden Years? The Incarceration of the Older Offender," *Geriatrics Today* 6 (2003): 32–35.

123. Criminal Code, S. 753.1 (1).

124. Marc Mauer, testimony before the U.S. Congress, House Judiciary Committee, on "Three Strikes and You're Out," (1 March 1994).

125. Canela-Cacho, Blumstein, and Cohen, "Relationship Between the Offending Frequency of Imprisoned and Free Offenders."

126. Stephen Markman and Paul Cassell, "Protecting the Innocent: A Response to the Bedeau-Radelet Study," *Stanford Law Review* 41 (1988): 121–170, p. 153.

127. James Stephan and Tracy Snell, *Capital Punishment, 1994* (Washington, DC: Bureau of Justice Statistics, 1996), p. 8.

128. Andrew Von Hirsch, *Doing Justice* (New York: Hill and Wang, 1976).

129. Ibid., pp. 15–16.

Chapter 5

1. Report of the State's Attorney for the Judicial District of Danbury on the Shootings at Sandy Hook Elementary School and 36 Yogananda Street, Newtown, Connecticut on December 14, 2012, Office of the State's Attorney Judicial District of Danbury Stephen J. Sedensky III, State's Attorney November 25, 2013; Lee Ellis, "A Discipline in Peril: Sociology's Future Hinges on Curing Biophobia," *American Sociologist* 27 (1996): 21–41.

3. Edmund O. Wilson, *Sociobiology: The New Synthesis* (Cambridge, MA: Harvard University Press, 1975).

4. Per-Olof Wikstrom and Rolf Loeber, "Do Disadvantaged Neighborhoods Cause Well-Adjusted Children to Become Adolescent Delinquents?" *Criminology* 38 (November 2000): 1109–1142.

5. Dalton Conley and Neil Bennett, "Is Biology Destiny? Birth Weight and Life Chances," *American Sociological Review* 654 (2000): 458–467.

6. Kevin M. Beaver, Michael G. Vaughn, Matt DeLisi, and George E. Higgins, "The Biosocial Correlates of Neuropsychological Deficits: Results from the National Longitudinal Study of Adolescent Health," *International Journal of Offender Therapy and Comparative Criminology* (December 2010) 54: 878–894.

7. Anthony Walsh and Lee Ellis, "Shoring Up the Big Three: Improving Criminological Theories with Biosocial Concepts," paper presented at the annual meeting of the Society of Criminology, San Diego, November 1997, p. 16.

8. Israel Nachshon, "Neurological Bases of Crime, Psychopathy and Aggression," in *Crime in Biological, Social and Moral Contexts*, eds. Lee Ellis and Harry Hoffman (New York: Praeger, 1990), p. 199.

9. *Time* (28 May 1979): 57.

10. Michael Krassner, "Diet and Brain Function," *Nutrition Reviews* 44 (1986): 12–15.

11. Kristina Cieslak, Jordyn Feingold, Daniel Antonius, Julie Walsh-Messinger, Roberta Dracxler, Mary Rosedale, et al., "Low Vitamin D Levels Predict Clinical Features of Schizophrenia," *Schizophrenia Research*, vol. 159, iss. 2/3 (November 2014): 543–545, doi: 10.1016/j.schres.2014.08.031.

12. Leonard Hippchen, ed., *Ecologic-Biochemical Approaches to Treatment of Delinquents and Criminals* (New York: Van Nostrand Reinhold, 1978).

13. J. Kershner and W. Hawke, "Megavitamins and Learning Disorders: A Controlled Double-Blind Experiment," *Journal of Nutrition* 109 (1979): 819–826; Diana Fishbein and Jerzy Meduski, "Nutritional Biochemistry and Behavioral Disabilities," *Journal of Learning Disabilities* 20 (October 1987): 505–512.

14. Stephen Schoenthaler and Walter Doraz, "Types of Offenses Which Can Be Reduced in an Institutional Setting Using Nutritional Intervention," *International Journal of Biosocial Research* 4 (1983): 74–84; Stephen Schoenthaler and Walter Doraz, "Diet and Crime," *International Journal of Biosocial Research* 4 (1983): 74–84. See also A. G. Schauss, "Differential Outcomes Among Probationers Comparing Orthomolecular Approaches to Conventional Casework Counseling," paper presented at the annual meeting of the American Society of Criminology, Dallas, November 1978; A. Schauss and C. Simonsen, "A Critical Analysis of the Diets of Chronic Juvenile Offenders: Part I," *Journal of Orthomolecular Psychiatry* 8 (1979): 222–226; A. Hoffer, "Children with Learning and Behavioral Disorders," *Journal of Orthomolecular Psychiatry* 5 (1976): 229.

15. H. Bruce Ferguson, Clare Stoddart, and Jovan Simeon, "Double-Blind Challenge Studies of Behavioral and Cognitive Effects of Sucrose-Aspartame Ingestion in Normal Children," *Nutrition Reviews Supplement* 44 (1986): 144–158; Gregory Gray, "Diet, Crime and Delinquency: A Critique," *Nutrition Reviews Supplement* 44 (1986): 89–94; Diana Fishbein, "The Contribution of Refined Carbohydrate Consumption to Maladaptive Behaviors," *Journal of Orthomolecular Psychiatry* 11 (1982): pp. 17–25.

16. Mark Wolraich, Scott Lindgren, Phyllis Stumbo, Lewis Steginik, Mark Appelbaum, and Mary Kiritsy, "Effects of Diets High in Sucrose or Aspartame on the Behavior and Cognitive Performance of Children," *New England Journal of Medicine* 330 (1994): 303–306.

17. Dian Gans, "Sucrose and Unusual Childhood Behavior," *Nutrition Today* 26 (1991): 8–14.

18. Benton, David. "The Impact of Diet on Anti-social, Violent and Criminal Behavior," *Neuroscience and Biobehavioral Reviews* 31 (2007) 752–774.

19. James Q. Wilson, *The Moral Sense* (New York: Free Press, 1993).

20. Lee Ellis, "Evolutionary and Neurochemical Causes of Sex Differences in Victimizing Behavior: Toward a Unified Theory of Criminal Behavior and Social Stratification," *Social Science Information* 28 (1989): 605–636.

21. Lee Ellis and Phyllis Coontz, "Androgens, Brain Functioning, and Criminality: The Neurohormonal Foundations of Antisociality," in *Crime in Biological, Social and Moral Contexts*, eds. Lee Ellis and Harry Hoffman (New York: Praeger, 1990), pp. 162–193, p. 181.

22. Alan Booth and D. Wayne Osgood, "The Influence of Testosterone on Deviance in Adulthood: Assessing and Explaining the Relationship," *Criminology* 31 (1993): 93–118; Lee Ellis, Shyamal Das, and Hasan Buker, "Androgen-promoted Physiological Traits and Criminality: A Test of the Evolutionary Neuroandrogenic Theory," *Personality & Individual Differences*, vol. 44, iss. 3 (February 2008): 699–709, doi:10.1016/j.paid.2007.10.003.

23. Booth and Osgood, The Influence of Testosterone on Deviance in Adulthood: Assessing and Explaining the Relationship."

24. Christy Miller Buchanan, Jacquelynne Eccles, and Jill Becker, "Are Adolescents the Victims of Raging Hormones? Evidence for Activational Effects of Hormones on Moods and Behavior at Adolescence," *Psychological Bulletin* 111 (1992): 62–107.

25. Booth and Osgood, "The Influence of Testosterone on Deviance in Adulthood"; Lee Ellis and Anthony W. Hoskin, "Criminality and the 2D: 4D Ratio: Testing the Prenatal Androgen Hypothesis," *International Journal of Offender Therapy & Comparative Criminology*, vol. 59, iss. 3 (March 2015): 295–312, doi: 10.1177/0306624X13503813.

26. Albert Reiss and Jeffrey Roth, eds., *Understanding and Preventing Violence* (Washington, DC: National Academy Press, 1993), p. 118.

27. Neil Boyd, *The Beast Within: Why Men Are Violent* (Vancouver : Greystone Books, 2000).

28. Anthony Walsh, "Genetic and Cytogenetic Intersex Anomalies," *International Journal of Offender Therapy and Comparative Criminology* 39 (1995): 151–166.

29. Walter Gove, "The Effect of Age and Gender on Deviant Behavior: A Biopsychosocial Perspective," in *Gender and the Life Course*, ed. A. S. Rossi (New York: Aldine, 1985), pp. 115–144.

30. For a review of this concept, see Anne E. Figert, "The Three Faces of PMS: The Professional, Gendered, and Scientific Structuring of a Psychiatric Disorder," *Social Problems* 42 (1995): 56–72.

31. Katharina Dalton, *The Premenstrual Syndrome* (Springfield, IL: Charles C. Thomas, 1971).

32. Julie Horney, "Menstrual Cycles and Criminal Responsibility," *Law and Human Nature* 2 (1978): 25–36.

33. Diana Fishbein, "Selected Studies on the Biology of Antisocial Behavior," in *New Perspectives in Criminology*, ed. John Conklin (Needham Heights, MA: Allyn and Bacon, 1996), pp. 26–38.

34. C. Neill Epperson, M.D., Meir Steiner, M.D., Ph.D., S. Ann Hartlage, Ph.D., Elias Eriksson, M.D., Peter J. Schmidt, M.D., Ian Jones, M.D., and Kimberly A. Yonkers, M.D. "Premenstrual Dysphoric Disorder: Evidence for a New Category for DSM-5" *Am J Psychiatry* 169(5) (May 2012): 465–475. doi: 10.1176/appi.ajp.2012.11081302.

35. Rosanna Langer, "That Time of Month:" Premenstrual Dysphoric Disorder in the Criminal Law—Another Look," *International Journal of Criminology and Sociology*, 1 (2012): 29–44.

36. Diana Fishbein, "Selected Studies on the Biology of Antisocial Behavior," in *New Perspectives in Criminology*, ed. John Conklin (Needham Heights, MA: Allyn and Bacon, 1996), pp. 26–38; Karen Paige, "Effects of Oral Contraceptives on Affective Fluctuations Associated with the Menstrual Cycle," *Psychosomatic Medicine* 33 (1971): 515–537.

37. Alexander Schauss, *Diet, Crime and Delinquency* (Berkeley, CA: Parker House, 1980).

38. C. Hawley and R. E. Buckley, "Food Dyes and Hyperkinetic Children," *Academy Therapy* 10 (1974): 27–32.

39. John Ott, "The Effects of Light and Radiation on Human Health and Behavior," in *Ecologic-Biochemical Approaches to Treatment of Delinquents and Criminals*, ed. Leonard Hippchen (New York: Van Nostrand Reinhold, 1978), pp. 105–183. See also A. Kreuger and S. Sigel, "Ions in the Air," *Human Nature* (July 1978): 46–47; Harry Wohlfarth, "The Effect of Color Psychodynamic Environmental Modification on Discipline Incidents in Elementary Schools over One School Year: A Controlled Study," *International Journal of Biosocial Research* 6 (1984): 44–53.

40. Oliver David, Stanley Hoffman, Jeffrey Sverd, Julian Clark, and Kytja Voeller, "Lead and Hyperactivity, Behavior Response to Chelation: A Pilot Study," *American Journal of Psychiatry* 133 (1976): 1155–1158.

41. Deborah Denno, "Considering Lead Poisoning as a Criminal Defense," *Fordham Urban Law Journal* 20 (1993): 377–400.

42. Terrie Moffitt, "The Neuropsychology of Juvenile Delinquency: A Critical Review," in *Crime and Justice: An Annual Review*, vol. 12, ed. Norval Morris and Michael Tonry (Chicago: University of Chicago Press, 1990), pp. 99–169.

43. Terrie Moffitt, Donald Lynam, and Phil Silva, "Neuropsychological Tests Predicting Persistent Male Delinquency," *Criminology* 32 (1994): 277–300; Elizabeth Kandel and Sarnoff

Mednick, "Perinatal Complications Predict Violent Offending," *Criminology* 29 (1991): 519–529; Sarnoff Mednick, Ricardo Machon, Matti Virkkunen, and Douglas Bonett, "Adult Schizophrenia Following Prenatal Exposure to an Influenza Epidemic," *Archives of General Psychiatry* 44 (1987): 35–46; C. A. Fogel, S. A. Mednick, and N. Michelson, "Hyperactive Behavior and Minor Physical Anomalies," *Acta Psychiatrica Scandinavia* 72 (1985): 551–556.

44. R. Johnson, *Aggression in Man and Animals* (Philadelphia: Saunders, 1972), p. 79.

45. Jean Seguin, Robert Pihl, Philip Harden, Richard Tremblay, and Bernard Boulerice, "Cognitive and Neuropsychological Characteristics of Physically Aggressive Boys," *Journal of Abnormal Psychology* 104 (1995): 614–624; Deborah Denno, "Gender, Crime and the Criminal Law Defenses," *Journal of Criminal Law and Criminology* 85 (1994): 80–180.

46. Adrian Raine, Patricia Brennan, Brigitte Mednick, and Sarnoff Mednick, "High Rates of Violence, Crime, Academic Problems, and Behavioral Problems in Males with Both Early Neuromotor Deficits and Unstable Family Environments," *Archives of General Psychiatry* 53 (1996): 544–549; Deborah Denno, *Biology, Crime and Violence: New Evidence* (Cambridge: Cambridge University Press, 1989).

47. Diana Fishbein and Robert Thatcher, "New Diagnostic Methods in Criminology: Assessing Organic Sources of Behavioral Disorders," *Journal of Research in Crime and Delinquency* 23 (1986): 240–267.

48. Lorne Yeudall, "A Neuropsychosocial Perspective on Persistent Juvenile Delinquency and Criminal Behavior," paper presented at the New York Academy of Sciences, 26 September 1979.

49. See, generally, Jan Volavka, "Electroence-phalogram Among Criminals," in *The Causes of Crime: New Biological Approaches*, ed. Sarnoff Mednick, Terrie Moffitt, and Susan Stack (Cambridge: Cambridge University Press, 1987), pp. 137–145; Z. A. Zayed, S. A. Lewis, and R. P. Britain, "An Encephalographic and Psychiatric Study of 32 Insane Murderers," *British Journal of Psychiatry* 115 (1969): 1115–1124.

50. Nathaniel Pallone and James Hennessy, "Brain Dysfunction and Criminal Violence," *Society* 35 (1998): 21–27; P. F. Goyer, P. J. Andreason, and W. E. Semple, "Positronic Emission Tomography and Personality Disorders," *Neuropsychopharmacology* 10 (1994): 21–28.

51. Diana Fishbein, "Neuropsychological Function, Drug Abuse, and Violence"; Adrian Raine, Monte Buchsbaum, and Lori LaCasse, "Brain Abnormalities in Murderers Indicated by Positron Emission Tomography," *Biological Psychiatry* 42 (1997): 495–508.

52. Pallone and Hennessy, "Brain Dysfunction and Criminal Violence," p. 25.

53. D. R. Robin, R. M. Starles, T. J. Kenney, B. J. Reynolds, and F. P. Heald, "Adolescents Who Attempt Suicide," *Journal of Pediatrics* 90 (1977): 636–638.

54. Raine, Buchsbaum, and LaCasse, "Brain Abnormalities in Murderers Indicated by Positron Emission Tomography."

55. Leonore Simon, "Does Criminal Offender Treatment Work?" *Applied and Preventive Psychology* (Summer 1998); Stephen Faraone et al., "Intellectual Performance and School Failure in Children with Attention Deficit Hyperactivity Disorder and in Their Siblings," *Journal of Abnormal Psychology* 102 (1993): 616–623.

56. Simon, "Does Criminal Offender Treatment Work?"

57. Ibid.

58. Terrie Moffitt and Phil Silva, "Self-Reported Delinquency, Neuropsychological Deficit, and History of Attention Deficit Disorder," *Journal of Abnormal Child Psychology* 16 (1988): 553–569.

59. Elizabeth Hart et al., "Developmental Change in Attention-Deficit Hyperactivity Disorder in Boys: A Four-Year Longitudinal Study," *Journal of Consulting and Clinical Psychology* 62 (1994): 472–491.

60. Eugene Maguin, Rolf Loeber, and Paul LeMahieu, "Does the Relationship Between Poor Reading and Delinquency Hold for Males of Different Ages and Ethnic Groups?" *Journal of Emotional and Behavioral Disorders* 1 (1993): 88–100.

61. Paul Verbrugge, Research and Statistics Division, Department of Justice Canada, "Fetal Alcohol Syndrome and the Youth Criminal Justice System: A Discussion Paper" 2004, 09, 10; Kenneth R. Warren and Brenda G. Hewitt, "Fetal Alcohol Spectrum Disorders: When Science, Medicine, Public Policy and Laws Collide," *Developmental Disabilities* 15 (2009): 170–175.

62. J. Conry and D. K. Fast, "Fetal Alcohol Syndrome and the Criminal Justice System" (Vancouver: Fetal Alcohol Syndrome Resource Society, 2000).

63. R. J. Williams, and S. P. Gloster, "Knowledge of Fetal Alcohol Syndrome (FAS) among Native in Northern Manitoba," *Journal of Studies on Alcohol*, 60 (1999): 833–836.

64. A. P. Streissguth, F. L. Bookstein, H. M. Barr, P. D. Sampson, K. O'Malley, and J. K. Young, "Risk Factors for Adverse Life Outcomes in Fetal Alcohol Syndrome and Fetal Alcohol Effects," *Journal of Developmental and Behavioral Pediatrics* 25 (4): 228–238.

65. Verbrugge, "Fetal Alcohol Syndrome and the Youth Criminal Justice System: A Discussion Paper," 2004.

66. Reiss and Roth, *Understanding and Preventing Violence*, p. 119.

67. Matti Virkkunen, David Goldman, and Markku Linnoila, "Serotonin in Alcoholic Violent Offenders," *The Ciba Foundation Symposium: Genetics of Criminal and Antisocial Behavior* (Chichester, England: Wiley, 1995).

68. van der Gronde T, Kempes M, van El C, Rinne T, Pieters T (2014) Neurobiological Correlates in Forensic Assessment: A Systematic Review. PLoS ONE 9(10): e110672. doi:10.1371/journal .pone.0110672

69. Lee Ellis, "Left- and Mixed-Handedness and Criminality: Explanations for a Probable Relationship," in *Left-Handedness: Behavioral Implications and Anomalies*, ed. S. Coren (Amsterdam: Elsevier, 1990): pp. 485–507.

70. Lee Ellis, "Monoamine Oxidase and Criminality: Identifying an Apparent Biological Marker for Antisocial Behavior," *Journal of Research in Crime and Delinquency* 28 (1991): 227–251.

71. van der Gronde T, Kempes M, van El C, Rinne T, Pieters T (2014) Neurobiological Correlates in Forensic Assessment: A Systematic Review. PLoS ONE 9(10): e110672. doi:10.1371/journal .pone.0110672

72. Lee Ellis, "Arousal Theory and the Religiosity—Criminality Relationship," in *Contemporary Criminological Theory*, eds. Peter Cordella and Larry Siegel (Boston, MA: Northeastern University, 1996), pp. 65–84.

73. Adrian Raine, Peter Venables, and Sarnoff Mednick, "Low Resting Heart Rate at Age 3 Years Predisposes to Aggression at Age 11 Years: Evidence from the Mauritius Child Health Project," *Journal of the American Academy of Adolescent Psychiatry* 36 (1997): 1457–1464.

74. Linda Li and Jianghong Liu, "The Effect of Pediatric Traumatic Brain Injury on Behavioral Outcomes: A Systematic Review," *Developmental Medicine & Child Neurology*. 55(1) (January 2013): 37–45, doi:10.1111/j.1469-8749.2012.04414.x.

75. Seena Fazel, Paul Lichtenstein, Martin Grann, and Niklas Långström, "Risk of Violent Crime in Individuals with Epilepsy and Traumatic Brain Injury: A 35-Year Swedish Population Study," 8(12) (December 2011): e1001150, doi: 10.1371/journal.pmed.1001150.

76. Gabriela Ilie1, Nigel E. Turner, Jurgen Rehm, and Michael D. Cusimano, "The Moderating Effects of Sex and Age on the Association between Traumatic Brain Injury and Harmful Psychological Correlates among Adolescents," *Public Library of Science* (PLoS), vol. 9, iss. 9 (1 September 2014): e108167.

77. David Rowe, "As the Twig Is Bent: The Myth of Child-Rearing Influences on Personality Devel-opment," *Journal of Counseling and Development* 68 (1990): 606–611; David Rowe, Joseph Rogers, and Sylvia Meseck-Bushey, "Sibling Delinquency and the Family Environment: Shared and Unshared Influences," *Child Development* 63 (1992): 59–67; Gregory Carey and David DiLalla, "Personality and Psychopathology: Genetic Perspectives," *Journal of Abnormal Psychology* 103 (1994): 32–43.

78. T. R. Sarbin and L. E. Miller, "Demonism Revisited: The XYY Chromosome Anomaly," *Issues in Criminology* 5 (1970): 195–207.

79. Sarnoff Mednick and Jan Volavka, "Biology and Crime," in *Crime and Justice*, ed. Norval Morris and Michael Tonry (Chicago: University of Chicago Press, 1980), pp. 85–159, p. 93.

80. For an early review, see Barbara Wooton, *Social Science and Social Pathology* (London: Allen and Unwin, 1959); John Laub and Robert Sampson, "Unraveling Families and Delinquency: A Reanalysis of the Gluecks' Data," *Criminology* 26 (1988): 355–380.

81. D. J. West and D. P. Farrington, "Who Becomes Delinquent?" in *The Delinquent Way of Life*, ed. D. J. West and D. P. Farrington (London: Heinemann, 1977), pp. 1–28; D. J. West, *Delinquency: Its Roots, Careers, and Prospects* (Cambridge, MA: Harvard University Press, 1982).

82. West, *Delinquency*, p. 114.

83. David Farrington, "Understanding and Preventing Bullying," in *Crime and Justice*, vol. 17, ed. Michael Tonry (Chicago: University of Chicago Press, 1993): 381–457; Sytske Besemer and David P. Farrington, "Conviction Trajectories of Fathers and Their Children," *European Journal of Criminology* 9(2) (2012): 120–141.

84. David Rowe and David Farrington, "The Familial Transmission of Criminal Convictions," *Criminology* 35 (1997): 177–201.

85. Mednick and Volavka, "Biology and Crime," p. 94.

86. Ibid., p. 95.

87. David Rowe, "Genetic and Environmental Components of Antisocial Behavior: A Study of 265 Twin Pairs," *Criminology* 24 (1986): 513–532; David Rowe and D. Wayne Osgood, "Heredity and Sociological Theories of Delinquency: A Reconsideration," *American Sociological Review* 49 (1984): 526–540.

88. Edwin J. C. G. van den Oord, Frank Verhulst, and Dorret Boomsma, "A Genetic Study of Maternal and Paternal Ratings of Problem Behaviors in 3-Year-Old Twins," *Journal of Abnormal Psychology* 105 (1996): 349–357.

89. Michael Lyons, "A Twin Study of Self-Reported Criminal Behavior"; Judy Silberg, Joanne Meyer, Andrew Pickles, Emily Simonoff, Lindon Eaves, John Hewitt et al., "Heterogeneity Among Juvenile Antisocial Behaviors: Findings from the Virginia Twin Study of Adolescent Behavioral Development," in the Ciba Foundation Symposium, *Genetics of Criminal and Antisocial Behavior* (Chichester, England: Wiley, 1995).

90. Kevin M. Beaver, J. Eagle Shutt, Brian B. Boutwell, Marie Ratchford, Kathleen Roberts, and J. C. Barnes, "Genetic and Environmental Influences on Levels of Self-Control and Delinquent Peer Affiliation Results from a Longitudinal Sample of Adolescent Twins" *Criminal Justice and Behavior*, vol. 36, no. 1 (January 2009): 41–60, doi: 10.1177/009385480832699.

91. Gregory Carey, "Twin Imitation for Antisocial Behavior: Implications for Genetic and Family Environment Research," *Journal of Abnormal Psychology* 101 (1992): 18–25; David Rowe and Joseph Rogers, "The Ohio Twin Project and ADSEX Studies: Behavior Genetic Approaches to Understanding Antisocial Behavior," paper presented at the annual meeting of the American Society of Criminology, Montreal, November 1987.

92. David Rowe, *The Limits of Family Influence: Genes, Experiences and Behavior* (New York: Guilford Press, 1995), p. 64.

93. R. J. Cadoret, C. Cain, and R. R. Crowe, "Evidence for a Gene–Environment Interaction in the Development of Adolescent Antisocial Behavior," *Behavior Genetics* 13 (1983): 301–310.

94. Barry Hutchings and Sarnoff A. Mednick, "Criminality in Adoptees and Their Adoptive and Biological Parents: A Pilot Study," in *Biological Bases in Criminal Behavior*, ed. S. A. Mednick and K. O. Christiansen (New York: Gardner Press, 1977).

95. For similar results, see Sarnoff Mednick, Terrie Moffitt, William Gabrielli, and Barry Hutchings, "Genetic Factors in Criminal Behavior: A Review," *Development of Antisocial and Prosocial Behavior* (New York: Academic Press, 1986), pp. 3–50; Sarnoff Mednick, William Gabrielli, and Barry Hutchings, "Genetic Influences in Criminal Behavior: Evidence from an Adoption Cohort," in *Perspective Studies of Crime and Delinquency*, ed. Katherine Teilmann Van Dusen and Sarnoff Mednick (Boston: Kluwer-Nijhoff, 1983), pp. 39–57.

96. Jamie Vaske, Danielle Boisvert, and John Paul Wright, "Genetic and Environmental Contributions to the Relationship Between Violent Victimization and Criminal Behavior," *Journal of Interpersonal Violence* 27(16): 3213–3235 2012, doi: 10.1177/0886260512441254 at http://jiv.sagepub.com.

97. Lawrence Cohen and Richard Machalek, "A General Theory of Expropriative Crime: An Evolutionary Ecological Approach," *American Journal of Sociology* 94 (1988): 465–501.

98. For a general review, see Martin Daly and Margo Wilson, "Crime and Conflict: Homicide in Evolutionary Psychological Theory," in *Crime and Justice: An Annual Edition*, ed. Michael Tonry (Chicago: University of Chicago Press, 1997), pp. 51–100.

99. Edward O. Wilson, *The Social Conquest of Earth* (New York: Liveright Publishing Co., 2012).

100. David C. Rowe, *Biology and Crime*, 2002

101. Ibid.

102. Lee Ellis, "The Evolution of Violent Criminal Behavior and Its Nonlegal Equivalent," in *Crime in Biological, Social and Moral Contexts*, eds. Lee Ellis and Harry Hoffman (New York: Praeger, 1990), pp. 63–65.

103. David Rowe, Alexander Vazsonyi, and Aurelio Jose Figuerdo, "Mating-Effort in Adolescence: A Conditional Alternative Strategy," *Personal Individual Differences* 23 (1997): 105–115.

104. Ibid., p. 101.

105. Margo Wilson, Holly Johnson, and Martin Daly, "Lethal and Nonlethal Violence Against Wives," *Canadian Journal of Criminology* 37 (1995): 331–361.

106. Lee Ellis and Anthony Walsh, "Gene-Based Evolutionary Theories of Criminology," *Criminology* 35 (1997): 229–276; Nigel Barber, "Evolutionary Explanations for Societal Differences and Historical Change in *Violent Crime and Single Parenthood Cross-Cultural Research*," vol. 41, no. 2: 123–148.

107. Byron Roth, "Crime and Child Rearing," *Society* 34 (1996): 39–45.

108. Deborah Denno, "Sociological and Human Developmental Explanations of Crime: Conflict or Consensus," *Criminology* 23 (1985): 711–741.

109. Glenn Walters and Thomas White, "Heredity and Crime: Bad Genes or Bad Research?" *Criminology* 27 (1989): 455–486, p. 478.

110. Edwin Driver, "Charles Buckman Goring," in *Pioneers in Criminology*, ed. Hermann Mannheim (Montclair, NJ: Patterson Smith, 1970), p. 440.

111. Gabriel Tarde, *Penal Philosophy*, trans. R. Howell (Boston: Little, Brown, 1912).

112. See, generally, Donn Byrne and Kathryn Kelly, *An Introduction to Personality* (Englewood Cliffs, NJ: Prentice Hall, 1981).

113. Veronique Mandal, "Schizophrenia: Widower Demands the Right to Know," *Windsor Star* (8 October 2002).

114. David Abrahamsen, *Crime and the Human Mind* (New York: Columbia University Press, 1944), p. 137; also see generally, Fritz Redl and Hans Toch, "The Psychoanalytic Perspective," in *Psychology of Crime and Criminal Justice*, ed. Hans Toch (New York: Holt, Rinehart and Winston, 1979), pp. 193–195.

115. August Aichorn, *Wayward Youth* (New York: Viking Press, 1935).

116. See, generally, D. A. Andrews and James Bonta, *The Psychology of Criminal Conduct* (Cincinnati: Anderson, 1994), pp. 72–75.

117. Paige Crosby Ouimette, "Psychopathology and Sexual Aggression in Nonincarcerated Men," *Violence and Victimization* 12 (1997): 389–397.

118. Robert Krueger, Avshalom Caspi, Phil Silva, and Rob McGee, "Personality Traits Are Differentially Linked to Mental Disorders: A Multitrait–Multidiagnosis Study of an Adolescent Birth Cohort," *Journal of Abnormal Psychology* 105 (1996): 299–312.

119. Seymour Halleck, *Psychiatry and the Dilemmas of Crime* (Berkeley: University of California Press, 1971).

120. Chinta Puxley, "Voice from God Told Man to Kill Passenger," *Toronto Star* (4 March 2009) p. A15.

121. Mike McIntyre, "Family Denounces Ruling Killer Not Criminally Liable," *Winnipeg Free Press*, 3 December 2010, p.A5; CBC News, "Greyhound Bus Killer Found Not Criminally Responsible" (5 March 2009) at http://www.cbc.ca/news/canada/manitoba/story/2009/03/05/mb-li-verdict.html (accessed 14 August 2011).

122. "Vince Li, Man in Bus Beheading, Granted Unsupervised Passes to Winnipeg—Manitoba Review Board Says It May Consider Letting Li Move to Group Home Later," CBC News (27 February 2015) at http://www.cbc.ca/news/canada/manitoba/vince-li-man-in-bus-beheading-granted-unsupervised-passes-to-winnipeg-1.2976618 (accessed 27 October 2015).

123. Richard Rosner, "Adolescents Accused of Murder and Manslaughter: A Five-Year Descriptive Study," *Bulletin of the American Academy of Psychiatry and the Law* 7 (1979): 342–351.

124. Richard Famularo, Robert Kinscherff, and Terence Fenton, "Psychiatric Diagnoses of Abusive Mothers: A Preliminary Report," *Journal of Nervous and Mental Disease* 180 (1992): 658–660.

125. Bruce Link, Howard Andrews, and Francis Cullen, "The Violent and Illegal Behavior of Mental Patients Reconsidered," *American Sociological Review* 57 (1992): 275–292; Ellen Hochstedler Steury, "Criminal Defendants with Psychiatric Impairment: Prevalence, Probabilities and Rates," *Journal of Criminal Law and Criminology* 84 (1993): 354–374.

126. Marc Hillbrand, John Krystal, Kimberly Sharpe, and Hilliard Foster, "Clinical Predictors of Self-Mutilation in Hospitalized Patients," *Journal of Nervous and Mental Disease* 182 (1994): 9–13.

127. Carmen Cirincione, Henry Steadman, Pamela Clark Robbins, and John Monahan, *Mental Illness as a Factor in Criminality: A Study of Prisoners and Mental Patients* (Delmar, NY: Policy Research Associates, 1991); see also Carmen Cirincione, Henry Steadman, Pamela Clark Robbins, and John Monahan, *Schizophrenia as a Contingent Risk Factor for Criminal Violence* (Delmar, NY: Policy Research Associates, 1991).

128. J. Monahan and H. J. Steadman, "Crime and Mental Disorder: An Epidemiological Approach," in *Crime and Justice: An Annual Review of Research*, eds. N. Morris and M. Tonry (Chicago: University of Chicago Press, 1983) pp. 145–189.

129. K. S. Douglas, L. S. Guy, S. D. Hart, "Psychosis as a Risk Factor for Violence to Others: A Meta-Analysis," *Psychological Bulletin*, 135 (5), 679–706.

130. Ibid.

131. S. Fazel, G. Gulati, L. Linsell, J. R. Geddes, and M. Grann, "Schizophrenia and Violence: Systematic Review and Meta-Analysis," Public Library of Science, Medicine.

132. Ibid.

133. K. S. Douglas, L. S. Guy, S. D. Hart, "Psychosis as a Risk Factor for Violence to Others: A Meta-Analysis." Richard Van Dorn, Jan Volavka, and Norman Johnson, "Mental Disorder and Violence: Is There a Relationship beyond Substance Use?" *Soc Psychiatry Psychiatr Epidemiol* (2012) 47: 487–503, doi 10.1007/s00127-011-0356-x.

134. Joseph Wolpe, and Joseph J. Plaud, "Pavlov's Contributions to Behavior Therapy: The Obvious and the Not So Obvious. *American Psychologist*, vol 52(9) (September 1997): 966–972.

135. Frances D. Horowitz, "John B. Watson's Legacy: Learning and Environment," *Developmental Psychology*, vol 28(3) (May 1992): 360–367.

136. Dennis J. Delprato, and Bryan D. Midgley, "Some Fundamentals of B. F. Skinner's behaviorism," *American Psychologist*, vol. 47, iss. 11 (November 1992): 1507.

137. This discussion is based on three works by Albert Bandura: *Aggression: A Social Learning Analysis* (Englewood Cliffs, NJ: Prentice Hall, 1973); *Social Learning Theory* (Englewood Cliffs, NJ: Prentice Hall, 1977); and "The Social Learning Perspective: Mechanisms of Aggression," in *Psychology of Crime and Criminal Justice*, ed. Hans Toch (New York: Holt, Rinehart and Winston, 1979), pp. 198–236.

138. David Phillips, "The Impact of Mass Media Violence on U.S. Homicides," *American Sociological Review* 48 (1983): 560–568.

139. UCLA Center for Communication Policy, *Television Violence Monitoring Project* (Los Angeles, 1995); Jonathan Freedman, "Television Violence and Aggression: A Rejoinder," *Psychological Bulletin* 100 (1986): 372–378; Wendy Wood, Frank Wong, and J. Gregory Chachere, "Effects of Media Violence on Viewers' Aggression in Unconstrained Social Interaction," *Psychological Bulletin* 109 (1991): 371–383.

140. K. A. Dodge, "A Social Information Processing Model of Social Competence in Children," in *Minnesota Symposium in Child Psychology*, vol. 18, ed. M. Perlmutter (Hillsdale, NJ: Erlbaum, 1986): 77–125.

141. Adrian Raine, Peter Venables, and Mark Williams, "Better Autonomic Conditioning and Faster Electrodermal Half-Recovery Time at Age 15 Years as Possible Protective Factors Against Crime at Age 29 Years," *Developmental Psychology* 32 (1996): 624–630.

142. L. Huesman and L. Eron, "Individual Differences and the Trait of Aggression," *European Journal of Personality* 3 (1989): 95–106.

143. Rolf Loeber and Dale Hay, "Key Issues in the Development of Aggression and Violence from Childhood to Early Adulthood," *Annual Review of Psychology* 48 (1997): 371–410.

144. D. Lipton, E. C. McDonel, and R. McFall, "Heterosocial Perception in Rapists," *Journal of Consulting and Clinical Psychology* 55 (1987): 17–21.

145. See, generally, Walter Mischel, *Introduction to Personality*, 4th ed. (New York: Holt, Rinehart and Winston, 1986).

146. See, generally, Hans Eysenck, *Personality and Crime* (London: Routledge and Kegan Paul, 1977).

147. Edelyn Verona and Joyce Carbonell, "Female Violence and Personality," *Criminal Justice and Behavior* 27 (2000): 176–195.

148. Hans Eysenck and M. W. Eysenck, *Personality and Individual Differences* (New York: Plenum, 1985).

149. David Farrington, "Psychobiological Factors in the Explanation and Reduction of Delinquency," *Today's Delinquent* (1988): 37–51.

150. Laurie Frost, Terrie Moffitt, and Rob McGee, "Neuropsychological Correlates of Psychopathology in an Unselected Cohort of Young Adolescents," *Journal of Abnormal Psychology* 98 (1989): 307–313.

151. David Lykken, "Psychopathy, Sociopathy, and Crime," *Society* 34 (1996): 30–38; Jack Pemment, "Psychophathy versus Sociopathy: Why the Distinction Has Become Crucial," *Aggression and Violent Behaviour* 18(5) (September 2013): 458–461; Paul Babiak, Jorge Folino, Jeffrey Hancock, Robert D. Hare, Matthew Logan, Elizabeth Leon Mayer et al., "Psychopathy: An Important Forensic Concept for the 21st Century," *FBI Law Enforcement Bulletin* (July 2012).

152. Avshalom Caspi, Terrie Moffitt, Phil Silva, Magda Stouthamer-Loeber, Robert Krueger, and Pamela Schmutte, "Are Some People Crime-Prone? Replications of the Personality–Crime Relationship Across Countries, Genders, Races and Methods," *Criminology* 32 (1994): 163–195; Heather M. Gretton, Robert D. Hare and Rosalind E. H. Catchpole, "Psychopathy and Offending from Adolescence to Adulthood: A 10-Year Follow-Up," *Journal of Consulting and Clinical Psychology* 72 (August 2004): 636–645.

153. Henry Goddard, *Efficiency and Levels of Intelligence* (Princeton, NJ: Princeton University Press, 1920); Edwin Sutherland, "Mental Deficiency and Crime," in *Social Attitudes*, ed. Kimball Young (New York: Henry Holt, 1931), chap. 15.

154. William Healy and Augusta Bronner, *Delinquency and Criminals: Their Making and Unmaking* (New York: McMillan, 1926).

155. Joseph Lee Rogers, H. Harrington Cleveland, Edwin van den Oord, and David Rowe, "Resolving the Debate Over Birth Order, Family Size and Intelligence," *American Psychologist* 55 (2000): 599–612.

156. Sutherland, "Mental Deficiency and Crime."

157. Travis Hirschi and Michael Hindelang, "Intelligence and Delinquency: A Revisionist Review," *American Sociological Review* 42 (1977): 471–586.

158. Deborah Denno, "Sociological and Human Developmental Explanations of Crime: Conflict or Consensus," *Criminology* 23 (1985): 711–741; Christine Ward and Richard McFall, "Further Validation of the Problem Inventory for Adolescent Girls: Comparing Caucasian and Black Delinquents and Nondelinquents," *Journal of Consulting and Clinical Psychology* 54 (1986): 732–733; L. Hubble and M. Groff, "Magnitude and Direction of WISC-R Verbal Performance IQ Discrepancies Among Adjudicated Male Delinquents," *Journal of Youth and Adolescence* 10 (1981): 179–183; Robert Gordon, "IQ Commensurability of Black–White Differences in Crime and Delinquency," paper presented at the annual meeting of the American Psychological Association, Washington, DC, August 1986; Robert Gordon, "Two Illustrations of the IQ-Surrogate Hypothesis: IQ versus Parental Education and Occupational Status in the Race–IQ–Delinquency Model," paper presented at the annual meeting of the American Society of Criminology, Montreal, November 1987.

159. James Q. Wilson and Richard Herrnstein, *Crime and Human Nature* (New York: Simon and Schuster, 1985), p. 148.

160. Ibid, p. 171.

161. Richard Herrnstein and Charles Murray, *The Bell Curve: Intelligence and Class Structure in American Life* (New York: Free Press, 1994).

162. H. D. Day, J. M. Franklin, and D. D. Marshall, "Predictors of Aggression in Hospitalized Adolescents," *Journal of Psychology* 132 (1998): 427–435; Scott Menard and Barbara Morse, "A Structuralist Critique of the IQ–Delinquency Hypothesis: Theory and Evidence," *American Journal of Sociology* 89 (1984): 1347–1378; Denno, "Sociological and Human Developmental Explanations of Crime."

163. Ulric Neisser et al., "Intelligence: Knowns and Unknowns," *American Psychologist* 51 (1996): 77–101, p. 83.

164. D. Andrews and J. Bonta, *The Psychology of Criminal Conduct*, 4th ed. (New York: Lexis Nexis Publishing, 2006).

165. M. Foucault, *Discipline and Punish: The Birth of the Prison* (Toronto: Vintage Books, 1979).

166. Susan Pease and Craig T. Love, "Optimal Methods and Issues in Nutrition Research in the Correctional Setting," *Nutrition Reviews Supplement* 44 (1986): 122–131.

167. Mark O'Callaghan and Douglas Carroll, "The Role of Psychosurgical Studies in the Control of Antisocial Behavior," in *The Causes of Crime: New Biological Approaches,* eds. Sarnoff Mednick, Terrie Moffitt, and Susan Stack (Cambridge United Kingdom: Cambridge University Press, 1987), pp. 312–328.

168. Reiss and Roth, *Understanding and Preventing Violence,* p. 389.

169. Kathleen Cirillo et al., "School Violence: Prevalence and Intervention Strategies for At-Risk Adolescents," *Adolescence* 33 (1998): 319–331.

Chapter 6

1. Conway Daly, "Beating Highlights Predicament of Canada's Homeless," Canadian Press, at http://www.canoe.com/ CNEWSLaw0201/11 _homeless-cp.html (11 January 2002).

2. Steven Messner and Richard Rosenfeld, *Crime and the American Dream* (Belmont, CA: Wadsworth, 1994), p. 11; Patrick C. Jobes, Joseph F. Donnermeyer, and Elaine Barclay, "A Tale of Two Towns: Social Structure, Integration and Crime in Rural New South Wales," *Sociologia Ruralis,* vol. 45, iss. 3 (July 2005): 224–244.

3. Edwin Lemert, *Human Deviance, Social Problems and Social Control* (Englewood Cliffs, NJ: Prentice Hall, 1967); and Sang-Weon Kim and William Alex Pridemore, "Poverty, Socioeconomic Change, Institutional Anomie, and Homicide," *Social Science Quarterly* (Blackwell Publishing), vol. 86 (December 2005 Supplement): 1377–1398.

4. Statistics Canada, "Low Income Cut-offs Before and After Tax by Community and Family Size, 2011 Constant Dollars, Annual (dollars)" at http://www.statcan.gc.ca/pub/ 75f0002m/2012002/tbl/tbl02-eng.htm (accessed 8 October 2015); and Armina Ligaya, CBC News Online, "The Debate over Canada's Poverty Line," (12 November 2007), at http:// www.cbc.ca/news/background/economy/ poverty-line.html (accessed 7 November 2011).

5. Family Service Toronto, "2009 Report Card on Child and Family Poverty in Canada: 1989–2009," at http://www.campaign2000.ca/ reportcards/national.

6. Myungkook Joo, "Long-term Effects of Head Start on Academic and School Outcomes of Children in Persistent Poverty: Girls vs. Boys," *Children & Youth Services Review,* vol. 32, iss. 6 (June 2010): 807–814.

7. Ibid.

8. Brooks-Gunn and Duncan, "The Effects of Poverty on Children"; Kevin K. Lee, "Urban Poverty in Canada: A Statistical Profile," *Canadian Council on Social Development* (April 2000): 2001, National Council of Welfare, *Poverty Profile 1999;* Campaign 2000, *2003 Report Card on Child Poverty in Canada.*

9. Jonathan Crane, "The Epidemic Theory of Ghettos and Neighborhood Effects on Dropping Out and Teenage Childbearing," *American Journal of Sociology* 96 (1991): 1226–1259; see also Rodrick Wallace, "Expanding Coupled Shock Fronts of Urban Decay and Criminal Behavior: How U.S. Cities Are Becoming 'Hollowed Out,'" *Journal of Quantitative Criminology* 7 (1991): 333–355.

10. Lee, "Urban Poverty in Canada: A Statistical Profile"; 2001, National Council of Welfare, *Poverty Profile 1999;* Statistics Canada, "1996 Census: Sources of Income, Earnings and Total Income and Family Income," *The Daily,* 12 May 1998.

11. Richard Sennett and Jonathan Cobb, *The Hidden Injuries of Class* (New York: Vintage Books, 1973).

12. Oscar Lewis, "The Culture of Poverty," *Scientific American* 215 (1966): 19–25.

13. Gunnar Myrdal, *The Challenge of World Poverty* (New York: Vintage Books, 1970).

14. Robin Armstrong, "Mapping the Conditions of First Nations Communities," *Canadian Social Trends* (Winter 1999): 14–18; see also British Columbia All Chiefs' Task Force Fact Sheet Aboriginal Poverty in Canada, at http://www .fns.bc.ca/pdf/ACTFPovertyFactSheet_02_2010 .pdf. (accessed 8 October 2015).

15. D. Wilson and D. Macdonald, "The Income Gap between Aboriginal Peoples and the Rest of Canada," Canadian Centre for Policy Alternatives (2010). at http://ywcacanada.ca/data/research _docs/00000121.pdf (accessed 8 October 2015).

16. Robin Armstrong, "Mapping the Conditions of First Nations Communities," *Canadian Social Trends* (Winter 1999): 14–18; see also British Columbia All Chiefs' Task Force Fact Sheet Aboriginal Poverty in Canada, at http://www .fns.bc.ca/pdf/ACTFPovertyFactSheet_02_2010 .pdf (accessed 8 October 2015).

17. James Ainsworth-Darnell and Douglas Downey, "Assessing the Oppositional Culture Explanation for Racial/Ethnic Differences in School Performances," *American Sociological Review* 63 (1998): 536–553.

18. National Institute of Child Health and Human Development Early Child Care Research Network, "Duration and Developmental Timing of Poverty and Children's Cognitive and Social Development from Birth through Third Grade," *Child Development,* vol. 76, iss. 4 (July/August 2005): pp. 795–810.

19. William Julius Wilson, *The Truly Disadvantaged* (Chicago: University of Chicago Press, 1987).

20. Kevin K. Lee, "Urban Poverty in Canada: A Statistical Profile" Canadian Council on Social Development, Ottawa, Ontario (April 2000); Robin Armstrong, "Mapping the Conditions of First Nations Communities," *Canadian Social Trends* (Winter, 1999).

21. See Charles Tittle and Robert Meier, "Specifying the SES/Delinquency Relationship," *Criminology* 28 (1990): 271–295, p. 293.

22. Wouter Steenbeek and John R. Hipp, "A Longitudinal Test of Social Disorganization Theory: Feedback Effects Among Cohesion, Social Control, and Disorder," *Criminology,* vol. 49, iss. 3 (August 2011): 833–871; and Ruth Kornhauser, *Social Sources of Delinquency* (Chicago: University of Chicago Press, 1978), p. 75.

23. Clifford R. Shaw and Henry D. McKay, *Juvenile Delinquency and Urban Areas,* rev. ed. (Chicago: University of Chicago Press, 1972).

24. E. Burgess, "The Growth of the City: An Introduction to a Research Project," in *The City,* eds. R. Park, E. Burgess, and R. McKenzie (pp. 47–62) (Chicago: University of Chicago Press, 1925).

25. Clifford R. Shaw and Henry D. McKay, *Juvenile Delinquency and Urban Areas,* rev. ed. (Chicago: University of Chicago Press, 1972). p. 52.

26. Ibid., p. 171.

27. The best known of these critiques is Kornhauser, *Social Sources of Delinquency.*

28. For a general review, see James Byrne and Robert Sampson, eds., *The Social Ecology of Crime* (New York: Springer Verlag, 1985).

29. Martin A. Andresen, "A Spatial Analysis of Crime in Vancouver, British Columbia: A Synthesis of Social Disorganization and Routine Activity Theory," *Canadian Geographer,* vol. 50, iss. 4 (Winter 2006): pp. 487–502.

30. D. Wayne Osgood and Jeff Chambers, "Social Disorganization Outside the Metropolis: An Analysis of Rural Youth Violence," *Criminology* 38 (2000): 81–117.

31. William Spelman, "Abandoned Buildings: Magnets for Crime?" *Journal of Criminal Justice* 21 (1993): 481–493.

32. Keith Harries and Andrea Powell, "Juvenile Gun Crime and Social Stress: Baltimore, 1980–1990," *Urban Geography* 15 (1994): 45–63.

33. Allison T. Chappell, Elizabeth Monk-Turner, Brian K. Payne, "Broken Windows or Window Breakers: The Influence of Physical and Social Disorder on Quality of Life," *JQ: Justice Quarterly,* vol. 28, iss. 3 (June 2011): pp. 522–540.

34. Steven Messner and Kenneth Tardiff, "Economic Inequality and Levels of Homicide: An Analysis of Urban Neighborhoods," *Criminology* 24 (1986): 297–317; Charis E. Kubrin, Jerald R. Herting, "Neighborhood Correlates of Homicide Trends: An Analysis Using Growth-Curve Modeling," *Sociological Quarterly,* vol. 44, iss. 3 (Summer 2003): p. 329.

35. G. David Curry and Irving Spergel, "Gang Homicide, Delinquency, and Community," *Criminology* 26 (1988): 381–407.

36. Darrell Steffensmeier and Dana Haynie, "Gender, Structural Disadvantage, and Urban Crime: Do Macrosocial Variables Also Explain Female Offending Rates?" *Criminology* 38 (2000): 403–438.

37. Robert Bursik, "Social Disorganization and Theories of Crime and Delinquency: Problems and Prospects," *Criminology,* 26 (1988), 521–539.

38. Stephen W. Baron, "Street Youth, Unemployment, and Crime: Is It That Simple? Using General Strain Theory to Untangle the Relationship," *Canadian Journal of Criminology & Criminal Justice,* vol. 50, iss. 4 (July 2008): 399–434.

39. Scott Menard and Delbert Elliott, "Self-Reported Offending, Maturational Reform, and the Easterlin Hypothesis," *Journal of Quantitative Criminology* 6 (1990): 237–268.

40. Steven A. Kohm, "Spatial Dimensions of Fear in a High-Crime Community: Fear of Crime or Fear of Disorder?" *Canadian Journal of Criminology & Criminal Justice*, vol. 51, iss. 1 (January 2009): pp. 1–30.

41. Bilan R. Wyant, "Multilevel Impacts of Perceived Incivilities and Perceptions of Crime Risk on Fear of Crime," *Journal of Research in Crime & Delinquency*, vol. 45, iss. 1 (February 2008): pp. 39–64.

42. Wesley Skogan, "Fear of Crime and Neighborhood Change," in *Communities and Crime,* ed. Albert Reiss and Michael Tonry (Chicago: University of Chicago Press, 1986), pp. 191–232.

43. Steven A. Kohm, "Spatial Dimensions of Fear in a High-Crime Community: Fear of Crime or Fear of Disorder?"; and Stephanie Greenberg, "Fear and Its Relationship to Crime, Neighborhood Deterioration, and Informal Social Control," in *The Social Ecology of Crime,* ed. James Byrne and Robert Sampson (New York: Springer Verlag, 1985), pp. 47–62.

44. Skogan, "Fear of Crime and Neighborhood Change."

45. Ibid.

46. Finn Aage-Esbensen and David Huizinga, "Community Structure and Drug Use: From a Social Disorganization Perspective," *Justice Quarterly* 7 (1990): 691–709.

47. Allen Liska and Paul Bellair, "Violent-Crime Rates and Racial Composition: Convergence over Time," *American Journal of Sociology* 101 (1995): 578–610.

48. Wesley Skogan, *Disorder and Decline: Crime and the Spiral of Decay in American Neighborhoods* (New York: Free Press, 1990), pp. 15–35.

49. Ralph Taylor and Jeanette Covington, "Neighborhood Changes in Ecology and Violence," *Criminology* 26 (1988): 553–589.

50. Allison T. Chappell, Elizabeth Monk-Turner, Brian K. Payne, "Broken Windows or Window Breakers: The Influence of Physical and Social Disorder on Quality of Life."

51. Leo Scheurman and Solomon Kobrin, "Community Careers in Crime," in *Communities and Crime,* ed. Albert Reiss and Michael Tonry (Chicago: University of Chicago Press, 1986), pp. 67–100.

52. Wilson, *The Truly Disadvantaged.*

53. Barbara Warner and Glenn Pierce, "Reexamining Social Disorganization Theory Using Calls to the Police as a Measure of Crime," *Criminology* 31 (1993): 493–519.

54. Karen Parker and Matthew Pruitt, "Poverty, Poverty Concentration, and Homicide," *Social Science Quarterly* 81 (2000): 555–582; Scot Wortley, "Justice for All? Race and Perceptions of Bias in the Ontario Criminal Justice System—a Toronto Survey," *Canadian Journal of Criminology* 38 (October 1996): 439–468.

55. Carolyn Rebecca Block and Richard Block, *Street Gang Crime in Chicago* (Washington, DC: National Institute of Justice, 1993), p. 7.

56. Lorraine Mazerolle, Rebecca Wickes, and James McBroom, "Community Variations in Violence: The Role of Social Ties and Collective Efficacy in Comparative Context," *Journal of Research in Crime & Delinquency*, vol. 47, iss. 1 (February 2010): pp. 3–30; and Felton Earls, *Linking Community Factors and Individual Development* (Washington, DC: National Institute of Justice, 1998).

57. Donald Black, "Social Control as a Dependent Variable," in *Toward a General Theory of Social Control,* ed. D. Black (Orlando: Academic Press, 1990).

58. Robert Bursik and Harold Grasmick, "The Multiple Layers of Social Disorganization," paper presented at the annual meeting of the American Society of Criminology, New Orleans, November 1992.

59. David Klinger, "Negotiating Order in Patrol Work: An Ecological Theory of Police Response to Deviance," *Criminology* 35 (1997): 277–306.

60. Rodney Stark, "Deviant Places: A Theory of the Ecology of Crime," *Criminology* 25 (1987): 893–911.

61. Delbert Elliott, William Julius Wilson, David Huizinga, Robert Sampson, Amanda Elliott, and Bruce Rankin, "The Effects of Neighborhood Disadvantage on Adolescent Development," *Journal of Research in Crime and Delinquency* 33 (1996): 389–426.

62. Mary L. Ohmer, Barbara D. Warner, and Elizabeth Beck, "Preventing Violence in Low-Income Communities: Facilitating Residents' Ability to Intervene in Neighborhood Problems," *Journal of Sociology & Social Welfare*, vol. 37, iss. 2 (June 2010): pp. 161–181.

63. Robert Bursik and Harold Grasmick, "Economic Deprivation and Neighborhood Crime Rates, 1960–1980," *Law and Society Review* 27 (1993): 263–278.

64. Joanna C. Jacob, "Male and Female Youth Crime in Canadian Communities: Assessing the Applicability of Social Disorganization Theory," *Canadian Journal of Criminology & Criminal Justice*, vol. 48, iss. 1 (January 2006): pp. 31–60; Denise Gottfredson, Richard McNeill, and Gary Gottfredson, "Social Area Influences on Delinquency: A Multilevel Analysis," *Journal of Research in Crime and Delinquency* 28 (1991): 197–206.

65. Bronwyn Dobchuk-Land, Owen Toews, and Jim Silver, "Neighbourhood-Level Responses to Safety Concerns in Four Winnipeg Inner-City Neighbourhoods: Reflections on Collective Efficacy," *Canadian Journal of Urban Research*, vol. 19, iss. 1 (Summer 2010): 18–33.

66. Robert Merton, *Social Theory and Social Structure,* enlarged ed. (New York: Free Press, 1968).

67. Albert Cohen, "The Sociology of the Deviant Act: Anomie Theory and Beyond," *American Sociological Review* 30 (1965): 5–14; and Eric P. Baumer and Regan Gustafson, "Social Organization and Instrumental Crime: Assessing the Empirical Validity of Classic and Contemporary Anomie Theories." *Criminology*, vol. 45, iss. 3 (August 2007): 617–663.

68. Steven Messner and Richard Rosenfeld, *Crime and the American Dream* (Belmont, CA: Wadsworth, 1994).

69. John Hagan, Gerd Hefler, Gabriele Classen, Klaus Boehnke, and Hans Merkens, "Subterranean Sources of Subcultural Delinquency Beyond the American Dream," *Criminology* 36 (1998): 309–340.

70. Robert Agnew, "Foundation for a General Strain Theory of Crime and Delinquency," *Criminology* 30 (1992): 47–87.

71. Ibid., p. 57.

72. Ibid.

73. Gregory Dunaway, "Strain, Relative Deprivation and Middle-Class Delinquency," in *Varieties of Criminology: Readings from a Dynamic Discipline,* ed. Greg Barak (Westport, CT: Praeger, 1994): 79–95; Nikos Passas, "Anomie and Relative Deprivation," in *The Future of Anomie Theory,* ed. Nikos Passass and Robert Agnew (Boston: Northeastern University Press, 1997): 62–94; and Giacinto Froggio, "Strain and Juvenile Delinquency: A Critical Review of Agnew's General Strain Theory," *Journal of Loss & Trauma,* vol. 12, iss. 4 (July–September 2007): 383–418.

74. Robert Agnew, Timothy Brezina, John Paul Wright, and Francis T. Cullen, "Strain, Personality Traits, and Delinquency: Extending General Strain Theory," *Criminology*, vol. 40, iss. 1 (February 2002): 43.

75. Robert Agnew and Helene Raskin White, "An Empirical Test of General Strain Theory," *Criminology* 30 (1992): 475–499.

76. Carter Hay, "Family Strain, Gender, and Delinquency," *Sociological Perspectives*, vol. 46, iss. 1 (Spring 2003): 107–135; Beverly Stiles, Xiaoru Liu, and Howard Kaplan, "Relative Deprivation and Deviant Adaptations: The Mediating Effects of Negative Self Feelings," *Journal of Research in Crime and Delinquency* 37 (2000): 64–90.

77. Robert Agnew, "Foundation for a General Strain Theory of Crime and Delinquency," *Criminology* 30 (1992): 47–87.

78. Ibid., p. 57.

79. John P. Hoffmann and Timothy O. Ireland, "Strain and Opportunity Structures," *Journal of Quantitative Criminology*, vol. 20, iss. 3 (September 2004): pp. 263–292.

80. Walter Miller, "Lower-Class Culture as a Generating Milieu of Gang Delinquency," *Journal of Social Issues* 14 (1958), 5–19.

81. Ibid., pp. 14–17.

82. Fred Markowitz and Richard Felson, "Social-Demographic Attitudes and Violence," *Criminology* 36 (1998): 117–138.

83. Jeffrey Fagan, *Adolescent Violence: A View from the Street,* NIJ Research Preview (Washington, DC: National Institute of Justice, 1998).

84. Albert Cohen, *Delinquent Boys* (New York: Free Press, 1955).

85. Ibid., p. 25.

86. Ibid., p. 28.

87. Ibid.

88. Ibid., p. 30.

89. Ibid., p. 133.

90. "Winnipeg Neighbourhood Hotbed for Crime," CBC News (27 September 2010) at http://www.cbc.ca/news/canada/manitoba/winnipeg-neighbourhood-hotbed-for-crime-1.953240 (accessed 16 October 2015).

91. Richard Cloward and Lloyd Ohlin, *Delinquency and Opportunity* (New York: Free Press, 1960).

92. Ibid., p. 171.

93. Ibid., p. 73.

94. James DeFronzo, "Welfare and Burglary," *Crime and Delinquency* 42 (1996): 223–230.

95. Hamilton Police Service, C.O.P.P. 2000: Challenging Our Patrol Priorities into the Next Century (June 1999).

Chapter 7

1. Charles Tittle and Robert Meier, "Specifying the SES/Delinquency Relationship," *Criminology* 28 (1990): 271–299, p. 274; Robert Agnew et al., "Socioeconomic Status, Economic Problems, and Delinquency," *Youth & Society* (2008), vol. 40, no. 2: 159–181.

2. Sheldon Glueck and Eleanor Glueck, *Unraveling Juvenile Delinquency* (Cambridge, MA: Harvard University Press, 1950); Ashley Weeks, "Predicting Juvenile Delinquency," *American Sociological Review* 8 (1943): 40–46.

3. Denise Kandel, "The Parental and Peer Contexts of Adolescent Deviance: An Algebra of Interpersonal Influences," *Journal of Drug Issues* 26 (1996): 289–315; Ann Goetting, "The Parenting–Crime Connection," *Journal of Primary Prevention* 14 (1994): 167–184; John Paul Wright and Francis T. Cullen, "Parental Efficacy and Delinquent Behavior: Do Control and Support Matter? *Criminology*, 39, 3 (2001): 677–705.

4. For general reviews of the relationship between families and delinquency, see Alan Jay Lincoln and Murray Straus, *Crime and the Family* (Springfield, IL: Charles C. Thomas, 1985); Rolf Loeber and Magda Stouthamer-Loeber, "Family Factors as Correlates and Predictors of Juvenile Conduct Problems and Delinquency," in *Crime and Justice: An Annual Review of Research*, vol. 7, eds. Michael Tonry and Norval Morris (Chicago: University of Chicago Press, 1986), pp. 29–151; Goetting, "The Parenting–Crime Connection"; Emma J. Palmer and Kirsty Gough, "Childhood Experiences of Parenting and Causal Attributions for Criminal Behavior Among Young Offenders and Non-Offenders," *Journal of Applied Social Psychology*, 37 (4) (2007): 790–806.

5. Joseph Weis, Katherine Worsley, and Carol Zeiss, *The Family and Delinquency: Organizing the Conceptual Chaos* (Monograph, Center for Law and Justice, University of Washington, 1982).

6. Susan Stern and Carolyn Smith, "Family Processes and Delinquency in an Ecological Context," *Social Service Review* 37 (1995): 707–731.

7. Lawrence Rosen and Kathleen Neilson, "Broken Homes," in *Contemporary Criminology*, eds. Leonard Savitz and Norman Johnston (New York: Wiley, 1982), pp. 126–132.

8. James Q. Wilson and Richard Herrnstein, *Crime and Human Nature* (New York: Simon and Schuster, 1985), p. 249.

9. L. Edward Wells and Joseph Rankin, "Families and Delinquency: A Meta-Analysis of the Impact of Broken Homes," *Social Problems* 38 (1991): 71–90.

10. Nan Marie Astone and Sara McLanahan, "Family Structure, Parental Practices and High School Completion," *American Sociological Review* 56 (1991): 309–320.

11. Joseph Rankin and L. Edward Wells, "The Effect of Parental Attachments and Direct Controls on Delinquency," *Journal of Research in Crime and Delinquency* 27 (1990): 140–165.

12. Ronald Simons et al., "A Cross-Cultural Examination of the Link Between Corporal Punishment and Adolescent Antisocial Behavior," *Criminology* 38 (2000): 47–79.

13. Robert Roberts and Vern Bengston, "Affective Ties to Parents in Early Adulthood and Self-Esteem Across 20 Years," *Social Psychology Quarterly* 59 (1996): 96–106.

14. Robert Johnson et al., "Parental Influences on Deviant Behavior in Early Adolescence: A Logistic Response Analysis of Age- and Gender-Differentiated Effects," *Journal of Quantitative Criminology* 11 (1995): 167–192; Nancy R. VanDeMark et al., "Children of Mothers with Histories of Substance Abuse, Mental Illness, and Trauma," *Journal of Community Psychology*, 33 (4) (2005): 445–459.

15. Judith Brook and Li-Jung Tseng, "Influences of Parental Drug Use, Personality, and Child Rearing on the Toddler's Anger and Negativity," *Genetic, Social and General Psychology Monographs*, 122 (1996): 107–128.

16. Thomas Ashby Wills, Donato Vaccaro, Grace McNamara, and A. Elizabeth Hirky, "Escalated Substance Use: A Longitudinal Grouping Analysis from Early to Middle Adolescence," *Journal of Abnormal Psychology*, 105 (1996): 166–180.

17. Heather Juby and David P. Farrington, "Disentangling the Link Between Disruptive Families and Delinquency," *British Journal of Criminology*, 41 (2001): 22–44. at http://www.fact.on.ca/news/news0103/410022.pdf (accessed 8 October 2015).

18. Shelley Trevethan, Sarah Auger and John-Patrick Moore, "The Effect of Family Disruption on Aboriginal and Non-aboriginal Inmates," Research Reports, Correctional Services Canada (2001). at http://www.csc-scc.gc.ca/research/r113-eng.shtml (accessed 8 October 2015).

19. Carolyn Smith and Terence Thornberry, "The Relationship Between Childhood Maltreatment and Adolescent Involvement in Delinquency," *Criminology* 33 (1995): 451–479.

20. Murray A. Straus, "Spanking and the Making of a Violent Society: The Short- and Long-Term Consequences of Corporal Punishment," *Pediatrics* 98 (1996): 837–843.

21. *The Forgotten Half: Pathways to Success for America's Youth and Young Families* (Washington, DC: William T. Grant Foundation, 1988); Lee Jussim, "Teacher Expectations: Self-Fulfilling Prophecies, Perceptual Biases, and Accuracy," *Journal of Personality and Social Psychology* 57 (1989): 469–480.

22. Eugene Maguin and Rolf Loeber, "Academic Performance and Delinquency," in *Crime and Justice: A Review of Research*, vol. 20, ed. Michael Tonry (Chicago: University of Chicago Press, 1995), pp. 145–264; Richard Thompson et al., "Early Adolescent Risk Behavior Outcomes of Childhood Externalizing Behavioral Trajectories," *Journal of Early Adolescence* (2) (2011): 234–257.

23. Jeannie Oakes, *Keeping Track: How Schools Structure Inequality* (New Haven, CT: Yale University Press, 1985); Marc LeBlanc, Evelyne Valliere, and Pierre McDuff, "Adolescents' School Experience and Self-Reported Offending: A Longitudinal Test of Social Control Theory," paper presented at the annual meeting of the American Society of Criminology, Baltimore, November 1990.

24. Harvey Krahn, "Streaming in the 10th grade in Four Canadian Provinces," Statistics Canada, 2000. at http://www.statcan.gc.ca/pub/81-004-x/2007002/9994-eng.htm (accessed 8 October 2015).

25. G. Roger Jarjoura, "Does Dropping Out of School Enhance Delinquent Involvement? Results from a Large-Scale National Probability Sample," *Criminology* 31 (1993): 149–172; Terence Thornberry, Melanie Moore, and R. L. Christenson, "The Effect of Dropping Out of High School on Subsequent Criminal Behavior," *Criminology* 23 (1985): 3–18.

26. Irving Janis, *Groupthink: Psychological Studies of Policy Decisions and Fiascoes* (Boston: Houghton Mifflin, 1982).

27. Delbert Elliott, David Huizinga, and Suzanne Ageton, *Explaining Delinquency and Drug Use* (Beverly Hills, CA: Sage, 1985); Helene Raskin White, Robert Padina, and Randy LaGrange, "Longitudinal Predictors of Serious Substance Use and Delinquency," *Criminology* 6 (1987): 715–740.

28. Robert Agnew and Timothy Brezina, "Relational Problems with Peers, Gender and Delinquency," *Youth and Society* 29 (1997): 84–111.

29. Scott Menard, "Demographic and Theoretical Variables in the Age-Period Cohort Analysis of Illegal Behavior," *Journal of Research in Crime and Delinquency* 29 (1992): 178–199.

30. Patrick Jackson, "Theories and Findings About Youth Gangs," *Criminal Justice Abstracts* (June 1989): 313–327.

31. Marvin Krohn and Terence Thornberry, "Network Theory: A Model for Understanding Drug Abuse Among African-American and Hispanic Youth," in *Drug Abuse Among Minority Youth: Advances in Research and Methodology*, ed. Mario De La Rosa and Juan-Luis Recio Adrados (Washington, DC: U.S. Department of Health and Human Services, 1993), pp. 29–46.

32. D. Wayne Osgood et al., "Routine Activities and Individual Deviant Behavior," *American Sociological Review* 61 (1996): 635–655.

33. Mark Warr, "Age, Peers, and Delinquency," *Criminology* 31 (1993): 17–40.

34. Sara Battin et al., "The Contribution of Gang Membership to Delinquency Beyond Delinquent Friends," *Criminology* 36 (1998): 93–116.

35. Terence Thornberry et al., "Delinquent Peers, Beliefs, and Delinquent Behavior: A Longitudinal Test of Interactional Theory," *Working Paper* no. 6, rev. (Albany, NY: Rochester Youth Development Study, Hindelang Criminal Justice Research Center, 1992), pp. 8–30.

36. Warr, "Age, Peers, and Delinquency."

37. David Fergusson, L. John Horwood, and Daniel Nagin, "Offending Trajectories in a New Zealand Birth Cohort," *Criminology* 38 (2000): 525–551.

38. Travis Hirschi and Rodney Stark, "Hellfire and Delinquency," *Social Problems* 17 (1969): 202–213.

39. T. David Evans, Francis Cullen, R. Gregory Dunaway, and Velmer Burton, Jr., "Religion and Crime Reexamined: The Impact of Religion, Secular Controls, and Social Ecology on Adult Criminality," *Criminology* 33 (1995): 195–224.

40. Lee Ellis and James Patterson, "Crime and Religion: An International Comparison Among Thirteen Industrial Nations," *Personal Individual Differences* 20 (1996): 761–768.

41. Edwin H. Sutherland, *Principles of Criminology* (Philadelphia: Lippincott, 1939).

42. See, for example, Edwin Sutherland, "White-Collar Criminality," *American Sociological Review* 5 (1940): 2–10.

43. See Edwin Sutherland and Donald Cressey, *Criminology*, 8th ed. (Philadelphia: Lippincott, 1970), pp. 77–79.

44. Sandra Brown, Vicki Creamer, and Barbara Stetson, "Adolescent Alcohol Expectancies in Relation to Personal and Parental Drinking Patterns," *Journal of Abnormal Psychology* 96 (1987): 117–121.

45. Craig Reinerman and Jeffrey Fagan, "Social Organization and Differential Association: A Research Note from a Longitudinal Study of Violent Juvenile Offenders," *Crime and Delinquency* 34 (1988): 307–327.

46. Sue Titus Reed, *Crime and Criminology*, 2nd ed. (New York: Holt, Rinehart & Winston, 1979), p. 234.

47. Gresham Sykes and David Matza, "Techniques of Neutralization: A Theory of Delinquency," *American Sociological Review* 22 (1957): 664–670; David Matza, *Delinquency and Drift* (New York: John Wiley, 1964).

48. Matza, *Delinquency and Drift*, p. 51.

49. Sykes and Matza, "Techniques of Neutralization"; see also David Matza, "Subterranean Traditions of Youths," *Annals of the American Academy of Political and Social Science* 378 (1961): 116.

50. Sykes and Matza, "Techniques of Neutralization."

51. Ian Shields and George Whitehall, "Neutralization and Delinquency Among Teenagers," *Criminal Justice and Behavior* 21 (1994): 223–235; Robert A. Ball, "An Empirical Exploration of Neutralization Theory," *Criminologica* 4 (1966): 22–32. See also M. William Minor, "The Neutralization of Criminal Offense," *Criminology* 18 (1980): 103–120; Robert Gordon, James Short, Desmond Cartwright, and Fred Strodtbeck, "Values and Gang Delinquency: A Study of Street Corner Groups," *American Journal of Sociology* 69 (1963): 109–128.

52. Robert Agnew, "The Techniques of Neutralization and Violence," *Criminology* 32 (1994): 555–580.

53. Jeffrey Fagan, *Adolescent Violence: A View from the Street*, NIJ Research Preview (Washington, DC: National Institute of Justice, 1998).

54. Norm Desjardins and Tina Hotton, "Trends in Drug Offences and the Role of Alcohol and Drugs in Crime," *Juristat* 24 (February 2004): 1; A. Synnott, *Shadows: Issues and Social Patterns in Canada* (Scarborough, ON: Prentice Hall, 1996).

55. Eric Wish, *Drug Use Forecasting 1990* (Washington, DC: National Institute of Justice, 1991).

56. Scott Briar and Irving Piliavin, "Delinquency: Situational Inducements and Commitment to Conformity," *Social Problems* 13 (1965– 1966): 35–45.

57. Lawrence Sherman and Douglas Smith, with Janell Schmidt and Dennis Rogan, "Crime, Punishment, and Stake in Conformity: Legal and Informal Control of Domestic Violence," *American Sociological Review* 57 (1992): 680–690.

58. Albert Reiss, "Delinquency as the Failure of Personal and Social Controls," *American Sociological Review* 16 (1951): 196–207.

59. Walter Reckless, *The Crime Problem* (New York: Appleton-Century Crofts, 1967), pp. 469–483.

60. Among the many research reports by Reckless and his colleagues are Walter Reckless, Simon Dinitz, and Ellen Murray, "Self-Concept as an Insulator Against Delinquency," *American Sociological Review* 21 (1956): 744–746; Walter Reckless, Simon Dinitz, and Barbara Kay, "The Self-Component in Potential Delinquency and Potential Non-Delinquency," *American Sociological Review* 22 (1957): 566–570; Walter Reckless, Simon Dinitz, and Ellen Murray, "The Good Boy in a High Delinquency Area," *Journal of Criminal Law, Criminology, and Police Science* 48 (1957): 12–26; Frank Scarpitti, Ellen Murray, Simon Dinitz, and Walter Reckless, "The Good Boy in a High Delinquency Area: Four Years Later," *American Sociological Review* 23 (1960): 555–558; Walter Reckless and Simon Dinitz, "Pioneering with Self-Concept as a Vulnerability Factor in Delinquency," *Journal of Criminal Law, Criminology, and Police Science* 58 (1967): 515–523.

61. Travis Hirschi, *Causes of Delinquency* (Berkeley: University of California Press, 1969).

62. Ibid., p. 231.

63. Ibid., pp. 66–74.

64. Michael Wiatroski, David Griswold, and Mary K. Roberts, "Social Control Theory and Delinquency," *American Sociological Review* 46 (1981): 525–541.

65. Patricia Van Voorhis, Francis Cullen, Richard Mathers, and Connie Chenoweth Garner, "The Impact of Family Structure and Quality on Delinquency: A Comparative Assessment of Structural and Functional Factors," *Criminology* 26 (1988): 235–261.

66. Bobbi Jo Anderson, Malcolm Holmes, and Erik Ostresh, "Male and Female Delinquent's Attachments and Effects of Attachments on Severity of Self-Reported Delinquency," *Criminal Justice and Behavior* 26 (1999): 435–452.

67. Patricia Jenkins, "School Delinquency and the School Social Bond," *Journal of Research in Crime and Delinquency* 34 (1997): 337–367.

68. For a review of exciting research, see Kimberly Kempf, "The Empirical Status of Hirschi's Control Theory," in *Advances in Criminological Theory*, eds. Bill Laufer and Freda Adler (New Brunswick, NJ: Transaction Publishers, 1992), pp. 111–129.

69. Peggy Giordano, Stephen Cernkovich, and M. D. Pugh, "Friendships and Delinquency," *American Journal of Sociology* 91 (1986): 1170–1202.

70. Denise Kandel and Mark Davies, "Friendship Networks, Intimacy, and Illicit Drug Use in Young Adulthood: A Comparison of Two Competing Theories," *Criminology* 29 (1991): 441–467.

71. Stephen Cernkovich, Peggy Giordano, and Jennifer Rudolph, "Race, Crime and the American Dream," *Journal of Research in Crime and Delinquency* 37 (2000): 131–170.

72. Velmer Burton et al., "The Impact of Parental Controls on Delinquency," *Journal of Criminal Justice* 23 (1995): 111–126.

73. Michael Hindelang, "Causes of Delinquency: A Partial Replication and Extension," *Social Problems* 21 (1973): 471–487.

74. Gary Jensen and David Brownfield, "Parents and Drugs," *Criminology* 21 (1983): 543–554. See also M. Wiatrowski, D. Griswold, and M. Roberts, "Social Control Theory and Delinquency," *American Sociological Review* 46 (1981): 525–541.

75. Leslie Samuelson, Timothy Hartnagel, and Harvey Krahn, "Crime and Social Control Among High School Dropouts," *Journal of Crime and Justice* 18 (1990): 129–161.

76. Alan E. Liska and M. D. Reed, "Ties to Conventional Institutions and Delinquency: Estimating Reciprocal Effects," *American Sociological Review* 50 (1985): 547–560.

77. Michael Wiatrowski, David Griswold, and Mary K. Roberts, "Social Control Theory and Delinquency," *American Sociological Review* 46 (1981): 525–541.

78. Linda Jackson, John Hunter, and Carole Hodge, "Physical Attractiveness and Intellectual Competence: A Meta-Analytic Review," *Social Psychology Quarterly* 58 (1995): 108–122.

79. President's Commission on Law Enforcement and the Administration of Youth Crime, *Task Force Report: Juvenile Delinquency and Youth* (Washington, DC: U.S. Government Printing Office, 1967), p. 43.

80. Howard Becker, *Outsiders: Studies in the Sociology of Deviance* (New York: Macmillan, 1963), p. 9.

81. Health Canada. Statement on Supreme Court of Canada Decision in R. v. Smith, July 7, 2015, at http://www.hc-sc.gc.ca/dhp-mps/marihuana/info/licencedproducer-producteurautorise/

decision-r-v-smith-eng.php (accessed 20 October 2015).

82. Laurie Goodstein, "The Architect of the 'Gay Conversion' Campaign," *The New York Times* (13 August 1998): A10.

83. Christy Visher, "Gender, Police Arrest Decision, and Notions of Chivalry," *Criminology* 21 (1983): 5–28.

84. Marjorie Zatz, "Race, Ethnicity and Determinate Sentencing," *Criminology* 22 (1984): 147–171.

85. Christina DeJong and Kenneth Jackson, "Putting Race into Context: Race, Juvenile Justice Processing, and Urbanization," *Justice Quarterly* 15 (1998): 487–504.

86. Joan Petersilia, "Racial Disparities in the Criminal Justice System: A Summary," *Crime and Delinquency* 31 (1985): 15–34.

87. Harold Garfinkle, "Conditions of Successful Degradation Ceremonies," *American Journal of Sociology* 61 (1956): 420–424.

88. Karen Heimer and Ross Matsueda, "Role-Taking, Role-Commitment and Delinquency: A Theory of Differential Social Control," *American Sociological Review* 59 (1994): 400–437.

89. Karen Heimer, "Gender, Race, and the Pathways to Delinquency: An Interactionist Explanation," in *Crime and Inequality*, eds. John Hagan and Ruth Peterson (Stanford, CA: Stanford University Press, 1995), pp. 32–57.

90. Heimer and Matsueda, "Role-Taking, Role-Commitment and Delinquency."

91. See, for example, Howard Kaplan and Hiroshi Fukurai, "Negative Social Sanctions, Self-Rejection, and Drug Use," *Youth and Society* 23 (1992): 275–298; Howard Kaplan and Robert Johnson, "Negative Social Sanctions and Juvenile Delinquency: Effects of Labeling in a Model of Deviant Behavior," *Social Science Quarterly* 72 (1991): 98–122; Howard Kaplan, Robert Johnson, and Carol Bailey, "Deviant Peers and Deviant Behavior: Further Elaboration of a Model," *Social Psychology Quarterly* 30 (1987): 277–284.

92. John Lofland, *Deviance and Identity* (Englewood Cliffs, NJ: Prentice Hall, 1969).

93. Frank Tannenbaum, *Crime and the Community* (New York: Columbia University Press, 1938), pp. 19–20.

94. Edwin Lemert, *Social Pathology* (New York: McGraw-Hill, 1951).

95. Ibid., p. 75.

96. Carl Pope and William Feyerherm, "Minority Status and Juvenile Justice Processing," *Criminal Justice Abstracts* 22 (1990): 327–336. See also Carl Pope, "Race and Crime Revisited," *Crime and Delinquency* 25 (1979): 347–357; National Minority Council on Criminal Justice, *The Inequality of Justice* (Washington, DC: National Minority Advisory Council on Criminal Justice, 1981), p. 200.

97. Scot Wortley, "Justice for All? Race and Perceptions of Bias in the Ontario Criminal Justice System," *Canadian Journal of Criminology* 38 (October 1996): 439–457; Scot Wortley, "Hidden Intersections: Research on Race, Crime, and Criminal Justice in Canada," *Canadian Ethnic Studies* 35 (2003): 99–117; Eric

Mills, ed., *Report of the Commission on Systemic Racism in the Ontario Criminal Justice System* (Toronto: Queen's Printer for Ontario, 1995).

98. Howard Kaplan and Robert Johnson, "Negative Social Sanctions and Juvenile Delinquency: Effects of Labeling in a Model of Deviant Behavior," *Social Science Quarterly* 72 (1991): 98–122.

99. Ruth Triplett, "The Conflict Perspective, Symbolic Interactionism, and the Status Characteristics Hypothesis," *Justice Quarterly* 10 (1993): 540–558.

100. Ross Matsueda, "Reflected Appraisals: Parental Labeling, and Delinquency: Specifying a Symbolic Interactionist Theory," *American Journal of Sociology* 97 (1992): 1577–1611.

101. Suzanne Ageton and Delbert Elliott, *The Effect of Legal Processing on Self-Concept* (Boulder, CO: Institute of Behavioral Science, 1973).

102. Christine Bowditch, "Getting Rid of Troublemakers: High School Disciplinary Procedures and the Production of Dropouts," *Social Problems* 40 (1993): 493–507.

103. Melvin Ray and William Downs, "An Empirical Test of Labeling Theory Using Longitudinal Data," *Journal of Research in Crime and Delinquency* 23 (1986): 169–194.

104. Sherman and Smith, with Schmidt and Rogan, "Crime, Punishment, and Stake in Conformity."

105. Charles Tittle, "Two Empirical Regularities (Maybe) in Search of an Explanation: Commentary on the Age/Crime Debate," *Criminology* 26 (1988): 75–85.

106. Robert Sampson and John Laub, "A Life-Course Theory of Cumulative Disadvantage and the Stability of Delinquency," in *Developmental Theories of Crime and Delinquency*, ed. Terence Thornberry (New Brunswick, NJ: Transaction Press, 1997), pp. 133–161; Douglas Smith and Robert Brame, "On the Initiation and Continuation of Delinquency," *Criminology* 4 (1994): 607–630.

107. Raymond Paternoster and Leeann Iovanni, "The Labeling Perspective and Delinquency: An Elaboration of the Theory and an Assessment of the Evidence," *Justice Quarterly* 6 (1989): 358–394.

108. B. Feld, and D. Bishop, *The Oxford Handbook of Crime and Juvenile Justice* (New York: Oxford University Press, 2012).

Chapter 8

1. Vincent Donovan, "Fracking Divides New Brunswick Communities: Advocates Say Shale Gas Will Boost Economy as Foes Warn of Harm to Drinking Water," *Toronto Star* (26 October 2013): A20; CBC News, "RCMP, Protesters Withdraw After Shale Gas Clash in Rexton: 40 Arrested, 5 Police Vehicles Burned But No One Seriously Injured in Violent Clash" (17 October 2013) at http://www.cbc.ca/news/canada/new-brunswick/rcmp-protesters-withdraw-after-shale-gas-clash-in-rexton-1.2100703 (accessed 14 October 2015); Ginabeth Roberts, "Shale Gas Protesters Sentenced to 15 Months," *Telegraph-Journal* (30 July 2014): A1; Ginabeth Roberts, "Protester Gets 200 Hours

of Community Service," *Telegraph-Journal* (25 November 2014): A5; Craig Babstock, "Rexton Demonstrators Mistreated by RCMP and While in Jail: Lawyer" *Telegraph-Journal* (2 November 2013): A3; Adam Huras, "Liberals Extend SWN Shale Licences," *Telegraph-Journal* (16 March 2015): A1; Adam Huras, "Panel Has Year to Report on Fracking Moratorium," *Telegraph-Journal* (25 March 2015): A1.

2. Michael Lynch, "Rediscovering Criminology: Lessons from the Marxist Tradition," in *Marxist Sociology: Surveys of Contemporary Theory and Research*, eds. Donald McQuarie and Patrick McGuire (New York: General Hall Press, 1994).

3. Michael Lynch and W. Byron Groves, *A Primer in Radical Criminology*, 2nd ed. (Albany, NY: Harrow and Heston, 1989), pp. 32–33.

4. Ibid., p. 4.

5. James Short and F. Ivan Nye, "Extent of Undetected Delinquency: Tentative Conclusions," *Journal of Criminal Law, Criminology, and Police Science* 49 (1958): 296–302.

6. See, generally, Robert Meier, "The New Criminology: Continuity in Criminological Theory," *Journal of Criminal Law and Criminology* 67 (1977): 461–469.

7. David Greenberg, ed., *Crime and Capitalism* (Palo Alto, CA: Mayfield, 1981), p. 3.

8. "Standing Up to the FLQ Terrorists," *Maclean's* (1 July 1999): p. 51.

9. William Chambliss and Robert Seidman, *Law, Order, and Power* (Reading, MA: Addison-Wesley, 1971), p. 503.

10. Ibid.

11. John Hagan and Celesta Albonetti, "Race, Class, and the Perception of Criminal Injustice in America," *American Journal of Sociology* 88 (1982): 329–355; Scot Wortley, "Justice for All? Race and Perceptions of Bias in the Ontario Criminal Justice System—A Toronto Survey," *Canadian Journal of Criminology* 38 (October 1996): 439–467.

12. Julian V. Roberts and Ronald Melchers, "The Incarceration of Aboriginal Offenders: Trends from 1978 to 2001," *Canadian Journal of Criminology* 45 (April 2003): 211–256; Akwasi Owusu-Bempa et al., "Years of Life Lost to Incarceration: Inequities Between Aboriginal and non-Aboriginal Canadians," *BMC Public Health 2014*, 14 (2014): 585, doi:10.1186/1471-2458-14-585,

13. Richard Quinney, "Crime Control in Capitalist Society," in *Critical Criminology*, eds. Ian Taylor, Paul Walton, and Jock Young (London: Routledge and Kegan Paul, 1975).

14. CBC News, "Dozens Arrested in Anti-capitalism May Day Protest in Montreal; Eighty-Four Protesters Arrested, Montreal Police Use Tear Gas to Disperse Demonstrators and Bystanders" (1 May 2015) at http://www.cbc.ca/news/canada/montreal/dozens-arrested-in-anti-capitalism-may-day-protest-in-montreal-1.3058316 (accessed 15 October 2015).

15. Richard Quinney, "Crime Control in Capitalist Society," in *Critical Criminology*, eds. Ian Taylor,

Paul Walton, and Jock Young (London: Routledge and Kegan Paul, 1975).

16. Ibid.

17. David McDowall, "Poverty and Homicide in Detroit, 1926–1978," *Victims and Violence* 1 (1986): 23–34; David McDowall and Sandra Norris, "Poverty and Homicide in Baltimore, Cleveland, and Memphis, 1937–1980," paper presented at the annual meeting of the American Society of Criminology, Montreal, November 1987.

18. Judith Blau and Peter Blau, "The Cost of Inequality: Metropolitan Structure and Violent Crime," *American Sociological Review* 147 (1982): 114–129; Richard Block, "Community Environment and Violent Crime," *Criminology* 17 (1979): 46–57; Robert Sampson, "Structural Sources of Variation in Race-Age-Specific Rates of Offending Across Major U.S. Cities," *Criminology* 23 (1985): 647–673.

19. David Jacobs and David Britt, "Inequality and Police Use of Deadly Force: An Empirical Assessment of a Conflict Hypothesis," *Social Problems* 26 (1979): 403–412.

20. Malcolm Homes, "Minority Threat and Police Brutality: Determinants of Civil Rights Criminal Complaints in U.S. Municipalities," *Criminology* 38 (2000): 343–368.

21. Alan Lizotte, "Extra-Legal Factors in Chicago's Criminal Courts: Testing the Conflict Model of Criminal Justice," *Social Problems* 25 (1978): 564–580.

22. Terance Miethe and Charles Moore, "Racial Differences in Criminal Processing: The Consequences of Model Selection on Conclusions About Differential Treatment," *Sociological Quarterly* 27 (1987): 217–237; Kent Roach and Jonathan Rudin (2000) "Gladue: The Judicial and Political Reception of a Promising Decision," *Canadian Journal of Criminology*, vol. 42, iss. (July 2000): 355–388.

23. Tracy Nobiling, Cassia Spohn, and Miriam DeLone, "A Tale of Two Counties: Unemployment and Sentence Severity," *Justice Quarterly* 15 (1998): 459–485; David Milward, "Locking up Those Dangerous Indians for Good: An Examination of Canadian Dangerous Offender Legislation as Applied to Aboriginal Persons," *Alberta Law Review*, vol. 51, iss. 3 (March 2014): 619–658.

24. Nancy Wonders, "Determinate Sentencing: A Feminist and Postmodern Story," *Justice Quarterly* 13 (1996): 610–648; Douglas Smith, Christy Visher, and Laura Davidson, "Equity and Discretionary Justice: The Influence of Race on Police Arrest Decisions," *Journal of Criminal Law and Criminology* 75 (1984): 234–249; Roberts and Melchers, "The Incarceration of Aboriginal Offenders: Trends from 1978 to 2001"; Alison Hatch and Karlene Faith, "The Female Offender in Canada: A Statistical Profile," *Canadian Journal of Women and the Law* 3 (1989): 432–456.

25. Thomas Arvanites, "Increasing Imprisonment: A Function of Crime or Socioeconomic Factors?" *American Journal of Criminal Justice* 17 (1992): 19–38.

26. Michael Leiber, Anne Woodrick, and E. Michele Roudebush, "Religion, Discriminatory Attitudes, and the Orientations of Juvenile Justice Personnel: A Research Note," *Criminology* 33 (1995): 431–447; Michael Leiber and Katherine Jamieson, "Race and Decision Making Within Juvenile Justice: The Importance of Context," *Journal of Quantitative Criminology* 11 (1995): 363–388.

27. Dragan Milovanovic, "Postmodern Criminology: Mapping the Terrain," *Justice Quarterly* 13 (1996): 567–610; Wortley, "Justice for All? Race and Perceptions of Bias in the Ontario Criminal Justice System—A Toronto Survey"; Commission on Systemic Racism in the Ontario Criminal Justice System, *Report of the Commission on Systemic Racism in the Ontario Criminal Justice System* (Toronto: Queen's Printer for Ontario, 1995); Zhongping Chen, "Chinese Minority and Everyday Racism in Canadian Towns and Small Cities: An Ethnic Study of the Case of Peterborough, Ontario, 1892–1951," *Canadian Ethnic Studies* (36) 1 (2004): 71–91.

28. Ian Taylor, Paul Walton, and Jock Young, *The New Criminology: For a Social Theory of Deviance* (London: Routledge and Kegan Paul, 1973).

29. See, for example, Larry Tifft and Dennis Sullivan, *The Struggle to Be Human: Crime, Criminology, and Anarchism* (Over-the-Water-Sanday, Scotland: Cienfuegos Press, 1979); Dennis Sullivan, *The Mask of Love* (Port Washington, NY: Kennikat Press, 1980).

30. Lynch and Groves, *A Primer in Radical Criminology*, p. 6.

31. This section borrows heavily from Richard Sparks, "A Critique of Marxist Criminology," in *Crime and Justice*, vol. 2, eds. Norval Morris and Michael Tonry (Chicago: University of Chicago Press, 1980), pp. 159–208; Barbara Sims, "Crime, Punishment, and the American Dream: Toward a Marxist Integration," *Journal of Research in Crime and Delinquency* 34 (1997): 5–24; Jeffery Reiman, *The Rich Get Richer and the Poor Get Prison* (New York: Wiley, 1984), pp. 43–44.

32. Ibid.

33. For a general review of Marxist criminology, see Lynch and Groves, *A Primer in Radical Criminology*.

34. Sims, "Crime, Punishment, and the American Dream."

35. Robert Bohm, "Radical Criminology: Back to the Basics," paper presented at the annual meeting of the American Society of Criminology, Phoenix, Arizona, November 1993, p. 2.

36. Ibid., p. 4.

37. Lynch and Groves, *A Primer in Radical Criminology*, p. 7.

38. W. Byron Groves and Robert Sampson, "Critical Theory and Criminology," *Social Problems* 33 (1986): 58–80.

39. Gregg Barak, "'Crimes of the Homeless' or the 'Crime of Homelessness': A Self-Reflexive, New-Marxist Analysis of Crime and Social Control," paper presented at the annual meeting of the American Society of Criminology, Montreal, November 1987.

40. Michael Lynch, "Assessing the State of Radical Criminology: Toward the Year 2000," paper presented at the annual meeting of the American Society of Criminology, Phoenix, Arizona, November 1993.

41. Steven Box, *Recession, Crime, and Unemployment* (London: MacMillan, 1987).

42. David Barlow, Melissa Hickman-Barlow, and W. Wesley Johnson, "The Political Economy of Criminal Justice Policy: A Time-Series Analysis of Economic Conditions, Crime, and Federal Criminal Justice Legislation, 1948–1987," *Justice Quarterly* 13 (1996): 223–241.

43. Mahesh Nalla, Michael Lynch, and Michael Leiber, "Determinants of Police Growth in Phoenix, 1950–1988," *Justice Quarterly* 14 (1997): 144–163.

44. Gresham Sykes, "The Rise of Critical Criminology," *Journal of Criminal Law and Criminology* 65 (1974): 211–229.

45. David Jacobs, "Corporate Economic Power and the State: A Longitudinal Assessment of Two Explanations," *American Journal of Sociology* 93 (1988): 852–881.

46. CBC News, "G20 Protest Violence Prompts Over 400 Arrests PM, Toronto Mayor Says 'Thugs' to Blame for Attacks," (26 June 2010) at http://www.cbc.ca/news/canada/g20-protest-violence-prompts-over-400-arrests-1.906583 (accessed 15 October 2015).

47. Richard Quinney, "Crime Control in Capitalist Society," in *Critical Criminology*, eds. Ian Taylor, Paul Walton, and Jock Young (London: Routledge and Kegan Paul, 1975), p. 199.

48. Ibid.

49. John Hagan, *Structural Criminology* (New Brunswick, NJ: Rutgers University Press, 1989), pp. 110–119.

50. Roy Bhaskar, "Empiricism," in *A Dictionary of Marxist Thought*, ed. T. Bottomore (Cambridge, MA: Harvard University Press, 1983), pp. 149–150.

51. Byron Groves, "Marxism and Positivism," *Crime and Social Justice* 23 (1985): 129–150; Michael Lynch, "Quantitative Analysis and Marxist Criminology: Some Old Answers to a Dilemma in Marxist Criminology," *Crime and Social Justice* 29 (1987): 110–117.

52. Alan Lizotte, James Mercy, and Eric Monkkonen, "Crime and Police Strength in an Urban Setting: Chicago, 1947–1970," in *Quantitative Criminology*, ed. John Hagan (Beverly Hills, CA: Sage, 1982), pp. 129–148.

53. William Chambliss, "The State, the Law, and the Definition of Behavior as Criminal or Delinquent," in *Handbook of Criminology*, ed. D. Glazer (Chicago: Rand McNally, 1974), pp. 7–44.

54. Timothy Carter and Donald Clelland, "A Neo-Marxian Critique, Formulation, and Test of Juvenile Dispositions as a Function of Social Class," *Social Problems* 27 (1979): 96–108.

55. David Greenberg, "Socio-Economic Status and Criminal Sentences: Is There an Association?" *American Sociological Review* 42 (1977): 174–175; David Greenberg and Drew Humphries, "The Co-optation of Fixed Sentencing Reform," *Crime and Delinquency* 26 (1980): 206–225.

56. Steven Box, *Power, Crime and Mystification* (London: Tavistock, 1984); Gregg Barak, *In*

Defense of Whom? A Critique of Criminal Justice Reform (Cincinnati: Anderson, 1980). For an opposing view, see Franklin Williams, "Conflict Theory and Differential Processing: An Analysis of the Research Literature," in *Radical Criminology: The Coming Crisis*, ed. J. Inciardi (Beverly Hills, CA: Sage, 1980), pp. 213–231.

57. Michael Rustigan, "A Reinterpretation of Criminal Law Reform in Nineteenth-Century England," in *Crime and Capitalism*, ed. D. Greenberg (Palo Alto, CA: Mayfield, 1981), pp. 255–278.

58. Rosalind Petchesky, "At Hard Labor: Penal Confinement and Production in Nineteenth-Century America," in *Crime and Capitalism*, ed. D. Greenberg (Palo Alto, CA: Mayfield, 1981), pp. 341–357; Paul Takagi, "The Walnut Street Jail: A Penal Reform to Centralize the Powers of the State," *Federal Probation* 49 (1975): 18–26.

59. Jack Gibbs, "An Incorrigible Positivist," *Criminologist* 12 (1987): 2–3.

60. Jackson Toby, "The New Criminology Is the Old Sentimentality," *Criminology* 16 (1979): 513–526.

61. Richard Sparks, "A Critique of Marxist Criminology," in *Crime and Justice*, vol. 2, eds. Norval Morris and Michael Tonry (Chicago: University of Chicago Press, 1980), pp. 159–208.

62. Carl Klockars, "The Contemporary Crises of Marxist Criminology," in *Radical Criminology: The Coming Crisis*, ed. J. Inciardi (Beverly Hills, CA: Sage, 1980), pp. 92–123.

63. Ibid.

64. Michael Lynch, W. Byron Groves, and Alan Lizotte, "The Rate of Surplus Value and Crime: A Theoretical and Empirical Examination of Marxian Economic Theory and Criminology," *Crime, Law, and Social Change* 18 (1994): 1–11.

65. Anthony Platt, "Criminology in the 1980s: Progressive Alternatives to 'Law and Order,'" *Crime and Social Justice* 21–22 (1985): 191–199.

66. See, generally, Roger Matthews and Jock Young, eds., *Confronting Crime* (London: Sage, 1986); for a thorough review of left realism, see Martin Schwartz and Walter DeKeseredy, "Left Realist Criminology: Strengths, Weaknesses, and the Feminist Critique," *Crime, Law, and Social Change* 15 (1991): 51–72.

67. John Lea and Jock Young, *What Is to Be Done About Law and Order?* (Harmondsworth, England: Penguin, 1984).

68. Ibid., p. 88.

69. Richard Kinsey, John Lea, and Jock Young, *Losing the Fight Against Crime* (London: Blackwell, 1986).

70. Martin Schwartz and Walter DeKeseredy, *Contemporary Criminology* (Belmont, CA: Wadsworth, 1993), p. 249.

71. Schwartz and DeKeseredy, "Left Realist Criminology."

72. For a general review of this issue, see Kathleen Daly and Meda Chesney-Lind, "Feminism and Criminology," *Justice Quarterly* 5 (1988): 497–538; Douglas Smith and Raymond Paternoster, "The Gender Gap in Theories of Deviance: Issues and Evidence," *Journal of Research in Crime and Delinquency* 24 (1987): 140–172; Pat Carlen,

"Women, Crime, Feminism, and Realism," *Social Justice* 17 (1990): 106–123.

73. Herman Schwendinger and Julia Schwendinger, *Rape and Inequality* (Newbury Park, CA: Sage, 1983).

74. Daly and Chesney-Lind, "Feminism and Criminology."

75. Janet Saltzman Chafetz, "Feminist Theory and Sociology: Underutilized Contributions for Mainstream Theory," *Annual Review of Sociology* 23 (1997): 97–121.

76. Ibid.

77. James Messerschmidt, *Capitalism, Patriarchy, and Crime* (Totowa, NJ: Rowman and Littlefield, 1986); for a critique of this work, see Herman Schwendinger and Julia Schwendinger, "The World According to James Messerschmidt," *Social Justice* 15 (1988): 123–145.

78. Kathleen Daly, "Gender and Varieties of White-Collar Crime," *Criminology* 27 (1989): 769–793.

79. Jane Roberts Chapman, "Violence Against Women as a Violation of Human Rights," *Social Justice* 17 (1990): 54–71; John Devaney, "Male Perpetrators of Domestic Violence: How Should We Hold Them to Account?" *Political Quarterly* Oct-Dec2014, vol. 85, iss. 4 (October–December 2014): 480–486, doi: 10.1111/1467-923X.12111.

80. James Messerschmidt, *Masculinities and Crime: Critique and Reconceptualization of Theory* (Lanham, MD: Rowman and Littlefield, 1993).

81. Suzie Dod Thomas and Nancy Stein, "Criminality, Imprisonment, and Women's Rights in the 1990s," *Social Justice* 17 (1990): 1–5.

82. John N. Edwards and Patricia Kluck, "Patriarchy: The Last Universal," *Journal of Family Issues*, vol. 1, iss. 3 (September 1980): pp. 317–337; Gwen Hunnicutt, "Varieties of Patriarchy and Violence Against Women: Resurrecting "Patriarchy" as a Theoretical Tool, *Violence Against Women*, vol. 15, iss. 5 (May 2009): 553–573.

83. Walter DeKeseredy and Martin Schwartz, "Male Peer Support and Woman Abuse: An Expansion of DeKeseredy's Model," *Sociological Spectrum* 13 (1993): 393–413.

84. Daly and Chesney-Lind, "Feminism and Criminology." See also Drew Humphries and Susan Caringella-MacDonald, "Murdered Mothers, Missing Wives: Reconsidering Female Victimization," *Social Justice* 17 (1990): 71–78.

85. Jane Siegel and Linda Meyer Williams, "Aggressive Behavior Among Women Sexually Abused as Children," paper presented at the annual meeting of the American Society of Criminology, Phoenix, Arizona, 1993, revised version.

86. Susan Ehrlich Martin and Nancy Jurik, *Doing Justice, Doing Gender* (Thousand Oaks, CA: Sage, 1996), p. 27.

87. Ruth Alexander, *The "Girl Problem": Female Sexual Delinquency in New York, 1900–1930* (Ithaca, NY: Cornell University Press, 1995).

88. Joan Sangster, "Girls in Conflict with the Law: Exploring the Construction of Female 'Delinquency'

in Ontario, 1940–60," *Canadian Journal of Women and the Law* 12 (2000): 1–31.

89. Meda Chesney-Lind, "Judicial Enforcement of the Female Sex Role: The Family Court and the Female Delinquent," *Issues in Criminology* 8 (1973): 51–69. See also Meda Chesney-Lind, "Women and Crime: The Female Offender," *Signs: Journal of Women in Culture and Society* 12 (1986): 78–96; "Female Offenders: Paternalism Reexamined," in *Women, the Courts, and Equality*, eds. Laura L. Crites and Winifred L. Hepperle (Newbury Park, CA: Sage, 1987): 114–139; "Girls' Crime and a Woman's Place: Toward a Feminist Model of Female Delinquency," paper presented at the annual meeting of the American Society of Criminology, Montreal, 1987.

90. Hagan, *Structural Criminology*.

91. John Hagan, A. R. Gillis, and John Simpson, "The Class Structure and Delinquency: Toward a Power-Control Theory of Common Delinquent Behavior," *American Journal of Sociology* 90 (1985): 1151–1178; John Hagan, John Simpson, and A. R. Gillis, "Class in the Household: A Power-Control Theory of Gender and Delinquency," *American Journal of Sociology* 92 (1987): 788–816.

92. Brenda Sims Blackwell, "Perceived Sanction Threats, Gender, and Crime: A Test and Elaboration of Power-Control Theory," *Criminology* 38 (2000): 439–488.

93. See, generally, Lynch, "Rediscovering Criminology," pp. 27–28.

94. Lori D. Moore and Irene Padavic, "Racial and Ethnic Disparities in Girls' Sentencing in the Juvenile Justice System," *Feminist Criminology*, vol. 5, iss. 3 (July 2010): 263–285.

95. See, generally, Stuart Henry and Dragan Milovanovic, *Constitutive Criminology: Beyond Postmodernism* (London: Sage, 1996).

96. Dragan Milovanovic, *A Primer in the Sociology of Law* (Albany, NY: Harrow and Heston, 1988), pp. 127–128.

97. See, generally, Henry and Milovanovic, *Constitutive Criminology*.

98. Bruce Arrigo and Thomas Bernard, "Postmodern Criminology in Relation to Radical and Conflict Criminology," *Critical Criminology* 8 (1997): 39–60; M. Allen, "Violence and Voice: Using a Feminist Constructivist Grounded Theory to Explore Women's Resistance to Abuse," *Qualitative Research* 11 (1) (2011): 23–45.

99. See, for example, Tifft and Sullivan, *The Struggle to Be Human*; Sullivan, *The Mask of Love*.

100. Larry Tifft, "Foreword," in Sullivan, *The Mask of Love*, p. 6.

101. Sullivan, *The Mask of Love*, p. 141.

102. Richard Quinney, "The Way of Peace: On Crime, Suffering, and Service," in *Criminology as Peacemaking*, eds. Harold Pepinsky and Richard Quinney (Bloomington: Indiana University Press, 1991), pp. 8–9.

103. Kathleen Daly and Russ Immarigeon, "The Past, Present, and Future of Restorative Justice: Some Critical Reflections," *Contemporary Justice Review* 1 (1998): 21–45.

104. Gene Stephens, "The Future of Policing: From a War Model to a Peace Model," in *The Past, Present and Future of American Criminal Justice*, eds. Brendan Maguire and Polly Radosh (Dix Hills, NY: General Hall, 1996), pp. 77–93; Jeff Latimer. *The Effectiveness of Restorative Justice Practices: A Meta-Analysis* (2010) at http://www.justice.gc.ca/eng/pi/rs/rep-rap/2001/rp01_1-dr01_1/p5.html (accessed 27 July 2011).

105. Barbara Tomporowski, Manon Buck, Catherine Bargen, and Valarie Binder (2010–2011). "Reflections on the Past, Present, and Future of Restorative Justice in Canada" *Alta. L. Rev.*, vol. 48 (2010–2011): 815–830.

106. Daly and Immarigeon, "The Past, Present, and Future of Restorative Justice," p. 26.

107. Kay Pranis, "Peacemaking Circles: Restorative Justice in Practice Allows Victims and Offenders to Begin Repairing the Harm," *Corrections Today* 59 (1997): 74.

108. Carol LaPrairie, "The 'New' Justice: Some Implications for Aboriginal Communities," *Canadian Journal of Criminology* 40 (1998): 61–79.

109. Adapted from Kay Pranis, "Peacemaking Circles."

110. *R. v. Gladue*. Supreme Court Judgments (23 April 1999) Report 1 SCR 688. Case number 6300, on appeal from British Columbia at http://scc-csc.lexum.com/scc-csc/scc-csc/en/item/1695/index.do?r=AAAAAQATQ2FuYWRhlEV2aWRlbmNllEFjdAE (accessed 21 October 2015).

111. Aaron Doyle and Dawn Moore (2011). *Critical Criminology in Canada*, Vancouver, BC: UBC Press.

112. Gillian Balfour, "Re-imagining a Feminist Criminology," *Canadian Journal of Criminology & Criminal Justice*, vol. 48, iss. 5 (September 2006): 735–752.

113. Eric Mykhalovskiy, "The Problem of 'Significant Risk': Exploring the Public Health Impact of Criminalizing HIV Non-Disclosure," *Social Science & Medicine*, vol. 73, iss. 5 (September 2011): 668–675, doi:10.1016/j.socscimed.2011.06.051.

114. Matthew G. Yeager, "Getting the Usual Treatment: Research Censorship and the Dangerous Offender," *Contemporary Justice Review*, vol. 11, iss. 4 (September 2008): 413–425, doi:10.1080/10282580802482645.

Chapter 9

1. Gerald Patterson and Karen Yoerger, "Developmental Models for Delinquent Behavior," in *Mental Disorder and Crime*, ed. Sheilagh Hodgins (Newbury Park, CA: Sage, 1993), pp. 150–159.

2. James Q. Wilson and Richard Herrnstein, *Crime and Human Nature* (New York: Simon and Schuster, 1985).

3. David Rowe, D. Wayne Osgood, and W. Alan Nicewander, "A Latent Trait Approach to Unifying Criminal Careers," *Criminology* 28 (1990): 237–270.

4. Lee Ellis, "Neurohormonal Bases of Varying Tendencies to Learn Delinquent and Criminal Behavior," in *Behavioral Approaches to Crime and Delinquency*, ed. E. Morris and C. Braukmann (New York: Plenum, 1988), pp. 499–518.

5. David Rowe, Alexander Vazsonyi, and Daniel Flannery, "Sex Differences in Crime: Do Means and Within-Sex Variation Have Similar Causes?" *Journal of Research in Crime and Delinquency* 32 (1995): 84–100.

6. Michael Gottfredson and Travis Hirschi, *A General Theory of Crime* (Stanford, CA: Stanford University Press, 1990).

7. Ibid., p. 27.

8. Ibid., p. 90.

9. Ibid., p. 89.

10. Alex Piquero and Stephen Tibbetts, "Specifying the Direct and Indirect Effects of Low Self-Control and Situational Factors in Offenders' Decision Making: Toward a More Complete Model of Rational Offending," *Justice Quarterly* 13 (1996): 481–508.

11. David Forde and Leslie Kennedy, "Risky Lifestyles, Routine Activities, and the General Theory of Crime," *Justice Quarterly* 14 (1997): 265–294.

12. Marianne Junger and Richard Tremblay, "Self-Control, Accidents, and Crime," *Criminal Justice and Behavior* 26 (1999): 485–501.

13. Gottfredson and Hirschi, *A General Theory of Crime*, p. 112.

14. Ibid.

15. Dennis Giever, "An Empirical Assessment of the Core Elements of Gottfredson and Hirschi's General Theory of Crime," paper presented at the annual meeting of the American Society of Criminology, Boston, November 1995.

16. Robert Agnew, "The Contribution of Social-Psychological Strain Theory to the Explanation of Crime and Delinquency," *Advances in Criminological Theory* 6 (1994): 211–213.

17. David Brownfield and Ann Marie Sorenson, "Self-Control and Juvenile Delinquency: Theoretical Issues and an Empirical Assessment of Selected Elements of a General Theory of Crime," *Deviant Behavior* 14 (1993): 243–264; Harold Grasmick, Charles Tittle, Robert Bursik, and Bruce Arneklev, "Testing the Core Empirical Implications of Gottfredson and Hirschi's General Theory of Crime," *Journal of Research in Crime and Delinquency* 30 (1993): 5–29; John Cochran, Peter Wood, and Bruce Arneklev, "Is the Religiosity–Delinquency Relationship Spurious? A Test of Arousal and Social Control Theories," *Journal of Research in Crime and Delinquency* 31 (1994): 92–123; Marc LeBlanc, Marc Ouimet, and Richard Tremblay, "An Integrative Control Theory of Delinquent Behavior: A Validation 1976–1985," *Psychiatry* 51 (1988): 164–176.

18. Byongook Moon, John D. McCluskey, and Cynthia Perez McCluskey, "A General Theory of Crime and Computer Crime: An Empirical Test." *Journal of Criminal Justice*, July 2010, 38 (4) April 2010: 767–772.

19. Christian Seipel and Stefanie Eifler, "Opportunities, Rational Choice, and Self-Control: On the Interaction of Person and Situation in a General Theory of Crime," *Crime & Delinquency*, 56 (2) April 2010: 167–197.

20. Xiaogang Deng and Lening Zhang, "Correlates of Self-Control: An Empirical Test of Self-Control Theory," *Journal of Crime and Justice* 21 (1998): 89–103.

21. Alex Piquero, Raymond Paternoster, Paul Mazeroole, Robert Brame, and Charles Dean, "Onset Age and Offense Specialization," *Journal of Research in Crime and Delinquency* 36 (1999): 275–299.

22. Carl Keane, Paul Maxim, and James Teevan, "Drinking and Driving, Self-Control, and Gender: Testing a General Theory of Crime," *Journal of Research in Crime and Delinquency* 30 (1993): 30–46.

23. David Brownfield and Ann Marie Sorenson, "Self-Control and Juvenile Delinquency: Theoretical Issues and an Empirical Assessment of Selected Elements of a General Theory of Crime," *Deviant Behavior* 14 (1993): 243–264; John Cochran, Peter Wood, and Bruce Arneklev, "Is the Religiosity–Delinquency Relationship Spurious? A Test of Arousal and Social Control Theories," *Journal of Research in Crime and Delinquency* 31 (1994): 92–123.

24. Velmer Burton, T. David Evans, Francis Cullen, Kathleen Olivares, and R. Gregory Dunaway, "Age, Self-Control, and Adults' Offending Behaviors: A Research Note Assessing a General Theory of Crime," *Journal of Criminal Justice* 27 (1999): 45–54; John Gibbs and Dennis Giever, "Self-Control and Its Manifestations Among University Students: An Empirical Test of Gottfredson and Hirschi's General Theory," *Justice Quarterly* 12 (1995): 231–255.

25. Carey Herbert, "The Implications of Self-Control Theory for Workplace Offending," paper presented at the annual meeting of the American Society of Criminology, San Diego, 1997.

26. Dennis Giever, Dana Lynskey, and Danette Monnet, "Gottfredson and Hirschi's General Theory of Crime and Youth Gangs: An Empirical Test on a Sample of Middle School Youth," paper presented at the annual meeting of the American Society of Criminology, San Diego, 1997.

27. Douglas Longshore, Susan Turner, and Judith Stein, "Self-Control in a Criminal Sample: An Examination of Construct Validity," *Criminology* 34 (1996): 209–228.

28. Deng and Zhang, "Correlates of Self-Control: An Empirical Test of Self-Control Theory."

29. Linda Pagani, Richard Tremblay, Frank Vitaro, and Sophie Parent, "Does Preschool Help Prevent Delinquency in Boys with a History of Perinatal Complications?" *Criminology* 36 (1998): 245–268.

30. Velmer Burton, Francis Cullen, T. David Evans, Leanne Fiftal Alarid, and R. Gregory Dunaway, "Gender, Self-Control, and Crime," *Journal of Research in Crime and Delinquency* 35 (1998): 123–147.

31. John Gibbs, Dennis Giever, and Jamie Martin, "Parental Management and Self-Control: An Empirical Test of Gottfredson and Hirschi's General Theory," *Journal of Research in Crime and Delinquency* 35 (1998): 40–70.

32. Vic Bumphus and James Anderson, "Family Structure and Race in a Sample of Offenders," *Journal of Criminal Justice* 27 (1999): 309–320.

33. Christopher Schreck, "Criminal Victimization and Low Self-Control: An Extension and Test of a General Theory of Crime," *Justice Quarterly* 16 (1999): 633–654.

34. Michael Benson and Elizabeth Moore, "Are White-Collar and Common Offenders the Same? An Empirical and Theoretical Critique of a Recently Proposed General Theory of Crime," *Journal of Research in Crime and Delinquency* 29 (1992): 251–272.

35. Ronald Akers, "Self-Control as a General Theory of Crime," *Journal of Quantitative Criminology* 7 (1991): 201–211.

36. Alan Feingold, "Gender Differences in Personality: A Meta Analysis," *Psychological Bulletin* 116 (1994): 429–456.

37. Gottfredson and Hirschi, *A General Theory of Crime*, p. 153.

38. Scott Menard, Delbert Elliott, and Sharon Wofford, "Social Control Theories in Developmental Perspective," *Studies on Crime and Crime Prevention* 2 (1993): 69–87.

39. Charles R. Tittle and Harold G. Grasmick, "Criminal Behavior and Age: A Test of Three Provocative Hypotheses," *Journal of Criminal Law and Criminology* 88 (1997): 309–342.

40. Douglas Longshore, "Self-Control and Criminal Opportunity: A Prospective Test of the General Theory of Crime," *Social Problems* 45 (1998): 102–114.

41. Otwin Marenin and Michael Resig, "A General Theory of Crime and Patterns of Crime in Nigeria: An Exploration of Methodological Assumptions," *Journal of Criminal Justice* 23 (1995): 501–518.

42. Bruce Arneklev, Harold Grasmick, Charles Tittle, and Robert Bursik, "Low Self-Control and Imprudent Behavior," *Journal of Quantitative Criminology* 9 (1993): 225–246.

43. Kevin Thompson, "Sexual Harassment and Low Self-Control: An Application of Gottfredson and Hirschi's General Theory of Crime," paper presented at the annual meeting of the American Society of Criminology, Phoenix, Arizona, November 1993.

44. Charles Tittle, *Control Balance: Toward a General Theory of Deviance* (Boulder, CO: Westview, 1995).

45. Marvin Krohn, Alan Lizotte, and Cynthia Perez, "The Interrelationship Between Substance Use and Precocious Transitions to Adult Sexuality," *Journal of Health and Social Behavior* 38 (1997): 87–103, p. 88.

46. G. R. Patterson, Barbara DeBaryshe, and Elizabeth Ramsey, "A Developmental Perspective on Antisocial Behavior," *American Psychologist* 44 (1989): 329–335.

47. Joan McCord, "Family Relationships, Juvenile Delinquency, and Adult Criminality," *Criminology* 29 (1991): 397–417.

48. Paul Mazerolle, "Delinquent Definitions and Participation Age: Assessing the Invariance Hypothesis," *Studies on Crime and Crime Prevention* 6 (1997): 151–168.

49. See, generally, Sheldon Glueck and Eleanor Glueck, *500 Criminal Careers* (New York: Knopf, 1930); Sheldon Glueck and Eleanor Glueck, *One Thousand Juvenile Delinquents* (Cambridge, MA: Harvard University Press, 1934); Sheldon Glueck and Eleanor Glueck, *Predicting Delinquency and Crime* (Cambridge, MA: Harvard University Press, 1967), pp. 82–83.

50. Sheldon Glueck and Eleanor Glueck, *Unraveling Juvenile Delinquency* (Cambridge, MA: Harvard University Press, 1950).

51. Ibid., p. 48.

52. Rolf Loeber and Marc LeBlanc, "Toward a Developmental Criminology," in *Crime and Justice*, vol. 12, ed. Norval Morris and Michael Tonry (Chicago: University of Chicago Press, 1990), pp. 375–473; Rolf Loeber and Marc LeBlanc, "Developmental Criminology Updated," in *Crime and Justice*, vol. 23, ed. Michael Tonry (Chicago: University of Chicago Press, 1998), pp. 115–198.

53. G. R. Patterson, L. Crosby, and S. Vuchinich, "Predicting Risk for Early Police Arrest," *Journal of Quantitative Criminology* 8 (1992): 335–355; Rolf Loeber, Magda Stouthamer-Loeber, Welmoet Van Kammen, and David Farrington, "Initiation, Escalation, and Desistance in Juvenile Offending and Their Correlates," *Journal of Criminal Law and Criminology* 82 (1991): 36–82.

54. Raymond Paternoster, Charles Dean, Alex Piquero, Paul Mazerolle, and Robert Brame, "Generality, Continuity, and Change in Offending," *Journal of Quantitative Criminology* 13 (1997): 231–266.

55. Magda Stouthamer-Loeber and Evelyn Wei, "The Precursors of Young Fatherhood and Its Effect on Delinquency of Teenage Males," *Journal of Adolescent Health* 22 (1998): 56–65; Richard Jessor, John Donovan, and Francis Costa, *Beyond Adolescence: Problem Behavior and Young Adult Development* (New York: Cambridge University Press, 1991).

56. Marvin Krohn, Alan Lizotte, and Cynthia Perez, "The Interrelationship Between Substance Use and Precocious Transitions to Adult Sexuality," *Journal of Health and Social Behavior* 38 (1997): 87–103, p. 88; Richard Jessor, "Risk Behavior in Adolescence: A Psychosocial Framework for Understanding and Action," in *Adolescents at Risk: Medical and Social Perspectives*, ed. D. E. Rogers and E. Ginzburg (Boulder, CO: Westview, 1992).

57. Deborah Capaldi and Gerald Patterson, "Can Violent Offenders Be Distinguished from Frequent Offenders: Prediction from Childhood to Adolescence," *Journal of Research in Crime and Delinquency* 33 (1996): 206–231; D. Wayne Osgood, "The Covariation Among Adolescent Problem Behaviors," paper presented at the annual meeting of the American Society of Criminology, Baltimore, November 1990.

58. Terence Thornberry, Carolyn Smith, and Gregory Howard, "Risk Factors for Teenage Fatherhood," *Journal of Marriage and the Family* 59 (1997): 505–522; Todd Miller, Timothy Smith, Charles Turner, Margarita Guijarro, and Amanda Hallet,

"A Meta-Analytic Review of Research on Hostility and Physical Health," *Psychological Bulletin* 119 (1996): 322–348; Marianne Junger, "Accidents and Crime," in *The Generality of Deviance*, ed. T. Hirschi and M. Gottfredson (New Brunswick, NJ: Transaction Press, 1993).

59. Robert Johnson, S. Susan Su, Dean Gerstein, Hee-Choon Shin, and John Hoffman, "Parental Influences on Deviant Behavior in Early Adolescence: A Logistic Response Analysis of Age- and Gender-Differentiated Effects," *Journal of Quantitative Criminology* 11 (1995): 167–192; Judith Brooks, Martin Whiteman, and Patricia Cohen, "Stage of Drug Use, Aggression, and Theft/Vandalism," in *Drugs, Crime and Other Deviant Adaptations: Longitudinal Studies*, ed. Howard Kaplan (New York: Plenum, 1995), pp. 83–96; Robert Hoge, D. A. Andrews, and Alan Leschied, "Tests of Three Hypotheses Regarding the Predictors of Delinquency," *Journal of Abnormal Child Psychology* 22 (1994): 547–559.

60. David Huizinga, Rolf Loeber, and Terence Thornberry, "Longitudinal Study of Delinquency, Drug Use, Sexual Activity, and Pregnancy Among Children and Youth in Three Cities," *Public Health Reports* 108 (1993): 90–96.

61. Rolf Loeber et al., "Developmental Pathways in Disruptive Behavior," *Development and Psychopathology* (1993): 12–48.

62. Amy D'Unger, Kenneth Land, Patricia McCall, and Daniel Nagin, "How Many Latent Classes of Delinquent/Criminal Careers? Results from Mixed Poisson Regression Analyses," *American Journal of Sociology* 103 (1998): 1593–1630.

63. Terrie Moffitt, "Natural Histories of Delinquency," in *Cross-National Longitudinal Research on Human Development and Criminal Behavior*, ed. Elmar Weitekamp and Hans-Jurgen Kerner (Dordrecht, Netherlands: Kluwer, 1994), pp. 3–65.

64. Michael Newcomb, "Pseudomaturity Among Adolescents: Construct Validation, Sex Differences, and Associations in Adulthood," *Journal of Drug Issues* 26 (1996): 477–504.

65. Rolf Loeber and Magda Stouthamer-Loeber, "Development of Juvenile Aggression and Violence," *American Psychologist* 53 (1998): 242–259.

66. Terrie Moffitt, "Adolescence-Limited and Life-Course-Persistent Antisocial Behavior: A Developmental Taxonomy," *Psychological Review* 100 (1993): 674–701.

67. David Fergusson, L. John Horwood, and Daniel Nagin, "Offending Trajectories in a New Zealand Birth Cohort," *Criminology* 38 (2000): 525–551.

68. Ronald Simons, Chyi-In Wu, Rand Conger, and Frederick Lorenz, "Two Routes to Delinquency: Differences Between Early and Later Starters in the Impact of Parenting and Deviant Careers," *Criminology* 32 (1994): 247–275; A. K. Ward et al., "Criminal Trajectories and Risk Factors in a Canadian Sample of Offenders," *Criminal Justice and Behavior* 37 (11): 1278–1300.

69. Mark Lipsey and James Derzon, "Predictors of Violent or Serious Delinquency in Adolescence and Early Adulthood: A Synthesis of Longitudinal Research," in *Serious and Violent Juvenile*

Offenders: Risk Factors and Successful Interventions, ed. Rolf Loeber and David Farrington (Thousand Oaks, CA: Sage, 1998).

70. G. R. Patterson and Karen Yoerger, "Differentiating Outcomes and Histories for Early and Late Onset Arrests," paper presented at the annual meeting of the American Society of Criminology, Phoenix, Arizona, November 1993.

71. Marshall Jones and Donald Jones, "The Contagious Nature of Antisocial Behavior," *Criminology* 38 (2000): 25–46.

72. See, for example, the Rochester Youth Development Study, Hindelang Criminal Justice Research Center, 135 Western Avenue, Albany, New York 12222.

73. David Farrington, "The Development of Offending and Antisocial Behavior from Childhood to Adulthood," paper presented at the Congress on Rethinking Delinquency, University of Minho, Braga, Portugal, July 1992.

74. Joseph Weis and J. David Hawkins, *Reports of the National Juvenile Assessment Centers: Preventing Delinquency* (Washington, DC: U.S. Department of Justice, 1981); Joseph Weis and John Sederstrom, *Reports of the National Juvenile Justice Assessment Centers: The Prevention of Serious Delinquency: What to Do* (Washington, DC: U.S. Department of Justice, 1981).

75. Julie O'Donnell, J. David Hawkins, and Robert Abbott, "Predicting Serious Delinquency and Substance Use Among Aggressive Boys," *Journal of Consulting and Clinical Psychology* 63 (1995): 529–537.

76. Terence Thornberry, "Toward an Interactional Theory of Delinquency," *Criminology* 25 (1987): 863–891.

77. Ross Matsueda and Kathleen Anderson, "The Dynamics of Delinquent Peers and Delinquent Behavior," *Criminology* 36 (1998): 269–308.

78. Thornberry, "Toward an Interactional Theory of Delinquency."

79. Ibid., p. 863.

80. Terrence Thornberry, Alan Lizotte, Marvin Krohn, Margaret Farnworth, and Sung Joon Jang, *Delinquent Peers, Beliefs, and Delinquent Behavior: A Longitudinal Test of Interactional Theory*, working paper no. 6, rev, Rochester Youth Development Study (Albany, NY: Hindelang Criminal Justice Research Center, 1992), pp. 628–629.

81. Robert Sampson and John Laub, *Crime in the Making: Pathways and Turning Points Through Life* (Cambridge, MA: Harvard University Press, 1993); John Laub and Robert Sampson, "Turning Points in the Life Course: Why Change Matters to the Study of Crime," paper presented at the annual meeting of the American Society of Criminology, New Orleans, November 1992.

82. Terri Orbuch, James House, Richard Mero, and Pamela Webster, "Marital Quality Over the Life Course," *Social Psychology Quarterly* 59 (1996): 162–171; Lee Lillard and Linda Waite, "'Til Death Do Us Part: Marital Disruption and Mortality," *American Journal of Sociology* 100 (1995): 1131–1156.

83. Mark Warr, "Life-Course Transitions and Desistance from Crime," *Criminology* 36 (1998): 183–216.

84. Pamela Webster, Terri Orbuch, and James House, "Effects of Childhood Family Background on Adult Marital Quality and Perceived Stability," *American Journal of Sociology* 101 (1995): 404–432.

85. John Hagan, Ross MacMillan, and Blair Wheaton, "New Kid in Town: Social Capital and the Life Course Effects of Family Migration on Children," *American Sociological Review* 61 (1996): 368–385.

86. Sampson and Laub, *Crime in the Making*, p. 249.

87. Raymond Paternoster and Robert Brame, "Multiple Routes to Delinquency? A Test of Developmental and General Theories of Crime," *Criminology* 35 (1997): 49–84.

88. Robert Hoge, D. A. Andrews, and Alan Leschied, "An Investigation of Risk and Protective Factors in a Sample of Youthful Offenders," *Journal of Child Psychology and Psychiatry* 37 (1996): 419–424.

89. Candace Kruttschnitt, Christopher Uggen, and Kelly Shelton, "Individual Variability in Sex Offending and Its Relationship to Informal and Formal Social Controls," paper presented at the annual meeting of the American Society of Criminology, San Diego, 1997; Mark Collins and Don Weatherburn, "Unemployment and the Dynamics of Offender Populations," *Journal of Quantitative Criminology* 11 (1995): 231–245.

90. Avshalom Caspi, Terrie Moffitt, Bradley Entner Wright, and Phil Silva, "Early Failure in the Labor Market: Childhood and Adolescent Predictors of Unemployment in the Transition to Adulthood," *American Sociological Review* 63 (1998): 424–451.

91. Erich Labouvie, "Maturing Out of Substance Use: Selection and Self-Correction," *Journal of Drug Issues* 26 (1996): 457–474.

92. Mark Warr, "Life-Course Transitions and Desistance from Crime," *Criminology* 36 (1998): 502–535.

93. Robert Sampson and John Laub, "Socioeconomic Achievement in the Life Course of Disadvantaged Men: Military Service as a Turning Point, circa 1940–1965," *American Sociological Review* 61 (1996): 347–367.

94. Daniel Nagin and Raymond Paternoster, "Personal Capital and Social Control: The Deterrence Implications of a Theory of Criminal Offending," *Criminology* 32 (1994): 581–606.

95. John H. Laub and Robert J. Sampson, *Shared Beginnings, Divergent Lives: Delinquent Boys to Age 70* (Cambridge, MA: Harvard University Press, 2003); Robert J. Sampson and John H. Laub, "A Life-Course View of the Development of Crime," *Annals of the American Academy of Political and Social Science*, 602 (2005) 12–45, 73–79; Robert J. Sampson and John H. Laub, "Life-Course Desisters? Trajectories of Crime among Delinquent Boys Followed to Age 70," *Criminology* 41 (2003): 319–339. See also Robert J. Sampson and John H. Laub "Seductions of Method: Rejoinder to Nagin and Tremblay's "Developmental Trajectory Groups: Fact or Useful Fiction?" *Criminology* 43 (2005): 905–913.

96. Ibid.

97. Ibid.

98. Frances T. Cullen, "Beyond Adolescence-limited Criminology: Choosing Our Future—The American Society of Criminology 2010 Sutherland Address," *Criminology*, 49(2) (2011): 287–330, doi: 10.1111/j.1745-9125.2011.00224.x.

99. Ibid.

100. J. C. Barnes, B. B. Boutwell, K. M. Beaver, C. L. Gibson, and J. P. Wright, "On the Consequences of Ignoring Genetic Influences in Criminological Research," *Journal of Criminal Justice*, 42 (2014): 471–482, doi: 10.1016/j.crimjus .2014.08.003; Örjan Falk et al, "The 1% of the Population Accountable for 63% of All Violent Crime Convictions," *Social Psychiatry & Psychiatric Epidemiology.*, vol. 49, iss. 4 (April 2014): 559–571, doi: 10.1007/s00127-013-0783-y; R. P. Wiebe, "Integrating Criminology Through Adaptive Strategy and Life History Theory" *Journal of Contemporary Criminal Justice*, 28(3) (2012): 346–365, doi: 10.1177/1043986212450231; David P. Farrington, "Integrated Cognitive Antisocial Potential Theory," in *Encyclopedia of Criminology and Criminal Justice* eds. Gerben Bruinsma and David Weisburd (New York: Springer-Verlag, 2014), pp. 2252–2564, doi: 10.1007/978-1-4614-5690-2_500.

Chapter 10

1. Tristin Hopper, "Unarmed Robber's Threat— 'I Have a Gun'—Was in Itself a Violent Act: Supreme Court Ruling," *National Post* (9 October 2014). at http://news.nationalpost.com/news/ canada/man-who-said-i-have-a-gun-during -robbery-committed-a-violent-act-even-though -he-was-unarmed-supreme-court (accessed 19 October 2015).

2. David Courtwright, "Violence in America," *American Heritage* 47 (1996): 36.

3. D. M. Mares, "Civilization, Economic Change, and Trends in Interpersonal Violence in Western Societies," *Theoretical Criminology*, 13 (4), 419–449.

4. Patrick White, "Corporal Nathan Cirillo, 'Canada's Son,' Laid to Rest, "*The Globe and Mail* (28 October 2014) at http://www .theglobeandmail.com/news/national/ the-funeral-for-corporal-nathan-cirillo/ article21347898 (accessed 19 October 2015).

5. Lynda Hurst, "10 Years Later, How a Massacre Changed Us All," *Toronto Star* (27 November 1999), pp. A1, A4.

6. Gisli Gudjonsson, Jon Fridrik Sigurdsson, Solrun Linda Skaptadottir, and Bora Helgadottir, "The Relationship of Violent Attitudes with Self-reported Offending and Antisocial Personality Traits," *Journal of Forensic Psychiatry & Psychology*, vol. 22, iss. 3 (June 2011): pp. 371–380; Richard Rogers, Randall Salekin, Kenneth Sewell, and Keith Cruise, "Prototypical Analysis of Antisocial Personality Disorder," *Criminal Justice and Behavior* 27 (2000): 234–255.

7. Dorothy Otnow Lewis et al., "Biopsychosocial Characteristics of Children Who Later Murder," *American Journal of Psychiatry* 142 (1985): 1161–1167.

8. Dorothy Otnow Lewis, *Guilty by Reason of Insanity* (New York: Fawcett Columbine, 1998).

9. Katherine Van Wormer and Chuk Odiah, "The Psychology of Suicide-Murder and the Death Penalty," *Journal of Criminal Justice* 27 (1999): 361–370; Vivian B. Lord and Michael W. Sloop, "Suicide by Cop: Police Shooting as a Method of Self-Harming," *Journal of Criminal Justice*, vol. 38, iss. 5 (September 2010), pp. 889–895.

10. Amy Murrell, Karen Christoff, and Kris Henning, "Characteristics of Domestic Violence Offenders: Associations with Childhood Exposure to Violence," *Journal of Family Violence*, vol. 22, iss. 7 (October 2007), pp. 523–532; Amy Holtzworth-Munroe and Gregory Stuart, "Typologies of Male Batterers: Three Subtypes and the Differences Among Them," *Psychological Bulletin* 116 (1994): 476–497.

11. Pamela Lattimore, Christy Visher, and Richard Linster, "Predicting Rearrest for Violence Among Serious Youthful Offenders," *Journal of Research in Crime and Delinquency* 32 (1995): 54–83; Leslie Gordon Simons et al., "Cognitive and Parenting Pathways in the Transmission of Antisocial Behavior from Parents to Adolescents," *Child Development*, vol. 78 iss. 1 (January 2007): 335–349.

12. Stephen Porter et al., "Profiles of Psychopathy in Incarcerated Sexual Offenders," *Criminal Justice and Behavior* 27 (2000): 216–233.

13. Albert Reiss and Jeffrey Roth, *Understanding and Preventing Violence* (Washington, DC: National Academy Press, 1993), pp. 112–113; K. S. Douglas, L. S. Guy, and S. D. Hart, "Psychosis as a Risk Factor for Violence to Others: A Meta-analysis," *Psychological Bulletin*, 135 (5) (2009): 679–706; S. Fazel, G. Gulati, L. Linsell, J. R. Geddes, and M. Grann, "Schizophrenia and Violence: Systematic Review and Meta-Analysis," *PLoS Medicine*, vol. 6, iss. 8 (August 2009): pp. 1–15; P. Gendreau, T. Little, and C. Goggin, "A Meta-analysis of the Predictors of Adult Offender Recidivism: What Works," *Criminology*, 34 (1996): 575–607.

14. Joan Kaufman, "Nature, Nurture, and the Development and Prevention of Antisocial Behavior Problems in Children," *Journal of the American Academy of Child & Adolescent Psychiatry* (April 2010): 300–301; Lindley Bassarath, "Conduct Disorder: A Biopsychosocial Review," *Canadian Journal of Psychiatry* 46 (September 2001): 609–616; Augustine Brannigan, William Gemmell, David J. Pevalin, and Terrance J. Wade, "Self-Control and Social Control in Childhood Misconduct and Aggression: The Role of Family Structure, Hyperactivity, and Hostile Parenting," *Canadian Journal of Criminology* 44 (April 2002): 119–142.

15. Robert Scudder, William Blount, Kathleen Heide, and Ira Silverman, "Important Links Between Child Abuse, Neglect, and Delinquency," *International Journal of Offender Therapy* 37 (1993): 315–323.

16. Charles Patrick Ewing, *When Children Kill* (Lexington, MA: Lexington Books, 1990), p. 22; and Ghitta Weizmann-Henelius et al., "Psychopathy and Gender Differences in Childhood Psychosocial Characteristics in Homicide Offenders—A Nationwide Register-based Study," *Journal of Forensic Psychiatry & Psychology*, vol. 21, iss. 6 (December 2010): 801–814.

17. Kathleen M. Heide, and Denise Paquette Boots, "A Comparative Analysis of Media Reports of U.S. Parricide Cases with Officially Reported National Crime Data and the Psychiatric and Psychological Literature," *International Journal of Offender Therapy & Comparative Criminology*, vol. 51 iss. 6 (December 2007): 646–675.

18. Lewis, *Guilty by Reason of Insanity*, pp. 11–35.

19. Sigmund Freud, *Beyond the Pleasure Principle* (London: Inter-Psychoanalytic Press, 1922).

20. Konrad Lorenz, *On Aggression* (New York: Harcourt Brace Jovanovich, 1966).

21. Amy Murrell, Karen Christoff, and Kris Henning, "Characteristics of Domestic Violence Offenders: Associations with Childhood Exposure to Violence," *Journal of Family Violence*, vol. 22, iss. 7 (October 2007): 523–532.

22. Michael Greene, "Chronic Exposure to Violence and Poverty: Interventions That Work for Youth," *Crime and Delinquency* 39 (1993): 106–124.

23. Marcus Felson, "Preventing Retail Theft: An Application of Environmental Criminology," *Security Journal* 7 (1996): 71–75; Marc Brandeberry, "$15 Billion Lost to Shoplifting," *Today's Coverage*, a newsletter of the Grocers Insurance Group, Portland, Oregon, 1997; C. Burrows, "Critical Decision Making by Police Firearms Officers: A Review of Officer Perception, Response, and Reaction," *Policing*, 1 (3) (2007): 273–283; and John MacDonald, Geoffrey Alpert, and Abraham Tennenbaum, "Justifiable Homicide by Police and Criminal Homicide: A Research Note," *Journal of Crime and Justice* 22 (1999): 153–164.

24. Statistics Canada, "Study: A Comparison of Urban and Rural Crime Rates," 28 June 2007, at http://www.statcan.gc.ca/daily-quotidien/070628/dq070628b-eng.htm.

25. Dana L. Haynie, and David P. Armstrong, "Race- and Gender-Disaggregated Homicide Offending Rates," *Homicide Studies*, vol. 10, iss. 1 (February 2006): 3–32 (see three tables on p. 27); and Marvin Wolfgang and Franco Ferracuti, *The Subculture of Violence* (London: Tavistock, 1967).

26. Marvin Wolfgang and Franco Ferracuti, *The Subculture of Violence* (London: Tavistock, 1967).

27. James M. Byrne and Jacob Stowell, "Examining the Link between Institutional and Community Violence: Toward a New Cultural Paradigm," *Aggression & Violent Behavior*, vol. 12, iss. 5 (September/October 2007): 552–563.

28. Susan E. Martin, Christopher D. Maxwell, Helene R. White, and Yan Zhang, "Trends in Alcohol Use, Cocaine Use, and Crime: 1989–1998. *Journal of Drug Issues*, vol. 34, iss. 2 (Spring 2004): 333–359; and Paul Goldstein, Henry Brownstein, and Patrick Ryan, "Drug-Related Homicide in New York: 1984–1988," *Crime and Delinquency* 38 (1992): 459–476.

29. "Research Report—Substance Abuse Linked to Violent Crimes," *Alcoholism & Drug Abuse Weekly*, 7 June 2004, vol. 16, iss. 22: 7-7.

30. Ted Myers, "Alcohol and Violent Crime Re-examined: Self-Reports from Two Sub-Groups of Scottish Male Prisoners," *British Journal of Addiction*, vol. 77 iss. 4 (1982): 399–413; and James Collins and Pamela Messerschmidt, "Epidemiology of Alcohol-Related Violence," *Alcohol Health and Research World* 17 (1993): 93–100.

31. Paul E. Bellair, Thomas L. McNulty, "Gang Membership, Drug Selling, and Violence in Neighborhood Context," *Justice Quarterly*, vol. 26, iss. 4 (December 2009): 644–669.

32. Mia Dauvergne, "Homicide in Canada, 2003," Statistics Canada: cat. no. 85-002-XPE, vol. 24, no. 8 (September 2004), p. 1.

33. Dominique Eve Roe-Sepowitz, "Comparing Male and Female Juveniles Charged with Homicide: Child Maltreatment, Substance Abuse, and Crime Details," *Journal of Interpersonal Violence*, vol. 24, iss. 4 (April 2009): 601–617; "Canadian Inmates Unhealthy and High Risk," *Canadian Medical Association Journal* 171 (2004): 227.

34. D. L. James, and L. E. Glaze (2006), *Mental Health Problems of Prison and Jail Inmates*, Washington, DC: U.S. Department of Justice.

35. Adam Cotter, "Firearms and Violent Crime in Canada, 2012," Statistics Canada cat. 85-002-X, *Juristat* (2014) at http://www.statcan.gc.ca/pub/85-002-x/2014001/article/11925-eng.htm (accessed 19 October 2015).

36. Martin Killias, John Van Kesteren, and Martin Rindlisbacher, "Guns, Violent Crime, and Suicide in 21 Countries, "*Canadian Journal of Criminology*, vol. 43 iss. 4 (October 2001): 429–448.

37. Mia Dauvergne and Leonardo De Socio, "Firearms and Violent Crime," Statistics Canada cat. 85-002-X, *Juristat*, vol. 28, no. 2 (2009).

38. Adam Cotter, "Firearms and Violent Crime in Canada, 2012."

39. Mia Dauvergne, "Knives and Violent Crime in Canada," *Juristat*, vol. 30, no.1 (Spring 2010), cat. no. 85-002-X.

40. Ibid.

41. Statistics Canada, "Homicide in Canada, 2013," *The Daily*, 1 December 2014.

42. Ibid.

43. Ibid.

44. J. Boyce, A. Cotter, and S. Perreault, "Police-reported Crime Statistics in Canada," 2013, *Statistics Canada*, cat. no. 85-002-X (2014).

45. Ibid.

46. William Green, *Rape* (Lexington, MA: Lexington Books, 1988), p. 5.

47. Susan Brownmiller, Against Our Will: Men, Women and Rape (New York: Simon and Schuster, 1975).

48. William Green, *Rape* (Lexington, MA: Lexington Books, 1988), p. 6.

49. Yuri Kageyama, "Court Orders Japan to Pay Sex Slaves," *Boston Globe* (28 April 1998), p. A2.

50. Marlise Simons, "Bosnian Serb Pleads Guilty to Rape Charge Before War Crimes Tribunal," *New York Times*, 10 March 1998, p. A8.

51. Anonymous, "Congo's Rape Rate 'Astounding,'" *Winnipeg Free Press*, 12 May 2011, p. A11.

52. Canadian Centre for Justice Statistics, "Sexual Assault in Canada 2004 and 2007" (Ottawa: Minister of Industry, December 2008) cat. no. 85F0033M, no. 19.

53. Statistics Canada, "Violence Against Women: Statistical Trends" (2 October 2006) at http://www.statcan.gc.ca/daily-quotidien/061002/dq061002a-eng.htm.

54. Angela Browne, "Violence Against Women: Relevance for Medical Practitioners," *Journal of the American Medical Association* 267 (1992): 3184–3189.

55. McLean, I. (2007). Climatic effects on incidence of sexual assault. Journal of Forensic and Legal Medicine, 14(1), 16–19.

56. Laura Woods and Louise Porter, "Examining the Relationship between Sexual Offenders and Their Victims: Interpersonal Differences between Stranger and Non-Stranger Sexual Offences," *Journal of Sexual Aggression*, vol. 14, iss. 1 (March 2008): 61–75.

57. Sarah Hauffe and Louise Porter, "An Interpersonal Comparison of Lone and Group Rape Offences," *Psychology, Crime & Law*, vol. 15, iss. 5 (June 2009): 469–491.

58. Shannon Brennan and Andrea Taylor-Butts, *Sexual Assault in Canada 2004 and 2007*, Canadian Centre for Justice Statistics (Ottawa: Minister of Industry, 2008) cat. no. 85F0033M, no. 19.

59. Ibid.

60. Janet Warren et al., "Crime Scene Analysis and the Escalation of Violence in Serial Rape," *Forensic Science International* 2 (1998): 56–62.

61. Pekka Santtila, Jenny Junkkila, and N. Kenneth Sandnabba, "Behavioural Linking of Stranger Rapes," *Journal of Investigative Psychology & Offender Profiling*, vol. 2, iss. 2 (June 2005): 87–103.

62. A. Nicholas Groth and Jean Birnbaum, *Men Who Rape* (New York: Plenum, 1979).

63. For other typologies, see Marita McCabe, and Michelle Wauchope, "Behavioral Characteristics of Men Accused of Rape: Evidence for Different Types of Rapists," *Archives of Sexual Behavior*, vol. 34 iss. 2 (April 2005): 241–253; and Raymond Knight, "Validation of a Typology of Rapists," in *Sex Offender Research and Treatment: State-of-the-Art in North America and Europe*, eds. W. L. Marshall and J. Frenken (Newbury Park, CA: Sage, 1997), pp. 58–75.

64. Ann Burnett et al., "Communicating/Muting Date Rape: A Co-Cultural Theoretical Analysis of Communication Factors Related to Rape Culture on a College Campus," *Journal of Applied Communication Research*, vol. 37, iss. 4 (November 2009): 465–485; see also R. Lance Shotland, "A Model of the Causes of Date Rape in Developing and Close Relationships," in *Close Relationships*, ed. C. Hendrick (Newbury Park, CA: Sage, 1989), pp. 247–270.

65. Cortney A. Franklin, "Physically Forced, Alcohol-induced, and Verbally Coerced Sexual Victimization: Assessing Risk Factors Among University Women," *Journal of Criminal Justice*, vol. 38, iss. 2 (March 2010): 149–159; and Diane Follingstad, Rebekah Bradley, James Laughlin, and Leslie Burke, "Risk Factors and Correlates of Dating Violence: The Relevance of Examining Frequency and Severity Levels in a College Sample," *Violence and Victims* 14 (1999): 365–378.

66. D. G. Kilpatrick, H. S. Resnick, K. J. Ruggierio, L. M. Conoscenti, and J. McCauley, *Drug-Facilitated, Incapacitated, and Forcible Rape: A National Study* (Charleston, SC: Medical University of South Carolina, National Crime Victims Research & Treatment Center, 2007).

67. Cortney A. Franklin, "Physically Forced, Alcohol-induced, and Verbally Coerced Sexual Victimization: Assessing Risk Factors Among University Women."

68. Crystal S. Mills and Barbara J. Granoff, "Date and Acquaintance Rape among a Sample of College Students," *Social Work*, vol. 37, iss. 6 (November 1992): 504–509.

69. Correctional Services of Canada, "The Safe Streets and Communities Act, 2012," at http://www.csc-scc.gc.ca/acts-and-regulations/005006-1000-eng.shtml (accessed 19 October 2015).

70. Julie Allison and Lawrence Wrightsman, *Rape: The Misunderstood Crime* (Newbury Park, CA: Sage, 1993) pp. 85–87.

71. Cited in Diana Russell, "Wife Rape," in *Acquaintance Rape: The Hidden Crime*, eds. A. Parrot and L. Bechhofer (New York: Wiley, 1991), pp. 129–139, p. 129.

72. Elaine K. Martin, Casey T. Taft, and Patricia A. Resick, "A Review of Marital Rape," *Aggression & Violent Behavior*, vol. 12, iss. 3 (May/June 2007): 329–347.

73. Jennifer A. Bennice and Patrick A. Resnick, "Marital Rape: History, Research and Practice," *Trauma, Violence, & Abuse*, vol. 4, no. 3 (July 2003): 228–246.

74. Lee Ellis and Anthony Walsh, "Gene-Based Evolutionary Theories in Criminology," *Criminology*, 35 (2) (May 1997): 229–276.

75. Ibid.

76. Laura Hensley Choate, "Sexual Assault Prevention Programs for College Men: An Exploratory Evaluation of the Men Against Violence Model," *Journal of College Counseling*, vol. 6 iss. 2 (Fall 2003): 166–176; see also Diana Russell, *The Politics of Rape* (New York: Stein and Day, 1975).

77. Kala Downs and Steven Gold, "The Role of Blame, Distress, and Anger in the Hypermasculine Man," *Violence and Victims* 12 (1997): 19–36.

78. Groth and Birnbaum, *Men Who Rape*, p. 101

79. Julie McCormack, Stephen M. Hudson, and Tony Ward, "Sexual Offenders' Perceptions of Their Early Interpersonal Relationships: An Attachment Perspective," *Journal of Sex Research*, vol. 39 iss. 2 (May 2002): 85.

80. Vanessa Vega, and Neil M. Malamuth, "Predicting Sexual Aggression: The Role of Pornography in the Context of General and Specific Risk factors," *Aggressive Behavior*, vol. 33 iss. 2 (March 2007): 104–117.

81. C. R. Bartol and A. M. Bartol, *Criminal Behavior: A Psychology Approach*, 9th ed. (Upper Saddle River, NY: Pearson Education, 2011).

82. Richard Felson and Marvin Krohn, "Motives for Rape," *Journal of Research in Crime and Delinquency* 27 (1990): 222–242.

83. Larry Baron and Murray Straus, "Four Theories of Rape: A Macrosociological Analysis," *Social Problems* 34 (1987): 467–489.

84. Christie Blatchford, "Crying Wolf," *National Post* (8 September 2001), pp. B1–B2.

85. Julian V. Roberts, and Renate M. Mohr, *Confronting Sexual Assault: A Decade of Legal and Social Change* (Toronto: University of Toronto Press, 1994); and Melanie Randall, "Sexual Assault Law, Credibility, and 'Ideal Victims': Consent, Resistance, and Victim Blaming," *Canadian Journal of Women & the Law*, vol. 22, iss. 2 (2010): 397–433.

86. Melanie Randall, "Sexual Assault Law, Credibility, and 'Ideal Victims': Consent, Resistance, and Victim Blaming."

87. Shannon Brennan and Andrea Taylor-Butts, *Sexual Assault in Canada 2004 and 2007*, Canadian Centre for Justice Statistics (Ottawa: Minister of Industry, 2008), cat. no. 85F0033M, no. 19; and Lise Gotell, "Canadian Sexual Assault Law: Neoliberalism and the Erosion of Feminist-Inspired Law Reforms," at http://ualberta.academia.edu/LiseGotell/Papers/279667/Canadian_Sexual_Assault_Law_Neoliberalism_and_the_Erosion_of_Feminist-Inspired_Law_Reforms.

88. Melanie Randall, "Sexual Assault Law, Credibility, and 'Ideal Victims': Consent, Resistance, and Victim Blaming," *Canadian Journal of Women and the Law* 22 (2010): 397–433.

89. Donald Lunde, *Murder and Madness* (San Francisco: San Francisco Book, 1977), p. 3.

90. S. Beattie, and A. Cotter, *Juristat: Homicide in Canada, 2009*, vol. 30, no. 3 (Fall 2010) (Ottawa: Minister of Industry) cat. no. 85-002-X.

91. Statistics Canada, "Canada's Crime Rate: Two Decades of Decline," *The Daily*, 2015. at http://www.statcan.gc.ca/pub/11-630-x/11-630-x2015001-eng.htm (accessed 19 October 2015).

92. Ibid.

93. Statistics Canada, "Homicide in Canada, 2013," *The Daily* (1 December 2014) at http://www.statcan.gc.ca/daily-quotidien/141201/dq141201a-eng.htm (accessed 19 October 2015).

94. Ibid.

95. S. Beattie, and A. Cotter, *Juristat: Homicide in Canada, 2009*, vol. 30, no. 3 (Fall 2010) (Ottawa: Minister of Industry) cat. no. 85-002-X.

96. See, generally, Marc Reidel and Margaret Zahn, *The Nature and Pattern of American Homicide* (Washington, DC: U.S. Government Printing Office, 1985).

97. Rui Yang and Sigurdur Olafsson, "Classification for Predicting Offender Affiliation with Murder Victims," *Expert Systems with Applications*, vol. 38, iss. 11 (October 2011): 13518–13526.

98. Krystal Mize, Todd Shackelford, and Viviana Shackelford, "Hands-on Killing of Intimate Partners as a Function of Sex and Relationship Status/State," *Journal of Family Violence*, vol. 24, iss. 7 (October 2009): 463–470; and Linda Saltzman and James Mercy, "Assaults Between Intimates: The Range of Relationships Involved," in *Homicide: The Victim/Offender Connection*, ed. Anna Victoria Wilson (Cincinnati: Anderson Publishing, 1993), pp. 65–74.

99. Angela Browne and Kirk Williams, "Exploring the Effect of Resource Availability and the Likelihood of Female-Perpetrated Homicides," *Law and Society Review* 23 (1989): 75–94.

100. Angela Browne and Kirk Williams, "Gender, Intimacy, and Lethal Violence: Trends from 1976 Through 1987," *Gender and Society* 7 (1993): 78–98.

101. Todd K. Shackelford, David M. Buss, and Viviana A. Weekes-Shackelford, "Wife Killings Committed in the Context of a Lovers Triangle," *Basic & Applied Social Psychology*, vol. 25, iss. 2 (June 2003): 137–143; and Richard Felson, "Anger, Aggression, and Violence in Love Triangles," *Violence and Victimization* 12 (1997): 345–363.

102. Statistics Canada, "Homicide in Canada, 2013."

103. David Boroff, "Ex–Gay Porn Actor Luka Magnotta, Known as the 'Canadian Cannibal,' Found Guilty in Slaying and Dismembering of Chinese Lover," *New York Daily News* (December 23, 2014) at http://www.nydailynews.com/news/crime/canadian-cannibal-found-guilty-grisly-slaying-article-1.2054628 (accessed 19 October 2015).

104. Christie Blatchford, "Luka Magnotta May Be a Sexual Sadist Who Got 'Strong Thrill' from Killing, Trial Told," *National Post* (23 December 2014).

105. Statistics Canada, "Homicide in Canada, 2013."

106. Sara Beattie and Adam Cotter, *Juristat: Homicide in Canada, 2009*, vol. 30, no. 3 (Ottawa: Minister of Industry, Fall 2010) cat. no. 85-002-X.

107. "RCMP Report Missing and Murdered Aboriginal Women, by the Numbers," The Canadian Press (27 February 2015) at http://www.rcmp-grc.gc.ca/pubs/abo-aut/mmaw-fada-eng.htm (accessed 27 October 2015).

108. Ibid.

109. Ibid.

110. Anonymous, "582 Native Women Listed Missing, Slain Report Adds 62 Names to Collection of Cases, Highlights Trauma to Aboriginal Families," *Toronto Star* (22 April 2010), p. 16.

111. "Matthew de Grood Charged in Calgary's 'Worst Mass Murder,'" Stabbings at House Party Near University of Calgary Campus Leave 5 Young People Dead," CBC News (15 April 2014) at http://www.cbc.ca/news/canada/calgary/matthew-de-grood-charged-in-calgary-s-worst-mass-murder-1.2610465 (accessed 19 October 2015).

112. Belea Keeney and Kathleen Heide, "Gender Differences in Serial Murderers: A Preliminary Analysis," *Journal of Interpersonal Violence* 9 (1994): 37–56.

113. Statistics Canada, CANSIM, Table 252-0013, "Crimes by Type of Offence," at http://www5.statcan.gc.ca/cansim/pick-choisir?lang=eng&searchTypeByValue=1&id=2520013 (accessed 11 November 2011).

114. Keith Harries, "Homicide and Assault: A Comparative Analysis of Attributes in Dallas Neighborhoods, 1981–1985," *Professional Geographer* 41 (1989): 29–38.

115. Jillian Boyce, Adam Cotter and Samuel Perreault, "Police-reported Crime Statistics in Canada, 2013," *Juristat*, Canadian Centre for Justice Statistics, cat. no. 85-002-X (23 July 2014) at http://www.statcan.gc.ca/pub/85-002-x/2014001/article/14040-eng.pdf (accessed 19 October 2015).

116. Ibid.

117. Harriet L. Macmillan et al., "Development of a Policy-relevant Child Maltreatment Research Strategy," *Milbank Quarterly*, vol. 85, iss. 2 (2007): 337–374.

118. Tracie O. Afifi et al., "Child Abuse and Mental Disorders in Canada," *Canadian Medical Association Journal* (22 April 2014), doi:10.1503/cmaj.131792.

119. Statistics Canada, "Family Violence in Canada: A Statistical Profile, 2013," *Canadian Centre for Justice Statistics*, Catalogue no. 85-002-X (15 January 2015) at http://www.statcan.gc.ca/pub/85-002-x/2014001/article/14114-eng.pdf (accessed 19 October 2015).

120. Glenn Wolfner and Richard Gelles, "A Profile of Violence Toward Children: A National Study," *Child Abuse and Neglect* 17 (1993): 197–212.

121. Nico M. Trocmé, Marc Tourigny, Bruce MacLaurin, and Barbara Fallon, "Major Findings from the Canadian Incidence Study of Reported Child Abuse and Neglect"; and Ruth Inglis, *Sins of the Fathers: A Study of the Physical and Emotional Abuse of Children* (New York: St. Martin's Press, 1978), p. 68.

122. Martin Daly and Margo Wilson, "Violence Against Step Children," *Current Directions in Psychological Science* 5 (1996): 77–81.

123. Sandra M. Stith et al., "Risk Factors in Child Maltreatment: A Meta-analytic Review of the Literature," *Aggression and Violent Behavior* (January 2009), 14 (1): 13–29.

124. Ibid.

125. R. Emerson Dobash and Russell Dobash, *Violence Against Wives* (New York: Free Press, 1979).

126. Julia O'Faolain and Laura Martines, eds., *Not in God's Image: Women in History* (Glasgow: Fontana/Collins, 1974).

127. Dobash and Dobash, *Violence Against Wives*, p. 46.

128. Ronald Cohen, Alan Rosenbaum, Robert Kane, William Warneken, and Sheldon Benjamin, "Neuropsychological Correlates of Domestic Violence," *Violence and Victims* 15 (2000): 397–410.

129. Neil Jacobson and John Mordechai Gottman, *When Men Batter Women: New Insights into Ending Abusive Relationships* (New York: Simon and Schuster, 1998). Other research studies also report a high correlation between spousal violence and stalking (criminal harassment), including P. Tjaden and N. Thoennes, "Prevalence and Consequences of Male-to-Female and Female-to-Male Partner Violence as Measured by The National Violence Against Women Survey," *Violence Against Women* 6 (2) (2000): 142–161; J. MacFarlane, et al. "Stalking and Intimate Partner Femicide," *Homicide Studies* 3 (4) (1999) 300–316.

130. Margo Wilson and Martin Daly, "Male Sexual Proprietariness and Violence Against Wives," *Current Directions in Psychological Science* 5 (1996): 2–7.

131. "Measuring Violence Against Women: Statistical Trends" (2013). The full report can be accessed at http://www.statcan.gc.ca/pub/85-002-x/2013001/article/11766-eng.pdf (accessed 22 October 2015).

132. Richard Rosenfeld, "Changing Relationships Between Men and Women: A Note on the Decline in Intimate Partner Homicide," *Homicide Studies* 1 (1997): 72–83.

133. Desmond Ellis and Lori Wright, "Estrangement, Interventions, and Male Violence Toward Female Partners," *Violence and Victims* 12 (1997): 51–68.

134. Federal Bureau of Investigation, *Crime in the United States, 1997* (Washington, DC: U.S. Government Printing Office, 1998), p. 28.

135. Jillian Boyce, Adam Cotter and Samuel Perreault, "Police-reported Crime Statistics in Canada, 2013," Statistics Canada, *Juristat*, 85-002-x (2014) at at http://www.statcan.gc.ca/pub/85-002-x/2014001/article/14040-eng.htm#a3 (accessed 19 October 2015).

136. Ibid.

137. Maire Gannon, *Crime Comparisons between Canada and the United States*, Statistics Canada (Canadian Centre for Justice Statistics, 2001), cat. no. 85-002-XIE, vol. 21, no. 11, pp. 5–6; Canadian Centre for Justice Statistics, "Firearms and Violent Crime in Canada," (2012) at http://www.statcan.gc.ca/pub/85-002-x/2014001/article/11925-eng.htm (accessed 22 October 2015).

138. Caroline Wolf Harlow, *Robbery Victims* (Washington, DC: Bureau of Justice Statistics, 1989), pp. 1–5.

139. Richard Felson, Eric Baumer, and Steven Messner, "Acquaintance Robbery," *Journal of Research in Crime and Delinquency* 37 (2000): 284–305.

140. James Calder and John Bauer, "Convenience Store Robberies: Security Measures and Store Robbery Incidents," *Journal of Criminal Justice* 20 (1992): 553–566.

141. Peter Van Koppen and Robert Jansen, "The Time to Rob: Variations in Time and Number of Commercial Robberies," *Journal of Research in Crime and Delinquency* 36 (1999): 7–29.

142. "'It's Still On:' Dana Martin Says He's Still Planning to Have Justin Bieber Murdered, and Other Things We Learned from His *Details* Profile," *National Post* (25 March 2013).

143. Section 264 (2), Criminal Code of Canada.

144. Shelly Milligan, "Criminal Harassment in Canada, 2009," *Juristat Bulletin* (3 March 2011), Statistics Canada cat. no. 85-005-X, p. 2.

145. Ibid.
146. Ibid.
147. Ibid.
148. Ibid.
149. Isabel Grant, "Intimate Partner Criminal Harassment Through a Lens of Responsibilization," Osgoode Hall Law School (2015) at http://digitalcommons.osgoode.yorku.ca/cgi/viewcontent.cgi?article=1082&context=olsrps (accessed 19 October 2015).
150. "Canadian Women Harassed by Former Partners Face Legal 'Catch-22,'" UBC News (11 March 2015) at http://news.ubc.ca/2015/03/11/canadian-women-harassed-by-former-partners-face-legal-catch-22 (accessed 19 October 2015).
151. Section 348.1, Criminal Code of Canada.
152. Mia Dauvergne, "Police-reported Robbery in Canada, 2008," Statistics Canada, Juristat (Spring 2010) 85-002-X at http://www.statcan.gc.ca/pub/85-002-x/2010001/article/11115-eng.htm#a5 (accessed 19 October 2015).
153. Melanie Kowalski, Home Invasions, Bulletin, Canadian Centre for Justice Statistics (June 2002) cat. no. 85F0027X1E.
154. Orest Fedorowycz, Breaking and Entering in Canada—2002 (Canadian Centre for Justice Statistics, Statistics Canada), cat. no. 85-002-XPE, vol. 24, no. 5.
155. Lucie Ogrodnik, "Seniors as Victims of Crime, 2004 and 2005," Canadian Centre for Justice Statistics, Statistics Canada, Catalogue no. 85F0033MIE, no. 14 (March 2007) at http://www.statcan.gc.ca/pub/85f0033m/85f0033m2007014-eng.htm (accessed 19 October 2015).
156. "Robbery," BC Crime Trends—Police & Crime, Summary Statistics, 1989–1998, Government of British Columbia, iss. 3 (March 2000): 3.
157. Jack McDevitt, "The Study of the Character of Civil Rights Crimes in Massachusetts (1983–1987)," paper presented at the annual meeting of the American Society of Criminology, Reno, Nevada, November 1989.
158. Ibid., p. 8.
159. Jack Levin and Jack McDevitt, Hate Crimes: The Rising Tide of Bigotry and Bloodshed (New York: Plenum, 1993).
160. Statistics Canada, "Police-reported Hate Crimes, 2012," The Daily (26 June 2014) at http://www.statcan.gc.ca/daily-quotidien/140626/dq140626b-eng.htm (accessed 19 October 2015).
161. Ibid.
162. Cheryl Edwards, "Workplace Violence: Evolving OHS Obligation," Occupational Safety Newsletter (January 2009) at http://www.cos-mag.com/legal/legal-columns/workplace-violence-evolving-ohs-obligation.html (accessed 19 October 2015).
163. Ibid.
164. Ibid.
165. Sylvain de Léséleuc, Criminal Victimization in the Workplace 2004 (Ottawa: Minister of Industry, February 2007) cat. 85F0033MIE, no. 13.
166. Hubert Herring, "The Good News About 'Going Postal,'" The New York Times (3 September 2000), p. A3.

167. J. Barling, K. E. Dupre, and E. K. Kelloway, "Predicting Workplace Aggression and Violence," Annual Review of Psychology, 60 (2009): 671–692.
168. Associated Press, "Gunman Wounds 3 Doctors in L.A. Hospital," Cleveland Plain Dealer (9 February 1993), p. B1.
169. James Alan Fox and Jack Levin, "Firing Back: The Growing Threat of Workplace Homicide," Annals 536 (1994): 16–30; and J. Barling, K. E. Dupre, and E. K. Kelloway, "Predicting Workplace Aggression and Violence," Annual Review of Psychology, 60 (2009): 671–692.
170. Canadian Bar Association 2010 National Administrative Law, Labour & Employment Law and Privacy & Access Law Conference November 26, 2010, Ottawa, Ontario. Presentation by Cheryl A. Edwards, LLB, "Workplace Violence & Harassment in Canada: Ontario's OHS Provisions in Perspective" at http://www.cba.org/cba/cle/PDF/adm10_edwards_paper_2.pdf (accessed 19 October 2015).
171. Mental Health Commission of Canada, Topics: National Standard for Workplace Violence (n.d.), at http://www.mentalhealthcommission.ca/English/issues/workplace/national-standard (accessed 19 October 2015).
172. Family Violence in Canada: A Statistical Profile, 2011 (Ottawa: Minister of Industry, 2011) cat. no. 85-224-X at http://www.statcan.gc.ca/pub/85-224-x/85-224-x2010000-eng.htm (accessed December 6, 2011).

Chapter 11

1. Andrew McCall, The Medieval Underworld (London: Hamish Hamilton, 1979), p. 86.
2. Ibid., p. 104.
3. James S. Frideres, First Nations in the Twenty-First Century (Toronto: Oxford University Press, 2011).
4. J. J. Tobias, Crime and Police in England, 1700–1900 (London: Gill and Macmillan, 1979).
5. Ibid., p. 9.
6. Marilyn Walsh, The Fence (Westport, CT: Greenwood Press, 1977), pp. 18–25.
7. John Hepburn, "Occasional Criminals," in Major Forms of Crime, ed. Robert Meier (Beverly Hills, CA: Sage, 1984), pp. 73–94.
8. James Inciardi, "Professional Crime," in Major Forms of Crime, ed. Robert Meier (Beverly Hills, CA: Sage, 1984), p. 223.
9. This section depends heavily on a classic book: Wayne La Fave and Austin Scott, Handbook on Criminal Law (St. Paul, MN: West Publishing, 1972).
10. La Fave and Scott, Handbook on Criminal Law, p. 622.
11. Jillian Boyce, Adam Cotter and Samuel Perreault, "Police-reported Crime Statistics in Canada, 2013," Juristat (July, 2014), cat. no. 85-002-X (Ottawa: Minister of Industry, 2014).
12. Global Hotels Amenities Survey, "Danish Hotel Guests Most Honest, but Canada Is Divided," (April 13, 2013) at http://www.newswire.ca/en/story/1145813/danish-hotel-guests-most-honest-but-canada-is-divided (accessed 20 October 2015); and Margaret Loftus, "Gone: One TV," U.S. News & World Report (14 July 1997), p. 61.
13. Andy Johnson, "Theft Ring up in Smoke: Cigarette Thieves Hit Here: Police," Evening Guide [Port Hope, Ontario] (14 July 2004), p. 1.
14. Jack Harris, BDO Dunwoody LLP "Combatting Employee Theft and Fraud," Okanagan Business Journal (2 May 2005).
15. Michael Winter, "Home Depot Hackers Used Vendor Log-on to Steal Data, E-mails," USA Today (7 November 2014) at http://www.usatoday.com/story/money/.../home-depot-hackers.../18613167; Francine Kopun, "Home Depot Confirms Data Breach; Home Depot Working with IT Security, Feds on Breach: Canadian Stores Part of Probe, but Online Purchases Not Affected," Toronto Star (9 September 2014), p. B.1.
16. Elizabeth Thompson, "Tax Computers Stolen in Laval, Probe Ordered," The Gazette (30 September 2003), p. A12.
17. Canadian Anti Fraud Centre Criminal Intelligence Analytical Unit, Annual Statistical Report 2013—Mass Marketing Fraud & ID Theft Activities, at http://www.antifraudcentre-centreantifraude.ca/english/documents/annual-2013-cafc.pdf (accessed 20 October 2015).
18. Norman A. Wilcox Jr. and Thomas M. Regan, "Unmasking Terrorist Identity Fraud," USA Today Magazine, vol. 134, iss. 2724 (September 2005): 24–26.
19. Dana Flavelle, "Stores Are Shopping for Ultimate Security; Canadian Retailers Are Losing an Estimated $8 Million a Day to Retail Theft But Many Are Starting to Fight Back in an Effort to Keep Costs under Wraps," Toronto Star (29 March 2008), p. 2.
20. Francine Kopun, "Organized Retail Crime Taking off in Canada," (12 December 2014) at at http://www.thestar.com/business/2014/12/12/organized_retail_crime_taking_off_in_canada.html (accessed 20 October 2015).
21. Mary Owen Cameron, The Booster and the Snitch (New York: Free Press, 1964).
22. Ibid., p. 57.
23. Lawrence Cohen and Rodney Stark, "Discriminatory Labeling and the Five-Finger Discount: An Empirical Analysis of Differential Shoplifting Dispositions," Journal of Research on Crime and Delinquency 11 (1974): 25–35.
24. Lloyd Klemke, "Does Apprehension for Shoplifting Amplify or Terminate Shoplifting Activity?" Law and Society Review 12 (1978): 390–403.
25. Peter Bowal, Ivan Via and Joshua Beckie, "Whatever Happened to ... David Chen and Citizen Arrests," Law Now: Relating Law to Life in Canada (5 September 2014) at at http://www.lawnow.org/whatever-happened-david-chen-citizen-arrests (accessed 20 October 2015).
26. Erhard Blankenburg, "The Selectivity of Legal Sanctions: An Empirical Investigation of Shoplifting," Law and Society Review 11 (1976): 109–129.

27. Jill Jordan Siedfer, "To Catch a Thief Try This: Peddling High-Tech Solutions to Shoplifting," *U.S. News & World Report* (23 September 1996): 71.

28. "Montreal Police Bust High-Tech Labs Making Fake Credit Cards," CBC News (12 January 2007) at http://www.cbc.ca/news/canada/montreal/strory/2007/01/12/mtl-fraud.htm.

29. RCMP, "Credit Card Fraud, Recognize It. What Is Credit Card Fraud?" at http://www .rcmp-grc .gc.ca/scams-fraudes/cc-fraud-fraude-eng.htm (accessed 6 August 2011).

30. Royal Canadian Mounted Police, "Scams and Fraud" at at http://www.rcmp-grc.gc.ca/scams -fraudes/index-eng.htm (accessed 20 October 2015).

31. Industry Canada, Office of Consumer Affairs (OCA), "Debit Card Fraud—Introduction" (16 November 2010) at http://www.ic.gc.ca/eic/ site/oca-bc.nsf/eng/ca01832.html (accessed 20 October 2015).

32. Sonja Puzic, "Massive Debit Card Scam Reached Far and Wide; EvenCredit Union CEO Fell Victim," *The Windsor Star* (18 February 2010), p. A3; Chris Kitching, "Sophisticated ATM Scam Cracked," *Toronto Sun* (20 September 2010) at http://www.torontosun.com/news/ canada/2010/10/01/15543316.html (accessed 20 October 2015); "Debit Card Fraud Suspects Nabbed in $1M Bank ATM Scam; Card Readers and Cameras Installed at Banking Institutions' ATMs to Read Card Data, PINs," (27 March 2014) at http://www.cbc.ca/news/ canada/montreal/debit-card-fraud-suspects -nabbed-in-1m-bank-atm-scam-1.2588825 (accessed 20 October 2015).

33. Government of Canada, Justice Laws Website, An Act to amend the Criminal Code (identity theft and related misconduct) S.C. 2009, c. 28, assented to 22 October 2009.

34. Barb Pacholik, "Chips Credited for Dip in Fraud; PINs Reduce Opportunity to Steal Data," *Leader Post* [Regina, Sask] (16 May 2015), p. B1.

35. Jillian Boyce, Adam Cotter and Samuel Perreault, "Police-reported Crime Statistics in Canada 2013," *Juristat* (July 2014), cat. no. 85-002-X (Ottawa: Minister of Industry, 2014).

36. Insurance Bureau of Canada. "Auto Theft" at http://www.ibc.ca/en/insurance_crime/auto _theft.

37. Mia Dauvergne, Statistics Canada, "Motor Vehicle Theft in Canada" (Ottawa: Minister of Industry, 2008) cat. 85-002-V.

38. Charles McCaghy, Peggy Giordano, and Trudy Knicely Henson, "Auto Theft" *Criminology*, 15 (1977), 367–381.

39. Kim Hazelbaker, "Insurance Industry Analyses and the Prevention of Motor Vehicle Theft," in *Business and Crime Prevention*, eds. Marcus Felson and Ronald Clarke (Monsey, NY: Criminal Justice Press, 1997), pp. 283–293.

40. David Carrigg, "B.C.'s Bait Car Program Wins Global Praise: Series: Stolen Lives: An In-Depth Look at the Dangerous World of Auto Crime," *The Province* [Vancouver, B.C] (6 October 2005), p. A10.

41. U.S. Department of Transportation, "NHTSA's Vehicle Theft Prevention" at http://www .nhtsa.gov/staticfiles/communications/pdf/ VehicleTheftPrevention.pdf... (accessed 20 May 2015).

42. Hazelbaker, "Insurance Industry Analyses and the Prevention of Motor Vehicle Theft," p. 289.

43. La Fave and Scott, *Handbook on Criminal Law*, p. 655.

44. Canadian Bankers Association, "Cheques—What You Need to Know," (19 January 2015) at http://www.cba.ca/en/consumer-information/40 -banking-basics/584-cheques-what-you-need -to-know (accessed 20 October 2015).

45. Edwin Lemert, "An Isolation and Closure Theory of Naive Check Forging," *Journal of Criminal Law, Criminology and Police Science*, 44 (1953): 297–298.

46. Linda Lee Larson, "'Check 21' Can Make Fraud Easier Be Alert to Changes in Check-Imaging Technology," *Fraud Magazine* (January/ February 2012).

47. Government of Canada, Canadian Anti-fraud Centre, "Anti-Virus Scams," at http://sunshinecoast .rcmp-grc.gc.ca/ViewPage.action?siteNodel d=1189&languageld=4&contentld=39983 (accessed 24 October 2015); The Canadian Anti-Fraud Call Centre, PhoneBusters, "Backgrounder: What Is Deceptive Telemarketing?" at http:// www .phonebusters.com/english/fraudprevention (accessed 31 October 2011).

48. Kevin Donovan, "Charity Scams Bust Public Trust," *Toronto Star* (2 June 2007) at http:// www.thestar.com/News/article/220756 (accessed 6 August 2011).

49. Jerome Hall, *Theft, Law and Society* (Indianapolis: Bobbs-Merrill, 1952), p. 36.

50. La Fave and Scott, *Handbook on Criminal Law*, p. 644.

51. Ibid., p. 708.

52. E. Blackstone, *Commentaries on the Laws of England* (London: 1769), p. 224.

53. Orest Fedorowycz, "Breaking and Entering in Canada—2002," *Juristat*, vol. 24, no. 5 (2004), Statistics Canada Catalogue no. 85-002-XIE.

54. S. Perreault and S. Brennan, Statistics Canada, "Criminal Victimization in Canada 2009," *Juristat*, 30 (2) (Ottawa: Minister of Industry, 2010) cat. 85-002-X.

55. Frank Hoheimer, *The Home Invaders: Confessions of a Cat Burglar* (Chicago: Chicago Review, 1975).

56. Richard Wright, Robert Logie, and Scott Decker, "Criminal Expertise and Offender Decision Making: An Experimental Study of the Target Selection Process in Residential Burglary," *Journal of Research in Crime and Delinquency* 32 (1995): 39–53.

57. Richard Wright and Scott Decker, *Burglars on the Job: Streetlife and Residential Break-ins* (Boston, MA: Northeastern University Press, 1994).

58. Simon Hakim and Yochanan Shachmurove, "Spatial and Temporal Patterns of Commercial Burglaries," *American Journal of Economics and Sociology* 55 (1996): 443–457.

59. Roger Litton, "Crime Prevention and the Insurance Industry," in *Business and Crime Prevention*, eds. Marcus Felson and Ronald Clarke (Monsey, NY: Criminal Justice Press, 1997), p. 162.

60. Graham Farrell, Coretta Phillips, and Ken Pease, "Like Taking Candy: Why Does Repeat Victimization Occur?" *British Journal of Criminology*, 35 (1995): 384–399, p. 391.

61. See, generally, Neal Shover, "Structures and Careers in Burglary," *Journal of Criminal Law, Criminology and Police Science* 63 (1972): 540–549.

62. Paul Cromwell, James Olson, and D'Aunn Wester Avary, *Breaking and Entering: An Ethnographic Analysis of Burglary* (Newbury Park, CA: Sage, 1991), pp. 48–51.

63. Statistics Canada, Cansim Table 252-0051, "Incident-based Crime Statistics, by Detailed Violations Annual," at http://www5.statcan .gc.ca/cansim/a26.

64. Nancy Webb, George Sakheim, Luz Towns-Miranda, and Charles Wagner, "Collaborative Treatment of Juvenile Firestarters: Assessment and Outreach," *American Journal of Orthopsychiatry* 60 (1990): 305–310.

65. Vernon Quinsey, Terry Chaplin, and Douglas Unfold, "Arsonists and Sexual Arousal to Fire Setting: Correlations Unsupported," *Journal of Behavior Therapy and Experimental Psychiatry* 20 (1989): 203–209.

66. Leigh Edward Somers, *Economic Crimes* (New York: Clark Boardman, 1984), pp. 158–168.

Chapter 12

1. Joe O'Connor, "Mysterious Canadian's life in the fast lane fuelled by penny stock scam: SEC," *National Post* (17 March 2014) at http://news .nationalpost.com/news/canada/mysterious -canadians-life-in-the-fast-lane-fuelled-by-penny -stock-scam-sec (access 21 October 2015).

2. Ibid.

3. Barrie Mckenna, "White-Collar Crime Hits More than a Third of Canadian Organizations," *The Globe and Mail* (24 February 2014) at http://www.theglobeandmail.com/report-on -business/white-collar-crime-rises-in-canada/ article17058885 (accessed 21 October 2015).

4. Stephen Ewart, "Ponzi Conviction Vital to Canada's Fight against White-Collar Crime," *Calgary Herald* (17 February 2015) at http:// calgaryherald.com/news/crime/ewart-ponzi -conviction-vital-to-canadas-fight-against -white-collar-crime) (accessed 21 October 2015).

5. Jeff Gray and Janet McFarland, "Crime without punishment: Canada's investment fraud problem," *The Globe and Mail* (24 August 2013) at http:// www.theglobeandmail.com/report-on-business/ crime-and-no-punishment-canadas-investment -fraud-problem/article13938792/?page=all) (accessed 21 October 2015).

6. Dwight C. Smith, Jr., "White-Collar Crime, Organized Crime and the Business Establishment: Resolving a Crisis in Criminological Theory," in *White-Collar and Economic Crime: A*

Multidisciplinary and Crossnational Perspective, eds. P. Wickman and T. Dailey (Lexington, MA: Lexington Books, 1982), p. 53.

7. See, generally, Dwight C. Smith, Jr., "Organized Crime and Entrepreneurship," *International Journal of Criminology and Penology* 6 (1978): 161–177; Dwight C. Smith, Jr., "Paragons, Pariahs, and Pirates: A Spectrum-Based Theory of Enterprise," *Crime and Delinquency* 26 (1980): 358–386; Dwight C. Smith, Jr., and Richard S. Alba, "Organized Crime and American Life," *Society* 16 (1979): 32–38.

8. Smith, "White-Collar Crime, Organized Crime and the Business Establishment," p. 33; Blythe Proulx, "Organized Criminal Involvement in the Illicit Antiquities Trade," *Trends in Organized Crime,* vol. 14, iss. 1 (March 2011): 1–29.

9. Mark Haller, "Illegal Enterprise: A Theoretical and Historical Interpretation," *Criminology* 28 (1990): 207–235.

10. John P. Wright, Francis T. Cullen, "The Social Construction of Corporate Violence: Media Coverage of the Imperial Food Products Fire," *Crime & Delinquency,* vol. 41, iss. 1 (January 1995): 20–36, Nancy Frank and Michael Lynch, *Corporate Crime, Corporate Violence* (Albany, NY: Harrow and Heston, 1992), p. 7.

11. Tomson H. Nguyen and Henry N. Pontell, "Mortgage Origination Fraud and the Global Economic Crisis, "*Criminology & Public Policy,* vol. 9, iss. 3 (August 2010): 591–612.

12. Nikos Passas and David Nelken, "The Thin Line Between Legitimate and Criminal Enterprises: Subsidy Frauds in the European Community," *Crime, Law and Social Change* 19 (1993): 223–243.

13. For a thorough review, see David Friedrichs, *Trusted Criminals* (Belmont, CA: Wadsworth, 1996).

14. Carole Gibbs, Edmund F. McGarrell, and Mark Axelrod, "Transnational White-Collar Crime and Risk," *Criminology & Public Policy,* vol. 9, iss. 3 (August 2010): 543–560.

15. Edwin Sutherland, *White-Collar Crime: The Uncut Version* (New Haven, CT: Yale University Press, 1983), p. 7.

16. Edwin Sutherland, "White-Collar Criminality," *American Sociological Review* 5 (1940): 2–10.

17. David Weisburd and Kip Schlegel, "Returning to the Mainstream," in *White-Collar Crime Reconsidered,* ed. Kip Schlegel and David Weisburd (Boston: Northeastern University Press, 1992), pp. 352–365.

18. K. Calavita, R. Tillman, and H. N. Pontell, "The Savings and Loan Debacle, Financial Crime, and the State," *Annual Review of Sociology,* vol. 23 (1997): 19–38.

19. Elizabeth Moore and Michael Mills, "The Neglected Victims and Unexamined Costs of White-Collar Crime," *Crime and Delinquency* 36 (1990): 408–418.

20. PriceWaterhouseCoopers, "The Global Economic Crime Survey, Economic Crime in a Downturn" (November 2009) at http://www.pwc.com/en_GX/gx/economic-crime-survey/pdf/global-economic-crime-survey-2009.pdf (accessed 21 October 2015).

21. "National Investment: Fraud Vulnerability Report," British Columbia Securities Commission (2012) at http://www.bcsc.bc.ca/uploadedFiles/News/News_Releases/2012_NIFVR_KeyHighlights_EN.pdf (accessed 21 October 2015).

22. Eric Beauchesne, "Fraud Strikes Half of Firms," *Calgary Herald* (9 July 2003), p. C1; Aaron Freeman and Craig Forcese, "Get Tough on Corporate Crime," *Toronto Star* (17 November 1994), p. A31; Doug Fischer, "Investigator Fears Fraud Cases Ignored," *Calgary Herald* (9 July 1994), p. A10.

23. Joe Chidley, "Camp Cupcake Has Nothing on Us," *Canadian Business,* vol. 77, iss. 20 (October 11, 2004): 4.

24. Jim Moran, "Thailand: Crime and Corruption Become Increasing Threat," *CJ International* 12 (1996): 5.

25. Sam Perry, "Economic Espionage and Corporate Responsibility," *CJ International* 11 (1995): 3–4; and Nikki Swartz, "Corporate Spying Costs $45 Billion," *Information Management Journal,* vol. 42, iss. 3 (May/June 2008): 16.

26. Marshall Clinard and Richard Quinney, *Criminal Behavior Systems: A Typology* (New York: Holt, Rinehart and Winston, 1973), p. 117.

27. Mark Moore, "Notes Toward a National Strategy to Deal with White-Collar Crime," in *A National Strategy for Containing White-Collar Crime,* eds. Herbert Edelhertz and Charles Rogovin (Lexington, MA: Lexington Books, 1980), pp. 32–44.

28. For a general review, see John Braithwaite, "White Collar Crime," *Annual Review,* 11 (1985): 1–25.

29. Tom Fennell, "Assumed Identities: English Police Charge a Canadian with Murder," *Maclean's* (16 December 1996), pp. 52, 54.

30. Mark Gollom, "'Mr. Big' Ruling a 'Game Changer' for Those Convicted in Sting Operations Up to 2008; The Tactic Has Been Used at Least 350 Times to Try to Solve Cold Murder Cases," CBC News (1 August 2014) at http://www.cbc.ca/news/politics/mr-big-ruling-a-game-changer-for-those-convicted-in-sting-operations-1.2724310 (accessed 21 October 2015).

31. Richard Quinney, "Occupational Structure and Criminal Behavior: Prescription Violation of Retail Pharmacists," *Social Problems* 11 (1963): 179–185; see also John Braithwaite, *Corporate Crime in the Pharmaceutical Industry* (London: Routledge and Kegan Paul, 1984).

32. "The Rise and Fall of Alan Eagleson," Canadian Broadcasting Corporation Archives, at http://archives.cbc.ca.

33. James Armstrong et al., "Securities Fraud," *American Criminal Law Review* 33 (1995): 973–1016.

34. Scott McMurray, "Futures Pit Trader Goes to Trial," *Wall Street Journal* (8 May 1990), p. C1; Scott McMurray, "Chicago Pits' Dazzling Growth Permitted a Free-for-All Mecca," *Wall Street Journal* (3 August 1989), p. A4.

35. John Greenwood, "Grmovsek Gets 39 Months for Insider Trading," *Financial Post* (7 January 2010) at at http://www.financialpost.com/related/topics/Grmovsek+gets+months

+insider+trading/2415865/story.html (accessed 21 October 2015).

36. Douglas Goold and Andrew Willis, *The Bre-X Fraud* (Toronto: McClelland & Stewart, 1997).

37. Jeff Gray, "After 17 Years, Bre-X Case Finally Closes," *The Globe and Mail* (23 April 2014) at http://www.theglobeandmail.com/report-on-business/industry-news/the-law-page/the-bre-x-case-finally-closes/article18124172/ (accessed 21 October 2015).

38. "The Bruce Carson Affair," *National Post* (7 April 2011), p. 5; Chantal Hebert, "Adscam and Culture of Entitlement," *Toronto Star* (4 August 2004), p. A4; Les Whittington, "Legal Tussle Stalls Inquiry," *Toronto Star* (10 November 2004), p. A20.

39. David Ljunggren, "Former Aide to Canadian PM Charged with Influence-peddling, *Reuters Canada* (27 July 2012) at http://ca.reuters.com/article/domesticNews/idCABRE86Q18H20120727 (accessed 21 October 2015).

40. Rosie DiManno, "Scandal Makes Case for Civilian Oversight," *Toronto Star* (23 January 2004), p. A20.

41. Allan Woods, "Officers Will Be Charged, Fantino Says," *National Post* (20 April 2004), p. A12; Tracy Huffman and John Duncanson, "Case Spotlights Police Probe," *Toronto Star* (6 November 2004), p. B1; John Duncanson and Tracy Huffman, "New Charges Laid Against Officers," *Toronto Star* (16 October 2004), p. A17.

42. David Bruser, "Police 'Unplugged' Corruption Probe, Lawyer Says; Claims Against Drug Squad Were Ignored, Court Told, as Damage Control Bid Was Under Way on Other Unit," *Toronto Star* (11 December 2009), p. GT1.

43. "Canada's Misbehaving Mayors: The Scandals Keep on Coming," *The Economist,* (20 June 2013): at http://www.economist.com/blogs/americasview/2013/06/canada-s-misbehaving-mayors (accessed 21 October 2015).

44. Ann Hui and Jill Mahoney, "Ford Brothers Face New Conflict-of-Interest Complaint in Court," *The Globe and Mail* (3 October 2014) at http://www.theglobeandmail.com/news/toronto/ford-brothers-face-new-conflict-of-interest-complaint-in-court/article20912455 (accessed 21 October 2015).

45. Daniel Dale, "Rob Ford: 'Yes, I Have Smoked Crack Cocaine,'" *Toronto Star* (5 November 2013) at http://www.thestar.com/news/crime/2013/11/05/rob_ford_yes_i_have_smoked_crack_cocaine.html (accessed 21 October 2015).

46. Robyn Doolittle and Greg McArthur, "Rob Ford Takes Leave as Recent Drug Videos Emerge," *The Globe and Mail* (30 April 2014) at at http://www.theglobeandmail.com/news/toronto/rob-ford-takes-leave-as-new-drug-video-emerges/article18354671 (accessed 21 October 2015).

47. Marlene Leung, "Ford Nation Still 'Stands by Their Man': New Poll," *CTV News* (22 November 2013) at http://www.ctvnews.ca/politics/ford-nation-still-stands-by-their-man-new-poll-1.1555428 (accessed 21 October 2015).

48. Anonymous, "Canada's Misbehaving Mayors: The Scandals Keep on Coming," *The Economist* (20 June

2013) at http://www.economist.com/blogs/americasview/2013/06/canada-s-misbehaving-mayors (accessed 21 October 2015).

49. Cited in Hugh Barlow, *Introduction to Criminology*, 2nd ed. (Boston: Little, Brown, 1984).

50. Charles McCaghy, *Deviant Behavior* (New York: Macmillan, 1976), p. 178.

51. Associated Press, "Business Fraud Prevails, May Worsen, Study Says," *Wall Street Journal* (17 August 1993), p. A4; Liane Greenberg and Julian Darling, "Employee Theft," in C.L. Cooper and D.M. Rousseau, eds. *Trends in Organizational Behavior*, vol. 3 (New York, NY: John Wiley & Sons, 1996), pp. 49–64.

52. J. Sorenson, H. Grove, and T. Sorenson, "Detecting Management Fraud: The Role of the Independent Auditor," in *White-Collar Crime: Theory and Research*, eds. G. Geis and E. Stotland (Beverly Hills, CA: Sage, 1980), pp. 221–251.

53. Canadian Health Care Anti-Fraud Association at http://www.chcaa.org

54. Charles Piper, "10 Popular Health Care Provider Fraud Schemes, 'Do No Harm' Isn't Their Motto," *Fraud Magazine* (January/February 2013) at at http://www.fraud-magazine.com/article.aspx?id=4294976280 (accessed 21 October 2015).

55. Joanne Levasseur, "Canadian Doctors' Improper Insurance Billings near $25M," *CBC News* (December 18, 2014) at at http://www.cbc.ca/news/canada/manitoba/canadian-doctors-improper-insurance-billings-near-25m-1.2877135 (accessed 21 October 2015).

56. Joseph Brean, "Medical Regulator Drops Charges Against Doctor," *National Post* (16 November 2011)_at http://news.nationalpost.com/news/canada/medical-regulator-drops-charges-against-doctor (accessed 21 October 2015).

57. Barbara Sibbald, "MDs Get Jail Terms, Fines as New Police Squad Targets Health Fraud," *Canadian Medical Association Journal* 163 (2000): 591.

58. Marnie Ko, "A Banker with Flash," *The Report/Newsmagazine* (National Edition) (9 September 2002): 33–35, at http://www.highbeam.com/doc/1G1-94199870.html (accessed 17 November 2011).

59. Tracy Huffman, "Jail Time Cut for ATM Fraud Pair," *Toronto Star* (11 September 2003), p. A6.

60. Anonymous. "Health Centre Clerk Charged in $1M ATM Fraud," *Calgary Herald* (12 November 2010), p. A15.

61. Canada Revenue Agency at http://www.cra-arc.gc.ca/convictions/ (accessed 21 October 2015).

62. Jamie Golombek, "What Does It Take to Be Jailed in Canada for a Tax Offence? *Financial Post* (8 January 2014) at http://business.financialpost.com/personal-finance/taxes/what-does-it-take-to-be-jailed-in-canada-for-a-tax-offence (accessed 21 October 2015).

63. Michael Maltz and Stephen Pollack, "Suspected Collusion Among Bidders," in *White-Collar Crime: Theory and Research*, eds. G. Geis and E. Stotland (Beverly Hills, CA: Sage, 1980), pp. 174–98; see also the Associated Press, "British Airways and Others Settle a Suit Over Price-Fixing," *The New York Times* (8 June 2011), p. 8.

64. Tim Carrington, "Federal Probes of Contractors Rise for Year," *The Wall Street Journal* (23 February

1987), p. 50; Tony Illia, "Guilty Pleas in Midwest Concrete Cartel Probe," *Engineering News-Record*, vol. 267, iss. 7 (12 September 2011): 18.

65. A. Freeman and C. Forcese, "Get Tough on Corporate Crime," *Toronto Star* (17 November 1994), p. A31.

66. Eradicating Ecocide. "The Solution: Proposal for Ecocide to Be the 5th International Crime Against Peace, *Eradicating Ecocide* (2011). at http://eradicatingecocide.com/ (accessed 3 October 20110.

67. Steven Edwards, "Madoff Gets 150 Years; Fraud Victims Cheer as Financier Sentenced in $65B Ponzi Scheme," *Star—Phoenix* (30 June 2009), p. C5.

68. Herbert Edelhertz and Charles Rogovin, eds., *A National Strategy for Containing White-Collar Crime* (Lexington, MA: Lexington Books, 1980), Appendix A, pp. 122–123.

69. Kathleen Daly, "Gender and Varieties of White-Collar Crime," *Criminology* 27 (1989): 769–793.

70. Donald Cressey, *Other People's Money: A Study of the Social Psychology of Embezzlement* (Glencoe, IL: Free Press, 1973).

71. Phone Busters, the Canadian Anti-Fraud Call Centre, at http://www.phonebusters.com.

72. Donald *Cressey, Other People's Money: A Study of the Social Psychology of Embezzlement* (Glencoe, IL: Free Press, 1973). p. 96.

73. Travis Hirschi and Michael Gottfredson, "Causes of White-Collar Crime," *Criminology* 25 (1987): 949–974.

74. Michael Gottfredson and Travis Hirschi, *A General Theory of Crime* (Stanford, CA: Stanford University Press, 1990), p. 191.

75. David Simon and D. Stanley Eitzen, *Elite Deviance* (Boston: Allyn and Bacon, 1982), p. 28.

76. This section relies heavily on Albert Reiss, Jr., "Selecting Strategies of Social Control over Organizational Life," in *Enforcing Regulation*, eds. Keith Hawkins and John M. Thomas (Boston: Klowver, 1984), pp. 25–37.

77. Raymond Michalowski and Ronald Kramer, "The Space Between Laws: The Problem of Corporate Crime in a Transnational Context," *Social Problems* 34 (1987): 34–53.

78. "Go Directly to Jail: White Collar Sentencing After the Sarbanes-Oxley Act," *Harvard Law Review*, vol. 122, iss. 6 (April 2009): 1728–1749; David Weisburd, Elin Waring, and Ellen Chayet, "Specific Deterrence in a Sample of Offenders Convicted of White-Collar Crimes," *Criminology*, vol. 33, iss. 4 (November 1995): 587–607; see also Steven Klepper and Daniel Nagin, "The Deterrent Effect of Perceived Certainty and Severity of Punishment Revisited," *Criminology* 27 (1989): 721–746.

79. Geis, "White-Collar and Corporate Crime," p. 154.

80. Norm Keith, *Corporate Crime and Accountability in Canada—From Prosecutions to Corporate Social Responsibility* (Markham, ON: LexisNexis Publishers, 2011).

81. Ellen Bressner and Shawn L. Graham, "Canada's First Criminal Conviction for Insider Trading," *Lexocology* at http://www.lexology.com/library/detail.aspx?g=9fea44e0-a422-42eb-9c89-5971e0f9c 223 (accessed 17 November 2011).

82. Frank Pearce and Steve Tombs, "Hazards, Law and Class: Contextualizing the Regulation of Corporate Crime," *Social and Legal Studies* 6 (1997): 79–107, p. 92.

83. See, generally, President's Commission on Organized Crime, "Report to the President and the Attorney General," *The Impact: Organized Crime Today* (Washington, DC: U.S. Government Printing Office, 1986) hereafter cited as *Organized Crime Today*; "2006 Annual Report on Organized Crime in Canada," *Trends in Organized Crime*, vol. 10, iss. 3 (September 2007): 76–88.

84. W. Shaw and V. Barry "Case: Ford Pinto: Business Ethics," in *Moral Issues in Business*, 8th ed. (Belmont CA: Wadsworth, 2001) at http://philosophia.uncg.edu/phi361-metivier/module-2-why-does-business-need-ethics/case-the-ford-pinto (accessed 21 October 2015).

85. Ibid.

86. Norm Keith, "After 10 Years, Bill C-45 Yields Few Prosecutions," *Occupational Safety Newsletter* (23 April 2014) at http://www.cos-mag.com/legal/legal-columns/3900-after-10-years-bill-c-45-yields-few-prosecutions.html (accessed 21 October 2015).

87. Frederick Martens and Michele Cunningham-Niederer, "Media Magic, Mafia Mania," *Federal Probation* 49 (1985): 60–68.

88. Stephen Schneider, *Iced: The Story of Organized Crime in Canada* (Toronto: John Wiley and Sons, 2009).

89. "The History of Cross-Border Smuggling," at http://www.canadiangeographic.ca/magazine/ja10/timeline/al-capone-smuggling.html (accessed 21 October 2015).

90. Ibid.

91. Criminal Code of Canada, section 467.1(1).

92. Criminal Intelligence Service Canada, "Backgrounder: Organized Crime in Canada, 2014," at http://www.cisc.gc.ca/media/2014/2014-08-22-eng.htm (accessed 21 October 2015); "2006 Annual Report on Organized Crime in Canada," *Trends in Organized Crime*, vol. 10, iss. 3 (September 2007): 76–88.

93. *Organized Crime Today*, pp. 7–8.

94. "Editorial: Organized Crime: Overview," *RCMP Gazette* 60 (1998): 3.

95. Criminal Intelligence Service Canada, *Annual Report*, 2009.

96. "Organized Crime Growing," *Blue Line Magazine*, February 2003, p. 16.

97. "CBC News In Depth: Biker Gangs in Canada," *CBC News* (15 April 2009), at http://www.cbc.ca/news/canada/story/2009/04/01/f-biker-gangs.html.

98. Criminal Intelligence Service Canada, *Annual Report*, 2009.

99. Donald Cressey, *Theft of the Nation* (New York: Harper and Row, 1969).

100. *Organized Crime Today*, p. 489.

101. Dwight Smith, *The Mafia Mystique* (New York: Basic Books, 1975).

102. Philip Jenkins and Gary Potter, "The Politics and Mythology of Organized Crime: A Philadelphia Case Study," *Journal of Criminal Justice* 15 (1987): 473–484.

103. Alan Block, *East Side/West Side* (New Brunswick, NJ: Transaction Books, 1983).

104. *Organized Crime Today*, p. 11.

105. Jenkins and Potter, "The Politics and Mythology of Organized Crime."

106. William Chambliss, *On the Take* (Bloomington: Indiana University Press, 1978).

107. Criminal Intelligence Service Canada, *Annual Report*, 2010.

Chapter 13

1. Criminal Code (R.S.C., 1985, c. C-46) Part VII Disorderly Houses, Gaming and Betting Definitions 197. (1)

2. "Owner of Swing Club Convicted," The *StarPhoenix* [Saskatoon, Sask] (23 July 1999), p. A4.

3. Clark Campbell, "Group Sex at Swingers Club Not Shocking, Defence Contends: Owner Charged: Investigator Quizzed on Porn Films He Has Viewed," *National Post* (27 Jan 1999), p. A9.

4. Lyne Casavant and James R. Robertson, "The Evolution of Pornography Law in Canada. Law and Government Division, Parliament of Canada (revised 25 October 2007) at http://www.parl.gc.ca/Content/LOP/researchpublications/843-e.htm (accessed 22 October 2015).

5. *R. v. Labaye*, [2005] 3 S.C.R. 728, 2005 SCC 80.

6. Edwin Schur, *Crimes Without Victims* (Englewood Cliffs, NJ: Prentice Hall, 1965).

7. Andrea Dworkin, quoted in "Where Do We Stand on Pornography?" *Ms* (January– February 1994), p. 34.

8. Jennifer E. Cobbina, and Sharon S. Oselin, "It's Not Only for the Money: An Analysis of Adolescent versus Adult Entry into Street Prostitution," *Sociological Inquiry*, vol. 81, iss. 3 (August 2011); 310–332.

9. Morris Cohen, "Moral Aspects of the Criminal Law," *Yale Law Journal* 49 (1940): 1017.

10. See Joel Feinberg, *Social Philosophy* (Englewood Cliffs, NJ: Prentice Hall, 1973), chap. 2, 3.

11. *United States v. 12 200-ft Reels of Super 8mm Film*, 413 U.S. 123 (1973) at 137.

12. Irving Kristol, "Liberal Censorship and the Common Culture," *Society* 36 (September 1999): 5.

13. Wayne La Fave and Austin Scott, Jr., *Criminal Law* (St. Paul, MN: West, 1986), p. 12.

14. Ibid.

15. Daphne Bramham, "Bountiful Polygamist Leader Files to Have Criminal Charge Quashed; Familiar Petition," *The Vancouver Sun* (28 February 2015), p.A16.

16. Howard Becker, *Outsiders* (New York: Macmillan, 1963), pp. 13–14.

17. Brad Badelt, "'Prince of Pot' Busted: Police Raid Seed Shop of Activist Marc Emery," *The Windsor Star* (30 July 2005), p. A13; Ian Mulgrew, "Prince of Pot's Prosecutor Declares Prohibition a Bust; Law Professor Declares That U.S. Marijuana Laws Endanger the Public—a week Before Marc Emery Is Sentenced," *The Vancouver Sun* (7 September 2010), p. A.7; Jonathon Gatehouse, "The Interview," *Maclean's* (18 August 2014), vol. 127, iss. 32: 14–15.

18. See, generally, V. Bullogh, *Sexual Variance in Society and History* (Chicago: University of Chicago Press, 1958), pp. 143–144.

19. Spencer Rathus, *Human Sexuality* (New York: Holt, Rinehart and Winston, 1983), p. 463.

20. Jeannie Marshall, "Put Aside Disgust, Revulsion': Lawyer for Dominatrix Says Moral Judgment Shouldn't affect judge's ruling," *The Ottawa Citizen* (1 September 1998), p. A5.

21. *Canada (Attorney General) v. Bedford*, 2013 SCC 72, [2013] 3 S.C.R. 1101

22. Bill C-36, *An Act to Amend the Criminal Code in Response to the Supreme Court of Canada Decision in* Attorney General of Canada v. Bedford *and to Make Consequential Amendments to Other Acts*, Assented to 6 November 2014, Parliament of Canada, at http://www.parl.gc.ca/HousePublications/Publication.aspx?Pub=Bill&Doc=C-36 (accessed 22 October 2015).

23. Richard Warnica, "Barely Illegal Why Vice Still Thrives; Four Months After New Laws Aimed at Ending Prostitution Were Enacted, the Vast Grey Market for Sexual Services in Canada Remains, Unsurprisingly, Intact," *National Post* (9 May 2015), p. A8; James Keller, "Sex Workers Say New Anti-Prostitution Law Still Puts Them in Danger," *The Canadian Press* (6 November 2014); Sandra Ka Hon Chu, Jenn Clamen, Richard Elliott, Katrina Pacey, and Tara Santini, "Reckless Endangerment: Q&A on Bill C-36: *Protection of Communities and Exploited Persons Act*" (June 2014) Canadian HIV/AIDS Legal Network, Pivot Legal Society and Stella, l'amie de Maimie at http://www.parl.gc.ca/Content/SEN/Committee/412/lcjc/Briefs/C-36/C-36_brief_Cdn_HIV-AIDS%28Supplementary%29_E.pdf (accessed 22 October 2015).

24. Statistics Canada, "Table 252-0051, Incident-based Crime Statistics, by Detailed Violations Annual (number unless otherwise noted)," (1 June 2015).

25. Federal/Provincial/Territorial Working Group on Prostitution, Report and Recommendation in Respect of Legislation, Policy and Practices Concerning Prostitution-Related Activities, Canada, December 1998.

26. C. Benoit and L. Shumka, *Sex Work in Canada* (2015) at http://www.understandingsexwork.co

27. Evan Wood et al., "Sex Trade Involvement Is Associated with Elevated HIV Incidence Among Injection Drug Users in Vancouver," *Addiction Research & Theory*, vol. 15, iss. 3 (June 2007): 321–325; Kathleen N. Deering et al., "A Peer-Led Mobile Outreach Program and Increased Utilization of Detoxification and Residential Drug Treatment Among Female Sex Workers Who Use Drugs in a Canadian Setting," *Drug & Alcohol Dependence*, vol. 113, iss. 1 (January 2011): 46–54.

28. Melissa Hope Ditmore, "Prostitution and Sex Work," in *Historical Guides to Controversial Issues in America* (Santa Barbara, CA: Greenwood, 2011).

29. E. van derMeulen, E. M. Durisin, and V. Love, *Selling Sex; Experience, Advocacy and Research on Sex Work in Canada* (Vancouver: UBC Press, 2013).

30. Sheila Jeffreys, *The Industrial Vagina: The Political Economy of the Global Sex Trade* (London: Routledge, 2009)

31. E. van derMeulen, E. M. Durisin, and V. Love, *Selling Sex; Experience, Advocacy and Research on Sex Work in Canada* UBC Press, Vancouver, B.C.

32. Kohm and Selwood, *Sex Work and City Planning*; J. Fraser, Report of the Special Committee on Pornography and Prostitution, vol 2 (Ottawa: Supply and Services, 1985).

33. Sam Cooper, "Fort Nelson Licenses Escort Services Despite Opposition, *The Province*, 14 April 2010, p. A9.

34. Sheila Jeffreys, *The Industrial Vagina: The Political Economy of the Global Sex Trade* (London: Routledge, 2009)

35. C. Benoit and L. Shumka, *Sex Work in Canada* (2015) at http://www.understandingsexwork.com

36. Treena Orchard, Sara Farr, Susan Macphail, Cass Wender, and Christine Wilson, "Expanding the Scope of Inquiry: Exploring Accounts of Childhood and Family Life Among Sex workers in London, Ontario," *Canadian Journal of Human Sexuality* 23(1) (2014): 9–18, doi:10.3138/cjhs.2323.

37. Bill McCarthy, Cecilia Benoit, and Mikael Jansson, "Sex Work: A Comparative Study," *Arch Sex Behav* (2014) 43:1379–1390, doi: 10.1007/s10508-014-0281-7.

38. Jane Scoular and Anna Carline, "A Critical Account of a 'Creeping Neo-Abolitionism': Regulating Prostitution in England and Wales," *Criminology & Criminal Justice* 14(5) (November 2014): , vol. 14, iss. 5: 608–626; Joan Reid and Alex Piquero, "Age-Graded Risks for Commercial Sexual Exploitation of Male and Female Youth," *Journal of Interpersonal Violence* 29(9) (June 2014): 1747–1777, doi: 10.1177/0886260513511535; Jane Dodsworth, "Sexual Exploitation, Selling and Swapping Sex: Victimhood and Agency," *Child Abuse Review*, vol. 23 (2014): 185–199, doi: 10.1002/car.2282; Kennedy Saldanha and Derek Parenteau, "Well, If You Can't Smile You Should Go Home!' Experiences and Reflective Insights on Providing Outreach to Young Sex Trade Workers," *Children and Youth Services Review*, 35 (2013): 1276–1283 doi. org/10.1016/j.childyouth.2013.04.015

39. Mark Ward, "Web Porn: Just How Much Is There? BBC News (1 July 2013) at http://www.bbc.com/news/technology-23030090 (accessed 23 October 2015); Inquisitr, "Study Shows Child Pornography to Be Largest Contributor to 'Dark Net' Usage" (2 January 2015) at http://www.inquisitr.com/1721824/study-child-pornography-dark-net-usage/#5hVheuQ2Ugk8yhED.99 (accessed 23 October 2015); Angus Crawford. "Dark Net 'Used by Tens of Thousands of Pedophiles,'" BBC News (19 June 2014) at http://www.bbc.com/news/technology-27885502 (accessed 23 October 2015).

40. Rosie DiManno, "Ontario's Former Deputy Education Minister Ben Levin Pleads Guilty to Child Pornography Related Charges," *Toronto Star* (3 March 2015); Leslie Ferenc, "Professor to Plead Guilty to Child Exploitation," *Toronto Star* (17 January 2015), p. A11.

41. Criminal Code of Canada, R. S.C., 1985, c. C-46 L.R

42. *Merriam-Webster Dictionary* (New York: Pocket Books, 1974), p. 484.

43. *Martin's Annual Criminal Code, 2012* (Aurora, ON: Canada Law Book, 2011), p. 311; Richard Barnhorst and Sherrie Barnhorst, *Criminal Law and the Canadian Criminal Code*, 4th ed. (Toronto: McGraw-Hill Ryerson, 2004).

44. James D. Griffith, Sharon Mitchell, Christian L. Hart, Lea T. Adams, and Lucy L. Gu, "Pornography Actresses: An Assessment of the Damaged Goods Hypothesis," *Journal of Sex Research*, 50(7) (2013): 621–632, doi: 10.1080/00224499.2012.719168; James Griffith et al. "Characteristics of Pornography Film Actors: Self-Report versus Perceptions of College Students," , vol. 42, iss. 4 (May 2013): 637–647.

45. Joshua B. Grubbs, Julie J. Exline, and Kenneth I. Pargament, "Internet Pornography Use: Perceived Addiction, Psychological Distress, and the Validation of a Brief Measure," *Journal of Sex & Marital Therapy*, 41(1) (2015): 83–106, doi: 10.1080/0092623X.2013.842192; Michael E. Levin, Jason Lillis, and Steven C. Hayes, "When Is Online Pornography Viewing Problematic Among College Males? Examining the Moderating Role of Experiential Avoidance," *Sexual Addiction & Compulsivity*, vol. 19, iss. 3 (July–September 2012): 168–180, doi. 10.1080/10720162.2012.657150; Vincent Egan and Reena Parmar, "Dirty Habits? Online Pornography Use, Personality, Obsessionality, and Compulsivity," *Journal of Sex & Marital Therapy*, 39 (2013): 394–409, doi: 10.1080/0092623X.2012.710182.

46. Stephanie Delaney, *Child Pornography and Sexual Exploitation of Children Online*, ECPAT International (September 2009) at http://www.ecpat.net/ei/Publications/ICT/Child%20Friendly_Child%20Pornography_FINAL.pdf (accessed 8 November 2011).

47. Ann Wolbert Burgess (ed.), *Child Pornography and Sex Rings* (Lexington, MA: Lexington Books, 1984).

48. Statistics Canada, "Table 252-0051, Incident-based Crime Statistics, by Detailed Violations Annual (Number Unless Otherwise Noted)."

49. Vanessa Vega1 and Neil M. Malamuth, "Predicting Sexual Aggression: The Role of Pornography in the Context of General and Specific Risk Factors," *Aggressive Behavior*, vol. 33 (2007): 104–117.

50. Drew A. Kingston, Neil M. Malamuth, Paul Fedoroff, and William L. Marshall, "The Importance of Individual Differences in Pornography Use: Theoretical Perspectives and Implications for Treating Sexual Offenders," *Journal of Sex Research*, 46(2–3) (2009): 216–232, doi: .1080/00224490902747701.

51. Eric W. Owens, Richard J. Behun, Jill C. Manning, and Rory C. Reid, "The Impact of Internet Pornography on Adolescents: A Review of the Research, *Sexual Addiction & Compulsivity*," (19) (2012): 99–122, doi: 10.1080/10720162.2012.660431; Eileen M. Alexy, Ann W. Burgess, and Robert A. Prentky, "Pornography Use as a Risk Marker for an Aggressive Pattern of Behavior Among Sexually Reactive Children and Adolescents," *J Am Psychiatr Nurses Assoc* 14(6) (2009): 442–453. doi: 10.1177/1078390308327137.

52. Neil Malamuth, Danile Linz, and René Weber, "The Internet and Aggression: Motivation, Disinhibitory and Opportunity Aspects," pp. 120–142, in *The Social Net*, 2nd edition, ed. Yair Amichai-Hamburger (Oxford: Oxford University Press, 2013.

53. *Martin's Annual Criminal Code, 2012* (Aurora, ON: Canada Law Book, 2011), p. 314; Barnhorst and Barnhorst, *Criminal Law and the Canadian Criminal Code*.

54. Ibid.

55. *Martin's Annual Criminal Code, 2012*; Barnhorst and Barnhorst, *Criminal Law and the Canadian Criminal Code*.

56. Criminal Code, Section 163 (8), *Martin's Annual Criminal Code, 2012*, p. 314.

57. Ibid.

58. *Protecting Canadians from Online Crime Act* (S.C. 2014, c. 31)

59. Katherine Marshall, "Gambling, 2011" cat. no. 75-001-X, Chart A, Net Revenue from Government-run Gambling at http://www.statcan.gc.ca/pub/75-001-x/2010108/pdf/11297-eng.pdf (accessed 23 October 2015).

60. Jason J. Azmier, *Gambling in Canada: Final Report and Recommendations* (Calgary: Canada West Foundation, 2001).

61. Statistics Canada (June 1, 2015). Table 252-0051, Incident-based Crime tatistics, by Detailecd Violations Annual (number unless otherwise noted)."

62. Brian J Cox, Nancy Yu, Tracie O Afifi, and Robert Ladouceur, "A National Survey of Gambling Problems in Canada," *Canadian Journal of Psychiatry*, vol. 50, iss. 4 (March 2005): 213–217.

63. Katherine Marshall "Gambling, 2011."

64. N. A. Dowling, and M. Brown, "Commonalities in the Psychological Factors Associated with Problem Gambling and Internet Dependence," *Cyberpsychology, Behavior, and Social Networking*, vol. 13, no. 4 (2010).

65. Jennifer N. Arthur, Robert J. Williams, and Yale D Belanger, "The Relationship between Legal Gambling and Crime in Alberta," *Canadian Journal of Criminology & Criminal Justice*, vol. 56, iss. 1 (January 2014): 49–84, doi: 10.3138/cjccj.2012.E51.

66. Ralph Weisheit, "Studying Drugs in Rural Areas: Notes from the Field," *Journal of Research in Crime and Delinquency* 30 (1993): 213–232.

67. David Hewitt, Gary Vinje, and Patricia Macneil (eds.), *Horizons Three: Young Canadians' Alcohol and Other Drug Use: Increasing Our Understanding* (Ottawa: Health Canada, 1995).

68. Health Canada, *Canadian Alcohol and Drug Use Monitoring Survey – Summary of Results for 2011* at http://www.hc-sc.gc.ca/hc-ps/drugs-drogues/stat/_2011/summary-sommaire-eng.php (accessed 23 October 2015).

69. Public Safety Canada—Substance Abuse at http://www.publicsafety.gc.ca/cnt/cntrng-crm/crrctns/sbstnc-bs-eng.aspx.

70. Irfan A. Dhalla et al., "Prescribing of Opioid Analgesics and Related Mortality Before and After the Introduction of Long-acting Oxycodone," *CMAJ* 181(12) (8 December 2009): 891–896, doi: 10.1503/cmaj.090784.

71. Connie I. Carter and Brittany Graham, "Opioid Overdose Prevention & Response in Canada," Policy Brief Series; Authorship Canadian Drug Policy Coalition/Simon Fraser University (2013) at http://drugpolicy.ca/wpcontent/uploads/2014/07/CDPC_OverdosePreventionPolicy_Final_July2014.pdf.

72. Jacques Gallant Fentanyl, "Use By Opioid Addicts on the Rise; Drug Addicts Are Turning to Highly Potent Fentanyl Now That Oxycontin Is No Longer Available," *Toronto Star* (1 August 2013) at http://www.thestar.com/news/gta/2013/08/01/fentanyl_use_by_opioid_addicts_on_the_rise.html (accessed 23 October 2015); Jason Van Rassel, "Provincewide Warning Issued as Officials Link Fentanyl to 100 Deaths Last Year," *Calgary Herald* (18 March 2015) at http://calgaryherald.com/news/crime/provincewide-warning-issued-as-officials-link-fentanyl-to-100-deaths-last-year (accessed 23 October 2015).

73. Global Commission on Drug Policy, "Taking Control: Pathways to Drug Strategies that Work," (September 2014) at http://www.globalcommissionondrugs.org/

74. "Former ONDCP Senior Advisor on Marijuana and Harm Reduction," *Alcoholism & Drug Abuse Weekly* (31 October 2011): 6–7 at doi: 10.1002/adaw; E. Chamberlain and R. Solomon, "Drug-Impaired Driving in Canada: Review and Recommendations, MADD Canada (2012) at http://www.madd.ca/media/docs/MADD-Canada_Drug-Impaired-Driving-Policy_November-2012.pdf.

75. James Inciardi, *The War on Drugs* (Palo Alto, CA: Mayfield, 1986), p. 2.

76. See, generally, David Pittman, "Drug Addiction and Crime," in *Handbook of Criminology*, ed. D. Glazer (Chicago: Rand McNally, 1974), pp. 209–232; Board of Directors, National Council on Crime and Delinquency, "Drug Addiction: A Medical, Not a Law Enforcement, Problem," *Crime and Delinquency* 20 (1974): 4–9.

77. Associated Press, "Records Detail Royals' Turn-of-Century Drug Use," *Boston Globe* (29 August 1993), p. 13.

78. Neil Boyd, *Canadian Law: An Introduction* (Toronto: Harcourt Brace Canada, 1998).

79. Gerald Hallowell, "Prohibition," at http://www.thecanadianencyclopedia.com, 2005.

80. Ibid.

81. McCaghy, *Deviant Behavior*, p. 280.

82. Gerald Hallowell, "Prohibition."

83. McCaghy, *Deviant Behavior*.

84. "Angus Reid Public Opinion: Majority of Canadians Would Legalize Marijuana, But Not Other Drugs," Vision Critical website at http://www.visioncritical.com/category/global-opinions-and-trends (accessed 1 November 2011).

85. CBC News, "CAMH Calls for Legalization of Marijuana; Current System 'Failing to Prevent

or Reduce the Harms' of Pot Use, Researcher Says," (9 October 2014) at at http://www.cbc.ca/news/canada/toronto/camh-calls-for-legalization-of-marijuana-1.2793460 (accessed 23 October 2015).

86. "Canada's High Court to Rule on Safe-Injection Site," *Canadian Press* (9 May 2011) at http://www.thestar.com/news/canada/article/987998-canada-s-high-court-to-rule-on-safe-injection-site (accessed 8 August 2011).

87. "Vancouver's Injection Clinic Gets Supreme Court Blessing to Stay Open," *Toronto Star* (1 October 2011) at http://www.thestar.com/news/article/1062370 (accessed 1 November 2011).

88. Jillian Boyce, Adam Cotter, and Samuel Perreault, "Police-reported Crime Statistics in Canada, 2013," *Juristat*, cat. no. 85-002-X, Canadian Centre for Justice Statistics Release date (23 July 2014); Statistics Canada, "Table 252-0051, Incident-based Crime Statistics, by Detailed Violations Annual (number unless otherwise noted)."

89. CBC News, "Date-Rape Drug Valued at $15M Seized in B.C" (26 January 2011) at http://www.cbc.ca/news/canada/british-columbia/story/2011/01/26/bc-record-ketamine-bust.html (accessed 23 October 2015).

90. Richard Curtis, "The Improbable Transformation of Inner-City Neighborhoods: Crime, Violence, Drugs, and Youth in the 1990s," *Journal of Criminal Law & Criminology*, vol. 88, iss. 4 (Summer 1998): 1233–1276.

91. Marvin Krohn, Alan Lizotte, Terence Thornberry, Carolyn Smith, and David McDowall, "Reciprocal Causal Relationships Among Drug Use, Peers, and Beliefs: A Five-Wave Panel Model," *Journal of Drug Issues* 26 (1996): 205–228.

92. R. Cloward and L. Ohlin, *Delinquency and Opportunity: A Theory of Delinquent Gangs* (Glencoe, IL: Free Press, 1960).

93. Lening Zhang, John Welte, and William Wieczorek, "Youth Gangs, Drug Use and Delinquency," *Journal of Criminal Justice* 27 (1999): 101–109.

94. See Elsbeth Tupker, "Youth and Drugs and Mental Health: A Resource for Professionals" (Toronto: Centre for Addiction and Mental Health, 2004).

95. Sally Weinrich and Sally Hardin, "Social Support and Psychological Correlates of High School Students Who Use Illicit Drugs," *American Journal of Health Studies*, vol. 13, iss. 1 (1997): 17.

96. Substance Abuse and Mental Health Services Administration, Office of Applied Studies, "The Relationship Between Mental Health and Substance Abuse Among Adolescents," *Analytic Series: A-9*, 1999.

97. Alison Bass, "Mental Ills, Drug Abuse Linked," *Boston Globe*, 21 November 1990, p. 3.

98. D. W. Goodwin, "Alcoholism and Genetics," *Archives of General Psychiatry* 42 (1985): 171–174.

99. For a thorough review of this issue, see John Petraitis, Brian Flay, and Todd Miller, "Reviewing Theories of Adolescent Substance Use: Organizing Pieces in the Puzzle," *Psychological Bulletin* 117 (1995): 67–86.

100. Jennifer O'Loughlin, "Variant Gene Causes Students to Become Addicted to Tobacco: McGill Study," *Telegram* (St. John's, Nfld.) (24 November 2004), p. A12.

101. Judith Brooks and Li-Jung Tseng, "Influences of Parental Drug Use, Personality, and Child Rearing on the Toddler's Anger and Negativity," *Genetic, Social and General Psychology Monographs* 122 (1996): 107–128.

102. Andrew Percy, Maeve Thornton, and Patrick McCrystal, "The Extent and Nature of Family Alcohol and Drug Use: Findings from the Belfast Youth Development Study," *Child Abuse Review*, vol. 17, iss. 6 (November/December 2008): 371–386.

103. Denise Kandel and Mark Davies, "Friendship Networks, Intimacy, and Illicit Drug Use in Young Adulthood: A Comparison of Two Competing Theories," *Criminology* 29 (1991): 441–471.

104. Robert John Zagar, Kenneth G. Busch, William M. Grove, and John Russell Hughes, "Summary of Studies of Abused Infants and Children Later Homicidal, and Homicidal, Assaulting Later Homicidal, and Sexual Homicidal Youth and Adults," *Psychological Reports*, vol. 104, iss. 1 (February 2009): 17–45.

105. D. Baer and J. Corrado, "Heroin Addict Relationships with Parents During Childhood and Early Adolescent Years," *Journal of Genetic Psychology* 124 (1974): 99–103.

106. John Wallace and Jerald Bachman, "Explaining Racial/Ethnic Differences in Adolescent Drug Use: The Impact of Background and Lifestyle," *Social Problems* 38 (1991): 333–357.

107. John Donovan, "Problem-Behavior Theory and the Explanation of Adolescent Marijuana Use," *Journal of Drug Issues* 26 (1996): 379–404.

108. Jeanette Østergaard, "Learning to Become an Alcohol User: Adolescents Taking Risks and Parents Living with Uncertainty," *Addiction Research & Theory*, vol. 17, iss. 1 (February 2009): 30–53.

109. Ibid.

110. Steve Sussman, Nadra Lisha, and Mark Griffiths, "Prevalence of the Addictions: A Problem of the Majority or the Minority?" *Evaluation & the Health Professions* 34 (1) (March 2011): 3–56; and Michael Newcomb and Mitchell Earleywine, "Intrapersonal Contributors to Drug Use: The Willing Host," *American Behavioral Scientist* 39 (7) (June 1996): 823–837.

111. Andrew Golub and Bruce Johnson, "The Multiple Paths Through Alcohol, Tobacco and Marijuana to Hard Drug Use Among Arrestees," paper presented at the annual meeting of the American Society of Criminology, San Diego, November 1997.

112. Inciardi, *The War on Drugs*, p. 60.

113. Mia Dauvergne, "Trends in Police-reported Drug Offences in Canada, Statistics Canada, *Juristat*, vol. 29, no. 2 (May 2009), cat. 85-002 _ X.

114. Josee Savoie, "Homicide in Canada, 2002," Statistics Canada, Canadian Centre for Justice Statistics, cat. no. 85-002- XIE, vol. 23, no. 8.

115. Ibid.

116. Kathryn Graham, Sharon Bernards, Sharon Wilsnack, and Gerhard Gmel, "Alcohol May Not Cause Partner Violence But It Seems to Make It Worse: A Cross National Comparison of the Relationship Between Alcohol and Severity of Partner Violence," *Journal of Interpersonal Violence* 26 (8) (May 2011): 1503–1523 and Besserer and Trainor, "Criminal Victimization in Canada, 1999."

117. Douglas B. Marlowe et al., "Targeting Dispositions for Drug-Involved Offenders: A Field Trial of the Risk and Needs Triage (RANT)™," *Journal of Criminal Justice*, vol. 39, iss. 3 (May 2011): 253–260; Mark A.R. Kleiman, and Lowry Heussler, "Crime-Minimizing Drug Policy," *Journal of Criminal Justice*, vol. 39, iss. 3 (May 2011): 286–288; and Charles Faupel and Carl Klockars, "Drugs–Crime Connections: Elaborations from the Life Histories of Hard-Core Heroin Addicts," *Social Problems* 34 (1987): 54–68.

118. Carrie Oser et al., "Criminality Among Rural Stimulant Users in the United States," *Crime & Delinquency*, vol. 57, iss. 4 (July 2011): 600–621; and Michael E. Ezell and Emily E. Tanner-Smith, "Examining the Role of Lifestyle and Criminal History Variables on the Risk of Homicide Victimization," *Homicide Studies*, vol. 13, iss. 2 (May 2009): 144–173.

119. M. Douglas Anglin, Barry S. Brown, Richard Dembo, and Carl Leukefeld, "Criminality and Addiction: Selected Issues for Future Policies, Practice, & Research," *Journal of Drug Issues*, vol. 39, iss. 1 (Winter 2009): 89–99.

120. Paul Goldstein, "The Drugs–Violence Nexus: A Tripartite Conceptual Framework," *Journal of Drug Issues* 15 (1985): 493–506; Marvin Krohn, Alan Lizotte, and Cynthia Perez, "The Interrelationship Between Substance Use and Precocious Transitions to Adult Sexuality," *Journal of Health and Social Behavior* 38 (1997): 87–103, p. 88; Richard Jessor, "Risk Behavior in Adolescence: A Psychosocial Framework for Understanding and Action," in *Adolescents at Risk: Medical and Social Perspectives*, ed. D. E. Rogers and E. Ginzburg (Boulder, CO: Westview, 1992).

121. Boyd, *Canadian Law: An Introduction*.

122. Ibid.

123. Ibid.

124. Ibid.

125. *Safe Streets and Communities Act* (S.C. 2012, c. 1) at http://laws-lois.justice.gc.ca/eng/annualstatutes/2012_1/page-1.html

126. *Martin's Annual Criminal Code, 2012*.

127. Department of Justice Canada "Impaired Driving," at http://www.justice.gc.ca/eng/pi/pcvi-cpcv/id-cafa.html (accessed 11 November 2011).

128. Andrew B. Whitford and Jeff Yates, *Presidential Rhetoric and the Public Agenda: Constructing the War on Drugs* (Baltimore, MD: Johns Hopkins University Press, 2009).

129. U.S. Department of State, 1998 International Narcotics Control Strategy Report (February 1999).

130. Clifford Krauss, "Neighbors Worry About Colombian Aid," *The New York Times* (25 August 2000), p. A3.

131. John Intini, "Guns in the Sun," *Maclean's*, vol. 120, iss. 21 (4 April 2007): 23–24; Stephen Maher, "Keep Eyes Open in Mexico, But Don't Think About It Too Much," *The Gazette* [Montreal, Que] (26 January 2012): A.15.

132. Jacqueline M. Drew, "Police Responses to the Methamphetamine Problem: An Analysis of the Organizational and Regulatory Context," *Police Quarterly*, vol. 14, iss. 2 (June 2011): 99–123; and Government of Canada, National Anti-Drug Strategy Enforcement at http://www.nationalantidrugstrategy.gc.ca/enf-app.html (accessed 11 November 2011).

133. John S. Goldkamp and E. Rely Vilcic, "Targeted Enforcement and Adverse System Side Effects: The Generation of Fugitives in Philadelphia," *Criminology*, vol. 46, iss. 2 (May 2008): 371–409; and Mark Moore, *Drug Trafficking* (Washington, DC: National Institute of Justice, 1988).

134. Carol Kaplan, *Sentencing and Time Served* (Washington, DC: Bureau of Justice Statistics, 1987).

135. Peter Rossi, Richard Berk, and Alec Campbell, "Just Punishments: Guideline Sentences and Normative Consensus," *Journal of Quantitative Criminology* 13 (1997): 267–283.

136. Marnie Wallace, "Crime Statistics in Canada, 2003," *Juristat*, 24, 6 (Ottawa: Statistics Canada, 2001), cat. no. 85-002-XIE.

137. CBC News, "Canadians Split on Pot, Death Penalty: Poll," at http://www.cbc.ca/news/canada/story/2010/03/18/ekos-poll018.html (accessed 11 November 2011).

138. Robert Davis, Arthur Lurigio, and Dennis Rosenbaum, eds., *Drugs and the Community* (Springfield, IL: Charles Thomas, 1993), pp. xii–xv.

139. Saul Weingart, "A Typology of Community Responses to Drugs," in *Drugs and the Community*, eds. Robert Davis, Arthur Lurigio, and Dennis Rosenbaum (Springfield, IL: Charles Thomas, 1993), pp. 85–105.

140. Earl Wyson, Richard Aniskiewicz, and David Wright, "Truth and DARE: Tracking Drug Education to Graduation as Symbolic Politics," *Social Problems* 41 (1994): 448–471.

141. Ibid.

142. Dennis M. Gorman, and Charles Huber Jr., "The Social Construction of "Evidence-Based" Drug Prevention Programs: A Reanalysis of Data from the Drug Abuse Resistance Education (DARE) Program," *Evaluation Review*, vol. 33, iss. 4 (August 2009): 396–414; and Dennis Rosenbaum, Robert Flewelling, Susan Bailey, Chris Ringwalt, and Deanna Wilkinson, "Cops in the Classroom: A Longitudinal Evaluation of Drug Abuse Resistance Education (DARE)," *Journal of Research in Crime and Delinquency* 31 (1994): 3–31.

143. Mareanne Zawitz, *Drugs, Crime, and the Justice System* (Washington, DC: U.S. Government Printing Office, 1992), pp. 115–122.

144. Canadian Human Rights Commission, *Policy on Alcohol and Drug Testing* (Ottawa: Canadian Human Rights Commission, 2002).

145. Christine B. Kleinpeter, Jo Brocato, and Jeffrey J. Koob, "Does Drug Testing Deter Drug Court Participants from Using Drugs or Alcohol?" *Journal of Offender Rehabilitation*, vol. 49, iss. 6 (August/September 2010): 434–444; Charlotte L. Powell, Deborah Bamber, and Marilyn M. Christie, "Drug Treatment in the Criminal Justice System: Lessons Learned from Offenders on DTTOs," *Drugs: Education, Prevention & Policy*, vol. 14, iss. 4 (August 2007): 333–345; and John Goldkamp and Peter Jones, "Pretrial Drug-Testing Experiments in Milwaukee and Prince George's County: The Context of Implementation," *Journal of Research in Crime and Delinquency* 29 (1992): 430–465; Chester Britt, Michael Gottfredson, and John Goldkamp, "Drug Testing and Pretrial Misconduct: An Experiment on the Specific Deterrent Effects of Drug Monitoring Defendants on Pretrial Release," *Journal of Research in Crime and Delinquency* 29 (1992): 62–78.

146. See, generally, Peter Greenwood and Franklin Zimring, *One More Chance* (Santa Monica, CA: Rand Corporation, 1985).

147. Anna Greaves, David Best, Ed Day, and Angela Foster, "Young People in Coerced Drug Treatment: Does the UK Drug Intervention Programme Provide a Useful and Effective Service to Young Offenders?" *Addiction Research & Theory*, vol. 17, iss. 1 (February 2009): 17–29.

148. Elizabeth Evans, Douglas Longshore, Michael Prendergast, and Darren Urada, "Evaluation of the Substance Abuse and Crime Prevention Act: Client Characteristics, Treatment Completion and Re-Offending Three Years After Implementation," *Journal of Psychoactive Drugs*, vol. 38 (November 2006 Supplement 3): 357–367.

149. The following section is based on material found in Jerome Platt, "Vocational Rehabilitation of Drug Abusers," *Psychological Bulletin* 117 (1995): 416–433.

150. Diane Riley, *Drugs and Drug Policy in Canada: A Brief Review and Commentary* (Ottawa: Canadian Foundation for Drug Policy, 1998).

151. Janice Tibbetts, "Marijuana Nation?: More Canadians Smoking Pot; More Than Half Support Legalization," *Leader Post* [Regina, Sask] (25 November 2004): A1.

152. Global Commission on Drug Policy (2014) Taking Control: Pathways to Drug Strategies that Work (September 2014) at http://www.globalcommissionondrugs.org; Patricia Erickson, Diane Riley, Yuet Cheung, and Patrick O'Hare, eds., *Harm Reduction: A New Direction for Drug Policies and Programs* (Toronto: University of Toronto Press, 1997).

153. Ethan Nadelmann, "America's Drug Problem," *Bulletin of the American Academy of Arts and Sciences* 65 (1991): 24–40.

154. Ibid., p. 24.

155. Ethan Nadelmann, "Should We Legalize Drugs? History Answers Yes," *American Heritage* (February/March 1993): 41–56.

156. Caitlin Elizabeth Hughes and Alex Stevens, "What Can We Learn from the Portuguese Decriminalization of Illicit Drugs?" *British Journal of Criminology*, vol. 50, iss. 6 (November 2010): 999–1022; Collis Parrett, "Illicit Drugs Policy: Legal and International Perspectives," Meanjin, vol. 61, iss. 2 (2002): 59.

157. David Courtwright, "Should We Legalize Drugs? History Answers No," *American Heritage* (February/March 1993): 43–56.

158. C. W. J. Maris, "The Disasters of War: American Repression versus Dutch Tolerance in Drug Policy," *Journal of Drug Issues*, vol. 29, iss. 3 (Summer 1999): 493–510; and Charles B. Rangel, "Why Drug Legalization Should Be Opposed," *Criminal Justice Ethics*, vol. 17, iss. 2 (Summer/Fall 1998): 2; and Kathryn Ann Farr, "Revitalizing the Drug Decriminalization Debate," *Crime and Delinquency* 36 (1990): 223–237.

Chapter 14

1. P. Paganini, P "83 Percent of TOR Hidden Service Traffic Flowed to Pedo Websites. Study Finds," *Security Affairs* (2015) at http://securityaffairs.co/wordpress/31690/cyber-crime/pedo-websites-tor-network.html (accessed 25 October 2015).

2. Ibid.

3. Ryan Mac, "Who Is Ross Ulbricht? Piecing Together the Life of the Alleged Libertarian Mastermind Behind Silk Road," *Forbes* (2 October 2013) at http://www.forbes.com/sites/ryanmac/2013/10/02/who-is-ross-ulbricht-piecing-together-the-life-of-the-alleged-libertarian-mastermind-behind-silk-road (accessed 25 October 2015).

4. Evander Smart, Silk Road's Ross Ulbricht sentencing details revealed. (2015). *The Cointelegraph* (3 June 2015) at http://cointelegraph.com/news/114463/silk-roads-ross-ulbricht-sentencing-details-revealed (accessed 25 October 2015).

5. Stew Magnuson, "Proliferation of Cheap 3-D Printers Raises Security Concerns," *National Defense*, 98(720) (2013): 14-14.

6. D. S. Wall, "Policing Cybercrimes: Situating the Public Police in Networks of Security within Cyberspace," *Police Practice & Research*, 2 (2007) 183–205, doi: 10.1080/15614260701377729 at http://www.cyberdialogue.ca/wp-content/uploads/2011/03/David-Wall-Policing-CyberCrimes.pdf (accessed 25 October 2015).

7. See Council of Canadian Academies, "Policing Canada in the 21st Century: New Policing for New Challenges Ottawa (ON): The Expert Panel on the Future of Canadian Policing Models, Council of Canadian Academies" at http://www.scienceadvice.ca/uploads/eng/assessments%20and%20publications%20and%20news%20releases/policing/policing_fullreporten.pdf (accessed 25 October 2015).

8. David O. Friedrichs, "Transnational Crime and Global Criminology: Definitional, Typological and Contextual Conundrums," *Social Justice*, 34(2) (2007): 4–18.

9. D. Plamer, and I. Warren, *Global Criminology* (Australia: Lawbook Co., 2015).

10. Louise Shelly, John Picarelli, and Chris Corpora, in *Beyond Sovereignty*, ed. Maryann Cusimano Love (Boston: Wadsworth, Cengage Learning, 2011); Susanne Karstedt, "Comparing Cultures, Comparing Crime: Challenges, Prospects and Problems for a Global Criminology, *Crime, Law & Social Change, 36* (2001): 285–308.

11. K Clark, "(Un)importance of Somali Piracy, *Crime Law and Social Change, 63* (2015): 269–280, doi: 10.1007/s10611-015-9565-7.

12. David Smith, "Somali Pirates Hijacking Fewer Merchant Ships," *The Guardian, 23* (2012) at http://www.theguardian.com/world/2012/oct/23/somali-piracy-declines (accessed 25 October 2015).

13. K. Clark, "(Un)importance of Somali Piracy."

14. Christopher L. Daniels, *Somali Piracy and Terrorism in the Horn of Africa* (Global United States: Scarecrow Press, 2012); N. Anyu and S. Moki, "S. Africa: The Piracy Hot Spot and Its Implications for Global Security," *Mediterranean Quarterly, 20*:3, doi: 10.1215/10474552-2009-017.

15. N. Anyu and S. Moki, "S. Africa: The Piracy Hot Spot and Its Implications for Global Security,"

16. "World Bank: Pirate Trails: Tracking the Illicit Financial Flows from Piracy off the Horn of Africa," at http://web.worldbank.org/WBSITE/EXTERNAL/TOPICS/EXTFINANCIALSECTOR/0,contentMDK:23491862~pagePK:210058~piPK:210062~theSitePK:282885,00.html; (accessed 25 October 2015).

17. E. A. Anderson, "It's a Pirate's Life for Some: The Development of an Illegal Industry in Response to an Unjust Global Power Dynamic," Indi*ana Journal of Global Legal Studies*, vol. 17 (2) (2010) at http://www.repository.law.indiana.edu/cgi/viewcontent.cgi?article=1425&context=ijgls (accessed 25 October 2015).

18. Stewart Bell, "Somali Militants Training Pirates; 'Relationship of Convenience': Canadian Report," *National Post* (3 December 2009): A.6.

19. David Pugliese and Louisa Taylor, "Somali Pirate Cash 'Coming to Ottawa'; Money May Also Be Going Back to Fund Hijackings, Expert Says," *The Ottawa Citizen* (30 April 2010): A1.

20. Stewart Bell and Sarah Boesveld, "Complicit in My Suffering"; Somali Man a Former Member of Terrorist Group: Officials," *National Post* (15 June 2015): A2; J. Bahadur, *The Pirates of Somalia: Inside Their Hidden World Paperback* (New York: Harper-Collins Publishers, 2011).

21. Joseph Brean, "In the Belly of the Beast; Canadian Freelance journalist recalls 15 terrifying months spent in Somalian captivity," *National Post* (13 June 2015), A3.

22. Josh Wingrove and Kim Mackrael, "Why So Many Somali-Canadians Who Go West End Up Dead," *The Globe and Mail* (22 June 2012) at http://www.theglobeandmail.com/news/national/why-so-many-somali-canadians-who-go-west-end-up-dead/article4365992/?page=all (accessed 2 November 2015).

23. David O. Friedrichs, "Transnational Crime and Global Criminology: Definitional, Typological and Contextual Conundrums," *Social Justice*, 34(2) (2007): 4–18.

24. Ibid.

25. David B MacDonald. "Five Reasons the TRC Chose the Words 'Cultural Genocide,'" *The Globe and Mail* (6 July 2015), p. A12.

26. Erin Hanson, "The Residential School System," Indigenousfoundations.arts.ubc.ca, University of British Columbia at http://indigenousfoundations.arts.ubc.ca/home/government-policy/the-residential-school-system.html (accessed 25 October 2015).

27. Anonymous, "Canada's Asbestos Shame," *Edmonton Journal* (29 September 2009), p. A14.

28. "Special Report: Stunning New Details About the Radioactive Poisoning of Russian Dissident Alexander Litvinenko," *The National*, CBC Television Toronto: Canadian Broadcasting Corporation (6 April 2015).

29. Geoff Ward, "The Slow Violence of State Organized Race Crime," *Theoretical Criminology* (2014): 1–16, doi: 10.1177/1362480614550119 at http://tcr.sagepub.com/content/early/2014/09/23/1362480614550119.full.pdf (accessed 25 October 2015).

30. Ibid.

31. Adam Walinsky, "America's Crime Crisis; An American Essayist Observes That U.S. Cities Have Been Abandoned to the Rule of Thugs. Millions of Citizens Live with Terror in Their Everyday Life. The Numbers Are Chilling," *The Gazette* [Montreal, Que] (15 July 1995), p. B1.

32. Geoff Ward, "The Slow Violence of State Organized Race Crime."

33. Ibid.

34. E. Mayroz, "Ever Again? The United States, Genocide Suppression, and the Crisis in Darfur, *Journal of Genocide Research*, 10(3) (September 2008): 359–388.

35. Laura L. Finley, "Examining the State and State-Corporate Crime Surrounding Major Sport Events," *Contemporary Justice Review*, 16, 2 (2013): 228–250, doi:10.1080/10282580.2013.798518

36. Erica Illingworth, "2016 Río Olympics: Impending Doom?" *Washington Report on the Hemisphere* 35, 3 (6 March 2015) at http://www.highbeam.com/doc/1P3-3640577501.html (accessed 2 November 2015).

37. S. Mackenzie, "Systematic Crimes of the Powerful: Criminal Aspects of the Global Economy," *Social Justice*, 33(1) (2006): 162–182.

38. R. Fergusson, "Risk, Responsibilities and Rights: Reassessing the "Economic Causes of Crime" Thesis in a Recession," *Youth Justice*, 13(1) (2013): 31–56.

39. Felicity Capon, Greek PM Tsipras holds IMF 'criminally responsible' for debt crisis 16 June 2015, *Newsweek* (Accessed 30 October 2015 from: at http://europe.newsweek.com/greek-pm-tsipras-holds-imf-criminally-responsible-debt-328802.

40. United Nations Office on Drugs and Crime (UNODC). 2011, Accessed 30 October 2015 from: https://www.unodc.org/unodc/en/frontpage/2011/October/illicit-money_-how-much-is-out-there.html

41. "What Is Money Laundering?" The Financial Action Task Force (FATF) at http://www.fatf-gafi.org/pages/faq/moneylaundering (accessed 26 October 2015).

42. Export Development Canada, "Financial Crime in International Trade" at http://www.edc.ca/EN/Promotions/Documents/financial-crime.pdf (accessed 26 October 2015).

43. United Nations Office on Drugs and Crime, "Criminals Rake in $250 Billion Per Year in Counterfeit Goods That Pose Health and Safety Risks to Unsuspecting Public" (26 July 2012) at https://www.unodc.org/unodc/en/frontpage/2012/July/criminals-rake-in-250-billion-per-year-in-counterfeit-goods-that-pose-health-security-risks-to-unsuspecting-public.html (accessed 2 November 2015).

44. "Fact Sheet," International Trademark Association at http://www.inta.org/TrademarkBasics/FactSheets/Pages/Counterfeiting.aspx (accessed 26 October 2015).

45. Canadian Intellectual property Council, "Counterfeiting in the Canadian Market: How Do We Stop It?" at http://www.inta.org/TrademarkBasics/FactSheets/Pages/Counterfeiting.aspx (accessed 26 October 2015).

46. L. L. Shelley, "The Diverse Facilitators of Counterfeiting: A Regional Perspective," *Journal of International Affairs*, 66(1) (2012): 19.

47. Ibid.

48. Daniele Lepido, "Knockoff Sellers Troll Luxury Ads on Facebook; Quarter of Top-End Sites Linked to Shams," *The Windsor Star* (15 November 2014), p. C9.

49. Kaliyaperumal Karunamoorthi, "The Counterfeit Anti-Malarial Is a Crime Against Humanity: A Systematic Review of the Scientific Evidence," *Malaria Journal* 13 (2 June 2014): 209 at http://www.ncbi.nlm.nih.gov/pmc/articles/PMC4064812 (accessed 30 October 2015), doi: 10.1186/1475-2875-13-209.

50. Intellectual Property Rights Crime, Frequently Asked Questions (accessed 30 October 2015 from: at http://www.rcmp-grc.gc.ca/fep-pelf/ipr-dpi/faq-eng.htm

51. Jeff Gray, "Lululemon Cracks Down on knockoffs," *The Globe and Mail* (19 July 2014), p. B4.

52. Canadian Intellectual Property Council, Counterfeiting in the Canadian Market: How Do We Stop It?" June 2012. Canadian Chamber of Commerce, Ottawa, Ontario.

53. Angelo Young, "How China's Alibaba Helps Counterfeit Goods Reach US Pirates," *International Business Times* (31 July 2015) at http://www.ibtimes.com/how-chinas-alibaba-helps-counterfeit-goods-reach-us-pirates-amazon-1798174 (accessed 26 October 2015).

54. Canadian Intellectual Property Council, "Counterfeiting in the Canadian Market: How Do We Stop It?" (June 2012) Canadian Chamber of Commerce, Ottawa, Ontario.

55. Canada Department of Justice, "Human Trafficking" at http://www.justice.gc.ca/eng/cj-jp/tp/legis-loi.html (accessed 26 October 2015); Government of Canada, *Immigration and Refugee Protection Act* at http://laws-lois.justice.gc.ca/eng/acts/I-2.5 (accessed 26 October 2015).

56. C. Bruckert, "Trafficking in Human Beings and Organized Crime: A Literature Review" at http://

www.rcmp-grc.gc.ca/pubs/ccaps-spcca/traffick-eng.htm (accessed 26 October 2015).

57. "UN Protocol to Prevent, Suppress, and Punish Trafficking in Persons, Especially Women and Children"athttp://www.unodc.org/unodc/en/treaties/CTOC/index.html (accessed 26 October 2015).

58. UNODC website at http://www.unodc.org/cld/index.jspx (accessed 26 October 2015).

59. Public Safety Canada, "Human Trafficking" at http://www.publicsafety.gc.ca/cnt/cntrng-crm/hmn-trffckng/index-eng.aspx (accessed 26 October 2015).

60. Ibid.

61. Public Safety Canada, "National Action Plan to Combat Human Trafficking: 2013–2014 Annual Report on Progress" at http://www.publicsafety.gc.ca/cnt/rsrcs/pblctns/2014-ntnl-ctn-pln-cmbt-hmn/index-eng.aspx (accessed 26 October 2015).

62. Lorine A. Hughes and Gregory J. DeLone, "Viruses, Worms, and Trojan Horses: Serious Crimes, Nuisance, or Both?" *Social Science Computer Review*, vol. 25, iss. 1 (Spring 2007): 78–98.

63. Vincent Kiernan, "2 Incidents Put More Than 200,000 Students at Risk of Data Theft," *Chronicle of Higher Education*, vol. 52 iss. 43 (30 June 2006): A21.

64. "Cybercrime: An Overview of Incidents and Issues in Canada," (2014) at http://www.rcmp-grc.gc.ca/pubs/cc-report-rapport-cc-eng.pdf (accessed 26 October 2015).

65. Erik Larson, "Computers Turn Out to Be Valuable Aid in Employee Crime," *Wall Street Journal* (14 January 1985), p. 1.

66. Clyde Wilson, "Software Piracy: Uncovering Mutiny on the Cyberseas," *Trial* 32 (1996): 24–31.

67. Susan W. Brenner, "'At Light Speed': Attribution and Response to Cybercrime/Terrorism/Warfare," *Journal of Criminal Law & Criminology* (Winter 2007) , vol. 97, iss. 2 (Winter 2007): 379–475.

68. "Stalking, Criminal Harassment and Cyberbullying," Canadian Bar Association, British Columbia Branch at http://www.cbabc.org/For-the-Public/Dial-A-Law/Scripts/Criminal-Law/206.aspx (accessed 26 October 2015).

69. Sheryl Smolkin, "The 10 Biggest Scams of the Year," *Toronto Star* (1 February 2013) at http://www.thestar.com/business/personal_finance/2013/02/01/the_10_biggest_scams_of_the_year.html (accessed 26 October 2015).

70. Ibid.

71. Eddie Thai and Katherine Baird, "Overview of the National Agenda to Combat Organized Crime," Public Policy Forum (May 2007).

72. Government of Canada website (at http://www.psepc.gc.ca) (accessed 30 October 2015).

73. SeniorBusters Program, at http://www.antifraudcentre-centreantifraude.ca/about-ausujet/index-eng.htm (accessed 30 October 2015).

74. Government of Canada, Canada's Anti-Spam Legislation, at http://fightspam.gc.ca/eic/site/030.nsf/frm-eng/MMCN-9EZV6S (accessed 30 October 2015)

75. Royal Canadian Mounted Police. Threat Assessment: Mass-Marketing Fraud The Canadian Perspective — Nov. 2007 at http://www.rcmp-grc.gc.ca/pubs/ci-rc/marketing-eng.pdf (Accessed 30 October 2015).

76. Stephen Schafer, *The Political Criminal* (New York: Free Press, 1974), p. 1.

77. Robert Friedlander, Terrorism (Dobbs Ferry, NY: Oceana, 1979).

78. Bruce Hoffman, *Inside Terrorism* (New York: Columbia University Press, 1998); and Walter Laquer, *The Age of Terrorism* (Boston: Little, Brown, 1987), p. 72.

79. National Advisory Commission on Criminal Justice Standards and Goals, Report of the Task Force on Disorders and Terrorism (Washington, DC: U.S. Government Printing Office, 1976), p. 3. and Section 83.1, Criminal Code Canada.

80. Austin T. Turk, "Sociology of Terrorism," *Annual Review of Sociology* 30 (2004): 271–86; and Paul Wilkinson, *Terrorism and the Liberal State* (New York: Wiley, 1977), p. 49.

81. Elisabeth Symeonidou-Kastanidou, "Defining Terrorism," *European Journal of Crime, Criminal Law & Criminal Justice*, vol. 12, iss. 1 (2004): 14–35; Eric Reitan, "Defining Terrorism for Public Policy Purposes: The Group-Target Definition," *Journal of Moral Philosophy*, vol. 7, iss. 2 (2010): 253–278; and Jack Gibbs, "Conceptualization of Terrorism," *American Sociological Review* 54 (1989): 329–340, p. 330.

82. For a general view, see Jonathan White, *Terrorism* (Pacific Grove, CA: Brooks/Cole, 1991).

83. Michael Barkun, "Leaderless Resistance and Phineas Priests: Strategies of Uncoordinated Violence on the Far Right," paper presented at the annual meeting of the *American Society of Criminology*, San Diego, November 1997.

84. Adnan R. Khan, "Who Killed Bhutto?" *Maclean's*, vol. 21, iss. 3 (28 January 2008): 24–29; Griff Witte, "Musharraf Denies Role in Bhutto Death; Pakistan President Insists Taliban Supporters Killed Her, Rejects Suggestion of Conspiracy," *Edmonton Journal* (4 January 2008), p. 4.

85. Stephen Engelberg, "Terrorism's New (and Very Old) Face," *The New York Times* (12 September 1998), p. A5.

86. Bruce Hoffman, *Inside Terrorism*.

87. Anonymous, "U.S. Abortionist Shot to Death at his Church; Attacked Before; Obama Health Secretary Has Ties to Slain Doctor," *National Post* (1 June 2009), p. A2.

88. Ted Robert Gurr, "Political Terrorism in the United States: Historical Antecedents and Contemporary Trends," in *The Politics of Terrorism*, ed. Michael Stohl (New York: Dekker, 1988).

89. Amnesty International, *Annual Report, 2011* (London, UK: May 2011).

90. This report on state action in Peru can be obtained on the Amnesty International website at http://www.amnesty.org/ailib/aipub/1996/AMR/2460396.htm.

91. Oliver Laughland, "FBI Director Stands by Claim That North Korea Was Source of Sony Cyber-Attack," *The Guardian* (7 January 2015) at http://www.theguardian.com/world/2015/jan/07/fbi-director-north-korea-source-sony-cyber-attack-james-comey (accessed 26 October 2015).

92. Ibid.

93. Kim Zetter, "An Unprecedented Look at Stuxnet, the World's First Digital Weapon," *Security* (11 November 2014) at http://www.wired.com/2014/11/countdown-to-zero-day-stuxnet (accessed 26 October 2015).

94. Katia Moskvitch, "The World's Five Biggest Cyber Threats," *BBC News* (26 April 2012) at http://www.bbc.com/news/technology-17846185 (accessed 26 October 2015).

95. Ibid.

96. Spiegel staff, "Embassy Espionage: The NSA's Secret Spy Hub in Berlin," *Der Spiegel* (27 October 2013) at http://www.spiegel.de/international/germany/cover-story-how-nsa-spied-on-merkel-cell-phone-from-berlin-embassy-a-930205.html (accessed 26 October 2015).

97. Tanya Basu, "Ashley Madison Faces $578 Million Class Action Lawsuit," *Time Magazine* (23 August 2015) at http://time.com/4007374/ashley-madison-578-million-lawsuit-canada (accessed 26 October 2015).

98. Mark Kennedy, "Kenney Says Homegrown Terrorism a 'Reality' in Canada," *Ottawa Citizen* (8 March 2015) at http://ottawacitizen.com/news/politics/kenney-says-homegrown-terrorism-a-reality-in-canada (accessed 26 October 2015).

99. Ibid.

100. Brent Smith and Gregory Orvis, "America's Response to Terrorism: An Empirical Analysis of Federal Intervention Strategies During the 1980s," *Justice Quarterly* 10 (1993): 660–681.

Index

Notes: Entries and page numbers in bold refer to key terms and the pages in the text on which they are defined. Page numbers followed by an *f* refer to figures; page numbers followed by a *t* refer to tables.

Chapter in Review

Learning Objectives

LO1 Identify the field of study of criminology.

LO2 Recognize the key theorists in the development of the discipline of criminology.

LO3 Summarize the major theoretical perspectives in criminology and the focus of each.

LO4 Identify the subareas that constitute the discipline of criminology.

LO5 Explain how the definition of behaviours as deviant or criminal can change over time.

LO6 Explain the origins of British common law and interpret its relationship to contemporary Canadian criminal law.

LO7 Analyze the relationship between *mens rea* and *actus rea* in the determination of criminal offences.

LO8 Evaluate the ethical issues in conducting criminological research with individuals who are engaged in criminal activities.

Key Terms

absolute liability crimes Illegal acts in which guilt does not depend on intent, or *mens rea*. They are usually acts that endanger the public welfare, such as violations of health and safety regulations.

actus reus An illegal or "guilty" act. It may be an affirmative act, such as killing, or a failure to act when legally required to do so.

anomie A lack of norms or clear social standards. Because of rapidly shifting moral values, the individual has few guides to what is socially acceptable or expected.

biosocial theory Approach to criminology that focuses on the interaction between biological and social factors as they relate to crime.

capital punishment The execution of criminal offenders; the death penalty.

Chicago School Group of urban sociologists who studied the relationship between environmental conditions and crime.

classical criminology The theoretical perspective suggesting that (1) people have free will to choose criminal or conventional behaviours; (2) people choose to commit crime for reasons of greed or personal need; and (3) crime can be controlled only by the fear of criminal sanctions.

Code of Hammurabi The first written *Criminal Code*, developed in Babylonia about 1780 B.C.

common law Early English law, developed by judges, that became the standardized law of the land in England and eventually formed the basis of criminal law in Canada.

conflict theory The view that human behaviour is shaped by interpersonal conflict and that those who maintain social power will use it to further their own ends.

conflict view The belief that criminal behaviour is defined by those in a position of power to protect and advance their own self-interest.

consensus view The belief that the majority of citizens in a society share common values and agree on what behaviours should be defined as criminal.

crime An act, deemed socially harmful or dangerous, that is specifically defined, prohibited, and punished under criminal law.

criminal law The written code that defines crimes and their punishments.

criminology The scientific study of the nature, extent, cause, and control of criminal behaviour.

deviance Behaviour that departs from the social norm but is not necessarily criminal.

excuse defence Criminal defence based on a lack of criminal intent (*mens rea*). Excuse defences include mental disorder, automatism, intoxication, and ignorance.

hybrid offence An offence where the crown attorney decides whether to try the case as a more minor summary conviction offence, or a more serious indictable offence.

indictable offence A serious offence punishable with maximum prison terms ranging from two years to life.

interactionist view The belief that those with social power are able to impose their values on society as a whole, and these values then define criminal behaviour.

interdisciplinary Involving two or more academic fields.

justification defence Criminal defence that claims an illegal action was justified by circumstances and therefore not criminal. Justification defences include necessity, duress, self-defence, and entrapment.

mandatory sentences A statutory requirement that a certain penalty shall be carried out in all cases of conviction for a specified offence.

mens rea A "guilty mind"; the intent to commit a criminal act.

Mosaic Code The laws of the ancient Israelites, found in the Old Testament of the Judeo-Christian Bible.

penology Subarea of criminology that focuses on the correction and control of criminal offenders.

positivism The branch of social science that uses the scientific method of the natural sciences and suggests that human behaviour is a product of social, biological, psychological, or economic forces.

precedent A rule derived from previous judicial decisions and applied to future cases; the basis of common law.

rational choice theory The view that crime is a function of a decision-making process in which the potential offender weighs the potential costs and benefits of an illegal act.

rehabilitation Treatment of criminal offenders aimed at preventing future criminal behaviour.

reliable Producing consistent results from one measurement to another.

social structure theory The view that disadvantaged economic class position is a primary cause of crime.

socialization Process of human development and enculturation. Socialization is influenced by key social processes and institutions.

sociological criminology Approach to criminology, based on the work of Quetelet and Durkheim, that focuses on the relationship between social factors and crime.

statutory crimes Crimes defined by legislative bodies in response to changing social conditions, public opinion, and custom.

summary conviction offence A minor offence punishable by a fine of up to $5000, six months in jail, or both.

utilitarianism A doctrine positing an action is right if it promotes the greatest happiness of the greatest number of people. Individuals who break the law threaten the ability of the rest of us to enjoy our freedom and the pleasures we work for. Punishment should increase the total amount of happiness in the world because it will prevent criminals from repeating their crimes and it deters others from committing crimes. Utilitarians believe that legal systems can be designed that maximize individual freedom and allow everyone to pursue their pleasures.

valid Actually measuring what one intends to measure; relevant.

white-collar crime Illegal acts that capitalize on a person's status in the marketplace. White-collar crimes may include theft, embezzlement, fraud, market manipulation, price fixing, and false advertising.

Quiz

1. What concept did Cesare Beccaria believe in?
   a. the Inquisition
   b. capital punishment
   c. hedonism
   d. utilitarianism

2. During the 19th century, phrenologists studied bumps on the skull and other researchers examined facial features and made associations between these features and the likelihood that one would engage in criminal behaviour. Which branch of criminology did they all belong to?
   a. contemporary
   b. sociological
   c. classical
   d. positivist

3. Who is credited with conflict theory's link to crime and criminology?
   a. Karl Marx
   b. Edwin Sutherland
   c. Emile Durkheim
   d. John Hagan

4. Which of the following did Emile Durkheim believe about crime in our society?
   a. It is a normal part of any society.
   b. It is based on a consensual relationship between victims and offenders.
   c. It is subjective.
   d. It is governed by biological forces.

5. Which of the following factors are considered by biological and psychological theorists when studying crime?
   a. treatment, diet, IQ and substance use
   b. temperament, treatment, hormones, and personality
   c. hormones, diet, personality, and intelligence
   d. disability, psychosis, behaviour, and diet

6. Consider the crime of sexually assaulting a child and the public response to it. Which of John Hagan's categories does it best fit into?
   a. social diversion
   b. social deviation
   c. conflict crime
   d. consensus crime

7. What is the most famous set of written laws of the ancient world known as today?
   a. Mosaic Code
   b. Code of Hammurabi
   c. Lex Talionis
   d. English Common Law

8. Which of the following elements must the Crown prove are present in order to show that a crime has taken place?
   a. *mens rea* and *mala in se*
   b. *actus reus* and *mala prohibitum*
   c. *mens rea* and *mala prohibitum*
   d. *mens rea* and *actus reus*

9. Joan has been caring for her neighbour's children before and after school for the past three years. According to Canadian law, she is responsible for assisting and protecting those in her care. Which guidelines outline her obligation?
   a. the relationship of the parties based on status
   b. a contractual relationship between Joan and the children/parents
   c. a common-law relationship dictated by precedent in case law
   d. civil statute relationship guidelines

10. What must the guilty action be in order to satisfy the requirements of *actus reus*?
    a. premeditated
    b. compelled
    c. voluntary
    d. malevolent

Answers: 1. d, 2. d, 3. a, 4. a, 5. c, 6. d, 7. b, 8. d, 9. b, 10. c.

Chapter in Review

Learning Objectives

LO1 Name three primary sources of crime statistics used in Canada.

LO2 Explain the benefits of the Crime Severity Index.

LO3 Identify the strengths and weaknesses of crime statistics.

LO4 Identify the important trends over time in the Canadian crime rate.

LO5 Identify major factors that influence the crime rate.

LO6 Define aging out or desistance.

LO7 Define racial profiling.

Key Terms

aging out (desistance) The fact that people commit less crime as they mature.

computerized crime mapping The use of police data and geographical information systems (GIS) computer programs to construct and analyze digital maps representing the spatial location of crimes, for the purpose of planning police use of resources to prevent and reduce crime.

Crime Severity Index A yearly crime report used by all police agencies in Canada that measures both volume and severity of crime across the country.

General Social Survey—Victimization Survey (GSS—VS) National study carried out in 1988, 1993, 1999, 2004, 2009, and 2014, by Statistics Canada, which surveys approximately 20 000 Canadians about their personal experiences of criminal victimization.

self-report surveys A research approach that requires subjects to reveal their own participation in delinquent or criminal acts.

street crimes Crimes such as robbery, assault, sexual assault, theft, and murder that often occur in public places, and are easy to detect.

suite crimes Crimes such as price-fixing, insider trading, embezzlement, and improper disposal of toxic waste that often occur behind closed doors in corporate boardrooms and offices, and are hard to detect.

UCR2 Revised crime-reporting system introduced in the mid-1980s. It collects detailed information about accused persons, victims, location, and weapons involved in each criminal incident. Most of the larger police agencies use the UCR and the UCR2.

Uniform Crime Report (UCR) A yearly crime report used by all police agencies in Canada.

TABLE 2.1

Factors Affecting the Validity of the Uniform Crime Reports

1. Many criminal incidents are never reported to the police. This is especially true of more minor crimes, but even a large percentage of sexual assaults and assaults are not reported. Victims may believe that there is nothing the police can do, or the crime was not important enough to go to the bother of reporting it. In other cases, the crime may have gone undetected. Sometimes victims are afraid to report a crime for fear of further reprisals from their victimizer. In rare cases, the victim may have died or disappeared. Biderman and Reiss (1967) coined the phrase the "dark figure" of crime to describe the many acts that take place that are, by definition, crimes, but never appear in the "official" statistics on crime.

2. Reports can vary in accuracy and completeness.

3. Sometimes, police agencies don't make a report, and the Canadian Centre for Justice Statistics has to "estimate" the amount of crime that would have occurred in that agency's jurisdiction.

4. Not all Canadian police agencies use the UCR2 form, although completion rates have improved greatly over time. In 2013, 154 police agencies across the 10 provinces and three territories reported complete data, covering approximately 99 percent of the Canadian population. Most agencies that do complete the UCR2 are urban, and so the data may not be representative regionally or nationally.

5. If an accused commits multiple crimes during one incident, only the most serious offence is recorded. For example, if a man sexually assaults, robs, and murders a victim, only the murder is recorded. Consequently, many lesser crimes go unreported.

6. All criminal incidents are not counted the same way. For example, one incident is counted for each separate occurrence of a property crime, such as theft, no matter how many victims are involved. But in the case of violent crime, one incident is counted for each victim involved in the occurrence.

Sources: Samuel Perreault, "Police-reported Crime Statistics in Canada," 2012 *Juristat* (July 2013) Statistics Canada Cat. no. 85-002-X; "Measuring Crime in Canada: Introducing the Crime Severity Index and Improvements to the Uniform Crime Reporting Survey 2009" Catalogue no. 85-004-X, Statistics Canada (April 2009) at http://www.statcan.gc.ca/pub/85-004-x/85-004-x2009001-eng.pdf; Martin A. Andresen, *The Science of Crime Measurement: Issues for Spatially-Referenced Crime Data* (New York: Routledge, 2014); Albert J. Reiss Jr., "On Exploring the 'Dark Figure' of Crime," *The Annals of the American Academy of Political and Social Science*, vol. 374, no. 1 (November 1967): 1–15, doi: 10.1177/000271626737400102.

Quiz

1. Which piece of information does the UCR play a primary role in summarizing?
   a. number of victims involved in a criminal incident
   b. race of offenders and victims
   c. number of criminal incidents in a jurisdiction
   d. gender of offenders and victims

2. Which resource is considered to be a valuable, comprehensive source of information about otherwise unknown crime data?
   a. Statistics Canada
   b. General Social Survey—Victimization Survey (GSS—VS)
   c. the *Juristat* report
   d. the Uniform Crime Report

3. If the General Social Survey—Victimization Survey (GSS—VS) were Canada's only source of information about crime frequency, what would we conclude from the results?
   a. Crime rates are high.
   b. Property crime rates are lower than violent crime rates.
   c. Crime rates are increasing.
   d. Crime rates are low.

4. Which of the following statements would a critic of self-report studies be most likely to make?
   a. Participants are not likely to be accurate in their recall of criminal events.
   b. Self-report studies are not conducted frequently enough to be helpful.
   c. Only offenders with the most extensive prior criminality are likely to be truthful.
   d. Males are less likely than females to be participants in self-report surveys.

5. Which of the following circumstances is correlated with increases in domestic assaults?
   a. Daylight savings time
   b. children leaving home to go to postsecondary institutions
   c. rising temperatures outside
   d. the death of a family pet

6. Which of the following factors would researchers such as Tittle say is most relevant to any discussion about a relationship between social class and crime?
   a. the fact that the wealthy have little interest in engaging in criminal activity
   b. the likelihood that poor, young people are biologically more likely to engage in criminal activity
   c. the existence of biases toward those of the lower class held by those in the criminal justice system
   d. that the wealthy are less likely to notice that they have been victims of crime

7. As a general rule, what is the believed peak age for property crime?
   a. 10–15 years
   b. 15–18 years
   c. 18–25 years
   d. 25–35 years

8. Which of the following offences are women more likely than men to be convicted of?
   a. fraud
   b. possession of stolen property
   c. public drunkenness
   d. common assault

9. What is the term used to describe the notion that as we grow older and more mature we tend to be less likely to commit crime?
   a. pseudomaturity
   b. transitional movement
   c. maturity hypothesis
   d. desistance

10. What response to chronic or repeat offending is most likely to lead to continued offending?
    a. prevention programs aimed at teenage offenders
    b. slow processing through the criminal justice system
    c. earlier eligibility for parole
    d. longer prison terms in more secure settings

Answers: 1. c, 2. b, 3. a, 4. a, 5. c, 6. c, 7. b, 8. a, 9. d, 10. d.

Learning Objectives

LO1 Define victimology.

LO2 Identify major problems faced by victims of crime.

LO3 Identify major risk factors for being victimized.

LO4 Explain the victim precipitation theory, lifestyle theories, and routine activities theory.

LO5 Describe how Canadian society has attempted to provide care for victims of crime.

LO6 Identify victims' services programs.

LO7 Explain the importance of advocacy for rights of victims.

LO8 Interpret the research on the effectiveness of programs designing to prevent victimization.

Key Terms

active precipitation Aggressive or provocative behaviour of victims that results in their victimization.

capable guardians Effective deterrents to crime, such as police or watchful neighbours.

compensation Financial aid awarded to crime victims to repay them for their loss and injuries; may cover medical bills, loss of wages, loss of future earnings, and/or counselling.

crisis intervention Emergency counselling for crime victims.

cycle of violence Victims of crime, especially childhood abuse, are more likely to commit crime themselves.

deviant place theory The view that victimization is primarily a function of where people live.

lifestyle theories The view that people become crime victims because of lifestyles that increase their exposure to criminal offenders.

motivated offenders People willing and able to commit crimes.

passive precipitation Personal or social characteristics of victims that make them "attractive" targets for criminals; such victims may unknowingly either threaten or encourage their attackers.

post-traumatic stress disorder Psychological reaction to a highly stressful event; symptoms may include depression, anxiety, flashbacks, and recurring nightmares.

routine activities theory The view that victimization results from the interaction of three everyday factors: the availability of suitable targets, the absence of capable guardians, and the presence of motivated offenders.

suitable targets Objects of crime (persons or property) that are attractive and readily available.

target hardening Making one's home or business crime-proof through the use of locks, bars, alarms, and other devices.

victim precipitation theory The view that victims may initiate, either actively or passively, the confrontation that leads to their victimization.

victim–offender reconciliation programs Mediated face-to-face encounters between victims and their attackers, designed to produce restitution agreements and if possible reconciliation.

victimologists Criminologists who focus on the victims of crime.

victimology The study of the victim's role in criminal events.

FIGURE 3.9

Routine Activities Theory

Lack of capable guardian
- Police officers
- Homeowners
- Security systems

Motivated offenders
- Teenage boys
- Unemployed
- Addict populations

CRIME

Suitable targets
- Unlocked homes
- Expensive cars
- Easily transportable goods

Quiz

1. What potential impact of experiencing serious violent victimization is specific to adolescence?
   a. the desire to stay in school longer to avoid the "real world" of work
   b. the inability of victims to pay for their own therapy because of their age
   c. difficulties in school leading to lowered earning potential in later life
   d. fewer youth moving out of their parents' homes in their adolescence

2. There is growing evidence that people who are crime victims also seem more likely to commit crime themselves. What term is used to refer to this phenomenon?
   a. cycle of violence
   b. crime inheritance
   c. learning the ropes
   d. violence precipitation

3. According to Statistics Canada, which of the following individuals is at greatest risk of being a victim of a serious crime?
   a. Suzy, who is a waitress at a busy downtown nightclub
   b. Tom, who is a waiter at a busy downtown lunch shop
   c. Mary, who manages a thriving daycare centre
   d. Tom, who works varied shifts at a factory

4. According to victimization data, after what age does victim risk rapidly diminish?
   a. after age 18
   b. after age 20
   c. after age 25
   d. after age 60

5. Statistically, most crime victims know the perpetrator. What type of crime tends to be the exception to this rule?
   a. robbery
   b. sexual assault
   c. theft
   d. murder

6. A young man has several drinks and then begins yelling insults at the spectators in front of him at a music concert. The spectators turn and begin yelling back and a fight breaks out. The young man is seriously injured and taken to hospital. Which theory places some of the responsibility on the young man for his victimization in the assault?
   a. lifestyle theory
   b. victim precipitation theory
   c. routine activities theory
   d. deviant place theory

7. According to statistics, teens are more likely to become victims of crime. Which is the most likely reason?
   a. Much of their time is spent "hanging out" with friends.
   b. They spend a great deal of time in vehicles.
   c. Much of their time is spent outdoors.
   d. Most of their day is spent away from adult supervision.

8. Which of the following combinations would present the ideal crime situation according to the routine activities theory?
   a. a teacher carrying a laptop through the halls of the school
   b. a bicycle left in a shed in the backyard of a suburban home
   c. an MP3 player left unattended on a table at a fast-food restaurant
   d. a cellphone left in a school locker over the weekend

9. What type of agencies organize victim witness assistance programs in Canada?
   a. counselling
   b. court-appointed
   c. volunteer
   d. governmental

10. What concept are reconciliation programs based on?
    a. the concept of "just desserts"
    b. the concept of restorative justice
    c. the concept of social ecology
    d. the concept of compensation

For additional study tools, go online to access MindTap for *CRIM*. There, you can

- Think like a criminologist with scenarios supplied
- Decide and justify those decisions with questions that reflect on chapter topics
- Analyze criminology in the media
- Prepare for tests with quizzes
- Use your interactive eBook
- and more

www.nelson.com/student

Answers: 1. c, 2. a, 3. a, 4. c, 5. a, 6. b, 7. a, 8. c, 9. d, 10. b.

Learning Objectives

LO1 State the major principles underlying rational choice theory and contrast it with positivist theory.

LO2 Explain the concept of situational crime prevention.

LO3 Explain general deterrence and critique its effectiveness in reducing the crime rate.

LO4 Explain specific deterrence and critique its effectiveness in reducing the crime rate.

LO5 Explain the logic of incapacitation as a means of crime reduction.

LO6 Outline the policy implications of choice theory.

© Luis Pedrosa/iStockPhoto

Key Terms

brutalization effect The belief that capital punishment creates an atmosphere of brutality that enhances rather than deters the level of violence in society.

choice theory The school of thought holding that people choose to engage in delinquent and criminal behaviour after weighing the consequences and benefits of their actions.

classical criminology The theoretical perspective suggesting that (1) people have free will to choose criminal or conventional behaviours; (2) people choose to commit crime for reasons of greed or personal need; and (3) crime can be controlled only by the fear of criminal sanctions.

crackdown The concentration of police resources on a particular problem area to eradicate or displace criminal activity.

defensible space The principle that crime can be prevented or displaced by modifying the physical environment to reduce the opportunity individuals have to commit crime.

diffusion of benefits An effect that occurs when efforts to prevent one crime unintentionally prevent another, or when

crime-control efforts in one locale reduce crime in other nontarget areas.

discouragement An effect that occurs when limiting access to one target reduces other types of crime as well.

displacement An effect of crime prevention efforts in which efforts to control crime in one area shift illegal activities to another.

edgework The excitement or exhilaration of successfully executing illegal activities in dangerous situations.

extinction The phenomenon in which a crime prevention effort has an immediate impact that then dissipates as criminals adjust to new conditions.

general deterrence A crime control policy that depends on the fear of criminal penalties, convincing the potential law violator that the pains associated with crime outweigh its benefits.

incapacitation effect The idea that keeping offenders in confinement will eliminate the risk of their committing further offences.

incarceration Confinement in jail or prison.

informal sanctions Disapproval, stigma, or anger directed toward an offender by significant others (parents, peers, neighbours, teachers), resulting in shame, embarrassment, and loss of respect.

just deserts The principle that those who violate the rights of others deserve punishment commensurate with the seriousness of the crime, without regard for their personal characteristics or circumstances.

offender-specific crime Theories of criminality that look at why people commit crime and the factors that explain criminality.

probation Sentence served in the community under the supervision of a probation officer and subject to certain conditions.

rational choice The view that crime is a function of a decision-making process in which the potential offender weighs the potential costs and benefits of an illegal act.

recidivism Repetition of criminal behaviour.

reintegrative shaming Brief and controlled shaming that is followed by forgiveness, apology, repentance,

and reconnection with the community.

seductions of crime The situational inducements or immediate benefits that draw offenders into law violations.

situational crime prevention A method of crime prevention that seeks to eliminate or reduce particular crimes in narrow settings.

specific deterrence The view that criminal sanctions should be so powerful that offenders will never repeat their criminal acts.

stigmatization Ongoing degradation or humiliation, in which the offender is branded as an evil person and cast out of society.

structuring crime According to the rational choice approach, the decision to commit crime, regardless of its substance, is structured by (1) where it occurs, (2) the characteristics of the target, and (3) available means.

three strikes and you're out American policy whereby people convicted of three felony offences receive a mandatory life sentence.

Quiz

1. In what school of criminology does rational choice theory have its roots?
   a. Marxist
   b. positivist
   c. classical
   d. sociological

2. What elements are critical to the rational choice perspective of crime?
   a. greed and the need for instant gratification
   b. degree of poverty and transient population in a region
   c. mental health of the offender and vulnerability of the victim
   d. skills possessed by the offender and the rewards of the offence

3. What does research suggest about whether or not street crimes are rational?
   a. Street crimes are irrational in that they generally result in arrest and conviction.
   b. Street crimes are rational in that only highly skilled offenders commit serious offences.
   c. Street crimes are rational in that the target and method of commission are carefully considered.
   d. Street crimes are irrational in that the majority of offenders only gain small rewards.

4. What term did sociologist Jack Katz use to describe immediate benefits, often a thrill or sense of superiority, which draw offenders into committing crimes?
   a. the seductions of crime
   b. the hedonistic approach
   c. the get-rich-quick scheme
   d. the winner-takes-all approach

5. What are target reduction strategies designed to do?
   a. narrow down the regions in which crime is likely to occur
   b. increase the sentences for young persons convicted of crime
   c. decrease the potential value of crime for the offender
   d. allow police departments to hire more officers

6. What does the concept of "general deterrence" suggest?
   a. Motivated people will violate the law if left free and unrestricted to do so.
   b. The decision to commit crime is affected by the perceived likelihood of punishment.
   c. If there are more suitable guardians for adolescents and children, there will be less crime.
   d. As people get older, they will commit fewer crimes due to responsibilities and maturity.

7. What factor could partially explain the fact that a young person in a tightly knit community is less likely to commit crime than a young person who lives in a transient community where few people know him or her?
   a. a lack of suitable targets
   b. the brutalization effect
   c. the idea of going to jail and missing out on community activities
   d. the perceived threat of informal sanctions

8. According to research, what type of specific deterrence is most effective in reducing recidivism rates?
   a. probation
   b. physical punishment
   c. incarceration
   d. mandatory community service

9. What has research shown about the direct benefits of incapacitation?
   a. The research has been inconclusive.
   b. Research indicates incapacitation actually increases the chance of reoffending.
   c. Research indicates incapacitation is an effective deterrent to criminal behaviour.
   d. Research indicates that the benefits of incapacitation have not been studied.

10. What term is used to refer to the fact that 38 percent of Canadians serving a life term will be years or older before they become eligible for parole?
    a. rehabilitative ageism
    b. elder confinement
    c. elder lock-up
    d. geriatric overload

Answers: 1. d, 2. a, 3. a, 4. d, 5. c, 6. b, 7. d, 8. a, 9. a, 10. d.

5 Chapter in Review

Learning Objectives

LO1 Explain the basic premises of trait theory.

LO2 Describe the major perspectives of biological trait theories.

LO3 Explain how fetal alcohol spectrum disorder (FASD) and criminality may be linked.

LO4 Explain the relationship between genetics and criminality.

LO5 Describe the major varieties of psychological trait theories.

LO6 Describe the relationship between mental illness and criminality.

Key Terms

androgens Male sex hormones.

antisocial personality Combination of traits, such as hyperactivity, impulsivity, hedonism, and inability to empathize with others, that make a person prone to deviant behaviour and violence; also referred to as sociopathic or psychopathic personality.

arousal theory The view that people seek to maintain a preferred level of arousal, but vary in how they process sensory input. A need for high levels of environmental stimulation may lead to aggressive, violent behaviour patterns.

attention deficit/hyperactivity disorder (ADHD) A developmentally inappropriate lack of attention, along with impulsivity and hyperactivity.

behaviour modelling Process of learning behaviour (notably aggression) by observing others. Aggressive models may be parents, criminals in the neighbourhood, or characters on television or in movies.

behaviour theory The view that all human behaviour is learned through a process of social reinforcement (rewards and punishment).

bipolar disorder An emotional disturbance in which moods alternate between periods of wild elation and deep depression.

cheater theory A theory suggesting that a subpopulation of men has evolved with genes that incline them toward extremely low parental involvement. Sexually aggressive, they use deceit for sexual conquest of as many females as possible.

cognitive theory Psychological perspective that focuses on mental processes—how people perceive and mentally represent the world around them and solve problems.

disorder Any type of psychological problem (formerly labelled neurotic or psychotic), such as anxiety disorders, mood disorders, and conduct disorders.

dizygotic (DZ) twins Fraternal (nonidentical) twins.

ego The part of the personality, developed in early childhood, that helps control the id and keep people's actions within the boundaries of social convention.

id The primitive part of people's mental makeup, present at birth, that represents unconscious biological drives for food, sex, and other life-sustaining necessities. The id seeks instant gratification without concern for the rights of others.

information-processing theory Theory that focuses on how people process, store, encode, retrieve, and manipulate information to make decisions and solve problems.

latent delinquency A psychological predisposition to commit antisocial acts because of an id-dominated personality that renders an individual incapable of controlling impulsive, pleasure-seeking drives.

meta-analytic studies A systematic method of evaluating statistical data based on results of several independent studies of the same problem. In effect, it is a "study of studies" on the same subject.

minimal brain dysfunction (MBD) An abruptly appearing, maladaptive behaviour, such as episodic periods of explosive rage.

monozygotic (MZ) twins Identical twins.

nature theory The view that intelligence is largely determined genetically and that low intelligence is linked to criminal behaviour.

neurophysiology The study of brain activity.

neurotic In Freudian psychology, a personality marked by mental anguish and feared loss of control.

neurotransmitters Chemical compounds that influence or activate brain functions.

nurture theory The view that intelligence is not inherited, but is largely a product of environment. Low IQ scores do not cause crime, but may result from the same environmental factors.

personality The reasonably stable patterns of behaviour, including thoughts and emotions, that distinguish one person from another.

premenstrual syndrome (PMS) The hypothesis that several days prior to and during menstruation, excessive amounts of female sex hormones stimulate antisocial, aggressive behaviour.

primary prevention programs Programs, such as substance abuse clinics and mental health associations, that seek to treat personal problems before they manifest themselves as crime.

psychodynamic (psychoanalytic) Theory originated by Freud that the human personality is controlled by unconscious mental processes developed early in childhood, involving the interaction of id, ego, and superego.

psychopath Psychologists believe that psychopathy is a psychological disorder that is a combination of genetic, biological, psychological, and environmental factors. A psychopath is an individual who does not feel guilt or show remorse for harming others; lacks empathy for the suffering of others; is deceptive and manipulative, and is impulsive and irresponsible. Research shows that psychopathy is related to neurological deficits.

psychotic In Freudian psychology, a personality marked by complete loss of control over the id, characterized by delusions, hallucinations, and sudden mood shifts.

schizophrenia A severe disorder marked by hearing nonexistent voices, seeing hallucinations, and exhibiting inappropriate responses.

secondary prevention programs Programs that provide treatment such as psychological counselling to youths and adults after they have violated the law.

social learning theory The view that people learn to be aggressive by observing others acting aggressively to achieve some goal or being rewarded for violent acts.

sociobiology View that inherited, biological traits explain the origin and development of social behaviours, including behaviours we have classified as deviant or criminal.

sociopath The term *sociopath* is increasingly reserved for behaviour that is believed to be the product of environmental conditions such as an abusive or neglectful home, poverty, lack of educational opportunity, and either low or high intelligence. A sociopath has a well-developed conscience, but follows a set of values and norms of right and wrong that are different than those of the dominant culture.

superego Incorporation within the personality of the moral standards and values of parents, community, and significant others.

testosterone The principal male hormone.

trait theory The view that criminality is a product of abnormal biological and/or psychological traits.

Quiz

1. What is the focus of criminal justice research conducted by sociobiologists?
   a. Criminal behaviour begins as poor impulse control in teenagers.
   b. Criminal behaviour is primarily a result of being raised in disorganized neighbourhood environments.
   c. Criminal behaviour is the result of social learning, which takes place in the peer group.
   d. Criminal behaviour is a function of unique personal traits further impacted by environment.

2. Which hormone has biosocial research found is linked to aggressive and antisocial behaviour?
   a. oxytocin
   b. testosterone
   c. estrogen
   d. peptides

3. What is the status of the link between PMS and crime?
   a. It has been well established.
   b. It has not been studied.
   c. It is questionable.
   d. It has been established for female juveniles only.

4. What does MBD stand for?
   a. maximum brain dysfunction
   b. minimal brain disorder
   c. maximum brain disorder
   d. minimal brain dysfunction

5. Tommy has been diagnosed with ADHD and is in Grade 3. What would be the best course of action to have a significant, long-term impact on his behaviour problems in the classroom?
   a. providing clear guidelines to Tommy about socially appropriate behaviour
   b. sending Tommy and his parents to family counselling
   c. enrolling Tommy in an early intervention reading program
   d. gradually moving toward a reduction in the use of Ritalin over his next year in school

6. Which of the following statements summarizes the research on twins, looking at a genetic basis to criminal behaviour?
   a. There is no evidence of a similar behaviour pattern between twins studied to date.
   b. There is a stronger similarity in the behaviour of monozygotic twins than between dizygotic twins.
   c. Dizygotic twins are found to be less criminal than non-twins studied to date.
   d. Only those monozygotic twins raised in criminal households exhibited criminal behaviour patterns.

7. Which of the following theories suggests that a subpopulation of sexually aggressive men has evolved who connect with young, unintelligent females to produce children who perpetuate their illegal, immoral ways?
   a. machismo theory
   b. cheater theory
   c. adultery theory
   d. deprivation theory

8. What is the most significant criticism of the gene–crime relationship?
   a. It has not been the subject of true scientific research.
   b. The findings are now outdated and no longer relevant.
   c. It is based largely on inadequate research designs and weak methodologies.
   d. It suggests that the weak and poor are more vulnerable to crime than other groups.

9. Which of the following areas of personality acts as a moral judge?
   a. id
   b. ego
   c. superego
   d. conscience

10. What has research determined about the relationship between IQ and criminality?
    a. Intellect has no bearing on crime links for males, but it does for females.
    b. There is a strong link between IQ and crime for first-time offenders under the age of 18 years.
    c. While there is a strong link between genetics and crime, there is no IQ–crime link.
    d. The IQ–crime link is tenuous at best and is the subject of continued research.

For additional study tools, go online to access MindTap for *CRIM*. There, you can

- Think like a criminologist with scenarios supplied
- Decide and justify those decisions with questions that reflect on chapter topics
- Analyze criminology in the media
- Prepare for tests with quizzes
- Use your interactive eBook
- and more

www.nelson.com/student

Answers: 1. d, 2. b, 3. c, 4. d, 5. c, 6. b, 7. b, 8. c, 9. c, 10. d.

6 Chapter in Review

Learning Objectives

LO1 Explain why sociology has been the main orientation of criminologists.

LO2 Explain why social structure theory supports the idea that those living in poverty are more likely to commit crimes.

LO3 State the three branches of social structure theories.

LO4 Explain the concept of "collective efficacy."

LO5 Discuss how strain theories interpret crime.

LO6 Explain the concept of "differential opportunity."

Martin Poole/The Image Bank/Getty Images

Key Terms

anomie theory View that anomie results when socially defined goals (such as wealth and power) are universally mandated but access to legitimate means (such as education and job opportunities) is stratified by class and status.

anomie According to Durkheim, anomie reflects a lack of norms or clear social standards. Because of rapidly shifting moral values, the individual has few guides to what is socially acceptable.

"Canadian Dream" The goal of accumulating material goods and wealth through individual competition; the process of being socialized to pursue material success and to believe it is achievable.

concentration effect As working- and middle-class families flee inner-city poor areas, the most disadvantaged population is consolidated in urban ghettos.

cultural deviance theory Branch of social structure theory that sees strain and social disorganization together resulting in a unique lower-class culture that conflicts with conventional social norms.

cultural transmission Process whereby values, beliefs, and traditions are handed down from one generation to the next.

culture of poverty A separate lower-class culture, characterized by apathy, cynicism, helplessness, and mistrust of social institutions, such as schools, government agencies, and the police, that is passed from one generation to the next.

delinquent subculture A value system adopted by lower-class youths that is directly opposed to that of the larger society.

differential opportunity The view that lower-class youths, whose legitimate opportunities are limited, join gangs and pursue criminal careers as alternative means to achieve universal success goals.

focal concerns Values, such as toughness and street smarts, that have evolved specifically to fit conditions in lower-class environments.

general strain theory (GST) The view that multiple sources of strain interact with an individual's emotional traits and responses to produce criminality.

institutional anomie theory The view that anomie pervades modern culture because the drive for material wealth dominates and undermines social and community values.

middle-class measuring rods The standards by which authority figures, such as teachers and employers, evaluate lower-class youngsters and often prejudge them negatively.

negative affective states Anger, frustration, and adverse emotions produced by a variety of sources of strain.

reaction formation Irrational hostility evidenced by young delinquents, who adopt norms directly opposed to middle-class goals and standards that seem impossible to achieve.

social class Segment of the population whose members are at a relatively similar economic level and who share attitudes, values, norms, and an identifiable lifestyle.

social disorganization theory Branch of social structure theory that focuses on the breakdown of institutions such as the family, school, and employment in inner-city neighbourhoods.

social structure theory The view that disadvantaged economic-class position is a primary cause of crime.

status frustration A form of culture conflict experienced by lower-class youths because social conditions prevent them from achieving success as defined by the larger society.

strain theory Branch of social structure theory that sees crime as a function of the conflict between people's goals and the means available to obtain them.

strain The anger, frustration, and resentment experienced by people who believe they cannot achieve their goals through legitimate means.

stratification Grouping based on economic or social class and characterized by the unequal distribution of wealth, power, and prestige.

subculture A set of values, beliefs, and traditions unique to a particular social class or group within a larger society.

transitional neighbourhood An area undergoing a shift in population and structure, usually from middle-class residential to lower-class mixed use.

underclass The lowest social stratum in any country, whose members lack the education and skills needed to function successfully in modern society.

Quiz

1. Which group of the Canadian population is hit especially hard by poverty?
   a. children
   b. the elderly
   c. those with mental illness
   d. single-parent families

2. What would a researcher be called who takes the position that crime rates are linked to class level and that those in lower classes are more likely to commit crime because of their economic struggles?
   a. a biosocial theorist
   b. a social structure theorist
   c. a cognitive theorist
   d. a Marxist theorist

3. Which of the following statements summarizes the perspective held by social disorganization theorists?
   a. Crime is a function of the conflict between people's goals and the means they can use to legally obtain them.
   b. Crime is a function of urban conditions: more uncertainty and less social structure equal higher crime rates.
   c. Criminality is a function of psychological predispositions, which determine the likelihood of offending.
   d. Criminality is a function of individual socialization: the larger one's social circle, the greater the likelihood of having delinquent connections.

4. Clifford Shaw and Henry McKay's work identified linkages between crime rates and various zones within urban centres. Which zones did Shaw and McKay identify as having the highest crime rates?
   a. suburban and rural zones
   b. inner-city and suburban zones
   c. inner-city and transitional zones
   d. transitional and suburban zones

5. What types of crime are experienced most often in neighbourhoods with low employment rates?
   a. aggravated assault and homicide
   b. armed robbery and muggings
   c. break and enters and rape
   d. fraud and embezzlement

6. What strategy can well-organized, low-crime neighbourhoods use to maintain order and structure?
   a. concentration effect
   b. population stabilization
   c. collective efficacy
   d. concentric zoning

7. Which of the following initiatives is an example of community engagement in the community policing model?
   a. gated communities
   b. mandatory curfews
   c. an increased police presence
   d. a neighbourhood association

8. Which of the following groups should have the lowest level of criminal behaviour, according to Robert Merton, because they have abandoned the success goal, which is at the root of criminal behaviour?
   a. conformists
   b. innovators
   c. ritualists
   d. retreatists

9. Which of the following concepts is the centrepiece of Richard Cloward and Lloyd Ohlin's theory that lower-class youths join gangs in order to belong and feel successful?
   a. relative deprivation
   b. differential association
   c. differential opportunity
   d. anomie

10. What is the impact of social welfare programs providing financial assistance directly to individuals and families in need?
    a. decreased drug use
    b. lower crime rates
    c. higher school attendance
    d. lower employment rates

For additional study tools, go online to access MindTap for *CRIM*. There, you can
- Think like a criminologist with scenarios supplied
- Decide and justify those decisions with questions that reflect on chapter topics
- Analyze criminology in the media
- Prepare for tests with quizzes
- Use your interactive eBook
- and more

www.nelson.com/student

Answers: 1. a, 2. b, 3. b, 4. c, 5. b, 6. c, 7. d, 8. c, 9. c, 10. b.

Chapter in Review

Learning Objectives

LO1 Describe how social process theories view criminality and explain why they have endured.

LO2 Debate the significance of family factors in predicting behaviour.

LO3 Demonstrate how the educational process and adolescent school achievement have been linked to criminality.

LO4 Evaluate the significance of peer relationships in relation to delinquency.

LO5 Differentiate between social learning theory and social control theory.

LO6 Contrast differential association theory and neutralization theory.

LO7 Describe how Travis Hirschi's contemporary social control theory explains why people obey the law.

LO8 Discuss why critics have charged that labelling theory lacks credibility.

Key Terms

commitment to conformity A strong personal investment in conventional institutions, individuals, and processes that prevents people from engaging in behaviour that might jeopardize their reputation and achievements.

culture conflict Result of exposure to opposing norms, attitudes, and definitions of right and wrong, moral and immoral.

deviance amplification Process whereby secondary deviance pushes offenders out of the mainstream of society and locks them into an escalating cycle of deviance apprehension, labelling, and criminal self-identity.

diversion programs Programs of rehabilitation that remove offenders from the normal channels of the criminal justice process, thus avoiding the stigma of a criminal label.

drift Movement in and out of delinquency, shifting between conventional and deviant values.

moral entrepreneur A person who creates moral rules, which thus reflect the values of those in power rather than any objective, universal standards of right and wrong.

neutralization techniques Methods of rationalizing deviant behaviour, such as denying responsibility or blaming the victim.

neutralization theory The view that law violators learn to neutralize conventional values and attitudes, enabling them to drift back and forth between criminal and conventional behaviour.

primary deviance A norm violation or crime with little or no long-term influence on the violator.

reflective role taking Assuming an identity based on the actual or perceived appraisals of others.

restitution Permitting an offender to repay the victim or do useful work in the community rather than face the stigma of a formal trial and a court-ordered sentence.

retrospective reading The reassessment of a person's past to fit a current generalized label.

secondary deviance A norm violation or crime that comes to the attention of significant others or social control agents, who apply a negative label with long-term consequences for the violator's self-identity and social interactions.

self-control A strong moral sense that renders a person incapable of hurting others or violating social norms.

social bonds The ties that bind people to society, including relationships with friends, family, neighbours,

teachers, and employers. Elements of the social bond include commitment, attachment, involvement, and belief.

social control theory The view that people commit crime when the forces that bind them to society are weakened or broken.

social learning theory The view that people learn to be aggressive by observing others acting aggressively to achieve some goal or being rewarded for violent acts.

social process theory The view that criminality is a function of people's interactions with various organizations, institutions, and processes in society.

social reaction theory (labelling theory) The view that people become criminals when labelled as such and they accept the label as a personal identity.

socialization Process of human development and enculturation. Socialization is influenced by key social processes and institutions.

stigmatize To apply negative labelling with enduring effects on a person's self-image and social interactions.

Quiz

1. Which of the following statements outlines the underlying principle of social process theories?
   a. All people are basically good and will remain law-abiding citizens for life.
   b. Everyone has the potential to become a criminal.
   c. Criminal behaviour is genetic, regardless of race or gender.
   d. People of the lower social classes are more prone to committing crime.

2. Parents of teenagers are often concerned about who their teens spend time hanging out with. What does research evidence indicate about what role parents should play in the lives of their teens in order to discourage involvement in criminal behaviour?
   a. Young people who attend school regularly are buffered against the influence of delinquent peers, so this should be a priority for parents.

b. Teens that are permitted to drink at home, in the company of their parents, are less likely to become addicted to alcohol later in life.

c. Parental involvement in time management balance for youths is important to keep youths from having time to engage in criminal behaviour.

d. Parents should be involved in peer selection since delinquent peers increase the likelihood of a young person engaging in and staying involved in delinquent activities.

3. According to social process theorists, which of the following youths is most likely to become a prosocial, positively contributing member of society?

a. the young person who has many friends and is popular at school

b. the young person whose parents remind her regularly to "be good"

c. the young person who is mentored by her family, church, and basketball team

d. the young person who has not missed a day of school and is now in Grade 10

4. Who developed the differential association theory?

a. David Matza

b. Travis Hirschi

c. Edwin Lemert

d. Edwin Sutherland

5. When asked why he assaulted the man at the bar, David commented that he shouldn't be in trouble because the man made him angry and he deserved what he got. What type of neutralization is this an example of?

a. denial of injury

b. denial of the victim

c. appeal to higher loyalties

d. denial of responsibility

6. What theory would suggest that regular school and church attendance along with strong family connections can buffer the likelihood that an individual would engage in criminal behaviour?

a. social learning theory

b. neutralization theory

c. social control theory

d. anomie theory

7. Travis Hirschi argues that the social bond a person maintains with society is divided into four main elements. Which of the following lists includes all of these bonds?

a. attachment, education, loyalty, and belonging

b. commitment, confidence, strength, and education

c. involvement, attachment, commitment, and belief

d. belief, involvement, self-concept, and religion

8. According to social reaction theorists, what are criminal careers based on?

a. race and gender

b. differential associations and educational streaming

c. social bonds and social reaction

d. negative social interactions leading to stigmatization

9. What is retrospective reading?

a. looking back over a criminal career and reflecting on where the cause of crime began

b. using a variety of tactics to justify criminal behaviour to avoid feelings of guilt

c. evaluating a person's behaviour according to an attached label rather than reacting to the actual behaviour

d. isolating the offender from the larger community by those who could make the most positive impact

10. Which of the following is a key criticism of social process theories?

a. They do not examine the role of agents of social control in criminal behaviour.

b. They do not explain geographical and seasonal fluctuations in crime rates.

c. They do not distinguish between criminal acts and criminal careers.

d. They focus on young male offenders and their gang activities but exclude female gangs.

Answers: 1. b, 2. d, 3. c, 4. d, 5. b, 6. a, 7. c, 8. d, 9. c, 10. b.

Learning Objectives

LO1 Discuss how social conflict theorists explain the existence of crime in a society.

LO2 Explain the purpose of the legal system according to conflict theorists.

LO3 Explain why Marxist criminologists view the justice system as an army.

LO4 Describe how Marxist criminologists explain crime.

LO5 Discuss how feminist criminologists view the role of patriarchy as a cause of both male and female criminal behaviour.

LO6 Explain how restorative justice is meant to prevent and control crime.

Key Terms

deconstructionist Approach that focuses on the use of language by those in power to define crime based on their own values and biases; also called *postmodernist*.

demystify To unmask the true purpose of law, justice, or other social institutions.

instrumental Marxist One who sees criminal law and the criminal justice system as capitalist instruments for controlling the lower class.

left realism Approach that sees crime as a function of relative deprivation under capitalism and favours pragmatic, community-based crime prevention and control.

marginalization Displacement of workers, pushing them outside the economic and social mainstream.

Marxist criminology The view that crime is a product of the capitalist system; also called *radical criminology*.

Marxist feminism Approach that explains both victimization and criminality among women in terms of gender inequality, patriarchy, and the exploitation of women under capitalism.

patriarchal Male-dominated.

peacemaking Approach that considers punitive crime control strategies to be counterproductive and favours the use of humanistic conflict resolution to prevent and control crime.

postmodernist Approach that focuses on the use of language by those in power to define crime based on their own values and biases; also called deconstructionist.

power The ability of persons and groups to control the behaviour of others, to shape public opinion, and to define deviance.

power–control theory The view that gender differences in crime are a function of economic power (class position, one- versus two-earner families), and parental control (paternalistic versus egalitarian families).

preemptive deterrence Efforts to prevent crime through community organization and youth involvement.

radical criminology The view that crime is a product of the capitalist system; also called Marxist criminology.

semiotics The use of language elements as signs or symbols beyond their literal meaning.

sentencing circle A peace-making technique in which offenders, victims, and other community members are brought together in an effort to formulate a sanction that addresses the needs of all.

social reality of crime The main purpose of criminology is to promote a peaceful, just society.

structural Marxist One who sees criminal law and the criminal justice system as means of defending and preserving the capitalist system.

surplus value The difference between what workers produce and what they are paid, which goes to business owners as profits.

Quiz

1. Which group became headline news after a campaign of terrorist activities in Canada during the late 1960s and 1970s?
   a. the Islamic Jihad
   b. the Irish Republican Army (IRA)
   c. Al Qaeda
   d. the Front de Libération du Québec (FLQ)

2. Who is responsible for defining crime, according to conflict theorists?
   a. those who enforce the law
   b. the social audience
   c. those in power
   d. those who commit crime

3. What is most commonly the cause of crime in a capitalist economic system?
   a. the desire of capitalists to distribute goods in a fair, impartial way
   b. the increase in the number of women holding powerful positions in the workforce
   c. workers being marginalized from middle-class social and living environments
   d. the inability of the lower class to neutralize deviance among young people in their communities

4. What focus does Marxist research tend to take?
   a. empirical research studies conducted across cultures and replicated regularly
   b. large examinations of the historical impact of crime and law on individuals and societies
   c. methodical analysis of data relevant to crime and criminals in specific jurisdictions
   d. story-telling anecdotes passed through generations about norms and morals

5. John Lea and Jock Young have developed a left realism perspective on crime. What is the viewpoint they take on crime?
   a. Feminism has historically created a disparity in sentencing as it relates to race and gender in the criminal justice system.
   b. The justice system is ruled by the upper classes and is unable to effectively deal with overall crime rates.
   c. Police and courts are unable to control crime because of inherent leniency.
   d. There is a need for control and order, but this must be balanced by social welfare programming.

6. When should preemptive deterrence efforts take place in order to impact crime rates?
   a. before prisoners are released from custody
   b. before police involvement is required
   c. once there have been "three strikes"
   d. as a part of probationary conditions

7. Joan Sangster investigated female delinquency in Ontario from 1940 to 1960. What did she find about young girls who were incarcerated in training schools?
   a. They were perceived as threats to the middle-class morals and values.
   b. They had become wards of the court, as they were homeless or orphaned.
   c. They had either or both severe physical or mental disabilities.
   d. They were incarcerated for longer periods than their male counterparts.

8. According to radical feminists, which condition triggers the onset of female delinquent and deviant behaviour?
   a. patriarchy
   b. discrimination
   c. exploitation
   d. gender bias

9. Which of the following statements best summarizes the impact of the double standard of sexual inequality on female adolescents in the justice system?
   a. Males are more likely to commit fewer but more serious offences than females.
   b. Females have a much narrower range of acceptable behaviours than males.
   c. Females receive lengthier custody dispositions than males.
   d. Females are viewed as easier to rehabilitate than males.

10. What would an advocate of the peacemakers' movement say about the criminal justice system?
   a. Criminals are subjected to repeated racism and discrimination within the criminal justice system.
   b. The criminal justice system is as violent and harsh as the acts of those it seeks to rehabilitate.
   c. The criminal justice system is organized around the end result of protecting the peace and order in a community.
   d. Criminal justice proceedings must be much more open to public observation and criticism.

Answers: 1. b, 2. c, 3. c, 4. b, 5. d, 6. b, 7. a, 8. a, 9. c, 10. b.

Chapter in Review

Learning Objectives

LO1 Describe how latent trait theorists explain criminality.

LO2 Explain what makes people commit crime according to Gottfredson and Hirschi.

LO3 Describe the two distinct elements of control according to Tittle's control balance theory and what happens when there is an imbalance.

LO4 Describe important developmental concepts of problem behaviour syndrome (PBS), pathways to crime, criminal trajectories, and continuity of crime, and explain how they help us understand how criminal careers evolve.

LO5 Describe briefly how the major theories of criminal development account for the onset, continuance, and desistance of crime.

Anne Kitzman/Shutterstock.com

Key Terms

adolescent-limited Offender who follows the most common criminal trajectory, in which antisocial behaviour peaks in adolescence and then diminishes.

authority conflict pathway Pathway to criminal deviance that begins at an early age with stubborn behaviour and leads to defiance and then to authority avoidance.

control balance theory A developmental theory that attributes deviant and criminal behaviours to imbalances between the amount of control that the individual has over others and that others have over him or her.

covert pathway Pathway to a criminal career that begins with minor underhanded behaviour, leads to property damage, and eventually escalates to more serious forms of theft and fraud.

desistence The process through which an individual's criminal behaviour subsides, or abruptly stops.

developmental criminology A branch of criminology that examines changes in criminal careers over the life course.

developmental theories The view that criminality is a dynamic process, influenced by social experiences as well as individual characteristics.

general theory of crime (GTC) A developmental theory that modifies social control theory by integrating concepts from biosocial, psychological, routine activities, and rational choice theories.

integrated theory A complex, multifactor theory that attempts to blend seemingly independent concepts into a coherent explanation of criminality.

interactional theory A developmental theory that attributes criminal trajectories to mutual reinforcement between delinquents and significant others over the life course—family in early adolescence, school and friends in mid-adolescence, and social peers and one's own nuclear family in adulthood.

latent trait A stable feature, characteristic, property, or condition, such as defective intelligence or impulsive personality, that makes some people crime-prone over the life course.

latent trait theories The view that criminal behaviour is controlled by a "master trait," present at birth or soon after, that remains stable and unchanging throughout a person's lifetime.

life-course persister One of the small group of offenders whose criminal career continues well into adulthood.

life-course theory Theory that focuses on changes in criminality over the life course; developmental theory.

overt pathway Pathway to a criminal career that begins with minor aggression, leads to physical fighting, and eventually escalates to violent crime.

problem behaviour syndrome (PBS) A cluster of antisocial behaviours that may include family dysfunction, substance abuse, smoking, precocious sexuality and early pregnancy, educational underachievement, suicide attempts, sensation seeking, and unemployment, as well as crime.

prosocial bonds Socialized attachment to conventional institutions, activities, and beliefs.

pseudomaturity Characteristic of life-course persisters, who tend to engage in early sexuality and drug use.

social capital Positive relations with individuals and institutions, as in a successful marriage or a successful career, that support conventional behaviour and inhibit deviant behaviour.

social development model (SDM) A developmental theory that attributes criminal behaviour patterns to childhood socialization and proor antisocial attachments over the life course.

turning points Critical life events, such as career and marriage, that may enable adult offenders to desist from crime.

Quiz

1. Which of the following concepts are latent trait theories based on?
   a. choice theories and conflict theories
   b. trait theories and choice theories
   c. trait theories and biosocial theories
   d. social reaction theories and choice theories

2. Your professor considers himself to be a latent trait theorist. What is he likely to say that he believes is the reason some people commit crime?
   a. Criminals carry a combination of traits that make them capable of committing crime, including low intelligence, low morality, and high testosterone levels.
   b. We are not all born equally capable of committing crime because of varying levels of intelligence.
   c. Some individuals are born with a predisposition to committing crime, but opportunity affects when and if they do so over time.
   d. Everyone is born with the desire and ability to commit crime, but not everyone has the moral structure to do so.

3. In what component of Michael Gottfredson and Travis Hirschi's work are the criminal offender and the criminal act considered separate concepts?
   a. general theory of crime
   b. control balance theory
   c. social development model
   d. interactional theory

4. What would a control balance theorist say is important to know about crime prevention?
   a. Harsher criminal penalties lead to reduced crime rates.
   b. Police and offenders are on opposite sides of attempts to maintain a crime balance within each community.
   c. Opportunity, when combined with a perceived excess or lack of control, leads to crime.
   d. Criminals do not spend all of their time engaged in criminal activities; they also have noncriminal interests.

5. According to developmental theorists, which of the following is the best predictor of future criminal behaviour?
   a. deviant peers and family members
   b. prosocial beliefs and morals
   c. mental health issues
   d. previous criminal behaviour

6. Which of the following theories links developmental stages with changes in criminal activity?
   a. cultural value theory
   b. social learning theory
   c. developmental trajectory theory
   d. life-course theory

7. What is the most important personal social factor related to persistent offending, according to developmental theorists Sheldon and Eleanor Glueck?
   a. gender
   b. race
   c. family relations
   d. social class

8. Sally is a young person who does not hand in schoolwork, is regularly late for curfew, and challenges her parents and teachers on any rules or consequences they present. Which of the following developmental pathways to crime is she most likely following?
   a. authority conflict pathway
   b. covert pathway
   c. behaviour syndrome pathway
   d. overt pathway

9. What is meant by the term *knifing off*?
   a. gang initiation
   b. the danger of being assaulted with a weapon in prison
   c. quitting a gang after years of membership
   d. the cutting of criminal ties

10. Which of the following results has been found in with known delinquents as they age into their 60s and 70s?
    a. Once a petty criminal, always a petty criminal.
    b. Even the most serious criminals age out of crime.
    c. Only low-risk offenders age out of crime.
    d. Ongoing negative peer influences are the critical factor in determining when and if criminal behaviour will stop.

Answers: 1. c, 2. c, 3. a, 4. c, 5. d, 6. c, 7. c, 8. a, 9. c, 10. b.

10 Chapter in Review

Learning Objectives

LO1 Describe the different types of interpersonal violent crime.

LO2 Contrast the various explanations for violent crimes.

LO3 Evaluate the significance of the changes in Canadian law in regard to rape.

LO4 Identify the different degrees of murder.

LO5 Explain the prevalence of assault that occurs in the family home.

LO6 Discuss why robbery is considered a violent crime.

LO7 Define and describe contemporary forms of interpersonal violent crime.

Key Terms

acquaintance rape Forcible sex in which offender and victim are acquainted with one another.

assault level 1 Applying, attempting to apply, or threatening to apply force, with intent and without consent, against another person, or openly wearing a weapon (or an imitation) and accosting or impeding another person.

assault level 2 Assault with a weapon, threatening to use a weapon (or an imitation), or assault causing bodily harm.

assault level 3 Aggravated assault involving wounding, maiming, disfiguring, or endangering the life of another person.

child abuse Physical, sexual, or emotional maltreatment or neglect that a child or adolescent may experience while in the care of someone he or she either trusts or depends on, such as a parent, sibling, other relative, caregiver, or guardian.

child neglect Failing to provide what a child needs for his or her physical, psychological, or emotional development and well-being.

date rape Forcible sex during a courting relationship.

disarming a peace officer Taking or attempting to take a weapon without consent from a peace officer engaged in the execution of his or her duties.

expressive violence Violence that vents rage, anger, or frustration.

first-degree murder The killing of another person that is planned and deliberate, the killing of a law enforcement agent, or killing that is related to committing or attempting other crimes that are particularly offensive to society (e.g., hostage taking, sexual assault, hijacking an airplane, etc.).

gang rape Forcible sex involving multiple attackers.

hate crime A violent act directed toward a particular person or group because of a discernible colour, race, religion, or ethnic origin.

homicide First-degree murder, second-degree murder, manslaughter, or infanticide. Deaths caused by criminal negligence, suicide, and accidental or justifiable homicide are not included.

infanticide The killing of an infant shortly after birth by the mother because she is not fully recovered from the effects of giving birth (e.g., in the case of postpartum depression) and her mind is disturbed.

instrumental violence Violence designed to improve the financial or social position of the criminal.

invitation to sexual touching Inviting, counselling, or inciting someone under age 16 to touch the body of someone else for a sexual purpose.

manslaughter Homicide, or the killing of another person, by committing an unlawful act with only a general intent (e.g., speeding and killing a pedestrian, giving a lethal punch in a sudden, provoked brawl).

marital exemption Traditional legal doctrine that a legally married husband could not be charged with raping his wife.

marital rape Forcible sex between people who are legally married to each other.

mass murderer One who kills many victims in a single, violent outburst.

murder Intentional killing of another person; recognized as having two classes: first-and second-degree murder.

robbery Every one commits robbery who

(a) steals, and for the purpose of extorting whatever is stolen or to prevent or overcome resistance to the stealing, uses violence or threats of violence to a person or property;

(b) steals from any person and, at the time he steals or immediately before or immediately thereafter, wounds, beats, strikes or uses any personal violence to that person;

(c) assaults any person with intent to steal from him; or

(d) steals from any person while armed with an offensive weapon or imitation thereof.

Source: Criminal Code of Canada, RSC 1985, c C-46.

second-degree murder Intentional killing of another person that is not first-degree murder.

serial killer One who kills a series of victims, usually over an extended period of time.

sexual abuse The exploitation of a child through rape, incest, or molestation by a parent or other adult.

sexual assault Anything from unwanted touching to rape.

sexual exploitation Sexual contact, even if consensual, between a person aged 16 to 18 and someone in a position of trust or authority, such as a minister, coach, employer, or teacher.

sexual interference Touching the body of a person who is under 16 years of age for a sexual purpose.

stalking An offence of criminal harassment, which is behaviour that causes another person to fear for his or her safety or for another person's safety: for example, repeatedly following a person, repeatedly communicating with a person, or watching a person's workplace or home.

subculture of violence Norms and customs that, in contrast to society's dominant value system, legitimize and expect the use of violence to resolve social conflicts.

Quiz

1. What term refers to violence used in order to improve the financial or social position of the criminal?
   a. expressive violence
   b. excessive violence
   c. instrumental violence
   d. institutional violence

2. Sigmund Freud believed that human aggression and violence are produced by two instinctual drives, one being *eros*. What is *eros*?
   a. the death instinct
   b. the life instinct
   c. the expressive instinct
   d. the instrumental instinct

3. Which of the following characteristics is commonly found in serial rapists and repeat sexual offenders?
   a. They tend to come from poor, disadvantaged homes.
   b. They are no more likely to have a major mental illness than those in the general population.
   c. They are highly likely to demonstrate a psychopathic personality.
   d. They are more likely to own a gun than those in the general population.

4. Tim grew up in a neighbourhood where fights and disorder are regular occurrences. How would a theorist who focuses on cultural values explain Tim's own violent behaviour?
   a. psychological normalization
   b. subculture of violence
   c. cultural desistence
   d. instinctual violence

5. In 1983, the Canadian government reformed the laws pertaining to marriage and rape. Which of the following changes was made?
   a. The definition of spouse was changed to include common-law partners.
   b. Assumed consent was defined.
   c. The marital exemption clause was removed.
   d. A spousal immunity from prosecution clause was added.

6. Given what research has indicated about the characteristics typically shared by males who are most likely to use violence in a dating relationship, which man is most likely to be a perpetrator?

   a. Alan, because he has recently been diagnosed with a personality disorder
   b. Paul, because he plays violent video games in most of his free time and watches pornography on occasion
   c. Carman, because he grew up in an abusive home where his parents regularly left him alone
   d. Stan, because he is quick to anger and insists that his girlfriend send him regular text messages as to her whereabouts

7. James has committed sexual assault. He is aggressive and callous and believes that violence is manly and that women deserve to be victimized. Which explanation of sexual assault applies to him?
   a. He is hypermasculine.
   b. He has a chromosomal abnormality (XYY).
   c. He has the desire to spread his genes to carry on his lineage.
   d. He grew up in a violent home and violence is normal to him.

8. What charge requires a killer to have intent but not premeditation or deliberation?
   a. first-degree murder
   b. second-degree murder
   c. voluntary manslaughter
   d. involuntary manslaughter

9. Which of the following best describes the typical robber?
   a. a professional who plans carefully for the largest reward using the most sophisticated methods to avoid detection
   b. an amateur who engages in some planning for targeting places or people lacking guardianship
   c. an alcoholic or drug addict who acts spontaneously to get funds to satisfy their addiction
   d. an opportunistic individual who is drawn in by the thrill of planning and executing and escaping detection

10. Which of the following was the most common motivation for the 1414 hate crime incidents reported by Canadian police services in 2012?
    a. bias based on religion
    b. bias based on race or ethnicity
    c. bias based on sexual orientation
    d. bias based on national origin

For additional study tools, go online to access MindTap for *CRIM*. There, you can
- Think like a criminologist with scenarios supplied
- Decide and justify those decisions with questions that reflect on chapter topics
- Analyze criminology in the media
- Prepare for tests with quizzes
- Use your interactive eBook
- and more

www.nelson.com/student

Answers: 1. a, 2. b, 3. c, 4. b, 5. c, 6. c, 7. a, 8. b, 9. b, 10. c.

Chapter in Review

Learning Objectives

LO1 List the major types of theft and fraud.

LO2 Identify the role "target hardening" strategies can play in reducing the incidence of shoplifting.

LO3 Identify the difference between "false pretences" and "fraud."

LO4 Define "break and enter" and explain why victims are likely to be revictimized.

LO5 List the motives for the crime of arson.

Stuart McClymont/Stone/Getty Images

Key Terms

arrest by owner of property The right of the owner or designate to arrest without warrant anyone found committing a criminal offence on or in relation to the owner's property.

arson The intentional or reckless damage by fire or explosion to property.

booster Professional shoplifter who steals with the intention of reselling stolen merchandise.

burglary (break and enter) Breaking into and entering a place with the intent to commit an indictable offence.

confidence game A swindle, usually involving a get-rich-quick scheme, often with illegal overtones, so that the victim will be too afraid or too embarrassed to call the police.

constructive possession A legal fiction that applies to situations in which persons voluntarily give up physical custody of their property but still retain legal ownership.

embezzlement (breach of trust) Taking and keeping the property of others, such as clients or employers, with which one has been entrusted.

false pretences Misrepresenting a fact in a way that causes a deceived victim to give money or property to the offender.

fence A receiver of stolen goods.

fraud Use of deceit or falsehood, whether or not it is a false pretence, to obtain property, money, or other valuables from a person or the public.

naïve cheque forgers Amateurs who cash bad cheques because of some financial crisis but have little identification with a criminal subculture.

occasional criminals Offenders who do not define themselves by a criminal role or view themselves as committed career criminals.

professional criminals Offenders who make a significant portion of their income from crime.

shoplifting The taking of goods from retail stores.

situational inducement Short-term influence on a person's behaviour, such as financial problems or peer pressure, that increases risk-taking.

snitch Amateur shoplifter who does not self-identify as a thief but who systematically steals merchandise for personal use.

systematic forgers Professionals who make a living by passing bad cheques.

target hardening strategy Locking goods into place or using electronic tags and sensing devices as means of preventing shoplifting.

target removal strategy Displaying dummy or disabled goods as a means of preventing shoplifting.

theft over $5000 Theft where the value of property stolen exceeds $5000; treated as an indictable offence.

theft under $5000 Theft where the value of the property stolen does not exceed $5000; treated as a hybrid offence for which the Crown can proceed by way of summary conviction or indictment.

theft Taking for one's own use the property of another, by means other than force or threats on the victim or forcibly breaking into a person's home or workplace.

Quiz

1. Which of the following groups do not perceive themselves to be criminals and yet they commit the majority of the property crimes each year?
   a. professional criminals
   b. career criminals
   c. occasional criminals
   d. persistent criminals

2. During the Middle Ages, thieves were pickpockets or con artists and smugglers avoided taxes. Which of the following did poachers do?
   a. stole from the church
   b. plotted against the monarchy
   c. vandalized property
   d. stole game

3. Professional theft typically refers to a form of criminal behaviour that is undertaken for monetary gain and with a high degree of skill. What form of criminal behaviour is this?
   a. violent
   b. homicidal
   c. nonviolent
   d. traditional

4. What type of situations prompted English judges to create the concept of constructive possession?
   a. forgery in the taking
   b. trespassing in commercial establishments
   c. theft of small amounts of money
   d. trespass in the taking

5. What group does the text report as being responsible for more than $2 billion in thefts from the retail sector each year?
   a. shoplifters
   b. employees
   c. professional thieves
   d. cheque and credit card forgers

6. When a store owner or employee encounters an individual stealing, what type of action is permitted?
   a. arresting the thief even without a warrant
   b. locking the thief in the office for the remainder of the store hours and then calling police
   c. pointing a weapon at the thief to ensure he or she does not escape
   d. detaining the thief using any means possible in order to teach him or her a lesson

7. What type of event is an example of "false pretences"?
   a. committing a robbery while in disguise
   b. providing false information to someone, which results in the person giving property or money to an offender
   c. providing false information to the police about one's identity, address, or business in a particular place at a particular time
   d. enabling a theft to take place in a workplace without stopping it, where possible, or reporting it after the fact to the police

8. Which of the following is the name of the system that installs in cars a hidden tracking device that gives off a signal, enabling police to pinpoint its location?
   a. the Rebound system
   b. the Bounce Back system
   c. the Ricochet system
   d. the Boomerang system

9. A few professionals make a substantial living by passing bad cheques. What term did Edwin Lemert use to refer to these professionals?
   a. amateurs
   b. systematic forgers
   c. embezzlers
   d. opportunistic criminals

10. The research of Neal Shover involved the qualities of the "good burglar." Who, according to Shover, may become a "good burglar"?
    a. Anyone can become a "good burglar" if he or she has the desire to commit the crime.
    b. Someone who has demonstrated to a criminal mentor that he or she is solid and capable of the training required may become a "good burglar."
    c. Only those who have committed other types of crimes are capable of successfully committing burglary.
    d. Only males are capable of being "good burglars."

Answers: 1. c, 2. d, 3. c, 4. d, 5. b, 6. a, 7. b, 8. d, 9. a, 10. b.

Chapter in Review

Learning Objectives

LO1 Differentiate between white-collar crime and organized crime and demonstrate how they are similar and how they are different.

LO2 Identify the various types of white-collar crime.

LO3 Describe some of the law enforcement strategies that

government is using to combat white-collar crime.

LO4 Describe major characteristics of organized crime and the groups involved in this criminal activity.

LO5 Interpret the debate about what is organized about organized crime.

SpeedKingz/Shutterstock.com

Key Terms

alien conspiracy theory The view that organized crime in the United States is controlled by the Mafia, centrally coordinated by a national committee that settles disputes, dictates policy, and assigns territory.

bank fraud To obtain money or property from a financial institution by false pretences, as by forgery or misrepresentation.

bucketing A form of stock-broker chiselling in which brokers skim customer trading profits by falsifying trade information.

chiselling Regularly cheating an organization, its customers, or both.

churning A form of stockbroker chiselling involving repeated, excessive, and unnecessary buying and selling of stock.

compliance strategies Fostering law conformity, cooperation, and self-policing

in the business community through the use of economic incentives and administrative agencies.

corporate crime A legal offence, such as price-fixing, restraint of trade, or hazardous waste dumping, committed by a corporate entity to improve its market share or profitability.

corporate culture view The view that some business organizations promote white-collar crime by maintaining a business climate that stresses profit over fair play.

deterrence strategies Detecting criminal violations, determining who is responsible, and penalizing the offenders to deter future violations.

enterprise Taking risks for profit in the marketplace.

front running A form of stockbroker chiselling in which brokers place personal orders

ahead of a large customer's order to profit from the market effects of the trade.

insider trading Buying and selling securities based on business information derived from a position of trust and not available to the general public.

La Cosa Nostra A U.S. syndicate of 25 or so Italian-dominated crime families who control crime in distinct geographic areas.

Mafia A criminal society that originated in Sicily, Italy, and is believed to control racketeering in the United States.

organized crime Illegal activities of people and organizations whose acknowledged purpose is profit through illegitimate business enterprise.

pilferage Employee theft of company property.

price-fixing A conspiracy to set and control the price of a necessary commodity.

restraint of trade A contract or conspiracy designed to stifle competition, create a monopoly, artificially maintain prices, or otherwise interfere with free market competition.

self-control view The view that white-collar crime, like all crime, is a product of low self-control.

white-collar crime Illegal acts that may include theft, embezzlement, fraud, market manipulation, restraint of trade, and false advertising; also known as commercial/business crime or economic offences.

Quiz

1. Which of the following involves illegal activities by people whose acknowledged purpose is to profit through an illegitimate business enterprise?
   a. organized crime
   b. restraint of trade
   c. white-collar crime
   d. embezzlement

2. According to Mark Haller, which of the following is a similarity between a chamber of commerce and an organized crime syndicate?
   a. They both plan counteroffensives on rivalling crime groups.
   b. They both form with the primary intent of bettering their communities.

    c. They both seek to remain hidden from public scrutiny.

    d. They both gather regularly to settle disputes between members.

3. How is corruption by public officials treated in China?

    a. It is encouraged and rewarded.

    b. It is punishable by death.

    c. It is ignored.

    d. It is relatively unheard of.

4. Joe is a bar owner who often substitutes lower-priced versions of alcohol to replace premium spirits in drinks but charges the premium prices. What category of white-collar crime is this an example of?

    a. professional chiselling

    b. stings and swindles

    c. securities fraud

    d. influence peddling and bribery

5. Several gas companies have joined forces to ensure that profits are high and consistent between them. Which of the following corporate crimes are they likely engaging in?

    a. influence peddling

    b. false trading

    c. restraint of trade

    d. negative tax evasion

6. Unsafe work environments are a form of corporate crime. What is the incidence of these events in Canada on a yearly basis?

    a. Statistics are not reliably kept on workplace deaths so comparison is difficult.

    b. Workplace deaths exceed street homicides in frequency each year.

    c. Street homicides far exceed workplace-related deaths in frequency and severity.

    d. Workplace deaths occur at a rate similar to street homicides each year.

7. Which of the following individuals has the dubious honour of having run the world's biggest "Ponzi scheme"?

    a. Ivan Boesky

    b. Bernard Madoff

    c. Michael Milken

    d. Ron Rewald

8. In 2003, the Canadian government passed an amendment to the Criminal Code, making organizations and anyone who directs the work of others criminally liable for safety offences. What is this amendment called?

    a. WHMIS

    b. *Bill C-45*

    c. *Health and Safety Act*

    d. Employer Responsibility Measure

9. How does the corporate culture theory explain the causes of white-collar crime?

    a. Corporations encourage "if you are not first, you are last" thinking, and the individuals who buy into this are more crime-prone than others.

    b. "Go along to get along" notions are promoted in corporations so that new employees are pressured into conforming to cultural norms.

    c. Offenders commit white-collar crimes because they have been hired into environments where it is the norm to "stay out of each other's business."

    d. "Greed is good" and "profit must come first" lessons are learned in corporations in the same way they are learned on the street by gang members.

10. Which of the following charges may now be laid against corporations or executives in the event that an employee dies in the workplace?

    a. manslaughter

    b. second-degree murder

    c. homicide

    d. criminal negligence

Answers: 1. a, 2. d, 3. b, 4. a, 5. c, 6. d, 7. b, 8. b, 9. d, 10. d.

Learning Objectives

LO1 Define a public order crime.

LO2 Describe the consequences of the implementation of *Bill C-36* for the control of prostitution and sex work in Canada; should we consider legalizing sex work in Canada?

LO3 Evaluate how we decide what is pornographic and understand how the law has changed to support

police in dealing with child pornography.

LO4 Know the impact, the good and the bad, of legal gambling in Canada.

LO5 Understand the role that substance abuse plays in criminal behaviour.

LO6 Think critically about whether Canada should legalize the possession of cannabis for personal use.

Pa/ZUMA Press/Newscom

Key Terms

moral entrepreneur A person who creates moral rules, which thus reflect the values of those in power rather than any objective, universal standards of right and wrong.

obscenity Material that links sex with undue exploitation, violence, or degrading or dehumanizing treatment, and has no redeeming social value.

pornography Books, magazines, films, tapes, pictures, or videos that graphically exploit sex or depict sex in combination with crime, horror, cruelty, or violence; includes any and all sexual exploitation of children.

Prohibition In Canada, the period from about 1915 to 1925 when the sale of alcohol

was prohibited; in the United States, the prohibition period was much longer, lasting from 1919 until 1933.

public order crime Behaviour that is outlawed because it threatens the general well-being of society and challenges its accepted moral principles.

sex work The consensual exchange of sexual services for money.

temperance movement The drive to prohibit the sale of alcohol in the United States and Canada, led by the Woman's Christian Temperance Union.

victimless crime Public order crime that violates the moral order but has no specific victim other than society as a whole.

Quiz

1. What are people called who seek to control or criminalize deviant behaviours?
   a. moralists
   b. moral entrepreneurs
   c. power seekers
   d. enthusiasts

2. What is the rationale for prostitution not being illegal in Canada?
   a. A charge may not be laid for a consensual act.
   b. Most prostitutes are too young to charge.
   c. Such laws would further victimize prostitutes.
   d. It is too difficult to find sufficient evidence in these cases.

3. There are three different perspectives that are utilized in an attempt to understand why individuals engage in sex work, according to van derMeulen, Durisin, and Love. Which of the following is NOT one of them?

    a. the perspective of sex work as a form of sexual slavery

    b. the perspective of sex work as being a sex-positive experience

    c. the perspective of sex work as a necessary evil

    d. the perspective of sex work as labour

4. What view do feminists who support sexual equality hold about prostitution?

    a. Women who engage in prostitution are engaging their free will and are not subjugated.

    b. Prostitution is a prime example of male domination and female subjugation.

    c. Prostitution must be viewed as a business transaction only.

    d. Those men who purchase sex for money are unable to engage in socially appropriate relationships.

5. What do the findings of various research studies into the use of pornography indicate is the relationship between violent behaviour and viewing pornography?

    a. Those who view more than five hours of pornography per week are much more likely to exhibit violent behaviour than others who view less or none.

    b. There is no clear link between obscene material and antisocial or violent behaviour.

    c. The link between violence and pornography viewing appears to pertain to young males under the age of 25 only.

    d. Convicted rapists report having viewed more pornography than the general population.

6. What is the role of lottery commissions in Ontario?

    a. lobbying the government to reduce the use of lotteries across the province

    b. designing new lotteries to be introduced for provincial revenue

    c. regulation of all legitimate lotteries and distribution of income

    d. meeting with young people to educate them on the dangers of gambling

7. In the late 1980s, which group of Canadians was granted the right to operate casinos to create jobs and provide income for the community?

    a. Lions Clubs

    b. Big Brothers and Big Sisters

    c. First Nations

    d. Anglican churches

8. According to the text, about how many homicides are committed by criminal offenders using drugs or alcohol at the time of their offences?

    a. one-quarter

    b. one-half

    c. two-thirds

    d. virtually all

9. Given the nature of the research results presented on drug control strategies, what approach should be used to have the most success in reducing drug use in a community?

    a. introducing prevention strategies to elementary school children

    b. introducing regular drug-testing programs across workplaces

    c. opening a methadone clinic

    d. providing drug users with employment supports

10. Which of the following outcomes is considered a potential consequence of harsher penalties for drug use?

    a. diffusion of distribution

    b. reduced usage by young people

    c. syndicated rings

    d. net widening

Answers: 1. b, 2. c, 3. b, 4. a, 5. a, 6. c, 7. c, 8. c, 9. a, 10. a.

14 Chapter in Review

Learning Objectives

LO1 Define what is meant by *global criminology* and describe how it differs from previous criminological theories.

LO2 Define the term *state crime* and explain how the activities of the state can be considered a crime.

LO3 Describe how the activities of large, multinational financial institutions can be considered as causes of crime.

LO4 Identify the role of the Internet in the spread of

transnational goods counterfeiting, and explain why goods counterfeiting is a serious form of crime.

LO5 Explain what human trafficking is, and describe its major purposes.

LO6 Explain how cyberbullying is considered a crime.

LO7 Identify the major types of terrorism.

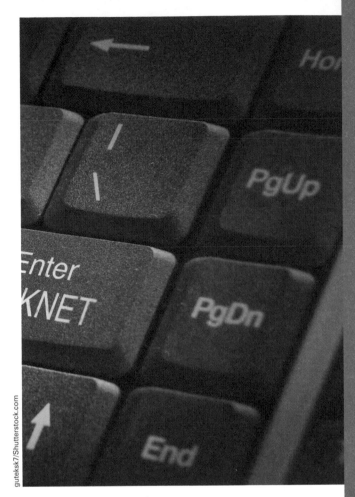
guteksk7/Shutterstock.com

Key Terms

genocide The attempt by a government to wipe out a minority group within its jurisdiction.

terrorism The illegal use of force against innocent people to achieve a political objective.

virus A computer program that disrupts or destroys existing programs and networks.

1. TECHNOLOGY AS INSTRUMENT

2. TECHNOLOGY AS TARGET

FIGURE 14.2

Two Types of Cybercrime as Defined by RCMP

Money laundering, Mass marketing fraud, Hacking for criminal purposes, Identity theft, Child exploitation, **Cybercrime**, Criminal botnet operations, Intellectual property infringements, Cyberbullying, Malware threats, Internet-based drug trafficking, Distributed denial of service, National security offences

Quiz

1. What is the TOR network?
   a. a network that promotes censorship of objectionable material
   b. a network designed by the National Security Agency (NSA)
   c. a network developed to directly tap into the servers of major corporations
   d. a network that allows clients to offer hidden services over the Dark Web

2. Which of the following comprised the single largest category within the Dark Web?
   a. websites that promoted terrorist activity
   b. forums that advocate for deposing political parties
   c. websites offering drugs and contraband
   d. sites for companies dealing in pornographic material

3. Islamic terrorism is considered to be the number one "global scourge." What is number two?
   a. human trafficking
   b. Deep Net revenge porn
   c. Somali piracy
   d. Dark Web pedophilia

4. According to the 2012 Canadian Chamber of Commerce report, what percentage of the counterfeit goods seized by Canadian authorities was manufactured in China?
   a. 90
   b. 80
   c. 70
   d. 60

5. A programmer working at a mail-order sales company had its computer round down odd cents in the company's sales-commission accounts and channel the round-downs into a dummy account he had established and could personally access. What was this programmer doing?
   a. super-zapping
   b. fraudulently impersonating
   c. activating a logic bomb
   d. salami slicing

6. What term is used to describe the most extreme form of state-sponsored terrorism?
   a. *jihad*
   b. genocide
   c. war crime
   d. enhanced interrogation techniques

7. Which of the following has been referred to as the world's first cyberweapon?
   a. the Stuxnet virus
   b. the Storm worm
   c. the North Korean hack
   d. the Chernobyl virus

8. Bill C-15A created the offence of "luring," which addresses the exploitation of children via the Internet. When was this bill passed?
   a. 2002
   b. 2005
   c. 2008
   d. 2011

9. For more than five years, Joe terrorized his fellow employees by creating and posting fake online profiles of them on numerous dating and child pornography sites. After a complex multi-force effort he was tracked down, charged, and found guilty of criminal harassment. What is the maximum penalty that he is facing?
   a. two years in jail
   b. five years in jail
   c. seven years in jail
   d. ten years in jail

10. After the breakdown of their marriage, Kevin uploaded all the naked pictures he had of his ex-wife, Becky, to a number of social media websites. Becky informed the police and Kevin was charged and found guilty of cyberbullying. What is the maximum sentence that Kevin can receive?
    a. ten years in jail
    b. five years in jail
    c. two years in jail
    d. one year in jail

For additional study tools, go online to access MindTap for *CRIM*. There, you can

- Think like a criminologist with scenarios supplied
- Decide and justify those decisions with questions that reflect on chapter topics
- Analyze criminology in the media
- Prepare for tests with quizzes
- Use your interactive eBook
- and more

www.nelson.com/student

Answers: 1. d, 2. c, 3. c, 4. b, 5. d, 6. b, 7. a, 8. a, 9. d, 10. b.

Synopsis OF CRIMINOLOGICAL THEORIES

Victimization Theories (Chapter 3)

Theory	Major Premise	Strengths
Victim precipitation	Victims trigger criminal acts by their provocative behaviour. Active precipitation involves fighting words or gestures. Passive precipitation occurs when victims unknowingly threaten their attacker.	Explains multiple victimizations. If people precipitate crime, it follows that they will become repeat victims if their behaviour persists over time.
Lifestyle	Victimization risk is increased when people have a high-risk lifestyle. Placing oneself at risk by going out to dangerous places results in increased victimization.	Explains victimization patterns in the social structure. Males, young people, and the poor have high victimization rates because they have a higher-risk lifestyle than females, the elderly, and the affluent.
Deviant places	People who live in deviant places are at high risk for crime. Victim behaviour has little influence over the criminal act.	Places the focus of crime on deviant places. Shows why people with conventional lifestyles become crime victims.
Routine activities	Crime rates can be explained by the availability of suitable targets, the absence of capable guardians, and the presence of motivated offenders.	Can explain crime rates and trends. Shows how victim behaviour can influence criminal opportunity. Suggests that victimization risk can be reduced by increasing guardianship and/or reducing target vulnerability.

Choice Theories (Chapter 4)

Theory	Major Premise	Strengths
Rational choice	Law-violating behaviour occurs after offenders weigh information on their personal needs and the situational factors involved in the difficulty and risk of committing a crime.	Explains why high-risk youths do not constantly engage in delinquency. Relates theory to delinquency control policy. It is not limited by class or other social variables.
Routine activities	Crime and delinquency are functions of the presence of motivated offenders, the availability of suitable targets, and the absence of capable guardians.	Can explain fluctuations in crime and delinquency rates. Shows how victim behaviour influences criminal choice.
General deterrence	People will commit crime and delinquency if they perceive that the benefits outweigh the risks. Crime is a function of the severity, certainty, and speed of punishment.	Shows the relationship between crime and punishment. Suggests a real solution to crime.
Specific deterrence	If punishment is severe enough, criminals will not repeat their illegal acts.	Provides a strategy to reduce crime.
Incapacitation	Keeping known criminals out of circulation will reduce crime rates.	Recognizes the role that opportunity plays in criminal behaviour. Provides a solution to chronic offending.

Synopsis CONTINUED

Biological and Psychological Theories (Chapter 5)

Theory	Major Premise	Strengths
Biosocial		
Biochemical	Crime, especially violence, is a function of diet, vitamin intake, hormonal imbalance, or food allergies.	Explains irrational violence. Shows how the environment interacts with personal traits to influence behaviour.
Neurological	Criminals and delinquents often suffer brain impairment, as measured by the EEG. Attention deficit/hyperactivity disorder and minimal brain dysfunction are related to antisocial behaviour.	Explains irrational violence. Shows how the environment interacts with personal traits to influence behaviour.
Genetic	Criminal traits and predispositions are inherited. The criminality of parents can predict the delinquency of children.	Explains why only a small percentage of youth in a high-crime area become chronic offenders.
Evolutionary	As the human race evolved, traits and characteristics have become ingrained. Some of these traits make people aggressive and predisposed to commit crime.	Explains high violence rates and aggregate gender differences in the crime rate.
Psychological		
Psychodynamic	The development of the unconscious personality early in childhood influences behaviour for the rest of a person's life. Criminals have weak egos and damaged personalities.	Explains the onset of crime and why crime and drug abuse cut across class lines.
Behavioural	People commit crime when they model their behaviour after others they see being rewarded for the same acts. Behaviour is reinforced by rewards and extinguished by punishment.	Explains the role of significant others in the crime process. Shows how family life and media can influence crime and violence.
Cognitive	Individual reasoning processes influence behaviour. Reasoning is influenced by the way people perceive their environment.	Shows why criminal behaviour patterns change over time as people mature and develop their reasoning powers. May explain the aging-out process.

Social Process Theories (Chapter 7)

Theory	Major Premise	Strengths
Social Learning Theories		
Differential association theory	People learn to commit crime from exposure to antisocial definitions.	Explains onset of criminality. Explains the presence of crime in all elements of social structure. Explains why some people in high-crime areas refrain from criminality. Can apply to adults and juveniles.
Neutralization theory	Youths learn ways of neutralizing moral restraints and periodically drift in and out of criminal behaviour patterns.	Explains why many delinquents do not become adult criminals. Explains why youthful law violators can participate in conventional behaviour.
Social Control Theory		
Hirschi's control theory	A person's bond to society prevents him or her from violating social rules. If the bond weakens, the person is free to commit crime.	Explains that onset of crime can apply to both middle- and lower-class crime. Explains its theoretical constructs adequately so they can be measured. Has been empirically tested.
Social Reaction Theory		
Labelling theory	People enter into law-violating careers when they are labelled for their acts and organize their personalities around the labels.	Explains the role of society in creating deviance. Explains why some juvenile offenders do not become adult criminals. Develops concepts of criminal careers.

Synopsis OF CRIMINOLOGICAL THEORIES

Synopsis OF CRIMINOLOGICAL THEORIES

Social Structure Theories (Chapter 6)

Theory	Major Premise	Strengths
Social Disorganization Theory		
Shaw and McKay's concentric zone theory	Crime is a product of transitional neighbourhoods that manifest social disorganization and value conflict.	Identifies why crime rates are highest in slum areas. Points out the factors that produce crime. Suggests programs to help reduce crime.
Social ecology theory	The conflicts and problems of urban social life and communities, including fear, unemployment, deterioration, and siege mentality, influence crime rates.	Accounts for urban crime rates and trends.
Strain Theory		
Anomie theory	People who adopt the goals of society but lack the means to attain them seek alternatives, such as crime.	Points out how competition for success creates conflict and crime. Suggests that social conditions and not personality can account for crime. Can explain middle- and upper-class crime.
Institutional anomie theory	Material goals pervade all aspects of North American life.	Explains why crime rates are so high in North American culture.
Relative deprivation theory	Crime occurs when the wealthy and poor live close to one another.	Explains high crime rates in deteriorated inner-city areas located near more affluent neighbourhoods.
General strain theory	Strain has a variety of sources. Strain causes crime in the absence of adequate coping mechanisms.	Identifies the complexities of strain in modern society. Expands on anomie theory. Shows the influence of social events on behaviour over the life course.
Cultural Deviance Theory		
Miller's focal concern theory	Citizens who obey the street rules of lower-class life (focal concerns) find themselves in conflict with the dominant culture.	Identifies the core values of lower-class culture and shows their association to crime.
Cohen's theory of delinquent gangs	Status frustration of lower-class boys, created by their failure to achieve middle-class success, causes them to join gangs.	Shows how the conditions of lower-class life produce crime. Explains violence and destructive acts. Identifies conflict of lower class with middle class.
Cloward and Ohlin's theory of opportunity	Blockage of conventional opportunities causes lower-class youths to join criminal, conflict, or retreatist gangs.	Shows that even illegal opportunities are structured in society. Indicates why people become involved in a particular type of criminal activity. Presents a way of preventing crime.

Synopsis

Social Conflict Theories (Chapter 8)

Theory	Major Premise	Strengths
Conflict theory	Crime is a function of class conflict. Law is defined by people who hold social and political power.	Accounts for class differentials in the crime rate. Shows how class conflict influences behaviour.
Marxist theory	Capitalist ownership of the means of production creates class conflict. Crime is a rebellion of the lower class. The criminal justice system is an agent of class warfare.	Accounts for the associations between economic structure and crime rates.
Instrumental Marxist theory	Criminals are revolutionaries. The real crimes are sexism, racism, and profiteering.	Broadens the definition of crime and demystifies or explains the historical development of law.
Structural Marxist theory	The law is designed to sustain the capitalist economic system.	Explains the existence of white-collar crime and business control laws.
Left realism	Crime is a function of relative deprivation; criminals prey on the poor.	Represents a compromise between conflict and traditional criminology.
Radical feminist theory	The capitalist system creates patriarchy, which oppresses women.	Explains gender bias, violence against women, and repression.
Power–control theory	Girls are controlled more closely than boys in traditional male-dominated households. There is gender equity in contemporary egalitarian homes.	Explains gender differences in the crime rate as a function of class and gender conflict.
Deconstructionism	Language controls the meaning and use of the law.	Provides a critical analysis of meaning.
Peacemaking	Peace and humanism can reduce crime; conflict resolution strategies can work.	Offers a new approach to crime control through mediation.

Integrated Theories (Chapter 9)

Theory	Major Premise	Strengths
Latent Trait Theories		
General theory of crime	Crime and criminality are separate concepts. People choose to commit crime when they lack self-control. People lacking in self-control will seize criminal opportunities.	Integrates choice and social control concepts. Identifies the difference between crime and criminality.
Control balance	An excess or lack of control makes people crime-prone.	Shows that control is a multidimensional concept.
Developmental Theories		
Social development model (SDM)	Weak social controls produce crime. A person's place in the structure influences his or her bond to society.	Combines elements of social structural and social process theories. Accounts for variations in the crime rate.
Interactional theory	Criminals go through lifestyle changes during their offending career	Combines sociological and psychological theories.
Age-graded theory	As people mature, the factors that influence their propensity to commit crime change. In childhood, family factors are critical; in adulthood, marital and job factors are key.	Shows how crime is a developmental process that shifts in direction over the life course.